W9-DFG-015

THE THEOLOGY OF CHRIST: COMMENTARY

CONTEMPORARY THEOLOGY SERIES

GENERAL EDITORS:

J. FRANK DEVINE, S.J.

RICHARD W. ROUSSEAU, S.J.

THE THEOLOGY OF CHRIST: COMMENTARY is one of the volumes in the Historical Theology section of this series.

The Theology of Christ: Commentary

READINGS IN CHRISTOLOGY

RALPH J. TAPIA

DEPARTMENT OF THEOLOGY
FORDHAM UNIVERSITY, NEW YORK

THE BRUCE PUBLISHING COMPANY / New York

Library of Congress Catalog Card Number: 70-87993

THE BRUCE PUBLISHING COMPANY, NEW YORK
COLLIER-MACMILLAN CANADA, Ltd., TORONTO, ONTARIO

Made in the United States of America

ACKNOWLEDGMENTS

We are grateful to the following for granting us permission to reprint copyrighted materials:

Abingdon Press, Nashville, Tennessee, for excerpts from Robert S. Paul's *The Atonement and the Sacraments,* © 1960, and from Sylvester Paul Schilling's *Contemporary Continental Theologians,* © 1966;

W. H. Allen Co., London, for excerpts from Henry Nutcombe Oxenham's *The Catholic Doctrine of the Atonement;*

Almqvist & Wiksell, Uppsala, Sweden, for excerpts from Per Beskow's *Rex Gloriae: The Kingship of Christ in the Early Church,* © 1962;

The Beacon Press, Boston, for excerpts from Adolf Harnack's *Outlines of the History of Dogma;*

Beauchesne et ses fils, Paris, for excerpts from Paul Galtier's *Saint Hilaire de Poitiers,* © 1960;

Buch-Kunstverlag Ettal, for excerpts from Keetje Rozemond's *La Christologie de Saint Jean Damascène,* © 1959;

Editions Henri Messeiller, Neuchâtel, for excerpts from Louis Perriraz' *Le Problème Christologique,* © 1956;

Wm. B. Eerdmans Publishing Company, Grand Rapids, Michigan, for excerpts from Ralph P. Martin's *The New Quest of the Historical Jesus,* edited by Carl Henry, © 1966;

Faith Press, London, for excerpts from John Meyendorff's *A Study of Gregory Palamas,* © 1964;

Fortress Press, Philadelphia, for excerpts from Paul Althaus' *The Theology of Martin Luther;*

Greek Orthodox Theological Review, for excerpts from Karekin Sarkissian's article "The Doctrine of the Person of Christ in the Armenian Church" (Winter 1964–1965) and from Stanley S. Harakas' article "Sergius Bulgakov and His Teaching" (Summer 1961, Winter 1961–1962);

Harper & Row, New York, for excerpts from J. N. D. Kelly's *Early Christian Doctrines,* © 1958 and 1960; for excerpts from James F. Peter's *Finding the Historical Jesus,* © 1965; for excerpts from J. N. D. Kelly's *Early Christian Creeds,* © 1960; for excerpts from W. Norman Pittenger's *The Word Incarnate,* © 1959; for excerpts from Francois Wendel's *Calvin: The Origins and Development of His Religious Thought,* translated by Philip Moiret, © 1963; and for excerpts from Martin Werner's *The Formation of Christian Dogma,* translated by S. G. F. Brandon, © 1957;

Harvard University Press, Cambridge, Massachusetts, for excerpts from Harry A. Wolfson's *The Philosophy of the Church Fathers,* © 1956; for excerpts from Heiko Oberman's *The Harvest of Medieval Theology,* © 1963, by the President and Fellows of Harvard College;

Hawthorn Books, Inc., New York, for excerpts from Francis Ferrier's *What Is the Incarnation?,* Vol. 24 in the *Twentieth Century Encyclopedia of Catholicism,* © 1962;

Helicon Press, Baltimore, for excerpts from L. Richard's *The Mystery of Redemption,* © 1965;

B. Herder Book Company, Inc., St. Louis, for excerpts from J. Tixeront's *History of Dogma,* Vol. III, © 1916, and from Bernard Otten's *Manual of the History of Dogmas,* © 1918;

Irish Theological Quarterly, for excerpts from Kevin McNamara's articles "The Psychological Unity of Christ, a Problem in Christology" (1956) and "Theodoret of Cyrus and the Unity of the Person in Christ" (1955);

J. H. Kok, Kampen, for excerpts from R. Allen Killen's *The Ontological Theology of Paul Tillich,* © 1956;

The Macmillan Company, New York, for excerpts from Gustaf E. Aulen's *Christus Victor,* © 1954, and from T. H. Clarke's *The Encounter with God,* © 1960, 1961, 1962;

Morehouse Publishing Company, for excerpts from Frank Gavin's *Some Aspects of Contemporary Greek Orthodox Thought,* © 1923;

Thomas Nelson and Sons, Ltd., London and New York, for excerpts from Robert S. Franks' *The Work of Christ,* © 1962;
Oliver & Boyd, Edinburgh, for excerpts from Gustaf Wingren's *Man and Incarnation: A Study in the Biblical Theology of Irenaeus,* © 1959;
Orthodoxy, for excerpts from A. Guirgis Waheeb's article "The Christology of the Coptic Church" (Winter 1961);
Oxford University Press, New York, for excerpts from Claude Welch's *God and Incarnation in Mid-Nineteenth Century German Theology,* © 1965;
Pantheon Books (Random House, Inc.), New York, for excerpts from Karl Adam's *The Christ of Faith,* © 1957;
The Paulist-Newman Press, New York, for excerpts from James Carmody and Thomas Clarke's *Christ and His Mission,* © 1966;
Presbyterian and Reformed Publishing Company, Nutley, N. J., for excerpts from Herman Ridderbos' *Bultmann,* © 1960;
Henry Regnery Company, Chicago, for excerpts from Eugene Portalié's *A Guide to the Thought of St. Augustine,* © 1960; and for excerpts from A. M. Henry's *The Mystery of the Incarnation* in *The Historical and Mystical Christ,* Vol. 5 of the *Theology Library,* © 1958;
S. A. L. E. Sodalitas, Milan, for excerpts from I. Tubaldo's *La Dottrina Cristologica di Antonio Rosmini,* © 1954;
S. C. M. Press, London, for excerpts from Thomas L. Torrance's *Karl Barth: An Introduction to His Early Theology 1910–1931,* © 1962;
Charles Scribners' Sons, New York, for excerpts from Donald M. Baillie's *God Was in Christ,* © 1945;
Sheed & Ward, Inc., for excerpts from Aloys Grillmeier's *Christ In Christian Tradition,* © 1965; from Jean Daniélou's *Origen,* © 1955;
The Society for the Promotion of Christian Knowledge (SPCK), London, for excerpts from E. G. Jay's *Son of Man, Son of God,* © 1965; from R. V. Sellers' *Two Ancient Christologies,* © 1954; from Sellers' *Council of Chalcedon;* and from George Prestige's *Fathers & Heretics,* © 1954;
Theology Digest, for excerpts from L. Malevez' article "The Christian Message and Myth: The Theology of Rudolf Bultmann" (Spring, 1962);
Theological Studies, for excerpts from Robert L. Faricy's article "Teilhard de Chardin's Theology of Redemption" (December 1966); and from Walter Burghardt's "Annotations on the Christology of Theodore of Mopsuestia" (September 1958);
The University of Fribourg Press, Fribourg, Switzerland, for excerpts from Tarsicius Van Bovel's *Recherches sur la Christologie de Saint Augustin,* © 1954; and from Raniero Cantalamessa's *La Christologia di Tertulliano,* © 1962;
Westminster Press, Philadelphia, for excerpts from John McIntyre's *The Shape of Christology,* © 1966.

EDITORS' INTRODUCTION
CONTEMPORARY THEOLOGY SERIES

This series begins with the presupposition that theology is necessary. It is necessary if Christian intelligence is to search for meaning in its dialogue with God, man and the world. Since Christian intelligence is not the exclusive possession of the theological specialist or the cleric, the search must be carried out in all those areas of life, secular as well as religious, including the college situation, where meaning is to be found.

This search is a peaceful one, for in some mysterious way it has already achieved its goal: the vision of faith and the fullness of love. Still it remains a relentless and universal search. Its inner certainty must radiate out not only to the edges of the mind, but also into the farthest recesses of the world. We could call it "lay" theology, but this word seems too pale a description for such an exciting enterprise of the Christian life.

In view of this the editors of this series are convinced that new questions had to be asked, new structures created and new books written. These books would be neither catechetical nor apologetic. They would be purely and simply theological. The primary audience would be believers but all thinking men would find them useful. In scope they would be broad enough to insure perspective. They would be scholarly enough to be intellectually relevant. They would avoid pedantry. In short, they would try to present a rich and deep understanding of Christian revelation in such a way that today's college students would be able to respond with a Christian faith and life that are both culturally mature and scientifically precise. Finally the authors of these books would be, for the most part, teachers in colleges and universities where much of the contemporary theological dialogue is now going on.

The series falls into four parts: biblical, historical, ecclesial and ethical. The divisions were not predetermined by the editors. They follow the shape of the most vigorous theological work now being done.

The books in the biblical section are intended to go beyond the traditional treatment of bible history and the now familiar perspectives of salvation history. They concentrate on various books of the Bible. Their method has been especially designed for college work. Tentatively, it might be called "exegetical theology." Every verse is not considered after the fashion of a commentary, nor are narratives developed as a biography, nor is there any attempt to create large theological syntheses. Rather the individual books are studied in chronological sequence; key passages are treated in detail and the rest are summarized. At the same time some attention is paid to the growing theological synthesis.

Since scholastic theology is already represented by individual works and sets of textbooks, the books in our historical section study dogmatic questions from a developmental point of view. In this way the editors hope to make the college students more aware of the great wealth of theological thinking that recent historico-theological studies have uncovered. This method, which is more inductive than deductive, should happily coincide with the thought processes of the college students. The three basic poles for synthesis are: God, Christ and Man. In each area the historical development will be studied and a significant number of basic source texts presented. The problems raised in these studies will range all the way from Augustinian pessimism to Teilhardian optimism.

The textbooks for the third part of the series will deal with issues of great contemporary importance. They will examine questions discussed by the Second Vatican Council. As the name implies, ecclesial theology must first concern itself with the Church, what the Church knows herself to be as expressed in the insights of the new Constitution of the Church and with the more significant of the Church's allied concerns: other world religions, American Protestantism, its history, its motivating forces and spirit, and finally, the new sacramental theology so enriched by the many magnificent liturgical advances. All of this growth has brought a wider and deeper appreciation of the nature of the Roman Catholic Church and her relationship rooted in understanding and love with the whole world.

The fourth and final section of the series is devoted explicitly to Christian moral response. The editors subscribe to the position that the proper place for the Catholic college or university to examine ethical questions is in a revelational rather than in a purely philosophical context. In addition to the "virtue" divisions of the *Summa* or the classic moral theology text, designed primarily for confessors, there is a need and a place for a "Christian ethics" that reflects the new insights which both biblical and dogmatic theology can provide. These books will strive to be openly Christian in spirit, eclectic in approach, up-to-date in scholarship and they will address themselves to those ethical problems which are most real to the modern American mind.

Finally, the editors would like to express their thanks to all those whose interest, advice and cooperation have made this series possible. To the individual authors who so graciously added to their heavy burden of academic responsibility by undertaking these books, we can only express the hope that their share in the shaping and influencing of the American Catholic community of today and of tomorrow will be far more meaningful to them than any meager thanks of ours.

The Editors,

REV. J. FRANK DEVINE, S.J.,
Boston College
REV. RICHARD W. ROUSSEAU, S.J.,
National Council of Churches

FOREWORD

The purpose of this book is to provide the college student a selective but comprehensive anthology of the views of contemporary authors on the development of Christology from the Apostolic period to the present.

Perhaps no other subject, outside that of man himself, has preoccupied Western thought so much in the past as the mystery of Christ. All of its aspects, static as well as dynamic, have been studied and discussed. Therefore, to do justice to the task, I have endeavored to select commentaries which touch upon all the various aspects of Christology and Soteriology: biblical, positive, speculative, cosmic, functional, psychological, etc. To avoid a onesided picture, I chose authors with different viewpoints from Catholic, Protestant, and Orthodox backgrounds. I tried to use works published in English, easily accessible to the student for further consultation, but I did not hesitate to make my own translations when I came to foreign authors whose work, as yet untranslated, I considered important to complete this volume.

CONTENTS

THE THEOLOGY OF CHRIST: COMMENTARY

INTRODUCTION[1]

The Development of Christology

The student of Christological development should be especially attentive to three points: First, the prevalence in any period, school or author of an Alexandrian or Antiochene outlook, a stress, that is, either on the unity of Christ or on the distinction and integrity of his human and divine natures. Secondly, the mode of discourse, conceptual and verbal, favored by the various sources at different periods and in different genres. Is the language that of rich religious imagery, or is it more abstract and technical, derived perhaps from the philosophical tradition? Is there an effort to "define" the constitution of the God-man (an "ontological" Christology), or is the primary concern to describe his role as Savior (a "functional" Christology)? Thirdly (where the approach is "ontological"), whether the Christological question is being placed concerning his basic structure (person, nature, hypostasis, etc.), or concerning the consequences of this basic structure, whether these consequences be more logical (for example, the question of whether we may call Christ an adopted Son of God) or more ontological (for

[1] This Introduction is an excerpt taken from "Summary and Appraisal" in *Christ and His Mission,* Vol. III of *Sources of Christian Theology,* edited and comments by James M. Carmody, S.J., and Thomas E. Clarke, S.J. (Westminster, Md.: The Newman Press, 1966), pp. 287–307. J. M. Carmody is a professor of theology at Le Moyne College, Syracuse, N.Y., and T. E. Clarke is professor of dogmatic theology at Woodstock College, Md. Both have written and edited other works such as *Word and Redeemer,* etc.

example, questions concerning the knowledge and grace of Christ).

The Christological question in the most proper sense, the question of how divinity and humanity are distinct yet united in the God-man, became central only at the end of the fourth century. It presupposed the settlement of two questions, concerning the true and integral humanity of Christ, and concerning his true and perfect divinity. From the earliest days both divinity and humanity had been called in question. About the end of the first century the Ebionites considered Jesus to be a mere man, and Paul of Samosata in the third century seems to have defended an Adoptionism which left room for a very loose union between Jesus and God. In the fourth century Arianism denied the perfect consubstantiality of Son and Father, thus reducing Christ, even in his "divine" aspect, to the status of the noblest of creatures. The earliest form of attack on the humanity of Christ was Docetism, the view, especially of the Gnostics, that his body, human birth, and sufferings were only apparent. In the fourth century Apollinarianism, along with Arianism, denied the spiritual component of the Savior's humanity by insisting that the divine Word assumed in Christ the function which the human mind fulfills in other men.

Each of these heresies was met in turn by firm opposition from the Church and her orthodox teachers. Ignatius of Antioch is already, in the post-apostolic Church, a vigorous opponent of Docetism, and shows how our salvation is essentially dependent upon the presence in the Savior of a true human body subject to suffering and death. Paul of Samosata is condemned by the synod of Antioch in 268. Arianism finally succumbs through Nicaea (325) and the great struggle of the fourth century, in which Athanasius and the Cappadocians are the champions of orthodoxy. Apollinarianism is condemned at Rome in 382 and in the first Council of Constantinople in 381; prominent among its adversaries were the Cappadocian Fathers as well as the school of Antioch, both of which groups argued from the soteriological consequences of denying a human mind in Christ.

And so, by the end of the fourth century, it is clear that true and perfect divinity, true and integral humanity, are to be found in the God-man. But now the real Christological question begins to be placed: what is the relationship of divinity and humanity in Christ? Are they to be conceived as related by indwelling? Do they constitute an identical nature? Is it the eternal Word who is born, suffers and dies, or are these human predicates to be ascribed to a man who, though intimately united with the Word and assumed by him, is distinct from him, as one "he" is distinct from another "he"? Such is the issue now raised between the two great Christological schools of Alexandria and Antioch. The former school, represented most prominently by Cyril of Alexandria, maintained a Word-flesh or "descending" Christology, according to which the Word takes to himself and makes his own a human body. One weakness of this school was that it made little room for the human mind of Christ in its conception of how Christ saved us. This weakness, discernible in such Alexandrians as Justin, Athanasius and Cyril, brought Apollinarius, as we have seen, to the point of denying a human mind in Christ. The strength of Alexandria was in its insistence on the unity of the God-man. He who died on the cross and he who is eternally born from the Father are one and the same he. Cyril insisted that this was not the same as saying that divinity died on the cross, and he was quite willing, when pressed, to use a two-nature terminology. Some of his followers, however, notably Dioscorus and Eutyches, pushed the union of natures to the point of identity.

In the school of Antioch, represented by Diodore of Tarsus, Theodore of Mopsuestia, Nestorius and John of Antioch, a quite different approach to Christ was taken. Reacting against the Apollinarist and Arian truncating of the humanity, they insisted that Mary's Son was perfect in soul and body. Fearful of enmeshing the Godhead itself in the limitations of human life, and suspicious of such expressions as *theotokos,* Nestorius brought this Antiochene Christology into open conflict with Alexandria. Cyril triumphed at Ephesus (431), but when John of Antioch, who did not share the extremism of Nestorius, refused to accept this decision, Cyril and John arrived at a compromise formulation in 433 which temporarily brought peace. After the death of Cyril, however, the dissatisfaction of his followers precipitated another crisis, which led to the Council of Chalcedon in 451. . . .

Historically, Chalcedon turned out to be far from definitive. The two later Councils at Constantinople testify to the continuation of basic differences. The fifth ecumenical Council in 553, which condemned the doctrine of Antiochenes long since dead, was an effort on the part of the emperor Justinian to bring reconciliation with the Monophysites. It brought no substantial doctrinal advance. In the following century, a similar effort at reconciliation led some to speak of one will and operation in Christ. Pope Honorius was drawn in by the movement, but eventually the sixth Council rejected the idea, and extended Chalcedon's two-nature doctrine to a doctrine of two wills and operations.

The theological context of these two Councils was formed by various attitudes toward Chalcedon itself. The Monophysites firmly rejected its two-nature doctrine, and claimed to be faithful to Cyril in so doing. Good scholars today maintain that the doctrine, as distinct from the terminology, of the Monophysites, is quite compatible with Chalcedon. There was, of course, the party which stoutly defended Chalcedon. But a *via media* also emerged, known today as neo-Chalcedonianism, which sought to resolve the conflict by employing *both* a one-nature and a two-nature terminology. In Christological speculation, perhaps the most significant advance was that of Leontius of Byzantium, with his teaching that the human nature of Christ, while not an *hypostasis,* is not *anhypostatos,* but is rather *enhypostatos*[2]; i.e., its subsistence in the Word eminently confers upon it all that it would otherwise have were it a merely human hypostasis. In the West, the most significant effort at Christological speculation is that of Boethius, whose celebrated definition of person was to form a base for the scholastic effort at penetrating the mystery of the Incarnation. The West also saw, at the very end of the patristic period, the relatively brief heresy

[2] Editor's note. *Hypostasis*—substance or subsistent being; *anhypostasis*—not a substance or subsistent being; *enhypostasis*—"within" a subsistent being.

of Spanish Adoptionism, a recurrence of the Nestorian tendency which had at least a semblance of support in the traditional Latin Christology, which had always been partial to *"Assumptus Homo"* formulations [i.e., to the Antiochene Christology wherein the eternal Son "assumed" into himself a man, Jesus].

Medieval speculation on the basic constitution of Christ assumed at first a form greatly influenced by logic or dialectics. Peter Lombard's listing of three opinions, which came to be known respectively as the *"Assumptus"* theory, the *"Subsistence"* theory, and the *"Habitus"* theory, became a classic *locus* for Christological inquiry. One can discern, in the various views, a continuation of the Alexandrian-Antiochene tensions. With the thirteenth century, metaphysics displaces logic as main source of the tools for speculation on the constitution of Christ. The Christological problem is now placed in terms of nature and person, but also of essence and existence, supposit and subsistence, etc. St. Thomas makes it clear that, among the three positions listed by Peter Lombard, only the *"Subsistence"* theory is orthodox. St. Thomas' own conception of the basic structure of Christ is more Alexandrian than Antiochene, and in this respect contrasts somewhat with that of Duns Scotus. The disciples of the two great medieval theologians have kept alive, in several speculative systems, the predominant emphases of the masters. One may say that, by and large, one aspect of the Catholic tradition leads from Cyril of Alexandria through Thomas Aquinas to the several Thomist Christologies of today, whereas another leads from Antioch and the Christology of the Latin Fathers through Duns Scotus to the views of modern Scotists and Suarezians. It would not be unfair to say that the former line has had the ascendancy; but the perseverance of the Antiochene strain may show that no system has as yet achieved a fully satisfactory explanation of the mystery. The Reformation, while it shied away from scholastic speculations, was concerned with the basic Christological question in connection with the articles of Christian faith and also with the Real Presence. The Reformers were at one among themselves and with their Catholic adversaries in accepting Chalcedon.

Logical Consequences of the Mystery: Communicatio Idiomatum. The mystery of the one and many in Jesus Christ has historically been approached under several different formalities. . . . Basic to all such questions is the general one of the so-called *communicatio idiomatum:* may we attribute divine properties to the man Jesus and human properties to the eternal Son of God? . . . As was to be expected, the Monophysites made a good deal of mutual predication of properties while the Nestorians considered it to be at best a loose way of speaking. The latter preferred the terminology of indwelling and *"Assumptus homo"*; before the conceptual and linguistic clarifications of late patristic and of medieval times such terminology is not unknown also in orthodox circles. Several of the Fathers, e.g., John Damascene, not only employ the *communicatio idiomatum* but formulate norms for its proper use. The Middle Ages, with its weakness for dialectics, pursued the question of proper speech about Christ in great detail, asking such questions as whether Christ as man was anyone or anything or nothing. The Reformers were led by the question of the Real Presence to discuss the *communicatio idiomatum,* which Luther understood very realistically as resulting in a certain ubiquity to the humanity of Christ; Calvin and Zwingli were more Antiochene in this regard.

Sonship, Natural and Adoptive. Another touchstone for Christological orthodoxy was the predication of sonship of Jesus Christ. How many sons of God were there in Christ? Might one speak of adoptive sonship with respect to the man Jesus or the human nature of the God-man? Adoptionism in various forms has always been a temptation. . . . Adoptionism is implicit in the Ebionite conception of Jesus as a mere man, and Paul of Samosata conceives that God (modalistically understood) adopted the man Jesus as his Son. Diodore of Tarsus seems to have held two sons in Christ, one the son of David, the other the Son of God. Both Theodore and Nestorius, however, reject the imputation of teaching a double sonship. . . . [The fault of the] later Adoptionism of eighth century Spain, . . . as Alcuin pointed out, was an inability to distinguish grace and adoption; the former predication does not attribute human personality to Jesus, but the latter does, since the very notion of adoption implies a person who is not a natural son. The first of the three opinions listed by Peter Lombard is implicitly Adoptionistic. Later scholastics, Durandus, Biel, Suarez and Vasquez, looking to safeguard the true humanity, have wished to speak of adoption in addition to natural sonship, or of a double natural sonship; these views have won little or no support. . . .

The Human Will and Operations of Christ. The Christological debates of the classic period centered about the basic notions of person, hypostasis, and nature. This was not to say that the more dynamic aspects of Christ's humanity, the sphere of the operational, volitional, and intellectual, were absent from the discussions. Certainly the presence of a human mind (*nous*) was central in the polemic against Arianism and Apollinarism. And one may recall the famous phrase of the *Tome* of Leo, "Each aspect (*forma*) performs its own acts in cooperation with the other . . . ," which aroused initial opposition at Chalcedon. But it was really only a few centuries after Chalcedon that the principle of duality of nature was explicitly extended into the realm of will and operation by a series of official declarations culminating in the sixth ecumenical Council at Constantinople in 681. This definition was the last major phase of the dialectic which, beginning at Ephesus in 431, had seen the emphasis swing from Alexandrian (Cyril and Ephesus) to Antiochene (Leo and Chalcedon), back to Alexandrian (second Constantinople), and finally to Antiochene in the action of 681 against the Monothelites. . . . What, one may ask, balanced off the affirmation of duality of wills and operations? Perhaps the notion, never solemnly defined but accepted by tradition despite a checkered career, of theandric operation, which contains, implicitly at least, the reminder that though human will and operation are distinct from divine will and operation in the God-man, it is one and the same person who is willing and acting through both natures. The medieval scholastics, especially St. Thomas, will further refine the relationship of humanity and divinity on this dynamic level by applying the notion of instrument to the humanity of Christ and its operations. . . .

The Knowledge and Consciousness of Christ. The implications of the Incarnation for the human knowledge of the God-man were in the Christian consciousness from the very beginning. And from the very beginning Christian theology had to wrestle with two series of New Testament texts, one attributing to Christ the fullness of knowledge, a unique intimacy with the Father, and extraordinary gifts of prophecy and clairvoyance, the other speaking of growth in wisdom, of wonder and ignorance, and even giving rise to the suspicion of error. Patristic reflection on these texts was conditioned very largely by current polemics as well as by basic Christological positions. Where the Arians appealed to the Scriptural assertions of the ignorance of the Son of Man as confirmation of their insistence that he was only the highest of creatures, the orthodox Fathers replied in various ways. Antioch could answer in terms of a complete human nature, body and soul, in which limitations of knowledge were possible; it is not surprising to find Theodore stressing the progress of Christ in knowledge. But even the Alexandrian Fathers, including Athanasius, were willing to admit ignorance in the human intellect of Christ, explaining it as part of the kenosis [or "emptying" of Christ's divinity, cf. Gal 2:19]. Sometimes, however, there is a greater reluctance to accept such limitations, and the pertinent Scripture texts are explained as not demanding more than a feigned or social ignorance. With the passage of time, the tendency was to extend, rather than limit, the perfection of human knowledge in Christ. This is seen, in the West, in Augustine, Fulgentius and Gregory the Great, and the tendency was continued in the Middle Ages, when the idea of the beatific vision in the earthly Christ and that of infused knowledge clearly emerged. Some scholastics were even led to diminish unduly the role of experiential knowledge. The doctrine of the threefold human knowledge, *scientia beata, infusa, experimentalis,* became common in the schools. The last century and the present have approached the human intellect of Christ from the viewpoint of consciousness and psychological personality. Protestant theologians have been quite willing to acknowledge a growth in Messianic and (when they held the divinity of Christ) divine consciousness; the same is true of Modernism. One finds the teaching Church in the last several decades wary of such conceptions, but Catholic theologians have remained free to discuss the question of a double psychological ego in Christ, and to maintain a growth in his conceptual self-awareness during his pilgrim phase. . . .

The Development of Soteriology

Christian reflection on the saving work of Christ has had a far different history than Christology in the narrow sense. No controversy in soteriology has assumed such major proportions as to require conciliar definition. The passages in Trent which speak of Christ's merit, satisfaction, and sacrifice, are rather incidental, at least as soteriological pronouncements, to other concerns. Lesser magisterial utterances are rather rare. The Christian consciousness, so divided where there was question of the basic structure of the God-man, is at one in acknowledging that he is the Savior of the world.

This does not mean that controversy has been absent from the scene. One may say that the history of soteriology has gradually disclosed the presence of two opposite tendencies. The first has looked upon the work of Christ from the viewpoint of a "descending" soteriology. Christ is seen as representing the Father in the world of men, and attention is focused on the direct effects of his life, teaching, and doctrine on men who come under his influence. Where this approach is exclusive, it takes the form of one of several "subjective" or "moral" theories of salvation in Christ. This first approach is characteristic of the Alexandrian school (which, however, does not exclude "objective" redemption), of Abelard, and of liberal Protestantism. It is in contrast with the viewpoint of an "ascending" soteriology, which looks at Christ as man facing the Father and representing the race of mankind in making amends for its sins. This approach, generally designated as "objective," is especially characteristic of the Western Fathers, of St. Anselm and generally of the post-medieval Catholic tradition. Like the "subjective" approach, it has various forms, which assume an extreme character when the innocent Christ is depicted as appeasing an angry God, feeling his wrath, or being guilty and punished in the literal sense in place of sinful men. One may say that Catholic orthodoxy desires an integral soteriology which will include both the descending and ascending aspects, both objective and subjective elements in man's redemption.

Besides looking in the development of soteriology for the above tendencies, the student should be aware of other questions: whether the saving act is attributed to God (the Father), to Christ in his divinity, or to Christ in his humanity; what kind of solidarity (moral, juridical, ontological) is conceived to exist between the Savior and the saved; what images and metaphors are used to express man's liberation from Satan; what divine attributes are stressed (love, mercy, justice, wisdom, power); what human analogues are employed (e.g., healing, teaching, rescue) in order to convey the rich and inexpressible mystery of our salvation in Christ.

Of the patristic period it may be said in general that we find a wide variety of soteriological images and analogies, based for the most part on Scripture while employing Platonic and Stoic conceptions as tools of expression. Anything like a treatise on soteriology distinct from other aspects of the Christian economy is absent. . . . Soteriology is a touchstone for Christological (and Trinitarian) orthodoxy. Three aspects of redemption are most prominent: (1) the enlightenment that has come to mankind in the darkness of sin through the divine Word, his teaching and example; (2) the restoration of man to immortality by the physical contact of divinity in the Word with the humanity of the Savior, which mystically contains all men; (3) the liberating victory of Christ over Satan achieved in accordance with justice and through the redemptive power of the blood of Christ.

The theme of redemption by illumination is especially prominent in the Fathers before Nicaea. This is so particularly of Justin, who employs his favorite conception of Christ as the Word to develop the theme, and Clement of Alexandria, for whom Christ is the divine teacher. Irenaeus centers his soteriology on the second-

Adam motif, in which, of course, his doctrine of recapitulation is most distinctive; he is followed especially by Methodius and Hippolytus. The victory over Satan is prominent, needless to say, in all the early Fathers, but it is Origen who gives the beginning of the theory of the devil's rights and of the notion that the blood of Christ was paid in ransom to Satan on behalf of enslaved man. The *Dialogue of Adamantius* vigorously rejects this conception, as will Gregory of Nazianzus later. It would be wrong to overlook, finally, the steady tradition which looks upon the death of Christ as a sacrifice; the influence of Scripture is strong here, as may be seen, for example, in Melito and Origen.

In the period between Nicaea and Chalcedon, so crucial for Trinitarian and Christological development, soteriology was always present as a normative force. What finally emerged from the controversies with Arians, Apollinarists, Nestorians, and Monophysites, was the conviction that our salvation depended upon the assumption (understood as a substantial union) of a true and integral humanity by the Word who is truly and perfectly God. In the East, this exigency was conceived not as a purely extrinsic one deriving from a choice by God of one of many possible ways of redemption, but as somehow inherent in the very creation of man according to God's image and the intrinsic corruption that had come to mankind as a result of Adam's sin. Athanasius is perhaps the leading exponent of this physico-mystical conception of our redemption; he is especially concerned to show how the experience of death by the God-man has destroyed death for all men. The Cappadocians likewise explain our salvation in these terms. For Gregory of Nazianzus, writing against Apollinarianism, the rule of redemption is the saving of like by like, so that our human minds, which were principally involved in sin, are saved only if Christ assumed a human mind. Gregory of Nyssa also applies his speculative genius to explaining the redemption by affirming inclusion of all men in Christ, conceived in Platonic terms. Cyril of Alexandria continues the tradition, and in him especially we see the link between the redemptive incarnation and our entry into its participation by baptism and the Eucharist. On a less profound level soteriology and the sacraments are linked in the catecheses of Cyril of Jerusalem. The school of Antioch, as represented by Theodore of Mopsuestia, places great stress on the freedom and obedience of the Savior, which liberated us from sin and death.

It must not be thought that the physico-mystical conception of redemption among the Greek Fathers was the effort of speculative minds to demythologize the Scriptural portrayal of salvation. The victory of Christ over Satan remains prominent, and this is conceived, notably by Gregory of Nyssa, in terms of ransom through the blood of Christ paid to Satan. His friend Gregory of Nazianzus rejects this notion, however. The notions of our salvation by way of sacrifice and of example also continue to be exploited.

In the Western soteriology of the period, there are indications, especially in Hilary (but also in Augustine and Leo), of influence from the Greek physico-mystical notion. But the West was more inclined toward the juridical and, though Tertullian did not apply his notion of satisfaction to salvation in Christ, the West does conceive of our redemption as an atonement wrought in justice. Augustine, as always, is an interesting figure, for he combines the descending and ascending aspects of redemption; the two aspects will tend to become separated in the Middle Ages. The descending aspect is expressed especially in his insistence on the example of God's humility, which cures the pride of man; the ascending aspect by his conception of the vicarious sacrifice of the God-man on our behalf. All the while the theme of victory over Satan and the payment of the ransom to him continues to be used in the Western Fathers.

In the Middle Ages, the ascending aspect of redemption achieves primacy, thanks especially to St. Anselm. Picking up St. Augustine's stress on vicarious sacrifice, and intent on excluding a gross conception of our redemption from Satan by the blood of Christ, the *Cur Deus homo* presents the classic development of the notion of satisfaction, arguing that only the death of a God-man was adequate to atone for the quasi-infinite offense offered to God by man's sin. A great deal has been written on this theory, and Anselm's work has been, with St. Thomas, the principal medieval influence on subsequent development. . . . It had shortcomings, however. . . . It was inevitable that it should provoke disagreement. It was Abelard who picked up the other facet of Augustine's soteriology, and exploited the saving power of the example of love given us by Christ. Since Abelard gave the appearance of rejecting objective redemption, he was opposed, notably by the Council of Sens and by St. Bernard. The latter himself placed great stress on the redemptive power of the example of Christ, but felt compelled to refute Abelard. He also advanced beyond Anselm by showing how the union of Christ with his mystical body lies at the base of vicarious satisfaction. This same stress on the solidarity of head and members is prominent in St. Thomas, who comes closer than Anselm to an integral synthesis. Since his Christology drew both from the Augustinian tradition and from the Greek Fathers, it was natural that he should incorporate into his soteriology elements of both traditions. . . .

Underlying the soteriology of St. Thomas there is a conception of solidarity between Christ, the head, and us, his members. But there is, more profoundly, a basic conception of God and of man's relationship with God which makes it possible to integrate the descending and ascending aspects of the redemption, and to indicate that it is a work both of divine communicative love and of divine justice. . . . Such a view might seem at first glance to weaken to the point of dissolution the notions of sin as offense, of satisfaction, of an objective redemption in which divine justice as well as divine love is manifested. But there are good grounds for thinking that we have here a demythologizing of Biblical, patristic and Anselmian soteriology which leaves the essentials of faith intact.

Not every type of mind, however, is willing to speak of salvation in the rather austere terms of St. Thomas (who himself does not always avoid the familiar metaphors). It was natural that the Reformers, feeling as they did about scholasticism, should wish to return to the Biblical and patristic images. Luther and Calvin did so in language which, if taken exactly, makes Christ the object of divine wrath and our substitute in bearing the punishment of sin. Though post-Reformation Catholic theology was too much under the influence of St. Thomas to accept such conceptions, a good many popular presentations of the atonement have had much in common with the Reformers. In the Protestant tradition, the liberal theologians of the last century, following the lead given earlier by Socinus (against whom Grotius had reacted), have tended to dismiss objective redemption entirely as leading necessarily to views incompatible with the love of God for mankind. Among Catholics, too, there has been a reaction against objective theories, and *Humani Generis* contains a brief warning against distorting the traditional notions of offense and satisfaction. More positively, there has been something of a return to the physico-mystical theme of the Greek Fathers, together with a desire to express our salvation in terms of sacramentality and sacrifice.

Creation and Redemption. New Testament soteriology had situated Christ the Savior in a threefold fashion: in the history of the chosen people, in the history of the entire human race (the Pauline theme of the second Adam), and within the entire cosmos which somehow participates in man's sin and redemption. This reference of Christ to humanity as a whole and to creation is never absent from the history of soteriology, though emphases and approaches will vary considerably. We have seen that Irenaeus intimately relates the first and the second Adam in his notion of recapitulation. St. Augustine does the same, but in the context of the Pelagian dispute, and hence with a special insistence on the difference between the graces (*adiutoria*) of the paradisiacal and Christian economies. The Greek Fathers intimately relate creation and redemption, exploiting for this purpose the Scriptural notion of man as created according to the image of God.

Since the Fathers generally are concerned only with the actual order of salvation, they affirm very strongly the redemptive purpose of the Incarnation, sometimes to the extent of saying that if Adam had not sinned, Christ would not have come. They also speak of the Incarnation and redemptive death of Christ as if it were the only means by which God could, in his wisdom, goodness and justice, repair the sin of man. This same stress on the necessity of the Incarnation is found in Anselm. But scholasticism will shortly, particularly in St. Thomas, make it clear that the necessity is an hypothetical one, that the incarnation is an exigency neither of God's nature nor of the nature of man, and that, even consequent upon the sin of man, God could have restored him, absolutely speaking, without the supreme condescension of sending his own Son to suffer and die.

Christian tradition had always insisted on the redemptive purpose of the Incarnation, and on the primacy of the God-man in the universe. Scholastic theology sought a further understanding of the revelation by seeking to relate these two truths. The question was put in its now classic form as the question whether, if Adam had not sinned, Christ would have come? St. Thomas and the tradition which follows him have given a negative answer, while Scotus and his followers have answered affirmatively. Each side has sought to safeguard one of the two indispensable elements of tradition, namely, that Christ came into the world to redeem us, and that Christ is the center and head of the entire creation. Centuries of dispute have led some on both sides to seek some middle ground, and sometimes to acknowledge that the question has been badly placed. If we avoid attributing to God any multiple-stage planning of the world, and if the focus is kept on the actual created order rather than on some hypothetical order, we may affirm that Christ has, indeed, the primacy in creation and in God's salvific plan, and that he has it not only as incarnate but as redeeming. Incarnation in the present order is essentially redemptive Incarnation. It is the Christ of Calvary and of the empty tomb who possesses the primacy. The sign of the cross, the "O *felix culpa*," is what is most distinctive of the Christian economy. And God has willed that the present order be the manifestation not merely of his infinite goodness, but of his mercy toward the unworthy. No title, perhaps, better expresses the role and status of Christ in the mystery of salvation than that of the second Adam, nobler than the first (because God-man), achieving his fulfillment by the road of humble obedience leading to death and resurrection, when he is endowed with perfect dominion over the whole of creation, so that he may bring it back to the Father.

I

CHRIST IN THE POST-APOSTOLIC TRADITION AND IN THE FIRST APOLOGISTS

1. A. Grillmeier, S.J.,[1] notes that the post-Apostolic Fathers' vision of Christ was not so much the product of New Testament writings, not even of the Synoptic Gospels, as a continuation of the all-pervading influence of the experience of Christ's great reality. Liturgy played a great part in bringing alive a direct link with the Lord of Glory who transcends all history. Although this age represents a period of transition between simple faith and Christology proper, it already begins to reflect upon the *Mysterium Christi:* "the one and the many."

Within the limits marked out on the one hand by the Synoptists and on the other by John and Paul, the christology of the New Testament itself already displays considerable diversity. We have, for example, the contrast between a Messianic christology (the Acts speeches, the Synoptic Gospels) and the Johannine idea of the Logos; the factors which determine a portrayal

[1] Aloys Grillmeier, S.J., is an eminent German theologian educated at the Universities of Frankfurt, Rome (Gregorian), and Freiburg, where he received his doctorate in 1942. He has since taught at several Jesuit institutions, and is presently professor of History

of Christ may be salvation history (Synoptics, Romans, Galatians), cosmology (Ephesians, Colossians 1:15ff), liturgy (Hebrews), or apocalyptic (Apocalypse). The picture of Christ given by the New Testament already shows sometimes predominantly Judaistic, elsewhere predominantly Hellenistic features. It would, however, be a mistake to remain completely skeptical about the essential unity of the christological tradition because of such differences. Common to all sources is a firm recognition of Jesus' transcendence and his central position in the salvation history. This clearly rests on living experience (primarily of the Resurrection, but also quite simply of the words and actions of the Lord) and finds its climax in belief in the Lordship of God and the divinity of Christ. This single recognition, or this single experience, is also the bond which links the post-Apostolic and the Apostolic age. The general tendency of contemporary scholarship is to regard the possession of Holy Scripture as the only psychological bridge between the two epochs. With regard to the Old Testament and the way in which it is used, this is to some extent correct. The role of the canonical books of the New Testament, and particularly the position of the Synoptic tradition, which may lay prime claim to transmitting the words and deeds of the Lord, is a question all on its own.

At the time of the Apostolic Fathers, the New Testament writings, even the Synoptic Gospels, did not yet have the normative character which they were to acquire in the course of the second century, when the Canon was being formed. A detailed examination of the use of the Synoptic Gospels by the Apostolic Fathers has produced the following conclusion: "In this period, even our three Synoptic Gospels play a completely subordinate role as a source for the citing of synoptic sentences."[2] We are still in a period when the real motive force behind the tradition was the all pervading influence of a great reality of experience, the Christ event that is the life and teaching of Jesus Christ. The written Synoptic Gospels were not the only expression of this event nor were they the only way in which the reality might be possessed. The Church knew that she was in full possession of the words and deeds of the Lord and of his whole history, even independently of the written Gospels. In the Apostolic age, this full possession formed the basis of teaching and preaching, the basis of the Church's formulation of her proclamation of Christ, even the basis of the written Gospels, themselves meant as an expression of the one Gospel. This phase of the Christian tradition was therefore dominated by

---

of Dogma at Frankfurt. He was a *peritus* at Vatican II. He has authored and edited many patristic and theological works: *Der Logos am Kreuz* (1956), "Christologie," *Lexikon Für Theologie und Kirche,* II, 1156–1166 (1958), "Doketismus," *ibid.,* III (1959), 470 ff., *Das Konzil von Chalkedon* 1–111 (1951–62), etc. It is from his book *Christ in Christian Tradition* (tr. by J. S. Bowden, New York: Sheed and Ward, 1965) that this excerpt is taken, selectively, from pp. 36–41, 123–124.

[2] H. Köster, *Synoptische Überlieferung bei den Apostolischen Vätern* (Berlin, 1957), p. 257. E. Massaux, however, asserts that the Fathers of the second century used a distorted text of the New Testament and this restricts the part of oral tradition. Investigating the *Didache,* J.-P. Audet achieves a similar result to Köster: *La Didache, Instructions Apôtres* (Paris, 1958), pp. 166–186; cf. F.-M. Braun, *Jean le théologien* (Paris, 1958).

the living, oral proclamation. If this was accompanied by a consciousness of the Scriptures—as was, in fact, the case from the very beginning—prime concern was with the Old Testament. Thus in the immediate post-Apostolic age there was a Christ-tradition, but this was as direct a source for the Apostolic Fathers as it had been for the written Gospels.

If this oral tradition is also an integral part of the nature of the Church, the consciousness of the position of Scripture in it can develop further. This was the case from Justin onwards; "he already 'uses' the Gospels to a great extent. In Justin's writings, the sources of the synoptic tradition are almost exclusively our Gospels, and therefore the history of the tradition is in Justin for the first time a history of the exposition of our Gospels."[3] A multilinear development now begins. In combating Gnosis and its "traditions" the Church increasingly reflected upon its "one" tradition. This meant being committed to the canon of New Testament writings, though not of course simply to the written word, and in addition the formation of the creed and the stress on the *regula fidei* in teaching and in preaching. Thus even the didactic formulas acquired a special significance, although it was precisely this age which still permitted a considerable variation in them. The special position of the formula, which is already evident in the New Testament (1 Cor. 15), meant that the "hearing of the faith" played a great part. "Faith from hearing" (cf. Rom. 10: 9–15) corresponds to the clearly defined word, the formula, the formulated tradition, and makes a link reaching back to the revelation which was completed in Christ. The place of the "hearing of the faith" is catechesis, the sermon coming within the framework of the liturgy, which, through its holy signs, actions and rites, is itself a powerful support to tradition and the source of a particular tendency toward conservatism. Here it fulfils another special function which cannot be valued highly enough for the life of the Church: if the formulated tradition runs the risk of historicizing the picture of Christ and the whole reality of faith and objectifying it so that it becomes too impersonal, the living liturgy has the task of providing and bringing alive a direct link with the Lord of glory, the *Christus praesens,* which transcends all history. It is peculiarly well suited for achieving the transition from the formula to the inner, spirit-governed faith which must support everything.

Throughout the early Christian period we notice a great simplicity in formulas. It was this simplicity alone which could secure uniformity of preaching amid the deficient theological education of most of the Church's spokesmen and, above all, could keep heresy away from the Church. It is astonishing how the Church of the "illiterates" was able to cope with the powerful onslaught of Gnosis in the second century. Hippolytus gives us an example of an encounter between faithfulness to the formula of the Church and newly emerging heresy which would certainly apply to Christian preaching in preceding years as

[3] H. Köster, *Synoptische Überlieferung,* p. 267. F. E. Vokes, *The New Testament Today,* Oxford Conference, September 11–15th, 1961, sees the same situation reflected in the Didache and therefore dates it after 150.

well. Noetus of Smyrna came forward and declared that the words of Scripture concerning Father, Son, and Spirit are really said only of One, of one person. Therefore in Christ, the Son of the Father did not take the form of a servant. This constituted an attack on the fundamentals of the Christian proclamation. The matter was brought before the presbyters of the Church of Smyrna. They were confronted for the first time with a difficulty toward the solution of which centuries were to labor. But the presbyters did not resort to high theology; they contented themselves with the simple formula which they had heard:

> We too worship only one God, but as we understand it. We too hold Christ to be the Son of God, but as we understand it—who suffered as he suffered, died as he died, and rose again the third day and ascended into heaven and sits at the right hand of the Father, and will come to judge the living and the dead. This we say as we have learned. Thereupon they convicted him (Noetus) and expelled him from the Church, because he was carried to such a pitch of pride that he founded a sect.[4]

From this we see that already at this time the single framework of a christological confession forms, so to speak, the backbone of the Church's tradition about Christ, something in which she can find support. We must always take into consideration the presence of such a christological confession with belief in the Godhead and manhood of the one Lord, if we are to understand the development of the Church's teaching about Christ.[5] The author of the "Little Labyrinth," transmitted to us in extracts by Eusebius, includes even the Apologists, who certainly signify a new departure in theology, the emergence of a *théologie savante,* without further ado among the first simple witnesses of the Church's belief. They too describe Christ as God and acknowledge him as God and man.[6] We should also notice the hymns of the early Christian period, the *carmen Christo quasi Deo dicere secum invicem,* which is referred to by Pliny[7] as a mark of the primitive Church.

Certainly the massiveness of the *Mysterium Christi* continued to remain the source of impulses leading to new formulas and efforts to give new expression to the inexpressible. Men were conscious that the *Mysterium* was something beyond words. We will further find that the Church grasped the totality of the picture of Christ more in a kind of spiritual intuition than in words and formulas. For this reason, expressions could vary even to the point of formulas which apparently contradicted each other. The Church measured newly emerg-

---

[4] Hippolytus, *Antinoetus* 1, ed. P. Nautin, *Hippolyte,* Contre les hérésis (Paris, 1949) 235[18]–237[3]. C. H. Turner, "The blessed presbyters who condemned Noetus," *Journal of Theological Studies,* 23 (1922), 28–35.

[5] It is not our task here to sketch the history of the Creed in itself. See the excellent chapter in H. E. W. Turner, *The Pattern of Christian Truth* (London, 1954), pp. 309–386; J. N. D. Kelly, *Early Christian Creeds* (New York: Harper & Row, 1950). A good survey of the creeds is found in the new edition of H. Denzinger, *Enchiridion Symbolorum,* revised by A. Schönmetzer (1963), Nos. 1–76.

[6] Eusebius, *History of the Church,* V 28, 4.5. Mention is made of Justin, Mitiades, Tatian and more especially of Melito of Sardis and Irenaeus.

[7] C. Plinius Sec. Min., *Epist.* lib. 10, 96, 7.

ing doctrines as much by her intuition as by her formula and made from them new fixed forms for her proclamation.

The incentive for this came less from within than from without, not least from the Church's encounter with the pagan world and its philosophy. The need to construct a *théologie savante* emerged from this encounter with pagan philosophy. Both the concepts and the language with which Christian doctrine was presented had to be developed further. The first aim was a clarification of the relation of Father and Son in the *Mysterium Christi*. Thus, the second century introduced the great task of the patristic period, that of achieving a better grasp of the data of revelation with the help of pagan philosophy. This proved to be both a powerful driving force to theological progress and a favorite starting point for heresies. It had important consequences for christology: the dynamic presentation of the mission of Christ in the economy of salvation was impregnated more and more with a static-ontological awareness of the reality of Christ as God and man. This is shown by the later creeds, as, for example, in the *homoousios* ("of one substance") of Nicaea, but also in formulas as early as Melito of Sardis and Tertullian. We can see, and it will become still clearer as we proceed, that here there was a special opportunity for metaphysics and therefore for the Greek way of thinking.

In this way the first phase of the oldest tradition was developed into something new, which has two main characteristics: the shaping of formulas and of a canon, and theological reflection. The post-biblical era of Christian theology, viewed as a whole, is a typical period of transition. Subsequent ages are inclined to value such periods lightly. The witnesses of the second century have not indeed yet the brilliance of the great names of the third, fourth and fifth centuries, the Patristic age proper. But their nearness to life is all the more valuable, as later we have the danger of abstract teaching. . . . Problems concerned with the popular image of Christ . . . are revealed even in the first christological heresies. The christology of the great Church, however, finds its real expression in the defenders of the divinity and manhood of Jesus against Docetism and Gnosis, Judaism and paganism. Here we are on the way from economic to ontological christology, or the doctrine of two natures, but at the same time, we also find the first influential examples of christocentric salvation history. Simple christological formulas stand alongside the first contacts of Christian theologians with pagan philosophy. No epoch of christology displays such numerous and different currents of thought as the second century. . . .

The second century is a link between the Apostolic age and the emergence of the christological problem proper and . . . (has) theological significance. This significance seems to us to lie in the following characteristics:

1. Nourished completely by the tradition of the primitive Church, its interpretation of the Old Testament, and more and more too, by the express use of the writings of the New Testament, this century made belief in Jesus Christ as true God and true man and belief in the *one* Christ prevail with equal weight in totally different strata of Church life. Jewish Christians and Gentile Christians, popular

christology and already more eminent spirits like Ignatius of Antioch, Justin and Irenaeus, put forward the same faith in Christ, despite all the differences. This faith sought expression in doctrine, in creed and in picture. The struggle against the Docetists and the Adoptionists gives rise to stronger stress on the Godhead and the manhood in Christ. The dispute with Gnosticism brings quite clearly into sight the basic features of the salvation history and the Christian Redeemer-figure.

2. Despite this emphatic delineation of the God-manhood of Jesus Christ, there is still no doctrine of two natures in the technical sense. Only Melito makes the first timid beginnings. The simple language of the Church's proclamation is retained, although it is in fact expressing just what the technical language of the two-nature doctrine is to say later. It is for precisely this reason that the second century, seen from the point of view of the history of tradition, is so valuable. Because the love of the Mysteries of the life of Jesus and the view of salvation history is still so much alive, because the unity of history is supported by typology and exegesis of the Old Testament, the portrait of Christ in the second century still seems dynamic, and not static, despite all the stress on Godhead and manhood and an often monotonous antithetical way of making christological statements.

3. Nevertheless, the second century is already brought up against the christological problem proper in two ways:

a) The problem of the relationship between the Father and the Logos emerges (Justin; the Apologists). . . .

b) Already round about 178, Celsus was putting quite pointedly the question how Godhead and manhood could be united in the one Christ. He confronted the theology of the Church with a dilemma—either Docetism or a change in the Godhead. In other words, either the Incarnation of Christ is only a semblance, or it means that the Godhead is changed: "Either God really changes himself, as they say, into a mortal body . . . or he himself is not changed, but makes those who see him think that he is so changed. But in that case he is a deceiver and a liar."[8]

So the second century is already confronted with problems as difficult as any generation of Christian theologians had to solve. The doctrine of the "one person in two natures," much abused because of its technical terms, was the only way out of the dilemma raised by Celsus. The question was whether God had really entered history while still remaining God, the same problem with which contemporary theology is still engaged, though in a different way, in its debate with R. Bultmann. The substance of Christianity was at stake.

2. A. Harnack[1] maintains that early Gentile Christianity's faith in Jesus found its expression in titles such as "angel," "servant," etc., which sprang from the fundamental idea that he was the "Christ" called by

[8] Cf. Origen, *Contra Celsum,* IV, 18.

[1] Adolf Harnack died in 1939. Professor of Church History at the University of Berlin, and Fellow of the Berlin Royal Academy, he is known above all for his *History of Dogma,* first published in Germany in 1885. This excerpt is from the *Outlines of the History of Dogma,* tr. by Edwin Knox Mitchell (Boston: Beacon Press, 1957), pp. 49–54.

God and entrusted with a task. Out of the usage of the title "Son of God" slowly grew the idea that Jesus belongs to the sphere of divinity. Facts appertaining to the real or imaginary history of Jesus were given exaggerated significance. Naive Greek philosophy began to exercise its influence.

Faith Knowledge was above all a knowledge of *God* as the only supernatural, spiritual and almighty being: God is the Creator and Ruler of the world and is therefore the Lord. But inasmuch as he created the world as a beautiful, well-ordered whole (monotheistic theory of nature) for the sake of man, he is at the same time the God of goodness and of redemption, and only through the knowledge of the identity of the Creator and Redeemer God does faith in God as the Father reach its perfection. Redemption, however, was necessary, because mankind and the world in the very beginning fell under the dominion of demons. A general and acceptable theory in regard to the origin of this dominion did by no means exist; but the conviction was fixed and universal, that the present condition and course of the world is not of God, but of the devil. Still, faith in the almighty Creator, and hope in the restoration of the earth did not allow *theoretical* dualism to make any headway and *practical* dualism dominated. The world is good and belongs to God, but the present course of it is of the devil. Thus men's thoughts oscillated between the conception of the world as a beautiful and orderly whole, and the impression of the present evil course of things, of the baseness of the sensuous and of the dominion of demons in the world.

Faith in Jesus Christ as the Redeemer was closely identified with faith in *God* as the Redeemer. Jesus is Lord (*Kyrios*) and Savior (*Sōtēr*) like God, and the same words were often used without indicating whether the reference was to him or to God; for in the Revealer and Mediator of salvation (Jesus), the Author (God) is represented (the purpose of salvation and the revelation of it coincide); prayer, however, was made to God through Christ. This title given to Jesus ("Christ") became indeed a mere name, since there was no real knowledge of the meaning of "Messiah." Therefore the Gentile Christians were obliged through other means to find expressions for the dignity of Jesus; but they possessed in the full eschatological traditions valuable reminiscences of the original apprehension of the Person of Jesus. In the confession that God has chosen and specially prepared Jesus, that he is the "Angel" and "Servant" of God, and that he shall judge mankind, and similar expressions, other utterances were made concerning Jesus, which sprang from the fundamental idea that he was the "Christ" called of God and entrusted with an office. In addition there was a traditional, though not common, reference to him as "The Teacher."

The title "Son of God" (not "Son of Man") was traditional, and was maintained without any wavering. Out of this grew directly the conception that Jesus belongs to the sphere of God and that one must think of him "as with God" (II Clem. 1). In this phrasing of it the indirect *theologia Christi, in regard to which there was no wavering,* found expression in classical forms. It is necessary to think of Jesus as one thinks of God, (1) because he is the God-exalted Lord and Judge, (2) because he brought true knowledge and life and has delivered mankind from the dominion of demons, from error and sin, or will deliver them. Therefore he is Savior, Lord our God, Son of God and God, Lord and God, but not *the* God. He is "our Hope," "our Faith," the High-Priest of our prayers, and "our Life."

Starting from this basis there were diverse theories in regard to the Person of Jesus, which, however, all bore a certain analogy to the naive and the philosophical Greek "theologies," but there were no universally accepted "*doctrines.*" We may distinguish here two principal types: Jesus was looked upon as the man whom God had chosen and in whom the Spirit of God (the Godhead itself) dwelt; he was, in accordance with his own testimony, adopted by God and clothed with authority (*Adoption Christology*); or Jesus was looked upon as a heavenly spiritual Being (the highest heavenly spiritual Being next to God), who became incarnate and after the completion of his work upon the earth returned to the heavens (*Pneumatic Christology;* the transition here to the *Logos Christology* was easy). These two different Christologies (the Deified man and the Divine Being appearing in the form of a man) were however brought closely together so soon as the implanted Spirit of God in the man Jesus was looked upon as the pre-existent Son of God (Hermas), and so soon as the title "Son of God," as applied to that spiritual Being, was derived from his (miraculous) incarnation—both, however, were maintained. Notwithstanding these transition forms the two Christologies may be clearly distinguished: In the one case the election (emphasis upon the miraculous occurrence at the baptism) and the exaltation to God are characteristic; in the other, a *naive* docetism; for as yet there was no two-nature theory (Jesus' divinity was looked upon as a gift, or else his human form as a temporary tabernacle). The declaration: Jesus was a mere man was undoubtedly from the beginning and always highly objectionable; likewise was the denial of the "incarnation" (*en sarki*); but the theories which identified the Person of Jesus with the Godhead (*naive modalism*) were not cast aside with the same assurance. A formal *theory* of the identity of God and Jesus does not seem to have been widespread in the Church at large. The acceptance of the existence at least of *one* heavenly, eternal, spiritual Being close to God was demanded outright by the Old Testament Scriptures, as men understood them, so that all were constrained to recognize *this,* whether or not they had any basis for reconciling their Christology with that heavenly Being.

The pneumatic Christology was always found wherever men gave themselves to the study of the Old Testament and wherever faith in Christ as the complete revelation of God was the foremost thought, i.e., it is found in *all* the important and educated Christian writers (not in Hermas, but in Clement, Barnabas, Ignatius, etc.). Because this Christology seemed to be directly demanded by the Old Testament as then expounded, because it alone united and reconciled creation and redemption, because it furnished the proof that the world and religion have the same Divine Source, because the most esteemed primitive Scriptures championed it, and, finally, because it gave room for the introduction of the Logos-speculation, it was the Christology of the future. The adoption Christology, however, proved itself insufficient over against the consideration of the relation of religion to the cosmos, to humanity and its history, as well as over against the Old Testament. And the advocates of the pneumatic Christology did not set it forth as a doubtful theologumenon; their expositions of it (Clement, Ignatius, Barnabas, Justin), on the contrary, indicate that they could not conceive of a Christianity without faith in the divine spiritual Being, Christ. On the other hand, in the liturgical fragments and prayers that have come down to us, we find little reference to the preexistence; it sufficed that Jesus is now the *Kyrios* to whom prayer may be addressed.

The representations of the work of Christ (Christ as teacher: Giving of knowledge, proclaiming of the new law; Christ as Savior: Giving of life, conquering of demons, forgiving of past sins in the time of error) were connected by some (following current tradition, using the Pauline Epistles) with his death and resurrection. By others they were affirmed without direct reference to these facts. Independent reflections upon the close union of the saving work of Christ with the facts set forth in his preaching are nowhere found; and yet the representation of the free endurance of suffering, of the cross, and of the blood of Christ, was accepted in many communities as a holy *mysterium,* in which the deepest wisdom and power of the Gospel is concealed (Ignatius), although the death on the cross and the forgiveness of sin were by no means everywhere (as in Clement, Polycarp and Barnabas) inseparably joined together (Hermas knows nothing whatever about such a union). The peculiarity and the individuality of the work of the historical Christ were moreover menaced by the idea that Christ had been the revealer of God in the Old Testament.

All the facts pertaining to the history of Jesus, the real and the imagined, received an exaggerated significance when reiterated in the work of instruction and when attacked by heretics. To the miraculous birth, death, resurrection, exaltation and return, was added definitely now the ascension on the fortieth day and, less definitely, the descent into hell, while the history of the baptism was more and more ignored. The reality of these occurrences was strongly emphasized; but they had not yet become "dogmas"; for they were neither inseparably connected with the idea of salvation, nor were they definitely outlined, nor was the *fantasie* restricted in its artistic exuberance.

3. M. Werner[1] believes that the primitive Christian Christ-Angel model continued to exercise great influence in Post-Apostolic Christology. It only had a decisive blow later on with the appearance of anti-Arian representations of Christ which reinterpreted the title "Son of God" in

[1] Martin Werner, professor of Systematic Theology and of the History of Doctrine and Philosophy at the University of Bern, is a well-known Protestant theologian and author. He has written several works, *Der protestantische Weg des Glaubens* (1955), *Die Entstehung des christlichen Dogmas* (1941), etc. It is from the translation of the latter (*The Formation of Christian Dogma,* by S. G. F. Brandon, New York: Harper and Bros., 1957) that this excerpt has been taken from pp. 131–137.

a literal sense. Angel-Christology and the Trinitarian Dogma of Nicaea are incompatible. Late Jewish angelology became a common presupposition to both Philonic Logos-ideology and Christian Logos-Christology.

The history of the Primitive Christian doctrine of Christ as a high angelic-being pursued its way in the Post-Apostolic period through successive stages. At first the view gradually subsided of its own accord and became problematical. Then, already profoundly shaken within, it had to endure finally a decisive assault during the Arian dispute of the fourth century. In that conflict it was bitterly attacked by the representatives of the new doctrine of Christ, which had emerged in the interval, and at last it was proscribed and suppressed as erroneous doctrine. This change of attitude was connected with the process of de-eschatologizing, which was brought about by the continuing delay of the *Parousia*. For the de-eschatologizing of the original doctrine of Christ's work of salvation indubitably entailed a corresponding change in the conception of the nature of his person. This necessarily followed from the fact that the nature of the personality of the Redeemer was conceived essentially in terms of the peculiar character of his mission and work.

It thus came to pass that the writers of the Post-Apostolic Church were no longer able to understand the most important Messianic designations and concepts. It was now thought possible to determine the meaning of the terms "Son of Man," "Christ" and "Son of God" directly from their literal sense. Accordingly, the title "Son of Man" was now no longer to signify the superhuman and supermundane, but just the humanity in Christ, and the person, whose son Christ was, became, from the time of Justin, the Mother, Mary. The designation "Christ" finally faded and dwindled away to the mere second half of the double name "Jesus Christ." Thus the way appeared open also to a reinterpretation, in a purely literal sense, of the title "Son of God." And it made it possible now, apparently, to conceive of the "Son" as being in some manner generated by the Father and like to Him in nature and substance.

But it was just at this point that further development was hindered by the subsequent effect of the oldest tradition, according to which the Christ was a heavenly being, of angelic kind. This meant that he was, in the last resort, a being, who in his supermundane essence was still, without question, subordinate to God. The memory of this ancient Christian conception was obviously preserved with care so long as the apocalypses, such as that of *Enoch,* were able to maintain their influence in Post-Apostolic Christianity. The fact was also clearly not without influence that within Judaism itself, or at least in certain Jewish circles during the Post-Apostolic period, the late-Jewish conception of the Heavenly Christ as a high angelic-being had been preserved and continued to be effective. . . . Post-Apostolic Christianity also adopted in this form the late Jewish conception of the Messiah as the highest leader of the angels of the supreme court of God in heaven. The assertion that Christ was the "angel of great counsel" of Isaiah 9:6 (in the Septuagint) is frequently met with in the Church writers of this period. It is expressly confirmed by Eusebius that this evaluation of Isaiah 9:6 as Scriptural evidence for the Angel-Christology, was derived from Jewish exegesis.[2] The "*angelus voluntatis tuae*" would even enter into the liturgy of the Eucharist.

Accordingly, in the Post-Apostolic period the appearance of angels in the Old Testament narrative, so far as they occurred in some way for the succour of men, had already begun to be interpreted as appearances of Christ. . . .

Lastly, the influence of the late Jewish speculation about the archangel Michael in the earlier period of Post-Apostolic Christianity helped to preserve the Angel-Christology; indeed it even provided new stimulus for the further development of Christology. In his day Wilhelm Bousset had already alluded to the fact, being the first to do so, in his writings about the "Antichrist." The figure of the archangel Michael had perhaps already influenced Philo's speculation about the Logos, and Philo had affected Christian authors of the Post-Apostolic period. In any case Philo did not identify the Logos with the Messiah, but with an archangel, and he predicated to him that which was appropriate to the archangel Michael. Thus the late Jewish speculation about Michael (which imparted Messianic traits to the archangel), the Philonic Logos doctrine, and the Post-Apostolic Logos-Christology appear in a sequence and indicate that the late Jewish doctrine of angels was their common presupposition. Hence, because the Christ of the oldest Christian dogma was a high angelic-being, as was the Philonic Logos, it was possible for him to be identified with the latter during the Post-Apostolic period in the course of the process of de-eschatologizing.

The Primitive Christian Angel-Christology caused its effect to be felt throughout the whole of Post-Apostolic Christianity, in the Logos-theology, Gnosis and Jewish Christianity, as also among the ordinary Gentile Christians.

The Christ, into whose status and being, according to the oldest teaching, Jesus had been raised and transformed by his resurrection, ranked also for Jewish Christianity of the Post-Apostolic period as a high angelic-being. According to the detailed account of Epiphanius, the Christ was reckoned by the Ebionites as one not generated but created by God and as the *Kyrios* over the angel-host, indeed the archangel appointed generally to be over all God's creatures. In particular, God had assigned to the archangel Christ the lordship in the "future aeon." That is the purest and most primitive form of the apocalyptic-eschatological Angel-Christology. With Elchasai Christ was called "Son of God," but he was set forth as an angel of human descent and of immense size and was understandably ranked as a "creature" (*ktisma*) of God. The Valentinians had characterized Christ as an angel-like being. The Valentinian Theodotus called Christ an "angel of the Pleroma," and told how that it was only from humility that he had appeared as a man and not as an angel. In this connection the angel-Christ was also called *Kyrios*. According to the account of Hippolytus, the Marcionite Apelles had ranked Christ as the fifth with four other supreme angels. With this Valentinian disciple

---

[2] Eusebius, *Praeparatio evangelica,* vii, 14 f.

of Marcion the angel Gabriel took the place of the Logos. Direct proof of the Gnostic identification of Christ with the angel Gabriel is forthcoming from the Gnostic *Book of Jeû* and the *Pistis Sophia.* In the *Sophia Jesus Christi* it is told how the Resurrected Redeemer had revealed himself as the "great angel of light."

But the literature of the Church also affords examples of the subsequent effects of the Angel-Christology. The *Epistola Apostolorum* causes Christ to appear as the angel Gabriel to Mary, and the archangels could represent the *Logos-Christus,* during his absence from the highest heaven, in the service which he rendered before God. The counterpart to this is afforded by an identification of Christ with the archangel Michael, an identification which is made in the *Shepherd of Hermas,* if not in a wholly consistent manner. In other respects also in *Hermas* the conception of Christ as a high angelic-being is clearly manifest. According to the early Christian writing *"Of the threefold fruits,"* Christ, as one of the seven archangels of God, was created "from fire" and exalted to the status of "Son." There is, incidentally, an ancient gem on which the seven archangels, of whom one is Christ, are indicated by name. The Angel-Christology recurs in some particularly popular variants in the edificatory literature of the apocryphal gospels. But the Church's theologians have also supplied examples. What has provided historians of doctrine for more than a century with an occasion for discussion has been the fact that Justin could conceive in one category the Logos-Son together with the "host of the other good angels, of like being to him," and that he set this angel-host, together with the Logos-Christ, before the (prophetic) Spirit. For Justin the Logos-Christ was, therefore, the *archistrategos,* the highest angel prince and leader of the angelic host. Christ figures as the *"princep exercitus angelorum"* in one of the Christological fragments of Melito. . . . In this connection an observation, published long ago but little regarded, should be recalled: "In Syria there was a solemn formula XMΓ (Christos, Michael, Gabriel), which can be recognized in epitaphs, on seal-stones, amulets, as well as on amphorae and such like, dating in part back to the fourth century."[3] It is thus possible on the ground of this trigram to describe the three names, Christos, Michael, Gabriel, as a trinitarian formula of the ancient Angel-Christology. . . .

We must devote special attention to the utterances of Methodius of Olympus. In the first place he often describes Christ as an archangel, once as the "first of the archangels." Then from him we learn of a piece of scriptural evidence for the Angel-Christology, which the Arians soon after brought into the field against the supporters of Nicaea and which demonstrably derived from the Gnostic exegesis of the Gospels. It concerns an explanation of the Parable of the Lost Sheep. Methodius sticks to the Matthean text (Mt 17:12–14), because herein the hundred sheep graze, not in the "wilderness" of the steppe, as with Luke, but on the mountains. These "mountains" are really heaven, the hundred sheep are the whole angelic-host, and the shepherd is the Logos-Christ, who leads as the *archistrategos* of the angelic-host, but who,

[3] Cf. W. Lucken, *Michael,* 1889, p. 118.

as an archangel, is himself one of these heavenly beings. But the hundredth sheep is Man, who originally belonged to the heavenly flock, but through the Fall had lost his way. Therefore the Logos-Archangel had left the heavenly host of the angels in order to rescue Man, who was lost upon earth.[4] That this exegesis goes back to the Valentinian interpretation of Luke[5] is evident from Irenaeus.

Of the subsequent existence of the Angel-Christology in the Latin West Novatian and Lactantius are preeminently the witnesses. Novatian calls Christ *angelorum omnium principem,* the chief prince of the angels.[6] Lactantius makes the equation: Christus-*spiritus-angelus.* In the *epiklesis* of the Mozarabitic Liturgy Christ is invoked as the "angel of peace and grace." We may mention here that the Holy Spirit was also often conceived of as an angel, e.g., in the *Ascensio Jesaiae,* by the Melchizedekites and by Elchasai. The original Angel-Christology was preserved longest among the sects. Trace of its further development can be followed from the Paulicians and Bogomils of the East to the mediaeval Catharists of the West. In the nineteenth century the Berlin Old Testament student, who was also editor of a church newspaper and an ecclesiastical politician, Ernst Wilhelm Hengstenberg, in his many-volumed work on the Christology of the Old Testament, concentrated upon the Early Christian identification of Christ with the angelic figures of the Old Testament, particularly the archangel Michael.

The significance of the Angel-Christology for the Post-Apostolic period, from the point of view of doctrinal history, lies in the fact that it stood in the way of the development of a homoousian doctrine of the Trinity in the later orthodox Nicene sense, owing to its fundamentally Subordinationist character. Angel-Christology and the Trinitarian dogma of Nicaea were in this respect absolutely incompatible. Hence the Angel-Christology was completely excluded on principle from the thought of the Church. . . .

4. K. Adam[1] finds in the *Shepherd of Hermas* the first traces of a primitive Christological speculation. This speculation is in line with that of later Apologists, namely, in terms of a duality and not of a trinity, and in terms of future Adoptionism. While the Apostolic Fathers were simply faithful witnesses to the Biblical proclamation, the Apologists used the dominant philosophy of the age to interpret it. Notwithstanding the many pitfalls of the Neoplatonic and Stoic doctrine of God, the Apologists held fast to their belief in Jesus' metaphysical status as the Son of God. Their soteriological estimation of Jesus' humanity led them to broach the question of its relationship to his divinity.

---

[4] Methodius, *Symposion,* i, 3; iii, 4; iii, 6.

[5] Irenaeus, *adv. haer.,* i, 8, 4.

[6] Novatian, *de trin.,* 11.

[1] Karl Adam has been one of the most influential Catholic theologians of the century. He was born in Bavaria in 1876 and was Professor of Theology at the Universities of Munich, Strasbourg, and Tübingen. His many works include *The Spirit of Catholicism, Christ Our Brother, The Son of God,* etc. This excerpt has been taken from pp. 179–183 of *The Christ of Faith,* tr. by Joyce Crick (New York: Pantheon Books, 1957).

Surveying the speculation of the early Fathers upon the mystery of Christ, we may recognize three stages in its development: the Christology of the Apostolic Fathers, the Apologists, and the theology subsequent to the Council of Nicaea.

The Apostolic Fathers. It is not difficult to understand why the Apostolic Fathers did little to interpret the Christological problem in the narrow sense; they were fully occupied with cherishing and protecting in the hearts of men the great new thing that was Christianity, and its faith in the Son of God become man. So what they had to say about the mystery of Christ was only a *paraphrase,* more or less detailed, of the Christology of the Bible. Some held more closely to the terminology of St. Paul, others to St. John, or they drew their formulations from both. St. John's pupil, Ignatius of Antioch, and the Epistle to Diognetus clung closely to the Johannine version; while Clement of Rome and the Pseudo-Barnabas are clearly followers of St. Paul. But even they are not completely faithful to the phraseology of their models. Clement follows the Epistle to the Hebrews in calling Christ "the image of divine majesty." And, like Paul, he commends humility by pointing out that the Lord Jesus Christ, the "sceptre of God's majesty," did not come in glory, although it was in his power to do so, but in lowliness (16.2). And Barnabas, with Paul's doctrine of Kenosis in mind, declares that man, who "could not bear the light of the fleeting sun, certainly would not endure the sight of essential glory, which is why Christ took on human nature" (7.2). Following St. John, Ignatius describes Christ as the Logos who was with the Father in eternity and was in recent times made manifest, who issued forth from the Father, and was with him, and had returned to him (*Epistola ad Magnesios,* 6.1; 7.2). "We have a physician, and he is flesh and spirit, begotten and unbegotten, God become flesh" (*Epistola ad Ephesios,* 7.2). Like his master John, he opposes the Judaic Christian Docetae, and stresses the true humanity of Jesus most emphatically. All the fundamental truths of Christianity—Christ's death for our salvation, his resurrection, and our redemption—stand or fall with the truth of his humanity. Docetism denied the power of Christ's crucifixion, the hope of resurrection, and the martyrdom of those who died for their faith. But Ignatius also uses Paul's terminology to confess: "This—Christ—is truly of David's line according to the flesh; and Son of God according to the will and the power of God" (*Epistola ad Smyrnenses,* 1.1). He is the New Man and, as such, takes all of those ready for salvation up into himself and makes of them his body. The Epistle to Diognetus in particular is strongly marked by the influence of St. John. Christ is the Logos sent into the world; the beloved, only-begotten Son of God, who was from the beginning and evermore shall be; who is for all time born anew in the hearts of the faithful; who enriches the Church and endows it with grace (11.3; 10.2). This makes comprehensible the accusation levelled by the pagans at the Christians that they worshipped a crucified man. In reply, the Fathers did not maintain that what they worshipped in Christ was only the Logos; they held fast to the doctrine that in the Crucified One they worshipped the Son of God.

The first traces of a primitive Christological speculation can be perceived in the Shepherd of Hermas. Like the later Apologists, Hermas too thinks in terms of a duality, not a trinity. It is true he is familiar with the idea of the three divine persons and, indeed, mentions them. But in his terminology, the third person of the Godhead, the Holy Spirit, is blended with the Son of God. To him, the Son is the Spirit of God working in the world. This Spirit of God is great and immeasurable. Every creature has been wrought by it. It fills the Apostles and the teachers, the Church and the faithful. In becoming man, it was united with the human form of a servant. Mary was visited by this Son-Spirit. It takes up its dwelling in this human figure. And as this human figure, this servant, acts in accordance with the divine Spirit dwelling in it; as it is obedient to it even unto death, so it too is raised to the status of Son of God. Hermas shows the first traces of what was later to become the Christology of Adoptionism and Nestorianism—the separation of the two Sons, the natural and the adopted, in Christ. But even Hermas insists that the divine Son-Spirit dwells in Christ the man, i.e., that it descended into the figure of a man, a servant. It is possible that his conception was influenced by Gnosticism. The Hebrew Gospel, which was written before the third century A.D., describes how the maternal power of the Holy Spirit descended upon Jesus at his baptism and made him the Son of God. The Ebionite Gospel and the Gnostic Gospel according to the Egyptians from the second century have a similar content.

The Apologists. Hermas is the transition to the second stage in the development of a systematic Christological doctrine, to the Christology of the Apologists Justin, Irenaeus, Hippolytus, Tertullian, and others. Where the Apostolic Fathers were only the faithful witnesses to the Biblical proclamation, the Apologists make the first hesitant attempt at conceptualizing and *interpreting* the Biblical annunciation of Christ with the aid of the dominant philosophy of the age. In the third and fourth centuries, this was Neoplatonic and Stoic. According to its doctrine, God is absolutely transcendent. He has no relationship at all to the world. In order to explain the creation of the world, some concept of a *mediator* between God and the world was needed as the creator of the world. This concept of God led Christian thought to define the Logos after the fashion of Subordinationism, i.e., as the divine being standing between the remote transcendent God and the world, as a mediator between the two. Because in this way the Logos is dependent upon its relation to the world, it entered into the temporal mode of being at least in the sense that its whole full essence came into being and received the designation "Son of God" only with the creation, or with Christ's incarnation. Previously it had been present only, as it were, in embryo. The spirit of the age favored this Subordinationist doctrine, which left its mark even upon Origen and the earlier Alexandrine school, even though they laid decisive stress upon the divinity of Jesus and its consubstantiality with the nature of the Father. This thought persisted until the Council of Nicaea (325), and, as far as the Holy Spirit is concerned, even afterwards. The influence of contemporary thought was not overcome until the Cappadocian Fathers, and not ultimately until Augustine and after him John of Damascus.

However, the Apologists did good service. Their finest achievement was their unfailing belief in the Lord's metaphysical status as the Son of God; and by their very clarification of John's concept of the Logos they prevented Christ from being ranged on the side of creation, and his status as the Son of God from being understood in ethical and theocratic terms after the fashion of the Judaeo-Christian Ebionites or the Dynamistic Monarchians. They finally overcame the theocratic image of the ancient Judaic Messiah.

The second achievement of their theorizing was in their concept of the Logos. Unlike the Stoics, they regarded it not simply as a cosmic principle but as the means of the revelation of our salvation; they regarded it as the creative founder of a new relationship to God, who as the Logos is indeed immanently at work in all men and at all times, but who has bound himself in an utterly unique union to human nature in Christ. Their Logos was at the same time Redeemer, and the bringer of all truth and grace. The cross was an essential part of this image. St. Justin Martyr (d. 165) already placed Jesus' death for our salvation at the heart of his theorizing (*Dialogus cum Tryphone,* 13.40, 54, *et al.; Apologia,* 1.32, 50), and Irenaeus (d. 202) dealt with Hellenistic Gnosticism, which denied Jesus' true humanity, and with the Judaeo-Christian Ebionites, who regarded Jesus only as a man endowed with grace, in emphasizing that an understanding of our redemption required the avowal both of Jesus' divinity and of his humanity (*Adversus Haereses,* 3.16 f).

This soteriological estimation of Jesus' humanity led the Apologists to broach the question of the relationship between Christ's divinity and his humanity; they were already posing the Christological problem in the narrow sense. That is their third achievement. Irenaeus, who deduced the doctrine of the two natures from the idea of redemption, also emphasized to the Gnostics the unity of the divine person. "One and the same is Jesus Christ, the Son of God, who through his suffering has reconciled us to God" (*Adversus Haereses,* 3.16, 19). He describes the union of God and man in Christ as a commingling, a *commixtio.* This expression survived for a long time in Christological speculation, although it did not entirely exclude a Monophysite interpretation. Even Augustine still speaks of a *"commixtus Deus homo"* ["God and man commingled"] but not without adding a *"quodammodo"* ["in some way or other"] (*De Trinitate,* 4.20, 30).

This expression *commixtio* still left a considerable vagueness, until it was expounded with greater precision by the keen dialectician Tertullian. He is the true creator of the phrase *"conjunctum in una persona"* ["conjoined in one person"], which was later to be established as the classic formula by Pope Leo I. In opposition to Praxeas the Patripassianist, he maintained that "we see in Christ a double status of being, which are not blended with one another, but united in one person, the God and the man Jesus. And in this union, the characteristic properties of each substance are preserved" (*Contra Praxeam,* 27). This is the essential achievement of African theology, especially of Tertullian: that as early as the third century it should have solved the Christological problem—at least as far as the terminology is concerned—in a precise formulation, and thus have given the Roman

Church the weapons to dispose of all the Monophysite and Nestorian interpretations. What Tertullian understood by *persona* is explained to us by his follower Hippolytus. In dispute with Noëtus he declares: "The flesh by itself could not persist without the Word, because it had its existence, its being in the Word" (ch. 15). According to this it is the person that gives to the human nature its independence and autonomy. The Logos takes on the human nature in such a way that it becomes its own. No longer does it subsist by itself, but it belongs now to the "I" of the Logos. This assertion of Hippolytus really anticipates the result of the coming disputes. But a gradual clarification was not achieved . . . until the disputes with Arius and Apollinaris, on the one hand, and with Nestorius, on the other.

5. J. N. D. Kelly[1] sees the Apologists more preoccupied with the meaning and function of the Logos in relationship to the Father than with the Gospel figure of Christ. Some of their expressions may appear objectionable in the light of post-Nicene formulations, but are orthodox in the thought-context of their time. This is particularly true of Irenaeus. His lack of abstract terms for "divinity" and "humanity" accounts for what would be later Nestorian expressions. The Apologists view redemption not only as liberation from error and bondage to demons, but also as atonement and recapitulation.

The Apologists and the Word. The Apologists were the first to try to frame an intellectually satisfying explanation of the relation of Christ to God the Father. They were all . . . ardent monotheists, determined at all costs not to compromise this fundamental truth. The solution they proposed, reduced to essentials, was that, as pre-existent, Christ was the Father's thought or mind, and that, as manifested in creation and revelation, He was its extrapolation or expression. In expounding this doctrine they had recourse to the imagery of the divine Logos, or Word, which had been familiar to later Judaism as well as to Stoicism, and which had become a fashionable cliché through the influence of Philo. Others had, of course, anticipated them. In the Fourth Gospel, for example, the Word is declared to have been with God in the beginning and to have become flesh in Christ, while for Ignatius Christ was the Father's Word issuing from silence. The Apologists' originality lay in drawing out the further implications of the Logos idea in order to make plausible the twofold fact of Christ's pre-temporal oneness with the Father and His manifestation in the world of space and time. In so doing, while taking up the suggestion of such Old Testament texts as Psalm 33:6 ("By the word of the Lord were the heavens made"), they did

[1] John Norman Davidson Kelly is Principal of St. Edmund Hall at Oxford University. He has been university lecturer at Oxford in patristic studies and also Canon of Chichester Cathedral and Prebendary of Wightring. He is the author of *Early Christian Creeds, Early Christian Doctrines,* and other works. It is from *Early Christian Doctrines* that this excerpt has been taken, selectively, from pp. 95–101, 145–149, 168–170. The book was published by Harper and Bros. (New York, 1958).

not hesitate to blend with them the Stoic technical distinction between the immanent word (*logos endiathetos*) and the word uttered or expressed (*logos prophorikos*).

Their teaching appears most clearly in Justin, although his theology is far from being systematic. His starting-point was the current maxim that reason (the "germinal logos"=*logos spermatikos*) was what united men to God and gave them knowledge of Him. Before Christ's coming men had possessed, as it were, seeds of the Logos and had thus been enabled to arrive at fragmentary facets of truth. Hence such pagans as "lived with reason" were, in a sense, Christians before Christianity. The Logos, however, had now "assumed shape and become a man" in Jesus Christ; He had become incarnate in His entirety in Him. The Logos is here conceived of as the Father's intelligence or rational thought; but Justin argued that He was not only in name distinct from the Father, as the light is from the sun, but was "numerically distinct too." . . .

Tatian was a disciple of Justin's, and like his master spoke of the Logos as existing in the Father as His rationality and then, by an act of His will, being generated. Like Justin, too, he emphasized the Word's essential unity with the Father, using the same image of light kindled from light. "The birth of the Logos involves a distribution, but no severance." . . .

The teaching of Theophilus of Antioch followed similar lines, although he frankly used the Stoic technical terms appropriate to the underlying system of ideas. . . .

A rather fuller account is given by Athenagoras. In a famous passage, after stating that the unoriginate, eternal and invisible God has created and adorned, and actually governs, the universe by His Word, he goes on to identify the Word as the Son of God. Repudiating the objection that there is something ridiculous in God's having a son, he protests that God's Son is not like the children of men, but is "the Father's Word in idea and in actualization." It was by Him, and through Him, that everything was made, and the Father and the Son form a unity. "The Son being in the Father and the Father in the Son by the unity and power of divine spirit, the Son of God is the Father's intelligence and Word" (*nous kai logos*). . . .

There are two points in the Apologists' teaching which, because of their far-reaching importance, must be heavily underlined, viz. (a) that for all of them the description "God the Father" connoted, not the first Person of the Holy Trinity, but the one Godhead considered as author of whatever exists; and (b) that they all, Athenagoras included, dated the generation of the Logos, and so His eligibility for the title "Son," not from His origination within the being of the Godhead, but from His emission or putting forth for the purposes of creation, revelation and redemption. Unless these points are firmly grasped, and their significance appreciated, a completely distorted view of the Apologists' theology is liable to result. Two stock criticisms of it, for example, are that they failed to distinguish the Logos from the Father until He was required for the work of creation, and that, as a corollary, they were guilty of subordinating the Son to the Father. These objections have a superficial validity in the light of post-Nicene orthodoxy, with its doctrine of the

Son's eternal generation and its fully worked-out conception of hypostases or Persons; but they make no sense in the thought-atmosphere in which the Apologists moved. It is true that they lacked a technical vocabulary adequate for describing eternal distinctions within the Deity; but that they apprehended such distinctions admits of no doubt. Long before creation, from all eternity, God had His Word or Logos, for God is essentially rational; and if what later theology recognized as the personality of the Word seems ill defined in their eyes, it is plain that they regarded Him as one with whom the Father could commune and take counsel. Later orthodoxy was to describe His eternal relation to the Father as generation; the fact that the Apologists restricted this term to His emission should not lead one to conclude that they had no awareness of His existence prior to that. Similarly, when Justin spoke of Him as a "second God" worshipped "in a secondary rank," and when all the Apologists stressed that His generation or emission resulted from an act of the Father's will, their object was not so much to subordinate Him as to safeguard the monotheism which they considered indispensable. The Logos as manifested must necessarily be limited as compared with the Godhead Itself; and it was important to emphasize that there were not two springs of initiative within the Divine Being. That the Logos was one in essence with the Father, inseparable in His fundamental being from Him as much after His generation as prior to it, the Apologists were never weary of reiterating. . . .

The Beginnings of Christology. Little enough can be gleaned from the Apologists, Justin apart, about Christology. Preoccupied with the Logos, they evince surprisingly little interest in the Gospel Figure. Tatian, it is true, speaks of Him as "God in the form of a man"; while Aristides, using language colored by the Spirit-Christology, states that "it is confessed that this Son of the most high God descended from heaven as holy spirit and took flesh from a virgin." For Melito He was "by nature God and man"; His pre-existence and complete identification with the Godhead were strongly stressed. Justin himself was usually content to reproduce the familiar affirmations of the rule of faith. He is satisfied that the Word became man by being born from the Virgin. As he expresses it, "He who was formerly Logos, and appeared now in the semblance of fire, now in incorporeal fashion, has finally by God's will become man for the human race." He pre-existed as God, and was made flesh of the Virgin, being born as man. His incarnation involved the assumption of flesh and blood, and Justin insists, in spite of the scandal thereby occasioned to Jewish critics, on the reality of the Messiah's physical sufferings. Yet He did not cease to exist as Word, being in fact at once "God and man."

Passages like these emphasize the reality of the two natures (what Melito of Sardis a little later, if we can trust our texts, was to call *Tas duo autou ousias,* literally "His two substances"), but throw no light on the manner of their co-existence in the one Person of Christ. The only explanation Justin hints at is one suggested by his doctrine of the germinal Logos (*logos spermatikos*). Since we agree, he argues, that the Logos manifested Himself in various forms to Abraham, Isaac and Moses (he is thinking of the Old Testament theophanies), why should we shrink from believing that He could be born as a man from the Virgin? The Logos, moreover, has been active in all men, imparting to them whatever goodness and knowledge they possessed. The idea lurking in his mind seems to be that His presence in Jesus Christ should be understood as similar in kind to this universal presence, though much greater in degree. Yet he does not follow up or develop the idea, and in any case leaves the presence of the Word in other men in all ages itself unexplained. Sometimes he speaks of His dwelling in them or being implanted in them like a seed, sometimes of them as living with the Logos, sometimes of their having a share or portion of Him.

There is, however, one crucial passage which has often been pointed to as providing an answer. This is Justin's statement that Christianity is manifestly superior to all other human teaching "for the reason that the rational principle in its entirety became the Christ who appeared because of us, body and Logos and soul" (*dia tou to logikon to holon ton phanenta di' hēmas Christon gegonenai, kai sōma kai logon kai psychēn*). The implication of the final clause, it has been suggested, must be that in Justin's view the Logos took the place in the man Jesus of the human rational soul (*Nous* or *pneuma*). If this interpretation is correct, Justin must have been a pioneer exponent of the "Word-flesh" type of Christology which we shall later be studying; and it is certainly the case that, one or two passages excepted, he shows little or no interest in Christ's human soul. The Stoic influences in his environment must have prompted him to regard the Logos as the governing principle, or *hēgemonikon*, in the God-man. On the other hand, the whole point of the passage is that the difference between Christ and ordinary men lies, not in any essential disparity of constitution, but in the fact that, whereas the Logos works in them fragmentarily or as a seed, He works in Christ as a whole. Indeed, if that had been what he intended, nothing could have been easier for Justin than to say quite frankly that the Logos had substituted Himself for the kind of soul ordinary men possessed. From this point of view it might be more plausible to regard the text cited as bearing testimony to Justin's belief that Christ's humanity was complete, including a soul (*psychē*) animated and enlightened by the Word, as well as a body. As a matter of fact, he has other passages, e.g. where he refers to the crucified Christ's surrendering His spirit (*pneuma*), or to His feelings when faced with His passion, which suggest that he may have allowed for His possession of a human soul. It is difficult, however, to feel any certainty where there is so little evidence to go upon; and while speculation opens up fascinating vistas, Justin's final conclusions on the matter must remain a mystery.

Although influenced by the Apologists, Irenaeus owed much more to the direct impact of St. Paul and St. John. In Christology his approach was conditioned negatively by his opposition to Gnosticism and Docetism, positively by his own tremendous vision of Christ as the second Adam, who summed up in Himself the whole sequence of mankind, including the first Adam, thereby sanctifying it and inaugurating a new, redeemed race of men. Thus he insists almost monotonously on the unity of the God-man, repudiating the Gnostic separation of the heavenly Christ from the man Jesus. As he read the Gospels and the rule of faith, it was the eternal Word Himself who became incarnate; and he never tires of applying the formula "one and the same" to the Lord Jesus Christ. His motive here was frankly soteriological; only if the divine Word entered fully into human life could the redemption have been accomplished. Similarly, as against Docetism, he argued for the reality of Christ's corporeal nature. He was "truly God" and "truly man"; if His flesh had differed in any respect (sinlessness excepted) from ordinary human flesh, the parallel between Him and the first Adam would not have been valid, and man's sinful nature could not have been reconciled to God. The Word Himself fashioned His own humanity in the Virgin's womb; and if it be asked why He did this instead of creating some altogether novel substance, the answer is that the humanity which was to be the instrument of salvation had to be identical with that which needed to be saved.

Thus Irenaeus, even more emphatically than Justin, is a representative of the view that at the incarnation the pre-existent Logos, who revealed Himself in the creation of the world and in the Old Testament theophanies, actually became man. The difference between them is that, while Justin accentuates the distinction between the Logos and the Father, even calling the former a "second God," for Irenaeus (here he is akin to Ignatius) He is the form in which the Godhead manifests Itself. A rather different Christology has been suspected to lie behind his habit of referring to "the God" and "His man" (e.g. "both confessing the God and firmly accepting His man"), as if the humanity were almost an independent person *vis-à-vis* the Word. But expressions like these do not betoken an incipient Nestorianism; they are simply examples of the vividly concrete language which Irenaeus was obliged to use because of his lack of abstract terms for "divinity" and "humanity." Two further points of interest deserve to be noticed. First, while it is not absolutely clear whether he attributed a rational human soul to the incarnate Lord (the question had not been posed in his day), the probability is that he did in so far as he thought about the matter at all. At any rate he was satisfied that human nature in its completeness includes such a soul, and that the Word became whatever human nature is. Secondly, there are passages in his writings which suggest that he was aware of some at any rate of the problems involved in the union of divinity and humanity. For example, he states that when the Lord was tempted, suffered and died, the Word remained quiescent, but cooperated with the humanity in its victory, endurance and resurrection. . . .

Man and His Redemption. When we inquire what effect the Apologists conceived Christ's coming to have had on fallen man, we find that only Justin provides anything resembling an answer, and that even his thought on the subject is shot through with ambiguity. Undoubtedly the principal purpose of the incarnation, when he views the matter as a philosopher, strikes him as having been didactic. Having forgotten the truth and having been inveigled into ignorance and positive error by the demons, men desperately need the restoration of the light they have lost. As "the new-lawgiver," or again, "the eternal, final law, the faithful covenant which replaces all laws and commandments," Christ imparts this saving knowledge. It was to bestow such illumination, in particular the realization of the oneness of God and the belief in the moral law, and to restore men by it, that the Logos in fact became man. . . . The conception of redemption as enlightenment among the Apostolic Fathers . . . reappears in the Apologists, but is given a firm, rational foundation in their doctrine of the Logos. Christ, we should observe, does not merely impart fresh knowledge; He at the same time breaks the spell of the devils who led men astray. God, states Justin, has finally destroyed principalities and powers by Him who became passible according to His will; the crucifixion has "shattered the might of the serpent, who instigated Adam's transgression." The aim of the incarnation, he points out, was the conquest of the serpent, who committed the initial sin, and of the fallen angels who imitated his example. At the temptation in the wilderness, or when He hung on the cross, and even at His birth, Christ wielded authority over the malefic spirits, and was proclaimed "Lord of the powers." So Justin thinks that he can perceive a continuation of the same victory in the power possessed by believing Christians to rout by exorcism "the demons who hold men captive."

If liberation from ignorance and error and from bondage to demons is one side of Christ's work, Justin recognizes another as well. He has a great deal to say about the cross, the presence of which he notices everywhere in nature and in all forms of life. It is "the chief symbol of His might and rulership," and was foretold in the Old Testament and even by Plato. The Word of God, he declares, "became man for our sakes, so that participating in our miseries He might heal them." Jesus Christ, our Savior, assumed flesh and blood for our salvation; He suffered in order to purify with His blood those who believe in Him. Thus we offer the eucharist in memory of the pains He endured on behalf of men; His death procures remission of sins and redemption from death. How this was achieved, Justin does not fully explain. In one important passage he argues that "by His blood and the mystery of the cross" Christ has acquired possession of mankind; thus His death can be said to redeem men in the sense that He has earned them for Himself by what He has suffered. In another passage with a passing allusion to Isaiah 53:5, he states that Christ suffered on our behalf so that by His stripes the human race might be healed. It was the Father's will that He should "take upon Himself the curses of all, for He knew that, after He had been crucified and was dead, He would raise Him up." In any case, because of what He endured, Christ has become the originator of a new humanity, regenerated by Him by water, faith and the cross. This last reference would seem to contain an anticipation of the idea of recapitulation which . . . Irenaeus actually attributes to Justin. Thoughts like these indicate that, however ready he might be on occasion to avail himself of the idiom of Hellenistic speculation, he remained all the time a churchman, with his feet firmly planted in the Church's living liturgical and Scriptural tradition.

6. G. Wingren[1] rejects the view that Irenaeus held that salvation is achieved by physical incarnation. He maintains that for him, Christ's recapitulation certainly commences with his incarnation and birth but lasts until the end of time. Regarding Christ's ontological constitution, Irenaeus maintains a precise distinction between God and man, but this distinction does not force him to contrast the two natures but rather is made to clarify his characteristic concept of "growth" and continuity in history.

Recapitulatio. For Irenaeus the One who is master over evil has lived, died, and risen again, and now rules at the right hand of the Father. His whole conception of creation and man's defeat is influenced by his belief in Christ. . . . Christ, as Irenaeus says, is nothing by himself, but what He is, He is for other people, for other men—for *man.* . . . In this . . . section, however, we shall be dealing only with the incarnate Christ Himself—as far as any such definition is possible. . . . This will give us the opportunity of opening the discussion on the concept of *recapitulatio.* . . . There are several aspects of it[2] . . . but the main point for our present consideration is first of all this: through the birth of Christ creation returns to its purity, the original form of creation is revealed in its perfectly developed form, and in Him Life enters into the world of Death.

Even although the actual words *anakephalaiōsis* or *recapitulatio* had been found in Justin, and, as was quite likely, had been borrowed from Justin by Irenaeus, we are unable with our present knowledge to derive this far-reaching doctrine of recapitulation which we find in Irenaeus from any source earlier than Irenaeus himself. The use of the terms *anakephalaiōsis* and *recapitulatio* is an attempt by Irenaeus to embody the whole of the biblical proclamation about the work of Christ in a single word. . . .

Recapitulation means the accomplishment of God's plan of salvation, and this accomplishment is within history, in a time sequence, and is not an episode at one particular point of time. It is a continuous process in which the *oikonomia, dispositio,* of God is manifested by degrees. First, and most important of all—and the basis of our whole salvation—is the event of the birth of Jesus when the Son of God became an actual man. Many other things are consequent on this basic fact—the conflict, death, and resurrection of Christ—but from one

[1] Gustaf Wingren was born in 1910. He is professor of Systematic Theology at the University of Lund, Sweden. He is the author of many theological works: *Luther on Vocation* (1957), *Theology in Conflict* (1958), *The Living Word* (1960), *Creation and Law* (1961), *Gospel and Church* (1964), etc. It is from his book *Man and the Incarnation: A Study in the Biblical Theology of Irenaeus* that this excerpt has been taken, selectively, from pp. 79–101. The book is a translation of R. MacKenzie (Edinburgh: Oliver and Boyd, 1959).

[2] From *Adversus Haereses,* III. xvii. 6 it is clear that Christ's progression through His birth, passion, resurrection, coming again, and the Last Judgment in its entirety, is *recapitulatio.* Of the work of recapitulation there still remain the *parousia,* the resurrection of the dead, and the judgment of the world. Christ awaits the proper time for this part of *anakephalaiōsis* ("*recapitulatio*") as He sits now as Lord and Head of the Church, *caput Ecclesiae.*

aspect what follows the primary event is simply a development of the resources of the power which was brought into the world through the child in Bethlehem. . . . The historians of dogma who maintain that in Irenaeus salvation is achieved through the physical incarnation, and that from this view Christ's ethical struggle has no significance, are in complete error. . . . What is involved in recapitulation . . . is, to be perfectly simple, everything that Christ has done or is doing, from His birth through His passion, death, and resurrection, the Church and the Consummation, up to the time when He shall have "delivered up the kingdom to the Father" for eternity (1 Cor 15:24). . . .

Recapitulation thus begins with the birth of Jesus of the Virgin Mary. The Son of God does not come into being at that point, for the world was created in Him. . . . But it is only the Incarnate One, the One who has been made flesh, who recapitulates. . . . Let us turn our attention to Christ becoming man.

It is characteristic of Irenaeus' exposition of the meaning of creation that he understands the world and man as having been created in the Son and the Spirit. The separation and the contrast between God on the one side and the world together with man on the other is due not to any distinction which has been in existence from the beginning between spiritual and material, but rather is attributable to the victory which evil has gained over man, the destruction of the order established by God by His enemy, and the effective rupture of man's relationship with God. In the incarnation there is to be seen the One in whom the world and man were created. In the birth of Jesus the source of life is made manifest in a world which had separated itself from the source of life and no longer was aware of its origin. Irenaeus holds creation and the incarnation together. The same force underlies both. In creation the whole of the universe comes into being, while in the incarnation it is a single, hidden human being who comes into existence, but in this one man there is to be found the purity which the whole world has lost. The need of the world which God has created is to be liberated from sin, and sin has no power over the man whom Mary bore. Men need only come to acquire what the incarnate Son possesses to be delivered from their bondage and return to the wholeness of creation. And it was precisely to bestow upon men the life which He Himself possessed that Christ was born into the world.

Since creation appears in its unspoiled state through the incarnation, there is therefore a similarity between Adam and Christ. Christ clothes Himself in the flesh of Adam. Adam has in fact been created in order to become like the Son. In the incarnation the Son enters His creation—He assumes flesh, and the flesh is Adam; who was created for Him, i.e. man. When God becomes incarnate, He becomes *man*. He gives His life, which is uncorrupted by any sin, to the human being, to man, who from the very beginning was destined to live eternal life without sin. Man therefore receives his fulfilment when the Son of God becomes through His human birth a man like us, or like Adam, with a human nature and lot, but without any evil contamination. Irenaeus quite explicitly states that in this connection recapitulation is integrally related to Adam, the first created man. That which occurs in the

Son's assumption of Adam ought to have taken place already in Creation—in Jesus Christ there appears the One who possesses everything that man as a creature ought to have, and nothing of what Adam brought upon himself as a result of his yielding to temptation. . . .

The Son of God had to invade humanity at the point where His enemy had gained a foothold, and there take up the struggle. Only if the Word was made flesh could the work of liberation be achieved. The concept of becoming man in Irenaeus develops immediately and naturally into the concept of conflict and victory. We cannot dispense with either of these concepts and maintain that one comprehends the whole meaning of both, nor can we play one against the other and maintain that any subsequent line of thought could contain both. The two ideas are inseparably related, and if they are isolated from one another they are both inadequate and incomplete.

Irenaeus lays a very great deal of emphasis on the fact that it is the Son from all eternity, and therefore *God Himself,* who assumes human flesh in Jesus. The One who has created everything from nothing enters into His corrupt creation in the incarnation in order to renew it. Irenaeus is no less vigorous in his consistent emphasis that the eternal Son of God became a *man,* and that there is nothing lacking in His humanity. . . . If there were, it would mean that the sinless One had not wholly entered the sphere from which sin was to be expelled. Sin is never in itself anything human, but on the contrary is the Devil's destruction of man as God made him. It is no limitation of Christ's humanity that He has no sin, but on the contrary His very freedom from sin qualifies Him for achieving the thing which is truly human, but which no other human being is capable of doing, for the whole of humanity is bound, captive, and unnatural.[3] . . .

The *Spirit* is life. The two hands of God at the creation of the world were the Son and the Spirit, and when man estranged himself from God by reason of his sin, he cut himself off from God's hands. But in the incarnation the hands of God lay hold of man again. The Son becomes flesh, and the Spirit makes His dwelling-place in a human body and soul. For this reason Jesus is called Christ, the One who is anointed with chrism, the anointing of the Spirit, just as a king is anointed for his rule over his people. Jesus Christ means the anointed Jesus, the anointed One, the One who is filled by the Spirit, Jesus Messiah. We notice here how far Irenaeus is from Hellenistic thought with its tendency to define human and divine as two mutually opposed substances or natures, and how close he is to Hebraic thought, of which it was a characteristic that the Son and Revealer of God was descended from the house of David and was born of an earthly dynasty. For Irenaeus, the name of Christ had very much the meaning of its Hebrew equivalent, Messiah—a man who was anointed as king. Christ's kingdom is a spiritual kingdom, and He is anointed with the Spirit. There is no distinction between

[3] There is a good definition of Adam and Christ in *Adversus Haereses,* v. xiv. 2. Adam and Christ are the same flesh in the possession of two different powers, that of Satan and that of God (cf. Col 1:22). The latter part of *Adversus Haereses,* III. xxv. 2 has the same essential meaning.

His humanity and His anointment, between Jesus and Christ, but the Spirit is incarnate in Jesus—in fact, we may say that the Spirit is incarnate in the same way as the body will be made a spiritual body in the resurrection, a *sōma pneumatikon*.[4] The man Jesus possesses the Spirit, and gives the Spirit, i.e. Life, to men. We shall see the point being discussed more clearly if we turn our attention to a different aspect of the idea with which we are dealing, i.e. to the idea of Christ as the *Verbum incarnatum*.

We find the same fundamental idea here too, for the *Verbum* is understood as a word which is spoken by God. The spoken word is never inactive or in equipoise between speaker and hearer. Simply because it is a *word*, it *issues* from someone and it is *received* by someone: Christ joins God and humanity together because He is the Word which God addresses to man. Irenaeus has an identical understanding of the Spirit in Christ—the Spirit is given by God to mankind in the anointed One, Jesus, and mankind is thereby united with God. The Spirit is like the Word in that both must proceed from the Savior to men, since both are creative—they are the hands of the almighty God, and they must be continually active. The Spirit proceeds from God in the incarnation, and moves directly to the Church, while the Word is addressed to men by God in the Incarnation, and nourishes the Church. We cannot say anything about Christ without also describing the Church, for Christ confers what He possesses, and the Church must extend. . . . It is of greater importance to notice how the Irenaean concept of the *Verbum incarnatum* makes any distinction between the divine and human natures of Christ impossible.[5]

The *Verbum* is God's and is divine, but it comes to man through being spoken by Jesus Himself and being heard as every other human word is heard. A man moves among his fellow-beings, speaks to them, and has dealings with them. In the case of the divine Word—the *Verbum*—there is no progression to a certain point at which it assumes human substance and then communicates the divine to mankind. Rather, the concept of the *Word* shatters the concept of substance, and a function or dialectic movement between God and men appears in place of the two static natures, and it is the spoken and heard Word which unites man to God. God is in His Word, His Son, and the Word, that is the divine Word, is operative in His divinity because it is heard, i.e. because it is human, material, and corporeal.[6] If

[4] The body which rises is wholly a *body*, despite the fact that it is spiritual. The change to such a "spiritual body" belongs to the Consummation. In the birth of Christ the movement was in the opposite direction. The Spirit became embodied. But the assumption in both cases is the same: the body and the Spirit are not opposed. The enemy of the Spirit is Satan, who is able to create great havoc in the body and "possess" it, but who in that very act of usurpation reveals himself to be an interloper who has no claim on the body.

[5] The starting-point of the discussion is the doctrine of the Word in the Prologue to the Gospel of St John, the doctrine of the Word which became flesh. See *Adversus Haereses* III. xi. 7–8, v. xvi. 1, and v. xviii, and also III. ix. 2. It is in this way that Irenaeus interprets the term *recapitulatio*.

[6] God addressed Adam in the cool of the day: "Where art thou?" (Gen 3:9), and the same question will be addressed to man through the *Verbum incarnatum* at the last day, although man may have hidden himself in his sin, . . . *Adversus Haereses* v. xv. 4.

the humanity within the *Verbum incarnatum* were to be eliminated the divinity would simultaneously be lost. For Irenaeus, the same immediate relation exists between the Spirit and the man Jesus, the Anointed One.[7] It should be borne in mind that both the Word and the Spirit are the hands with which God has created the heavens and the earth. Everything which exists has proceeded from the Son (the Word) and the Spirit (Wisdom). These creative hands are involved anew in creating in Christ, and in particular in laying hold on man in order to fashion him according to the decree of God, and in recapitulating the previous creation of Adam.[8] . . .

Imago and Similitudo. The characteristic confusion of divine and human . . . in Irenaeus's use of the concept of *"imago et similitudo Dei"* makes it possible for us to offer some kind of interpretation. We might expect that in regard to the incarnate Christ Irenaeus would say, first, that He is like God, that He is the image of God, and also that He is like Adam and had assumed the form of Adam—and these two diametrically opposed propositions ought, presumably, to be interchangeable, for Adam was created in the image of God, and therefore He who is the image of God ought *eo ipso* to be like Adam. In fact, the writings of Irenaeus confirm to a remarkable degree that this presupposition is justified. In this we are confronted with a major difficulty—are divine and human the same thing for Irenaeus, and is Christ true God *because* He is true man? If not, then what is the difference between divine and human?

It has been said that man's likeness to God is certainly mentioned in the account of creation, but it is not "demonstrated,"[9] for the *Logos,* in whose image man was formed, was not yet visible and had not been made flesh. It was for this reason too that man forthwith lost his likeness to God, and his yielding to temptation meant that evil had destroyed the image of God. But when the *Logos* became flesh, He secured the image and likeness by making the image of God visible and by Himself becoming what man, who had been fashioned after Him, was himself, and also by transforming man into the likeness of the invisible Father. Since the Son is a manifestation of God and at the same time an actual becoming real of the original man who was created in the image of God, the incarnation presents a double aspect to us, or a double "demonstration": it is *God* who reveals Himself, but in this very act of His self-disclosure it is also revealed what *man* ought to be, and indeed what sort of man he actually is in his unfallen state. We can see in other words what in man's actual status is God's pure and uncorrupted creation, and what is the destruction or deterioration of that creation by evil. The Son is the image of the Father.[10] But the Son is also man's antetype, the model or pattern after whom man was

[7] It is for this reason that Irenaeus continually opposes those who "divide the Lord" into two substances, . . . *Adversus Haereses* III. xvii. 5. Cf. II. xxx. . . . See also III. xviii. 3. . . . This criticism of the Gnostics constantly recurs.

[8] Cf. *Adversus Haereses* III. xxx–xxxi. 1. . . . On the Incarnation as the union of the Word with the flesh of Adam, see *ibid.,* I. I. 20.

[9] *Adversus Haereses* V. xvi. 1. This is one of the few passages where *eikov* and *homoiosis* are distinguished.

[10] Cf. the somewhat obscure words of *Adversus Haereses* IV. xxx.

formed, at the time when he was created from the dust of the earth. As the Incarnate One He reveals God for the very purpose of redeeming man. We do not possess God in His majesty by His becoming man in Jesus Christ, but we do have Him in His goodness and love. It is not within the power of man to find out God, despite His participation in manhood, but Jesus gives man power to *believe,* and in so doing makes him the child of God. It was for this purpose that the Lord came—to establish communion between God and man.

But while Irenaeus maintains this profound connection between divine and human, he also preserves the distance between Christ and man in the clearest possible way. Since man was created in the likeness of the Son, the Son therefore stands over him and is specifically distinct from him. The definition of the incarnation is that God has become man. There is in the incarnation something that is essentially different from what we find in creation, even when creation is at its most perfect. That which became a reality in the incarnation is not present even as a potentiality in man. He is destined to be like God, but he has never been destined to be God. Out of all mankind only Jesus Christ is God. When the eternal Son of God was born as man, what also took place was that, simultaneously with this event of God's becoming man, the actual human being whom Mary bore, and in whom the fullness of God dwelt bodily, was in his actual birth a pure being, free from sin, and therefore the perfection of humanity as such. And this fulfilment of humanity was due to the fact that God became man in Christ, a principle which is to be completely distinguished from any question of human perfectability as such, and He became man since only God can defeat the Devil, i.e. remove man's enemy from man. It is essential for any understanding of the relationship between the divine and the human in the Incarnate Christ that we should see that the contrast between God and Satan is one which is immediately related to our condition. To emphasize the point which we are making more sharply: Christ is man because He is God, but other men cannot be true men because they are subject to Satan, the destroyer of our humanity.

In Christ we see the *imago* and *similitudo* of God. In the beginning man was created in the *imago* and *similitudo* of God, but man was only a child, and, even before the Fall, did not achieve the *imago* and *similitudo.* In the incarnation man takes flesh and blood in accordance with the purpose which God has for him, and in Christ we see on earth man in his full maturity and development. From one point of view Jesus is the perfection of human nature. If man who had been created by God had developed in his unfallen condition as God intended, he would have become like the man Christ. In the humanity of the incarnation we are confronted with a humanity which surpasses that of Creation, but which is nevertheless the humanity of creation. "Growth" links identity with change, progression, and development. The full-grown man is different from the child, and yet the same. . . . Christ, as man, is the man whom God created in his developed and full-grown form if we try at the same time to bear in mind the contrast which we have stressed above between God and evil, Life and Death, the Creator and Satan. These two ideas—

first, of growth, and second, of the conflict between God and His adversary—are to be clearly distinguished. Man is a living being, protected by the power of God from the onslaught of death, and a growing personality who is wounded by the adversary but protected by the Father. In the Fall man's growth and life are arrested; in the incarnation they are triumphantly revived, for death must of necessity yield to God Himself, and God becomes man in Christ.

God and Man. Up to this point there has been a certain lack of precision throughout our study in defining the relationship between the divine and human in Christ, a lack which we have noticed in Irenaeus himself at this point, for there are times when he seems to be asserting Christ's divinity as over against His humanity while elsewhere he appears to reverse the process, and we get the impression that if we were to insist on his providing us with a clear definition of Christ's divinity as distinct from His humanity, we should be forcing him into the position of having to set Christ's divinity and humanity over against one another in order to give a sufficiently clear answer to our question, in so doing destroying what is central to his theology. It will be necessary to have a less sharply defined distinction between God and man if we are not to lose sight of the specifically Irenaean concept of "growth"—a continuity in history which has no distinct lines of division, and no break, distinction, or discontinuity at any point of its line of progression. And yet this would be a misleading impression to convey of what Irenaeus is in fact saying, for he continually maintains a precise distinction between God and man, though the distinction is such that it does not force him to contrast the two substances, divine and human, but in actual fact rather clarifies his concept of "growth."

7. L. Richard[1] suggests that only a superficial view of the theology of the early Church would support the idea that the Church lacked a defined doctrine of redemption. Early professions of faith, Ignatius of Antioch, the author of the Epistle to Diognetus, and especially Irenaeus are eloquent witnesses of that belief. Irenaeus' doctrine of redemption contains practically all the aspects later developed by Anselm.

Faith in the redemption accomplished by Christ is so fundamental in primitive Christianity, and the texts of the New Testament which express it are so numerous, that the Fathers of the Church and the Christian writers frequently treated this subject. But the images they used and the viewpoints they presented are so varied that Christian literature on the redemption seems at first glance to be an impenetrable thicket, in which the prin-

[1] Louis Richard died in 1956 shortly after he had reviewed or completely recasted his former work *Le dogme de la Redemption,* which first appeared in 1932 in the *Bibliotheque Catholique des Sciences Religieuses.* It is from the English translation of the revised edition, under the title *The Mystery of Redemption* by Frank B. Noriss, S. S. (Baltimore: Helicon Press, 1965), that this excerpt is taken, pp. 127–141.

cipal paths are visible only to the practiced eye.

Historians, following their first impression, have maintained that the early Church did not have any clearly defined doctrine on the redemption. In his *Cur Deus homo,* St. Anselm, using the material afforded by the Latin tradition (expiation, sacrifice, redemption), would construct the doctrine of satisfaction for sin offered to God by Christ in accepting the death of the cross and thus meriting our salvation. This "objective" concept, set forth in precise terms, touched up, resumed and worked over by the medieval scholars, would become the orthodox expression of the redemption in the Catholic Church. It was even kept by the Reformation churches until it was criticized for departing from the data of Scripture and reason. After this time, this so-called "objective" concept of the redemption was opposed, in Protestantism, by a "subjective" concept: Christ revealed the Father, the God of love, who calls us to believe and be converted. The redemption is no longer based on the satisfaction offered to God by Christ, but on what is accomplished in the person at Christ's invitation. Abelard prepared the way for this theological view, but it was not until the "age of enlightenment" that it was formulated in more precise terms—not without a lively reaction from the supporters of the orthodox view. Such is the schema presented by the most influential of Protestant historians, like Ritschl and Harnack.

More thorough and more intelligent studies of the thought of the early Fathers, undertaken by both Protestants and Catholics, have led to very different conclusions:

> It is completely inaccurate to see in the theology of the primitive Church a sort of groping beginning of the doctrine of the redemption. . . . It is no longer simply a question of an accumulation of assorted concepts placed side by side. As a matter of fact, in the midst of all the differences we come across one basic idea. . . . The primitive Church had one great leitmotif which was constantly reappearing, that of *Christus victor,* of Christ fighting with and triumphing over the "tyrants," the powerful enemies of God: sin, death, and the devil. . . . The redemption is seen as one single divine action, continued and uninterrupted.[2]

These last words mean that the accomplishment of this divine action is not conditional on a human action going up from earth to heaven, so much as that of Christ offering to the Father, as man and "head" of mankind, the perfect satisfaction which the forgiveness of sins demanded.[3] In this doctrine of the oblation of Christ, Aulén acknowledges, on the historical plane, a line which "is admittedly of vast importance and influence [in Latin Christianity], but still only a side-track"[4] which, for him, means theologically negligible.

We should be grateful to the Protestants for giving prominence to the primacy of the initiative of divine love

[2] Gustaf Aulén, *Christus Victor,* p. 23 of the French edition, dated 1949. This statement is not contained in the English edition, *Christus Victor: An historical study of the three main types of the atonement,* trans. A. G. Hebert (New York: Macmillan, 1931), to which all subsequent page numbers refer.

[3] *Ibid.,* p. 171.

[4] *Ibid.,* p. 31.

and the victory of God, in Christ, over all the obstacles raised by the creature's revolt in order to reconcile the world to himself. But we cannot disregard the traditional position in which the death of Christ on the cross is the perfect sacrifice offered to God to expiate the sins of men. This understanding is not only Latin; it is a universal tradition which goes back to the Scriptures and ends by finding expression in the idea of satisfaction. . . . "Satisfaction" does not interrupt the saving action in which, according to Aulén, the incarnation would be only "the necessary presupposition of the Atonement."[5] On the contrary, it proceeds from it as a natural consequence: Since God decided to reconcile mankind to himself in Christ becoming incarnate, dying and rising for us, mankind has been called, in the Person of its mediator, to atone for its fault, to render to God, by him and in him, that perfect glorification which was denied by sin.

The First Centuries

Profession of Faith in Christ the Savior. The faith of the primitive Church in the redemption was expressed in the very act of baptism which incorporated the neophyte into the Church precisely in order to enable him to share, through the remission of his sins, in the salvation obtained by Christ. Baptism was administered by a triple immersion in which the subject answered, by an act of faith. . . .

"Do you believe in Christ Jesus, the Son of God, who was born by the Holy Spirit of the Virgin Mary, died and was buried, was raised living from the dead on the third day, ascended into heaven, was seated at the right hand of the Father, and will come to judge the living and the dead?" "I believe."[6]

This profession of faith at the time of baptism was the basis of what we call the "Apostles' Creed," which was formulated during the first centuries.

The act of faith addressed to Christ the Savior proclaims the divine fact which accomplished the salvation of man by God. For it is clear that Christ's coming, passion, death and resurrection were accomplished "for us, for our salvation." This is stated explicitly in the liturgy—especially in the celebration of the Eucharist where the initiation of the neophyte is completed[7] and would later be affirmed expressly in the Niceno-Constantinopolitan Creed, which was based on the ancient baptismal creed of Jerusalem or Caesarea and is used by the Church in the Mass. The entire mystery of the redemption is centered in this relationship between Christ and ourselves.

The Christians constantly renewed their faith in the mystery of Christ the Redeemer by sharing in the celebration of the Eucharist.

The Fathers of the Second Century and Irenaeus

St. Ignatius. In the post-apostolic era, what more moving witness could be cited than St. Ignatius, bishop of Antioch, who wrote his letters to the

[5] *Ibid.*, p. 168.

[6] On this double meaning of the formula for baptism, cf. St. Justin, *Apol. I,* 61, 3, 10 and 11; cf. also Hippolytus of Rome, *The Apostolic Tradition,* 21.

[7] St. Justin's description of baptism (*Apol. I,* 61 and 66, 1–2) explicitly mentions this redemptive activity of Christ.

churches while he was being taken to Rome to be put to death?

Jesus Christ . . . suffered "in order to save us" (Sam 2:1). He "died for us, rose because of us" (Rom 6:1). The cross is "a scandal for the unbelieving, but for us salvation and eternal life" (Eph 18:1).

It is to the fruit of his cross, to his holy and divine passion, that we owe our life. It is thus that, by his resurrection, he has raised his standard over the centuries, in order to gather his saints and his faithful, from the bosom of Judaism as well as from among the Gentiles, into one and the same body, which is his Church (Sam 1:2).

Thus Christ has overthrown the kingdom of the devil. . . .

Epistle to Diognetus. The letters of St. Ignatius express the mystical outbursts of a soul inflamed with love for Christ with whom he is soon going to be reunited through martyrdom. The *Epistle to Diognetus,* of unknown author and uncertain date, strives to convince a sincere pagan and sets forth the essence of the Christian dogma for him: God the Creator, Revealer and Savior. It recalls God's goodness and patience toward the crimes of men.

> When our wickedness was at its height and it was perfectly clear that the reward which awaited it was punishment and death, then came the time which God had chosen for manifesting his goodness and his power: What an abundance of divine goodness and love for men! . . .
>
> Pitying our sad state, he took upon himself our sins. He himself handed over his own Son as a ransom for us, the Holy One for transgressors. . . .
>
> What else could cover our sins except his justice? In whom could we, wicked and ungodly as we were, be justified, except in the only Son of God? . . . The wickedness of many has been buried in the justice of one, and the justice of one justifies many transgressors!
>
> In times past he first had to convince us that our nature was powerless to obtain life; now he has shown us the Savior who has the power to save even those who could not be saved.[8]

St. Irenaeus

> It is true that we do not find in him [Irenaeus] the brilliant style of Tertullian, the philosophical erudition of Clement or Origen, or the religious depth of Augustine. Yet of all the Fathers there is not one who is more thoroughly representative and typical, or who did more to fix lines on which Christian thought was to move for centuries after his day. His strength lies in the fact that he did not, like the Apologists and the Alexandrians, work along some philosophical line of approach to Christianity, but devoted himself altogether to the simple exposition of the central ideas of the Christian faith itself.[9]

These words of a Protestant theologian concerning the second bishop of Lyons, the most distinguished witness of Catholic Tradition in the second century, open his historical study of "the Christian notion of redemption," which is undeniably, for Irenaeus, the center of the Christian faith.[10]

---

[8] *Epistle to Diognetus,* IX, 26; trans. and annotated J. A. Kleist (*Ancient Christian Writers* [Westminster, Md.: The Newman Press], vol. 6). Between the outside limit of 120 and 210, H. I. Marrou readily attributes this work to Pantene, toward the end of the second century.

[9] G. Aulén, *Christus Victor,* pp. 32–33.

[10] St. Irenaeus' great work, *Adversus Haereses,* is found in vol. VII of Migne's *Greek Patrology,* col. 433–1224. For an English translation of the entire work, cf. *Five books by*

> The Word of God, Jesus Christ our Lord, because of his immense love for us, became what we are, in order to enable us to become what he is (*Adv. Haer.*, preface to Book 5, M.G. 1120). The Word of God was made man, and the "Son of God" was made the "Son of man," so that man might enter into communion with the Word of God, and by receiving adoption, become a son of God (3, 19, 1, 139).

These formulas, inspired especially by St. John, attest that the incarnation is "the cornerstone of Irenaeus' theology,"[11] the foundation upon which everything rests, and that the salvation of man accomplished by Christ is essentially a mystery of the *agape* of God who, in order to unite man to himself, united himself to man by the incarnation of the Word.

But St. Irenaeus was well aware that Christ had to meet and overcome the hostile powers which enslaved man. If "the Word of God was made man, . . . it was in order to kill sin, annihilate death and give life to man" (3, 18, 7, 938). Thus the incarnation and the redemption are "in the closest relation to one another."[12]

St. Irenaeus condemned the radical dualism of the Gnostics and Marcion, which contrasted a demiurge, the creator of this material and evil world and the author of the Law, with the good God manifesting himself in Jesus with a gospel which reserved salvation to the "spiritual ones." He placed himself in the historical perspective of the Bible in which, through a gradual process, God the Creator and Savior invited his free creatures to respond to his love, in order to become united with him and to share in his immortality. It was the proud refusal of the creature to answer this invitation which had introduced evil and death into the world: first the sin of Satan, "the apostasy," then the sin of our first parents, committed at Satan's instigation. The Old Testament is the history of God's interventions: the promise of victory over Satan, the election of Israel, prophecies and theophanies in which St. Irenaeus sees the Word of God preparing himself and mankind for the incarnation, willed since the beginning. . . .

With this point of view, St. Irenaeus took up and made use of the contrast—comparison between the two Adams, which St. Paul had already expressed. . . .

St. Irenaeus was fond of this term "to recapitulate" by which St. Paul had expressed the *entire* plan of God realized in Jesus Christ (Eph 1:10). And to recapitulate is also to bring "to a head" again, from the beginning, in order to make God's plan succeed; to take up again and bring to perfection what Adam had destroyed. For Jesus, then, to recapitulate is to bear in himself the long line of men who are powerless to free themselves from sin, all of mankind, in order to obtain for them the salvation of which he is the principle, since he is God made

---

St. Irenaeus . . . against heresies, trans. J. Keble (Oxford: Parker, 1872). For an English version of the valuable little work *Demonstratio predicationis apostolicae,* which was rediscovered in 1904 in an Armenian version, see *Ancient Christian Writers,* vol. 16 (trans. J. P. Smith). A general survey of St. Irenaeus' soteriology will be found in the thesis (Theological Faculty of Lyons) of J. Chaine, *Le Christ Rédempteur d'après saint Irénée* (Le Puy, 1919).

[11] G. Aulén, *op. cit.,* p. 36.

[12] *Ibid.,* p. 35.

man. "God, recapitulating [*recapitulans*] in himself the original pristine man, has killed sin, annihilated death and given life to man" (3, 18, 7, 938).

It was Christ's obedience to the Father unto death (followed by his victory over death) which obtained "reconciliation" for us sinners by atoning for the disobedience of Adam, with whom we were one. . . .

Furthermore Christ, who came like a second Adam in the historical order, was in reality, in the intention of God, the First, the true Adam in whom all are called and can be saved, beginning with the Adam of Genesis.

Thus the first Adam was only a shadow of the Adam who was to come, the Word made flesh. As Irenaeus saw it, creation was subject to a law of growth, of progress.[13]

Adam and Eve, according to St. Irenaeus, were still spiritually children (3, 22, 4, 959; R, 224, and *Dem.*, 12–14; RSR, 1916, p. 377f.; *Patrologia Orientalis,* 12, 762f.) when they gave in to the temptation of the serpent who seduced them. Satan promised them that *they would be like gods,* and he brought them death (3, 23, 1, 90). By his unfaithfulness, Adam opened the way for the power of Satan, who is the "apostasy" drawn up against his Creator. Christ had to free us from his domination—hence the dramatic character of the victorious struggle of Christ.[14]

We see that St. Irenaeus uses the biblical image of the ransom paid by Christ for the liberation of captives. He even adds the detail of designating the one who, by means of his victory in the beginning, holds men under his power. It has been claimed that he thus sketched the theory of the "rights of the devil," to whom Christ, in order to free us, paid a just ransom by handing over himself. This is a misunderstanding of his thought, for he expressly denies that the devil has any rights over sinful men.[15]

Christ's struggle with the devil

[13] "Irenaeus showed a surprising preference for the words *paulatim* and *adsuescere*. . . . Maturation, the slow process of becoming accustomed to something—these are so many variations of the one theme of the growth of man throughout his life" (M. Aubineau, S.J., "Incorruptibilité et divinisation selon saint Irénée," *Recherches de Sciences Religieuses* (*RSR*) XLIV [1956], 46).

[14] For the exegesis of this . . . cf. P. Galtier, "La Rédemption et les droits du démon dans saint Irénée," *RSR,* II (1911), 1–24; "Les droits du démon et la mort du Christ," *RSR,* III (1912), 345–355; J. Rivière, "Le démon dans la théologie rédemptrice de saint Irénée," *RSR, IV* (1913), 57–60; P. Galtier, "La mort du Christ et la justice envers le démon," *ibid.,* 60–73; A. d'Alès, "La doctrine de la récapitulation en saint Irénée," *RSR,* VII (1916), 202–211; J. Rivière, *Le dogme de la Rédemption, études critiques et documents* (Louvain, 1931), Part II, III (in which an article from the *Bull. d' Anc. Littér. ed d' Archéol. chrét.,* I [1911], 169–200, answering Galtier's first article, is reproduced and completed), pp. 109–112, 115–119, 121–129; F. Cavallera, *Bull. Litt. Ecclés.* (Toulouse), XXXVI (1935), 84–85; J. Rivière, *Le dogme de la Rédemption dans la théologie contemporaine* (Albi, 1948), pp. 50–54. . . .

[15] J. Rivière, who did not understress the "relief given to Satan" by the theology of St. Irenaeus, concludes one of his works in this way: "The *justice* which he strives . . . to show in the entire unfolding of the work of salvation is nothing other than the wisdom of God; and, if the devil serves to make it appear so readily under one of its aspects, it never does constitute a subject of application" ("Le 'droit' du démon sur les pécheurs avant saint Augustin," *Recherches de Théologie Ancienne et Médiévale,* III, [1931], 118. Cf. his *Le dogme de la Rédemption, Études critiques et documents* pp. 118–121; 129–130; 137–141). The etymological sense of *lytron* is sometimes lost sight of, as is shown in

began with the temptation in the desert and lasted throughout his entire ministry. The high point of the struggle occurred in the passion, on Calvary, for the devil instigated the death sentence. But the apparent defeat of Christ, who handed himself over freely for us, was actually his victory, as was made known in his resurrection. It is sometimes said that, for St. Irenaeus, Christ won his victory over the devil and over death, much more than over sin. But for him sin and death are indissolubly connected. Sin is the greatest evil, an abuse of the freedom which is God's great gift. It places man in opposition to God and separates him from him, but, for that very reason, affects the whole man. "Communion with God is light and life . . . separation from God is death" (5, 27, 2, 1196).

Throughout his writings, St. Irenaeus sees the work of Christ the Savior as a divine work of love and of the victorious power of God in Christ. Only God the Word, by becoming incarnate in this world which is certainly his work but which has been invaded by the evil forces of sin, death and the devil, could conquer these forces and make his victory become ours. . . .

But if St. Irenaeus sees Christ's mediation as first coming down from God to man, he does not deny that it also goes up from man to God. This descending and ascending at least appear in his thought when he repeats St. Paul's parallel between the two Adams and the opposing solidarity which we have with each one for the benefit of the second. . . .

It is true that St. Irenaeus did not expound a doctrine of expiatory sacrifice offered by Christ in his death on the cross. Rather he expounds a doctrine of ritual sacrifice offered to God, not because God has any need of it, but in order that we might not be ungrateful to God, the author of all good. The sacrifices demanded by the Law of Moses signified an interior sacrifice. They were imperfect and were replaced by the oblation of the new covenant instituted by Christ at the Last Supper, when he declared the bread to be his body and the wine to be his blood. This spotless victim announced by the prophet Malachy (1:11) is offered to God by the Church throughout the world. The relationship of the Eucharist to the cross is implied by the words of the Last Supper rather than explicitly stated (4, 17 and 18, 1019–1029). . . .

several texts of St. Justin, for example; likewise, *redimere* and *auferre* are often used synonymously in the Latin version of Irenaeus. Cf. P. Galtier, "La mort du Christ et la justice envers le démon" *RSR*, IV (1913), 65f., note 1. But see J. Rivière, *op. cit.*, pp. 135–136.

II

CHRISTOLOGICAL DEVELOPMENTS IN THE THIRD CENTURY

1. **A. Grillmeier, S.J.,[1] points out how as Christian faith moved into speculative theology (*théologie savante*), the fundamental proposition of its content, the confession that Jesus was God, had to be the first one to exact demonstration. He rejects the view which sees here the beginnings of a chronic Hellenization of Christian dogmas, although he admits that the Church made a discerning use of contemporary concepts and language. Clement and Origen in Alexandria, and Tertullian in Africa represent the height of this movement. Clement's merit lies in having identified the personal preexisting Logos with the historical person of Jesus Christ. Origen is above all the theologian of the soul of Christ.**

The Foundation of Christology as Speculative Theology and the Emergence of Hellenism

The foundations for the further development of christology were laid in the East (by Origen) and in the West (by Tertullian) during the first half of the third century. Justin had, of course, already done some preliminary work. The controversy with Gnos-

[1] Cf. Ch. I, n. 1. This excerpt is from *op. cit.*, pp. 125–127, 159–172, selectively.

ticism had made the Church all the more conscious of the value of a closed biblical and apostolic tradition within the framework of the *regula fidei*. This consciousness is to become a constant corrective in the trinitarian and christological struggles of later times, and is further strengthened by the introduction into theology of the "argument from the Fathers." At the same time, the Church found herself driven to thinking through the traditional material of her belief more deeply, whether from an inward interest in the Christian revelation or from the demands of the controversy with Judaism and paganism. The hour had come for the birth of speculative theology, of theological reflection, of *théologie savante*. The confession of Jesus Christ as the Son of God, the *novum* of the Christian faith (cf. Irenaeus, *Adv. Haer*. IV 28, 2), demanded of Christian theology a twofold demonstration, first that it was compatible with Jewish monotheism, and secondly that it was different from pagan polytheism. The solution of this problem depended on the possibility of combining in God a true unity with a true distinction (between Father, Son and Spirit). At the same time, Christians became more and more conscious of what it meant to assert that God had been made incarnate.

As a result of Gnosis, Christian theologians also saw themselves compelled both to show how their belief in God the Father and God the Son, the Incarnate, fitted into the whole pattern of the relationship between God and the world and to construct a Christian picture of the world and of history. Here christology had its chance of becoming the cardinal point of a *Weltanschauung*. And here Christian theologians made a contribution which can and must be placed alongside the great cosmological systems of Platonism, Stoicism and Neo-Platonism. As a result of these systems, above all Stoicism, Middle Platonism, and finally Neo-Platonism, the theologians were also stimulated to make speculations, and they began to see the possibility of making a first attempt at solving the problems mentioned above. The Gnostic doctrine of emanation must not be forgotten in this context.

The procession of the Son and the procession of the world, creation and incarnation: for all this the acknowledged systems offered some help, but it was only very limited. The Christian problems burst the bounds of any one system. If this was not realized, if an attempt was made to apply any of these systems to the Christian revelation without correction, the result was of necessity a false one. An identification of the Neo-Platonic triad of *Hen* (the One), *Nous* (Mind or Intelligence) and *Pneuma* (Spirit or Soul) with the Christian triad of a Father, Logos and Spirit inevitably led to a denial of the transcendent-immanent character of this Christian triad, i.e. to Arianism. A transference of the Stoic teaching of expansion and contraction to the procession of the Son and the Spirit led to no less dangerous consequences. So the history of Christian theology, now beginning, was often like a movement made up of two steps forward and one back. Hardly any speculative attempt at interpretation succeeded at once. Corrections had to be made continually in the light of the Church tradition. If these were refused, the result was a real paganizing and Hellenizing, and thus a debasing, of the Christian revelation. Where the analogical character of the speculative concepts, or even of the popular pictures with which this revelation was expressed, was not consciously borne in mind, the peculiar element of a transcendent reality could never be preserved.

Over against this, the Church's dogmas of the Trinity and the Incarnation are an attempt to maintain the mystery inherent in the basic data of the Christian revelation by a limited use of Hellenistic or contemporary concepts and language and to avoid the distortions of Hellenization. To see the chronic Hellenization of Christianity in these dogmas themselves (Adolf Harnack) is to mistake the first intention of the dogmatic statements.

The process thus described begins with the Logos doctrine of the Apologists and reaches its first heights in Tertullian, Clement of Alexandria and Origen. . . .

The Alexandrines

The special center of christological reflection in the Greek-speaking world of the third century is Alexandria. It is to maintain its leading role for a long while. Wherever Alexandrian theology penetrated, the picture of Christ has been lastingly influenced by it. For in it the doctrine of the Logos and the incarnation occupy a central position, even if they are at the same time seen through a special Alexandrine prism, in Clement from an ethical point of view, in Origen from the viewpoint of the *Imago* doctrine and mystical knowledge.

(*a*) *Clement of Alexandria.* Like Justin, Clement begins with the Old Testament theophanies, in which he sees a preparation for the Incarnation. The Incarnation itself, however, is something completely new, just as there are also a new people of God and a New Testament (*Paed.* I 59, 1). The incarnate Logos as Logos retains his transcendence, which he has in common with the Father—an advance on Justin and the Apologists, who had exaggerated the transcendence of the Father and based the possibility of a mission of the Logos on his diminished transcendence. His entry into history, however, makes him its center and completes the Old Testament theophanies. His coming is the sign of the Father's love for men (*Paed.* I 8, 2; *Protr.* 116, 1). In him a new sun rises on the world (*Paed.* I 88, 2), the sun of the revelation of the Father which alone brings us the true light of the knowledge of God (*Protr.* 113, 3). The incarnation is the Son's step into visibility (*Strom.* V 39, 2; 16, 5). The Logos begets himself—Clement applies Luke 1:35 to the Logos—without thereby becoming twofold. He remains identical with himself. He is one and the same who is begotten of the Father in eternity and becomes flesh (*Exc. Theod.* 7, 4; 8, 1). The Gnostic multiplicity of Logoi and redeemer figures is thus strictly repudiated. Clement stands by the Prologue of St. John's Gospel. This gives his christology a clear line and focus in contrast to the Gnostic dissolution. Of course in Clement the relationship between the inner begetting of the Logos in God and the Incarnation is as unexplained as in the early theologians considered hitherto. The starting point of the mission of the Son into the world is the begetting of the Logos as the *Imago* of the Father, as his *prosopon* (Strom. V 34, 1). "The prosopon of the Father, is the Logos, by whom God is made visible and manifest" (*Paed.* I 57, 2). The Son as incarnate is thus the *prosopon* of the Father, but is so because he is already the *Imago* of the invisible God from eternity (*Strom.* V 38, 7). By virtue of his being begotten of the eternal *Nous* he is already "revealer" by nature. So closely, however, do eternal begetting and incarnation seem to be linked together that the first only takes place because the second lies in the purpose and the love of God (*Q. div. salv.* 37, 1–2). The inner *oikonomia* of God is coupled with the outer one, just as cosmos and salvation are conjoined. Clement progresses from the idea of creation and Incarnation to the idea of the Church (*Paed.* I 27, 2). In the Church, the school of the divine pedagogue, Christ is our Father, Mother, Guardian and Nourisher (cf. *Paed.* I 42, 1–3). In that the Christ becomes the abode of the Logos through the baptism, he is made like to the Logos and God (*Paed.* III 1, 5). Risen like the sun in the incarnation, he will become the sun of the soul and escort it on his chariot to the Father (*Protr.* 121, 1; cf. *Protr.* 118, 4, picture of Odysseus' ship).

The fact that in contrast to the surely predominant impersonally and cosmologically defined Logos-concept of Middle Platonism Clement identifies the personal pre-existent Logos with the historical person Jesus Christ shows his essential distinction from all non-Christian Logos and pneuma doctrines, however much they may have influenced him. As Clement is so enamoured of the Logos idea, the emphasis of the descent of this Logos into the flesh is especially marked (*Strom.* V 105, 4). . . . This *katabasis* (descent) becomes a presence which can be comprehended by the senses (*ibid.* V 38, 6), . . . a being bound to the flesh. We will now look at this picture of Christ as a unity of Logos and *sarx* (flesh) rather more closely.

The unity in tension between the Logos and the flesh is the predominant factor. It is true that Clement has repeatedly been suspected of docetism, but he consistently maintains the reality of the human nature of Christ, though at the same time his tendency to spiritualize seems to make the reality of the incarnation merely relative. Attempts have also been made to interpret the figure of Christ which Clement presents as the union of the Logos with a mere unsouled fleshly nature, a position where the special significance of the Logos in Alexandrine christology would become manifest. Put in these terms, however, such an interpretation is mistaken. The tradition of Christ's soul is clearly still so vigorous that even the teaching of animation through the Logos cannot obscure it.

Nevertheless, we find in Clement precisely that element of the non-Christian Logos doctrine which leads to the total obscuring of the distinction between Logos and soul in his christology. His teaching on *pathē* (passion) is an indication of this. Clement distinguishes two kinds; the one is necessary for the preservation of the body (*Strom.* VI 9, 71), the other is a suffering of the soul. The latter in particular must be subdued in a Christian if he is to be a Gnostic; in Christ, *pathē* of the soul are quite unthinkable. On the other hand, bodily sufferings are necessary for the ordinary man because of the "economy," to maintain bodily life. But from either point of view Christ is without suffering. He does not need the automatic, bodily impulses to maintain his (always real) bodily life. On the contrary, these are replaced by the indwelling "holy power." In him, therefore, *apatheia* ("passionlessness") is complete because the indwelling Logos can itself perceive those necessities which are brought to the notice of the ordinary man by the impulses which the creator Logos imparts. Without doubt we can trace here a strong Stoic element—that doctrine of the *hēgemonikon* (ruling principle). Clement knows it, and knows it, moreover, in its original Stoic form, even though he expands it by adding biblical concepts. The *logistikon* (power of thought) and *hēgemonikon* is the fundamental basis for the organic unity of a living being, its *systasis* (*Strom.* VI 135, 1–4), the seat of the free will, decision and the power of thought. It is so to speak the soul of the soul.

Now if the *hēgemonikon* in its inmost being is none other than the Logos, or that part of man's being which has the greatest participation in the Logos, the christological significance of this Stoic anthropology is immediately clear, as too is the indication of the danger to the traditional christology. Clement speaks of the "governing power" of the Logos. Now if this Logos, entire and personal, has taken up its dwelling in Christ, according to Clement's Stoic-Philonic doctrine of the soul, it must also be the predominant *hēgemōn* of Christ's human nature. When the original appears, the copy must lose its place and function. The lower soul of Christ, then, remains throughout as a tool in service of the *logos hēgemōn* ("ruling Word"), as it is also the mediatrix between *hēgemonikon* and body, and lies like a covering around the inmost kernel, the "inner man."[2] But in Christ, the "inner man" is the Logos, which in Clement's christology becomes the all-predominating physical principle. The power of the Logos makes a transforming intervention in the physical body of the Lord. . . . The Logos is the "sunbeam" in the depths which must be distinguished from the bodily nature, the *corpus quod erat extrinsecus,* and it is certainly regarded as the real "inner man" that is within Christ. In such a christology the human soul of Christ can achieve no theological significance, though to claim that "a positive understanding of the redemptive meaning of the incarnation in Jesus is completely lacking in Clement"[3] seems to us to be too harsh. His whole christology is not to be identified with a number of speculations influenced by Gnosticism and philosophy.

(*b*) Origen. . . . Origen . . . is not primarily interested in the ontological constitution of Christ. He sees Christ above all as mediator of the mystical union of the soul with the hidden God, as mediator between Church and God, and all this from the viewpoint of the union in knowledge and in love. Logos, soul of Christ, the humanity of the Lord, are seen in the service of that movement in which God goes out from himself and returns to himself. The Platonic pattern of antitype-type shows the poles between which this movement takes place and in addition

[2] The expression "inner man" (*ho anthrōpos ho endon*) should be noted. Henceforward it is to play a great role. Clement, like other representatives of the christological use of "outer" and "inner" man, goes right back to Paul, who for his part speaks in the language of his time. From this, an anthropological framework develops in the writers of the Church.

[3] A. Wintersig, *Die Heilsbedeutung der Menscheit Jesu in der vornicünischen griechischen Theologie* (Tübingen, 1932), p. 72.

helps to make clear the tension there is between them. The whole drive is from symbol to reality (truth). Despite the extent to which Origen's christology incorporates the traditional doctrine of Christ, his Godhead and manhood, and of body and soul, it is completely moulded by his subjective interests and thought-patterns and hence by his mysticism. This is why his doctrine of *epinoia* ("perception") could become so central for his interpretation of Christ. . . . The Son, then, is the revelation of the Father and his mediator toward the world. From his begetting onwards he exists for mankind. In him the transcendent properties of the Father take form, as the expression of an objective, inexpressible reality. By means of participation, Christians too for their part can express the perfections of Christ and further the unfolding of the *epinoiai*. By means of the knowledge of the perfections of Christ they themselves ascend to the Father. . . .

Origen now also takes up his interpretation both of the relationship between the Godhead and the manhood of Christ and of the place of the soul of Christ into his doctrine of the mystical ascent of the soul. The Logos is the image of God, but the soul of Christ is the image of the Logos. . . . But the way to the Logos-God is by means of the *"Logos incarnatus."* Christ's manhood is the starting point of the ascent. It is not that the ascending one has to leave it completely behind. Even Christ in his ascension into heaven did not leave behind his manhood, as some assume. These are combated by Origen. With the progress of the ascent of the soul the manhood of Christ becomes more and more, and finally in the eternal vision completely, transparent for the Godhead. In the Logos, of course, all the secrets of God are first contained. He reveals the Father. The manhood of Christ, like Holy Scripture, is like a filter through which the Godhead is imparted in accordance with the receptive capability of man. Christ is a spiritual nourishment appropriate for all. Hence the doctrine of the different forms under which Christ is perceived. This may not be interpreted as Docetism. . . .

This is where the whole problem of the appreciation of the Incarnation in Origen is raised. Even in Origen, the Incarnation is the real new element of the New Testament. . . . [For Origen] the incarnation means the real arrival of the Logos. Even if the corporeality of Christ has in some respects the more negative function of a filter and appears to lose its positive significance as medium of revelation in the view of eternity, nevertheless the whole possibility of this view and the ascent to it even in Origen depend on the fact of the Incarnation. It thus remains forever valid and remains so above all in the reality of the Church. Although Origen's symbolism and his doctrine of the ascent seem to make the Incarnation (and the corporeality) of Christ relative, it still has true saving significance and truly brings about salvation and thus also has true historicity. . . .

Origen is, above all, the theologian of the soul of Christ. Here he takes up genuine biblical traditions and helps in a number of ways to guarantee their continuance. At the same time, however, he subjects these selfsame traditions to a heightened danger. His teaching on the soul of Christ was overloaded with peculiar anthropological and christological concepts which were at a later date either given up or at least strongly contested. The soul of Christ has a special function in Origen's reflections on the conjunction of Godhead and manhood.

Unity in Christ is achieved through the mediacy of the soul of Christ between sarx and Logos, which the Platonic dualism of Origen is otherwise unable to unite. This soul, however, has already been united from eternity with the divine Logos in complete understanding and love of God. Indeed it has already existed from eternity, before the body was created. But what is the relationship between soul and Logos? The two are directly conjoined through direct vision in love (*De Princ.* II 6, 3). The soul is related as spirit to spirit. By complete union with the Logos the soul of Christ becomes, as it were, the living view of God and the perfect love of God. This provides for Origen the highest and most inward mode of union, in which the human soul of Christ becomes fully divinized and is aglow throughout as iron in the fire (*ibid.*, II 6, 6). From Origen's metaphysic of the action of the spirit we must conclude that the unity so formed is meant as a really *ontic* unity, a conjunction which does not merely rest on the power of the subjective moral act, as, say, with the adoptionism which he has described earlier. But the fact is that the unity of the God-man is only *meant* to be an ontic unity, and is not really proved to be such. Basically, this explanation of Origen's leads along a false trail and confuses essential being with its (spiritual) actions. When all is said and done Christ is in danger of being still only a "quantitatively" different exceptional case of the universal relationship of the "perfect" to the Logos, however mystically deep Origen may wish to make the relationship between Logos and soul in the God-man. Incidentally, it is interesting to see that the problem of unity in Christ is stated quite explicitly as such, and is described as being a mystery. . . . Even as a Platonist Origen is none the less conscious of the Christian *Mysterium*.

Though Origen spoke above all as a Platonist in his explanation of the mediacy of the soul of Christ, it is as a Stoic that he goes on to talk of the *hēgemonikon*. He, too, knows of it, and transfers it to the heart. This *hēgemonikon*, i.e. the *nous* (intelligence) or the *pneuma logikon* (rational soul) is the "inner man which is called rational" (*De princ.* IV 4, 9). Has Origen brought this "inner man" and the Logos in Christ so near together that the latter now becomes the *hēgemonikon* in the human nature of Jesus? The final grounds on which a difference is to be assumed between the indwelling of the Logos in "Peter" or "Paul" and in Christ is this—that in Christ the Logos is completely in control. With Origen's Christ this control is exercised primarily in the moral sphere. But once the Stoic term "*hēgemonikon*" has been taken over and has been associated with the Logos terminology which has likewise been enriched from the Stoic, the final result must be a picture of Christ in which unity is based on the working of the divine *hēgemōn*. Here Origen could ultimately be on the way to a metaphysical interpretation of the unity of Christ by means of the concept of "person." For the real personality of a man is rooted in his *hēgemonikon*. On the other hand, this conception of the Logos-Hegemon together with his doctrine of the soul of Christ was logically to lead Origen to assume a double personality of Christ. For the soul of Christ was conceived as a center of activity. The lack of the concept of "person" is a clear fact.

At the same time he could well debar himself from an approach to the understanding of the unity of person in Christ because this unity is transferred into the sphere of physical action and finally is not really anything more than a "natural" unity, that is to say, a unity like the unity between two constituent parts which go together to form one reality. Origen himself, it is true, did not draw these consequences; nevertheless, he exposed himself to the charge that his system left no room for a full appreciation of the humanity of the Lord. Even the essential act of the human Christ, his redemptive death, has been said to be devalued. It is thus possible to note two opposed tendencies in this christology. One would follow the path of the Church's tradition toward a distinction of the two natures, so that even the idea of indwelling emerges as a theological interpretation of the unity in Christ. The other would urge the obliteration of the human element in the Lord.

Be this as it may, Origen is himself a key witness to the traditional teaching of the soul of Christ, even though he has mixed it with strong philosophic elements. The newly discovered *Dialektos* (ed. Scherer) is of great importance for Origen's christological anthropology. He distinguishes in Christ body, soul, spirit, and in addition to these, the divine *pneuma*. Moreover, Origen already advances that argument which is to play a great part in the anti-Apollinarian controversy. . . . "The whole man would not have been redeemed had he not assumed the whole man" (*ei mē holon ton anthrōpon aneilēphei*).

Conclusion

It is clear from this survey that the rise of christological reflection was a very slow process. The main emphasis was laid on the theological interpretation of the relationship of Father and Son, though this was seen to be closely connected with the incarnation. Over against the Gnostics and the Docetists, the theologians of the Church had above all to stress the duality of the two natures in Christ and their reality. True, the first reflections on the problem of the unity of Godhead and manhood are made. The Fathers know that the incarnate Logos is "one and the same." But this unity is more intuitively seen than speculatively interpreted. It can—with the sublimity of the *Mysterium Christi* in the Christian faith—also be no more than a matter of the first repulse of the attacks which, for example, Celsus had made against the Christian doctrine of the incarnation. For the interpretation of the unity in Christ, the Fathers fall back on the Stoic *krasis* (control) doctrine. Here they bequeathed posterity a legacy which was to burden theology for a long time. In fact, in this way the path of a *unio secundum naturam*, the Monophysite solution, was trodden. Even if the concept of person emerges for the first time, it is not yet made the basis of the solution of the problem of Christ. And when in addition "person" is sought metaphysically in "individuality," the centering of theological reflections on this concept will first go on to create the real difficulties which are later manifest in the Nestorius dispute. So about 250, we have merely a first, confused beginning of speculative christology. But this also has a very positive side: the foundation of christology is the tradition and the simple proclamation of the Church. It still shines clearly through the different speculative attempts at interpretation.

2. J. Danielou, S.J.,[1] sees Origen's treatment of the dogmas of the incarnation and redemption as part of his theology of the Logos. Origen represents the nature of the Logos as inferior to the Father but superior to the *logikoi,* creatures of the spiritual world. His emphasis on the sacramentality of the incarnation and its relevance to the spiritual life may erroneously lend credence to the accusation of Docetism in his views. Redemption is for him not only victory over evil but also a process of education.

The importance of the incarnation and the redemption to Origen's theological system has been questioned by Hal Koch and De Faye respectively. In Hal Koch's opinion, the incarnation mattered little to Origen, because the principal part in the history of the universe was played by the Logos.[2] In De Faye's opinion, the redemption was not of great importance, because Christ's function was essentially to reveal the truth: his death on the cross did not come within the field of thought envisaged.[3] But a study of the sources leads one to modify these views: they give too narrow an idea of Origen's outlook. The part played in history by Christ's humanity is given the greatest prominence in the commentaries of the New Testament, and Christ's contest with the powers of evil—the central idea in the dogma of the redemption in the second and third centuries—occupies an important place in Origen's work as a whole. What is true in the other view is that these dogmas form part of a wider whole, the theology of the Logos, which is an essential element in Origen's system. We will therefore begin by studying the nature of the Logos, whom Origen regards as being between the Father and the *logikoi.* It is one of the most difficult of his concepts. After that, we will look at the part played by the Logos in the economy of salvation and consider the problems arising out of the incarnation and the significance of the concept of Christ's passion as a victory over death.

THE FATHER, THE LOGOS, THE *Logikoi*

. . . [Origen] regards the relationship between the Logos and the Father as parallel to the relationship between the creatures of the spiritual world and the Logos. It is one of the factors in his system where the influence of

---

[1] Jean Danielou, S.J., is a well-known French theologian, a *peritus* at Vatican II. He is professor of Theology at the Institute Catholique in Paris. He is also the editor of the series *Sources Chretiennes* and the author of many works, *Christ and Us, Lord of History,* etc. It is from his book *Origen* (New York: Sheed and Ward, 1955) that this excerpt has been taken, pp. 251–273.

[2] Hal Koch, *Pronoia und Paideusis* (Leipzig, 1932), p. 63.

[3] De Faye, *Origène* (Paris, 1923–28), p. 230.

Middle Platonism is most clearly discernible. . . . In the many passages where Origen describes the Logos in relation to the Father and the *logikoi,* he represents him as inferior to the Father and superior to the *logikoi.* . . . He says in the *Commentary on St. John:* ". . . God is the true God and the other gods are fashioned after his image; they are like copies of the prototype. But here again, the Logos is the original model of all these copies. The Logos dwells with God and has existed from the beginning, because he is God."[4] . . .

This passage brings us right to the heart of the question as Origen sees it. We note, first, the contrast between God with the article—the sole *autotheos,* God in his own right—and the other gods, who are *theoi* only by participation. This is based on Philo. . . . In this sense, God alone is *alēthinos theos* ("true God"), and consequently he is transcendent with respect to the Son. Origen's aim in maintaining this is to reassure those who, in their anxiety to avoid polytheism, fall into modalism or adoptionism; but he does it at the cost of attributing to the Son the same sort of divinity that all other created spirits who are *theoi* possess. However—and this is the second point—though the Son is classed with the *theoi,* he transcends them all. He alone of them dwells with the Father. He is of higher rank than they are. He alone knows the Father in his entirety, he alone does the Father's will in every detail.[5] His divinity is not his in his own right—he has it as a gift from the Father; but once he has it, he is the Source from which all other divinization proceeds. Thus, if he is in a different category from the Father, he is also in a different category from the *logikoi.*

The two relationships, then—the Father's to the Son and the Son's to the *logikoi*—are to some extent analogical. . . .

If the Son and the Spirit transcend all *logikoi,* they are themselves transcended to a still greater extent by the Father. They thus form an intermediate category, which though much nearer to the Father than to the rest of creation, is still separate from him because their essence, power and other attributes are different from his. . . . [Origen's theory of the Logos] . . . is obviously tainted with subordinationism. The only point on which he wavered was the question of the proportion between the two sets of differences—those separating the Father from the Son and those separating the Son from creatures. . . . He says that the Father is at a greater distance from the Son than the Son is from the rest of creation. In the *Commentary on St. Matthew,* however, we find the opposite idea.[6] . . .

It is a hierarchical view of things, the Logos being entirely dependent on the Father and the other *theoi* depending in turn on the Logos. Origen looks out onto a world of created spirits, whom he sees as surrounding the Logos and sharing in his life. It is the Stoic theory over again—the Logos is everywhere in the cosmos and individual *logoi* are mere sharers in his properties—but with the difference that Origen shifts the world of the *logoi* into a region that was in exist-

[4] *Commentary on St. John,* 2, 2.
[5] *Ibid.,* 32, 28; 10, 35.
[6] *Commentary on St. Matthew,* 15, 10.

ence before the cosmos began. "In so far as a man possesses wisdom, he shares in the life of Christ, who is Wisdom."[7] An essential feature of the theory is that the world of the *logikoi* is coeternal with the Logos. This is one of the points where Origen's theology is deeply embedded in his cosmology. Some of his predecessors—Tertullian and Hippolytus, for example—did not regard the *logikoi* as eternal; but then, they did not think that the Logos was eternal either: he came on the scene, according to them, when the cosmos was created. Origen very properly reacted against this idea. To his mind, there never was a time when the Logos did not exist. On that point he could be used in the anti-Arian controversy. . . .

The essence of the reasoning used by Origen to justify his idea of the Logos as the intermediary between the first God and the spiritual cosmos is the argument that between absolute unity and the multiplicity of creatures there must be a being who is one and yet shares in that multiplicity.[8] This brings us to a point of first-rate importance to Origen's theory, for in the last resort it is the multiplicity in the Logos that makes his dealings with the *logikoi* possible, since it enables him to adapt himself to their diversity. The argument will be found set out in the *Commentary on St. John*[9] . . . [where we find] the main factors in the theory. In the first place, there are various different facets in the Word, various *epinoiai* ("thoughts") or *thēōrēmata* ("idea"). Some of these *epinoiai,* such as the names Wisdom, Word, Truth and Life, denote the Word as he is eternally in himself; others are bound up with the economy of the Redemption. Consequently, it is evident that there will be degrees of excellence among them: to the sick the Word will appear as Healer, to those who need guidance he will show himself the Shepherd; his self-revelation as Wisdom and Life will be kept for the perfect. In essence, Origen's theology of the Word is simply a catalogue of the different *epinoiai,* the "unfathomable riches of Christ" (Eph 3:9). . . .

Origen protests against those who treat the name "Word" as if it were the only name the Son of God possessed, and he takes the opportunity of giving a further catalogue. . . .

As there are so many sides to his personality, Jesus can manifest himself to men in different ways, according to their capacity for seeing him. "Not all who see Christ receive an equal degree of light from him. The amount of light they receive depends on the amount they are capable of receiving." The Logos is here envisaged in relation both to theology and to the spiritual life. The spiritual life—which is essentially what the life of the *logikoi* is—is a process of feeding on the Logos.[10] . . .

The Word adapts himself to the capacities of the men he is dealing with. There is a whole gamut stretching from the beginner, who has only a natural knowledge of him, i.e., who knows nothing of his Godhead, to the soul admitted to a sight of the dark mysteries of his divinity. . . .

[7] *Commentary on St. John,* 1, 34.
[8] *Commentary on St. John,* 1, 20.
[9] *Ibid.,* 1, 23.
[10] *Homily on Genesis,* 1, 8.

However suggestive this theology of the Logos may be in some respects, the fact that Origen pressed it into the mould of Middle Platonism means that it is distorted on two essential points and that the value of his teaching about the Trinity and about grace is thereby seriously diminished. In the first place, through his idea of the superiority of the Father to the Logos, he falls into the error of subordinationism. He holds that Father and Son are different not just because they are different Persons but because they have different natures. Consequently, the Son merely shares in the Godhead instead of possessing it absolutely. . . . Contrariwise, he does not allow difference enough between the Logos and the *logikoi*. On that point he was influenced by the Stoic idea that the Logos is imminent in all individual *logikoi*. . . . It is true that because of their sins spirits may, in his opinion, be incapable of living a fully spiritual life unless the Word helps them; they will need his assistance for that. But even so, the spiritual life is still only the development of that participation in the life of the Logos which is rooted in all spirits by nature. Hence the difference between them and the Logos can only be one of degree. And that destroys the essentially gratuitous character of grace considered as a sharing in the life of a transcendent Trinity.

Origen does not devote much space in his writings to the incarnation. There is one short chapter on it in the *De Principiis* (2, 6). The reason is that there never was a time when the Word was not acting on the human race. But at any rate—and this is what De Faye does not realize—the incarnation does represent the pre-eminent instance of the Word's intervention in human affairs. Origen begins by reminding his readers of the Word's remarkable attributes and then shows what an extraordinary thing it was that he should come down and live among men. "We have seen so much to admire," he says, "in the nature of God's Son, but we are struck dumb with wonder when we reflect that possessing, as he did, this most sublime of natures, he divested himself of the majesty surrounding him, became Man and lived among men."[11] . . .

[Origen tries] to find a place for [the incarnation] in his system. It will be remembered that in his opinion the soul exists from all eternity. The same will be true, then, of Christ's soul too. . . . Thus the soul of Jesus—which he mentioned himself when he said that nobody could rob him of it (John 10:18)—was attached to him inseparably and irrevocably in his capacity of Wisdom, Word of God, Truth and true Light, ever since it was assigned to him at the beginning of creation.[12] . . .

"This soul has always been immersed in the Word," he says, "in some such way as that. Hence it can feel nothing, will nothing, do nothing but God." It is noteworthy that the solutions here given by Origen were afterwards applied to other problems. The first is found in connection with the Immaculate Conception. The second was used by Cyril for the Incarnation; but as used by Origen himself, it applies to the eternal relationship between the Word and his soul before the Incarnation.

[11] *De Principiis,* 2, 6, 6.
[12] *Commentary on St. John,* 1, 32; 20, 12, 19.

If Origen lays so little stress on the incarnation of the Word, the reason is to be found in his peculiar attitude to the visible, which he regards as no more than a sacramental of the invisible. That applies to the Saviour's humanity as well: it is simply a means of approach to the Logos, who is the real food of the soul. And in this connection Origen again makes use of the idea that the visible phenomena of Christianity are shadows and prophecies of things yet to come. "It seems to me," he says, "that the prophet Jeremiah realized what nature it was that Christ took for our salvation and what his other nature was—the nature of divine Wisdom—when he said: 'Christ the Lord is the breath of our mouths, and we shall live among the nations in his shadow' (cf. Lam 4:20)." . . .

The theology of the incarnation here merges with exegesis of the New Testament and the theology of the sacraments. All three spheres are dominated by Origen's idea of the relationship between the visible and the invisible. He by no means belittles the visible. He is no more a Docetist in his theology of the incarnation than he reduces everything to the spiritual in his theory of the sacraments. He believed that Christ really did become incarnate. But just as in his theory of the Eucharist he lays little stress on the visible eating and makes much of the invisible feeding on Christ, so here he does not dwell for long on the historical aspect of Christ, because he is in a hurry to examine its spiritual significance. . . . The spiritually minded man tries to "reach the Word who became flesh for those who live in the flesh."[13] Following the same line of thought, Origen draws a contrast between natural or fleshly knowledge of Christ and spiritual knowledge of Christ. It will be seen that this is the same principle as the one governing his exegesis of the New Testament—the one that leads him to distinguish between the sensible and the spiritual sides of the Gospels and ask what good an explanation of the sensible side is if it does not lead to the spiritual. Thus, his position is the same whether the question at issue is the material side of worship, the literal meaning of Scripture, or the visible humanity of Christ: he affirms the reality of all three, but at the same time he regards them only as starting-points.

As for the invisible essence hidden behind the visible phenomenon, the Incarnate Word, there are two different aspects of that. The historical Christ is a sacrament of the Christ who presides over the inner life and is present unseen in the Church and in souls; he is also a sacrament of the glorious Christ who will be revealed at the end of time. The first of the two is the one more often found: we are often told that we must go beyond Christ's humanity and get at his hidden divinity. But it is the other that figures in the passage . . . about living among the nations in Christ's shadow. It might be, Origen there said, that the thing which cast the shadow would be known at the time of revelation, when the saints gaze on God face to face, as they deserve. The passage has a familiar ring. It was in fact Origen's *leitmotiv* in his explanation of the figurative meaning of Scripture. Here again, then, the theology of the incarnation comes into

[13] *Commentary on St. Matthew,* 12, 4.

line with exegesis, for it too recognizes a spiritual Gospel, which is the mystery of Christ living in the Church and in souls, and a divine, eternal Gospel, which is the mystery to be accomplished at the end of time. "The prophet said in this connection: 'Christ the Lord is the breath of our mouths, and we shall live among the nations in his shadow.' We shall do that when God does us the wonderful service of bringing all the saints from the temporal Gospel to the eternal Gospel, as John calls it in the Apocalypse (Apoc 14.6)."[14] . . .

[Origen] does not dwell on the externals of Christ's life, nor does he lay much stress on the eschatological side, the comparison between the two "parousias," a theme to which Justin had given such prominence. What he was out to do was to discover the relevance of the mysteries of Christ's life to the life of the soul. He regarded Christ's whole life as one great sacrament, which continued to operate, invisibly, in the Church. The mysteries of Christ's life were still being enacted in the Church. What Christians had to do, then, was to go behind the external details of the historical Christ's behaviour and try to discern the spiritual activity of the Christ who lives in the soul. . . .

The Redemption

Origen's teaching about the Redemption has perhaps given rise to a greater volume of adverse criticism from the moderns than any other theory of his. De Faye says: "Nothing could be more incoherent and contradictory than his teaching about the Redemption."[15] On the one hand, we find him echoing the tradition handed down by previous writers—St. Paul and the apologists—to whom the essence of the Redemption had seemed to lie in Christ's victory over the powers of evil who had been holding mankind in captivity. It is an extremely important factor in Christian tradition. On that point, then, Origen is obviously a strong supporter of the traditional belief. On the other hand, he regards the world as the scene of an educative process carried on by the Logos, who as Master and Healer was gradually inducing all free creatures to return to the good. De Faye and Koch think this a purely philosophical outlook and consider that it runs counter to the other. We must begin by observing that the idea of a divine process of education did not come to Origen from a philosophical source; he got it from the Bible and the Church. It corresponds to one aspect of Christian dogma. The Christian view is that the world is the scene at once of history and of drama. Any theological system which excluded one or the other of these would be incomplete. That the two aspects should never quite coincide is only to be expected: it is characteristic of mysteries that the formulas we invent to express them can never exhaust their essence. That is equally true of the Eucharist, the Redemption, the Trinity and the Church.

We must therefore add a further statement—that the idea of the Redemption as something pedagogical came to Origen from Tradition and the Bible. Koch is thus wrong in regarding it as due simply to the influence of philosophy. His mistake

[14] *De Principiis,* 4, 3, 13.
[15] *Op. cit.,* vol. III, p. 210.

arises from his Protestant outlook, which makes him think of salvation as justification or pardon coming from without[16] and not as the rebirth of liberty. But this latter concept provides a means of reconciling both the aspects found in Origen's theory. On the one hand, Christ's death had to set our freedom free from the tyranny of sin that was weighing upon it, as Augustine was later to show with such force. But freedom, though recovered, still had to turn freely to God, and thus the idea that there is an educative side to the Redemption remains valid. That is not where Origen is wrong. His mistakes lie in some of the details of his educative theory—he is wrong in applying it to all spirits without exception, devils included; wrong in supposing that the process of education continues in successive worlds; wrong about the ultimate universality of forgiveness, because he bases it on a philosophical theory (the theory that evil cannot be eternal), whereas he ought to have stayed, as we all have to, on the threshold of the mystery. That is the way the question ought to be stated. Since its two aspects emerge one after the other, we will examine each in turn and show in both cases what comes from Tradition and what belongs to Origen's own system, as we did with his other tenets.

I shall keep the title "doctrine of the Redemption" for the first part of the programme. The viewpoint here is that mankind was under the yoke of the powers of evil until Christ came on earth. The powers in question are the whole of that company of bad angels . . . and particularly the wicked angels who had been ruling over the nations. Christ's life is considered to have been a struggle with these opposing powers from the beginning. The *dynamis* ("power") in him—he himself is the *megalē dynamis* ("great power")—weakened the opposing powers right from the time of the incarnation. . . .

What finally ousted the powers of evil was Christ's passion and resurrection. . . . "The cross of our Lord Jesus Christ can be regarded," Origen says, "from two points of view." It was obvious to the eye that the Son of God was crucified; what was not obvious to the eye was that the devil too was nailed to the cross, with his princedoms and his powers. . . .

Origen explains the meaning of the Passion. . . . He shows "how for love of us the Father gave up his Son to the powers of evil and they in turn gave him up to men, to be put to death. Death, his enemy, was to hold him in his power, as he holds all who die with Adam (cf. I Cor 15:22)." . . .

It will be seen that what emerges from this is the essence of St. Paul's teaching on the Redemption, which Origen very ably lays bare. The devil and death are one and the same thing, one and the same evil power. This evil power thought it had triumphed over Christ, its enemy, but its apparent victory was in reality a defeat, for by dying himself and rising from the dead, Christ destroyed death's power and thus outwitted the devil. The outwitting of the devil was much stressed by the Fathers. The doctrine has also been much criticized, because its underlying meaning has not been perceived. It is only an echo of the ironical question: "Where then, death, is thy victory?" (1 Cor 15:55), flung

[16] *Op. cit.,* p. 19.

out by St. Paul after Death had been fooled. . . .

All the same, the victory Christ won on the cross will first have to be applied to the individual soul, and the powers of evil must be ousted afresh in each individual case. "All who are crucified with Christ despoil the principalities and powers and expose them in open show, triumphing over them through the cross (cf. Col 2:15); or rather, all that is done in them by Christ."[17] The martyr especially is regarded as continuing what Christ achieved when he mastered death and the devil and gave the human race its freedom. . . . It shows, too, how profitable martyrdom is, shows what its *ōpheleia* ("gain") is. The evil spirits are well aware of the blessings martyrdom brings to Christians; they dread it so much that they strive to slow down persecution.[18]

It may be observed in this connection that Origen's theology of the Redemption is in keeping with what one would expect from a Christian living in the age of the martyrs. Consequently, it reflects the outlook of the Christian community in those early times, with its awareness of the struggle going on against the powers of evil entrenched in idolatry. The Origen we see here is Origen the ordinary Christian. As a matter of fact, a considerable part of his theology could be said to fit into the same context. As he was both martyr and doctor, his theology may be considered to share in the charismata of both. That is perhaps what gives it its special individuality. It cannot be reduced to either of them alone; they both flow in it together. A whole sphere of his thought has its character determined by his experience of the Christian life. And it is that experience that colours his theology of the Redemption. . . .

3. P. Beskow[1] points out that although early Alexandrian theology envisioned Christ primarily as a revealer of divine truth, it did not neglect the consideration of Christ as King. Clement and Origen played a considerable role in spreading the concept of Christ's Kingship. Under the influence of Philo they developed a Hellenistic ideal of His Kingship. Origen's New Testament exegesis included many texts dealing with Christ as King. The more traditional eschatological concepts are developed in his commentaries on the New Testament, while his works on the Old Testament contain a theology more strikingly spiritual in character.

It has often been pointed out that the royal aspect of Christ is not expressed so clearly in Clement and Origen as in the NT and the oldest Church tradition. Theologians in the highly Hellenized milieu of Alexandria did not think in terms of eschatology. Philo had interpreted the OT in such a way as to minimize the importance of a historical process; he was not the

[17] *Commentary on St. Matthew,* 12, 25.

[18] *Celsus,* 8, 44.

[1] Per Beskow is a Swedish theologian; he is the author of *Rex Gloriae: The Kingship of Christ in the Early Church* (Uppsala: Almqvist & Wiksell, 1962). This excerpt has been taken from this book, selectively, from pp. 212–230.

first Jewish theologian in Alexandria to do so. The Biblical figures are made to function as symbols of a super-earthly and superhistorical reality. Even Moses, who receives a central position in Philo's thought, is really no more than an expression in time of the eternal Law.

Clement, following in Philo's footsteps, wished to present Christianity as the perfect philosophy and as a saving gnosis; for him, Christ was mainly the Revealer, the Philosopher and the Teacher. (That Christ is the Revealer of Divine truth is of course an important aspect of NT Christology but is given a Hellenistic accent in Alexandrian theology.) The NT doctrine of Christ as the eschatological King and Judge of the world, on the other hand, has little significance in Clement's work.

It is only natural, therefore, that the Alexandrian Christ has often been set up in contrast to the fourth-century theology of Christ as King. A number of art historians have pointed out that Alexandrian theology is also clearly reflected in the art of the period: the sarcophagi and catacomb paintings of the third century show Christ sitting, in the manner of the ancient philosophers, with a scroll in his hand, discussing with his disciples. Not until the beginning of the fourth century, when other motives began to dominate, did the majestic characteristics of the image of Christ become more apparent.

The distinction between Christ the Teacher and Christ the King should not however lead us to a one-sided estimation of the Alexandrian theologians' image of Christ. Clement and Origen also played a considerable part in spreading the concept of the Kingship of Christ, as it began to make its mark on the young Byzantine Empire. It is true that Clement (and to some extent Origen also) makes no use of those forms of literature with which the royal ideology seems to have been particularly connected during the sub-Apostolic age. We have few examples of exegesis of OT texts, such as we find in the anti-Jewish polemic of Justin Martyr and Irenaeus. Apocalyptic descriptions are entirely absent; little interest is shown in matters of liturgy. We do however find elements in the Alexandrian theologians which seem to be missing from the older tradition. We find a Hellenistic ideal of Kingship, taken over from Philo, and an incipient Hellenistic-inspired political metaphysic. While expositions of the NT are extremely rare in the early post-Apostolic age, we find a rich deposit of NT exegesis in Origen; this includes expositions in which Jesus appears as King.

Clement of Alexandria. Despite having little interest in politics as such, Clement's views on Kingship show that he was very much dependent upon Philo's political writings, even if he has also studied other political authors. . . .

"The King is to the state as God is to the world," [wrote Philo]. Clement, in common with Philo and the Pythagorean philosophers, makes the category of Kingship refer to various stages of rule. God and the Logos rule over the world-all, the lawgiver-king rules over the people, and the wise man rules himself. These various forms of rule are interdependent, in a ladder of hierarchy: the wise man gains his knowledge from the wiser lawgiver, who in turn represents the Logos of God. Consequently, when Christ is represented as King in Clement's works, he is described in terms of the lawgiver.

The concept of "the universal Kingship" is developed in a number of passages of the *Stromateis*. According to the philosophers, it is only the wise king, lawgiver, or general who is righteous, holy and God-fearing.[2] The wise man *par excellence* is Moses, not only for Philo but also for Clement; he is prophet, lawgiver, tactician, general, statesman and philosopher.[3] These functions are hierarchically interrelated; the task of the tactician is a part of the general, which is part of that of the King. It is not only legislation and justice, but also divinity, which is summed up in the principle of Kingship. The Kingship thus stands at the head of the hierarchy of values, and includes in itself all other functions.[4] According to this passage, the King is the one who determines the laws, and has the power of reason, enabling him to rule voluntary servants,[5] just like the Lord, who rules over those who believe in him and in Christ, and under whose feet God has placed all things.

The common Hellenistic concept of the wise man as King recurs in a number of passages of Philo's works, and it is certain that Clement has taken over the idea from him, though he refers to Plato and other Greek philosophers as well.[6] . . .

It has been claimed by historians of religion that Philo's views were derived from Hellenistic syncretism; but this is an unwarranted conclusion, and recent years have seen greater emphasis placed on his Jewish and OT background. . . . The character of the Israelite King as righteousness incarnate has been stressed. . . . This idea of the King as *nomos empsychos* ("law ensouled") is thus an excellent example of the way in which OT-Jewish and Greek material is interwoven in Philo; so much so, that it is a hazardous undertaking to attempt to distinguish its various original components.

It is characteristic of Philo that his suprahistorical *Weltanschauung* leaves no room for the Messianic idea. Moses, who is depicted as the ideal King, and given all the epithets usually reserved for the Messiah, stands instead at the focus of Philo's system. Moses is thus called King and priest and above all lawgiver. . . .

The image of Christ in the early Church was coloured by the Messianic expectations of Palestinian Judaism. Both the apocalyptic world of concepts and the Messianic interpretation of the OT were taken over by Jesus and, after him, by the Church, in the conviction that the prophecies had been fulfilled and that the eschatological King had come. But Alexandrian theology was connected with an entirely different Jewish tradition. It was presumably not only Philo who substituted Moses for the Messiah at the heart of his theology; we may suppose it to have been a general

---

[2] *Stromateis,* I, 168, 4. The wise man is called *nomos empsychos* ("ensouled law") in *Stromateis* II, 18, 4.

[3] *Ibid.,* I, 158, 1.

[4] *Ibid.,* I, 158–159.

[5] It is a general principle in Hellenistic political philosophy that one of the characteristics of the true kingship is to rule, unlike the tyrant, over voluntary subjects.

[6] In *Stromateis* II, 18.1–19.4. Clement refers to Plato's *Euthydemos* and the *Statesman,* in which the wise man is called royal, even when a private citizen, and to Pindar, Speusippus, and Chrysippus. In Philo the idea is found particularly in Mut. 151f., Post. 127–129, Sobr. 56f., and Somn. II. 243f.

tendency in Alexandrian Judaism. Consequently the Christian Church in Alexandria came to represent Christ as the new and consummate Moses. This tendency can be discerned as early as in the Epistle to the Hebrews, which appears to have originated in Alexandria.[7]

The parallelism between Moses and Christ is presented all the more clearly in the work of Clement, who describes both in the same terms and connects the same idea with both. In one extended passage he describes Moses as a Hellenistic ideal king, and supplies Moses with all the epithets normally reserved for such a king.[8] He is not only a wise king and lawgiver; he is even called *nomos empsychos.*[9]

According to Clement, Christ has the same qualities, though they are even more pronounced than in Moses' case: Christ is the true King, high priest and lawgiver. Christ has proved himself to be King, since he was addressed as such by the unbelieving Jews, by little children and by the prophets; his Kingdom is so great that he was able to refuse the offer of the world and all its gold when it was made by the adversary. He is the one and only High Priest, since he alone knows the nature of true worship; he is the King of peace, Melchizedek, who is best fitted to lead the human race. He is lawgiver, since it was he who proclaimed the Law through the mouths of the prophets, and he who taught, in the clearest possible terms, what we ought to do and what we ought not to do.[10]

Moses was the mouthpiece of the Logos for men. Christ is himself the Logos incarnate. In this Clement goes far beyond Philo. But when he describes Christ's royal qualities, he is so close to Philo's description of Moses that it is virtually impossible to distinguish the two. It is significant that in the passage we have just summarized, Clement appears to refer to the three-fold ministry of King, priest and prophet. Although he does not mention the prophet, his description of the lawgiver fits in with the character of the prophet.

Similarly, both Moses and Christ are called "shepherd": a title which in Alexandrian theology is particularly important as referring to the Logos.[11]

The titles of shepherd and King are synonymous in the Near East and in the OT. Philo, too, uses the two synonymously. The title of shepherd is given not only to Kings and wise men (Kings of course being wise men as well), but also to God, the King of the world-all. . . . The hymn which concludes Clement's *Paedagogus* is a particularly expressive description of Christ as Shepherd and King; here he enumerates the titles of Christ, and returns time and time again to the words "Shepherd" and "King."[12] It is probable that there are connections between this and an older tradition of hymn-writing, and that the epithets given to Christ by Clement refer back to an early liturgical usage.

---

[7] C. Spicq, *L'Epitre aux Hébreux* 1 (Paris, 1952), pp. 64 ff. In Spicq's view Heb. is directly dependent upon Philo, *op. cit.,* pp. 39–91.

[8] *Stromateis,* I, 158–168.

[9] *Ibid.,* I, 167, 3.

[10] *Ibid.,* II, 21.1–5.

[11] *Protrepticus,* 116.1.

[12] *Paedagogus,* III, 101.3.

Origen. There are certain standard difficulties encountered in . . . every attempt to describe Origen's theology; this is no less true of the attempt to give an overall picture of Origen's doctrine of the Kingship of Christ. His general presentation varies, between a more or less traditional Biblical theology and Platonic speculation, depending upon the part of his work to which we turn. There is little about Christ as King in either *Contra Celsum* or *De principiis;* the commentaries and homilies, on the other hand, contain a number of sayings on the Kingship of Christ. . . . It is clear that the fact that we have here a more traditional type of theology than in *Contra Celsum* and *De principiis* is due to the different character of the works in question. It is however possible, even within the framework of the Biblical theology, to come across different estimations of the Kingship of Christ. The more traditional eschatological concepts are to be found mainly in the *Commentaries on St. Matthew and St. John,* while the OT homilies and the *Commentary on the Song of Songs* contain a theology strikingly spiritual in character. . . . In his *Commentary on the Song of Songs* he links the royal theme with the theme of the bridegroom, symbolizing the relationship between Christ and the individual believer.

The oldest preserved commentaries on the text of the NT are to be found in Origen; these are of particular interest for us, since they provide the earliest examples of an exposition of the actions and words with which Jesus manifests himself as the Messiah. Apart from unimportant passages in Justin and Irenaeus, the only pre-Origen commentary on the NT which we possess is a highly fragmentary commentary on John by the Valentinian theologian Heracleon. It is probable that Origen was inspired to undertake his commentaries by Heracleon, and he has also taken over a proportion of Heracleon's exegesis, in a more or less modified form.

The traditional Christian idea that the Kingship of Christ was made manifest above all at the Ascension is also to be found in Origen, largely in his exposition of the descriptions in Matthew and John of Jesus' entry into Jerusalem.[13] The entry is, according to Origen, an anticipation of the Ascension of Christ, his entry into the heavenly city. The Zion which rejoiced and the Jerusalem which proclaimed the good tidings (Zech 9:9) cannot in Origen's view be identical with the earthly Jerusalem, over which Jesus wept—the town which murdered the prophets and crucified Christ. The prophecy refers instead to the heavenly Zion (Heb 12:22) and the Jerusalem above, which is free (Gal 4:26).[14] The ass and the foal symbolize the Jews and the Gentiles, who are freed by Christ from their bonds and led into the heavenly city.[15]

Origen has taken over these allegori-

[13] *Commentary on St. Matthew,* 16, 14–19; *Commentary on John,* 10, 28–32 (18).

[14] *Commentary on St. Matthew,* 16, 15.

[15] *Commentary on St. John,* 10.29 (18). . . . When the true Jerusalem received Jesus, when he ascended on the *hupozugion* which was his body, the earthly Jerusalem—which was a shadow of the heavenly—and its Temple, were destroyed. We find the same contrast in the *Commentary on St. Matthew,* 12.20. Jesus was killed in the Jerusalem here below, but after his resurrection reigns on Mt. Zion and in the Jerusalem which is the city of the living God (here the Latin version has a quotation from Ps. 2.6).

cal interpretations from earlier traditions, of which no more than a few traces remain. In the *testimonia* tradition the entry into Jerusalem is seen only as the fulfilment of Zech 9:9 and Gen 49:11. Irenaeus on one occasion represents the entry into Jerusalem as the coming of the expected King, but says nothing about it being an anticipation of the Ascension.[16] The background of Origen's exegesis must be sought instead in Alexandrian theology. Clement has a passage in which he represents the entry into Jerusalem as anticipating the Ascension.[17] A similar interpretation of the same event is to be found in Heracleon; the resemblance between this interpretation and those of Clement and Origen is striking, though the former is dominated by Heracleon's Valentinian theology. . . .

Although we know that Clement and Origen were not entirely uninfluenced by Gnostic exegesis, it would nevertheless be quite wrong to regard this interpretation as originally Gnostic. It is entirely in accord with the parallelism between the heavenly and the earthly Jerusalem, which is already to be seen in Judaism, and which is reflected in the NT, and particularly in those passages quoted by Origen: Gal 4:26 and Heb 12:22, as well as Rev 21–22. . . . We have already pointed out that in *testimonia* there is a tendency to interpret the processional Psalms as referring to the Ascension. The King, entering the Temple in procession, is taken to be a *typos* of Christ enthroned in the heavenly sanctuary. It is fully in agreement with this interpretation when Origen interprets the entry into Jerusalem as prefiguring the coming Ascension. . . .

Origen, as he himself admits, took over the typological interpretation of the ass and the foal as the Jews and the Gentiles from an earlier exposition.[18] . . . The fact of there being two animals was used by the allegorizers in order to represent Christ as *hēniochos* ("driver"): He is the Logos, who yokes the two races of man and leads them into the holy city.

The prophecy of the coming prince of peace, who is to cast chariots and horses out of Jerusalem and destroy the bows of war (Zech 9:10) is taken by Origen and given a special interpretation agreeing with his exposition of Jesus' entry into Jerusalem. Before the coming of Christ, the heavenly Jerusalem was ruled by the spiritual powers of darkness in the heavenly places (Eph 6:12), but these were cast out when he entered, just as he cast out the merchants from the Temple after his entry into Jerusalem (Matt 21:12 par.).[19] . . . One element in the enthronement of Christ is that his enemies are laid beneath his feet. "He has disarmed the principalities and powers of the spiritual world."

As the entry of Jesus into Jerusalem prefigures the coming Ascension, so the episode in which Jesus is mocked is taken to prefigure the coming Kingship. The crown of thorns and the mantle do not however give rise to any presentation of the Kingship. The reed which Jesus held in his hand is reminiscent of the broken reed upon which we supported ourselves before we believed (Is 36:6).

[16] *Adversus Haereses,* IV, 11.3.
[17] *Protrepticus,* 121.1.
[18] *Commentary on St. John,* 10.29 (18).
[19] Origen, *Commentary on St. John,* 10.29.

Jesus took the reed, and gave us in its place the sceptre of the Kingdom of Heaven, of which it is written: "The sceptre of thy kingdom is the sceptre of righteousness" (Ps 44 (45):7). There follow two quotations in which the word *hrabdos* ("sceptre") is the key-word: I Cor 4:21 and Ex 12:11; the technique used is reminiscent of Justin's, with one difference—that Origen also makes use of NT quotations among his proof-texts.

Origen saw the Kingship of Christ as manifested in his Ascension, which at the same time was his enthronement. This view is particularly prominent in his commentary on Matt 20.20 ff., the pericope in which the mother of the sons of Zebedee comes to Jesus with the request that her sons may be allowed to sit, one on the right hand and one on the left hand of Jesus in his Kingdom. Origen points out that her request is typical of the kingdoms of the world, in which it is accounted an honour to sit together with the king, dressed in his finery and bearing his regalia.

In this context Origen produces a large number of proof-texts from the OT and the NT, showing what is meant by the *sessio* of Christ. . . . Origen goes on to say that the throne of God is spiritual, and so is the throne of Christ. The fact that Christ is seated at the right hand of Power must also be understood spiritually. To imagine that it would be possible to sit at the right and left hand of the throne of Christ is therefore both worldly and absurd. That Christ has been installed in his Kingship and has received power must be understood as meaning that he has destroyed sin, which ruled in our mortal bodies (cf. Rom 6:12) and ruled over every evil *archē* ("principle") and *exousia* ("power") and *dynamis* ("dominion"); this is the meaning of Christ's enthronement on the throne of his glory. . . .

It is mainly in the homilies and the commentaries on the books of the OT that Origen places sayings having to do with the Kingship of Christ in the context of Philonic allegory.[20] . . .

In these allegorical expositions Origen often returns to the theme of "royalty"; it is seldom that he is referring to the Kingship of Christ when he does so. He took over instead the idea of the wise man as king, which we have previously encountered in Philo and Clement. . . . The parallelism between the "princes" and the "nobles" he interprets as referring to two kinds of people; the princes dug and the kings delved: the kings are thus those who delve the deepest and penetrate the secrets of God. In connection with this Origen sets out what royalty implies: Christians are called "a royal people" (cf. 1 Pet 2:9). The Apostles and those who rule the churches are even more entitled to be called kings, and the Lord is thus called "the King of kings," since he rules over kings. Origen also mentions the fact that Paul calls the Christians in Corinth kings, though ironically, in 1 Cor 4:8. His exposition closes with a summary. True kings and rulers are necessary to take away the earth from the well, i.e. take away the superficial meaning of the letter of Scripture and penetrate to the inner rock, which is Christ, and bring out

[20] *Commentary on St. John,* 10.28 (18). An interpretation of Jerusalem as the individual into which Christ makes his entry is found as far back as Orac. Sib. 8.324 ff.

the spiritual meaning like living water. Kings are thus those who have driven out the rule (*regnum*) of sin from their bodies and have accepted the reign of righteousness in their limbs. To be great in the Kingdom (Matt 5:19) means to be a king. . . . Origen wishes to represent the wise man, i.e. the Christian, as king. Since Christ rules over all Christians, he is the King of kings: this spiritualized interpretation becomes common in later allegorical Scripture exposition, influenced as it was by Origen. . . .

The allegorical interpretation of the Kingship of Christ is especially noticeable in Origen's commentaries on the Song of Songs. . . . The writings of Hippolytus and Origen on the Song of Songs are practically contemporaneous. It is uncertain whether there has been any influence exercised in one or other direction, though it seems that Hippolytus is more likely to have influenced Origen than vice versa.

In his commentary Hippolytus has a Christological interpretation of the poem according to which the bridegroom is Christ and the bridal-chamber is the Church. The King in S. of S. 1:4 and 1:12 is thus obviously Christ.[21] But at the same time we find that there has been some influence from Philo, in Hippolytus' psychological interpretation of the text of Scripture.

This tendency is even more marked in Origen, according to whom Solomon is a pattern of Christ, partly as King of peace, partly because the Queen of the East came to hear his wisdom. . . . The idea of Christ as King of peace also occurs on a number of occasions in the commentary to S. of S. 1:4.[22] . . .

A link with the *testimonia* tradition's representation of Christ as King is found in the use of the exposition of Ps. 44 (45) in connection with the exegesis of S. of S.; there is no doubt that Ps. 44 was of great importance for the interpretation of the Kingship of Christ and the Church as his bride, and for the growing Marian typology. However, the description of Christ as King in the context of a bride-bridegroom mysticism lies outside the development which we are describing here.

4. H. A. Wolfson[1] maintains that it was concern over the preservation of God's utter unity that gave rise to unorthodox views regarding the relationship of the preexisting Christ to God and of the born Christ to God. Differences of method and opinion led to controversy. He studies the two basic non-Catholic alternatives concerning the preexisting Logos and the two main unorthodox views regarding the Christ born of Mary.

Philosophic scrutiny into established Christian beliefs brought to light certain inherent difficulties. Especially were such difficulties revealed in the belief about the relation of the preexistent Christ to God and also about

[21] Hippolytus, *Commentary on the Song of Songs,* 3.1.

[22] Origen, *Commentary on the Song of Songs,* Prologue.

[1] Harry Austryn Wolfson, a native of Russia, is Nathan Littauer Professor (Emeritus) of Hebrew Literature and Philosophy in Harvard University. He has authored several philosophical and religious works, *Philo, Philosophy of Spinoza, Religious Philosophy,*

the relation of the born Christ to God. In each of these beliefs a certain inconsistency appeared. But inconsistencies in beliefs which were accepted as true were inconceivable. And so the need for a solution became urgent. In this search for a solution, two main methods suggested themselves. One was to harmonize the inconsistencies; the other was to eliminate one of the recalcitrant elements. But if the method employed happened to be that of elimination, the further question arose as to which of the recalcitrant elements should be eliminated. Differences of method and of procedure led to differences of opinion and hence to controversies. All these controversies started within the body of Christianity which called itself catholic and among persons who held positions of authority within the Church. They all argued from commonly admitted premises, they all supported themselves by proof-texts of commonly recognized Scriptures, and they all claimed to represent the ancient tradition of Christianity. But the controversies were not allowed to go on as free individual discussions. Councils were called to decide which side was right. The decision of right and wrong was arrived at by majority vote. Those who won retained to themselves the name catholic. Those who were voted down were anathematized and declared as heretics. Thus a statutory Catholicism of Christianity emerged to take the place of the consentaneous catholicism which had fought and won its victory over Gnosticism.

This is the history of Christianity for over three centuries and a half. . . .

Heresies with Regard to the Preexistent Christ

The problems arising from the relation of the preexistent Christ to God had their origin in the two conflicting elements which orthodox Christianity tried to harmonize. On the one hand, there was the original Jewish belief in the unity of God, which is reaffirmed in the New Testament and constantly repeated by the Fathers in their assaults upon the polytheism of the heathens. On the other hand, there was the newly arisen belief that the Logos was God or that both the Logos and the Holy Spirit were Gods. Already by the time of Justin Martyr, with the very first attempts at the rationalization of Christian beliefs, this inconsistency became apparent and the search of a solution began.

The solution advanced by the orthodox Fathers . . . is a solution by harmonization, an attempt to combine, as Gregory of Nyssa characterizes it, the monotheism of the Jews and the polytheism of the Greeks. The method of harmonization used by them was to thin down the Jewish monotheism as a concession to Greek polytheism. The unity of God was not to mean, as insisted upon by Philo, absolute unity; it was to mean relative unity, or else it was to mean unity of rule.

But within the then catholic Christianity there were those who felt that in the New Testament there was no warrant for a triune God such as would have to lead to an attenuation of the principle of the unity of God. The scriptural injunction, both of the

etc. It is from his book *The Philosophy of the Church Fathers* (Cambridge, Mass.: Harvard University Press, 1956) that this excerpt has been taken, selectively, from pp. 577–599.

Old Testament and of the New Testament, that God is one, to them, was to be understood in the Philonic sense, and generally in the Jewish sense, that He is absolutely one. Beside God so conceived as one neither the Logos nor the Holy Spirit could be conceived by them as God. In the New Testament they found no statement by which they felt themselves compelled to believe that the Logos and the Holy Spirit were each God, and this despite Paul's description of the preexistent Christ, whom he also called the Holy Spirit, as being equal with God, and John's description of the Logos as being God. However, already in the New Testament, in the baptismal formula as well as in the Epistles of Paul, both the Son and the Holy Spirit have been associated with God the Father as objects of invocation and prayer and praise. There was thus already an established Trinitarian formula, which, they felt, must be preserved. This, they admitted, constituted the fundamental faith of Christianity: catholic Christianity in its true sense. But once one had confessed his belief in the Trinity, one was free to conceive of that Trinity in a way in which it would not infringe upon the unity of God in the strict sense of the term. And so they felt that the true meaning of the Logos and the Holy Spirit could not be that which through some misunderstanding had become current in the Church. Their true lost meaning had to be searched after and rediscovered. And in their search for this true lost meaning of the Logos and the Holy Spirit two alternatives suggested themselves. First, the Logos has no reality as a being distinct from God; it is only a power of God and hence it is God himself, its distinction from God being only as that of a mode of His manifestation to us. And what is true of the Logos is true also of the Holy Spirit. This view is usually referred to as Modalism, though in the case of some of its exponents, those who use the term "name" as a description of the Logos, the term Nominalism would be a more appropriate description of their view. However, the difference that one may discern between Modalism and Nominalism was not a conscious issue with those Fathers who were battling against the reality of the Logos. Second, the Logos, though admitted to have a real existence, was conceived to have been created by God out of nothing, and consequently, like everything else created by God, is not to be thought of as God. And what is true of the Logos is true also of the Holy Spirit, though in the case of the Holy Spirit its creation may have come about by the intermediacy of the Logos. This view shall be referred to as Creationalism. We thus have two solutions of the difficulty by means of elimination. One eliminates the reality of the Logos but retains the description of it as God, using this description in the sense of its being identical with God. The other eliminates the description of the Logos as God but retains its description as a real being, using this description in the sense of its being a creation of God.

The difficulty faced by faithful Christians with regard to what had already become the orthodox conception of the preexistent Christ, on the score of the unity of God, and the refuge they sought from it in the two alternative positions of Modalism and Creationalism is depicted by Origen. . . . The same difficulty faced by faithful Christians is also referred to by Tertullian. . . .

A reference to the first of these two alternative solutions is to be found, before the time of Origen, in a work by Justin Martyr, which was composed at about the middle of the second century. Justin Martyr himself had solved the problem of triunity by interpreting the unity of God as preached in the Old and the New Testaments in the sense of unity of rule, a conception of unity which to him did not exclude the existence of the Logos as a real personal being and as God. But there were others, he says, who, while admitting with him that there was a preexistent Christ called Logos, took that Logos to be a "power" which is "indivisible and inseparable from the Father, just as they say that the light of the sun on earth is indivisible and inseparable from the sun in the heavens."

Who were those people who denied the reality of the Logos and took it to be only a power of God? Some scholars take them to be a "class of Jewish theologians" or "Jews of Alexandrian culture," or those who reflect "Jewish notions"; or, more specifically, followers of Philo. . . .

While those to whom Justin Martyr refers cannot be identified, a little later, toward the end of the second century and the beginning of the third, representatives of this view appear under the names of Praxeas, Noetus, Epigonus, Cleomenes, Callistus, Sabellius, Paul of Samosata, and Commodian. Out of this list of names we shall take as our subject of discussion Praxeas, Noetus, Sabellius, Paul of Samosata, and Commodian.

All of them insist upon the unity of God in the absolute sense of the term. Concerning Praxeas and his followers it is said that "they will have the two to be but one, so that the Father shall be deemed to be the same as the Son," for "He himself, they say, made himself a Son to himself." Concerning Noetus it is said that "he thinks to establish monarchy by asserting that the Father and the Son so-called are one and the same, not another from another but himself from himself." Concerning Sabellius it is said that he maintained that "Father and Son are the same" and "in hypostasis one." Concerning Paul of Samosata it is said that he believed that "God the Father and the Son and the Holy Spirit are one God, that is to say, one person. And Commodian, speaking for himself, says almost in the words quoted above as representing the views of Praxeas and Noetus: "God is omnipotent, one, having been created out of himself" and "Hereupon the Father went into the Son, one God everywhere," by which he means that the Father and the Son are one person, for he immediately continues: "nor would He have been called Father had He not been made Son."

All of them similarly maintain that the term Logos is not to be taken as a real personal being. Concerning Praxeas and his followers it is said that they will not allow the Logos "to be really a substantive being, by having a substance of His own, in such a way that He may be regarded as an objective thing and a person, and so be able, as being constituted second to God the Father, to make two, the Father and the Son, God and the Word," for they will say, "what is a word, but a voice and sound of the mouth, and, as the grammarians teach, air when struck against, intelligible to the ear, but for the rest a sort of void, empty, and incorporeal thing." Concerning Noetus, it is said that "he thinks to establish monarchy by asserting the Father and the Son so-called are one and the same, not another from another, but himself from himself, and that He is called by the name of Father and Son according to the change of times." Concerning Sabellius it is said that he maintained that "the Father is Son and again the Son Father, in hypostasis one, in name two," or that the terms Father and Son and Holy Spirit are but actions (*energiai*) or names (*onomasiai*) and are to be compared to "the light and the heat and the circular form in the sun." Concerning Paul of Samosata it is said that he held that "God's Logos and His Holy Spirit are eternally in God [the Father], just as man's own reason (*logos*) is in his heart; the Son of God has no subsistence of his own; it subsists in God [the Father]." And Commodian speaking for himself describes God as one "who is called Father and Son and Holy Spirit."

So much for the first of the two alternative unorthodox solutions of the problem of triunity, the one which retained the description of the Logos as God but denied its reality. We shall now take up the other alternative unorthodox solution, the one which retained the reality of the Logos but discarded the description of it as God. The first unorthodox solution of the problem of triunity, in so far as it discarded a second stage of existence in the Logos, that of its real existence, may be regarded as a reversal of Philo's view of the Logos; the second solution, as we shall see, is a reversion to the original view of Philo. This second solution is that which is identified with the name of Arius.[2] . . .

Heresies with Regard to the Born Christ

Just as the controversies within catholic Christianity with regard to the relation of the preexistent Christ to God arose as a reaction against the orthodox combination of two contradictory elements, described by Gregory of Nyssa as the monotheism of the Jews and the polytheism of the Greeks, so also the controversies with regard to the relation of the born Christ to God similarly arose, we shall now try to show, from the orthodox attempt to combine two contradictory conceptions of Jesus, the Jewish and the pagan, or the Ebionitic and the Docetic.

From the earliest times in the history of Christianity these two non-Catholic views about the relation of the born Christ to God existed by the side of its gradually developing catholic view. Ebionism represents the view of the original Jewish followers of Jesus, who conceived of him as a mere human being upon whom, as the promised Messiah, "the spirit of the Lord" rested, "the spirit of wisdom and understanding, the spirit of counsel and might, the spirit of knowledge and the fear of the Lord." Docetism represents a view introduced by pagan converts to Christianity who, after the analogy of pagan deities who assumed the appearance of some human being, conceived of Jesus not as a real human being but as God who only appeared in human form. These two conceptions of the born Christ, as we have seen, are to be found among the Gnostics:

[2] The views of Arius are discussed in Ch. III, n. 3.

the Ebionitic in Cerinthus, Carpocrates, and Justinus; the Docetic in Simon, Menander, Saturninus, Basilides of Irenaeus, Marcion, and, in a modified form, in Apelles. The catholic Christian conception of the born Christ may be considered as a combination of these two extreme conceptions. Jesus was not a mere appearance of God in human form; he was a real man; but he was not a mere man; he was also God. He was, as Tertullian puts it, "both man and God, the Son of man and the Son of God." As man, he had a complete human nature besides his complete divine nature; as God, the person in him was only that of the Logos: the humanity in him was not a person. It is this view, which had been implicit in the orthodox teachings of catholic Christianity from its very beginning, that ultimately found expression in the formula of one person and two natures, the one person in him being the person of the Logos in him and the two natures being the natures of the Logos and the man in him.

But just as the harmonization of what Gregory of Nyssa described as the Jewish monotheism and the Greek polytheism in the conception of the preexistent Christ roused opposition to it within catholic Christianity among those who insisted upon a rigid conception of the unity of God, so also the view interposed between Jewish Ebionism and pagan Docetism in the conception of the born Christ roused opposition to it within catholic Christianity, again among those who insisted upon a rigid conception of the unity of God. If there is to be one God, they argued, then Jesus can be no God, not even in part. And just as in the problem of the preexistent Christ, the opposition to the catholic conception of him fell into two groups, one making the preexistent Christ a mere mode of God and the other making him a mere creature of God, so now in the problem of the born Christ the opposition to the catholic conception of him fell also into two corresponding groups, one making the born Christ a mere appearance of God and the other making him a mere man. That it was the attempt to preserve the unity of God in its strict sense that gave rise within catholic Christianity to these two contrasting views with regard to the born Christ is attested by Novatian in a passage where, after referring to the Old and the New Testament as the source of true faith, he proceeds to say: For both they who say that Jesus Christ himself is God the Father and they who would have him to be only man have gathered thence (from Scripture) the sources and reasons of their error and perversity, because, when they perceived that it was written that 'God is one,' they thought that they could not otherwise hold such an opinion than by supposing that it must be believed either that Christ was man only or really God the Father." In this passage, the expression "Christ was man only" reflects the Ebionitic alternative, whereas the expression "really God the Father" reflects the Docetic alternative.

Thus Docetism and Ebionism, which were never part of catholic Christianity, were about to be brought into catholic Christianity by zealous catholic Christians. It was not, however, Docetism and Ebionism in their purest form that were to be brought into catholic Christianity, but each of them in some modified form, a sort of neo-Docetism and neo-Ebionism. For, while like the old Docetism of the type we have met with in Simon, this new kind of Docetism took the incarnation to mean the transformation of God into the mere appearance of man, still, unlike the old Docetism as represented in Simon, which took the suffering of Jesus to be also a mere appearance, it took the accounts of the suffering of Jesus to be literally true. And since to them Jesus, whose suffering was real, was not a real man but God the Father in the appearance of man, it follows that it was God the Father himself who experienced all the real suffering that is ascribed to Jesus. It is for this reason that they are not called Docetists but rather Patripassians, that is to say, those who believed that it was the Father himself who suffered in the passion of Jesus. But Patripassianism, as it was well said, "was a higher form of Docetism" or had an "affinity" with Docetism. Similarly, while, like the old Ebionism of the type which we have met with in Cerinthus, this new kind of Ebionism took the incarnation to mean the indwelling of God or His Logos in Jesus as in any righteous man, still, unlike the Ebionism as represented in Cerinthus, it attributed some miraculous element to the birth of Jesus, either by making the indwelling to have begun with his birth or by making his birth to have been from a virgin.

One would expect that logically Modalists in the problem of the preexistent Christ would be Docetists in the problem of the born Christ, and some Modalists indeed met this logical expectation and were Docetists. Similarly one would expect that logically Creationalists in the problem of the preexistent Christ would be Ebionites in the problem of the born Christ, and again, some Creationalists were Ebionites. But it also happens that some who preserved the unity of God in the problem of the preexistent Christ by resorting to Modalism tried to preserve the unity of God in the problem of the born Christ by resorting to Ebionism. We thus have three groups. One group was led from Modalism to a modified form of Docetism. A second group was led from Modalism to a modified form of Ebionism. A third group was led from Creationalism to a modified form of Ebionism. We shall try to illustrate this generalization by concrete examples.

The first group, that which was led from Modalism to a modified form of Docetism, is represented by Praxeas, Noetus, and Commodian, who in their views of the relation of the Logos to God, as we have seen, were Modalists.

Praxeas and his followers are reported to have said that "in the course of time, then, the Father forsooth was born, and the Father suffered,—God himself, the Lord almighty, whom in their preaching they declare to be Jesus Christ." Noetus is reported to have said that God the Father "was He who appeared and underwent birth from a virgin and dwelt as a man among men, and acknowledged himself to those who saw him to be a Son by reason of the birth that had taken place, but did not conceal from those who could receive it that he was also the Father, and that he also suffered . . . and died and did not die." Commodian similarly says of the crucified Christ that "He was indeed not a man, but He was a God" and he speaks of God as "having suffered" and as "capable of suffering."

Hippolytus, following his habit of tracing Christian heresies to pagan philosophers, tries to find the origin of the Noetean Christology in Heraclitus. The Noetean Christology in its broader implications means to Hippolytus that God who is one and the same in reality assumes many forms in appearance, so that, though "invisible" and "unbegotten" and "immortal," He took on the appearance of one who is "visible" and "begotten" and "mortal," when He wished to take on that appearance. Such a conception of God, a God who is one in reality but who appears to us in more than one form, maintains Hippolytus, is implied in a statement which he quotes from Heraclitus, as follows: "God is day and night, winter and summer, war and peace, surfeit and hunger, . . . but He takes various shapes, just as [fire], when it is mingled with spices, is named according to the savor of each." Irrespective of the question whether the Noetan Patripassianism was derived, as asserted here by Hippolytus, from Heraclitus or whether it was derived from the general mythological belief in the transformation of gods into the form of human beings, it is quite clear that Hippolytus took the Patripassianism of Noetus as a sort of Docetism. And what he says of Noetus would be true of all the other Patripassians.

The second group, that which was led from Modalism to a modified form of Ebionism, is represented by Paul of Samosata, who in his view of the relation of the preexistent Christ to God, as we have seen, was a Modalist. Paul of Samosata is reported to have said of Jesus that "he was in his nature an ordinary man" or "a mere man." But, while Jesus was a mere man, he was a superior man, for, as he says, "the constitution of Christ differs from that of ours" and wisdom, that is, the Logos, he says by implication, came to dwell in Jesus at his birth. The superiority of Jesus was thus not acquired; it was native. It was a free grace to him from God. Jesus may be said to have belonged to that class of men who are described by Philo as those whom "even before their birth God endows with a goodly form and equipment, and has determined that they shall have a most excellent portion" and among whom he includes Noah, Melchizedek, Abraham, Isaac, Jacob, and Moses. To Paul of Samosata, however, Jesus was superior even to these, for, using the term wisdom for the Logos and with evident reference to the statement just quoted from Philo, he says, God had ordained that "wisdom should not so dwell in any one else, for it was in the prophets, to a still higher degree in Moses and in many men of eminence, but to a still higher degree in Christ." But following the view of those Fathers who distinguished between the Logos and the Holy Spirit, he says concerning Jesus that subsequently, at his baptism, "having been anointed with the Holy Spirit, he was named Christ." But neither the indwelling of wisdom or Logos in him which started at his birth nor the descent of the Holy Spirit upon him at his baptism did make Jesus a God. With regard to the indwelling of the Logos in Jesus, he maintains that its union with Jesus left him still a mere man. "Jesus Christ is one thing, and the Logos is another thing." The union between them is "according to knowledge and communion and not according to a substance subsisting in a body. Wisdom was not begotten together with the humanity substantially, but according to quality. Mary did not bear the Logos . . . she bore a man like us," that is to say, like wisdom, the Logos was not begotten together with the humanity substantially but only according to quality. Similarly with regard to the descent of the Holy Spirit upon him, he maintains, as we have seen, that it only proclaimed him a Christ.

The third group, that which was led from Creationalism to neo-Ebionism, is represented by Arius and his followers [to be discussed later]. . . .

The case of Sabellius deserves special attention. Though his view on the preexistent Christ, as we have seen, is definitely Modalistic, his view on the born Christ is open to doubt as to whether it is Docetic or Ebionitic. In the teachings reported in his name, he is never quoted as saying that Jesus was God or that it was God who suffered, but neither is he quoted as saying that Jesus was a mere man. Whatever statements are quoted in his name on the relation of the born Christ to God lend themselves to opposite interpretations.

He is, for instance, reported to have used the expressions "the man which the Logos wore (*ephoresen*)" and "the flesh which the Logos wore (*ephoresen*)." These expressions undoubtedly suggest an analogy between the body of Jesus and a garment. Generally the analogy of garment . . . whether used with reference to the relation of the body of Jesus to the Logos in him or with reference to the relation of body to soul in man in general, always implies that the body, whether in its relation to the Logos in Jesus or in its relation to the soul in man, is a real body. But at the same time it also implies that the Logos to which the body of Jesus is related is a real being and similarly the soul to which the body of man is related is also a real being. But we already know from his view on the preexistent Christ that the Logos to him is not a real being. Consequently the Logos, which in the passage quoted is said to have worn the man or the flesh, is not a real being. The question, therefore, may be raised whether in the same passage the terms man and flesh, which the Logos is said to have worn, like the term Logos, are similarly not used by him in the sense of a real being or whether, unlike the term Logos, these terms are used by him in the sense of a real being. In the former case, his two expressions, "the man which the Logos wore" and "the flesh which the Logos wore" would be interpreted Docetically to mean that God transformed himself into the mere appearance of man or flesh. In the latter case, they would be interpreted Ebionitically to mean that God came to indwell in the real man or flesh of Jesus as He does in any real righteous person. . . .

A similar vagueness is to be found in a restatement of the view of Sabellius by Basil. . . .

We have thus seen that . . . there is no evidence to show whether Sabellius' view on the born Christ was Docetic or Ebionitic.

Two eminent students of the history of doctrine assume, without sufficient evidence, we believe, that Sabellius' view on the born Christ is Docetic. Thus Dorner is inclined to reject a certain interpretation of Sabellius' view on the plurality in the work of God on the mere ground that it would imply Ebionism and Sabellius' Christology is described by him as "simply a higher potence of Docetism" or as that in which Patripassianism "attained its most perfect form and expression." Similarly with evident reference to Sabellius' statements quoted above about the Logos wearing the man or the flesh, he says that the statements to the effect that "the Logos was clothed with the man Jesus" show that Sabellius "was far from sharing the Ebionism of elder writers, or of Paul of Samosata." But, as we have seen above, these statements lend themselves either to a Docetic or to an Ebionitic interpretation. Moreover, on finding that the statement "not the Logos was the Son, but this man was the only-begotten Son of God" attributed to Sabellius implies that the personality of Jesus is derived from the humanity alone, he rejects this implication of the statement, again, on the mere ground that it "would lead to Ebionism, contrary to the fundamental view of Sabellius," and hence proceeds to argue that the statement must have some other meaning. Thus also Harnack similarly assumes a Patripassian and hence Docetic interpretation of Sabellius' Christology and so, on the basis of a remark of Epiphanius that "the Sabellians derived their whole heresy and its strength from certain Apocrypha, especially the so-called Gospel of the Egyptians," he infers that "it confirms the view that the Christology of Sabellius cannot have been essentially different from the older, the so-called Patripassian doctrine."

But whatever Sabellius' view may have been it is clear that the various forms of modified Docetism we have discussed followed logically from Modalism and that the various forms of modified Ebionism we have discussed followed also logically either from Modalism or from Creationalism and that ultimately the opposition of all these neo-Docetic and neo-Ebionitic views to the orthodox view of two natures arose out of a desire to preserve the principle of the unity in its strict sense.

Then we meet, however, with two heretical views on the relation of the born Christ to God, one a still further modified Docetism and the other a still further modified Ebionism, which have no logical basis in an attempt to preserve the strict conception of the unity of God which, in connection with the preexistent Christ, had given rise to Modalism and Creationalism. They are held by men who in their views on the relation of the preexistent Christ to God are strict followers of the orthodox view. Their deviation from orthodoxy on the problem of the relation of the born Christ was due to theological considerations of a different kind.[3]

5. R. Cantalamessa[1] remarks that Tertullian's Christology is more in line with Antiochian than Alexandrian thinking. He sees him as greatly responsible for that dual nature mentality which later rose against

[3] These are the views of Apollinaris and Nestorius. They will be discussed in the next chapter.

[1] Raniero Cantalamessa, O.F.M.C., a native Italian, is Assistant Professor of Ancient Christian Literature at the Catholic University of the Sacred Heart in Milan. He has published various articles dealing with patristic studies "Meliton de Sardes," "La Primitiva Esegesi Cristologica di Rom. 1, 3–4 e Luc. 1, 35." It is from his book *La Cristologia di Tertulliano* (University of Fribourg, Switzerland, 1962) that this excerpt is taken, pp. 193–196.

Monophysism. He rejects Harnack's view that Tertullian's doctrine of "two substances or natures," which prevailed in Christian thought from the end of the second century on, was an adaptation of Gnostic and Valentinian dualism. The context of Tertullian's Christology is one of opposition to Gnosticism and Marcion.

Regarding Christ's divinity, Tertullian does not teach a gradual generation of the Word in his *Apology*. On the other hand, this theory is clearly taught in *Adversus Hermogenem* and in *Adversus Praxean*. The procession of the Word occurs in three successive stages parallel to the three stages through which creation takes place: *"cogitatio"* ("thought"), *"dispositio"* ("disposition"), and *"perfectio"* ("perfection"). The Word as "Son" and as a distinct person is not eternal; he begins with the creation of the world. He is of the same substance of the Father, but he does not possess that substance in the same measure as the Father (*modulo alter*). He is God in the same way as the Father, but not in the same measure. . . .

The parallelism which he establishes and smoothly pursues between the "god of the philosophers" and the God-Father of the Christians and between the intermediate divinities and the Son offers a reason for the continuation and accentuation of trinitarian subordinationism in the historical level of the incarnation. Side by side with a trinitarian subordinationism, one may see a "Christological subordinationism" in Tertullian. . . .

Among the different titles given to Christ in trinitarian contexts, the title *"Spiritus Dei"* is a relevant one. This is a technical name, exclusively used for the Son, which enfeebles Loof's contention of a binitarian theory in Tertullian's theology.[2] In Tertullian, unlike Theophilus of Antioch and Irenaeus, *"Sophia"* ("wisdom") is also a title exclusively used for the Second Person. . . .

The incarnation of the Word was real and not merely visionary. The Word, however, did not "transform" himself into flesh; rather, he revested himself with and assumed flesh from Mary's womb. Preexistence and incarnation are presupposed in Tertullian's exegesis of Phil 2:6 ff. . . .

Tertullian gave great weight to the Savior's humanity in contrast to Gnostic and Marcionist docetism. Yet, at the same time, he affirmed the transcendence of his humanity in the realm of holiness when compared with our holiness. Tertullian was the first Christian author to speak clearly and extensively about the human and rational soul of Christ, attributing to it a redemptive function. Notwithstanding his traducianistic views, he makes Christ's soul the product of direct divine action. . . .

He used numerous formulae to express the two natures in Christ. However, that of *"duae substantiae"* is definitive. He uses the term *"substantia"* with the stoic meaning of *"ousia"* ("essence") in the sense of a body—*sui generis*. This special kind of body is also understood in the stoic sense. Apparently, he discovered the formula *"duae substantiae"* in Melito of Sardis. . . .

---

[2] F. Loofs, *Paulus von Samosata,* Leipzig, 1924, 211/8. (Cantalamessa discusses this matter fully in his *op. cit.,* pp. 51 ff.)

The doctrine of Tertullian on the two natures is derived directly from the Scripture, in particular from the two well-known Christological texts of Rom 1: 3–4 and Jn 1: 14. The importance which this doctrine achieved at the end of the second century must be attributed not to the widely spread presupposition that it was a formulation of Gnostic and Valentinian dualism but to the reaction against Marcionistic Docetism which it instilled. . . .

The union of the two substances in Christ is treated in the light of stoic theories concerned with the physical union of bodies. Tertullian rejects the type of union which would imply a "confusion" of the substances and adopts, more or less openly, the *krasis di' holōn* ("compenetration through wholes"), i.e., the union in which both the substances and their properties remained unaltered. The union of the two natures in Christ is, consequently, a result achieved more from the physical than from the metaphysical point of view. . . .

The expression *"una persona"* in the formula *"duplex status in una persona"* is not understood in the sense of the future Chalcedonian definition, that is, in a strictly Christological sense, but rather in a trinitarian sense. The expression should be understood as in the context of *"in una persona Trinitatis."* The term *"persona"* in Tertullian's theology does not mean "juridical person," nor "face or visage," nor even "interlocutor." It has, or it tends to have already, a "philosophical" meaning. Hence, "persona" means a "particular individual," or, as the author states, a "personal substance" (Val. 4, 2). Tertullian incorporated the term *"persona"* into his theological language from profane usage. . . .

While continuing the use of the *communicatio idiomatum* as those before him had done, Tertullian insists more emphatically on the principle of the "distinct activity" of the two natures. This is the basis of an argument which will become classic in Christology, namely, the two series of operations in Christ: the "passions" of the flesh and the "actions" of the Spirit. The term and concept of *"proprietas,"* which will also have an important role in the future Christological controversies, is borrowed from the stoic categories and stands for the essential quality which gives distinct characteristics and prerogatives to any substance. Notwithstanding the analytic character of Tertullian's Christology, Christ's unity as a person and as a being is never compromised. This remains true even when he speaks of the *"homo Christi."* Christ's unity is explicitly affirmed. . . .

Were we to define Tertullian's Christology in contrast with future controversies we would say that it is a Christology which is prevalently dual-natured and analytic. This orientation was greatly influenced by external factors. His Christology was formulated almost entirely in the context of his polemics with the Gnostics and Marcion. Therefore, it was formulated under the constant preoccupation of affirming the reality of the Savior's humanity and the permanence of the two distinct substances. We believe that the personal unity of Christ is never compromised. It is true that the main concern of Tertullian's Christology lies primarily in the distinction of the two natures rather than in the unity of the person. He moves more in line with the future Antiochian school than with the Cyrillian and Alexandrian school. Limited as it might be, this is an accomplishment of his Christology. The "Nestorian" heresy condemned at Ephesus is, indeed, pernicious, but the Eutychian heresy rejected at Chalcedon is no less disastrous to the proper understanding of Christ and his redemptive work.

6. R. V. Sellers[1] looks at the legalistic mentality proper of the West as greatly influencing the soteriological thought of the early Latin Fathers. The ideas on redemption of the Easterners failed to strike their imagination. Their attention is focused primarily on Calvary, on the Lord's meritorious death. This is the purpose of the incarnation. Their Christology, however, keeps balanced the two fundamental principles of confession and of inquiry, namely the unity of Christ, and the distinction of natures.

As is well known, unlike their brethren in the East, the Westerns have no real interest in speculation. Rather, they are jurists and administrators, who, trained in Roman law and rhetoric, are primarily concerned with the matter of ecclesiastical organization, and all that it involves. Moreover, brought up under the influence of the idea of the Roman *imperium,* they think of God rather in terms of sovereignty than in those of being.

Through the influence of Tertullian and Cyprian, the Christian religion in the West was being carried more and more into the legal sphere, and the Church had come to be regarded as "the institute of salvation." In the Scriptures she possessed the *lex Dei*—the *lex sacra,* the *lex divina*—in which was to be found what God enjoined and what he forbade; in addition, she possessed her *lex fidei,* which Rule of Faith summed up the *lex evangelica* and the *traditio catholicae ecclesiae,* handed down from the Apostles themselves. Thus in clearest terms the Christian was taught the doctrines necessary to salvation, and at the same time protected against the pernicious outcome of the vain curiosity of the heretics. . . .

Against the same intellectual background the Westerns developed their conception of sin. For them, sin is a crime against the sovereignty of God which calls for satisfaction. Such words as "debt," "guilt," "merit," and "compensation" appear again and again in Tertullian, who teaches that God is Master and Creditor, while man is slave and debtor. . . . But, he goes on, the way of reconciliation is open, and through acts of penitence,[2] themselves "the price at which the Lord himself has determined to award pardon," and a "compensation" offered to him, we can make satisfaction.[3] And, as we should expect, Cyprian's views are similar to those of his master.[4]

[1] Robert Victor Sellers, D.D. is professor of Biblical and Historical Theology in the University of London. He is the author of several historical and doctrinal studies: *Eustathius of Antioch, Two Ancient Christologies,* etc. It is from his book *The Council of Chalcedon* (London: S.P.C.K., 1953) that this excerpt has been taken, selectively, from pp. 182–203.

[2] Tertullian, *De Poenitentia,* 7.

[3] *Ibid.,* 9; see also *de jejunio,* 3.

[4] *De lapsis* and *de opere eleemosyna,* passim.

Closely related to this teaching on the sacrament of penance is the teaching of the Westerns on the atoning work of Jesus Christ. Surrounded by the political absolutism of a State which was determined that its code of laws should be enforced, the Western theologians came to regard God as essentially will, whose law in spiritual matters was likewise supreme. Hence they find themselves face to face with this question: How can man escape the severe condemnation which God in his justice must mete out to him on account of his disobedience to the divine injunctions? Their answer is that God must intervene and vindicate his law: satisfaction must be made, and the debt paid, through the coming of One who will take man's guilt upon himself, and in his perfect obedience offer himself willingly as a sacrifice on man's behalf. In this way, man's forgiveness—and forgiveness is ever the desired end according to Western soteriological thought—could be secured.

Thus we can easily understand why theories of the Atonement, prevalent in the East, failed to strike the imagination of the West. The conception that man's salvation amounts to his deification could not thrive on Western soil, and it is only because of contact with Eastern ideas that it appears in Hilary and Leo. Nor does the Antiochene conception of man's moral perfection in a future life make any direct appeal to Western teachers, though it is implicit in doctrine. Rather, they focus attention, not so much (like the Alexandrians) on the meaning of the incarnation, or (like the Antiochenes) on that of the Resurrection, as on that of Calvary, as they lay stress on the forgiveness which it brings. Certainly they are at one with the Easterns in maintaining the traditional idea that Christ has redeemed us from the powers of evil—an idea which they develop in picturesque detail and, true to their upbringing, seek to justify on legal grounds—but for them the *totum Dei opus* is to be seen in the Lord's meritorious Death. To this end had the Son of God become man that, as man's representative, he might pay the debt, and remove man's guilt through an expiatory sacrifice. . . .

In a word, then, the Westerns see the need of the coming of a Mediator between God and man, himself at once God and man. Towards the close of the days when as yet Latin was not distinct from Greek theology, and each had to pursue its course according to its native peculiarities, Irenaeus had declared that, if man is to be saved, God must unite man to himself, since, "unless man had overcome man's antagonist, the enemy would not have been justly overcome, and unless it had been God who had granted the salvation, we could never have possessed it so surely"[5]; and his doctrine, so clearly expressed in the New Testament itself (Tim 1: 5, 6) was carried forward in its simplicity by successive generations of Latins. Tertullian, who can say that "nothing is so worthy of God as the salvation of man,"[6] speaks of Christ as "that most faithful Mediator between God and man, who

[5] Irenaeus goes on: "It became the Mediator between God and man, by his relationship to both, to bring both into friendship and concord; and, while presenting man to God, to reveal God to man" (*Adversus Haereses.*, III, xviii., 7; see also xix., 6).

[6] *Adversus Marcion.*, ii., 27.

reconciles both God to man and man to God", since he has united in his own self flesh and Spirit;[7] Cyprian in the *Testimonia* produces passages from the Old Testament as proof that Christ was constituted both God and man, "in order that he might be Mediator between us and the Father,"[8] and, continuing the work of Tertullian, Novatian in his *de Trinitate* sets out to refute the heretics by showing that Scripture proclaims the Saviour of our race as being, not man only, or God only, but both God and man,[9] and describes his Mediatorship as 'a most profound and recondite sacrament', in that the incarnate Logos links together earthly things with heavenly, joining God to man and man to God.[10] . . .

It will be obvious that, when these soteriological ideas are carried forward into Christology, the two root principles of Christological confession and Christological enquiry, as we are calling them, at once emerge: the Mediator, the God-man, is one Person, and in him are to be seen, as they are presented to the human mind, the two natures or substances of Godhead and manhood. Unlike the Easterns, the Latins keep these two principles in balance.

Vincent of Lerins claims that Tertullian may be called the Origen of the West. . . . Convinced that in Jesus Christ God himself has indeed experienced the human life in order to redeem us, he sets at the forefront of his teaching the fundamental truth that in him the divine Logos[11] became man. In this Witness and Servant of the Father, who unites in himself man and God (*miscente in semetipso hominem et Deum*),[12] he affirms:

> God has held converse with man that man might learn to act as God; God has put himself on a level with man, that man might be able to be on a level with God; God was found little, that man might become exceeding great.[13]

---

[7] *De Resurrectione,* 63. Cf. Hippolytus: "In order that he might be shown as having in himself each *ousia*—the ousia of God and that of men . . . it was necessary that Christ, in becoming the Mediator between God and man, should receive from both an earnest of some kind" (from a work entitled, *Balaam's Blessings;* the fragment has been preserved by Leontius, *c. Nestor. et Eutych.,* i; *P. G.,* lxxxvi., i., 1312A).

[8] *Testimonia,* ii., 10.

[9] *De Trinitate,* x., xi.

[10] *Ibid.,* xxiii.

[11] It is outside our purpose to consider Tertullian's doctrine of the Logos, though we may notice that one aspect of his teaching indicates that, like Paul of Samosata at Antioch and Novatian and Hippolytus at Rome, and Lactantius (who also hailed from Africa), he can be regarded as a representative of what Loof calls the "Economic Trinitarian" tradition in the early history of Christian doctrine: the Logos, from the first immanent in God as His Reason, is put forth (*prolatum*) as his *Sermo* when God moves in the fulfilment of his creative purpose, and, seemingly, is known as Son when he assumes manhood in Jesus Christ (see Loofs, *Paulus von Samosata,* esp. pp. 211ff, 41 n, 143f). . . .

[12] *Adversus Marcion,* ii, 27. Cf. Hippolytus: "For there is also one Servant of God, by whom we too receiving the regeneration through the Holy Spirit desire to come all to one perfect and heavenly man. For whereas the Logos was without flesh (*asarkos ōv*), he put on the holy flesh from the holy Virgin, wearing for himself like a bridegroom a robe in the suffering of the Cross, that by mingling (*sugkerasas*) his own power with our mortal body, and by mixing (*mixas*) the incorruptible with the corruptible, and the strong with the weak, he might save perishing man" (*de Christo et Antichristo,* 3f).

[13] *Adversus Marcion,* ii, 27.

And, Tertullian insists, this union of the Logos with manhood—a real manhood, that is, consisting of a body and a human rational soul[14] in the *homo Deo mixtus*[15] has not been effected through any change in respect of the divine element. . . . So is he still the same Logos, though now, for our salvation, he has assumed the incarnate state. And, Tertullian maintains, just because Jesus Christ is thus one Person (*una persona*), at once divine and human . . . the Christian is not ashamed to confess that "the Son of God was born," or that "the Son of God died."[16] . . .

Thus, with its implications, the first of the two principles fundamental to the Church's doctrine of the Person of Jesus Christ is already established in the West. Later teachers had but to follow the course mapped out for them by the pioneer.

Novatian, for instance, teaches that the Son of God, the *Verbum Dei,* who was *in substantia* (*Dei*) before the foundation of the world, descended from heaven, and was incarnate (*incarnatum*) by the Holy Spirit who came upon the Virgin.[17] Thus the Son of God linked to himself (*sibi annectit*)—took up unto himself (*in se suscepit*) and associated with and joined to himself (*sibi sociavit et iunxit*)—the Son of Man, and, "by his connection and mingling of association" (*connexione sua et permixtione sociata*), made him Son of God who is not so by nature.[18] He, then, who before the descent was *sine carne* is now revealed *in carne,*[19] and he who was "before Abraham" is now, as man, "of Abraham".[20] Nothing could be plainer: for Novatian, though the expression *una persona* may not appear in his extant works, in Jesus Christ the divine Logos, who existing eternally in and with the Father, has condescended to live the human life through an inseparable union with a manhood like ours. . . .

Again, the Westerns insist on the necessity of making use of the *communicatio idiomatum,* in order to bring out the cardinal truth of the Gospel; and this they do to the full. Thus Novatian teaches that one must confess that "the Son of God was born," since Christ is in the form of God, and that "God died," since, "if Christ is God, and Christ died, then God died."[21] Cyprian appeals to Scripture in support of the affirmation that the Son of God, who had been from the beginning, had to be begotten again according to the flesh.[22]

---

[14] See, for instance, Tertullian's argument in *de carne Christi,* 3–10.

[15] *Apol.* 21; *de carne Christi,* 15. Irenaeus, too, speaks of the *commixtio et communio Dei et hominis* (*Adversus Haereses,* IV., xx., 4), and Hippolytus (*de Christo et Antichristo,* 3f), writes in the same way. Yet these teachers are utterly opposed to the conception of the "*confusion*" of the natures: like the Alexandrians, they use the term "mixture"—which, clearly, has reached them from the East—only in order to enforce the doctrine of the indivisibility of the union of the divine and human elements in Jesus Christ.

[16] See, for instance, *de carne Christi,* 5. The use of the principle of the *communicatio idiomatum* by Hippolytus is particularly noteworthy: his statements in *c. Noetum* 18 may well be set beside those of Leo in his *Tome.*

[17] *De Trinitate,* xvi, xxiv.

[18] *Ibid.,* xxiv.

[19] *Ibid.,* xiii.

[20] *Ibid.,* xi.

[21] *Ibid.,* xxii, xxv.

[22] *Testimonia* II, 8.

Our conclusion, then, . . . is that, as resolutely as the Alexandrians, these uphold the truth fundamental to the Gospel, namely, that Jesus Christ, the Mediator who is at once God and man, is one Person—the Son of God himself, made man for man's salvation. We would now see how they arrive at the same results as the Easterns when they proceed to attempt to investigate this mystery of God incarnate.

We must not expect the Western teachers to offer, like Cyril, a scientific explanation of the process of enquiring into the mystery of the Son of God made man; for their primary interest lies rather in the practical affairs of the Church than in matters of speculation. Nevertheless, clear evidence is forthcoming that they appreciate the value of the process, and that their formula "two substances" [*duae substantiae*: "two existent things," that is, or "two objective entities" (*res*)] is—theoretically speaking—arrived at as they "see" Godhead and manhood, each with its distinct properties, inseparately united in the one Person of Jesus Christ. Thus in an important doctrinal passage in the *Adversus Praexean* Tertullian writes:

"We see a twofold condition (*videmus duplicem statum*) which is not confounded but conjoined in one Person, God and man—Jesus."[23] . . . [The same views were expressed by Novatian.][24] From these passages it will be clear that the Westerns most definitely uphold the principle of "recognizing the difference" of the natures. . . . But they also make it plain that these teachers take the preliminary step, and, like the Alexandrians and the Antiochenes in the East, first "see," "understand" or "recognize" that in the *una persona* of Jesus Christ are the *duae naturae* (or *duae substantiae*) of Godhead and manhood.

Consequently, we ask: How do the Western theologians sum up the truth, thus laid bare, that the Son of God made man consists of these two, and different, elements? In this connection, it should be noted, earlier teachers use the proposition *ex,* and say that Jesus Christ is *unus ex utroque.* Thus Tertullian, who is wont to use the terms "Spirit" and "flesh" when referring to the two "substances" in Jesus Christ, teaches that these exist *in uno,* and that *ex his* he is constituted, each remaining in its reality: *Neque caro Spiritus fit neque Spiritus caro: in uno plane esse possunt. Ex his Jesus constitit: ex carno homo, ex Spiritu Deus* ("Nor does the flesh become Spirit, nor the Spirit flesh; yet they can plainly be in one. From them is Jesus constituted: man from flesh, God from Spirit."[25] Similarly Novatian insists that, as the Scriptures proclaim, Jesus Christ possesses both the Divine and the human element, and that their reality must not be denied.[26] Hence, he teaches, Jesus Christ is both *ex homine* and *ex Deo*: he is *ex utroque.*[27] . . . We can safely say that the "*unus ex utroque*" of the earlier Latin theologians represents the importation into the West of the . . . *ek duo eis* ("one from two") tradition in the East. . . .

We can now resume our enquiry into the teaching of the Latins on the need of "recognizing the difference" of

[23] *Adversus Praexeon,* 27; Cf also c. 29. . . .
[24] *De Trinitate,* xxi.
[25] *Adversus Praexeon,* 27.
[26] *De Trinitate,* xxi.
[27] *Ibid.,* xi.

the natures in Christ; for, like their brethren in the East, they well appreciate that this important Christological principle must be upheld in order to exclude the idea of "confusion." Here again Tertullian is the pioneer. . . . He insists that the Word continued in his own proper form (*perseverando in sua forma*) when he became flesh, and was not changed into flesh.[28]

Similarly, in the *de carne Christi,* Tertullian employs the principle of seeing the two substances as "the one" and "the other," as he would expose Marcion's error of "cutting away" all the suffering of Christ. . . .

Novatian, too, is constantly insisting that the *distinctio,* as he calls it, between what belongs to Christ as Son of God and what is his as Son of Man must be firmly upheld in the interest of sound belief. In two interesting chapters of his *de Trinitate* he points out that Sabellianism and Docetism, though each contained excellent arguments in support of the doctrine of Christ's Godhead, arose from the fundamental error of refusing to recognize the Scriptural proofs of the reality of his manhood. The Sabellians, he declares, would not have exaggerated his divine honours above measure, and dared to think that he is God the Father himself, and the Docetists would not have "so far embraced his Godhead . . . as to withdraw from him the whole manhood which he took upon him," lest a human nativity should diminish in him the power of the divine Name, had these heretics seen in him, who in his own self united God to man and man to God, the tokens of each element (*utriusque partis pignora*)[29]; since, once such a "distinction" is made, Jesus Christ is easily shown to be God and man. And earlier in the work,[30] when he is proving that Christ is neither a Christ in imagination nor a mere man, but the divine Son of God who links to himself (*sibi annectit*)[31] the Son of man, and is therefore both divine and human, Novatian illustrates how, in accordance with Scripture, the "distinction" should be made. As man (*qua homo*) Christ is of Abraham, "Son of David," and "under the Law"; as God (*qua Deus*) he is before Abraham, "David's Lord," and "Lord of the Sabbath." As man, he is condemned; as God, he judges quick and dead. As man, he was born subsequent to the world, after man and in subjection to others; as God, he was before the world, before all and greater than all. As man, he ascended into heaven; as God, he came down thence. Both imperfections, which prove human frailty, and works which affirm divine power, must be believed, says this able theologian, and both must be "seen"[32] if one's faith is to be true and complete.

But it should be understood that while the Latin theologians thus distinguish the natures, and see each with its distinct properties, they do not consider that Christ acts now in his divine, now in his human nature. For them, rather, as for the Alexandrians, and, as we would argue, for the Antiochenes—even if the point is not often brought out—all the actions and sayings reported of Christ in Scripture are

---

28 *Adversus Praexeon,* 27.
29 *De Trinitate,* xxiii.
30 *Ibid.,* x, xi.
31 *Ibid.,* xxiv.
32 *Ibid.,* xi.

those of the one Person of the Mediator, the God-man, who is the Logos made flesh." . . .

Thus, like the Alexandrians and, as we could claim, like the Antiochenes, the Westerns, their Christology also soteriologically determined, start from the fundamental doctrine that the Person of the Mediator, the Son of God made man, is one, and proceed to lay down that in him "are made known," and therefore are to be "recognized," the two substances of Godhead and manhood. Though they may not offer either formulas which sum up the truth of the unity of Christ's Person, or a scientific explanation of the principle of "recognizing the difference" of his natures, it is clear that in its main outline their Christology differs not one whit from that of Cyril.

III

THEOLOGICAL INTERPRETATIONS OF CHRIST FROM NICAEA TO CHALCEDON

1. M. Werner,[1] in line with his presuppositions about dogma and Hellenization in general, sees in this period the evolution of the dogma of Christ's divinity, not as a divinization of Christ as Man, but as a deification of Christ as angel. The late Jewish and primitive Christian doctrine about Christ became translated into religious Hellenic metaphysical terms. The Gnostic framework originally rejected was now accepted. The Gnostic identity of "nature of God" and of "Logos" prepared the way for the Nicaean *homoousia.*

THE TRANSITION TO THE DOGMA OF THE DIVINITY OF CHRIST

In the development of the dogma of Christ's divinity the decisive motive was provided by the Church's newly formulated doctrine of Redemption. The champions of the new Christology expressly used in its defence the argu-

[1] Cf. Ch. 1, n. 3. This excerpt is from *op. cit.*, pp. 213–224.

ment that the very possibility of Redemption presupposed the divinity of the Redeemer. The case for Modalism had already been argued along this line, and the old protagonist of Nicaea, Athanasius, will follow it whole-heartedly in his fight against the Arians. Thus he will assert that Christ could only have provided mortal man with immortality by being himself the divine creator of man.[2] Athanasius will also give the argument a somewhat negative turn: not only a mere man, but even an angel could never have achieved the Redemption in the form of a new creation of man.[3]

This formulation of Athansius serves to remind us that, in the transition to the new dogma of Christ's divinity, the issue was not one of the exaltation of a man to divine status, but that of the deification of an angelic-being. The presupposition of the new dogma was the old Angel-Christology of Primitive Christian tradition. This original doctrine of the Christ was translated from the religious metaphysic of late-Jewish apocalyptic, in terms of which Primitive Christianity had thought, into the religious metaphysic of Hellenistic philosophy and religion. Such a translation was feasible for the following reason. According to the late-Jewish and Primitive Christian view, there was a transcendent creator-deity, who surpassed all predicates of absoluteness in his decrees, and beneath him there stood the hierarchically graded angel-world. This order of things corresponded to the essentials of Hellenistic monotheism, pre-eminently that of late-Platonic philosophy, which had adjusted itself to the old polytheistic tradition of the popular religion. Celsus explained this compromise to the Christians and declared: "He, who honours and worships all the gods (appertaining to the one god), does not grieve the (one) god, to whom they all appertain."[4]

Post-Apostolic Gentile Christianity came also generally to identify its view of God as the "Father of All" with the late-Jewish, as well as with the monotheism of Hellenistic philosophy. Thus there was formed within the Church the settled belief in the one eternal transcendent Creator-God, "the same for all men." The Apologists of the 2nd century had transmitted to the Christian doctrine of God the predicate of absoluteness from philosophical monotheism. But there was little possibility of the divinity of Christ being understood in terms of a conception of God of this order. The *deus invisibilis* of the philosophical doctrine of God could, for example, never appear in a terrestrial *milieu*. An eclipse of his true being such as this would imply would be tantamount to the surrender of his absoluteness. Indeed Tertullian once went as far as to declare that, even if the Holy Spirit asserted that there had been a visible appearance of God the Father, he would himself not believe it.[5] However, in the concept of God, relative to the compromise effected between the polytheism of popular religion and philosophical monotheism, there existed the possibility of a transition to the dogma of Christ's divinity. The theology of the Church did indeed set its face against polytheism, but not in a truly radical sense. . . .

---

[2] Athanasius, *De Incarnatione* 20.
[3] *Ibid.*, 13.
[4] Celsus, *apud* Origen, *Contra Celsum*, viii, 13.
[5] Tertullian, *adv. Prax.* 16

Attention must be given to the fact that, and the way in which, support was sought in the Old Testament for the new dogma of Christ's divinity, conceived as it was in terms of the corresponding concept of God in Hellenistic religion. The theologians of the Church were aware that in the Old Testament, together with the proclamation of Israelite-Jewish monotheism, there were still remains of other estimates of diety. Origen, in his discussion with the pagan Celsus, came on more than one occasion to speak about the Old Testament's designating angels as "gods." He had in mind particularly the passage of Psalm lxxxi, I, 6 (LXX), which was an abiding source of wonderment for the theologians of the Early Church. The Old Testament thus endorsed the relative concept of deity in the non-Christian religions which was now being employed in the formation of new Christological doctrine.

It is in terms of the evident tendency of the new development that the peculiarities of its long protracted course are to be explained. It is thus intelligible how the first phase, i.e. the effective transition from the Angel-Christology to the dogma of Christ's divinity, could have been easily accomplished and without opposition. Indeed one already encounters frequently in this transitional phase Christological statements which appear to have a naive Modalistic meaning. Christ appears as "God absolutely,"[6] as "my God,"[7] as "my Lord and my God,"[8] as "our God."[9] However despite such Modalistic-sounding expressions, it is often not a case of a conscious equating of the divine element of Christ with God, the "Father of All." Statements also appear from time to time which clearly presuppose the distinction of the two. On the other hand in the *Acts of John* there is notably no attempt at qualification and Jesus is addressed in prayer directly with the formula: "Thou alone art God and none other."[10] Here, as also with Marcion, the Syriac *Didaskalia,* and certain Montanists, a true Modalism is evident.

These symptoms of an early, sporadic, but spontaneously appearing Modalistic outlook prove how easily Post-Apostolic thought could change over from the traditional Angel-Christology to the conception of the divinity of Christ. . . . From the comparative point of view the concept of God, which at this stage included the new doctrine of Christ's divinity, was primarily only the Hellenistic equivalent of the concept of Christ in the Angel-Christology of late Judaism and Primitive Christianity, minus its specifically eschatological complexion.

But that factor, which here made the Christology so easy, conjured up for the future those fundamental difficulties which were to render the long doctrinal conflict inevitable. Through the transition from the Angel-Christology to the dogma of the divinity of Christ, Christology came now to constitute a special problem of the concept of God. In the provocative question about the relationship of Christ's

[6] Ignatius, *Smyrn.* i, I.
[7] Ignatius, *Rom.* 6, 3.
[8] John xx, 29; *Apoc. Petri,* 16.
[9] Ignatius, *Rom. inscr.*
[10] *Acta Johannis,* 77 (Lipsius-Bonnet, ii, 1, p. 189); see also *Acta Thomae,* 25 (Lipsius-Bonnet, ii, 2, p. 140).

divinity to the divinity of the "Father of All" was contained the new problem of the equation of the two different concepts of God, which were involved therein. . . .

We have now to trace out the efforts which were made to master this new problem. In this connection Arianism has only to be considered in so far as it effectively conditioned the development of the new Christological dogma. The adoption of the concept of *homoousia* is not involved here. Catholic theology had indeed achieved the *homoousia* formula in opposition to Arianism. And this had the effect of finally invalidating the Primitive Christian Angel-Christology, which in Arianism was putting up its last fight for existence, having long fallen victim to the process of de-eschatologising. . . .

Arianism, however, in defending its own position, had forced the new "homoousian" theology to a conscious effort at defining and differentiating the already existent doctrine of the Two Natures. . . .

The Significance of the Idea of the Divine Sonship

The designation of Christ as a pre-existent being was handed on to Post-Apostolic Christianity in the form of the "Son of God" directly through the teaching of Paul. . . . In the Post-Apostolic period, before the time of Justin, the Pre-existent One was designated "Son of God" already in the Johannine writings, and by *Barnabas* and Hermas. In so far as there were doctrinal variations in this connection, they existed simply as a result of the differences between the older Jewish Christian and the Pauline interpretations of Christ and the attempts at reconciliation which they soon prompted. . . .

Things were situated differently from the beginning of the 3rd century. Then serious controversies broke out over the question whether the Pre-existent One was the "Son." The occasion was the appearance of Monarchianism. Any one who refused to recognise a pre-existent "Son" was rejected as a heretic by the Church even before the time of Marcellus of Ancyra and Photinus of Sirmium in the 4th century.

What appeared as a new factor in the Post-Apostolic conception of the divine sonship of Christ was the interpretation, according to which the "Son of God," as such, should be the "Begotten" of God, the Father of all. A misunderstanding of the Messianic doctrine of late Judaism and Primitive Christianity was involved here. . . .

But the new interpretation of the concept "Son of God" did correspond to the mythological thought of Hellenistic folk-religion, as is sufficiently attested by the Christian philosopher Justin, when he, by way of example, draws an analogy between Christ, the "Son of God" and the sons of Zeus. However that may be, it now became a factor of importance that the "Son of God" idea, according to the new interpretation, could be utilised to illustrate and prove the new dogma of the divinity of Christ. The new interpretation had first appeared in the oldest form of Gnosticism. Gnosticism, as Epiphanius rightly maintained later, had virtually abandoned the idea of Creation and in its place had made the concept of generation the basic concept of its cosmological system. . . .

The Post-Apostolic Church had to define its attitude to the fundamental position of Gnosticism. In the first place the idea of generation by sexes was felt to be shocking. . . .

Later the Modalists raised the fundamental question, in what sense could one speak at all of a "beginning" and a "being begotten" in connection with God? And the Arians made their position clear by rejecting the thesis of divine generation as a piece of untenable anthropomorphism. Athanasius could only answer them by suggesting that the generation of man is one thing and the divine generation another.[11] The problem was occasionally taken up and dealt with, in inevitably gross terms, by the popular apologetic of devotional writings. The question was thus formulated: was God then married, that one could ascribe to him the generation of a Son?

The notion of the generation of a Son from God the Father could thus not be taken over into the doctrine of the Post-Apostolic Church, without at the same time safeguarding against the Gnostic presentation of it. . . . What happened here in the course of the Church's dispute with Gnosticism was a repetition of what had happened frequently in the development of Christological doctrine on other important points. A Gnostic theory was rejected, but sooner or later it was annexed by the Church to its own set of fundamental notions. . . .

Irenaeus had actually already taken up the term *eadem substantia* with his Gnostic opponents, but it did not occur to him to avail himself theologically of this important heretical formula. For him it savoured too much of the heresy of Gnosticism. But the time was not far off when the Church would find itself compelled to adopt this very idea of *homoousia* from Gnosis and to use it. Later still notable opposition showed itself, especially in the East, towards that which Gnosticism offered as the means of doctrinal advance. . . .

With the concept of generation, adopted on Gnostic instigation, it became possible for the theology of the Church to explain the new estimate of the divinity of Christ as stemming directly from God, the Father of all. But the problem still was that of safeguarding the recognition of this twofold divinity in the Father and Son. . . .

It thus transpired that in reality, in terms of the generation-concept itself, by means of which it was sought to derive the divinity of the Son as homogeneous from that of the Father, there was implicit a difference of divinity between them. It was the distinction between the begetting, but himself unbegotten, Father and the Son, who was the begotten. This distinction was already established by the 2nd century. However, it was first experienced and dealt with as a serious problem in the 4th century in consequence of the progressive development of Christology. Before all else it was seized upon and fashioned into an argument by the "heretics." In the Pseudo-Clementine writings the thesis is maintained: "That which is begotten is not comparable to the unbegotten or that which is self-begotten." For the Anomoeans of the 4th century the thesis was a powerful argument against the new orthodoxy of Nicaea, which was embarassed

[11] Athanasius, *de decr. Nic. Syn.* 10 f. (MG, xxv, 433).

thereby. With what hopelessly confused formulae the Nicaean party at first entered into the debate with the Arians is to be seen in the case of Alexander of Alexandria. For he could say of the Son that he exists "independently of God (the Father), continually begotten, in a state of unbegottenness." Marcellus of Ancyra could congratulate himself on his own peculiar doctrinal position, because it enabled him to cut uncompromisingly through the tangle, for in the Bible neither the prophets, the evangelists nor the apostles had spoken of a distinction between an "unbegotten" and a "begotten" God. This sound conclusion meant in fact a recognition that the Apostolic and Primitive Christian Messianic name "Son of God," attested by the New Testament, had originally nothing to do with the notion of an act of generation by God. Origen sought a solution by employing the concept of an "eternal generation" of the Son. . . . In the following period it became customary to infer the eternal generation from the thesis that the attribute of Fatherhood belonged to the eternal and unchanging being of God. Hence appeared, as a new *motif,* the endeavour of the "homoousian" theology of Nicaea to equate the divinity of the Son in every respect with that of the Father. The attribute of eternity appertained to the Son's divinity as it did to the divinity of the Father. Thus there came to be ascribed to the Son, as well as to the Father, "unoriginateness." Accordingly, occasion was given for the contention of Arius: if the Son is in an effective sense eternal as the Father, then he must really be not the Son but the Brother of the Father.

A) The Alexandrian School: Logos-sarx Christology

2. A. Grillmeier, S.J.,[1] notes that fourth century Christology does not involve itself yet in the deeper interpretation of the inner unity of Christ of Ephesus and Chalcedon. The controversy in the Arian and Apollinaristic issues revolves around the components of the person of Jesus, namely true divinity and complete humanity. The problematic was the preservation of God's transcendence in the midst of the highest degree of immanence in Christ. He explains how Alexandrian thought came to depart from the Origenistic Logos-anthropos view of Christ.

Toward Fourth Century Christology

The interpretation of the basic christological truths in the tradition, begun by the Apologists and continued by the Alexandrines Clement and Origen, without doubt exerted a far-reaching influence. . . . We would now draw attention to the first theological interpretations of the person of Christ. The interpretations take the form of "frameworks," or unitary principles for the explanation of the nature or the person of Jesus Christ. We will term briefly the "Logos-sarx" and the "Logos-anthropos" frameworks. The tension between these two ways of interpreting the person of Jesus

[1] Cf. Ch. 1, n. 1. This excerpt is from *op. cit.,* pp. 175–182, 241–242, selectively.

Christ dominates the history of christology from Origen to the Council of Ephesus (431). This is not to assert that the whole development may be subsumed under these two heads without remainder; it does not even mean that the presence of such theological frameworks was as firmly realized as was the case with the later scholastic systems.

This contrast between Logos-sarx and Logos-anthropos christology does not entirely coincide with the usual distinction between "Alexandrine" and "Antiochene" christology. Useful as such a classification of christological views may be, it does only partial justice to the real state of affairs. The historical reality is far more complicated than the division between Alexandria and Antioch might suggest.

For any understanding of the development during the fourth century it is important to realize that with few exceptions (probably to some degree Gregory of Nyssa and Nemesius) there was still no deeper recognition of the real problem of patristic christology, namely *how* the inner unity of God and man in Christ was to be interpreted. This is the centre of the controversy at Ephesus and even here there is trouble because of an unclear presentation of the problem. The fourth century is above all concerned with the nature or the person of Jesus Christ—the question with the Arians is that of his Godhead, with both Arians and Apollinarians that of his complete manhood (body and soul). *In actual fact,* of course, the question of the unity in Christ has already been raised and "solved" at the same time. For the denial of a soul in Christ is at least partly conditioned by the desire to express the unity of God and man in Christ. The relationship of Logos and sarx in Christ is analogous to the unity of the body and the soul in man. It was not for nothing that this anthropological analogy was applied so strongly; for the theologians of the time it was the supreme example of the unity of two substances. At the same time, it was also of supreme religious significance because the whole relationship between God and the world seemed to be expressed in the unity of Logos and sarx in Christ. The incarnation was, in fact, the greatest expression of the relationship of God to his creation. It was the task of fourth-century theology, in its christology, to preserve the transcendence of God while still demonstrating this highest degree of his immanence. This is where the real problem of the Arian and Apollinarian heresies lay. Their mistake was that they applied philosophical frameworks to the interpretation of Christ without having made the necessary corrections. . . . The Logos-sarx framework in its chief historical forms . . . differs quite considerably. We have two heretical forms, those of Arianism and of Apollinarianism. But there was also an orthodox Logos-sarx christology, at least in the sense that the "soul" of Christ played no part in the interpretation of his nature and his soteriological action, his life and his death. It was manifestly still no "theological entity" or "theological factor," even if it was for these theologians a "physical entity" in the sense that there was a consciousness of its physical reality. We may represent St. Athanasius as an advocate of this middle line and point to his following. With the defeat of Arianism (as a christology) and Apollinarianism, even this group disappeared, as precisely the reality of the soul of Christ or the complete manhood of the Lord was raised to the status of an article of belief. We will, however, be able to observe traces of it right into the fifth century. Thus in the fourth century developments lead to the full recognition of the "Logos-anthropos" framework. Only then does the question of the inner unity of Godhead and complete manhood in Christ arise—the subject of the Nestorian controversy. . . .

The classical period for the interplay of the two frameworks is the fourth century. It seems to begin with earlier Arianism and the opposition to it from Eustathius of Antioch, and reaches its climax with later Arianism and Apollinarianism and their opponents

But what happened between the death of Origen (253–4) and Nicaea (325)? Here there are many blank patches on the patristic map. How did it happen that the christological legacy of Origen, incomplete though it may have been, could partly have been lost? Origen in particular we have seen as a theologian of the soul of Christ; indeed, apart from Tertullian no theologian before Nicaea spoke of it so clearly. How then could it come about that on Alexandrian soil in particular the recognition of a created soul was obscured or even excluded?

There can be no doubt that the "Affair of Paul of Samosata" is a distinctive event in the history of christology. . . . Paul appears to have represented a "divisive" christology, and his opponents in the Church, among whom the Presbyter Malchion played a leading role, a "unitive" christology. According to the Synodal Letter preserved in part by Eusebius (H.E. 7. 30), Paul denied the divinity of Christ which he had earlier allowed. Christ had not "come down from heaven" but was "from below." According to witnesses of a later period (*Contestatio Eusebii* of 428, *Timothy Aelurus, Severus of Antioch*) Paul put forward a christology of the indwelling of the "Logos" in a man (with body and soul). Malchion, on the other hand, appears to have put forward a christology the terminology of which had already progressed quite considerably. He saw in Christ a unity of Logos and sarx corresponding to the unity between body and soul in a human being. The Logos is in Christ what the soul is in man. Malchion would see that this guaranteed a strict unity in Christ. If Paul, on the other hand, allowed a soul in Christ, Malchion would have felt him to be renouncing the possibility of assuming a strict unity in Christ. Thus the Apollinarian solution of christology would be anticipated as early as the third century. If . . . we can accept the tradition about Paul of Samosata as genuine, it would be possible that we had here the common root of Arianism, Apollinarianism and some aspects of the christology of the Alexandrian Church. Naturally the different development of the three branches of this Logos-sarx christology would have to be taken into account. In any case, their mutual relationship is an important problem in the history of the dogma of the third and fourth centuries. . . .

What happened to the Origenistic tradition in the circle of his pupils and their followers? There is, of course, still no sign of a Logos-sarx christology in *Gregory Thaumaturgus* (died c. 270), *Dionysius of Alexandria* (died 264/5), *Theognostus* (writing between 250 and 280) and *Pierius* (writing 281/2–300) the "new Origen." But a pupil of Pierius, the presbyter *Pamphilus* (died 309/10), makes an important observation in his *Apology for*

Origen. Origen's teaching that Christ had assumed a human soul had become a stumbling block for some people. The presbyter, of course, does not waste words on the extent of such a "scandal,"[2] but in any case we have here a noticeable, open opposition which may well have been associated with hostility to Origen's doctrine of the pre-existence of souls.

We can already establish a negative attitude towards Origen in *Peter of Alexandria* (died 311), especially towards Origen's teaching of the pre-existence of the soul. Does this influence the actual picture of Christ? Peter was a renowned witness of the Christian faith and was even quoted at the Council of Ephesus, but we are unable to answer the question because of the regrettably few remains of his writings. It is nevertheless striking that in two of the best known of Origen's opponents, *Methodius of Olympus* (died c. 311) and *"Adamantius,"* as, moreover, in St. Athanasius' teacher *Alexander of Alexandria* (died 328), a more or less pronounced form of the "Word-flesh" christology may be discerned. It is probably because of his opposition to Origen that Methodius, who fought against Origen's doctrine of the pre-existence of souls and in particular of the soul of Christ, was occasioned to leave Christ's soul unnoticed in his picture of Christ. He maintains a complete silence over it, though in view of his dependence upon Origen elsewhere he must have known of the teaching of the *Peri Archon* (cf. *Symposion* 7. 8 with *De Princ.* II 6, 4). Some formulas seem to combine a Logos-anthropos and a Logos-sarx framework: "For this was Christ: man filled with the pure and perfect Godhead, and God comprehending man (3. 4)" . . . "And so God, moistening His clay once again and modelling the same man again unto honour, fixed and hardened it in the Virgin's womb, united and mingled it with the Word, and finally brought it forth dry and unbreakable into the world . . . (3. 5)."

According to some authors there may, however, be one still more decisive influence in the history of a Logos-sarx christology, especially on St. Athanasius. H. G. Opitz drew attention to the relationship between *Athanasius and Eusebius of Caesarea* (died 339).[3] F. L. Cross has pointed it out once again.[4] Eusebius' journey to Alexandria in 311 would have been particularly important. The principal works for a comparison between Athanasius and Eusebius would be the early writings of the former (*Contra Gentes* and *De Incarnatione*) and the *Theophaneia* and *De ecclesiastica theologia* of the latter. Closer investigation, however, does not seem to uphold these suppositions. Nevertheless, Eusebius' christology is clearly conceived within the pattern of the Logos-sarx framework. Though he is a pupil of Pamphilus and an Origenist in his christology, his picture of Christ shows decisive alterations when compared with that of Origen. It reveals only the Logos, which is joined to the flesh (without a soul).[5] It is in just

---

[2] Pamphilus, *Apol. pro Orig.*: cd. C. H. E. Lommatzsch (Berolini, 1846) 24, 373f. . . .

[3] H. G. Opitz, *Untersuchungen zur Überlieferung der Schriften des Athanasius* (Berlin-Leipzig, 1935) 197.

[4] F. L. Cross, *The Study of St. Athanasius* (Oxford, 1945), 13–15.

[5] On the christology of Eusebius see H. de Riedmatten, *Procès de Paul de Samosate,* 65–81. He shows that all references to the soul of Christ in Eusebius are associated with

this conjunction with the flesh that the Logos, primarily understood as revealer, shows himself to be an individual hypostasis, distinct from the Father. Eusebius sees this as a refutation of the Trinitarian teaching of *Marcellus of Ancyra* (died about 374) (*Eccl. Theol.* 1. 20). At the same time he accuses Marcellus of having made Christ into a "mere man" by having him composed of body and soul, for in this way Christ is not different from the human nature of an ordinary man. By his teaching Marcellus is renewing the heresy of Paul of Samosata (*ibid.* 15–22).

The lack of a soul in Christ and the replacement of it by the Logos are, then, necessary for Eusebius if the transcendence of Christ is to be proved. Arguing from the modalism of Marcellus he suggests different possibilities of interpreting Christ: Christ is either the Father incarnate, or—if this be not allowed—a mere man (with body and soul), or a mere fleshly nature without a soul. These would be the possible interpretations for the trinitarian teaching of Marcellus. But if—and this is without doubt Eusebius' own view—the Logos in Christ actuates the flesh in the same way as a soul, then he is proved a distinct hypostasis from the Father. That this Logos-sarx christology is in fact the view of Eusebius is shown conclusively in his *Demonstratio Evangelica* (10. 8; cf. *Theophaneia* 3. 41). Here he ranges himself alongside the advocates of the so-called Logos Descensus, i.e. the teaching which holds that at the death of Christ it is not the soul of Christ but the Logos that descends to the underworld.[6] The death of Christ is not the separation of soul and body but of Logos (sometimes *dynamis*) and sarx, an interpretation which we are still to meet frequently. If despite this the "soul" (*psychē*) of Christ is sometimes mentioned, it is only in connection with scriptural quotations, and such passages should be interpreted in the light of the whole of the christological framework.

scriptural quotations. Otherwise Eusebius is an outspoken advocate of the Logos-sarx theology. De Riedmatten would also assume a real influence of the Synod of Antioch (268) and its Logos-sarx framework on the followers of Eusebius. A. Bigelmair, *Zur Theologie des Eusebios von Caesarea* (Kempten-München, 1914) 13, 17, 18 also regards Eusebius as an advocate of this christology; H. Berkhof, *Die Theologie des Eusebius von Caesarea* (Amsterdam, 1939); A. Weber, APXH, *Ein Beitrag zur Christologie des Eusebius von Cäesarea* (Rom 1964, diss., typescript). This study is a most valuable contribution to the christology of Eusebius and its position in the history of Nicene theology. W. starts from *Prov.* 8. 22ff. and its exegesis in Eus. He demonstrates well the relationship of Eusebius' christology to the pre- and post-Nicene tradition (Justin, Irenaeus, Origen, Eusebius of Emesa, Athanasius, Hilary, Ambrose and esp. Marcellus of Ancyra). Eusebius is the end-point of the pre-Nicene doctrine of *oikonomia* (combining the development of the Trinity with creation and salvation-history) rather than the beginning of the post-Nicene distinction between *oikonomia* and *theologia* (Athanasius). He is no Arian, although with the Arians he recognizes only Logos and sarx in Christ (with no human soul) (so A. Weber in ch. III, 3). This is all the more important as Eusebius is a historian who is reflecting the doctrine of the sources before him rather than advancing his own thought. So the position of Eusebius in the history of the Logos-sarx christology is exceptional, especially as we have no direct testimony from the Arians of the first generation about their rejection of a human soul in Christ. So, too, Dr. M. Tetz in a letter to the author, 17.11.63.

[6] See A. Grillmeier, "Der Gottessohn im Totenreich," *Zeitschrift für Katholische Theologie,* 71 (1949) 1–53, 184–203.

To preserve the transcendence of the Logos within this framework, Eusebius has to loosen the unity between Logos and sarx. Whatever happens to the flesh (birth, suffering, death) has no effect on the Logos, for although he takes over the place of the soul in Christ he nevertheless remains the all-fulfilling Logos (*Dem. Ev.* 7. 1). Here Eusebius comes close to a "divisive" christology, but it is quite distinct from the Antiochene Logos-anthropos christology. We will find this self-same position once again in *Eusebius of Emesa.* Here, however, the original aim of Eusebius' christology is reversed. He denies the soul of Christ only from the fear of the adoptionism of Paul of Samosata. On the other hand, however, the positive significance of the Logos-sarx christology is evident; it is meant to be an interpretation of the transcendence and inward unity of Christ. The counterpart to Eusebius of Caesarea is *Eustathius of Antioch,* who, in his pre-Nicene writing *De Engastrimytho,* follows the christology of Origen, but elsewhere reveals himself to be an anti-Origenist. . . .

The Logos-sarx christology, as it was put forward in Apollinarianism, had at its disposal not only an already well-developed terminology but also a theological "framework" which could offer a consistent explanation of the person of Christ. . . .

Apollinarius, therefore, at first had the initiative. As far as we can still see from the tradition, he must be credited with having introduced into christology, or having brought to bear on the discussion, the three most important concepts which occur in the Chalcedonian Definition, *physis, hypostasis* and *prosōpon.* These concepts were eventually taken over by the Council of Chalcedon itself, but they were canonized in a refined and clarified sense. A christology with a "Word-man" framework will now develop. Of necessity it seems to lead to a loosening of the unity in Christ and so it was vigorously opposed by its counterpart. The problem to be solved, then, was how to combine this "Word-man" framework with as deep and inward a conception of the unity of Christ as was possessed by the other side. It only became really acute, however, when belief in the divinity of Christ (against the Arians) and his soul (against both Arians and Appollinarians) was brought out into the open.

The development took place in quite clearly distinguishable stages, and different groups contributed to the process. The so-called Antiochene christology developed from the struggle against the Logos-sarx framework, but its origins and early stages seem, remarkably enough, to lie within the sphere of this framework. . . . With the progress of christological reflection, the philosophical presuppositions of the Fathers and the theologians are most influential, particularly in the conception of the unity of Christ. First of all, the usual conceptions of and analogies to the unity of two substances are unconsciously applied to the unity of Christ. Here the different parties begin from different philosophical presuppositions (Platonic, Neo-Platonic, Stoic, Aristotelian) or even from a mixture of different systems. Their task should have been to uncover these different philosophical frameworks, but this kept on being neglected. The mistake became all the more deep-seated because for a long time there was no clear presentation of the christological problem. The more the question of the unity of God and man presents itself . . . the more the chief concern is to make clear the levels on which unity and distinction are to be sought in Christ. The important complexities of this period are a result of the difficulty of separating these two levels.

3. J. N. D. Kelly[1] explains how the Arian concept of God's absolute transcendence carried the inescapable corollary of Subordinationism. The production of the Word was needed because creation could not bear the direct action of the uncreated God. The Origenistic influence is clear. The Nicene Creed was the reply of orthodoxy. Its characteristic formula *homoousion*, of the same substance as the Father, although not patently biblical, was chosen because it clearly conveys the meaning of the dogma that the Son shares fully the divine essence.

The Arian Theology. The outbreak of the Arian debate is probably to be placed somewhere in 318,[2] when Arius was presiding as priest over the church of Baucalis. The broad lines of his system, which was a model of dovetailed logic, are not in any doubt. Its keystone was the conviction of the absolute transcendence and perfection of the Godhead. God (and it was God the Father Whom he had in mind) was absolutely one: there could be no other God in the proper sense of the word beside Him. The carefully drafted profession of faith[3] which he sent to bishop Alexander from Nicomedia,[4] always recognized as classic authority for his teaching, opened with the emphatic words: "We acknowledge one God, Who is alone unbegotten, alone eternal, alone without beginning, alone true, alone possessing immortality, alone wise, alone good, alone ruler, alone judge of all, etc." This God was unengendered, uncreated, from everlasting to everlasting: Himself without source, He was the source and origin of whatever else existed. The being, substance, essence of the unique God was absolutely incommunicable. For God to communicate His essence or substance to another being would imply that He was divisible and subject to change. Moreover, if another being were to share the divine nature in any valid sense, there would be a plurality of divine Beings, whereas God was by definition unique. Thus everything else that existed must have come into existence by an act of creation on His part, and must have been called into being out of nothing.

The inescapable corollary of this was the drastic subordination of the Son or Word. God desired to create the world, and for this purpose He employed an agent or instrument. This was necessary because, as one of the exponents of the Arian theology,

[1] Cf. Ch. 1, n. 5. It is from his book *Early Christian Creeds* (London: Longmans, 1960) that this excerpt was taken, from pp. 231–239.

[2] This traditional date, instead of autumn 323 as proposed by E. Schwartz (*Nachricht. Gött.* 1905, 297), has been shown still to be best supported (cf. H. G. Opitz, *Zeitschrift für die neutestamentliche Wissenschaft,* xxxiii, 1934, 131 ff.; N. H. Baynes, *Journal of Theological Studies* (J.T.S.) xlix, 1948, 165–8).

[3] Cf. St Athan., *De syn.* 16 (*P.G.* 26, 708 f.) . . .

[4] W. Telfer has rendered Arius' flight to Nicomedia doubtful (*J.T.S.* xxxvii, 1936, 60 ff.).

Asterius the Sophist, put it,[5] the created order could not bear the weight of the direct action of the increate and eternal God. Hence God brought into existence His Word. But, first of all, the Word was a creature, a *ktisma* or *Poiema* as the Arians were for ever reiterating, Whom the Father had brought into existence by His fiat. True, He was a perfect creature, and was not to be compared with the other creatures, but that He was to be ranged among other derivative and dependent beings they had no doubt. He was "the first-begotten of all creation," the Pauline text being interpreted to mean that He was included among creation. And, like all other creatures, He had been created out of nothing. To suggest that He participated somehow in the essence of the Godhead was, hinted Arius with a mischievous touch, to lapse into a species of Manichean perversion.[6]

Secondly, as a creature the Word must have had a beginning, only the Father being without beginning (*anarchos*). "He came into existence before the times and the ages," said Arius in his letter to Eusebius of Nicomedia,[7] naturally, because He was the creator of "the times and the ages" just as much as of all the rest of the contingent order, and so was "begotten outside time." But, continued Arius, "before He was begotten or created or defined or established, He was not." Having been created by God, He was necessarily posterior to God. Hence the familiar and repeatedly used Arian slogan, "There was when He was not." Hence, too, their exasperated protests against the orthodox countercry, "God from everlasting, the Son from everlasting; the Father and the Son together always,"[8] and their rejection out of hand of the idea that the Son could eternally coexist with the Father. Thirdly, it followed from all this that the Son could have no real knowledge of His Father. Being Himself finite, He could not comprehend the infinite God: indeed He had no full comprehension of His own being. "The Father," remarked Arius in a passage cited[9] by St. Athanasius, "remains ineffable to the Son, and the Word can neither see nor know His Father perfectly and accurately . . . but what He knows and sees, He knows and sees in the same way and with the same measures as we know by our own powers." The same point was rammed home on many occasions.[10] A fourth consequence was that the Son was liable to change and sin. Arius himself in his more formal writings[11] seems to have declared that the Word remained immutable and morally impeccable, but he more than once let it out that it was by His own resolute act of will that He retained His moral perfection.[12]

It might be asked in what sense the

---

[5] Cf. St Athan., *Or. con. Ar.* 2, 24; see also *De decret. Nic. syn.* 8 (*P.G.* 26,200; 25, 437).

[6] Cf. his profession of faith cited above. For the Manichaean idea that God was light, i.e. a material substance, and Jesus Christ a fragment of the divine light, see St Aug., *Confess.* 3, 7, 12; 5, 10, 20 (*P.L.* 32, 688; 715f.).

[7] In St Epiphan., *Pan Haer.* 69, 6 (Holl III, 157). . . .

[8] Cf. the letter to Eusebius just cited.

[9] *Ep. ad episc. Aeg. et Lib.* 12 (P.G. 25, 565).

[10] Cf. St. Athan., *Or. con. Ar.* 1, 6; *De syn.* 15; St Alexander in Socrates, *Hist. Eccl.* 1, 6, (*P.G.* 26, 24; 708; 67, 48).

[11] Cf. his letter to St. Alexander (in St Athan., *De syn.* 16: *P.G.* 26, 708f. . . .

[12] Cf., e.g., St Athan., *Or. con. Ar.* 1, 5 (*P.G.* 26, 21).

Word was God's Son if He was cut off from Him and subordinated to Him in all these ways. Arius and his friends continued to use the words "begotten," "Son," etc. They even exploited the ideas they conveyed in order to insinuate the necessary priority of the Father to the Son, and drew full profit[13] from the current confusion between "begotten (*yennētos*)," which it was agreed on all hands that the Son was, and "contingent (*yenētos*)," which the orthodox denied the Son was. But they declined to draw the inference which the orthodox drew, that if He was really Son, the Word must share to the full His Father's nature. In fact, they did not attach more than a metaphorical significance to the term. The Word, in Arius' eyes, was not the authentic but the adoptive Son of the Father: "He is called Son or Power by grace."[14] He had been promoted to that position because the Father had foreseen the meritorious and perfect life He would, by His own free acts of will, lead. The net result was that the Trinity, or divine Trias, was described, in speciously Origenistic language, as consisting of three Persons.[15] But the three Persons were three utterly different beings, and did not share in any way the same substance or essence as each other. Only the Father was "true God," the title being ascribed to the other two in an almost figurative sense.

The Reply of the Nicene Creed. Such in outline was the Arian theological position. With its main features before us, we can begin to appreciate the full import of the special clauses in the Nicene creed, at least in so far as they sought to rebut Arianism. We may pass over ONLY-BEGOTTEN (*monogenē*), although much ink has been expended in the discussion of it, because it was accepted by all parties in the Arian quarrel and no special dogmatic significance was read into it. Let us look, however, at the first of the anti-Arian interpolations, the clause that is, FROM THE SUBSTANCE OF THE FATHER (*Toutestin ek tēs ousias tou patros*), which was inserted immediately after the words BEGOTTEN FROM THE FATHER, ONLY-BEGOTTEN, and was clearly intended to give a more precise interpretation to BEGOTTEN FROM THE FATHER. What we have here is a deliberately formulated counterblast to the principal tenet of Arianism, that the Son had been created out of nothing and had no community of being with the Father. The Arians had been perfectly willing to acquiesce in the description "begotten from the Father", so long as they were at liberty to interpret it in a sense consistent with their theory of the Son's origin by a creative fiat of the Godhead. To exclude any such interpretation, our clause nails up the thesis that, so far from being produced like the creatures out of nothing, the Son was generated out of the Father's very substance or being. The implication which this carried with it was that He shared the divine essence to the full. This latter thought was driven home in the all-important phrase OF THE SAME SUBSTANCE AS THE FATHER (*homoousion tó patri*), which was in-

[13] Cf. his letter to Eusebius of Nicomedia (in St Epiphan., *Pan. Haer.* 69, 6; Holl III, 157). . . .

[14] In St Athan., *Or. con. Ar.* 1, 9 (*P.G.* 26, 29).

[15] Cf. *ωστε τρεις εισιν ὑποστάαεις* in Arius' letter to St. Alexander (in St Athan., *De Syn.* 16: *P.G.* 26, 709) . . .

serted a couple of lines further down.

The phrase FROM THE SUBSTANCE OF THE FATHER was not, however, an entire novelty. The sentence, "He is sprung from the Father's substance," . . . had been used, as St. Athanasius himself later pointed out[16] toward the end of the third century by Theognostus in his *Hypotyposes.* Moreover, the idea it conveyed was one which the Arians had strenuously and persistently denied, often in language approximating to that now employed. Arius himself, in his well-known letter to St. Alexander, had branded the proposition that the Son was *homoousios* with the Father as savouring of Manichaeism, and in his *Thalia* had sung:[17] "He is not equal to Him (the Father), nor for that matter of the same substance . . . the Father is alien to the Son in substance." Again, he had said:[18] "He is not from the Father, but came into existence out of nothingness, and Himself has nothing in common with the Father's substance; . . ." and, "The substances of the Father and of the Son and of the Holy Spirit are different and have no share in each other.[19] He was always insisting that the Word was utterly unlike (*anomoios kata panta*) the Father's essence or being. His great friend and champion, Eusebius of Nicomedia, was entirely at one with him, and in his letter[20] to Paulinus of Tyre had repudiated the very words "derived from His essence." . . .

The next anti-Arian clause is TRUE GOD FROM TRUE GOD (*Theon alēthinon ek theou alēthinou*). It has already been stated that the absolute uniqueness of the divine Father was one of the staple Arian articles. To bring out His uniqueness the heretics pressed the Saviour's words in *Jn.* 17, 3, "This is life eternal, that they should know Thee the only true God", into their service, trying to squeeze out of them every drop of meaning. Eusebius of Caesarea, who quoted the text with effect in a letter,[21] added that the suggestion of the words was "not that the Father alone is God, but that He alone is true God, and the addition of the word 'true' is most necessary". The Word of God, he admitted, was "God," but not "true God." Arius too, according to a report of St Athanasius,[22] had remarked, "Nor is the Word true God. . . . If He is called God, He is none the less not true God, but is God by favour, like all the others, and is called so in name only." Our clause had the effect of laying it down that the Son was truly God in whatever sense the Father was God. As a matter of fact, however, it was not much appealed to by either side in the controversy. When pressed, the Arians were prepared to concede that the Son was "true God," for that He was God in a certain sense they readily agreed, and that He was "true" was obvious from the fact that He was a real existent. St. Athanasius drew attention to this quibbling interpretation of theirs when criticizing the way they

[16] *De decret. Nic. syn.* 25 (*P.G.* 25, 460). Cf. M. J. Routh, *Reliquiae Sacrae,* Oxford, 1846, III, 411.

[17] In St Athan., *De syn.* 15 (*P.G.* 26, 708).

[18] In St Athan., *Or. con. Ar.* 1, 9 (*P.G.* 26, 29).

[19] *Ibid.* 1, 6 (*P.G.* 26, 24).

[20] In Theodoret, *Hist. eccl.* 1, 6 (Parmentier, 28). . . .

[21] To Euphration, cited at Sess. V of the Second Council of Nicaea. See Mansi XIII, 317. It is printed by H. G. Opitz as *Urkunde* 3.

[22] *Or. con. Ar.* 1, 6 (*P.G.* 26, 24).

wriggled out of every attempt to tie them down to an orthodox definition.[23]

The sentence BEGOTTEN NOT MADE (*gennēthenta ou poiēthenta*), which was the next characteristically Nicene article, was not one from the implications of which the Arians could escape so easily. They were, as has been previously indicated, eager enough to employ such language as BEGOTTEN, but the meaning they put upon it was indistinguishable from MADE. The Word was a creature, a perfect creature admittedly and in a class altogether apart from other creatures, but He had been brought into existence by the divine decree out of nothing. To suggest that He had in any real sense been born implied subjecting the Godhead to a kind of necessity. They liked to stress that his coming into being had depended on an act of the Father's will.[24] The orthodox rejoinder was to insist on taking the word BEGOTTEN in its full acceptation, and to point out[25] that it was nonsense to talk of God being subjected to necessity if His very nature was to beget. In answer to the objection that then the Father must, since it is natural for fathers so to be, be prior to the Son, they had recourse to Origen's well-known teaching of the eternal generation of the Son by the Father. The Godhead had never been without His Word or His Wisdom: so the Father had never been other than Father, and had never been without His Son. The Son and the Father must therefore have coexisted from all eternity, the Father eternally begetting the Son. . . .

It was in the fourth characteristic phrase of the creed, the words OF ONE SUBSTANCE WITH THE FATHER, (*homoousion tō patri*), that the full weight of the orthodox reply to Arianism was concentrated. . . .

There were four chief grounds for hostility to it, and each of them carried different degrees of weight with different people. First, there were many who thought that the term must entail a materialistic conception of the Deity, the Father and the Son being regarded as parts or separable portions of a concrete substance. Secondly, if the Father and the Son were taken as being of one substance, it seemed to many that Sabellianism with all its perils must lurk round the corner. Thirdly, the semi-Arians made the point at the council of Ancyra (358) that the word had already been condemned by sound and orthodox bishops at the Antiochene synod (268) which had dealt with Paul of Samosata. Fourthly (and this consideration worked upon the minds of many who were far removed from Arianism proper), the word CONSUBSTANTIAL, no more than the phrase FROM THE SUBSTANCE OF THE FATHER, was not to be found in Holy Scripture, and thus the tradition that the binding formulae contained in the Church's creeds should be expressed in inspired language was violated. The orthodox had their answers to all these cavils. They would have preferred a more Scriptural term, but they had discovered that every Scriptural title or image that was put forward was immediately twisted by the Arian minority to suit their own purposes. St. Athanasius was later to argue[26] that, if the word did not appear in Holy Writ, the meaning it

---

[23] *Ep. ad Afr.* 5 (*P.G.* 26, 1040).
[24] Cf., e.g., *hypoustēsanta idiō thelēmati* in Arius' letter to St. Alexander (*P.G.* 26, 709).
[25] Cf., e.g., St Athan., *Or. con. Ar.* 3, 62 ff. (*P.G.* 26, 453 ff.).
[26] *De decret. Nic. syn.* 21 (*P.G.* 25, 453).

stood for did. . . . As for the Antiochene fathers who had anathematized Paul's use of the word, they had understood it, he argued, in a purely materialistic sense.[27] He vigorously denied that the word implied that the essence of the Father was divided, or that the Son was a portion of the Father, on the analogy of human generation. The divine essence was, of course, indivisible, and as such it must be wholly possessed by the Son.

As if the Arian theology had not been placed under a total ban in the creed itself, the anathemas return to the attack with renewed vigour and particularization. All the phrases singled out for condemnation are typical Arian catchwords or slogans: most of them had been repeated again and again by Arius himself in his ill-fated *Thalia*. To a certain extent they repeat the analogous anathemas appended to the profession of faith published by the council held at Antioch earlier in the year.

4. K. Adam[1] sees the rise of Apollinarism as a second attempt within the Logos-sarx scheme to explain the union of Christ's divinity with his humanity. Aware of the Aristotelian principle that two complete natures cannot compound themselves into one, it explained the incarnation by having the Logos take the place of the *nous* of the soul of Christ. Its condemnation did not suppress the Logos-sarx scheme. Cyril based on it the beginning of his speculation. His main achievement, however, consists in having perfected it with insights borrowed from the Antiochian position during the course of the Nestorian controversy.

The first attempt to reconcile Jesus' divinity with his low human estate by regarding the latter as mere outward appearance was rejected at the very beginning of Christianity. The Church's consciousness of faith clung just as firmly to the Lord's true humanity as it did to his true divinity. This alone withdraws the image of Christ from the oppressive realm of the pagan mythologies and theogonies. The pagan gods that had come down to earth had absorbed all their human quality into their divinity. They were not God become flesh, but gods upon earth whose human form was mere outward appearance. In contrast to this, the Christian faith firmly maintained that Christ was not a god upon earth, but God become flesh.

The Logos-sarx Christology of Arius and Apollinaris. The second attempt to approach a solution to our question derived from Arius and Apollinaris. . . .

Apollinaris, Bishop of Laodicea (d. about A.D. 390), formulated a far more profound theory of the unity of humanity and divinity in Christ, taking the same Logos-sarx scheme as his point of departure. The object of his speculations was to make as close as possible the union of true divinity and true humanity in Christ, which, he recognized, were both truly essential parts of Christ's nature. This union seemed closest to him if the divinity and humanity in Christ complemented each other so as to constitute one nature and being, if together they composed a single divine-and-human na-

[27] *De syn.* 45 (*P.G.* 26, 772).
[1] Cf. Ch. 1, n. 4. This excerpt is from *The Christ of Faith*, pp. 29–37.

ture. However, he concluded, drawing upon Aristotle, two complete perfected natures are not able to compound themselves into any such unity of nature (*dyo teleia en genesthai ou dyñatai*). They cannot interpenetrate each other, but only exist side by side. If all the same a true unity of nature should be established, it could be only by diminishing, as it were, the human nature of Jesus at its highest point. He tried to clarify this with the aid of trichotomistic psychology, which distinguishes in man's soul a lower, sensuous soul (*psyche, anima sensitiva*) and a higher, spiritual principle (*poneuma, nous anima intellectiva*). In the incarnation, the Logos takes the place of this spiritual soul. The incarnation is brought about by the joining of the divine Pneuma and the sarx, living but deprived of its higher spirit, into a union. In agreement with the Alexandrian tradition, which arose under the influence of Stoicism, Apollinaris regarded the Logos as the really effective principle in Jesus' higher spiritual life, and thus as the dominating, animating, fundamental power in Jesus' humanity too. Thus Christ was bound to transience and the earth only in his organic, sensuous being. His spiritual thinking and willing were divine, the wisdom and omnipotence of the Logos. He had but a single consciousness: the divine. Thus Christ is a "heavenly human" in so far as he derives his body from the Virgin but his soul from the Logos. These two parts are related to each other as parts of a whole, and are therefore together *mia physis mia ousia, en prosōpon,* expressions which for Apollinaris are almost identical. But it is the Logos that controls all life in Christ. In this sense, Apollinaris speaks of the "one nature of God-Logos become flesh," an expression later taken up by Cyril and used in a somewhat different sense. This was the only way Apollinaris believed he could save the unity of the image of Christ and avoid a split of Christ's self-consciousness into human and divine. On the other hand, this seemed to him the only certain and dependable way of explaining the redemption of mankind. For if Christ thought and willed purely as a man, he could not be denied freedom of decision, and must also have had the freedom to sin. But this would mean the end of all the certainty of redemption, which, according to Paul and John, had from eternity been part of the divine ordinance for salvation. For in the last resort it would depend upon the free decision of Jesus' human thought and will, something accidental. The great divine dispensation in its entirety, above all the mystery of the incarnation, would be dependent upon the good will of Jesus' humanity. And this would be unworthy of God and his wisdom.

Apollinaris' theory is distinguished—to its advantage—from that of Arius by the fact that it recognizes in Christ not merely the human body but also a human soul. But by depriving this soul of its dominant spiritual principle, the nous, it can hardly claim to speak of a fully human nature in Christ. In order to establish in Christ a true unity of nature, Apollinaris denatures the humanity of Jesus. It remained something incomplete, a fragment, at bottom near to what the animals have, an animal soul. This was a great threat to the whole divinity and sublimity of Christ's humanity. What would Christ's example have to say to man if it were based not on the anguished struggling of the human will, but on the all-holy Logos? How could man's innermost will have been redeemed by Christ if Christ's own will had been not human but divine? This was and is an axiom of soteriology: *quod non est assumptum, non est sanatum.* If the entire human thought and volition were not assumed into the divine person, it could not be led by the latter to experience any objective purification and salvation. We may well say: "The two heretical forms of the Logos-sarx Christology, Arianism and Apollinarianism, were probably the most dangerous invasion of Hellenistic ideas into the traditional conception of Christ"... Apollinarianism bears the first seeds of the later heresy of Monophysitism, which laid the gilding of divinity onto the picture of Christ so thickly that the Lord's human traits disappeared completely and Christ reverted to the ranks of pagan mythologies.

Apollinarianism could not be combated from the position of Alexandrine theology. Even the great Athanasius puts so little stress on the human soul in Jesus that it never becomes the express object of theological avowal in his scheme. He recognizes and worships the pattern of the human soul so exclusively in the Logos that the image of the Logos, Christ's human soul, retreats completely. The Logos itself is represented as the animating and energizing principle of Christ's body, the physical source of all his actions as living man. In a more moderate form than Apollinaris, Athanasius too is bound to the Logos-sarx pattern of thought. Indeed, we may say that even later, the Eastern Church never completely threw off her bondage to this pattern.

The great achievement of the theology of Antioch was that it overcame Apollinarianism; indeed, it was in dispute with the heresy that the school first developed. It countered the Logos-sarx scheme with a Logos-Anthropos scheme. . . . With this doctrine [it was] able to point out the inadequacy of the Arian and Apollinarian Christology.

At the Synods of Alexandria and Rome, Apollinarianism was condemned. The first Council at Constantinople (381) pronounced its solemn sentence (Denzinger, 86). Since then, Church theology has expressly emphasized that God became flesh *mediante anima,* through the mediation of the human soul, and not in place of the human soul. The rejection of Apollinarianism anticipated the later rejection of fully developed Monophysitism, Monotheletism, and Monenergism.

It is true that terminologically the expressions "became flesh" and "incarnation" remained in use. Didymus the Blind in particular used them so frequently and recklessly in his early period that theologians were tempted to range him close to Apollinarianism. St. Augustine, too, was fond of the phrase *caro Christi,* but he always used it in the sense of the entire humanity of Jesus. The early Scholastics remained faithful to this usage of Augustine's. The high age of Scholasticism, however, preferred the unambiguous phrase "made man." Since then, theology has no longer spoken of an *assumptio carnis* alone, but of the *assumptio carnis et animae,* i.e., *hominis.*

The disputes with Apollinaris had made the following dogma clear: Both divinity and perfect humanity are in Christ. This humanity is fully conscious of itself and its peculiar spirituality. It is in no sense replaced by the Logos. The unity of divinity and humanity in Christ may not be brought about by any diminishing or denaturing of humanity in Christ. This prepared the way for the realization that the union of divinity and humanity in Christ can take place only *secundum personam,* not *secundum naturam.* It cannot be that divine powers poured themselves, as it were, with natural necessity, into the humanity of Christ and transformed it into divinity. Rather, Christ's human nature remained completely unabsorbed after the union. What the Logos imparts to Christ's human nature can be only the identity of the second person, the consciousness of being this person, the independence, the autonomy. It is true, this conclusion did not come fully to light until the disputes with Monophysitism. The question that this heresy raised was this: If Christ is truly God, and in body and soul wholly man, and if both parts of his being, divine and human, remain undiminished, how can the *unus Christus,* the unified self, arise, and how can this unified self be more precisely defined? . . .

Where the Alexandrians from their point of departure were disposed to overstrain the unity of person in Christ into a unity of nature, the school of Antioch was inclined to extend the duality of natures to a duality of persons. It is only natural that even Cyril should, at the beginning of his speculation, base it on the traditional Logos-sarx scheme and even go on undisturbed to use Apollinarian formulations. Only in the course of the disputes with Nestorius did he come to recognize that for its part Alexandrian theory did not do justice to the peculiar importance of Christ's human soul and its deeds. It was the particular achievement of his speculation to unite the insights of both schools, and thereby to furnish a sufficiently clear basis for further correct development of the truths of Christology.

The characteristics of his speculation can be summed up briefly: The process of incarnation had its starting point not in the human but in the divine self. Christ the man did not become the Logos—that would be an apotheosis after the fashion of pagan mythologies—but rather the Logos became man. The subject of the union is solely the Logos-self. Thus we can speak only of a single self in Christ, the divine self of the Logos. Even after the incarnation, there is only one self in Christ. "One and the same is Christ." This Logos has assumed human nature to such an extent that it possesses human nature physically (*henōsis physikē*) in its being, and not through some moral act of faith and love on the part of human nature. The union of God and man in Christ is accomplished once and for all in the incarnation. It does not depend upon free will or a moral act. This formula of Cyril's, *henōsis physikē,* is not to be understood in the sense that the later Monophysitism ascribed to it, that the union of both natures took place *secundum naturam divinam* so that all the characteristics of the divine nature of themselves poured into the humanity and completely absorbed it. The formula rather means: The union is not accidental and dependent upon will, brought into being through a voluntary act of human nature, but is permanent, unique, brought into being by the fact of the incarnation. The self of the Logos is thus not the result but the permanent principle of the union, which already existed before any moral act that Christ was capable of, and is so close that the divine and the human in Christ can be separate only theoretically in idea. In reality it is one and the same divine self that performs not only the divine but also the human deeds, so that both divine and human actions are equally expressions of Christ. This is the *communicatio idiomatum.* From the self in Christ named after his divine nature, one can adduce human actions, and from the self in Christ called after his human nature, one can adduce divine actions. I can avow: The Logos became man and suffered, just as I can affirm: The crucified one is the prince of life. I may say this because the subject of my avowal is always one and the same: the self of the eternal Word. This is why our worship is due not simply to the Logos in Christ but to the whole Christ, including his humanity, because this humanity belongs to the Logos and is not to be separated from it. This is why Mary is truly the mother of God, because the living being that she bore is the Son of God become man.

This powerful emphasis on *henōsis physikē,* which Cyril derived from the Alexandrian tradition, preserves the image of Christ from all antinomies and stresses the divine basis of Christ's life, the mighty fact that God himself, the second divine person, is the true bearer of all human and superhuman characteristics and powers of the Lord. At last the *verbum caro factum est* of St. John, and the believing conviction that the selfsame historical Jesus is also the Son of the living God, was once again given lucid expression and clear spiritual perception.

It is true, the liberating word had not yet been uttered, that the union was not a *unio secundum naturam* but only *secundum personam.* Cyril had not yet attempted to draw a clear distinction between nature and person, or to establish that existence as person is not an essential part of nature, but that existence as person can rather be distinguished from existence as nature, and that it is hence conceivable, and indeed really the case, that in Christ a human nature can certainly exist, but not a human person. Since Cyril had not gone as far as this, the suspicion could still arise that at root the Alexandrians taught the assumption of human nature into divine nature in such a way that the divine nature could absorb and assume even human qualities and powers. This possibility was first grasped at a later date by Monophysitism. . . .

5. R. V. Sellers[1] places the Cappadocians in line with the tradition of Athanasius and other Alexandrian theologians. He finds that their doctrine is faithful to what he calls the principles of Christological confession and inquiry. Although he admits that their terminology and concepts lack precision at times, their views are far removed from Nestorianism or Eutychianism. Strong opponents of Apollinarism, they defend the presence of the complete manhood in Christ, but with the rest of Greek theologians they fail to bring this principle to all its conclusions.

[1] Cf. Ch. 2, n. 6. This excerpt is from his book *Two Ancient Christologies* (London: S.P.C.K., 1954), selectively, from pp. 65–80.

The coming of the Laodicene marks the beginning of a fresh stage in the development of the Alexandrine doctrine concerning Christ's Person, for now its exponents are provided with carefully worded phrases which sum up the essentials of their faith. . . . The Cappadocian Fathers—Basil of Caesarea († 379), his brother Gregory of Nyssa († *c.* 394), and Gregory of Nazianzus († 390)—. . . stand as representatives of the Alexandrine Christological tradition, inheriting what had been said by Origen and by Athanasius. . . . Lacking the clear-cut expressions of Apollinarius, their language is at times unsatisfactory; moreover, they introduce conceptions concerning the Lord's manhood which can be pronounced heterodox. Nevertheless, it seems impossible to deny that they would uphold the same two Christological principles which had been upheld by those who had gone before. . . .

The Cappadocians lay all emphasis on the thought that God Himself has intervened in the Person of Jesus Christ in order to establish man in newness of life, and so to "deify" him.[2] Such is "the Gospel mystery" Man, they proclaim, is a fallen creature, and the Incarnation has been rendered necessary by the Fall. The point is worked out by Gregory of Nyssa who is preeminently the thinker among them. Like Athanasius, he is indebted to Methodius of Olympus, and, starting from the conception of the universality of sin, sees that the redemption must consist in the lifting up of the whole human race from its present evil state—and, to raise up fallen man, to restore to him the gift of life, and to effect his ransom, God, he teaches, who might have issued some direct command, "submitted Himself to the condition of a human body, was born, and died, and rose again, and in this way accomplished His object."[3] *Cur Deus homo?* The Bishop's answer is that the Incarnation was the best way in which God's attributes of power, goodness, wisdom and righteousness could be manifested,[4] that only thus could men be delivered from the state of death, itself the result of sin, which began in one man,[5] and that man is redeemed as the beginning of the Resurrection-life extends through the Redeemer to the whole of humanity.[6] But is Gregory thinking of a process which is purely physical? Does he mean that the redemption is effected as the divine nature pervades the whole of human nature? Does he mean that both in the Redeemer and, through Him, in the redeemed the human is so transfused with divine qualities, as a result of the "commingling," that it is human no longer? Certainly he speaks of the "lump" of humanity, and uses the mixing of liquids to illustrate his doctrine con-

[2] Cf. Greg. Naz. *Orat.* xxx. 14 (he is speaking of Christ's intercession for us): "He still pleads even now as man for my salvation; for He continues to wear the body which He assumed till He has made me God by the power of the Incarnation." Basil's statement that souls cleansed from every spot, and illuminated by the Spirit, themselves become spiritual and, "abiding in God", become "like to God" and, highest of all, are made God (*de Spiritu Sancto,* 23) shows what these teachers understand by man's "deification" —it is an essentially spiritual process. . . .

[3] *Orat. Catech.* xv.

[4] *Ibid.* xvii ff.

[5] *Ibid.* viii.

[6] *Ibid.* xvi.

cerning the Lord's manhood, but what has been said in the case of Athanasius seems applicable here: realistic categories are being used to describe what is understood as a moral and spiritual process.[7]

Upon these ideas concerning God and man and man's redemption, the Cappadocians built their Christology. While from the point of view of their expressions they can be regarded as the successors of the Origenists, their doctrine is, rather, akin to that of Athanasius—the one in whom soteriology and Christology are inseparably brought together. With them, as with him, the two cardinal principles are seen in their soteriological bearing—though, as we say, we miss here that clearness of thought which might have been expected now that the Christological problem is to the fore.

For man and his salvation, these teachers hold, God has Himself become man as Jesus Christ, the divine Logos having assumed a nature like ours. The Logos Himself, says Gregory of Nazianzus, "came to His own image, and took on Him flesh for the sake of our flesh, and mingled Himself with an intelligent soul for my soul's sake, purifying like by like; and in all points except sin was made man."[8] And this becoming man, they say, has not involved any change in respect of the divine existence of the Logos. . . . The Logos, then, though He has united man's nature to Himself, is still the same Person, the only difference being that He who was once *simplex* is now, through His becoming man, *compositus*.

Further, the Cappadocians, it seems, appreciate that, in order to become man, the Logos must accommodate Himself to human conditions. In this connection, a passage in the *adversus Eunomium* of Gregory of Nyssa is of distinct value. Eunomius was saying that "if he can show that God, who is over all, who is the unapproachable Light, was incarnate, or could be incarnate, came under authority, obeyed commands, came under the laws of man, bore the Cross, then let him say that light is equal to The Light." Thus, as Gregory says, Eunomius, who, as is clear, would distinguish between the Son as "light" and the Father as "The Light,"[9] was ranking the Son with Creation, not worshipping Him equally with the Father, and, seeing in the Cross evidence of weakness, holding that He could not have experienced His sufferings had He not had a nature capable of such suffering. The Cappadocian then gives his answer to the Anomoean: it is, in effect, that one can posit an incarnation of One who is truly God because—a truth "surprisingly wonderful"—He accommodates Himself to conditions

[7] Cf. Dorner's verdict that Gregory's is "a strictly ethical estimate of Christianity" (Person of Christ, I, ii. p. 514).

[8] *Orat.* xxxviii. 13.

[9] The above translation of the quotation from Eunomius (taken, in the main, from that in *Nicene and post-Nicene Fathers,* vol. v, p. 176) is based on the Φ reading in Jaeger's text (*Gregorii Nysseni Opera,* Berlin, 1921)—*Ison to phōti phōs*. It is unlikely that this would have formed from the π reading, *Ison to phōti* ("the Light is equal to the Light," as in trans. in *N. and p.-N.F.*), while the converse is not unlikely. The Φ text is comprehensible. Eunomius has declared the Ingenerate to be *aprositon phōs* in contradistinction to diffused *phōs:* He is thus to be called *to phōs,* but the Son *phōs* just as Asterius argues that the Son is called in Scripture *dynamis* and *sophia* distinguishing His being from *hē dynamis tou theou etc.*

external to His nature. Clearly, it is the answer of one who would maintain the Hebraic conception of God against one who was to no small extent being influenced by ideas essentially Greek. . . .

At the same time, we must not read too much into this evidence, for, beside . . . passages which seem to point to the recognition of the thought that the Logos limited Himself in order to become man, we must set others which show that these teachers hesitate to make full use of the idea of a self-emptying.[10] As we say, none of the theologians of the Early Church attempted to work out this doctrine.

In their insistence on the fundamental truth that in Jesus Christ the Logos Himself has become man, the Cappadocians firmly uphold the doctrine of the unity of the Person of the Incarnate. Adopting current expressions,[11] they speak of the union of the divine and the human in Him as a "composition," a "mixture," a "commingling." But it should not be thought that the use of these words points to the presence of the Eutychian view of our Lord's Person. Rather do these teachers speak in this way in order to give the lie to the idea of dividing Christ into a duad of Sons through emphasizing the thought of the closeness of the union. Their point is that the union of the Logos with human nature is such that it is utterly impossible to consider that in Jesus Christ there can be two Persons, one divine, the other human, each having His own individual existence. Thus Gregory of Nyssa affirms that the text "God hath made that same Jesus whom ye have crucified, both Lord and Christ" (Acts ii. 36) should not be taken as meaning that one (*allos*) suffered, and another (*eteros*) was honoured by exaltation. What is said here, he declares, refers to one Person (*en prosōpon*), to whom both the sufferings and the honour are to be ascribed.[12] Gregory of Nazianzus is equally emphatic . . . Nestorianism is expressly condemned.[13] . . . (Yet)

[10] Thus, interpreting the text "Of that day and hour . . ." (Mt xxiv. 36), Gregory of Nazianzus can say that it is "only the Father" who knows the hour of the Parousia, the Son being ignorant of it apart from the Father's communication (*Orat.* xxx. 16). The same interpretation is preferred by Basil (*Ep.* ccxxxvi, 2).

[11] Origen and the Origenists had already used these terms. . . . They were also being used at this time by Apollinarius and his followers (see above, p. 52). It may be noted, too, that the term "mixture," which was being used by Epiphanius (*Anchor.* 81), . . . is to be found in Irenaeus (*Adv. Haeres.* III. xx. I—(?*Homo*) *Commixtus Verbo Dei*), in Tertullian (*Apol.* 21—*Homo Deo mixtus*), and in Cyprian (*de Idol. Van.* II—*Deus cum homine miscetur*). The same word was to be employed later on by Leo of Rome, what he says plainly revealing his reason for adopting it: "This wonderful child-bearing of the holy Virgin produced in her offspring one Person, truly divine, truly human; not in such a way that . . . there could be a dividing of Person, but in such a way that one nature was blended (*misceretur*) with the other" (*Sermo* xxxviii, *in Nativ. Dom.* iii).

[12] *Adv. Eunom.* v. 3.

[13] This is undoubtedly the case, even if—and this illustrates the point that these have no precise Christological formulas . . .—their language is at times quasi-Nestorian. See the passages from Greg. Naz. collected by A. J. Mason, who comments: "If his language were taken according to its strict grammatical sense, it might sometimes be pressed to mean that in the Incarnate Saviour a human person co-existed with the Eternal Word" (*The Five Theological Orations of Nazianzus,* pp. xvi ff.). For an illustration of the quasi-Nestorian language of Gregory of Nyssa, see his *adv. Eunom.* v. 5. It may be noted, too, that this writer, when speaking of the "union," often uses the term *synapheia*—the term favoured by the Antiochenes.

while rejecting the teaching of "two Sons," Gregory would not go to the other extreme and teach the confusion of the two natures.

There are two natures, God and man (*pyseis men gar dyo theos kai anthropos*), as also body and soul are; but there are not two Sons or Gods; there are not two men in one because Paul speaks of an inner and an outer man.[14] Clearly, then, these stand with Origen and his followers, with Apollinarius and Cyril, as upholders of a scheme of doctrine which is inherently anti-Nestorian: they will not countenance teaching which, as the Bishop of Nazianzus puts it, shirks the begetting of the Logos in the flesh.

It has to be observed, too, that the Cappadocians hold that all the acts and sayings recorded of Jesus Christ in the scriptures are to be attributed to this one Person—the Logos who has assumed flesh. Gregory of Nazianzus especially is emphatic on this point. Thus in the third (*de Filio*) of his *Five Theological Orations* we find such expressions as these: He who hungered was He who fed thousands and is the Bread that giveth life; He who thirsted is He who promised that fountains should flow from those who believe; He who was weary is He who is the Rest of the heavyladen; He who is called a Samaritan and demon-possessed is He who saves him that fell among thieves; He who prays is He who hears prayer; He who weeps is He who causes tears to cease; He who asks where Lazarus was laid is He who raises him; He who is sold is He who redeems the world; He who as a sheep is led to the slaughter is He who is Shepherd of Israel and of the whole world; He who is nailed to the tree is He who restores us by the Tree of Life; He who died is He who gives life and by His death destroys death.[15] . . . He would agree with the other Gregory in saying that "while not attributing our salvation to a man, we do not admit that the divine nature is capable of suffering and mortality."[16] So he makes a distinction between what belongs to Christ in His eternal being, and what belongs to Him as He has become flesh. . . . In all this, it will be understood, the Bishop of Nazianzus is but emphasizing a doctrinal principle which has an important place in the Christology of the Alexandrine school of thought. As we have said, the representatives of this school do not think that the Incarnate acts and speaks now in His divine, now in His human, nature: everything, whether divine or human, they hold, is performed by the one Person,[17] the God made man, and His acts and sayings are those of God—though not of God as He is eternally (for in His divine nature God is impassible), but of God who, while remaining what He was, has entered into a novel state through the Incarnation, having become *theos pathētos* for us men and for our salvation.

Let us see how the second main principle of the Alexandrine Christology has its place in the teaching of the Cappadocians. As has been pointed out, it would be a mistake to suppose

[14] It is interesting to find that the Antiochenes appealed the Pauline text (2 Cor. iv. 16) in support of their assertion that it is necessary to "separate" the natures. Perhaps, then, Gregory was mindful of this fact when he wrote the words quoted above.

[15] *Orat.* xxix. 20.

[16] *Adv. Eunom.* vi. 1.

[17] Cf. the direct statement to this effect in Greg. Nyss., *adv. Eunom.* v. 3.

that their language indicates the presence of Eutychian ideas. Gregory of Nazianzus, for instance, who does not hesitate to employ the terms "mixture" and "commingling" and—without a word of explanation—boldly speaks of the "deification" of the human element by the divine,[18] directly refutes the notion of "confusion." The body of the Lord, he says in his letter to Cledonius, "has not been swallowed up by the Son, as the Manichees fable, . . . neither has it been poured out, and dissolved in the air like a voice or a stream of perfume, or a flash of lightning."[19] In Jesus Christ, he affirms there are two natures (*dyo physeis*).[20] He is twofold (*diplous*)[21] and, accordingly, One "out of two" (*ek dyo*).[22] Further, we must note that this teacher makes use of the principle of "recognizing the difference of the natures" in their union in the one Person of Jesus Christ.[23] That this is the case is seen when we enquire into his interpretation of Scripture. . . . Clearly, in all this Gregory is but following what had been laid down by Athanasius—namely, that if one "recognizes what is proper to each," it is impossible to "entertain low ideas concerning the Logos." At the same time, he explicitly rejects the Eutychian doctrine: it is "not by nature" that the two express the One.

But it is a weakness in the Christology of his namesake of Nyssa that this Cappadocian does not sufficiently appreciate the necessity of defending the faith against the idea of "confusion." As is well known, there are times when he puts forward the doctrine that in Jesus Christ there is but one, and that a divine, nature. By the commingling, he declares, the body in which the Lord underwent the Passion is made to be *oper hē analabousa physis estin*,[24] the Lord's human nature

[18] Thus in the well-known passage in Gregory's *Oratio de Epiphania seu Nativitate* (*Orat.* xxxviii. 13) we have the expression: *to men theose, to de etheōthe*. But in view of what he says elsewhere—and this, it should be remembered, is a highly rhetorical passage—it seems clear that the Bishop does not mean that the human has been transformed into the divine nature as a result of the union. It may be supposed, then, that had his thoughts been fully developed, Gregory would have offered the explanation of the statement which was put out by John of Damascus—namely, that such words are used "not according to a change of nature, but according to the economic, that is, the hypostatic, mind . . . and the interpenetration of the natures with one another" (*de Fid. Orth,* iii. 17, *P.G.* xciv. 1069A).

[19] *Ep.* ci.

[20] *Ibid.*

[21] *Orat.* xxx (*Theol. Orat.* iv). 8; *Orat.* xxxviii. 15.

[22] *Orat.* ii. 23, xxxviii. 3, and *Ep.* ci, where we have εν ἐκ δύο . . .

[23] It is interesting to find that Amphilochius of Iconium († after 394), who was regarded as the most prominent ecclesiastic in the East after his friends Basil and Greg. Naz., upholds the same principle. Thus the fragment of his discourse on "My Father is greater than I," which is preserved in the *Dialogues* of Theodoret, begins: "Distinguish me now the natures—that of God and that of man . . . I am speaking of God and man." Then, explaining the text on this principle, he goes on: "Sometimes I call Myself equal to the Father, and sometimes I say that the Father is greater—not contradicting Myself, but showing that I am God and man, for God is of the lofty, and man of the lowly." One may note—as illustrating the point that these theologians sometimes use quasi-Nestorian language—that Amphilochius here speaks of assigning the lowly titles *tō ek Marias anthrōpō* (Theodoret, *Dialogues,* i, ii, ed. Schulze, *Op.* IV. pt. i. pp. 66, 152; *P.G.* xxxix. 109A, Frag. XII; cf. also Frags. II, VII, XI—preserved by Theodoret, *Dial.* iii, ed. Schulze, IV. pt. i. pp. 248 f—*P.G. xxxix.* p. 100B ff.).

[24] *Adv. Eunom.* v. 3.

he likens to a drop of vinegar mingled with the sea[25] . . . and in another place he expressly says that the flesh "no longer remains in its own limitations and properties, but is taken up into that which is overwhelming and transcendent."[26] All the same, Gregory of Nyssa can hardly be called the forerunner of those who, in a later age, were deserving of the name "Monophysite," and, as is often said[27] it is likely that, influenced by the teaching of Origen, he considered that it was only after the Resurrection that the human in Christ was changed into the divine. For his doctrine here has another side. Thus we find him saying: "The contemplation (*theōria*) of the properties of the flesh and of the Godhead remains without confusion so long as each of these is contemplated by itself" (*eph eautōn*).[28] Again, in a passage in which he defends the position that the Logos was subject to suffering "in the flesh," he says that the pain, slumber, need, trouble, wounds and death which Christ endured were real, and that they belong to the flesh which has its "peculiar attributes," his point being that "just as it is not possible to contemplate the peculiar attributes of the flesh as existing in the Logos that was from the beginning, so also we may not conceive those which are proper to the Godhead as existing in the nature of the flesh."[29] Certainly Gregory's use of the word "contemplate" in this connection is unfortunate, since it can give the impression that in his view the natures are different, not in reality, but only in thought, but it seems legitimate to argue from such passages that he is aware of the principle of "recognizing the difference of the natures," and, indeed, would apply it. Moreover, it is worthy of note that in his *Dialogues* Theodoret of Cyrus—who, as leading representative of the Antiochene doctrinal tradition, is determined to safeguard the reality of the Lord's human nature in its union with the Logos—can appeal to the Bishop of Nyssa in support of his *"Inconfusus,"* and adduce quotations from his writings in which the distinction is made between what is divine in Christ, and what is human.[30]

We can say, then, that the Cappadocians uphold the principle that in Jesus Christ the Logos has become "man." But do they mean by this that the manhood which He has assumed is at once both representative and individual? Now it cannot be doubted that, like Athanasius, these teachers stand for the conception that the Incarnate is the Representative Man, altogether like ourselves. He is the firstfruits of all human nature, who presents it to its God and Father.[31] Indeed, they could hardly be more definite on this point. In his celebrated letter to Cledonius, the Bishop of Nazianzus proclaims that if the Lord had been without a mind, only the half of us would have been saved; rather is He *totus homo,* and, the whole man being mingled with the Godhead, the whole of our nature is

[25] *Ibid.* v. 5 (similarly, *Antirrhet.* 42).
[26] *Adv. Eunom.* v. 5 . . .
[27] For a different view, see Raven, *Apollinarism,* p. 267.
[28] *Adv. Eunom.* v. 5.
[29] *Adv. Eunom.* VI. 1.
[30] *Dial.* ii, ed. Schulze, IV. pt. i, pp. 150 f.
[31] Cf. Greg. Nyss., *adv. Eunom.* ii. 8.

saved. . . .[32] There is no need to say more on this subject: that these teachers upheld the conception of the representative character of Christ's manhood is abundantly clear.

But do they so clearly maintain the individual character of that manhood? They say that the redemption could not have been real had not the Logos taken to Himself a manhood complete with a human rational soul. Do they, then, see in the Incarnate a manhood which possesses its own faculty of self-determination? Has it, according to them, its own individuating quality? . . .

B) The Antiochian School: Logos-anthropos Christology

1. R. V. Sellers[1] sees the Antiochians closer to the Bible and to Judaism than the Alexandrians. Their Christological system evolves in the light of three fundamental postulates: the oneness of God which is made known in three hypostases, the essential difference and distance between God and man, the concept of man as a moral being responsible for his fate. Their soteriological preoccupations greatly influenced their Christology.

A very different intellectual background confronts us when we pass from the Christological thought of the Alexandrians to that of the Antiochenes. That theirs is a moral rather than a philosophical outlook is not surprising when we take into account their close connection with Judaism. . . . Moreover, though the earlier representatives of this tradition, Paul of Samosata and Eustathius of Antioch were deprived by the local Hellenists, their work as pioneers lived on, and found its fulfilment in the teaching of Theodore of Mopsuestia (†428), who, following in the steps of Diodore of Tarsus († before 394) and Flavian of Antioch (†404), systematized the thought of the school. Consequently, the later classical Antiochenes, Theodoret of Cyrus (†458) being the last and most learned of them, are dependent on him whom they venerated as "The Interpreter" for much of their teaching.

An investigation of the ideas fundamental to their Christological system will reveal the extent of the debt which the Antiochenes owe to the Old Testament.

Thus, in the first place, in their theology they start, not, like the Alexandrians, from a trinitarian conception of God, but from the conception of his unity,[2] and, in the light of the divine acts of creation and redemption, maintain that the one God whom Israel worshipped is now made known in the three *hypostases* or *proposa* of the Father, the Son, and Holy Spirit.[3]

---

[32] *Ep.* ci.

[1] Cf. Ch. 2., n. 6. This excerpt has been taken from his book *The Council of Chalcedon,* selectively, from pp. 158–181.

[2] Thus it may be said that the Trinitarian doctrine of the school of Antioch "is the doctrine of God *in* God, just as the doctrine of Alexandria was a doctrine of God *of* God" (F. W. Green, "The Later Doctrine of the Trinity," in *Essays on the Trinity and the Incarnation,* ed. A. E. J. Rawlinson, p. 264).

[3] Thus Theodore of Mopsuestia in his *ad Baptizandos,* or *de Interpretatione Symboli trecentorum decem et octo Patrum,* ed. A. Mingana, "The Commentary of Theodore of

In earlier days, when the concept of Sonship, carrying with it the thought of eternal and personal existence, had yet to be fully brought out, Paul of Samosata, as has been argued, seems to have regarded the Logos as the Reason and Word of God which, in him from the first, was "begotten," and came into personal existence when God moved in the fulfilment of his creative purpose.[4] And after the Arian controversy, when the classical Antiochenes could reap the fruits of the labours of those who, both in their own and in other schools of thought, held firmly to the *homoousios,* and the doctrine of the Son's co-eternity with the Father was fully established, the background is still the same: like Paul of Samosata before them—and like him, too, in that they were daily confronted with the monotheistic belief of their Jewish neighbours—Theodore and Theodoret start from what is laid down in the Shema.[5] There is one divine *ousia,* to which the name "God" is given,[6] they proclaim; and in it are seen three *hypostases*—three individual existences, that is—which, though differing in "manner of subsisting,[7] fully and equally partake of it. The Son, eternally begotten of the unbegotten Father, is "out of," "with" and "in[8] the Father,"[9] and "out of" the Father,

Mopsuestia on the Nicene Creed," *Woodbrooke Studies,* vol. V. pp. 28f: "Through the prophets we only understood God and the being to whom an uncreated nature belongs, but the teaching of our Lord Jesus Christ gave us also with certainty the persons in whom is Divine nature. This is the reason why our blessed Fathers placed first the doctrine of the belief in one God, as it was written in the Old Testament, in order to destroy the error of polytheism, and then imparted to us the knowledge of the persons according to the teaching of Christ."

[4] According to the letter of the Synod which condemned him, Paul said: "This one (him born of David) the Virgin bore through the Holy Spirit, but That one, the Logos, God begat without a virgin, and (indeed) without any one, there being no one but God; and thus the Logos came into existence. . . . Paul's "there being no one but God" is important as illustrating his insistence on the unity of God: the Logos, when begotten, is still "in God," and cannot be separated from him, the Father and the Logos in him being one God. Cf. the saying attributed to Paul by Epiphanius, *Haeres.* 65. 1. "God is one . . . the Father, and the Son, in Him as logos is in man, are one God . . . 'The Lord thy God is one Lord.'" Hence, if Paul used the term *homoousios* at the Synod, it seems that he used it in the sense that the Logos is of the same *ousia* as the Father—of the same divine content.

[5] Theodore (e.g. *ad Baptiz.;* ed. Mingana, pp. 25, 27, 36) and Theodoret (see the important chapter *de Principio* in his *Graec. Affect. curat.* ii; ed. Schulze, IV. i. pp. 743ff), are constantly appealing to Deut. vi. 4. For Paul's use of the text, see the saying attributed to him by Epiphanius, *Haeres.* 65. 1. . . .

[6] Thus Theodoret: the names "Lord" and "God" signify the divine nature (*Quaest in Deut.* vi; ed. Schulze, I. i. p. 262); "God" is the name of "the single nature" (*Ep.* cxxx; *ibid.,* ii. vi. p. 1215).

[7] I.e., the Father is unbegotten, the Son begotten, and the Holy Spirit proceeds. See Theodoret, *Graec. Affect. curat.* ii, *Haeretic. Fabul. compend.* v. 3. (ed. Schulze, IV. ii. pp. 756ff, IV. i. pp. 388ff).

[8] When these teachers speak of the Son as being "in" the Father, what they have in mind, it seems, is the notion that he is "in the bosom of the Father" (John 1. 18—a text to which they constantly appeal): between the Father and the Son there is a communion of being which is unceasing; the Son is in the Father eternally (cf. Theodore, *ad. Baptiz.;* ed. Mingana, pp. 32, 38).

[9] The three prepositions are constantly appearing in Antiochene expositions of the doctrine of the Trinity. See, for instance, Theodore, *ad Baptiz.;* ed Mingana, pp. 24, 30, 31, 32, 42, 44, 53. . . .

"in" whom also he is, the Holy Spirit proceeds:[10] Thus for them, as for Israel under the Old Covenant, there is one divine self-consciousness[11]—though, in the light of the revelation in Jesus Christ, they say, we now understand what is meant when we read, for instance, "And *God* said, Let us make man in *our* image, after *our* likeness."[12]

Secondly, we must notice that, fundamental to the thought of the Antiochenes, is the doctrine of the essential difference between God the Creator and man the creature[13]; over against God in his immortality, incorruptibility and impassibility is set mortal, corruptible and passible man. But whence is this doctrine derived? There are passages in the writings of these teachers from which it might be inferred that they regard Divinity and Humanity as two antithetical *ousiai*. . . . But upon closer investigation it is seen that they speak in this way only as they would enforce a conception to which they had been led by their study of the Old Testament. . . . God alone . . . the one God made known in three *hypostases,* has an uncreated *ousia,* while every other form of existence has of necessity a created *ousia.*[14] This thought, it should be understood, lies at the very heart of the teaching of the Antiochenes,[15] and is the ultimate ground of their insistence of the "two natures" in Jesus Christ, and the necessity of "dividing"

---

[10] See, for instance, Theodoret, *Graec. Affect curat.* ii; ed. Schulze, IV. ii. p. 757.

[11] The Antiochenes plainly teach that there is one divine *ousia,* which, shared by three *hypostases,* is omnipotent, omniscient and omnipresent, and possesses one will and one activity. Thus Theodoret (*Interpret. in Ps.* cxxxviii. 7; ed. Schulze, I. ii. p. 1533), and . . . (*in Ps.* ci. 28; *ibid.,* p. 1322). In the same connection we may note this teacher's use of the analogy of the human soul. The human soul, says Theodoret, possesses a rational and a vital principle; the soul begets the spoken word, and with the spoken word perpetually proceeds breath. Yet, he goes on, this human analogy has its limitations, since both spoken word and breath are "without *hypostasis,*" whereas in the Trinity there are three *hypostases,* united without confusion, and each personally subsisting (*Quaest. in Gen. i, Interr.* xx; ed. Schulze, I. i. p. 28; see also *de Prov.* x; *ibid.,* IV. i. p. 660, and *Graec. Affect. curat.; ibid.,* IV. ii. p. 757).

[12] *Quaest. in Gen.* i, *Interr.* xix; ibid. I. i. p. 23.

[13] It is noteworthy that the conception of the difference between the uncreated being of God and the created being of man had been upheld from very early days. See Theophilus, *ad Autol.* ii. 10.

[14] See esp. Theodoret, *Quaest. in Gen.* i. *Interr.* iv; ed. Schulze I. i. p. 9, where the principle is enunciated. . . . (similarly, *ibid.,* p. 10). We may also note that this teacher is constantly making use of Ps. 148 to prove, against the Arians, that the Son and the Holy Spirit have not a created nature: it is the whole of creation, he argues, which sings this hymn of praise to the Creator, and neither Person is mentioned as taking part in it (*Interpret. in. Ps.* cxlviii; *ibid.,* I. iii. p. 1576). The principle, too, has a foremost place in the *Expositio rectae fidei* (*P.G.* vi. 1212C)—a pseudo-Justinian work which can now be attributed to Theodoret (*J.T.S.,* vol. xlvi. no. 183–184).

[15] But according to the Antiochenes, the difference between the Creator and the creature, does not mean that God cannot come into touch with man, or that man cannot enjoy communion with God. On the contrary, God, who dwells in all things "according to *ousia,*" and is omnipotent in his operations "according to activity," dwells "according to good pleasure" in "those who are eager to cling to him," bestowing upon them "the best and highest will of the Divine" (cf. the well-known passage in Theodore, *de Incarn.* vii. ed. H. B. Swete, *Theodore of Mopsuestia on the Minor Epistles of St. Paul,* ii. pp. 293f), and the God of all things "seeks the fellowship of faith" (Theodoret, *interpret. in Ep. ad Rom.* ix. 29; ed. Schulze, III. i. p. 109).

or "separating" them. But, as we are arguing, though the doctrine may be expressed in terms borrowed from their Greek neighbours, it is theirs just because, in the first instance, the ancient Scriptures are theirs.

Thirdly, these teachers are supremely interested in man the moral being, and in particular concentrate on his power of self-determination.[16] But it is important to notice that the conception of man as a free spirit is never considered in isolation, but always against the background of the thought of God's good purpose for him: they may be called anthropologists, but their anthropology is intimately associated with their ethical and soteriological ideas. . . . But when in his freedom man disobeyed the Divine commandment, he was compelled to suffer the penalty; henceforward, death became his lot, and the harmonious conjunction of heaven and earth was broken. . . .

Furnished with these ideas, the Antiochenes set out to offer their explanation of the Christian message of salvation. . . . Their Christology has its foundation in their soteriological thought. They argue, it seems, in this way: Because man has followed Adam in his disobedience to the divine law, his is now a state of mutability and corruption; if, then, order is to be restored, a new stage *katastasis*[17] in the world's history must be set up; and the coming of this new stage involves the creation of a new Man, who, succeeding where Adam failed, will be the *bonorum principium immutabile;* but, since man, being what he is, is unable to free himself from the chains of disobedience, God himself must intervene, and, through creating, and uniting to himself, the new Man, bring into being the "Man-God,"[18] that man may be re-established in obedience to God's will, and heaven and earth re-united in perfect harmony.

It is nothing less than this, the Antiochenes declare, which has taken place through the coming of Jesus Christ. . . . And what these teachers mean by the "Economy of our Lord Jesus Christ" is that in him the divine Logos, the Second Person of the Trin-

---

[16] The *de natura hominis* of Nemesius of Emesa (who flourished at the beginning of the fifth century) is an outstanding example of the anthropological interest of the Antiochenes. Man, says Nemesius, is "the truly rational being," who in his freedom will be either an earthly or an heavenly man: he may incline to bodily things, choosing the life of creatures devoid of reason, or follow "the blessed and divine life which befits him" (*de Nat. Hom.* i, *P.G.* xl. p. 512). Similarly, Theodoret describes man as "a reasonable and mortal being" (*Dial.* ii.; ed. Schulze, IV. i. p. 107), and insists that he is free either to allow his appetites (*epithymia*) to gain the upper hand, or to follow the dictates of his heart (*thymos*)—which God in his wisdom has joined with human impulses—when these get out of control; but if he does not allow the rational element in him (*ho logiamos ho nous*) to play its part through keeping the lower element in harmony with the higher, then disaster will follow—charioteer, horses and chariot will be cast into the depths (*Graec. Affect. curat.* v; *ibid.*, p. 827; see also *Interpret. in Ep, ad Rom.* v. p. 15; *ibid.*, III. i. pp. 76f).

[17] Thus Theodore clearly distinguishes between the two stages in the history of creation: the first is the stage of mutability and mortality, resulting from the Fall, the second that of immutability and immortality (cf. *in Gen.*, *P.G.* lxvi. p. 634)—a theme which is constantly recurring in his *ad Baptiz.* (ed. Mingana, *op. cit.*, esp. pp. 19f).

[18] Nestorius uses the expression, the "Man-God": "He (the Logos) has received his (the Man's) *prosōpon* as something created, in such wise as not originally to be man, but at the same time Man-God by the Incarnation of God, who in him is what God was in the first man" (*Bazaar of Heracleides,* trans. Driver and Hodgson, p. 60).

ity, has assumed "the form of a servant," and united it to himself, and that, as a result of this union, the divine image is now restored to man,[19] and heaven, and earth are once more brought together. This "form of a servant," they hold, was itself specially created[20] through the agency of the Holy Spirit and the Virgin Mary, that it might be the instrument of the Logos in establishing the renewed order of obedience to God's will; and, in that it observed all the divine commandments, though tried to the uttermost,[21] and willingly faced a death totally undeserved, the debt which man owed to God through his disobedience has been paid,[22] and a new order, not of law but of grace, has come into existence. Moreover, they go on, "the form of a servant," having been raised from the dead—and the Resurrection is described by Theodore as "the end of all the Economy of Christ"[23] it has triumphed over corruption and mortality, and continues for ever in the state of stability which it possessed from the first.[24] Hence they can proclaim that as men are in Christ they are new creations, and already made partakers of those good things which are laid up for them in a future life. For then death and corruption will have ceased, and man, once more the head of a restored creation through him who is by right *princeps in omnibus,*[25] will enjoy immutability of soul, and, in his perfect obedience, sin no more.

After this survey of the ideas funda-

---

[19] Cf. Nestorius: "God the Logos was made man that he might therein make the humanity the likeness of God, and that he might therein renew [the likeness of God] in the nature of humanity; and thereupon he renewed his material elements and showed him [to be] without sin in the observance of the commandments, as though he alone sufficed for renewing him who had originally fallen by the transgression of the observance of the commandments . . . (*Bazaar of Heracleides,* trans. Driver and Hodgson, pp. 212f; similarly, p. 62).

[20] Cf. in this connection the use made by Eustathius of Prov. 8. 22 ("*Creavit me initium* . . .") . . . Similarly in the same work (*Discourse on Prov.* 8. 22) we find this: "What wonder, or worthy of astonishment, that we say: 'Of old the Man of Christ was known by God, and in the depths of the Divine Mind fixedly fitted?' " (F. Cavallera, *Le Schisme d' Antioche,* Frag. 34, 35; see also the present writer's *Eustathius of Antioch,* p. 73, n. 8).

[21] Thus speaking of the trials of "the form of a servant," Nestorius can say that 'there was not the least room for Satan to introduce disobedience (*Bazaar of Heracleides,* trans. Driver and Hodgson, p. 72).

[22] Though the "classic" theory of the Atonement holds the field among the Antiochenes, theirs is also the penal conception that through the Death voluntarily undergone, Christ has paid the debt, and suffered the penalty due to us for our sins. See, for instance, Theodore, *in Gal.* 3. 12, 4. 4, 5, ed. Swete, *op. cit.,* i, pp. 42, 62, *ad Baptiz.* ed. Mingana, pp. 63, 69f; Nestorius, *Bazaar of Heracleides,* trans. Driver and Hodgson, p. 172; and esp. Theodoret, *Interpret. Ep. ad Rom.* i, 17, iv. 25, viii. 4, *ad Coloss.* ii. 14; ed. Schulze, III. i. pp. 22, 52, 81, 488, and, even more striking, *de Prov.* x; *ibid.,* pp. 660ff.

[23] So Theodore, *ad Baptiz;* ed. Mingana, p. 75. Thus if the Alexandrians lay stress on the Incarnation, and the Westerns on the Cross, the Antiochenes lay stress on the Resurrection of Jesus Christ.

[24] Nestorius speaks of "the likeness of a servant which was without sin in its creation" (*Bazaar of Heracleides,* trans. Driver and Hodgson, p. 213).

[25] So Eustathius (*P.G.* xviii. 696, Frag. 2). But it should be noted that like his successors, this early Antiochene does not divide the one Christ: The Man of Christ is *omnium creaturarum Dominator propter divini Verbi commistionem* (*ibid.,* 693, Frag. 2).

mental of Christological teaching of the Antiochenes, we can now proceed to consider the teaching itself, . . . their doctrine is founded upon the same two cardinal principles of Christological confession and enquiry.

It is easy to understand why ardent anti-Nestorians should consider that those brought up in the Syrian doctrinal tradition were denying the central truth of the Gospel through dividing the one Christ into a duad of Sons. For, they could argue, was it not only too clear that these proclaimers of "two natures" were personalizing the natures. . . .

But one after another, the representatives of the school of Antioch most emphatically deny such charges. Theirs they declare, is the faith which was laid down at Nicaea,[26] and what the Fathers said, they also say.[27] Again and again they expressly assert that, whatever their enemies may think, they do not preach the doctrine of "two sons"; rather, they retort, the "dividing" of the one Person of Jesus Christ into two is as much to be abhorred as the "confusing" of his natures;[28] and any such notion as that he is *homo purus*,[29] or that his manhood existed "as that of another beside the Logos," they utterly reject.[30] . . .

We must bear in mind that they possessed no Apollinarius who could sum up their doctrine in carefully worded phrases, and that no theologian arose among them of the same caliber as Cyril; moreover, though concentrating on the doctrine of "two natures" in order to overthrow the idea of "confusion," they were too apt to pay but little attention to the other aspect of their doctrine; for there seems no doubt that Cyril was justified in remarking that they were "a little in the dark"[31] in regard to their teaching on the union. Yet there is ample evidence to show that though, generally speaking, they do not express themselves with sufficient clarity, they are in fact at one with the Alexandrians in proclaiming that Jesus Christ is the divine Logos, the Second Person of the Trinity made man.

In the first place, we have to reckon with the fact that their Christology is soteriologically determined; as we have tried to show their argument is that God himself must take the initiative if

---

[26] Thus, after the deadlock which succeeded the Council of Ephesus (431) the Antiochenes proposed as the basis of reunion with Cyril and his party the general acceptance of the Creed of Nicaea and Athanasius, *ad Epictetum*.

[27] E.g. Theodoret, *Ep.* cli; ed. Schulze, IV. ii. pp. 1312ff.

[28] Thus Theodoret sees but little difference in impiety between those "who contract into one of the two natures of the Only-begotten" and those who "divide our Lord Jesus Christ, the Son of the living God, the divine Logos made man" into two Sons—though he doubts whether there were "any such" (*Ep.* cxliii; *ibid.*, p. 1238). Similarly, just as those who divide the one Christ into two Sons transgress from the road trodden by the holy apostles, so the maintainers of "one nature" fall head-long into the opposite ravine. (*Ep.* cli; *ibid.*, p. 1310). See also *Dial.* ii; *ibid.*, IV. i. p. 109.

[29] Theodore of Mopsuestia, it may be said, speaks for all the representatives of the Antiochene school in his answer to the charge that they were teaching "a mere man," and therefore should be called "*hominicolae*" . . . (*de Incarn.* vi; ed. Swete, *op. cit.*, ii. p. 293).

[30] See the reply of Andrew of Samosata to Cyril's Anaths. vii. xi. (*Apol. adv. Orient;* ed. Pusey, VI. pp. 308, 352; quoted in this writer's *Two Ancient Christologies*, pp. 153f). Similarly Theodoret in his letter to the monks of Constantinople (*Ep.* cxlv; ed. Schulze, IV, i. p. 1256 . . .

[31] Cyril, *ad. Eulog.*, *P.G.* lxxvii, 225B.

man is to be re-established in obedience to the Divine will. Accordingly, in their Christology—and here we should not be misled by their constant use of the terms of "Christ," "Son" and "Lord," since these are the names which, following Scripture, they give to the incarnate Person, who is at once divine and human—they start from the cardinal truth that in Jesus Christ it is the Logos himself who, with the Father and the Holy Spirit from whom he cannot be separated, has wrought this great redemptive act[32] through "uniting the Man to himself" *hēnōsev auton heautō*. This expression is particularly noteworthy; it is used by Cyril himself when he explains what is meant by the "incarnation" of the Logos,[33] and we could quote example after example to show that the Antiochenes, one and all, also use it.[34] Consequently, it seems reasonable to conclude that at the heart of their system, though but rarely brought out, lies the conception of the personal union of the Logos with our nature. But we can go farther than this. From Eustathius onwards, these teachers refer to "the Man" (which is their term for "manhood") as the *suum* of the Logos, which he made his own *a prima statim plasmatione,*[35] and as Theodore also says, dwelt in him "as in a Son";[36] and, beginning with Flavian, the teacher of Theodore, the classical Antiochenes can say that the Logos "allowed" the manhood to experience what belongs to it.[37] Moreover, like the Alexandrians, they speak of a "complete union,"[38] and insist that it is one which is altogether indivisible.[39] And it is equally significant that, while they are always careful to point out what is not to be inferred from these confessions, they agree with the Alex-

---

[32] One of the best illustrations of the soteriological background of the Christology of the Antiochene teachers is found in Theodoret, *de Prov.* x; ed. Schulze, IV. i. pp. 660f. We may also note his remark when commenting on II Kings 6. 6 . . . (*ibid.*, I. i. p. 525).

[33] See, for instance, *adv. Nestor, praef.* ii, ii. 8 (ed. Pusey, VI. pp. 93, 117), *Apol. adv. Orient,* xi. (*ibid.*, p. 392), *Ep.* ii *ad Nestor., P.G.* lxxviii. 45BD, *Ep.* iii *ad Nestor., ibid.,* 109C.

[34] See *Two Ancient Christologies,* pp. 152f.

[35] So Theodore of Mopsuestia, *c. Apoll.* iii. (ed. Swete, *op. cit.,* ii. p. 314).

[36] According to Theodore—whose, as is well known, is the doctrine of a "union according to good pleasure" . . . can say that 'the union of the natures according to good pleasure effects in respect of both one title, will, activity, authority, majesty, lordship, dignity and power, which can in no way be severed' (*Ep. ad Domnum, ibid.,* p. 338). The union, then, according to this teaching, has not its ground in the moral relationship of sameness of will, but sameness of will is the outcome of the union. Hence the divine indwelling in Jesus Christ is far different from that in apostles and righteous men; for in him, the Logos dwelt *ōs en yiō,* the indwelling being such that he "united to himself" (*de Incarn.* vii, *ibid.,* p. 296).

[37] For references, see *Two Ancient Christologies,* pp. 85f, 102, n. 1, 145–151.

[38] The phrase *hē akra enōsis* is found in the reply of Andrew of Samosata to Cyril's Anathematisms (*Apol. adv. Orient.* iv. xi; ed. Pusey, VI. pp. 290, 292, 354) and in Theodoret, *Dial.* ii. (ed. Schulze, IV. i. p. 116)—the very phrase, which is used by Apollinarius and Cyril is used by Nestorius: *hē akra syna pheia.*

[39] It should be observed that when the Antiochenes use the analogy of the union of body and soul in the individual man, they lay stress on the "otherness" of these elements. See for instance, Theodore, c. Apoll. iv; ed. Swete, *op. cit.,* ii, p. 318, and Theodoret, *Dial,* ii, iii; ed. Schulze, IV. i. pp. 107, 177ff. On the other hand, the Alexandrians, while pointing to the "otherness" of body and soul, use it as their primary illustration of the unity of Christ's Person.

andrian teachers that in virtue of the union of God and man in Christ—which union "causes the names to be common"[40]—the Virgin can be called "Theotokos," and it can be said that the Logos endured "two births," as well as that "God suffered and died."[41] But how could they thus accept the principle of the *communicatio idiomatum* if they did not first accept the fundamental Christological principle that Jesus Christ is the Logos made man, one Person, at once God and Man?

Certainly, they distinguish between "Logos" and "Christ," and, claiming that the latter name signifies in Scripture him in whom we see the union of Godhead and manhood,[42] insist that in accordance with this usage one should call the Virgin "Christotokos," and say that "Christ" suffered and died.[43] But it should be understood that in all this they are safeguarding the doctrine of the impassibility of the Divine. . . .

As we have urged, the Antiochenes were so engrossed in their defence of the "two natures" against teaching which, they were convinced, implied "the abominable confusion" that they did not turn their mind to the more fundamental aspect of their belief. Yet there were times of crisis when they were compelled by their opponents to explain their position. . . .

Certainly the Antiochenes differ from the Alexandrians in that, emphasizing the fundamental difference between the uncreated and the created nature, they see in the Incarnation a Divine self-emptying which operates only so far as human limitations will allow, whereas the latter, ever impressed by the thought that man's deification is the end of the work of Christ, see in it the elevation of our nature to the conditions of the divine life in the Person of the Logos—but both are at one in confessing that in Jesus Christ the eternal Son of God came down from heaven, and was made man for our salvation.

We can now proceed to examine the Antiochene doctrine of the two natures of our Lord, as we would show that this aspect of their thought has its ground in what we are calling the principle of Christological enquiry.

One after another, these teachers affirm that in Jesus Christ exist the two elements of real Godhead and real manhood: in him these elements (to use the Chalcedonian word) are "made known" objectively, and must be "recognized" subjectively, if the truth concerning his Person is to be upheld. As we should expect, on this point the Antiochenes are particularly insistent. "The Church," says Theodoret, "following the foot-prints of the Apostles, contemplates in the Lord Jesus Christ perfect Godhead and perfect manhood;[44] in the one Christ we contemplate the manhood through the sufferings, and we apprehend the Godhead through the miracles."[45] Nestorius states that "two perfect na-

[40] Cf. Theodoret, *Ep.* cxxx; *ibid.,* IV. ii. p. 1217.

[41] See *Two Ancient Christologies,* pp. 166ff.

[42] We should notice that Apollinarius of Laodicea speaks in the same way: (Lietzmann, *op. cit.,* Frag. 119, p. 236).

[43] For what seems one of the best illustrations of this aspect of the Antiochene teaching, see Nestorius, *Sermo* x; ed. F. Loofs, *Nestoriana,* esp. pp. 269ff.

[44] *Ep.* cxlv (ed. Schulze, IV. ii. p. 1249).

[45] *Ep.* cli (*ibid.,* p. 1301).

tures, both without confusion and without division, must be observed (*videantur*) in our Lord Jesus Christ,"[46] and that "we recognize the manhood of the Child, and the Godhead."[47] Before him, Theodore of Mopsuestia in his confession of faith had declared: "We confess one Son and Lord Jesus Christ, through whom all things were made, apprehending chiefly the divine Logos, who is Son of God according to *ousia*, and at the same time having in mind that which was taken."[48] And before "The Interpreter," Eustathius had said the same: at the time of the Temptation, the devil, "regarding the Person (*prosōpon*) of Christ, saw on the one hand, within in fact and in deed, God and true Son of God by nature, and on the other, without, he saw revealed clothing him, a Man, pure undefiled and spotless, a most beautiful example of a temple, consecrated, inviolate.[49]

And, they insist, the Godhead and manhood thus "seen" in the one Person of our Lord are real, the properties of each being fully preserved. They refer to them not only as "natures" and *ousiai*, but also as *hypostases* (= *substantiae*),[50] and in this way lay additional emphasis on their reality; for the notion of "confusion" they will not tolerate. The Godhead, they teach, remains Godhead in its immutability and impassibility, and the manhood remains real manhood, consisting of a body and a soul, the soul giving to the body its vital force, and itself possessing to the full the power of self-determination. Indeed, intent on bringing out these truths, they maintain that, since "there is no *hypostasis* without its *prosōpon*,"[51] both the Godhead and the manhood in Christ are seen each with its *prosōpon*—each, that is, as possessing its "appearance," its "individuality" and its "person"; for it would seem that these teachers, and especially Nestorius, use the term in a variety of meanings in their Christology.[52] It will be obvious that in all this they would enforce doctrines which lie at the heart of their system: they insist that the natures are "two," and remain "two,"[53] as they see in the formula "two natures" an expression of their fundamental belief that there is an essential difference between the Creator and the creature; and they strenuously resist not only the error of Apollinarius of Laodicea,[54] but also any thought which seemed to them to imply the denial of Christ's human

[46] Loofs, *op. cit.*, p. 330 (Syriac, p. 380).
[47] *Ibid.*, p. 328.
[48] Swete, *op. cit.*, ii. p. 330.
[49] *De Engastr.* x; ed. Jahn, p. 40; *P.G.* xviii. 633B.
[50] For an account of the terminology of the Antiochenes, see *Two Ancient Christologies*, pp. 180f. . . .
[51] "It cannot be said that a *hypostasis* is without its *prosōpon*," says Theodore of Mopsuestia (*de Incarn.* viii; ed. Swete, *op. cit.*, p. 299. Similarly, Nestorius: "The *prosōpon* does not exist without the *ousia* (*Bazaar of Heracleides*, trans. Driver and Hodgson, p. 170). This axiom was generally accepted, and was to be used both by the Monophysites as they argued against the Chalcedonian faith, and by Leontius of Byzantium as, through his doctrine of the *enhypostasia*, he sought to explain it.
[52] See *Two Ancient Christologies*, pp. 156ff.
[53] The Antiochenes would say that the natures are forever "two." Thus Theodore, *ad Baptiz.* (ed. Mingana, p. 90); "The natures will remain two, because they are "two."
[54] For attacks against the doctrine of Apollinarius, see for instance, Theodore, *ad Baptiz.* (*ibid.*, pp. 55ff); Theodoret, *Dial.* i; ed. Schulze, IV. i. pp. 73f; *Epp.* civ, cxlv.

rational soul,[55] just because theirs is the root conception that, if man is to be redeemed, a Second Adam must come to his aid, who will freely undergo the temptations of this life, and triumph over them through an obedience which is voluntary from start to finish.

Consequently, they at once raised the alarm when, as they firmly believed, the very foundations of orthodoxy were being removed through the introduction of the idea of "confusion." We notice their outcry when Cyril published his Twelve Anathematisms: his "hypostatic" and "natural" union were to them proof positive that he was trying to revive the "Apollinarian" error. Again, for them the formula of the Alexandrian orthodoxy, "one incarnate nature of the divine Logos" meant "such a mingling of the two natures that they are themselves deprived of the *hypostases* which each possess";[56] and the other watchword of their opponents, "after the union, one nature," carried with it the impiety of "alienating each nature from its properties by commixture and confusion.[57] Similarly, they were suspicious of the "out of two," especially since it seemed but another tool in the hands of the framers of the "new heresy": it was not that they expressly rejected it,[58] but rather that they did not favour its use, lest it should be taken as signifying *alterum rursus praeter naturas quod ex ipsis est.*[59]

Thus we arrive at the outstanding feature of the doctrine of the Antiochenes: they never fail to assert that it is only as one "divides" the natures in Jesus Christ that a real guarantee is afforded against the introduction of the idea of confusion . . .

The conclusion is obvious: when these teachers pronounce that it is necessary to "divide" the natures, they mean no more than that, if the Eutychian error is to be avoided, one must see them in their difference. In other words they are but employing the principle upheld by all the early Christologians as the sure means whereby the doctrine of the reality of our Lord's natures could be safeguarded. . . .

So we come to the question: How do the Antiochene theologians use this principle? They see in Christ the two natures or *ousiai* or *hypostases* of Godhead and manhood, each with its *prosōpon*[60]—its "appearance," its "individuality" and its "person"—an attribute to each its own: to the Godhead, and so to "the God" [in Christ] belong the miracles and whatever is God-befitting; to the manhood, and so to "the Man," birth, growth, suffering

[55] As early as Eustathius, we may note, the Antiochenes were insisting on the reality of Christ's human rational soul (see *P.G.* lxxxvi. 2037, 2040).

[56] So Nestorius, Loofs, *op. cit.*, pp. 209f (Syriac p. 369).

[57] *Ibid.*, p. 329 (*ibid.*, p. 379).

[58] Thus Theodoret can confess that Christ is *eis ex amphion* (*Dial.* ii; ed. Schulze, IV. i. p. 119). Similarly, *ex utraque substantia* appears in the third of the Counter-Anathematisms attributed to Nestorius.

[59] So Eutherius of Tyana, in his criticism of Cyril's letter to John of Antioch (*Synodicon,* cci). Cf. Theodoret, *Dial.* ii: "Orthodox" asks "Eranistes," when the latter has said that he accepts "out of two natures" but rejects "two natures," whether he is thinking of a compound—like that of gold and silver, or of lead and tine (ed. Schulze, *op. cit.,* IV. i. p. 101).

[60] See the explicit statement of Theodore of Mopsuestia, *de Incarn.* viii; ed. Swete, *op. cit.,* ii. p. 299.

and death. Similarly in their exegesis they enquire whether a particular text has to do with divine or with the human *hypostasis* and—especially in the case of the sayings of our Lord—refer the words to the appropriate "natural and hypostatic *prosōpon*."[61] . . . Both the earlier and the later Antiochenes follow the rule which appears in Theodoret: we "contemplate two natures" in the Lord Christ, and "apply to each its own properties";[62] we ascribe the words of humiliation as to Man *hos anthrōpō,* and as to God *hos Theo* the God-befitting words of exaltation.[63]

But this does not mean that the Antiochenes teach that in Jesus Christ there are two parallel *prosopa.*[64] We readily agree that they do not carefully explain that when they are attributing this to the Logos, and that to the Man, they are but "recognizing the difference"—and, as we have tried to show, this Christological principle, if it is not to be misused, must always be seen in its relation to the fundamental doctrine that the Person in whom the natures are united is one. Nevertheless, it is certain that those many statements of theirs which at first sight seem to indicate that they are teaching "two Sons," must be viewed in such a context if we are not to do them no small injustice. It would not have been so readily assumed, for instance, that for Theodore of Mopsuestia the union of God and man in Christ is a purely moral union like that of man and wife, had it been perceived—as indeed the context shows—that when he uses this analogy he is discussing the natures, and would emphasize their difference.[65]

It seems clear, then, that so far as fundamentals are concerned, there is no difference between the Christological teaching of the Antiochenes, and that of the Alexandrians, though, when set beside that raised by the latter, the Antiochene doctrinal structure must appear crude and unfinished. Nevertheless, approaching the problem of Christ's Person from the moral, rather than from the philosophical point of view, these make their own contribution as they emphasize the doctrine of his two natures and what this involves; . . . the Council of Chalcedon accepted their work.

2. G. L. Prestige[1] suggests that as a whole the school of Antioch was as orthodox and contributed as much to sound belief as the schools of Alexandria and Cappadocia. The real theological bond between all the Antiochians was not the specifically Nestorian strain of thought, but a

[61] Nestorius uses the phrase: *Bazaar of Heracleides,* trans. Driver and Hodgson, p. 86.

[62] *Dial.* ii; ed. Schulze, IV. i. p. 103.

[63] *Ep.* xii; *ibid.,* IV. ii. p. 1086.

[64] Cf. Theodotus, Bishop of Antioch (420–429), . . . in a fragment preserved by the Chalcedonians from his lost work, *c. Synousiastas, P.G.* lxxxvi. i. 1836A2.

[65] *De Incarn.* viii. ed. Swete, *op. cit.,* ii. p. 299: [We may note that this was one of the passages adduced at the Fifth General Council as proof of Theodore's "Nestorianism." . . .]

[1] George Lennard Prestige, D. C. died in 1955. He was the Chancellor of St. Paul's Cathedral in London. He authored several works in Patristic Theology: *God in Patristic Thought, St. Basil the Great and Apollinaris of Laodicea, Fathers and Heretics.* It is from this last book, that this excerpt has been taken from pp. 133–138. The book was published in London: S.P.C.K., 1954.

stress on the entire reality and completeness of Christ's human nature. The broad outlines of this Christology were blocked in by Eustace and Diodore.

. . . When modern writers discuss the distinctive qualities of the school of Antioch, they sometimes tend to suggest that the principal link between its members was the specifically Nestorian strain of thought, which created difficulties in envisaging the unity of God and man in Christ. But that is not in fact an accurate presentation of the matter. So far as our knowledge extends, only three of the leaders of the school either experienced or created any such difficulties. The real theological bond between all the Antiochenes was their clear perception of the full and genuine human experience which the incarnate Son historically underwent; they shrank in horror from the idea that He was not in all respects as truly kin to us as He was kin to God; they emphasised the Gospel evidence of His human consciousness and moral growth, and would not have it thought that His human life was merely the illusory exhibition on earth of an action which in sphere and method was exclusively celestial. It might be said that they pinned His human nature down to this earth to which, in a true and vital sense, it belonged. But by no means all of them viewed His humanity in such isolation as to endanger the unity of His person. No proof of such an attitude emerges from the fragments of Eustace; the pastoral and unspeculative mind of Chrysostom is far removed from any risk of such declension; and Theodoret, who defended Nestorius even after John of Antioch had thrown him over, manifests no sign of intellectual strain in the effort to hold the unity of Christ together. These are among the greatest of the school: there are others of less prominence on whom the same verdict could be passed. When Antiochene theology is said to have a natural trend towards Nestorius, the judgment is only true in the sense that disproportionate pressure on the truths specially valued at Antioch was bound to lead to consequences of which Nestorius is the unhappy example. Taken as a whole, the school of Antioch was just as orthodox as the school of Alexandria or that of Cappadocia, and contributed as much to sound belief as either of the others.

The broad outlines of Antiochene Christology were blocked in by Eustace with an insight that seems almost prophetic, at a time when theology was wholly concerned with Trinitarian problems, a complete generation before attention was seriously diverted to problems arising from the incarnation of the Redeemer. The substance of his teaching about Christ is easy to observe in the fragments preserved by Theodoret in the three dialogues entitled "Eranistes" (Schulze vol. iv., to the pages of which the following references apply). Eustace insists explicitly on the reality of Christ's human soul (56B), and is anxious throughout the writings quoted to oppose the Arian contention that the sufferings of Christ were endured in His heavenly character. He therefore maintains consistently that Christ's humiliations belong to Him specifically as son of Mary; they are not evidence that His heavenly nature was subjected to the domination of physical circumstance; though He assumed the form of a slave, as the apostle said, yet in His godhead He remained free, untouched and uncontrolled by material conditions (*e.g.*, 57B, 235D.). He distinguishes firmly between "Him who anoints" and "him who is anointed"; the former is "God by nature, begotten of God," the latter is "beautified by exquisite construction, from the godhead that dwelt in him," but his virtue is not innate, but "acquired," the fruit of moral effort (57D–58A).

Eustace bestows on Christ's manhood several different titles. He calls it the "shrine" of God the Son (*e.g.*, 57C, compare St. John ii. 19), or His "tabernacle" (*ib.*, compare St. John i. 14), or His "house" (235C, compare Proverbs ix. 1). Again he calls it the "human instrument" which the divine Word assumed for the purpose of redemption (136A, B). Frequently he calls it simply "the man." Stress must not be laid on any one of these descriptions to the exclusion of the rest. If "the man" sounds Nestorian, the phrase "human instrument" sounds no less Apollinarian, particularly when it is observed that Eustace sometimes refers to the manhood simply as "the body" (57D, 236C). He has no special doctrinal bias; he is merely employing language current both in his own time and later, not as the catchword of a party, but to illustrate the many-sided truth. Similarly the relation between God the Word and His manhood is variously described. He "took up and wore" the human instrument (136A). He "occupied Himself [or, carried on His life] inside" the body (236C). In the same way He "wore" His man, like a garment (57D), and "inhabited" His man, like a sanctuary and shrine (134A). The subject is normally the divine personality, working in and through the human agency. But that the human element possesses a true and characteristic life is indicated not only by calling it "the man," and by ascribing to it "a soul of the same stuff as our souls," but also by the plain statement that "the man lives from the power of God, that is, because he occupies himself conjointly with the divine spirit, for He that is believed on within him is the Power of the Most High" (236B); and by consequence, after the victory won, the man is exalted to heaven and installed "on a common throne with the most divine spirit, on account of the God that dwells in him continuously" (134A).

All that this amounts to is that the human experience of the Redeemer was a real experience and not an artifice or fantasy, while at the same time it was the experience of God. On the one hand, Eustace asserts, the divine word in His own nature continued in the bosom of the Father; the divine Wisdom did not cease to contain the whole creation; being immaterial and invisible, He did not in His heavenly character sustain the nails and the tomb. On the other, His man, compact of diverse members, was crucified and rose again, and was made Lord and Christ, and called the Lord of glory. Yet there are no two Sons being preached. In the same sermon Eustace refers the whole action to the single person of God the Son. Quoting Christ's claim that no one took His life from Him, for He had power both to lay it down and to take it back again (St. John x. 18), Eustace proceeds: "Though He had power, as God, to do both, He acceded to those who without counsel tried to destroy His shrine, and in raising it up He rebuilt it more magnificently; it is proved on unimpeachable testimony that He Himself by His own act raised up and rebuilt His own house" (234c–235b). He repeats the last statement elsewhere: "The Word and God gloriously raised up the shrine of Himself" (237c). The divine spirit of Wisdom had two spheres of action; "He both lived inside the body, and rode upon the heavens and contained the earth and mastered the abyss" and "performed all normal acts as God." He was not contained exclusively within the physical limitations of His manhood like water in a cup, but "being a divine and ineffable Power He embraces and strengthens both what is quite interior and what is quite external to His shrine" (236c, d).

Nor does Eustace stop at affirming the unity of Christ's person; he throws out a pregnant suggestion as to the basis of the unity. As God the Son, he says, is the image of the Father, so is the man whom He wore the image of the divine Son, though in a different material. St. Paul did not claim (Rom. viii. 29) that we are foreordained to be conformed to the Son of God, but to the image of His Son; and reason supports the apostle's phraseology. "For the immaterial spirit of Wisdom is not conformed to physical men, but His impress is, the man who has been made body by the spirit and wears members of like number with every one else and is clad in similar shape" (134d–135a). This argument is much more important than it looks at first sight. It means, not that the man Christ Jesus is as like God the Son as the Son Himself is like the Father; but that, making due allowance for the different medium of expression, the man is identically the same with the divine Son, just as the being of the Son is actually the same as that of the Father. The word "image," as used in Trinitarian theology, implies that the Son is a second complete presentation of exactly the same reality as the Father; that is the truth, not only to which Hosius bore witness at Nicaea and for which Athanasius made a good confession for half a century after Nicaea, but for maintaining which Eustace himself was deposed from his bishopric by the Arians. His use of the word "image" and of the analogy with the holy Trinity is therefore most significant. It implies that Christ's man—"the dominical man," as Augustine and many Greek Fathers called Jesus—is nothing less than a reproduction on earth in human material of God the Word, the eternal Son in heaven; a translation into human terms of the actual godhead: an earthly presentation of what God Himself would be, and was, when He should deign to be a man. The divine nature was not debased or diminished in its own sphere by the incarnation, as the Arians falsely asserted, but God received an exact expression of His own perfection in the finite medium of physical existence. He ceased not to be all that He had ever been, but He condescended to undergo a process of limitation by which He became that which hitherto He had not been.

This interpretation is further confirmed by a passage in Eustace's only work that has survived complete, the exegetical treatise on the Witch of Endor. The devil, he says, "regarded the figure[2] of Christ; he saw there, on the inward side, God in fact and deed, God's true Son by nature; and he saw

[2] The word used is *prosōpon,* that is, the object which He constituted for perception, His "presentation"; compare *God in Patristic Thought,* p. 157.

revealed, clothing Him on the outside, a pure, undefiled and stainless man, a beauteous example of a shrine, consecrated, inviolate" (*de engastr.* 10). In this one sentence Eustace sums up his whole doctrine of Christ. There is only one Christ; He is both a single person and a single object of perception. But those who have the eyes to see can perceive in Him two distinct depths of reality. Outwardly He appears on earth a man, the very fairest flower of human development. But within, He is yet more than that; the human figure is the finite expression of the immeasurable truth of God.

Eustace, then, the father of the Antiochene school of Christology, was sound in thought by any rational standard of theological orthodoxy, having many links with the greatest and most reputable Christian thinkers, and exhibiting no private inclination towards intellectual impiety. He enjoyed a wide angle of vision and saw the truth from many sides; but no one ever accused him of seeing it double. Diodore, the next outstanding Christian teacher of Antioch, did nothing to dissatisfy the dominant Cappadocian orthodoxy of his day, but fell completely foul of Apollinaris, the substance of whose mind was definitely not Cappadocian but Alexandrine. This fact again is profoundly significant. Alexandria had put unity in the forefront of its theological speculation. Cappadocia, on the other hand, though it fully accepted the conclusions of Alexandrine unity, continued to flirt with pluralism; Basil and his friends found in Athanasian unity rather the goal of their mental pilgrimage than the base of their campaign, and the historical reason for their attitude is simply that they arrived at Nicene orthodoxy by the road of Semi-Arian Conservatism. Diodore followed a similar course; although at Antioch he fought Arianism to a standstill, the early theological influences that shaped his mind were of the pragmatical type that emphasised distinct facts without looking too deep into their interior for a unifying principle. Diodore's mental constitution, in fact, was what is sometimes called Aristotelian rather than Platonistic; such sharp antitheses are apt to prove very misleading, but the description serves to suggest his bent.

When he approached Christology, he grasped the subject from the dualistic end, and seems to have shown a good deal less caution than Eustace in his handling of it. He remarked, for instance, that God the Word had no intention of calling Himself David's son but David's Lord; it was His "body" that He chose to have called the son of David. Again, he said: "The Son before the ages is perfect in His kind; perfect too is the Davidic one, the son of David whom the Son of God assumed. You will ask, Do I then preach two Sons? I do not say two sons of David, for I never called God the Word David's son; nor do I say two Sons of God in real being, for I do not assert two Sons out of the being of God; I say that the pre-eternal God the Word has inhabited in him of David's seed." Diodore does not, at least in the extract given, deny the charge of preaching two Sons, though his words suggest that what he meant to convey was rather a double Sonship; the same comment may justly be made upon his further statement that "the man out of Mary is son by grace, God the Word is Son by nature." (The text is to be found apud Leont. Byz. *c. Nest. & Eut.* 3.) But we only possess the few shreds of Diodore's doctrinal writings which his later critics pared off as evidence of his alleged Nestorianism, and it is therefore quite impossible to form a proper estimate of his real teaching, or to judge how fully he balanced his separatist tendencies with more constructive statements. We can only say that in 381, in the decree by which the Emperor confirmed the decisions of the second General Council, Diodore was named as the standard of orthodoxy for the churches in his own region; that he died full of years and of honour; that Apollinaris's attack on him received no support until more than thirty years after his death; and that, of his two great disciples, though Theodore of Mopsuestia was certainly the immediate source of almost everything that Nestorius taught, yet Chrysostom can hardly anywhere be matched for the passionless propriety of his doctrine.

Nevertheless, it is plain from the quotations given that Diodore would not find it easy to issue a direct denial of the accusation which Apollinaris brought against him. He did maintain a distinction between two Sons, though it is extremely improbable that he meant by it anything essentially different from what Eustace had previously laid down. His fault lay not in what he meant to express or even in what he actually said, so much as in his failure to guard adequately against the inferences to which his language gave momentum. This failure was accentuated in Diodore's disciple Theodore.

3. J. L. McKenzie, S.J.,[1] is not convinced by the arguments of those who impugn Theodore of Mopsuestia's orthodoxy. On the contrary, he maintains that the Christology of Theodore was substantially orthodox but accidentally defective in its terminology and in some aspects of its details. Objectivity would demand that the charge of heterodoxy be not made simply because he failed to give a fully precise answer to a question which was never proposed to him in the terms of Ephesus.

Francis A. Sullivan, S.J., of the Gregorian University, has given us a new synthesis of the Christology of Theodore of Mopsuestia[2] This synthesis is the first to appear since the article of Amann in 1946[3] The book exhibits high competence in the handling of the material and in theological thinking. Sullivan has based his conclusions on a study of all the existing remains of the writings of Theodore of Mopsuestia and he has consulted all the recent literature on the subject. The importance of the work needs no emphasis; it is an indispensable tool for anyone who wishes to study Theodore's Christology in detail . . .

The synthesis discusses Theodore's

[1] John L. McKenzie, S.J. is a well-known Scripture scholar. He has been professor at the Jesuit College of West Baden, and is presently teaching at the University of Chicago. He is the author of several books and articles, *The Two-Edged Sword, The Power and the Wisdom, Myths and Realities, Authority in the Church,* etc. This excerpt is from his article "Annotations on the Christology of Theodore of Mopsuestia" in *Theological Studies* (September 1958) from pp. 345–373, selectively. Fr. Sullivan's reply to this article was published *ibid.*, vol. 20 (1959), pp. 264–279.

[2] *The Christology of Theodore of Mopsuestia* (Rome, 1956).

[3] DTC 15/1, pp. 235–279.

concept of the Incarnation. Here Sullivan concludes that for Theodore the Incarnation was most frequently conceived in terms of inhabitation: the Word did not become man, but became in a man. The third part deals with the unity of person; here Sullivan proposes that, while the language rather clearly indicates that Theodore considered that the two natures exist in one *prosopon,* actually it implies that this single person was created by the Incarnation itself and is therefore distinct from the person of the Word. On this basis, then, Sullivan's conclusion is that Theodore, like Nestorius, did not understand that the one *prosōpon* in which the two natures are united "is actually the Divine Person of the Word," and that therefore is "ample justification for the verdict of the 'Doctor of the Incarnation': that Theodore of Mopsuestia was the Father of Nestorianism."[4]

I cast no aspersions on the integrity or the technical competence of Sullivan's work when I say that I do not believe he has demonstrated his thesis. This judgment is not made in haste. It is based on an examination of the texts cited by Sullivan, as well as an examination of the larger context of Theodore's writings in which these passages appear and of other texts of those passages which are preserved in Syriac versions without depending exclusively on the translations of Sachau, Tonneau, or Vosté; this, it seems, is the least we can do when a man's theological reputation is involved, even if the man has been dead fifteen hundred years. And perhaps what I wish to say about the book is best summed up by saying that the book is an argument in defense of a thesis rather than an impartial examination of the evidence. . . . I suggest that Theodore's Christology is no more and no less than what we should expect it to be in a man who lived in his time and his theological milieu. The Christology of Theodore is not the Christology of Ephesus and Chalcedon; nor do I think we should expect it to be. Neither is his terminology that which was elaborated in these Councils and in the theological discussions which took place before, during, and after them. The greatest single defect in Theodore's terminology is without doubt his lack of a clearly defined understanding of *hypostasis.* It is, however, no more than fair to ask where Theodore might have attained this understanding, which was the result of subsequent discussions. Sullivan attributes to Athanasius a Christology which did not have that degree of clarity and precision which Sullivan claims for it. The language of Athanasius, like the language of Theodore, was to a large extent determined by the heresies which he opposed. Actually, one may consider that the movement of Athanasius away from Arianism opened the door at least slightly for the error of Apollinaris; and Theodore, in refuting both the Arians and Apollinaris, moved not only back towards the center, but too far in the other direction, as did Athanasius, and—I think one may say—Cyril of Alexandria, whose insistence on the unity of person permitted his followers and successors to pervert his doctrine into a unity of nature.

Possibly we shall have to renounce any effort ever to reach the true mind of Theodore. The condition in which his writings have been preserved certainly makes it extremely difficult.

[4] Sullivan, *op. cit.,* p. 284.

Further examination may disclose his mind more clearly, but at the present moment it seems doubtful to this writer. But the opposite hypothesis which I suggest is that Theodore had a Christology which was substantially orthodox but accidentally defective in its terminology and in some of its conceptions in detail. These defects were not such as to render his Christology unorthodox or even to permit the legitimate deduction of an unorthodox Christology from his principles. Hence one finds in his writings certain inconsistencies, as Sullivan has pointed out in abundance. There are explanations of doctrine which are not mere parrotings of orthodox formulae but statements in his own language; and these statements exhibit none of the basic defects which Sullivan attributes to him in his synthesis of Theodore's thought. With these—sometimes on the same page—we find other pages which are simply not correct in their use of philosophical terms . . . these incorrect passages, which read against the larger context of Theodore's writings, can be fitted into a basically orthodox Christology. Theologians who deal with these problems, it seems, deal with them on an antecedent presumption which is either favorable or unfavorable. In this respect greater objectivity is an ideal which all who study the matter should consider seriously. But I think a minimum of objectivity would demand that we do not charge Theodore with heterodoxy, or even with heterodox tendencies, because he fails to give a fully correct and precise answer to a question which was never proposed to him in the terms in which it was proposed to the Council of Ephesus. Sullivan has quoted and examined a great many passages of Theodore's writings. It will seem strange to many readers that at the end he has so little evidence to support his thesis. The reader will wonder that Theodore is able to speak of Christology so often without betraying the fundamental defects outlined in Sullivan's synthesis.

The defects of Theodore's terminology, . . . can often be ultimately reduced to his use of biblical texts. Sullivan has stated that Theodore's favorite formula is that the Word is in man or dwells in man. Theodore certainly does use this formula frequently; he can support it by Colossians 1:19, 2:9. But perhaps an even more favorite formula is the form of God and the forms of a slave, based on Philippians 2:7. Both of these biblical texts are more easily open to a Nestorian misconception than "The Word was made flesh" (Jn 1:14), as long as "flesh" is understood to mean "man." But I do not need to refer to the difficulties which were created in theology by the use of this biblical term "flesh." Hence Theodore, in selecting his terms, without feeling the necessity of emphasizing other texts—a necessity which he had no reason to feel from the theological discussions with which he was familiar—may easily use metaphors drawn from these passages which later theologians found it impossible to use. In fact, if the standards so strictly applied to Theodore were applied to the New Testament, one could easily show that these passages and others in the new Testament themselves exhibit a defective Christology. Of course they do not; but those who study these questions must bear in mind that the terminology of the New Testament is not the terminology of Ephesus and Chalcedon either, and that a theologian like Theodore, who was so familiar with the New Testament, is more likely to draw on the New Testament for his language than on a theological definition of terms of which he had never heard.

Sullivan remarks[5] that a question of the justice of Theodore's condemnation by the Fifth Ecumenical Council arises because of the Council's employment of evidence which was distorted, and on this page he promises that he will return to the question of the justice of the condemnation. Later, however, he professes that he is not dealing with the justice of the condemnation,[6] and I find no fulfilment of the promise to return to the question except almost at the end of the book . . .[7] The justice of the condemnation is upheld because Theodore actually was the father of Nestorianism, although not for the reasons which were adduced before the Council.

But this is the conclusion of Sullivan's thesis which I cannot accept. It is misleading to put the question as if the unity of subject was already settled when the Nestorian controversy arose. Nestorius did not assert simply that the two natures are united in one *prosōpon,* but that each of the natures before the union constituted a distinct *prosōpon.* Of such a view Sullivan has adduced no evidence whatever in the writings of Theodore of Mopsuestia; and I have adduced passages in this article which are in direct contradiction to such a view. The contradiction is not explicit because the question did not arise in Theodore's mind in these terms; but these passages are enough to raise a serious doubt about what Sullivan says concerning which side Theodore would take in this conflict of ideologies. One may question whether a man who asserts that there is only one Son, that He is the true Son, that the Incarnate Word Jesus Christ, divinity and humanity, is adored with a single act of adoration, who speaks of one subject as begotten of the Father, redeeming by His sufferings, raising from the dead and raising others from the dead, would have agreed with Nestorius that in the Incarnate Word there is not one subject but two. Hence I affirm that Sullivan's conclusion that Theodore would certainly agree with Nestorius is not a historical judgment. One would have to invoke a much more massive manipulation of the Syriac versions than Sullivan admits to exclude these "positive and sound elements" from his thinking.

Neither on historical evidence can I affirm that Theodore would have disagreed with Nestorius. On this question Theodore never had to stand up and give his vote. Quite possibly—Sullivan is certain—his dyophysism and his preference for speaking of the nature of the Word rather than the person of the Word would have driven him to support Nestorius; it is far more probable, I think, that his insistence on the unity of subject would have driven him to repudiate duality of person. He had in his own Christology the materials to correct its defects and to take his stand with the defenders of the doctrine that in the Incarnation there is only one *hypostasis* of the Word.[8]

---

[5] Sullivan, p. 112.

[6] *Ibid.,* p. 158.

[7] *Ibid.,* p. 284.

[8] I could not obtain the article of Paul Galtier, S.J., "Théodore de Mopsueste: Sa vraie pensée sur l'Incarnation," *Recherches de science religieuse* 45 (1957) 161–86, 338–60, until this article was ready for the press. Some of the passages treated here are

4. A. Grillmeier, S.J.,[1] takes into account the most recent scholarship on the question of Nestorius' true position, and gives an outline of the different views. He seems to favor the position which tends to understand and vindicate Nestorius from the charge of heresy. However, he claims that Nestorius' teaching was no substantial contribution to the development of Christology.

Ecclesiastical Kerygma, Theology, and the Orthodoxy of Nestorius

It is not strictly our task to decide the question of Nestorius, the deposed Patriarch of Constantinople. Nevertheless, an accurate description of his role in the evolution of the christological tradition may be an immediate contribution to his theological rehabilitation. The more we can show the orthodoxy of his thought, the more ecumenical contact will be possible with the Nestorian Church of today, though Nestorius himself would probably not claim to be the father of a new community. In his letter to the inhabitants of Constantinople he expresses his disapproval of the teaching of his more extreme followers, a fact which is not usually noticed: "leur enseignement et le nôtre n'est pas le même."[2]

As our survey on Nestorius in the light of dogmatic teaching and historical research shows, two different positions may be adopted in passing judgement on the case of the Patriarch. A stand may be made, first, on the kerygma or dogma of the Church; secondly, on the researches of theological scholarship. We will attempt a brief definition of the relationship between these two positions.

1. Nestorius and the Kerygma (or Dogma) of the Church

The kerygma of the Church is the presentation of the beliefs held by the Church at the time in question. This kerygma confessed Mary as "Mother of God" (Theotokos) and spoke of the "suffering God" (*Deus passus*) as an expression of the fact that the true Son of God was born, as man, from Mary and died on the cross. This kerygma was not the result of theological speculation, but of the belief and confession of the Church according to the Apostolic tradition. Nestorius, though his own intentions were good, made the mistake of halting a kerygmatic evolution whose age and theological value he did not fully appreciate.[3] In the great confusion caused

---

discussed by Galtier. With a dry understatement he says of Sullivan's work that he is not "partout de son avis." His conclusion is diametrically opposed to Sullivan. . . .

[1] Cf. Ch. 1, n. 1. This excerpt is taken from *op. cit.*, selectively, from pp. 369–372, 496–505.

[2] Nestorius, *Lettre aux habitants de Constantinople*, tr. F. Nau, *Le Livre d'Héraclide de Damas* (Paris, 1910), 374 nos. 6 and 8.

[3] This Nestorius did so to speak *ex cathedra*, that is on the kerygmatic level, as bishop of his church. But he himself was more moderate than some of his followers, e.g. the Antiochene presbyter Anastasius whom he permitted to preach against the title "Theotokos." Cf. Socrates, H. E. 7. 32: *PG* 32, 808–9. According to Cyril of Alexandria, the most excessive follower of Nestorius was the Bishop Dorotheus, who in full assembly cried: "If anyone says that Mary is *Theotokos*, let him be anathema" (*Acta Conc. Oecum.* I, 1, 5, p. 11, no. 3). But even here we may presume that "Theotokos" in the abusive sense

on the kerygmatic level, the Church's reaction followed the laws of the kerygmatic tradition. This remains true, even if we have to complain of Rome's inaccurate information of the passionate feeling of Cyril of Alexandria. The Nestorian criticism of the use of "Theotokos" was felt by those who knew the tradition of the Church to be an unjust rejection of a legitimate kerygma and a *skandalon oikoumenikon.*[4] The faithful were *skandalidsomenoi.*[5] In other words, a central feature of the faith and preaching of the Church had been attacked in the sight and hearing of simple believers and their bishops. Matters were the more serious because "Theotokos" was a key word by faith in the Incarnation.[6]

We now know that this state of alarm was created on Nestorius' side by his imprudence and lack of clarity in theological thought, and on that of St. Cyril largely by personal, church-political and terminological concerns, while Pope Celestine had insufficient knowledge of the true situation and the intentions of the Patriarch of Constantinople. If Nestorius and Cyril could have been compelled to discuss their differences calmly and to define their terms with precision, under the supervision of a strict and impartial arbiter who could have kept them under control until they had explained themselves clearly, there is little doubt that they would have found themselves in substantial agreement theologically, though separated *toto caelo* as far as the prestige of their respective archiepiscopal sees was concerned. But, unfortunately, history does not always take the shortest path to the solution of its difficulties.

In this state of alarm, the Nestorian rejection of "Theotokos" was considered by the Church in the context of all its possible systematic or historical consequences, even if only *grosso modo*. An investigation was made to discover all the consequences which this denial might *objectively* have (a doctrine of two Sons, of two persons in Christ). All possible lines were drawn to other heresies of earlier periods (Adoptionism, Judaism). In this way an objective, impersonal picture of heresy was formed, which was then assigned to Nestorius as its originator. All this results in a "popular" image of a heresy, and a heretic, which chiefly corresponds with the demands of the Church's preaching rather than with those of historical accuracy. The

---

of the Apollinarians is meant. The mistake was to attribute this sense to all uses of the title. Only in the course of the dispute did Nestorius come to see more and more the orthodox sense of "Theotokos." He was then ready to allow it, but mostly with reservations caused by his anti-Arian and anti-Apollinarian attitude. Thus explicitly in *Ep.* 3 *ad Celest.;* F. Loofs, *Nestoriana* 181[17-20]. In his "Second Homily on the Temptations of Jesus" he even uses this title without explanation. See F. Nau, *Le livre d'Héraclide de Damas* (Paris, 1910) 345[7]; Milton V. Anastos, "Nestorius was orthodox": *Dumbarton Oaks Papers* 16 (1962) 122, n. 6. Nestorius did not know the full tradition of "Theotokos." Otherwise he could not have affirmed that "Theotokos" is not to be found in the Fathers (*Liber Heraclidis: ed.* P. Bedjan, *Le livre d'Héraclide de Damas,* Paris-Leipzig, 1910) 220. Cf. the testimonies quoted by Socrates, H. E. 7. 32: *PG* 67, 812 AB, who censures the ignorance of the Patriarch (809B) about the writings of the Fathers.

[4] Cyril Al., *Ep.* 2 *ad Nestor., ACOI* 1, 1, p. 24[23-4].

[5] *Ibid.* 24[25]; similarly *Ep.* 8: *PG* 77, 60B.

[6] E. Schwartz, "Zur Vorgeschichte des ephesinischen Konzils. Ein Fragment": *Historische Zeitschrift* 112 (1914) (237–63) 249 calls "Theotokos" a "cult-word." It would be better to speak of a liturgical use of the title.

Church reacts to the *impia kerygmata* of the Bishop of Constantinople, which are felt to disturb the faith of the "oikoumene" and does so by affirming her own kerygma, *"ex cura pastorali."*[7] In the belief of his contemporaries, the condemnation of Nestorius removed an "ecumenical scandal." A *αἵρεσις* was eradicated by a *καθαίρεσις*.

2. *The Position of Historical Research*

It is the task of theological scholarship to take into consideration all factors which could serve to explain the case of Nestorius. These factors include not only the psychological, philosophical and theological presuppositions of Nestorius and his opponents, but also the circumstances of civil and ecclesiastical politics. Scholarship may rightly put the question, "Was Nestorius a Nestorian?" and show a concern for his person. It must therefore make good the neglect of his contemporaries and undertake a detailed analysis of the christological concepts and intentions of Nestorius and his opponents. At the time of the Council of Ephesus, the Church did not possess a theological method which would make possible a scientific judgment on the kerygmata of Nestorius. There was neither the ability nor the inclination to investigate the Patriarch's basic ideas and concepts. Modern scholarship is on the way towards filling this gap and is performing an "ecumenical" task now vigorously inculcated by the Second Vatican Council. . . .

The Nestorius-Question in Modern Study

As no agreement has been reached upon the verdict to be passed on Nestorius it is necessary to outline in brief the position of modern study. When we come to a theological assessment of Nestorius it is, of course, significant that the condemnation expressed at Ephesus has in later times frequently been confirmed: by Pope Hormisdas in his *Libellus professionis fidei* of 517; by the Second and Third Councils of Constantinople in 553 and 680–681; by the Lateran Council under Martin I in 649; by Eugenius IV in the Decree for the Jacobites (4. II. 1442; 1441 *stilo Florentino*); by Benedict XIV in the constitution *Nuper ad nos* of 1743; in most recent times by the Ephesus Encyclical of Pope Pius XI, *Lux Veritatis* (AAS 1931, 493–517); and finally by the Chalcedon Encyclical of Pope Pius XII, *Sempiternus Rex Christus* (AAS 1951, 625–44). These documents deliberately contain no scholarly discussion of the teaching of Nestorius. Indeed, this could only begin once the sources had been made available. For this reason we are to expect no essential change in the verdict on Nestorius even from the Reformers, though this change has been said to be noticeable as early as Luther . . . Luther finds

[7] Cf. Celestin., *Ep. ad. Nestor.* (Summer 430, after the Synod of Rome): ACO 12, 9^{27}: *"Ubi est diligentia pastoralis?"* For the importance of this term *diligentia* and, consequently of the objection contained in the question, see: H. Jaeger, "La preuve judiciaire d'après la tradition rabbinique et patristique" in: *La Preuve* (Collections Jean Bodin: Editions de la Librairie Académique de Bruxelles) . . . Nestorius sincerely acted out of pastoral care, though in an imprudent manner. The accusation of "imprudence"—as in the case of Eutyches—would have applied better to the action of Nestorius than the accusation of negligence. Cf. Socrates, *loc. cit.*

the chief error of Nestorius in his denial of the *communicatio idiomatum* and finally says of the Decree of Ephesus: "Es hat auch dis Concilium viel zu wenig verdampt an dem Nestorio"; in other words, this Council dealt with Nestorius far too lightly (*Luther-Werke* T. 50, Weimar, 1914, 590; *ibid.* 581–92). In his *De duabus naturis in Christo* Chemnitz too does no more than arrive at the traditional verdict on Nestorius.

Only in the seventeenth century was a new basis for scholarship laid by Johann Garnier in his naturally very disordered and incomplete edition of *Marius Mercator* (two volumes, Paris, 1673). . . . At the same time criticism of the traditional verdict on Nestorius begins. For the first time the question "Was Nestorius a Nestorian?" is asked. Walch gives an excellent survey of this in his *Historie* Vol V, 817-37. . . . The work of the Calvinist J. Bruguier of Lille is particularly important; in a book published anonymously in Frankfurt in 1645 he sets out to prove Nestorius orthodox and Cyril as the heretic. . . .

The Catholic authors maintain a negative attitude, in particular Dionysius Petavius, who, in the sixth book of his Treatise on the Incarnation, attacks the anonymous work (*Dogmata Theologica,* ed. Fournials T. VI, 1–105). He refers to other well-known authors of his time. Lenain de Tillemont, too, reaches the same conclusion in the fourteenth volume of his *Memoires pour servir à l'histoire ecclésiastique des six premiers siècles* (Paris, 1709), . . . The *Annali Ecclesiastici* of Baronius (T. I, Rome, 1683 for the year 428 and after) sharpen the tone against Nestorius. Richard Simon draws attention to the oriental sources (*Critique de la Bibliothèque des auteurs Ecclésiastiques . . . du Elies Du-Pin* T. I, Paris, 1730, 171–3; posthumous). On the other hand, Walch's *historie,* mentioned above, 838–936, gives an example of a theoretical and practical endeavour towards a new understanding of Nestorius and points to similar attempts. According to Walch both Nestorius and Cyril teach rightly, but both should have tempered their language (861). But the author still has insufficient means at his disposal to criticize the term *prosōpon* in Nestorius. This tendency of Walch is still followed by J. A. Dorner, *Entwicklungsgeschichte der Lehre von der Person Christi* (T. II, Berlin, 1853, 60–86). He is inclined to attribute a teaching of two persons to Nestorius (p. 63).

With the end of the nineteenth and the early years of the twentieth century a new phase in the study of Nestorius begins. This is concerned with two fields of research:

1. *The editions of the text.* F. Loofs in *Nestoriana* (Halle, 1905) gathers together the texts known up to his time, thereby taking up once again the work of Garnier. But the most significant event was the discovery and publication of the so-called *Liber Heraclidis,* the (second) apology of Nestorius preserved in a Syriac translation. F. Loofs in Theologische Literaturzeitung 51 (1926) 193–201, and Louise Abramouski, *Untersuchungen zum L. H. des Nestorius,* Corpus Script. Christ. Orientalium, 242, sub-22, give a report on the find. . . .

2. *The new description of Nestorius' teaching.* A further twentieth-century contribution to the study of Nestorius is the repeated attempts at a new description of his teaching. Even before the *LH* had been made available, J. B. Bethune-Baker began, with the help of

a transcript of the work placed at his disposal, to vindicate the teaching of Nestorius: *Nestorius and his Teaching, A fresh examination of the evidence* (Cambridge, 1908). The main chapter deals with the terms presumed to have been used by Nestorius (Ousia, Hypostasis, Prosopon), with the repudiation of the "Theotokos" title, and above all with the question "Did Nestosius postulate two persons in Christ?" (82–100). Bethune-Baker thinks that the unity of Prosopon in Nestorius represents no merely moral unity. Nestorius' *Bewährungslehre* (that is, the theory that Christ earned his exaltation to Sonship through his obedience and virtue) is given a very positive assessment (121–39). His teaching on the Incarnation is then compared with that of Cyril by means of two lengthy quotations from the *LH* (148–70). Nestorius is to be shown as a defender of the orthodox teaching which was then defined at the Council of Chalcedon (189–96). Cyril is blamed for one or two objectionable expressions which would, however, be capable of an orthodox interpretation. This is principally clear from the analysis of the formula of the "hypostatic union" (171–88).

With this work, Bethune-Baker introduces the second epoch of efforts to rehabilitate Nestorius. Whether in so doing he has been influenced by the results of earlier scholarship cannot be seen from his work. More restrained in his judgements, but nevertheless strongly dependent upon Bethune-Baker, is L. Fendt in his Strasbourg Dissertation *Die Christologie des Nestorius* (Kempten, 1910). In considering the position of scholarship we can give wide recognition to the conclusions of Fendt (the pupil of Albert Ehrhard), at that time still a Roman Catholic. With him, Catholic scholarship too begins to adopt a milder approach to the Nestorius-question. Of course, it was for this reason that J. B. Junglas, *Die Irrlehre des Nestorius* (Trier, 1912), was subject to severe censure. In seeking a partial vindication of Nestorius he argued that the heretical element in his work was not so much in the *prosōpon* doctrine as in the *Bewährungslehre.* This might result in an unfortunate shifting of accent. In judging the case of Nestorius we must begin with the *prosōpon* concept; this is the point from which the *Bewährungslehre* is to be judged. The parts of the acts which were read out at the Council before the condemnation of Nestorius do not speak of this *Bewährungslehre,* but of the unity in Christ as it is expressed in the *communicatio idiomatum.* Several more Catholic theologians move in the direction of a deeper desire to understand Nestorius and towards at least a partial vindication of his person and his theology, especially I. Rucker, *Das Dogma von der Persönlichkeit Christi und das Problem der Häresie des Nestorius. Die Quintessenz der syr. Nestorius-Apologie, genannt Liber Heraclidis (Damasceni)* (Oxenbrunn, 1934). This attempt to work out a new and yet correct interpretation of the christology of Nestorius did not, however, succeed (cf. A. Denefft, Schulastik 10, 1935, 548–60).

E. Amann gives a better groundwork for the solution of this problem. His article "Nestorius" in DTC XI, 1, 76–157, with great care seeks to explain the positive and the negative, the psychological and doctrinal elements in the Nestorius case. In these pages we have the best description and interpretation of Nestorius hitherto. Less balanced, but still worth noting because of the material it contains, is the study of the same author, "L'affaire Nestorius vue de Rome," in Review des Sciences Religieuses 23 (1949) 5–37, 207–44; 24 (1950) 28–52, 235–65. As the title states, an attempt is made here to explain the handling of the Nestorius affair by Rome. E. Amann advances many important documents and important matter for their interpretation. But his tendency to rehabilitate Nestorius and to attack Cyril and his party, now more emphatic in comparison with his earlier work, did not remain uncontradicted. Cf. L. Ciccone, DivThom 54 (1951) 33–55. It should be noted that the article did not receive a last revision.

The latest advances from the Catholic side towards the solution of the Nestorius question have been made by L. I. Scipioni, O.P., in his work *Ricerche sulla Cristologia del 'Libro di Eraclide' di Nestorio. La formulazione e il suo contesto filosofico* (Fribourg, 1956) and by the writer in the paper already quoted: Schol 36 (1961) 312–56. Similarly, from the Orthodox side, we have Milton V. Anastos, "Nestorius was orthodox": Dumbarton Oaks Papers 16 (1962) 119–40. Scipioni's problem is not whether Nestorius was a Nestorian; his purpose is to go beyond earlier scholarship in giving an analysis of the whole of the *LH* rather than merely giving an investigation of individual theological terms. Unfortuately he has not seen the necessity of first making a complete literary critical analysis, but his sober method is the right way to the solution. The important things about his work are the new emphasis on Nestorius' insistence on the unity of Christ, "the firm and undiscussed starting-point" of his christology (170), stress on Nestorius' anti-Apollinarianism and an account of the philosophical background of his doctrine. L. I. Scipioni holds that the prime contributory factor was the Stoic teaching of *krasis*. We largely follow his interpretation, adding a separate inquiry on the Nestorius of the time between 429–436 and recalling the Cappadocian background. In putting forward this theme Scipioni had already been anticipated by R. Arnou, "Nestorianisme et Néoplatonisme. L'unité du Christ et l'union des 'Intelligibles'" in Gregorianum 17 (1936) 116–31. Whereas I. Rucker (*op. cit.*) and also H. A. Wolfson, *The Philosophy of the Church Fathers* I (Cambridge, Mass., 1956) 451–63 had made Nestorius an Aristotelian, R. Arnou stamps him as a Neo-Platonist. But by recourse to the Stoa, L. I. Scipioni was able to show that the unity *prosōpon* in Nestorius lies not so much in the moral as in the metaphysical realm. His investigation is limited to the *LH* as "a systematic treatise, in which Nestorius has attempted an organic presentation of his thought" (13). While he here rightly concedes to Nestorius a more or less full approximation to orthodoxy, he leaves on one side the Nestorius of the documents which were condemned at Ephesus (13). Does Scipioni thus concede a development in the teaching of Nestorius? R. Seeberg had already made such a distinction between an earlier and a later Nestorius in the second edition of his *Lehrbuch der Dogmengeschichte, Band* 2 (Leipzig, 1910) 202. Such a development is, of course, possible, but is not easy to define, especially as Nestorius in the *LH* is given to referring back to earlier propositions and expressions of his own. There seems to be no substantial progress, especially if the spurious parts of the *LH* are excluded. Abramowski gives an accurate description of this evolution (*ibid.* 213–24) and we have tried to do the same.

In contrast to these studies, which have a more or less marked tendency to seek to understand or to vindicate Nestorius, two other writers are concerned to expound the traditional view of the relationship between Cyril and Nestorius. So especially M. Jugie, *Nestorius et la controverse nestorienne* (Paris, 1912); *idem, Theologia dogmatica christiana orientalis* Tome V (Paris, 1935) 76–211; *idem.*, Art. "Nestorio e Nestorianismo," in *Enciclopedia Cattolica* VIII (1952) 1780–84. Jugie finds a firm starting-point for his criticism of Nestorius in the later dogmatic concepts such as person and hypostasis, and finds in his writings an explicit doctrine of two persons and two hypostases. In dealing with the later Nestorius, however, he makes particular reference to the "Counter-anathemas" which from the time of E. Schwartz have no longer been accepted as genuine, *Die sogenannten Gegenanathematismen des Nestorius, Sitzungsberichte der Bayrischen Akademie der Wissanschafter* (Munich, München, 1922) Heft 1. The study of C. Pesch, *Nestorius als Irrlehrer. Zur Erläuterung einer wichtigen theologischen Prinzipienfrage* (Paderborn, 1921), employs a similar method and arrives at the same results. According to Nestorius, God and man are joined only in a moral union "which is based on mutual love and knowledge" (91. 21). P. Bedjan and F. Nau had already passed judgement in this way in the introductions of their editions of the *LH;* the latter also in his study *Nestorius d'après les sources orientales* (Paris, 1911) and "St. Cyrille et Nestorius," *Revue de L'Orient Chrétien* 15 (1910) 355–91; (1911) 1–51.

In Anglican theology most writers have concurred in the verdict of J. F. Bethune-Baker, in particular R. V. Sellers, *Two Ancient Christologies* (London, 1940): "From all this it seems clear that Nestorius is hardly deserving of the title 'Nestorian,' and that this is a legitimate conclusion is borne out by statements of his which show that for him Jesus Christ is very God incarnate" (164). The same author makes a similar attempt to draw together Nestorius and Cyril in his work *The Council of Chalcedon* (London, 1953). In his work *Fathers and Heretics* (London, 1948) 120–49, G. L. Prestige also puts forward compelling arguments for a better assessment of Nestorius. He sees clearly the limitations of the christology of Nestorius: "the unorthodoxy of Nestorius was not a positive fact but a negative impotence; like his master Theodore, he could not bring within the framework of a single, clearly conceived personality the two natures of Christ he distinguished with so admirable a realism. . . . The orthodoxy of Nestorius was positive: with his peculiarities of presentation once for all eliminated, the substance of his doctrine was accepted as the faith of Christendom at the Council of Chalcedon in 451" (143 f.). According to G. L. Prestige there are only small differences within the Antiochene school. For Aubrey R. Vine, *The Nestorian Churches* (London, 1937) 21–36, it was really Theodore of Mopsuestia who formed the Antiochene christology as it was condemned in Nestorius. It is correctly said that Nestorius never fully understood the idea "which '*communicatio idiomatum*' was meant to convey" (35). J. W. C. Wand, *The Four Great Heresies* (London, 1955) 89–109, sees both the positive element and the inadequacy in Nestorius' christology: "Nestorius was right, of course, in asserting a singularity of person, but wrong in saying that it could be made up of an earlier duality of persons, for two persons who were *ex hypothesi* already perfect and complete could not without diminution make a third" (98 f.).

The modern Protestant approach to the "Nestorius affair" found most pointed expression in the four lectures which F. Loofs gave at the University of London in 1913 and published under the title *Nestorius and his place in the History of Christian Doctrine* (Cambridge, 1914). First of all he describes the newly awakened interest in Nestorius and the tragedy of his life (26–60), going on to outline his teaching (60–94) and finally his place in the history of dogma (94–130). For Loofs, Nestorius is orthodox by the standard of the Council of Chalcedon but not by the standard of the Second (553) and Third (680–681) Councils of Constantinople. Nevertheless, in his teaching Nestorius stands in a better and more complete tradition than Cyril. Loofs then describes this dogmatic background with his own particular terminology and insight; it is formed by a general christological framework common to all Christians and occurring in both East and West. This framework presupposes no mystic, immanent doctrine of the Trinity and no *henōsis kata physin* with their mythologies, but is economic (viz. temporarily) -trinitarian and monotheistic. Here Loofs, of course, supports his positions with constructions which have not gained wide acceptance. For this reason this attempt represents no solution of the Nestorius question. . . . A. v. Harnack, *Lehrbuch der Dommengeschichte II*[1] (Tübingen, 1931[5]) 355–68, and W. Koehler in his *Dogmengeschichte* (Zürich-Leipzig, 1938) 158 f. speak quite moderately on the Nestorius question. In his *Lehrbuch der Dogmengeschichte II*[3] (Erlangen-Leipzig, 1923) 210–42, R. Seeberg, elsewhere so concerned to reach a balance, passes a very sharp verdict. In his view, "Nestorius offered a presentation of the Antiochene christology which is the clearest, simplest, and nearest to the Church's understanding that we possess. There is nothing 'heretical' in his thought. . . . None of the great 'heretics' of the history of dogma bears this name as undeservedly as Nestorius" (219 f.). Of course, R. Seeberg overlooks the role of Theodoret and the other moderate Antiochenes. Other historians have still more pointed expressions (cf. H. Ristow, "Der Begriff ΠΡΟΣΩΠΟΝ in der Thelogie des Nestorius," in *Aus der byzantinistischen Arbeit der Deutschen Demokratischen Republik I* (Berlin, 1957) 218–36; the survey of the position of Nestorius scholarship given there on 219–21 is very defective. Cf. also C. Pesch, "Zur neueren Literatur über Nestorius," 115, in the additional volume to the *Stimmen aus Maria Laach* (Freiburg, 1914). All these assessments of Nestorius and the Nestorius question given by the Protestant side are developed and surpassed by the excellent passage "Zur Christologie des Nestorius in der *Zweiten Apologie* und in den übringen *Nestoriana*" which occurs in the study of L. Abramowski, often quoted here: *Untersuchungen zum L.H.*, 208–29; cf. 183–99: "Die Christologie des Ps. Nestorius." By any standard this study by L. Abramowski prepares the basis for a balanced judgment on Nestorius and the Nestorius question.

5. K. McNamara[1] believes that it was in the person of Theodoret of Cyrus that the specifically Antiochene approach to the Incarnation received due recognition, exercising decisive influence in the Chalcedonian definition. As to the question of his alleged Nestorianism, his expressions are truly misleading. It seems that he not only failed to make a formal identification of the person of Christ with that of the Word, but he also failed to grasp at least the metaphysical dependence of the human nature on the Word.

"For it is not a little thing that is at stake but the supreme question of all."[2]

It was in these words that Theodoret, fifth century bishop of the Syrian see of Cyrus and illustrious Antiochene exegete, emphasized the vital importance for Christianity of the issues around which centred the great Christological controversies of his day. The several phases of the Nestorian-Monophysite crisis were, it is well known, marked by much of that acrimony and party spirit which, in time of intense intellectual crisis, so easily pass for genuine zeal for truth. In this respect Theodoret himself was not altogether free from blame. . . . Once he had entered the fray, however, and assumed by common consent of the Antiochene party that position of leadership for which his natural endowments fitted him, he could scarcely have remained unaffected by the intense party spirit prevalent on all sides.

Yet it was no party spirit, but considerations far more worthy of a scholar and a bishop, that played the decisive role in enticing him to interrupt his beloved pastoral duties in order to cross swords with Cyril of Alexandria. What chiefly motivated him then, and continued to support him during the long period of controversy that went on intermittently down to the time of Chalcedon, was the conviction, expressed in his words quoted above, that the central doctrine of the Catholic faith was in danger of being misunderstood and destroyed. In the interests of that doctrine he was prepared to bear witness before all the world to the faith that was in him. This he did, for the greater part of two decades, with a sincerity that shines through the mists of controversy, as it must have lit his own way in the dark moments of condemnation and deposition, when Dioscorus and his *Latrocinium* seemed to have effected the final triumph of heresy.

In staunchly defending the doctrine of Christ's complete and distinct human nature against the Monophysite heresy, Theodoret unquestionably rendered invaluable service to the Church. With the rise of Eutyches and the open emergence of Monophysitism, there fell upon the shoulders of Theodoret the mantle which St. Cyril had worn as defender of orthodoxy in the Nestorian con-

[1] Kevin McNamara is professor of Dogmatic Theology at St. Patrick's College in Maynooth, Ireland. He is also the editor of a recently published collection on Mariology, and a regular contributor to the *Irish Theological Quarterly*. It is from his article entitled "Theodoret of Cyrus and the Unity of Person in Christ," published in that *Quarterly* (Vol. 22, 1955), that this excerpt is taken, pp. 313–328.

[2] *Acta Conciliorum Oecumenicorum,* I, 4, 2, p. 134.

troversy. But now the roles of Alexandria and Antioch were reversed, and it was an Alexandrian not an Antiochene whose teaching threatened to destroy the traditional belief in the Incarnation doctrine. At such a time it was providential that the Church had at hand a theologian whose training and Christological outlook made him the implacable foe of any doctrinal tendency which minimized the human nature of Christ. At Ephesus the Alexandrian School had had its day of justification and triumph, but the advent of Eutyches ushered in the hour of the Antiochene theology, the positive values of which were now to be vindicated. In the person of Theodoret the specifically Antiochene approach to the Incarnation, with its emphasis on the human aspect of Christ, received a long-delayed recognition, and was enabled to play a role of the highest importance in the dogmatic definition of Chalcedon.

There were many, however, who could not forget that Theodoret was the disciple of Theodore and friend of Nestorius, and were unable to satisfy themselves that on the subject of Christ's unity he was altogether free from the error for which Nestorius had been condemned. Even at the Council of Chalcedon, where the Antiochene theology received its just measure of recognition, suspicion of Theodoret was strong enough to withhold from him acceptance as a "magister orthodoxus" until he agreed to repudiate publicly Nestorius and his teaching. The reluctance with which Theodoret finally pronounced anathema against Nestorius is apparent from the Acts of the Council[3] and is more than sufficient to justify the conditions imposed on him by the Fathers. Twenty years after the condemnation of Ephesus, Theodoret apparently was not convinced in his heart that Nestorius had been heretical in his subjective belief.

The fact is a significant one and in itself would pose a curious problem. Was Theodoret, one is led to ask, despite his realization of the gravity of the issue at stake, the sincerity of his purpose, and the indubitable benefits he conferred on the cause of Christian doctrine in combating the error of Eutyches, himself deficient or even in error in this very doctrine which from one point of view he so ably defended? Did his Christology sufficiently safeguard the unity of Christ's person? The question becomes even more pressing when one turns to an examination of Theodoret's writings, for there one finds a Christology which has many points of contact with that of Nestorius. Finally, one recalls that the fifth General Council of the Church, held at Constantinople in 553 A.D., condemned the writings of Theodoret in so far as they were directed "against the right faith and the twelve chapters of St. Cyril and the Council of Ephesus," and so far as they defended Nestorius and Theodore of Mopsuestia.[4] The prevailing spirit at the Council was, it is true, markedly anti-Antiochene and hardly such as to win a favorable interpretation of doubtful passages in Theodoret. It is also true that the condemnation refers only to a particular phase of Theodoret's controversial activities and cannot be taken, even for that limited phase, as

[3] Mansi VII, 185ff. Cf. P.C. da Mazzarino, *La Dottrina di Theodoreto di Ciro sull Unione Ipostatica* (Rome, 1941), pp. 149–52.

[4] Mansi IX, 290-7.

deciding the question of his subjective belief. It is nevertheless a further reason for asking the question: was Theodoret Nestorian, at any rate, in the early years of his theological career?

Of the writers who have examined this problem, the majority have acquitted Theodoret of sharing in the heresy of Nestorius. If one accepts their verdict one is faced with the question as to how precisely the thought of Theodoret and Nestorius differed. It cannot be deemed a satisfactory answer to this question to say, as M. Jugie does, that while Nestorius was heretical in his concept of the incarnation Theodoret was so only in expression. This is a hypothesis which demands considerably more evidence than M. Jugie offers. From the outset one suspects it of being an oversimplification of an intricate and delicate problem which can scarcely be solved in terms of a rigid classification into heretical and orthodox, and certainly not in terms of the unqualified descriptions "one person in Christ," "two persons in Christ. . . ."

As is to be expected in an Antiochene writer, Theodoret insists above all on the existence in Christ of two integral, distinct natures. . . . He teaches that God the Word is of the same substance as the Father, but is a distinct *hypostasis* or *idiotes.* In union with the human nature God the Word remains unchanged, since He is by nature immutable.

Treating of Christ's manhood, Theodoret repeatedly defends its reality and integrity, particularly its possession of an intellectual soul. He admits, however, that Christ's human intellect was ignorant of certain matters and that there was a real increase in Christ's knowledge with the passage of time. Here he is on common ground with Nestorius[5] and Theodore.[6] In the matter of Christ's moral perfection, however, his views are notably different from theirs, since he avoids any suggestion that Christ was subject to concupiscence.[7] Yet he retains, at least in the early years, the old Antiochene idea of the gradual achievement by Christ of ever more perfect virtue. "Who then," he asks, "is he who was perfected by toils of virtue and was not perfect by nature? Who is he who learned obedience by experience and before his experience was ignorant of it? . . . Not God the Word. . . . It is on the contrary that which was assumed by Him."[8] He does not give us to understand, however, that there was ever a period in Christ's life when temptation involved for Him a real possibility of sinning. Here again there is an important difference between his thought and that of Theodore and Nestorius, in reading whom one cannot escape the impression that they regarded sin as a real possibility for Christ.[9] It is one of the points which show most clearly how tenuous had become the bonds of unity of person in their Christology, how much out of harmony was their teaching with the great truth contained in the

---

[5] *Bazaar of Heracleides* (Ed. Driver-Hodgson), Oxford, 1925, p. 63.

[6] *De Incarnatione, P.G.* 66, 980.

[7] *De Incarnatione, P.G.* 75, 1433. Cf. Nestorius, *loc. cit.;* Theodore, *De Incarnatione,* 991.

[8] *Reprehensio,* 10, *P.G.* 76, 436 f. Date of composition is 431.

[9] Nestorius, *Heracleides,* p. 214; Theodore, *In Luc.* 4: I, *P.G.* 66, 720-1; *De Incarnatione* 15, *P.G.* 66, 991-2.

words of St. John, "and the Word was made flesh and dwelt among us."

The tendency which is here seen to such disadvantage in Theodore and Nestorius is no doubt the same that leads Theodoret to speak of the perfecting of Christ in virtue, but the fact that he refuses— as far as we can see— to contemplate the possibility of sin for Christ is not without some significance. It entitles us to say that he is more alive—we shall not say to the *divinity of Christ,* but to the *meaning of the divine in Christ* than was either Theodore or Nestorius. In this light it is interesting to compare Theodoret's reference, quoted above, to Christ's growth in perfection through obedience to the divine will, which occurs in his reply to the tenth anathema of St. Cyril, as a comment on Hebrews 5: 8, with his later handling of the same passage in his commentary on the Epistle. There he says simply that the perfecting of Christ refers to his Resurrection and transition to immortality, and takes the words "learned obedience by the things he suffered" as an "hyperbolical" statement by the Apostle, since in reality Christ was obedient before He suffered.[10] Here we find an even more sensitive awareness of the implications of the union of the Word with a human nature, an even greater care to dissociate any idea of imperfection from the assumed nature. We have here a clear indication that Theodoret's thought, in the course of his theological career, underwent a certain development which removed him some degrees further from the most dangerous of the positions adopted by Theodore and Nestorius. Whether or not that development freed him—if he needed to be freed—from the fundamental weakness of the Antiochene position, is something that remains to be determined.

Turning now to Theodoret's explicit teaching on the unity of person in Christ, we find that he vigorously professes his belief in that unity. Christ, he says, is both God and man,[11] He is one Son since the Word and the man are one and the same. . . . Christ therefore is but one *prosōpon* or person.[12] This word is one of four technical terms used by Theodoret in the context of the incarnation. The others are *physis, ousia* and *hypostasis.* The two former terms mean "nature" and "essence" respectively, and so Theodoret expresses the traditional doctrine that there are in Christ real Godhead and real manhood by the phrases "two *physeis*"[13] and "two *ousiai.*"[14] He also uses the phrase "two *hypostaseis.*[15] It seems clear that *hypostasis* for Theodoret conveys the idea of real and true existence,[16] and so when he says that there are "two *hypostaseis*" in Christ, he means that there are two distinct realities. There remains the term *prosōpon.* What idea had Theodoret in mind when he said that Christ was but "one *prosōpon*"? It

[10] *In Hebr.* 5: 8, *P.G.* 82, 712-3. Date of composition is between 435 and 449. . . . ?
[11] *Graecarum affectionum curatio,* 6, *P.G.* 83, 985.
[12] *Reprehensio,* 3, 404.
[13] *Ep.* 130, *P.G.* 83, 1345.
[14] *De Incarnatione,* 9, *P.G.* 75, 1428.
[15] *Reprehensio,* 3, *P.G.* 76, 404.
[16] Thus he says that light is distinguished from darkness in that the latter has not an *hypostasis* (*ou gar hyphestēkēn, anypostaton de Chrema esti*), *Quaestio 7 in Genes., P.G.* 80, 88. f. R. V. Sellers, *The Council of Chalcedon* (London, 1953), p. 138, n. 7.

would be a mistake to conclude immediately that he had in mind an idea identical with our philosophical concept of person, i.e. an independent subject of attribution. *Prosōpon* was undoubtedly the ordinary term used by Theodoret,[17] as also by Theodore[18] and Nestorius[19] to refer to the individual person, and as such brought with it the idea of real concrete unity. But it was not attended by any clearly-defined concept of ontological independence. It placed the emphasis rather on the person as he appeared to the onlooker.

It has been suggested that the modern idea which comes closest to the Antiochene concept of *prosōpon* is that of "personality" in the modern, psychological sense of that term. The suggestion is undoubtedly a valuable one as showing the direction in which we should adjust our philosophical concept of person, with its clear-cut metaphysical character, in order to arrive at an understanding of what *prosōpon* meant for the Antiochenes. We should bear in mind, however, that the word was used by them in contexts where in ordinary nonphilosophical parlance today the word "person" would be employed rather than "personality" with its pronounced psychological nuances. If then we agree to accept "personality" as representing the meaning of *prosōpon* for the Antiochenes, we must not exclude from its connotation the idea of the concrete unity of an individual rational being—an idea which can scarcely be absent whenever a person is considered as a distinct and separate individual, even though he be considered primarily from the psychological point of view. It may even be more clearly present to consciousness when the phrase "one *prosōpon*" is used for the express purpose of excluding the division of the natures in Christ . . . "it is right to confess one *prosōpon,* one Son and one Christ."[20] . . . Here "one *prosōpon*" has the same meaning as one Son: the idea of the substantial unity of a rational being, if not the dominant one, is nevertheless certainly present. To say that Christ is but one *prosōpon* means therefore, for Theodoret, that the "personality" which results from the combination and harmonious blending of divine and human qualities in Christ is a single concrete being, possessing a unity no less real than that of any other person, except that in Him there are two real and distinct natures.

There is no question then but that Theodoret firmly intended to preserve the unity of person in Christ, and that he had in mind real unity of being. Nevertheless it is extremely difficult to reconcile with this position Theodoret's language concerning the human nature. In common with Diodore of Tarsus, Theodore, and Nestorius he often refers to the human nature in concrete rather than abstract terms, describing it as "the man," "the assumed man," "the Son the man."[21]

---

17 E.g. *Eranistes,* 3, *P.G.* 83, 236 *auton ton prosopon.*

18 E.g. *Commentary on the Eucharist,* ed. Mingana, (Cambridge, 1933), pp. 113f.

19 E.g. *Heracleides,* pp. 132, 133 ("those *prosopa* who were taking the place of those who were absent from the Council"), 233 ("for 'is the same' indicates one and the same *prosōpon*").

20 *Reprehensio,* 3, *P.G.* 76, 404.

21 *De Incarnatione,* 11, 30, *P.G.* 75, 1430, 1472; *Expositio rectae confessionis.* 12, *P.G.* 6. 1229.

While language such as this can be paralleled in the writings of many illustrious teachers in both the Eastern and the Western Church, its habitual use by an author gives grounds for suspecting that he does not grasp the dependent character of the human nature in relation to the Word in Christ. In Theodoret's case this suspicion is confirmed by his regular practice of predicating human attributes of the human nature as if it were an independent subject of attribution.[22]

In Theodoret's concept of the Incarnate Word, the divine and human natures are accorded an equal status as subjects of attribution for their respective properties. We are also tempted to conclude that each is looked on as an independent subject or subsisting nature. Here, however, we must recall that Theodoret was able to think of the person of Christ as endowed with the real unity of an individual *prosōpon.* We can scarcely conceive how he could have done so if his idea of the human nature was accompanied by any pronounced concept of subsistence. It is nevertheless true that, when thinking and writing of the human nature as the subject of its own attributes, his idea of it could have approached our idea of a subsisting nature, while lacking the clear outlines of that concept. It is apparently only along lines such as these that we can hope to reach a solution of the problem of Theodoret's Christology—the problem of reconciling his concept of Christ's unity with his failure to grasp the dependent character of the human nature. The theory of a human nature vaguely conceived as subsisting is certainly in harmony with what has already been said concerning Theodoret's mental image of a *prosōpon.* In that concept external appearances and psychological qualities occupied a large place, thereby impeding the mind from penetrating to any clear idea of ontological independence. The same consideration is applicable—perhaps even with greater force—to Theodoret's concept of the human nature considered as the subject of its own attributes. In all this problem the dominant ideas for Theodoret were those of real existence, the distinction of two perfect natures, and real unity visibly expressed in the striking harmony of divine and human qualities in Christ. In so far as the idea of subsistence was present it was not clearly distinguished from that of real existence of a concrete nature. Expressed in other terms this means that the idea of "ownership"—for us the key concept where unity of person is concerned—was very much attenuated in Theodoret. In his mind, "to own," "to possess as an ultimate subject," was not clearly distinguished from the idea "to be the immediate source or principle of." Thus while he accords to the human nature a similar position to that of the Word—a position which, viewed from a truly metaphysical point of view and in its logical implications, is incompatible with unity of person in Christ—he can still in his own mind think of Christ as a real quasi-substantial unity of two individual, distinct natures.

A point of considerable interest in regard to Theodoret's use of concrete terms to describe the human nature is that it is confined to the earlier years of his theological career. In the years immediately following the Nestorian controversy, at a date which cannot be

[22] *Reprehensio,* 10, *P.G.* 76, 436 f.

determined exactly, Theodoret abandoned this usage. Does this mean that somewhere about the year 433 Theodoret's thought concerning the human nature underwent a radical change? This was the theory adopted by Bertram in his study of Theodoret's Christology, but it harmonizes ill with Theodoret's declared conviction that his earlier thought is completely in line with that of his later years.[23] . . . What most clearly demonstrates, however, that Theodoret's thought remained essentially unaltered, despite his abandoning of the concrete descriptions of the human nature, is his unchanged attitude to the "communication of idioms." . . .

The theological basis for the "communication of idioms," by which both divine and human properties are predicated of one person, named from either nature, is that the person of the Word, existing from eternity in the divine nature, has made its own the human nature with all its attributes. It is for this reason that Catholic theology defends such propositions as: God was born, suffered, died, etc., or: Mary is the Mother of God (*Theotokos*). Theodoret, one can see immediately, fails to grasp this principle. He is never at ease in the presence of such statements. He admits that they can be justified "because of the union,"[24] because the "temple," of which alone the human attributes can truly be predicated, is united to God.[25] It is true that from about the year 448 onwards he accepts the title "theotokos" without qualification,[26] but he had for long insisted on the need for adding "anthropotokos. . . ."

Theodoret's final admission of "theotokos" without qualification cannot be interpreted to mean that he had now come to realize that the person of Christ was the identical person of the Word. Such an interpretation is excluded by his consistent refusal to admit such expressions as: God suffered, God the Word suffered.[27] . . .

To describe Mary as "theotokos" was merely to express a certain relationship between her and Christ, and came very near to being a simple statement of Christ's divinity. On the other hand, the immediate effect produced on the mind by the statement that God has suffered was an association of the two ideas, "God" and "suffering," rather than the idea that Christ was God. Hence propositions of this kind were to be avoided, that is to say, absolute accuracy of statement was to be preserved when speaking of the human attributes concerned. For Theodoret such accuracy meant that they could be predicated only of the human nature. He had not, even at this stage, come to view the incarnation from the point of view of the identity of person in Christ and the Word: that truth was still effectively, if not completely, outside his mental horizons.

Had Theodoret then, it is pertinent to ask, strayed in some degree from the traditional line of thought on the Incarnation? When one compares his position with that of earlier witnesses to tradition, one will find it difficult to

---

[23] *Ep.* 109, *P.G.* 83, 1304; *Ep.* 62, *ibid.*, 1265.
[24] *Reprehensio,* 12, *P.G.* 76, 449.
[25] *Ibid.*, I 393.
[26] *Ep.* 83. *P.G.* 83, 1269, 1273.
[27] *Eranistes,* 3. *P.G.* 83, 221.

deny that he had. That everything in the human nature of Christ belonged to God the Word and therefore could be predicated of Him was an integral part of the Christian tradition from the beginning.[28] It was from this principle that there developed, through Athanasius and the Cappadocians to St. Cyril and the post-Chalcedonian theologians, the doctrine that the principle of personality in the God-man was to be found in the Word, and the further conclusion, elaborated by Leontius of Byzantium in the sixth century, that the human nature existed not of itself but in the *hypostasis* of the Word.[29] Prior to the fourth century there is no trace of hesitation in predicating human attributes of God the Word. The rise of the Appolinarian heresy, however, which denied the existence of a human intellect in Christ, recognizing the Logos as the sole principle of His intellectual activity, caused the "communication of idioms" to be viewed with some suspicion. This was especially true at Antioch where the integrity of Christ's human nature was constantly to the fore. In the Antiochene milieu the predication of human attributes of God the Word gradually came to be recognized as the characteristic stock-in-trade of Apollinarian and other Monophysite writers. In their anxiety to prevent the integrity and distinct character of Christ's manhood from being lost sight of, however, many of the Antiochenes—there are exceptions—lost sight of the real meaning of the truth expressed in the "communication of idioms."

This was the heritage Theodoret received from his master Theodore, and it fully explains his refusal to predicate human attributes of God the Word. . . .

The reason for this failure was Theodoret's inability to distinguish—at any rate at the level of articulate conscious ideas—between the Word of God under the aspect of person and under the aspect of nature, just as he was unable to make a similar distinction in regard to the human nature. Thus his concept of the Incarnate Word was a "symmetrical" one—two natures juxtaposed (and of course united in one *prosōpon*), without the idea of the metaphysical dependence of the human nature on the divine. . . .

It may well be, of course, that Theodoret, as the influence of various factors played on him with the passage of time, came nearer to a true appreciation of the traditional "communication of idioms," and was led to some less confused, though still unclear, idea of the distinction between nature and person. . . . Such a vision however can only have been fleeting and uncertain, for Theodoret's problem, as far as available evidence goes, remained with him to the end. . . . Theodoret's (later) statement that the "body" is not that of anyone other than of the only-begotten Son of God does not therefore bring him any

---

[28] Cf. Tixeront, *History of Dogmas* I, pp. 144 ff., pp. 271 ff. Striking examples of the "communication of idioms" by early writers are: "the blood of God," St. Ignatius of Antioch, *Ad. Ephes.,* 1, 1, *P.G.* 5, 644; "ipsum Verbum Dei incarnatum suspensum est super lignum," St. Irenaeus, *Adv. Haeres.,* 5, 18, 1, *P.G.* 7, 1172; "the blood of the Logos," Clement of Alexandria, *Paedagogus,* 3, 2, 19, *P.G.* 8, 409.

[29] Leontius, *Contra Nestor. et Eutych, P.G.* 86, 1269–1396; *Contra Severum, P.G.* 86, 1901–6.

nearer to a formal identification of the person of Christ with the person of the Word.[30]

Because he failed to make this identification, Theodoret's christology never came to its due perfection. Even apart from making this identification consciously, however, he could still have avoided the Nestorian tendency, if he had been able to keep in view the metaphysical dependence of the human nature on the Word. The least one can say is that he did not do so sufficiently, because of a defect in the particular tradition in which he was formed.

One cannot then, it seems, recognize any deep line of division between Theodoret and Nestorius on the subject of the unity of person in Christ. That there were at all times important points of difference between them is nevertheless true; it is even possible that by the time of the Council of Chalcedon a fairly wide divergence had developed. On that point, however, one's judgment will depend on the significance one attaches to the doctrinal development of Theodoret discussed above, and also, of course, on the exact position one assigns to Nestorius at the time of the Council of Ephesus and on possible developments of that position between Ephesus and Chalcedon. That, however, is a separate question, with many difficulties of its own.

6. J. N. D. Kelly's[1] study of the soteriology of the Greek fathers leads him to state that, despite appearances, the various theories about redemption during the patristic age should not be regarded as mutually incompatible, but rather as different aspects which elucidate the same great truth. They are complementary of each other. In this light he discusses Athanasius, the Cappadocians, Chrysostom, Eusebius, and Cyril of Jerusalem.

The Clue to Soteriology. The student who seeks to understand the soteriology of the fourth and early fifth centuries will be sharply disappointed if he expects to find anything corresponding to the elaborately worked out syntheses which the contemporary theology of the Trinity and the Incarnation presents. In both these latter departments controversy forced fairly exact definition on the Church, whereas the redemption did not be-

[30] Fr. Grillmeier (in *Das Konzil von Chalkedon,* Vol. I, p. 100) thinks we should interpret the above statement, together with the assertion (*Ep.* 146, *P.G.* 83, 1393) that Jesus Christ is not a person other than the Son completing the Trinity, as indicating a distinct advance by Theodoret towards an appreciation of the true position of the Logos in Christ. The reference to the Trinity, however, appears to affirm what was no more than a traditional Antiochene position. We find the statement exactly paralleled in Theodore ("Quomodo itaque possible est quartam personam super has addere illam quae assumpta est servi formam?" *Ep. ad Artemium, P.G.* 66, 1012), and so it can scarcely represent a personal development in Theodoret. In regard to the statement that the body belongs to the Word, we can, I think, find a parallel for it in one of Theodoret's early works, where he speaks of the "form of God" appropriating the sufferings because of the Union (*Reprehensio,* 12, *P.G.* 76, 449. . . .)

[1] Cf. Ch. 1, 5. It is from his book *Early Christian Doctrines* that this excerpt has been taken, selectively, from pp. 375–386.

come a battleground for rival schools until the twelfth century, when Anselm's *Cur deus homo* (*c.* 1087) focussed attention on it. Instead he must be prepared to pick his way through a variety of theories, to all appearance unrelated and even mutually incompatible, existing side by side and sometimes sponsored by the same theologian.

Three of these are particularly significant, and it will make for clarity if we set them down at the threshold of our discussion. First, there was the so-called "physical" or "mystical" theory (we have already come across it in Irenaeus) which linked the redemption with the incarnation. According to this, human nature was sanctified, transformed and elevated by the very act of Christ's becoming man. Often, though not quite correctly, described as the characteristically Greek theory, it cohered well with the Greek tendency to regard corruption and death as the chief effects of the Fall. In its strict form it tended to be combined with the Platonic doctrine of real universals, in the light of which it was able to treat human nature as a generic whole. Secondly, there was the explanation of the redemption in terms of a ransom offered to, or a forfeit imposed on, the Devil. The former version goes back to Irenaeus and Origen; the latter began to emerge in our period with the growing realization of the incongruity of attributing any rights to the Devil in the matter. Thirdly, there was the theory, often designated "realist," which directed attention to the Saviour's sufferings. Making more of sin and the punishment due for it than of its tragic legacy, this placed the cross in the foreground, and pictured Christ as substituting Himself for sinful men, shouldering the penalty which justice required them to pay, and reconciling them to God by His sacrificial death.

Faced with this diversity, scholars have often despaired of discovering any single unifying thought in the patristic teaching about the redemption. These various theories, however, despite appearances, should not be regarded as in fact mutually incompatible. They were all of them attempts to elucidate the same great truth from different angles; their superficial divergences are often due to the different Biblical images from which they started, and there is no logical reason why, carefully stated, they should not be regarded as complementary. In most forms of the physical theory, for example, the emphasis on the incarnation was not intended to exclude the saving value of Christ's death. The emphasis was simply the offshoot of the special interest which the theologians concerned had in the restoration in which, however conceived, the redemption culminates. Similarly, the essential truth concealed behind the popular, often crudely expressed imagery of a deal with Satan was the wholly Scriptural one (cf. Acts 26, 18) that fallen man lies in the Devil's power and salvation necessarily includes rescue from it.

There is a further point, however, which is not always accorded the attention it deserves. Running through almost all the patristic attempts to explain the redemption there is one grand theme which, we suggest, provides the clue to the fathers' understanding of the work of Christ. This is none other than the ancient idea of recapitulation which Irenaeus derived from St. Paul, and which envisages

Christ as the representative of the entire race. . . .

Athanasius. The dominant strain in Athanasius' soteriology is the physical theory that Christ, by becoming man, restored the divine image in us; but blended with this is the conviction that His death was necessary to release us from the curse of sin, and that He offered Himself in sacrifice for us. Both aspects are sometimes combined in a single context, as when he writes,[2] . . . "The Word became flesh in order both to offer this sacrifice and that we, participating in His Spirit, might be deified."

Let us look more closely at the former aspect. The effect of the Fall was that man lost the image of God and languished in corruption. Hence the prime object of the incarnation was his restoration. . . . The Word being the principle of life, the principle of death is reversed in us and the precious gift of incorruptibility (*aphtharsia*) lost at the Fall is restored.[3] Hence the redemption can be described as a re-creation carried out by the Word, the original author of creation.[4]

Athanasius' language often suggests that he conceived of human nature, after the manner of Platonic realism, as a concrete idea or universal in which all individual men participate. From this point of view, when the Word assumed it and suffused it with His divinity, the divinizing force would be communicated to all mankind, and the incarnation would in effect be the redemption. Such is the clear implication of numerous passages. . . . The stress laid on the kinship of His body with ours, and on the consubstantiality which exists between all men, points in the same direction. There is little doubt that Athanasius' Platonism tended at times to lose touch with his Christianity. His more considered teaching,[5] however, is that divinization through the Word does not come naturally to all men, but only to those who are in a special relation to Him. To be more precise, we are divinized by intimate union with the Holy Spirit, Who unites us to the Son of God, and through Him to the Father. . . . This brings us to the second aspect of his teaching. . . . "It still remained to pay the debt which all owed, since all, as I have explained, were doomed to death, and this was the chief cause of His coming among us. That is why, after revealing His Godhead by His works, it remained for Him to offer the sacrifice for all (*hyper pañton tēn thusiañ*), handing over the temple of His body to death for all, so that He might rescue and deliver them from their liability for the ancient transgression, and might show Himself superior to death, revealing His own body as immortal as a foretaste of the incorruption of all. . . . Because both the death of all was fulfilled in the Lord's body, and death and corruption were annihilated because of the Logos Who indwelt it. For there was need of death, and a death had to be undergone for all, so that the debt of all might be discharged.[6] His underlying thought is that the curse of sin, i.e. death, lay heavy on all mankind; it was a debt

[2] *De incarn.* 9.
[3] E.g. *de incarn.* 8; *c. Ar.* 3, 33.
[4] *Ad Adelph.* 8 .
[5] Cf. *de incarn.* 27–32.
[6] *Ibid.* 20.

which had to be paid before restoration could begin. On the cross Christ, the representative man, accepted the penalty in His own body, and died. Thus He released us from the curse, procured salvation, and became our Lord and king.[7] To describe this the traditional language came readily to Athanasius' pen. Christ's death, he wrote,[8] was a sacrifice which He offered to the Father on our behalf. It was "the ransom (*lytron*) for men's sins,"[9] and Christ not only heals us, but bears the heavy burden of our weaknesses and sins.[10] On the surface the doctrine is one of substitution, but what Athanasius was seeking to bring out was not so much that one victim was substituted for another, as that "the death of all was accomplished in the Lord's body."[11] In other words, because of the union between His flesh and ours, His death and victory were in effect ours. Just as through our kinship with the first Adam we inherit death, so by our kinship with "the man from heaven" we conquer death and inherit life.[12]

Fourth-century Greek Fathers. Next to Athanasius the chief exponent of the physical theory in the fourth century was Gregory of Nyssa. Here and there, admittedly, hints of it appear in other writers. Basil, for example, emphasizes[13] that if the Lord had possessed a nature different from ours, "we who were dead in Adam should never have been restored in Christ." . . . Through becoming incarnate, writes[14] Gregory Nazianzen, "He takes me wholly, with all my infirmities, to Himself, so that as man He may destroy what is evil, as fire destroys wax or the sun's rays the vapours of the earth, and so that as a result of this conjunction I may participate in His blessings." John Chrysostom explains[15] that it is precisely because the Word has become flesh and the Master has assumed the form of a servant that men have been made sons of God. But their most characteristic ideas move in a different orbit. For Gregory of Nyssa, however, the incarnation, culminating in the resurrection, is the sovereign means for restoring man to his primitive state. His theory[16] is that the effect of the Fall has been the fragmentation of human nature, body and soul being separated by death. By becoming man, and by dying and rising again in the human nature which He assumed, Christ has forever reunited the separated fragments. Thus, just as death entered the world by one man, so by one man's resurrection the principle of life has been given back to us.[17] His argument, we observe, depends on the classic antithesis between the first and second Adams. Like Athanasius, too, he translates the Biblical idea of solidarity into

[7] C. *Ar.* 2, 76: cf. ib. 1, 60; 3, 33.
[8] *Ibid.* 1, 41; 2, 7; *de decret.* 14.
[9] C. *Ar.* 1, 45.
[10] *Ibid.* 3, 31.
[11] *De incarn.* 20.
[12] C *Ar.* 1, 44; 2, 61; 2, 67.
[13] *Ep.* 261, 2.
[14] *Or.* 30, 6: cf. ib. 2, 23–5.
[15] *In Ioh. hom.* 11, 1.
[16] *Or. cat.* 16; *antirrh.* 55.
[17] *Or. cat.* 16.

the language of Platonic realism. The whole of human nature, he claims,[18] constitutes as it were a single living being . . . so that the experience of a part becomes the experience of the whole. In this way all mankind is seen to share in what Christ achieves by His resurrection.[19] . . .

Christ's death, we notice, was integral to the scheme, and so Gregory had no difficulty in applying the Biblical language of sacrifice to it. Christ is the good shepherd who gives his life for the sheep, at once priest and victim. . . . If the underlying idea in this is expiation, Isaiah 53, 4 suggested that of substitution, and Gregory was able to speak[20] of Christ making our sufferings His own and submitting to the stripes due to us. At the same time, since the Fall placed man in the power of the Devil, he liked to envisage the redemption as our emancipation from him. As Gregory developed this aspect, his chief concern was for God's justice; hence his reiteration that it was through his own free choice that man fell into the Devil's clutches. The Devil, therefore, had a right to adequate compensation if he were to surrender him, and for God to have exercised *force majeure* would have been unfair and tyrannical. So He offered him the man Jesus as a ransom. When Satan saw Him, born as He was of a virgin and renowned as a worker of miracles, he decided that the exchange was to his advantage. What he failed to realize was that the outward covering of human flesh concealed the immortal Godhead. Hence, when he accepted Jesus in exchange for mankind, he could not hold Him; he was outwitted and caught, as a fish is by the bait which conceals the hook.[21] There was no injustice in this, Gregory tried to show,[22] for the Devil was only getting his deserts, and in any case God's action was going to contribute to his own ultimate benefit (Gregory shared[23] the doctrine of his master, Origen, that in the final restoration the pains of the damned, Satan included, would come to an end).

Precisely the same theory of the Devil's right to keep mankind in bondage until given adequate compensation found support with his elder brother Basil. All men, he taught,[24] are subject to the authority of the prince of this world, and only Christ can claim (cf. John 14, 30) that "he hath nothing in me." Hence a ransom is necessary if their deliverance is to be effected, and it cannot consist in any ordinary human being. The Devil could hardly be induced to hand over his captives by receiving a mere man; in any case such a man would require redemption himself. What is needed is someone who transcends human nature —in fact, the God-man Jesus Christ.[25] Gregory's grotesque imagery of the bait and hook, we observe, is absent here, and Basil does not seem to press the theory. In the same context he oscillates between interpreting Christ's

---

[18] *Ibid.* 32.
[19] Cf. *antirrh.* 16; 55.
[20] *Antirrh.* 21.
[21] *On cat.* 22–4.
[22] *Ibid.* 26.
[23] *Ibid.* 26, 35.
[24] *Hom. in ps.* 7, 2.
[25] *Ibid.*, 48, 3 f.

death as a ransom paid to the Devil and as a sacrifice offered to God. On the other hand, the whole conception of rights belonging to the Devil and of the Son of God being handed over to him was subjected to an important extremely damaging critique by Gregory of Nazianzus. . . . Gregory went on to show that Christ's blood was not, strictly speaking, a ransom paid to God the Father either, since it is inconceivable that He should have found pleasure in the blood of His only Son. The truth rather is that the Father accepted it, not because He demanded or needed it, but because in the economy of redemption it was fitting that sanctification should be restored to human nature through the humanity which God had assumed. As for the Devil, he was vanquished by force.

The cogency of objections like these must have been felt and it is not surprising that John Chrysostom's account of the transaction was less vulnerable to attack. According to this,[26] the Devil was strictly within his rights in dealing despitefully with men; they had sinned, thereby placing themselves under his jurisdiction. But in sowing the seed of conspiracy in Judas's heart and in lifting his hand against the sinless Christ, he exceeded his rights. In fact, he brought down well-merited sanctions on his own head, and being thrust forth from his empire he lost his hold over those whom he kept in bondage. So the bizarre conception of just claims which could only be circumvented by a palpable ruse practiced on the Devil by God Himself faded into the background, and attention was focused on his scandalous abuse of his powers.

Neither the physical theory, however, nor the mythology of man's deliverance from the Devil represents the main stream of Greek soteriology in the fourth century. For this we have to look to doctrines which interpreted Christ's work in terms of a sacrifice offered to the Father. We saw that both Athanasius and Gregory of Nyssa, while viewing man's restoration as essentially the effect of the incarnation, were able to find a logical place for the Lord's death conceived as a sacrifice. This aspect is forcibly presented by Athanasius' contemporary, Eusebius of Caesarea. Christ appropriated our sins, he argues,[27] and accepted the punishment we deserved; His death is a substitutionary sacrifice. And He was able to identify Himself with our sins and the penalties attached to them because, as very man, He shared our nature. But teaching like this fits awkwardly into Eusebius' system, according to which the function of the Word is to reveal eternal truths rather than to accomplish saving acts. A much more representative witness to the soteriology of the period is Cyril of Jerusalem. Writing for a popular audience, he stresses the unique importance of the passion. It is the cross which brings light to the ignorant, deliverance to those bound by sin, and redemption to all.[28] By offering Himself as a ransom Christ has appeased God's wrath towards sinful men.[29] Innocent himself, He has given His life for our sins.[30] Again the idea is that

---

[26] *In Ioh. hom.* 67, 2 f.; *in Rom. hom.* 13, 5.
[27] *Dem. ev.* 1 10; 10, 1.
[28] *Cat.* 13, 1.
[29] *Ibid.* 13, 2.
[30] *Ibid.* 13, 3–6; 13, 21–3.

of substitution based on the Saviour's kinship with us; as the new Adam He can take responsibility for our misdeeds. Cyril's freshest contribution is the suggestion that the universal efficacy of His sacrifice is explained by the measureless value attaching to His Person. "It was not someone of no significance," he states,[31] "who died for us. It was no irrational beast, no ordinary man, not even an angel. It was God incarnate. The iniquity of our sins was not so great as the righteousness of Him Who died for us. Our transgressions did not equal the goodness of Him Who laid down His life on our behalf."

Similar teaching appears in Basil, Gregory of Nazianzus and John Chrysostom. . . . Chrysostom teaches[32] that mankind stood condemned to death by God, and was indeed virtually dead; but Christ has delivered us by handing Himself over to death. Whereas the sacrifices of the old Law were incapable of achieving this, Christ has saved us by His unique sacrifice.[33] He has done this, Chrysostom makes it clear, by substituting Himself in our place. Though He was righteousness itself, God allowed Him to be condemned as a sinner and to die as one under a curse, transferring to Him not only the death which we owed but our guilt as well.[34] And the sacrifice of such a victim was of surpassing efficacy, being sufficient to save the entire race.[35] He died for all men, to save all, so far as He was concerned; for the death was a fair equivalent (ἀντίρροπος) in exchange for the destruction of all.[36] In dying His object was to save all; and if in fact not all have achieved salvation the reason lies in their refusal to accept Him.

[31] *Ibid.* 13, 33: cf. ib. 13, 2.
[32] *In Gal. comm.* 2, 8.
[33] *In Hebr. hom.* 15, 2.
[34] *In 2 Cor. hom.* 11, 3 f.; *in Eph. hom.* 17, 1.
[35] *In Gal. comm.* 2, 8.
[36] *In Hebr. hom.* 17, 2.

IV

THE CHALCEDONIAN FAITH AND ITS FURTHER CLARIFICATIONS

1. F. Ferrier[1] considers the lack of precision in Cyril's terminology one of the main causes responsible for the Christological controversies which followed his death in 444. The situation would have been different if the clarification made by Proclus of Cyzicus had been generally adopted. Eutyches' role and doctrinal position are mostly the product of his stubborness and mediocrity. The Chalcedonian faith comes to us immediately not so much from Cyril, the patriarch, as from Leo the pope.

The formulas used by St Cyril in his twelve anathemas to state the truth about the mystery of the Incarnation were far from satisfying all the bishops. At Antioch the patriarch John and his group of disciples only reached an understanding with St Cyril in 433, and though John accepted Mary's

[1] Francis Ferrier is the author of *L'Incarnation,* first published in France in 1960. It was translated into English by Edward Sillem under the title, *What is the Incarnation?*, Vol. 24 of the *Twentieth Century Encyclopedia of Catholicism* (New York: Hawthorn Books, 1962). It is from this book that this excerpt is taken, pp. 50–61.

title of Mother of God, "he nevertheless continued to teach an uncommingled union of divinity and humanity in Christ," which was far too vague a statement about the union to satisfy Cyril's standards of theological exactitude. Cyril's victory, unfortunately, was not as complete as he had imagined. The followers of Nestorius went into hiding and endeavoured to pass unnoticed for the time being, but the predominant fear of the majority of the Eastern bishops was not the growth of Nestorianism: fear of a revival of Apollinarianism was their primary anxiety.

The anti-Nestorian movement had had powerful support from the monasteries, but now a heretical movement of monastic origin was about to break upon the world, and it was to win the support of hosts of monks as it developed into one of the most stubborn of heretical movements since Arianism. By an irony of fate the anathemas of St Cyril, the instrument that had contributed so much to the triumph of the faith at Ephesus, were to become the occasion of this new heresy, which was sprung on the Church after St Cyril's death in 444. The driving personality behind the heretical party was now to be Dioscorus, the patriarch of Alexandria; the combined efforts of the party were soon to be directed to bludgeoning Flavian, the patriarch of Constantinople, and the entire Eastern Church to their support . . . This new heresy is known as Monophysitism because it taught that in Christ there is only one nature (*monos physis*).

The spread of Monophysitism was intimately associated with the person of a monk called Eutyches with whose preaching it originated, with the story of the intrigues in which he became entirely involved, and with an ambiguous kind of formula, reminiscent of that which St Cyril had borrowed from Apollinaris, describing Christ as "the one nature of the God-Logos become man." St Cyril had written as follows in a letter to Nestorius:

> When we consider in our understanding the realities of which the one Son of God and Lord Jesus Christ is formed, we say that they are two natures; but after the union, as there is no separation of the natures, *we believe that the nature of the Son is one,* and that he is man and incarnate. If anyone says that he who is incarnate and made man is the Word of God, all suspicion of change is removed, for he remains what he was, and the union without confusion of natures is also professed by us.[2]

In using this kind of formula Cyril had in mind both the permanence of the Person of the Word, after as before the Incarnation, and the newness of his presence in the flesh taken from the Virgin Mary. In using the word "nature" he unfortunately gave ground for the Antiochene theologians to accuse him of the much dreaded Apollinarianism, but Cyril had been able to defend and explain his formula against all his accusers. He had been able to show that he used *nature* in this formula to mean what we shall call "person." But when St Cyril died and the interpretation of words like these was undertaken by a comparatively simple-minded person who was incapable of entering into the subtleties of his theology, it was inevitable that his doctrine about the union of two natures in the one Person of Christ would become seriously distorted.

[2] St Cyril, Letter XL.

Just before Eutyches began popularizing his version of St Cyril's doctrine, Proclus of Cyzicus, who in 434 had succeeded the aged Maximian as patriarch of Constantinople, had pointed out the ambiguity in the use of the word "nature" by many of the Greek-speaking theologians, and had introduced a new terminology, which from his time onwards the Greeks began to adopt. Proclus, replying to some Armenian messengers who had come to ask him questions both about Apollinarianism and Nestorianism, stated that the orthodox doctrine of the Incarnation of the Word could be expressed concisely in the following propositions:

> We confess that the Divine Word, one of the Persons in the Trinity, was made man:
> We confess one *hypostasis* of the incarnate Word of God.

By using the word *hypostasis,* and speaking of "*one hypostasis* of the Incarnate Word" (in place of St Cyril's "one nature of the Incarnate Word"), Proclus showed clearly that he was in full agreement with St Cyril and all those who had defended the Virgin Mary's title, "Mother of God," and he also introduced an exceedingly useful clarification in the expressions of Cyril's own theology. Till this time the Greeks had used two words, *physis,* nature, and *hypostasis,* hypostasis, to speak of a person. But they had invariably used the first term, nature, equivocally, and even the precise St Cyril had used it sometimes to mean person or self, and at other times to mean nature or essence; furthermore, they had used the word "nature" to mean sometimes essence in the abstract (manhood) and at other times essence in the concrete (human nature as realized in James or John). Proclus suggested that the term hypostasis should be used to denote an essence, that is, what kind of reality an individual thing is. Thus hypostasis concerns "who"; nature or essence concerns "what." By adopting this usage the old ambiguous formula adopted by St Cyril, "the one nature of the God-Logos become flesh," is changed to "the one hypostasis or person of the God-Logos becomes flesh"; had this change been made earlier, many of the misunderstandings which had bedevilled the discussions between the rival schools of Alexandria and Antioch might have been removed. Though this new terminology was adopted rapidly, the actual situation was so complex that there was no chance of confusion being removed instantaneously as though by magic. The Greeks, lovers of subtleties, warmed more than any Westerner can appreciate to the possibility of theological jousts; they could never let any change for the better take place quietly without a fray.

Eutyches was an ardent disciple of St Cyril. Cyril had evidently held him in esteem and had sent him a copy of the acts of the Council of Ephesus. He certainly prided himself on his knowledge of St Cyril's theology and work, but it is equally certain that he had little understanding either of the great doctor's thought or of the theological formulas associated with his name. He took his stand on the text of the famous anathemas, the wording of which Cyril had recast for the sake of making terms with John of Antioch, and of convincing the Antiocheans that his insistence on the unity of Christ's Person in no way impaired the reality of his two natures. Eutyches, however, was one of the many Alexandrian supporters of the saint who regretted this (so-called) compromise he had made for the purpose of making peace with John in 433, and who wished to defend Cyril now that he was dead by adhering literally to the text of the original formulas he had used against Nestorius. But he misinterpreted the meaning of these formulas so seriously as to say that in Cyril's doctrine Christ was not one in nature, or consubstantial, with us in his manhood. He held that the human nature that Christ took was absorbed into the divine nature in some way and so changed after the Word became flesh (or as the Word became flesh), because it was absorbed by the divine nature "like a drop of oil in the sea." Eutyches thus launched a new trend of theological opinion which reacted against Nestorianism in the direction of Apollinarianism in that it emphasized the reality of the divinity of Christ at the expense of his human nature. But it went far beyond the position of Apollinaris, who had at least accepted the reality of Christ's physical human nature, to the extreme limit of the oldest Christological heresy of Docetism, for Monophysitism denied that Christ's human nature *remained* a human nature once it had been united to the Word. He held, then, that Christ is one Person with one nature. In holding that the human nature was absorbed by the divine nature in such a way that Christ had only one nature, that of the incarnate God-Logos, Eutyches was in fact saying that Christ's human nature could only have been apparent. There were other problems. If Christ's human nature was not consubstantial with ours, how could it have been taken by the Word from the Virgin Mary, and how can we honour Mary as the Mother of God? If Christ did not owe anything to her as to his Mother, to whom did he owe the apearance of his human nature? Eutyches' answers to questions like these were confused. The least that could be said was that he was not clear in his own mind about the definitions of the Council of Ephesus. His confusion of thought was made quite plain when he appeared, after many summons and with the assurance of the patrician Florent, a friend of Theodosius who stood bail for him, before a synod held at Constantinople in 448 to try him. It was only possible to obtain a confused statement from him:

> I do not say that the body of the man became the body of God, but I speak of the human body of God, and I say that the Lord was made flesh of the Virgin. . . . I acknowledge that before the union of the divine and human natures, there were two natures, but after the union I do not recognize more than one.[3]

St Leo the Great taught, in the famous letter he sent to Flavian (known as the *Tome of Leo*, written 449) in which he condemned Eutyches, that it is not merely inexact, but positively incorrect to speak of two natures *before* the union, because the human nature Christ assumed did not exist before the Word was conceived as man. Before the Annunciation the Word alone existed as God. The bishops assembled at the synod of Constantinople had not noted this important point. Nonetheless, the synod under the direction of Flavian, the patriarch of Constan-

[3] See G. Bardy, *Histoire de l'Eglise,* IV, p. 216. Also Karl Adam, *The Christ of Faith,* pp. 38–40.

tinople, stated the doctrine of the universal Church in a formula which is thoroughly Leonine in character: "after the Incarnation Christ had two natures in one hypostasis of person; there is one Christ, one Son and one Lord." The synod condemned Eutyches and deprived him of his dignity of archimandrite.

Eutyches was thoroughly out of his depth, but instead of submitting to the synod he persisted in his doctrine and took as his line of defence the astonishing plea that his formula, if not the same as, bore at least a remarkable resemblance to those of St Cyril so that he could not be in the wrong. He made a demonstration of being at one with St Cyril by appealing first of all to the pope, then to the protection of the new patriarch of Alexandria, Dioscorus, and finally, opening a program of intrigues at the palace of the emperor to win support for his cause. The emperor, Theodosius II, befriended Eutyches, and as the final result of all his maneuvers the emperor decided to call another Council at Ephesus in August 449 where he appointed Dioscorus to act as supreme judge and arbiter. The pope, St Leo, met this emergency by sending three legates to preside at the Council, but when they appeared they were not allowed to read the letter, the famous *Tome,* St Leo had sent to Flavian, saying that Eutyches had been justly condemned at the synod of Constantinople. Dioscorus dictated how the deliberations of the Council were to be conducted, and enforced his will with threats of imperial sanctions against any bishop who opposed Eutyches. The imperial Praetorian guards were in attendance to see that Dioscorus had his way. The Council rehabilitated Eutyches, and condemned Flavian together with Eusebius of Dorylaeum, who had raised the opposition to Eutyches' heresy in the first place. When the meeting eventually became a tumult Eusebius and one of the papal legates, Hilary, managed to get away, and, after narrowly escaping capture, they eventually reached Rome to report what happened to Leo. The luckless Flavian was beaten up and dragged away from the altar to be trampled upon by the mob which probably included soldiers and monks. He died of his wounds three days later on his way to exile. Such, in brief, is the story of the famous "Robber Council of Ephesus."

At this crucial juncture in the course of events Theodosius died and in 450 he was succeeded by the devout Pulcheria who later married Marcian. The empress immediately came to terms with the pope and they decided between them to rectify the disaster by putting the whole matter of the union of the two natures in Christ once more before the bishops assembled at another General Council. But St Leo only agreed to the Council as necessary for the sake of ensuring peace, and on condition that the truths of faith he had himself set forth in the *Tome* he had sent to be read at Ephesus, and the doctrine that had been stated at the synod of Constantinople, were accepted as beyond all doubt and not included on the agenda as requiring discussion. He appointed as legates three bishops and two priests: among the bishops was Julian of Cos, a Greek who had lived for a long time at Rome, and who was particularly well qualified to act as a mediator. Though convoked at first to meet at Nicaea, the Council actually opened in the neighbourhood of Constantinople, at Chalcedon, on October 8, 451.

Two sessions sufficed to clear Flavian of all the accusations of heresy that had been brought against him, and to expose the infamy of Dioscorus' conduct at the Robber Council. At the third session Dioscorus was convicted of abusing his authority and deposed. At the fourth the attention of the Fathers turned to the theology of the Incarnation, but, in accordance with the directives of the pope, there was no debate about the truths stated by him in his *Tome*. Paschasius, the papal legate who presided over the Council, declared: "The Council has as its rule of faith what has been defined at the Council of Nicaea and what the 150 bishops assembled at the Council of Constantinople by the great Theodosius confirmed; it accepts the statement that Cyril made of the faith at Ephesus, and that which the venerable Leo, bishop of all the Churches, has given of it in his letter condemning the heresies of Nestorius and Eutyches. Such is the faith of this Council and such is the faith to which it binds itself without suppressing or adding anything."

All the bishops welcomed this declaration that the doctrine of Pope Leo was one with that of the earlier Councils and of St Cyril, and agreement was within sight of being reached when a number of bishops from Egypt, spurred on by their partisan allegiance to the memory of Cyril, raised the whole issue once again in a characacteristically polemical manner. They stated that if the Council professed in the clear-cut way of Pope Leo's *Tome* the presence of two natures in Christ after the union, they feared a return of Nestorianism with a vengeance. They were, of course, grounding their fears on their own confusion in the use of the terms "nature-essence" and "nature-hypostasis or person." Quite understandably, the Latin bishops, whose terminology was more exact and whose outlook was more realistic, were by now exasperated by the anticipation of further wrangling on the part of a minority of Greek bishops. But this last-minute intervention only showed how necessary it was to find a formula of faith that all could accept. Thus a series of secret meetings and discussions was undertaken by a commission composed of the papal legates, six oriental bishops and several influential members of the group from Alexandria. Dioscorus himself was well and truly condemned, but it was necessary to win the support of the self-styled "Cyrillians" to a formula of faith, and above all to the teaching of St Leo contained in the *Tome,* which had clarified and done away with the ambiguities of Cyril's twelve anathemas. The formula of faith that was eventually adopted at this great Council marks a major step forward in the theology of the Incarnation in that it put an end to such one-sided interpretations of the doctrine of St Cyril as those embodied in the errors of Nestorius and Eutyches, and it stated the Catholic faith precisely and plainly. . . .

This formula despite, or rather because of, its length left nothing unconsidered nor hanging vaguely in the air. It gave a precise and definite answer to all the difficulties which had been raised during the past thirty years, and which had led so many into the most lamentable errors. The crux of the mystery is stated to be that in the one Person of Christ, the Word of God, there are two natures which are radically different from each other, the one uncreated and the other created. It is worth noting that, on the question as to how these two natures are united, the Council said nothing about the point St Leo had made in his *Tome* condemning Eutyches, namely that of the two natures one alone pre-existed, that of the Word. It was, however, obviously important to insist that Christ's human nature never existed on its own before it was assumed by the Word, to safeguard the unity of Person in Christ. The Council did this by saying that Christ is complete *in* two natures; it avoided saying that he came to be *from* the uniting of the two. The so-called "Cyrillians" were, however, not enthusiastic in their acceptance of this great formula; even after accepting it, they continued to voice certain difficulties and, as far as they were concerned, the peaceful settlement was, alas, something of a compromise. Three days later the Council disbanded after a final session to proclaim its faith and manifest its gratitude to God for the successful accomplishment of its work. The Fathers acclaimed the faith of all in the Incarnate Word of God, and its debt to the emperor and his wife. Christian tradition, however, for which emperors and empresses count for little in the making of conciliar decisions and definitions, has retained above all the memory of the saying ascribed to the assembly of the Fathers after they had heard the reading of the *Tome* hailing the doctrine of Leo: "Peter has spoken through the mouth of Leo: such is the faith." The beginning of the letter of homage that the bishops sent to the pope by the legates acknowledges his authority quite explicitly:

> You have come to us: you have been for us the interpreter of the voice of Blessed Peter, and you have procured for all the blessing of his faith. We have been able to manifest the truth to the children of the Church in the communion of one and the same spirit.

Thus the Catholic doctrine of the Incarnation has come down to us through the ages, and it comes immediately not so much from St Cyril the patriarch, as from St Leo the pope. However final the teaching of the Council of Chalcedon has been, it is sad to have to say that it achieved so much that a certain artificiality in the concluding peace settlement was almost unavoidable. The progress made by the Council is clear for us all to see today, but at the time it was far from being shared by all in the same fruitful manner, especially for some of the Greek-speaking theologians and Eastern Christians. Worst of all, Monophysitism was not dead: it survived the condemnation of Chalcedon, in particular in parts of Africa where the attachment to the terminology of St Cyril, still badly understood, blinded many to the progress that the theology of the Catholic Church had made. In Palestine numbers of monks rallied to the support of Dioscorus and Eutyches almost as soon as the Council had finished.

2. J. McIntyre[1] maintains that the formula of the Chalcedonian definition does not appear to correct what he considers Cyril's violation of the

[1] John McIntyre was born in 1916 in Scotland. He was professor of Theology at St. Andrew's University in Sydney from 1946 to 1956. Since then he has been professor of Divinity at the University of Edinburgh. It is from his book *The Shape of Christology* (Philadelphia: Westminster Press, 1966), that this excerpt has been taken, pp. 83, 93–101.

generally accepted metaphysical principle of "no physis anhypostatos." The two possibilities by which the vacuum may be filled are represented in the views of Leontius of Byzantium and Ephraim of Antioch. The author prefers the latter's views.

The Two-Nature Model. It will have become clear by now that in a quite fundamental way the model is the controlling element in the development of any discipline. It determines how we shall handle the given from which the discipline takes its beginning. It dictates the method we follow in imposing form and structure upon the given. It regulates our discussions with one another upon the validity or invalidity of statements made within the given. . . .

Beginning with the two-nature model I should like to indicate its main constituent features. The feature that is most obvious is, of course, the description of the person of Jesus Christ as both human and divine. . . .[2]

The Chalcedonian Definition. This is what is thought to be the classical expression of it (the two-nature model in Christology).

> Therefore, following the holy fathers, we all unanimously teach that Jesus Christ is to be confessed to be one and the same Son, our Lord Jesus Christ, the same perfect in Godhead, the same perfect in manhood, and the same truly man, consisting of a rational soul and body, of one nature with the Father in respect of his Godhead, and of one nature with ourselves in respect of his manhood. . . . One and the same Christ, Son, Lord, Only-begotten, to be acknowledged in two natures (which exist in him) without confusion, without change, without division, without separation; the difference in nature being in no way removed as a result of the union, but rather the property of each nature being preserved and concurring in one person (*prosōpon*) and *hypostasis.*

It is now commonly acknowledged that this document is at its most explicit when it excludes the heresies. No Eutychean or Nestorian could find much comfort here. But when we try to advance beyond the negatives into a definition of the positive view which is offered there is not much to guide us, within the document itself. Clearly the unity which we took to be part of the two-nature is here affirmed. It is *one and the same* Son who is the subject of our confession and acknowledgment; no suggestion here of a Duad of Sons, or of two Christs. Even when it is said that there are two natures with two series of properties, nevertheless these properties concur in a single person and a single hypostasis. This fact can not be too often repeated, in reply to critics of Chalcedon who aver that it presents a dualistic view of Jesus Christ. In an almost literal sense, its first and its last words about Jesus Christ are that he is *one.*

As we have just seen, going on to look for the other features of the two-nature model, it is equally explicit that in Jesus Christ the two natures, human and divine, exist to their fulness. As eternal Son, he is consubstantial with the Father; here is the fulness of Godhead in no way diminished by reason of the incarnation. In his human nature, he is identical in essence with

[2] McIntyre goes on to discuss now the *Biblical Picture of Jesus, the Aristotelian Sources of the Two-Nature Model,* and *Eutychianism.*

ourselves. The presence in him of deity in no way reduces his human nature to an illusion. It is possible in reference to Jesus to deploy two series of properties and to affirm them equally of the single person.

When we continue beyond that point and endeavour to identify the person to whom the two natures are attributed, it would almost certainly appear that it is the hypostasis of the divine nature of the Logos, who is the subject of the incarnational situation. I must say "almost certainly" because however closely you look at the text it is difficult to see what the document really intends. This much is clear: there is no question of there being a second hypostasis or person. In other words, there cannot be a human hypostasis. This interpretation of the situation is at this point reinforced by reference to Cyril in whose writings it is somewhat clearer that the human nature of Jesus Christ is a *physis anhypostatos.* Whether Cyril tries to correct this patent violation of the principle of "no *physis anhypostatos*" as H. R. Mackintosh suggests, it has to be admitted that no attempt is made within the four corners of the Chalcedonian definition to make any such correction. It is for this reason that popular criticisms are levelled at the Chalcedonian definition: it offers an impersonal view of the human nature of Christ (*anhypostasia*). For us "impersonal" means hard, callous, indifferent, even unloving; and it is a term with pejorative connotations, and in this context even damning implications. However, if we do apply it to Chalcedon—and there is no real evidence to suggest that we should—it is to be construed logically; or at most ontologically, as signifying that the human *physis* of Jesus Christ had no human *hypostasis.* It is assumed in the definition—a point that might be questioned—that this lack does not reduce the true humanity of Christ.

What must, I think, be said however is that so firmly is the "no *physis anhypostatos*" principle rooted in the minds of all participants in the christological controversies of the fifth and sixth centuries that the vacuum which was created by the indecision of Chalcedon on the matter of an *hypostasis* for the human nature was one to be abhorred. It is a matter of consequent interest to discover how it was filled. Two possibilities existed and they were adopted. Curiously enough, they have both acquired importance for our modern handling of the two-nature model.

Leontius of Byzantium. The first is traditionally associated with the name of Leontius of Byzantium (*c.* 485–543). That interpretation of the Chalcedonian definition which denied that the human *physis* of Jesus Christ had an *hypostasis* came to be known as *anhypostasia;* and it was in contradistinction to that view that Leontius sought to solve the same problem with his theory of *enhypostasia.* . . . [*We know*]how the "no *physis anhypostatos*" principle had operated to give both Eutycheanism and Nestorianism; and how, also, the Chalcedonian position because of its failure to conform to the principle was in a rather unstable position. We . . . [*know*] how the original principle of "no *physis anhypostatos*" derives very directly from the *Categories* of Aristotle, with a variation, in specific nomenclature. Leontius, in giving the two-nature model his cash-values draws more heavily upon the reserves of Aristotelian logic. He does so in two stages. First, to begin with, he elaborates considerably upon what is involved in the term "nature" (*physis*). Following the Aristotelian conception of definition as *per genus et differentiam* he holds that *physis* is to be defined in terms of genus, species and essential qualities and properties. These terms all apply to what we would call the universal, i.e. "nature" is that which the particular entity shares with all the fellow-members of the genus. *Hypostasis,* on the other hand, carries the reference to the principle of self-existence, particular and individual existence, of the sort the single entity has over against the logical group. The individual instance is distinguished from the other members of the group by peculiar characteristics of its own, *idiōmata aphoristika,* some of which are separable accidents (*symbebēkota chōrista*) and others are lasting (*symbebēkota achōrista*). So far nothing that makes any great difference to the basic interpretation of the two-nature model has been contributed by Leontius. Secondly, he affirms, in line with the Chalcedonian definition, that the human nature of Jesus Christ has no *hypostasis* of its own, but adds that it is not on that account *anhypostatos.* In fact, it is a *physis enhypostatos,* an enhypostatic nature; it finds its *hypostasis* in *(en)* the *hypostasis* of the Logos. Through the union with the divine nature, and as a result of not having an *hypostasis* of its own, the human nature is not absorbed. Its integrity is preserved through its sharing in the *hypostasis* of the Logos. The distinguishing characteristics of the particular man who Jesus was are then attributed to the divine *hypostasis* as well as the essential qualities of the species (man) to which he belongs. In this way he has secured a form of Chalcedonianism against the principle that it is impermissible, even impossible, to affirm a *physis* without an *hypostasis.*

This view was destined to have such a normative effect upon subsequent christology, both in the seventh century and in our own time, that it might be important to draw attention to three *prima facie* defects which it seems to have.

First, there is the criticism which Harnack made[3] so long ago, and it is echoed by H. R. Mackintosh,[4] that "A pious Apollinarian monk would probably have been able to say with regard to the *hypostēnai en tō Logō:* Apollinaris says pretty much the same thing only in somewhat more intelligible words." It is not unusual to substantiate this charge of Apollinarianism by pointing out, as does W. N. Pittenger[5] that on enhypostatic terms, the human nature of Christ has consequently no strictly personal center; there is no ego around which the human life may move and upon which its experiences can "home." So the question has to be raised whether we may rightly ascribe to Jesus Christ the fulness of humanity, or whether in fact E. L. Mascall is correct in saying (though the very phrase is a self-condemnation) that Christ's human nature is an abstraction. Clearly the enhypostatic theory is not Apollinarianism in the strict sense. For, while Leontius affirms that the Logos takes human nature, Apollinaris speaks more

[3] *History of Dogma* (ET) (Williams and Norgate 1898) IV, pp. 233–4 n. 3.
[4] *The Person of Jesus Christ,* p. 218.
[5] *The Word Incarnate,* Nisbet 1959, pp. 100–3.

specifically of the *flesh*. There are sentences like: "He who was once without flesh is now revealed in flesh as God incarnate (*Theos ensarkos*); but he remains still one and the same person," and again, "in Jesus Christ there is a unification of flesh with Godhead into one person."[6] Leontius' position therefore only resembles that of Apollinaris in so far as both of them omit from Christ's person the human ego. Even if we were to come at the question from the side of the trichotomic anthropology which Apollinaris employs, and to affirm that while Jesus Christ has a human body and mind, the human spirit is replaced by the Logos; we could find no clear parallel to anything in Leontius. It would perhaps also be a little premature to follow too closely Pittenger's interpretation of *hypostasis* as a center of human experiences; for, as we shall see later, it is not immediately justifiable to translate what is a strictly logical concept into psychological terminology. What we could say, however, is that if the *hypostasis* is an essential part of what we associate with humanity (even if it is not strictly a part of human nature as *physis*), then in respect of his humanity, Christ is not completely one with us.

A second criticism, which might be raised against the *enhypostasia* of Leontius concerns the relation of the divine *hypostasis* to the human *physis*. In the Aristotelian paradigm of this relation, the *prōtē ousia* is the individual in which the *deutera ousia* is particularized, or at least it is the subject of the particularized form of the *deutera ousia* or the universal. In other words, the *prōtē ousia* is not just a blank area in which we stick the stamps of the *deutera ousia;* and we are at liberty to choose whichever stamps we wish for the purpose. On the contrary, it is so closely and integrally related to and congruous with the *deutera ousia* that it is understandable and describable only in terms of the latter. When we substitute for the *prōtē ousia-deutera ousia* relation that of *hypostasis-physis,* then we see just how difficult it is to remove the human *hypostasis* in the belief that the divine *hypostasis* can function in its place. The particularity and individuality of the man Jesus would be removed. In fact, it would be impossible to differentiate the *man* Jesus from the man Peter or the man John unless, in some way, the human *hypostasis* were retained.

A third criticism of *enhypostasia,* and one which could be the most serious of all, follows. If the *hypostasis* is understood to be so linked to the *physis* humanity that the latter cannot exist except as particularized in the several *hypostasis* then the redemption of the whole man is placed in jeopardy. For there is another important christological principle which we have not so far stated, which runs: "What Christ did not take, he did not redeem."[7] If, therefore, the *hypostasis* forms part of what it means to be human, then surely man's redemption requires that the *hypostasis* in a man be redeemed as well as his *physis*. It was this principle, too, which was the final basis for the rejection of Apollinarianism: because Christ did not take the spirit of man, but only his

[6] The quotations in this sentence appear in Sellers' *The Council of Chalcedon,* respectively on pages 138 and 140.

[7] Greg. Naz., *Ep.* ci.

body and mind, the spirit of man was placed beyond the range of Christ's redemptive power. At this same point, any doctrine involving *anhypostasia* would be open to criticisms of being a defective basis for soteriology. In a very real sense any christology stands or falls by the soteriology which it makes possible, or implies.

Barth on enhypostasia. The enhypostatic christology has come to figure so centrally in Barthian theology that it may not be inappropriate to consider what Barth himself has said on the subject.[8] Drawing upon such writers as Hollaz, Polanus and Heidegger, Barth says that *hypostasis* meant the independent existence, the *propria subsistentia* of Christ's humanity. The human essence is adopted by the Logos and taken into unity with himself. Barth also feels that to say that it was a *homo,* a particular man, that was united with the Logos and not *humanitas* would allow a degree of autonomy to the human nature which would endanger the whole of christology. Barth does not explain the reason for his rejection of such autonomy, but one might guess either that it would imply Nestorianism, or that it would assign an unduly high place to the creature alongside the redeemer in the incarnation. Man would be a corredemptor. Barth is, however, aware of something rather like the difficulties we have been mentioning which the enhypostatic theory raises for the right presentation of the human nature of Jesus Christ. . . .

Barth seems to think that what the *enhypostasia,* presupposed in the enhypostatic doctrine, denies is the autonomous existence of the humanity of Christ. But it is more than doubtful not only whether the *propria subsistentia* is rightly translated as "independent existence," and whether any christologian, even the most extreme Nestorians, ever thought of the human nature as autonomous. Accordingly Barth goes on in fact to mention what the anhypostatic theory would deny, namely, that the *humanum* exists in Jesus Christ in the form of an actual man. (One wonders if Barth would accept *prosōpon* as a fair translation of the term, and admit that there are then two *prosopa* in Jesus Christ.) Barth makes a final break with the logic out of which the whole enhypostatic theory has been constructed when he says that Jesus Christ is a real man only as the Son of God: for it is no longer possible to see the original *prōtē ousia—deutera ousia* distinction on which that theory rests in the relation of a "real man" to the Son of God. Barth, I should say, is right in insisting upon the fact that in Jesus Christ the *humanum* exists in the form of an actual man (though how, having said so, he can still believe that in Jesus it was not a *homo, i.e.* a particular man, but *humanitas* that was united with the Logos, is difficult to understand). But if he still wishes to avoid both Nestorianism and Docetism then he must revise his definition of the human *hypostasis* (as equivalent to "independent existence") and of its relation to the human nature and to the divine *hypostasis.*

Ephraim of Antioch. It has always been of interest to me both that the quite radical difficulties which have been mentioned above in connection with the enhypostatic interpretation of the Chalcedonian definition have not inhibited the widespread development

[8] *Church Dogmatics* IV/2 (ET), (Edinburgh: T. & T. Clark, 1958), pp. 49f.

of this theory and that a possible modification of a theory which goes a long way to meeting some of the difficulties has not been presented in this setting. I am referring to Ephraim of Antioch, whose views have been preserved for us in the writings of Photius of Tyre, . . . He maintains customary Chalcedonian positions, for example, that Jesus Christ is of one nature with the Father in respect of Godhead, and of one nature with men in respect of his humanity; that the two natures are not to be divided, for "two natures does not mean two *hypostaseis*." But what I would consider to be his originality emerges when he tries to explain the "two natures in the union which is according to *hypostasis*"[9] by saying that while the two natures as such are not confused or compounded one with the other, the two *hypostaseis* are. Accordingly the *hypostasis* of Jesus Christ is a fusion of the human and the divine *hypostasis*: it is *synthetos hē hypostasis*. I am not interested to argue the authenticity of Photius' review of Ephraim's theories, or even the validity of Ephraim's other theological assertions. But it does seem that his theory of the *synthetos hē hypostasis,* the composite *hypostasis,* meets not a few of the difficulties created by the enhypostatic theory.

For example, first of all, by insisting upon the presence, in the composite *hypostasis,* of the human *hypostasis* it secures the wholeness of the humanity which Jesus Christ took, and firmly avoids the docetic and Apollinarian tendencies of the enhypostatic theory. Jesus Christ is a real man, not simply *humanitas* or the *humanum,* so really man, in fact, that it was possible for someone to write a purely human account of his life and death. In view of the different ways in which subsequent writers e.g. W. N. Pittenger, have come to use the two-nature model, this advance on *anhypostasia* and *enhypostasia* which doctrinally guarantees the integrity of the human nature of Jesus, is a genuine gain. On the strictly technical side it serves to protect Chalcedon from the common charge that it operates with an "impersonal" view of the human nature of Jesus Christ.

Next, if we follow up the soteriological approach to Ephraim's theory, we could argue that it also secures the totality of the atonement of man. There is no hidden corner of his person, no aspect of his whole being which escapes the redemptive power of God. All has been taken, and all has been redeemed. Thirdly, it meets Barth's criticism that if we allow that the Logos took not only *humanitas* but also *homo,* then we affirm the autonomy and the independence of human nature. For, if the human nature has an *hypostasis* which is conjoined with that of the divine nature, there is an end of independent existence and autonomy. God brings the human nature and its *hypostasis* under his control as its creator and redeemer.

Fourthly, Ephraim's theory has this additional advantage that it answers to the way in which we speak about the events of the incarnation. If we were to ask, "Who is the subject of the stories which the Gospels record? Who took the loaves and the fishes and with them miraculously multiplied fed the multitude? Who suffered and died on Calvary? Who, indeed, was raised from the dead?," there could be but a single answer, "Jesus Christ," and not "the

[9] Quoted by R. V. Sellers, *op. cit.*, p. 323, *q.v.* for an interesting account of Ephraim.

Son of God, *simpliciter.*" The latter phrase, "the Son of God" would appear as the subject in a sentence answering the question, "Who was incarnate?" Answer: "The Eternal Son of God." But after the incarnation, it is the God-man who is subject of what subsequently happens. In the end, this fact explains why it is so artificial, if not entirely erroneous, to try to assign some of the experiences to one nature, and some to the other. The God-man may "have access" to certain experiences because he is divine, and to others because he is human; but ultimately it is he himself, and not either of his natures, who has the experiences and is the subject of them.

3. E. G. Jay[1] analyzes the most relevant criticisms that modern authors raise against the Chalcedonian definition. He recognizes in them a certain validity, particularly in their examination of the terminology used. However, he maintains that the definition preserved the essential meaning of the event of Jesus as the Christ. He sees the definition as the most eloquent expression of the two-nature model in Christology.

. . . we shall . . . state our objections which are frequently made to the Chalcedonian Definition. . . .

1. *It is negative.* The Chalcedonian Definition of Christ's person purports to protect the New Testament teaching, and the conviction of the Christian Church, that in Christ God was reconciling the world to himself, and that he is truly God and truly man. The Definition was constructed to exclude what were believed to be errors which made it impossible to hold that God had in fact acted in Christ for man's total salvation. Here arises the first, and perhaps the least serious, of the criticisms. It is that it is negative, and therefore of little use to those who seek positive help in understanding the person of Jesus. "Properly speaking," says Bishop J. A. T. Robinson, "it is not a solution but a statement of the problem."[2] This has long been recognized. As long ago as 1891 Bishop Charles Gore wrote of the dogmatic decrees of the Councils that they were "only limits, negatives which block false lines of development, noticeboards which warn us off false approaches, guiding us down the true road to the figure in the Gospels."[3] This, however, is hardly a criticism. A negative function may well be useful, and lead to a positive value. Chalcedon certainly on the negative side rules out Nestorianism and Eutychianism, marking them as "false approaches" to an understanding of Christ. It can be *criticized* for this only by those who want to reintroduce these teachings. No theologian today may want to introduce Eutychianism. But there is reason to suppose that some would like to revive an Adoptionism not unlike that which was implied in Nestorianism.

---

[1]E. G. Jay, Ph. D., is the Dean of the Faculty of Divinity and Professor of Historical Theology at McGill University. It is from his book *Son of Man, Son of God* (London: S.P.C.K., 1965) that this excerpt is taken from pp. 74–80.

[2] J. A. T. Robinson, *Honest to God* (S.C.M., Westminster Press, 1963), p. 65.

[3] Charles Gore, *The Incarnation of the Son of God* (Scribners, 1891), p. 118 (1905 ed.).

2. *It is expressed in out-dated philosophical language.* It is a more serious criticism that the orthodox definition uses the concepts and terminology of Greek philosophy which are no longer accepted. It is pointed out that it was a philosophy which used static terms: it sought to understand an object by means of definition, putting it into its proper class and differentiating it from other instances of the same class by noting its particular "accidental" qualities. Such definition was often assumed to provide the fullest possible knowledge. This was the "science" of the ancient world. But when Christian thinkers sought for terms in which to express their faith they could hardly do otherwise than employ those used by the serious thinkers of their day. "If people thought at all, they could only think in that kind of medium."[4] Thus we find them using such terms as "essence" or "substance" and "accident," "nature" and *hupostasis, genus, species* and *differentia.* These terms are not used in contemporary science and philosophy. Nobody imagines that we can understand an object by placing it in its proper *genus* and noting its differences from other members of that *genus,* or by a consideration, of some aspect of the object called its "substance" or "nature." Such concepts seem mere abstractions to the modern mind. Speaking broadly, modern philosophy views reality dynamically, and not statically; and modern science studies an object in its functions. From the point of view of modern science it could with justice be said that the categories of thought used by the Fathers of the first five centuries are bankrupt: they produce nothing in the way of positive knowledge. William Temple in his contribution to *Foundations* in 1912 spoke of the Chalcedonian Definition as "a confession of the bankruptcy of Greek Patristic theology." Later he modified this sweeping condemnation, but still maintained that the formula marks "the definite failure of all attempts to explain the Incarnation in terms of Essence, Substance, Nature, and the like."[5] As Paul Tillich says, the conceptual tools used by the Chalcedonian Fathers were inadequate.[6] Yet he can say that the formula of Chalcedon "was true to the genuine meaning of the Christian message" and that "it saved Christianity from a complete elimination of the picture of Jesus as the Christ."[7]

If the philosophical concepts and terminology of the Chalcedonian formula are out of accord with modern modes of thought, they are equally strange to ancient Hebraic modes. In his contribution to *Soundings,* Canon H. W. Montefiore writes: "The biblical revelation is not expressed in philosophical terms, because the Jews did not think philosophically. They were concerned not with ontological definition but with dynamic function and with personal relationship.'[8] The Old Testament attempts no philosophical discussion of the nature of God. It is

---

[4] G. L. Prestige, *God in Patristic Thought* (S.P.C.K., 1956), p. xvii. On this point pp. xiii-xviii repay study.

[5] William Temple, *Christus Veritas* (Macmillan, 1924), p. 134.

[6] Paul Tillich, *Systematic Theology,* vol. II (Nisbet: University of Chicago Press, 1957), p. 161.

[7] *Ibid.,* p. 163.

[8] *Soundings,* ed. A. R. Vidler (Cambridge, 1962), chapter 7, "Towards a Christology for Today" by H. W. Montefiore, p. 157.

concerned with what God has done and will do. The New Testament also is primarily concerned "with what Christ did for men, and with the difference that this makes to our relations with God and with one another."[9] Montefiore quotes two other theologians, Gregory Dix and Oscar Cullmann, who insist that biblical christology is a christology of function rather than of status, although they admit that when the Gospel was preached to Greeks, the question of Christ's status and nature was inevitably raised "because that was the only way in which Greeks could think."

It is, therefore, a frequent criticism of Chalcedon that it used concepts which were alien alike from the biblical witness to Christ and from the modern way of thinking. Yet there is a readiness to admit that it could not have been otherwise. Even so independent a thinker as Tillich can say that the definition preserved the essential meaning of "the event of Jesus as the Christ." The implication of this, it seems to many, is that we should seek a fresh formula which will express the truth of Christ's person in concepts at once more modern and more biblical. It is suggested that we need dynamic concepts which will lead to knowledge of his person through an understanding of his activity, rather than static concepts which attempt to "place" him by defining his nature.

3. *It is dualistic.* But some modern theologians are not prepared to give even so much approval to the Chalcedonian Definition. They have attacked it as implying, through its insistence on the two natures, a duality of persons little different from the Nestorianism it purports to exclude. Harnack, quoting the Tome of Leo, says, "The proposition . . . 'each nature in communion with the other does what is proper to it' actually makes two subjects out of one."[10] H. R. Mackintosh speaks of Chalcedon's "blank unrelieved insistence upon the eternal parallelism of two natures," and says that such "a twofold personality is not merely something that we fail to understand; it is something we see quite well to be impossible. In fact a being in whom now the God acts, now the man, is equally repellent to faith and theory."[11] But such criticisms are not altogether fair to the Chalcedonian Fathers. They certainly affirmed that Jesus Christ is Son of God and Lord "recognized in two natures," and this was later elaborated as implying "two wills and two activities." But, in spite of some unwary sentences, they did not mean that Jesus willed and acted alternately in his divine nature and in his human nature. For them (and the Definition by its repetition of the phrase "one and the same" insists on it), there is one agent, the Son of God incarnate, and all the thoughts, words, and actions are the thoughts, words, and actions of that one agent.

The charge of dualism is partly to be explained by the fact that several of the key words of the Definition are employed differently today. This is especially true of "Person," as translating the Greek *hupostasis,* and "Nature" as translating *phusis.* "Person"

---

[9] *Ibid.*

[10] A. Harnack, *History of Dogma,* vol. IV (English translation), (Williams and Norgate, 1893), pp. 223–4.

[11] H. R. Mackintosh, *The Doctrine of the Person of Christ* (Scribners, 1912), p. 296.

(*hupostasis*) in the Chalcedonian sense did not connote consciousness, will, capability, energy, or function, all of which were thought of as belonging to the *nature* of a thing. It meant rather a unique individualization which makes a "nature" concrete in a particular instance. It was a cold and somewhat colorless word which could be used of inanimate things as well as of living beings. The modern sense of the word "person" may be said to go back to Descartes' *cogito ergo sum,* I think, therefore I exist. A person is a center of consciousness. This, however, has been felt to be an inadequate definition, pointing solely to the passive side of personality as a receiving center of mental impressions. Some idealist philosophers have urged that personality is more truly defined in terms of will. Perhaps a putting together of the two points provides a modern definition of personality which would be generally accepted: personality consists in consciousness and will. A person is constituted when an entity establishes a relationship with the external world passively in consciousness, and actively in volition.

But in the thought of fifth-century philosopher-theologians consciousness and will were allotted not to the person (*hupostasis*), but to the "nature." To one who holds a modern idealistic view of personality the Chalcedonian doctrine appears, therefore, to be a doctrine of two persons. He will want to say to the Chalcedonian Fathers "What you call a nature I call a person. Your doctrine of Christ's two natures is really a doctrine of two persons, two streams of consciousness, and two wills, which simply does not make sense to me. And your '*hupostasis,*' which your Latin brothers translated *persona,* and which in our translations we render 'person,' is a needless complication, an abstraction without content."

We can, perhaps, begin to understand why it seems to some that Chalcedon is "a confession of the bankruptcy of Greek Patristic theology." The Greek theologians had come to an impasse. Their insistence on the true divinity and full manhood of Christ as well as the unity of his person testifies to their loyalty to the New Testament picture of Jesus, but the concepts they used and the terms in which they expressed themselves had brought them to the point at which questions were raised to which no intellectually satisfying answer was forthcoming, nor perhaps could be forthcoming.

4. *It raises unanswerable questions.* One instance of the kind of question which Chalcedon raises is mentioned by Professor Donald Baillie in his *God was in Christ.*[12] He is discussing modern attempts to restate the doctrine of "two natures, one *hupostasis,* and that the *hupostasis* of the Word." One such attempt[13] is the suggestion that in the Incarnation the divine Logos who is the subject of divine experience enters into human experience, and thus becomes also the subject of human experience. The difficulty Baillie sees is that if "the only 'subject' of the experience was God the Son, there seems to be no room left for what we surely find in the Gospel story: Jesus as a man having experience of God in faith and prayer, where God is not the 'subject' but the object." In other words,

[12] Scribner's, 1948, pp. 86–7.

[13] By Leonard Hodgson, in *Essays on the Trinity and the Incarnation,* ed. A. E. J Rawlinson (Longmans, 1928), p. 383.

what was happening when Jesus was praying? Was he praying to himself?

The Chalcedonian doctrine that it is the divine Logos who is the experiencing subject in the Incarnation raises other difficult questions, some of which occur to the simplest people. If Jesus was God must he not have known that he would not give in to temptation? Was not temptation much easier, then, for him to resist than for us? He must also have known that he would triumph over death. Were not his sufferings, therefore, more endurable for him than ours for us? There is an even more subtle question in connection with the consciousness of Jesus. If he was the eternal Word of God must he not have known it? We cannot without verging on the nonsensical think of one who is God without knowing that he is God. Now, since there is clearly personal continuity between the Babe of Bethlehem and the adult Jesus, are we to say that in his mother's arms he knew that he was the eternal Word? If he did not, could we think of him as in fact being the Word? If he did, can we think of his manhood as being like ours in all essentials?

Such questions are difficult to answer. One attempt to answer some of them was the kenotic (from the Greek *kenō,* to empty) theory of comparatively recent years. Bishop Charles Gore, who taught a cautious kenotic doctrine, put it thus: "The Incarnation is the supreme act of self-sacrificing sympathy, by which one whose nature is divine was enabled to enter into human experience. He emptied himself of divine prerogatives so far as was involved in really becoming man, and growing, feeling, thinking, and suffering as a man."[14] As Gore realized, a kenotic doctrine also raises problems, and Kenoticism has evoked heavy criticism.[15]

Bishop Frank Weston in *The One Christ*[16] is critical of kenotic theories, but his own restatement is not dissimilar: The Logos in assuming manhood is the subject or "ego" of all the experiences of the Incarnate, but he recognizes a "law of self-restrant."[17] He voluntarily restricts his divine consciousness and powers to the measure of the manhood at each stage of its growth.

These restatements of orthodox doctrine, though they take cognizance of modern theories of personality, still abound in difficulties. We have new terms, for example "ego" for *hupostasis,* "consciousness," for *phusis,* but the old questions remain.

4. J. Tixeront[1] studies the different forms of Monothelitism and their various stages of development. He examines the struggles, often influenced by

[14] Charles Gore, *Belief in Christ* (Murray, 1922), p. 226.

[15] See D. M. Baillie, *op. cit.,* pp. 94–8. But it appears to the present writer that Baillie's criticisms are directed at a kenoticism of the type of Thomasius, and miss the mark so far as Gore's version of it is concerned. For a sympathetic view of the kenotic theory, see Vincent Taylor, *The Person of Christ in New Testament Teaching* (Macmillan, 1958), c. 19, "Christology and the Kenosis."

[16] Longmans, 1907.

[17] *Ibid.,* p. 151 (2nd ed., 1914).

[1] J. Tixeront died in 1925. He was a professor at the University of Lyons and later of Toulouse. He authored many works, such as *Apologetical Studies, Handbook of Patrology, Holy Orders and Ordination.* This excerpt is taken from his book, *History of Dogmas* (St. Louis: B. Herder, 1916), Vol. III, pp. 164–179.

politics, which orthodoxy had to undergo to preserve the faith of the Fathers. He sees in the final rejection of Monothelitism the end of Christological controversies in Eastern Christianity.

Monothelitism . . . The Monothelite teaching . . . is rather confused and can hardly be understood without some previous explanations.

Orthodox Christology holds that the Divine Logos so united the human nature to Himself as to appropriate it to Himself and make it His own. Hence the actions and passions of that nature are referred to Him, as to the center of imputability; it is the Word Incarnate who acts and suffers in that nature and through it. But this must be carefully circumscribed. The human nature is not, in the hands of the Word, what an instrument is in the hands of an active principle, an ax, for instance, in the hands of a workman. For the personality, taken apart from the nature, has in itself no activity and is not a dynamic principle; it is a mere mode of being of the nature, the mode of existing apart by itself and constituting one independent physical whole. The personality is a *condition* necessary in order that the nature may exercise its activity, for an *anypostatos* nature can neither exist nor act; but the personality does not set that activity a-going. The actions and passions of the nature are referred to the person, not because the personality taken by itself is the main effective cause thereof, but because the concrete person comprises both the nature and the personality, i.e., expresses the whole to which the actions and passions of the nature—a part improperly so called of that whole—must be referred.

Therefore, when we say that the Word Incarnate acts and suffers in and through His human nature, what do we mean? Simply that the human nature, which exists in the Word as in its hypostasis or personality, acts and suffers, and that these actions and passions are rightly attributed to the concrete whole, to the person of the Incarnate Word. The same reasoning holds in regard to the divine nature of the Word, and thus we see that the divine and human activities and operations of Jesus Christ must be considered as forming two *parallel*[2] series. both of which have indeed the condition of their existence in the personality of the Word, but proceed from each of the two natures as from their true efficient principle.[3] These series, I say, are *parallel,* and not *subordinate:* the human activity is not physically subordinate to the divine activity, because it is not the divine *nature,* but the *person* of the Word, a mere subsisting relation, that has made the humanity its own. If, then, there is a harmony between these two activities, when exercised, that harmony is not obtained mechanically, as it were, but results from the free and spontaneous

[2] The word *parallel* must not be taken here in the strict geometrical sense, since the two series have a common meeting-point in the Word; the following remarks sufficiently illustrate my meaning.

[3] This is really what St. Leo meant to say in the famous phrase: "Agit enim utraque forma cum alterius communione quod proprium est." The word *forma* has the drawback of being abstract, but it shows aptly that the natures are, in Jesus Christ, the active principles. The activity of each nature is exercised "cum alterius communione," because the two natures are united in the Word.

consent of the man ordering his resolutions and actions in conformity with the divine will and actions.

These principles were altogether forgotten or purposely ignored by the Monothelites. Under the influence of Severian Monophysitism, which insisted always and everywhere on the person of the Word, or of Eutychian Monophysitism, which sublimated the human nature into the divine nature of Jesus Christ, and also, if we go back still further, under the influence of Apollinarianism, according to which Christ's humanity, being deprived of a human soul, was but a useless organ in the hands of His Divine nature, the Monothelites regarded the person of the Word as an active principle moving the human nature at its will, or making the latter, through the *idiōpoiēsis,* a property of the divine *nature.* The two activities—divine and human—are not exercised *coordinately,* but the human is *subordinate* to the divine, and, to use Sergius' words, is exercised only "when and how and inasmuch as the divine Word wills."

This dependence, however, may be conceived more or less absolutely, and the question is how the Monothelites understood it.

It may be assumed that the human faculties, including the will, no longer perform any spontaneous acts, but only act at the command and under the impulse of the divine will, which moves them and applies them to action, while the human will, which is also moved, merely transmits the divine impulse to the other faculties. The human will being thus reduced to a passive state, there is in Christ but one will *hen thelema,* the divine or hypostatic *thelema,* and only one operation, *mia energeia,* if considered in its primary source.

There is no doubt that this error was professed by Sergius and his partisans. . . . It is evident that these authors denied in Jesus Christ, as man, all spontaneity and free-will action. . . .

The question may be solved in a still more radical way by denying to the humanity of Jesus Christ any capacity of its own to act, making it a mere inert substance in which the divine activity is diffused and exercised almost as the human body receives its life and motion from the soul. The dynamic principle is one, and therefore the *energeia,* the action and operation of that principle, is one also. This view is called *Monenergism.* It seems that many Monothelites rejected this radical explanation of the unity of operation in Jesus Christ. It has been remarked that, except at the very beginning, Sergius, whilst insisting on the unity of will, merely demands that nothing be said either of the unity or the duality of the *energeia;* moreover, he does not seem to have denied, in the humanity of Jesus Christ, the existence of natural faculties capable of acting. It is probable, however, that several of his partisans did not imitate his reserve. In fact, Apollinarianism, from which Monothelitism evidently springs, had taught that in Jesus Christ the Word was the strength, the energy, the mover, whereas the humanity, or rather the body, was the passive element, that which was moved, the organ . . . Besides, the comparison of the union of the divine and human elements in Christ with that of the body and soul in man, on which the Monothelites insisted, led naturally to this conclusion, and in fact many must have drawn it.

There is a third way to conceive the unity of operation and will in Jesus Christ, viz., by considering all His acts as proceeding from one mixed theandric nature, and sharing the theandric character of the same. Some Eutychians may have thus understood the *energeia theandrikē* of Pseudo-Dionysius; but that was not the case with most Monothelites.

This, then, was the exact meaning of the formulas put forth by Sergius and the Emperor to win over the Monophysites: there is in Jesus Christ only one will and one truly spontaneous and free activity, the divine activity and will. Granting the existence of a human nature, its activity is completely subordinate to that of the divine; the humanity in the hands of the Logos is merely a docile instrument which He uses and which is devoid of any initiative of its own.

It is against this false concept of Christ's humanity that orthodox theologians took up the cudgels.

The Dyothelite Reaction up to the Lateran Council of 649. Pope Honorius . . . died October 12, 638. His successor, Severinus, who ruled only two months, may have had time enough to condemn Monothelitism. At any rate, John IV, who replaced him, had it condemned by a council held at Rome in January, 641 and conveyed the sentence to Heraclius. The latter died on February 11 of the same year, leaving the throne to his two sons. Heraclius Constantine and Heracleon. The Pope profited by this opportunity to send to them almost immediately an important letter explaining the true doctrine and asserting the orthodoxy of Pope Honorius.[4] He said that after Sergius had informed Honorius that some taught the existence of two contrary wills in Jesus Christ, the Pope had justly condemned that error. Man, who is born in sin and experiences the law of the flesh, has two opposing wills: *duas autem dico mentis et carnis invicem reluctantes;* but this is not the case with Jesus Christ, who was born innocent and without concupiscence: in His sacred humanity there was but one *human* will; and this was precisely what Honorius had meant to say. Instead, the Patriarch Pyrrhus and his followers represent him as attributing to Jesus Christ only one will, common both to the divinity and the humanity. This is a misrepresentation;[5] and besides, that view cannot be upheld. The unity of will would imply that either the Savior's divinity or His humanity is incomplete, according as one admits that that will is human or divine, or that the two natures are but one nature, should one admit that the only will and operation come both from the divinity and the humanity. In conclusion, the Pope asked the emperors to withdraw the Ecthesis.[6] . . .

Pope John IV died, October 12,

---

[4] Mansi, X, 682–686, and *P. L.*, LXXX, 602–607. The letter is dated from the year 641.

[5] The reader will observe that John IV defends Honorius only on the subject of the unity of the will. He does not extenuate his predecessor's prohibition to speak of one or two operations, nor his assertion that Holy Writ teaches nothing on the subject. Moreover, he sees in the text of Honorius the assertion of one *human* will in Jesus Christ. Honorius had in fact insisted upon the absence of concupiscence in Jesus Christ, but his conclusion was that, likewise, there was in Him but one divine and human will *as regards the willed object.* In truth, Honorius needed no defense on this last point.

[6] The *Ecthesis* was Heraclius' decree of 638 upholding one will in Christ. The *Typus* was Constans' decree proscribing all formulae in 648.

642, and Theodore was elected in his stead (November 24, 642). But the papal policy remained the same. . . .

In the year 648, the Emperor, at Paul's (Pyrrhus' successor) suggestion, published another edict—the *Typus*.

The *Typus* was intended to impose silence on both parties and to end the controversy by suppressing it. Monothelitism and Dyothelitism were dealt with on equal terms; all Christians were urged to abstain altogether from discussing whether there were in Christ one or two operations, one or two wills. The Ecthesis was withdrawn; but no one was to be molested on account of his former views, and severe punishments were enacted against offenders.

Had it been published some twenty years sooner, the *Typus* might have restored the peace; but now it was too late; the quarrel had become too bitter and called for an authoritative decision; silence was no longer possible. The discussion not only continued, but the debate took a wider range, and Rome prepared to strike a heavier blow.

Theodore, who died on May 14, 649, was succeeded, in the month of July, by Martin I, who had been apocrisiarius at Constantinople and knew the character of those with whom he had to deal. No sooner had he become pope than, spurred on by the abbot Maximus, he gathered at the Lateran, from October 5 till October 31, 649, a council of five hundred bishops, in which Monothelitism was closely examined, and which later on came to be regarded almost as a general council. The Pope did not hesitate to come forward personally, and spoke a great deal. In the fifth session, the teaching of the Monothelite documents that had been read in the third, was compared with that of the Fathers and of heretics who had been already condemned.[7] The outcome was a condemnation of the new error, couched in a profession of faith and twenty anathematisms. The profession of faith was that of Chalcedon, with this addition: ". . . Et duas eiusdem [Christi] sicuti naturas inconfuse, ita et duas naturales voluntates, divinam et humanam, et duas naturales operationes, divinam et humanam. . . ." The same doctrine was reproduced in the anathematisms, the second of which asserted the spontaneity of Christ's suffering for us, and thus marked the importance of the controversy from the soteriological point of view. The eighteenth was directed against Theodore of Pharan, Cyrus of Alexandria, Sergius, Pyrrhus, Paul of Constantinople, against the Ecthesis and the *Typus*.

The Sixth General Council . . . Pope Eugene . . . replaced Pope Martin on August 10, 654. He tried to reach an agreement and sent apocrisiaries to Constantinople. They were so cleverly deceived that they accepted a hybrid teaching recognizing in Jesus Christ three wills—two natural wills and an hypostatic will. This was again placing the principle of the Savior's human activity in the Word. On their return to Rome, the Pope's delegates were very coldly received. But Eugene died

[7] Three series of Patristic texts were brought forward to prove (1) that, according to the Fathers, the operation and the will spring from the nature, and not from the hypostasis, and consequently that the number of natures determines that of operations and wills; (2) that the Fathers ascribed to Christ two free-wills; and (3) that they ascribed to Him two natural operations.

on June 2, 657, and under the rule of his successors, . . . a sort of *modus vivendi,* based on mutual silence, was agreed upon with Constantinople, where the patriarchs were rapidly succeeding each other.

Once more, the Emperor's death put an end to the crisis. In the year 668, Constantine IV Pogonatus succeeded Constans II, who had been assassinated. He did not urge the acceptance of the *Typus,* and, as early as 678, asked Pope Agatho to send legates to Constantinople to examine peacefully and in good faith the question in dispute. . . .

He intended the meeting to be merely a conference for a quiet discussion of Monothelitism. But . . . the conference became a council, the 6th General Council.[8] It lasted from November 7, 680, to September 16, 681, and held eighteen sessions. . . .

The definitive sentence was promulgated in the 18th session, September 16, 681.[9] After reproducing the creeds of Nicaea and Constantinople, the Fathers of the Council accepted the letters of Agatho and his council to the Emperor, and repeated the creed of Chalcedon, with this addition: "We also declare that there are in Christ two natural *thelēseis* or *thelēmata,* and two natural operations, without separation, conversion, division or mixture, according to the teaching of the holy Fathers. And the two natural wills are not opposed to each other—God forbid—as the impious heretics said, but His human will follows, and it does not resist and oppose, but rather is subject to the divine and almighty will. For the will of the human nature [of Jesus Christ] necessarily moved, but also subjected itself to the divine, as the most wise Athanasius says." At the end, sentences of deposition and anathema are pronounced against all who are refractory, whether priests or laymen . . .

The condemnation pronounced by the 6th General Council was the deathblow of Monothelitism. The heresy revived from 711 to 713, through the exertions of the Emperor Philippicus, who had been a pupil of the monk Stephen; but only a short while. After it had been cut off from Monophysitism, in which it had its root, and deprived of the help of the secular power, Monothelitism could no longer maintain itself. It fell, and its fall brought the Christological controversies to a close in the East. These controversies had lasted for about three centuries; and it was through a sort of successive and regular balancing that the Church upheld, against the radical views that had been proposed, both the personal unity and the integrity of Christ's human nature. While the 5th General Council had confirmed the work of Ephesus, the 6th had resumed the principles of Chalcedon, and again proclaimed Jesus perfect in His manhood and endowed with a human will. Even merely verbal Monophysitism had not the last word, which proves that, contrary to what has been asserted, it was not the adequate and authentic expression of Greek piety.[10]

---

[8] Cf. the acts in Mansi, XI.

[9] Mansi, XI, 624–697.

[10] As is well known, Honorius' letters and his condemnation by the 6th General Council have given rise to heated controversies on the subject of papal infallibility and the right of a general council to judge the Pope. It belongs, of course, to dogmatic theology to solve these problems. However, I may be allowed to state that, to my mind, the difficulty

5. K. Rozemond[1] projects John of Damascus as the most genuine and eloquent representative of Eastern theology after Chalcedon. He put the final touch to Christological thought in the East. His Christology accords a preponderant place to the divinity of Christ's person. Yet this vision of Christ's divinity did not diminish the part played by the humanity which He assumed in its fullness. The Damascene writes both as a theologian and as a contemplative.

In 451 the council of Chalcedon gave the Church its great formulation on Christ: perfect in His divinity, perfect in His humanity; truly God and truly man; of the same essence as the Father and of the same essence as men; recognized as of two natures without admixture, change, division, or separation. Besides these definitions which underline with such insistance the duality in Christ, the council affirmed with just as much precision and force the unity of Him Whom it confessed to be God and man by proclaiming Him the one and the same Christ and by putting the accent on the fact that the two natures are united in a single person and a single hypostasis. For the first time here the words hypostasis and person are identified in a document of such importance, and this identification accorded to the conception of the unity of the person of Christ a new stability and metaphysical profundity. Moreover, the definitive distinction of the words hypostasis and nature permitted, in the interior of the personal and hypostatic unity of Christ, a radical distinction of human and divine natures.

Such is the mystery that the council transmitted to the reflection of subsequent centuries; the unity of the person-hypostasis of Christ and the perfection of the two natures which constitute this hypostasis. This is the formulation which during the centuries will hold the whole attention of Eastern theological thought. This thought, after having discovered and examined thoroughly the questions involved, will give its answers after a long maturation.

At the very heart of the difficulty which the council introduced by its double definition—having one person-hypostasis and two complete natures—it also gave a reference point from which all reflection must proceed: the subject concerning which these two opposed truths are stated, the person of Christ. Before proclaiming their definition of the person of Christ, the Fathers of the council had to name Him, and they did this in clear and simple terms. They called Him, Whose two natures united in a single person and hypostasis [they confessed,] ". . . one and the same Son, Our Lord Jesus Christ . . . ," ". . . one and the same Christ, the Only-begotten, Son, Lord . . . ," ". . . one and the same Only-begotten Son, Word of God, Lord Jesus Christ . . ." These titles

has been exaggerated. Honorius' mistake was one of practical judgment, due to lack of perspicacity and reflection, rather than a doctrinal error . . . cf. J. Chapman, *The Condemnation of Pope Honorius* (London, 1907).

[1] Keetje Rozemond, sister of the Order De Grandchamp, is the author of *La Christologie de Saint Jean Damascène* (Buch-Kunstverlag Ettal, 1959). It is from this book that this excerpt is taken, from pp. 1–3, 104–105.

point out to us the irreducible foundation of Christological reflection for the Fathers of the council of Chalcedon as well as for later theologians: the One who is the object of theological researches is first recognized as Son, Lord, Only-begotten, Word. Before proclaiming whatever He might be regarding the constitution of His person, the Fathers simply addressed Him with titles, which, since the first ages of the Church (as found in the epistles of St. Paul and the Gospel of St. John) proclaim him to be God.

Florovskij, in his book on the Fathers of the fifth and sixth centuries, has written in this regard:

> There is, in the definition of Chalcedon, an unexpressed and paradoxical aspect. Already by the very arrangement of the statement it is clear that the divinity of the Word is considered as the hypostatic center of the divine-human unity, "One and the same Christ, Son, Lord, Only-begotten recognized in two natures . . . , one and the same Only-begotten Son." . . . But . . . the unity of the hypostasis is not directly defined as the hypostasis of the Word. It is from this, that the greatest obscurity springs concerning His human "nature." What does the acknowledgment of a "nature" but not of a hypostasis signify? Can it be perhaps that there is an "anhypostatic nature?" Historically such was the principal opposition of Chalcedon. In it the absence of a human hypostasis —in the sense known precisely from the "anhypostasicity" of the human nature in Christ—is clearly confessed. And it is NOT explained how this is possible. It is precisely in this point that the definition approaches closely the theology of St. Cyril. The acknowledgment of human "anhypostasicity" is the acknowledgment of the asymmetry of the divine-human unity . . .[2]

Let us keep here the term asymmetry that Florovskij used to designate the priority of Christ's divinity. This asymmetry, therefore, is at the basis of Eastern Christology since in its principal document—the one which perhaps most accentuates the duality of Christ's natures—Christ Himself is designated by His divine names.

Often the very great place given to Christ's divinity in the Christological thought of the East has been regarded as a subsequent development or even a deviation. Some tendencies more or less monophysite could have been taken up again in theology since the middle of the fifth century under the verbal protection of the council of Chalcedon, which was, however, diophysite. Such is the assumption, for example, in the whole line of historical development of Harnack in the second volume of his history of dogmas. This view can find some basis in reality. There was some excess in the thought and piety from the fifth to the seventh centuries . . . but to possess a correct view of Greek theology following the council of Chalcedon, one must begin by establishing this truth: the preponderant place accorded to the divinity of Christ's person has its basis in the dogma itself, such as it has been proclaimed by the Fathers of the council. If one does not begin by underlining this, the perspective from which one would study Christology after the fifth century would be fundamentally wrong. Behind the definition of Christ's humanity and divinity, there is the contemplation of Christ as God, and it is against this back-

[2] G. V. Florovskij, *Vizantinskii Otsi* V-VIII v., pp. 25–26.

ground that the Fathers and subsequent councils direct their efforts when reflecting on the complete humanity of Christ. This must be kept in mind.

This fundamental vision of Christ's divinity in Eastern theology will also be the center of . . . the Christology of St. John Damascene. However, it is necessary to closely examine the complete notions of his dogmatics on Christ's humanity at first in order to refute all suspicion of heresy that his stress put upon divinity can give rise to, and especially in order to show clearly the Damascene's view of that vast and total comprehension of the salvation that Christ has given us through His incarnation. However, the guideline which strikes one immediately on the first reading of his work, is his primordial centering of attention on Christ as God. It would be necessary to analyze the vision of divinity in all the difficult questions that our doctor has treated in his work, to see each time how he has made an effort to keep this vision without diminishing the part played by the fullness which Christ has assumed.

How was the vision of Christ as God, which was that of the Greek Fathers of the council of Chalcedon, taken up by St. John Damascene? . . .

Before being able to understand the researches of Damascene on the person of Christ, one must try to see why the Fathers, and St. John Damascene in particular, devoted so much careful attention and labor to Christology. The work of the Saint himself has furnished us with some indications for the answer . . . His detailed studies made about the constitution of the person of Christ had but one central motive: to establish that Christ as God had assumed the whole of human nature so that the whole of human nature might be saved by and through Him, especially that which was the cause of man's fall, his will, the root of his disobedience. This soteriologic interest is directly linked to the Gospel message. . . .

St. John Damascene deepened our knowledge of Christ's divinity. In his investigations devoted to the union of the two natures, the greatest place is always reserved for His divinity. With this vision of the greatness of the divine nature, the doctor penetrated the most difficult questions of Christ's mystery: In what sense can one say that He Who is the very Wisdom of God possesses but a limited knowledge? How can He Who was God complain of being abandoned by God? How does the Life come to death? Damascene's confession then becomes impressive, which proclaims that His divinity remains united to His humanity even in the lowest conditions which followed the fall of man.

The doctrine of the two natures displays itself in the work of St. John Damascene in a form so full, so complete, so mature, that one can consider it as a work of art. Certain problems could be posed, such as those which are reflected in the theological investigations of the nineteenth and twentieth centuries. But it should be stressed that even today, the Christology of this Byzantine doctor is worth knowing and studying with attention. It gives a structure of thought that can possess more clarity than one might believe, in regard to actual problems in the area of Christology. The effort demanded to understand the philosophic and dogmatic expression, tied, at least in part, to his historical age, is worth the trouble in order to perceive the central truths of this Christology. . . .

St. John Damascene expresses a vision of Christ valid for the whole Church. It is because of his love for it that he wrote his dogmatic works. He made known to the Church, guardian of the richness of tradition, the treasures of its dogma and theology. He gathered together the teaching of the centuries concerning Christ while meditating upon His revelation in the Gospel. By this fidelity to tradition, he entered into the deepest current of the Church, into its life guided by the Holy Spirit. He was aware that he must be totally dependent on the Spirit of God in order to be able to grasp the mystery of Christ.

The doctrinal work of the Fathers served him as a protective bulwark. His ideal is the person the Church worships. In this sense, St. John Damascene is one of the richest manifestations of the Spirit which animates the Church, because he unites in his work both dogmatic thought and contemplation. . . .

V

CHRISTOLOGY IN THE WESTERN FATHERS

1. P. Galtier, S.J.,[1] portrays St. Hilary's doctrine of the Incarnation as a consistent profession of orthodox faith formulated against the background of the heresies he attacked, mainly Arianism. The obscurity of his language renders his thought difficult to understand at times. He emphasizes the reality of the divinity and humanity in Christ. However, he speaks of a celestial body formed by the Word in the womb of Mary. He equally insists upon the unity of His personality: the same Son of God is the Son of Man.

Introduction. What St. Hilary denounces as the fundamental error of the Arians is that they attribute to the Word, as such, all that which is of the "dispensation"—all of the consequences of the flesh to which He is united.

[1] Paul Galtier, S. J. is one of the most relevant theologians of this century. He taught Dogmatic Theology for many years at the Gregorian University in Rome. He is the author of many patristic and theological works, *De Incarnatione ac Redemptione, De SS. Trinitate, Le Saint Esprit en nous d'après les Pères grecs, L'unité du Christ,* etc. It is from his book *Saint Hilaire de Poitiers* (Paris: Beauchesne, 1960) that this excerpt is taken from pp. 109–129, 169–171.

According to the orthodox position, the union contracted by the Son of God with His humanity is the closest union possible. This union permits and requires that we attribute to Him in a very real sense all that which was formed in the womb of the Virgin. Thus we may say that He was born of her. Yet, this birth does not imply that the Son Himself became a constituent or integrating part of the man formed in this manner. Despite his birth of a Virgin, nothing is lacking to this man which enters into the constitution of an ordinary man. Only that at the very moment of his conception, the Son of God united Himself to him, or appropriated him to Himself in such a way that He can attribute to Himself all that is found in man. It is not that He became . . . the immediate principle of his activity. On the contrary, all that is in Him of life and of activity, of sensitivity, of wonders and of sufferings has its principle in that which makes Him a man. To be or to belong to the Son of God does not negate in Him His being wholly in the human realm; man did not become God. Of Himself He is completely man; but He is not only man. He is the Son of God who, in uniting Himself in the above mentioned manner, became man. By doing this, He did not cease to be that which He is by nature from all eternity. He only took on, in time, a second nature. From this emerges the fact that both He and we may attribute to Him all that is appropriately human. But it is not according to the attributes which can be predicated of Him in this manner that it is possible to determine His real nature.

Such is the conception of the "dispensation" or of the Incarnation, through which the irreductible opposition of orthodoxy to Arians is manifested. St. Hilary does not cease to insist upon it. While for the adversaries of His faith, Christ is neither truly Gor nor fully man, for St. Hilary He is essentially and fully both. . . .

St. Hilary's Doctrine of the Incarnation. Above all, it contains the faith in Christ as being truly and really God: he who ignores this will not have life. Either to deny that Christ is God the Spirit or to doubt that He is the flesh of our body is equally erroneous.[2] This faith implies the truly real Incarnation of the Word, the eternal Son of God. Engendered from all eternity in the bosom of the Father, He was also born, in time, of the Virgin Mary. The two generations are to be equally believed. The Church upholds this belief against Sabellius, and also against those who, like Arius, see only in the Word a mere creature, and, finally, against Photin, the modern Ebion. St Hilary explains all that His new birth implies for the only begotten of the Father. This birth causes Him to share all that every infant coming into the world has to undergo. Having descended to the womb of the Virgin, He progressively took the form of a human body: *"in corpusculi humani formam . . . accrescit."* He who made and sustains the universe comes into existence through childbirth: *"humani partus lege profertur."* His voice makes heaven and earth tremble, and one hears Him wail like a child. The immense and the incomprehensible which is hidden from sight, from the senses and from the touch, is sleeping in a

[2] *De Trinitate,* IX, 3 (PL, X, 282 B).

crib.[3] This is the real mystery of our faith: the mystery of the unity of Christ. He excludes in Christ all division. The Church does not divide the Christ Jesus as if Jesus were not Himself Christ. She does not make a distinction between the son of man and the Son of God lest some one believe that the Son of God is not also the son of man.[4] On the contrary, she maintains that the Word of God was born as a man while conserving His own nature. Thus it is equally true that He is *"in forma Dei"* and also *"in forma servi."* That which is said of His human nature is also said of His sufferings, His death, and His resurrection. They are all part of one and the same Christ. One cannot divide Christ concerning any of these realities.

Furthermore, He Who rose from the dead, rose from the dead Himself. It is true, that ordinarily the resurrection is attributed to the Father; but the Son, by virtue of His community of nature, effected Himself the work of the Father. By attributing to Himself the power to do away with and to retake His soul, Christ presents Himself as being the author of His resurrection. In the action of God raising Christ to life again, one also discovers the action of Christ effecting by Himself that which God effects. It is granted that in the man-God death was the work of man and the recalling to life was the work of God; nevertheless, one cannot distinguish between He Who died and He Who rose from the dead. The divine nature is recognized, therefore, in the power to recall life; the assumption of humanity is recognized in death. . . .[5]

However, this unity is not effectuated, as the Arians suggest, by the insertion in the human element of the divine element to complete it. On the contrary, St. Hilary recognizes a distinct and complete being in this human element. This is a "man"—a true man—who was united to the Son of God. Thus in every page of St. Hilary's work there appears the issue, one may say, of an *"assumptus homo."* This is the expression which he uses to designate that which in more abstract language may be called "humanity"—the human nature of Christ. This expression has the advantage of contradicting at the same time the doctrine of both Arius and Photin. If it is to a complete man that the Son of God united Himself, He did not have to complete that man by His union with him. On the other hand, if the man born of Mary has been assumed by the Son of God, it is because this man has another existence, other than His own —an existence which was anterior to Him.

This expression is also an advanced contradiction to Apollinaris. If the assumed man was, like us, really man, then Christ, Who has all that which makes Him truly divine and also all that which makes Him truly human, must have a human soul.[6]

Concerning this point, St. Hilary further states that, like the soul of all men, Christ's soul was created immediately by God. . . .[7]

Therefore . . . the man conceived by

---

3 *Ibid.*, II, 25 (PL, X, 66 C).
4 *Ibid.*, X, 52 and 66 (PL, X, 384 B and 394 B).
5 *Ibid.*, IX, 10, 12 and 14 (PL, X, 289 A–C, 291 A–C and 292 B – 293 B).
6 *Ibid.*, X, 19 and 23 (PL, X, 357 A–B and 361 A).
7 *Ibid.*, X, 20 (PL, X, 358 A).

the Virgin is entirely from the Holy Spirit. In her, the Word framed Himself His own body and He gave to Himself His soul. It is this man, formed in this manner, who bears the name of Jesus: *"Jesus enim ejus hominis, qui ex Maria natus est, nuncupatio est,"* as St. Hilary would state in his commentary to Ps. 65. He also states the same thing in *De Trinitate. . . .*[8]

In the same manner, it is because of His humanity that we must understand whatever refers to an inferiority of nature in Christ. Such is the case of His obedience to His Father. . . .[9] Such is the case of His demand for His glorification, addressed to His Father. Such is the instance of His confession of inferiority of His nature and of superiority of the Father. . . .[10]

All this leaves no doubt concerning the distinct nature of the *"homo assumptus."* By the same token, he quickly halted the attempts of the Arians to render the dependance, the weaknesses and the infirmities of Christ accountable to the Word. . . .

A literal interpretation of the words of St. Hilary could lead one to believe that he, too, was guilty of "dividing" Christ. However, as strongly as he affirms the presence of a complete man in Christ, the Bishop of Poitiers excludes all suspicion that this man might be someone other than the Son of God Himself. We have already stated how he affirms the identity of Him who was born man while being God. It is the identity of Him Who rose from the dead, and Who rose from the dead by Himself. He does not cease to inculcate this identity. This man "whose birth (*partus*) is of the Virgin and whose conception is of the Spirit"[11] is the son of man who "came down from heaven." Such is the very mystery of the "assumed man" (*suscepti hominis sacramentum*), who was simultaneously on earth and in heaven; the Word became man while remaining that which He was.[12] The son of man is, therefore, none other than the Son of God. . . .[13]

Thus it is that the same person had God for a Father and also had God for God at the same time: having been born of Him, He had Him for a Father; having been formed from the flesh of the Virgin, He had Him for a God. . . .[14]

This faith allows for "a harmonious arrangement" of the Incarnation, but it "does not bring about a division in Christ," neither does it distinguish the son of man from the Son of God, nor does it absorb one in the other. The Church does not divide Christ into three parts: Word, body and soul. For her everything is the Christ-man. In the unity of her faith she takes care not to lead some to believe that Christ is anything other than Jesus or to teach that Jesus is other than Christ.[15]

---

[8] *Tractatus in psalmum* 65, C.S.E.L., vol. XXII, p. 257; *De Trinitate* XI, 17 (PL, X, 411 A).

[9] *Ex opere historico fragmentum* XI, 3 (PL, X, 712 A); Ed. A. Feder C.S.E.L., vol. XLV. II. A., Series A, p. 45.

[10] *De Trinitate,* IX, 56 (PL X, 327 A).

[11] *Ibidem,* X, 17 (PL, X, 356 A).

[12] *Ibidem,* X, 16 (PL, X 354 B – 355 B).

[13] *Ibidem,* X, 19 (PL, X, 357 A–B).

[14] *Ibidem,* XI, 17 (PL, X, 411 A).

[15] *Ibidem,* X, 52 (PL, 384 B).

St. Hilary challenges these *"tripartientes Christum"* at the same time that he challenges those who reduce Christ to be but an ordinary man. Neither of these heretical positions could explain how the same One could, on the cross, commend His soul to His Father and promise paradise to the good thief; how, the same One could have complained of having been abandoned and, at the same time, speak of paradise where He reigns. In order to explain this, one must admit that the same One, at the same hour, dies while He reigns and gives testimony Himself to do both of these things. Faith in the unity of Christ, however, explains everything: He complained of being abandoned because He is man, and He Who dies says that He reigns in paradise because He is God.[16]

Against the "dividers" of Christ, he defends his position with the words of St. Paul[17] identifying the Jesus crucified with Him who is the wisdom of God. . . .

St. Hilary tried to dispell any misunderstanding by precising the distinction to be made in this unique being, the Word Incarnate: it is the distinction between some of the words and some of the actions of Christ which reveal one or the other of His natures. He begins by reflecting upon what the Arians consider regarding the Word Himself (*"de se ipso"*): they consider the words spoken by Him, and, in a sense, these words can be understood as concerning His nature as the Word.[18] However, St. Hilary quickly points out that the Incarnate Word is not only this nature. Here, then, the two fundamental distinctions are brought to light: they are the two distinctions which should generally guide the interpretation of the words and actions of Christ.

First of all the distinction of His constitutive elements entail the distinction in His words. Since Jesus Christ is man and God—One Who did not start to be, when He became man —and since, in becoming man, He did not cease to be God, He has to admit in His own words the same mystery as that of His makeup.[19]

Therefore the distinction of the different states or stages in which one can and must understand Christ is to be made. This distinction completes the previous distinction.

It is because Christ did not commence to be when He became man that St. Hilary argues that it is according to time (*secundum tempus*), that one may distinguish the man from the God. From this viewpoint, one may distinguish those which are the words of the one or of the other. Again, as one confesses Him to be God and to be man, one discerns those which are the words of God and those which are the words of man. Finally, aware of this union of man and God, one realizes what should be understood simul-

[16] *Ibid.,* X, 61–62 (PL, X, 391 A – 392 A).

[17] *I Cor.,* I, 23.

[18] . . . *De Trinitate,* IX, 6 (PL, X, 285 A). Dom Coustant in his edition points out that in this text the word *"nature"* may be understood here as "person," as in other places. It can be understood, he adds, of a nature that has become His. Our interpretation is based, however, in what is said in the following number, where Christ is said to speak and act according to His human nature, without concealing that it is of His being to be God . . . *Ibid.,* IX, 7 (PL, X, 286 A).

[19] *De Trinitate,* IX, 6 (PL, X, 285 A). The word *"generis"* frequently expresses in the language of St. Hilary, what we call "essence" or especial "nature."

taneously of the whole man–God. . . .[20]

Thus, St. Hilary concludes, "since it is a different matter to be God before being man, and something else, to be simultaneously God and man, and finally, after having been man and God, to be entirely man and entirely God, one must be careful not to confuse the mystery of the "dispensation" with the diversity of origins and natures. In the mystery of this man, the language which concerns Him before His birth is one thing, the language which appertains to Him before dying is another thing, and the language which concerns Him when He is already eternal is finally another thing."[21]

In a word, one may distinguish three periods or three stages in what can be called the story, the career, or, at least, the total consideration of either the Incarnate Word or of the man-God . . .[22] St. Hilary tries to safeguard the unity of Christ despite his insistence on these distinctions. . . .

St. Hilary maintains that even when Christ appears as man and behaves as man, it is, again, the power of His divine nature which intervenes and has the initiative. It is a positive fact that His birth, His sufferings, and His death are realities of our nature; but He performed all these realities by virtue of His nature, because it is He who is the cause of His birth; it is He Who, not being able to suffer, wanted to suffer; it is He, life itself, Who died. . . .[23]

The explanation, the justification, is laborious. The imprecision of vocabulary renders the understanding difficult, but the meaning is clear. One may interpret what was previously said as the intercommunion of the divine and human in the operations of the Incarnate Word. Here, one may see, above all, the unification. Through this unification, the actions —human as well as divine—belong to the Word, and the human actions are produced under the impulse of, and on account of the intervention of the divine. St. Hilary concludes that all, birth, suffering, and death of Christ, are part of the plan of salvation, elaborated for us before the constitution of the world. The Son of God had to be born as man, so that man could find himself forever in God. And thus it happened that that which belongs to us (*homo noster*) persists in God, and that the sufferings of our weak nature are found associated with God.[24] This is, therefore, how the unification of the divine and the human are realized in the Word Incarnate: He is in Himself the meeting point and the link. In the work of our salvation, both cooperate; but the initiative of it belongs always to the divine. . . .

We thus have reached the central and culminating point of the Christology of St. Hilary. It is from this point of view, that its general features appear strongly drawn. One sees anticipated in them the future definitions of Chalcedon. Irreducibly distinct, the divine and the human are found to be so closely united in Christ that one could not dream of dividing them without destroying the conception which faith imposes. If St. Hilary speaks of

---

[20] *Ibid.*, IX, 6 (PL, X 285 A).
[21] *Ibid.*, IX, 6 (PL, X 285 B).
[22] *Ibid.*
[23] *De Trinitate,* IX, 7 (PL, X, 236 A).
[24] *Ibid.*, IX, 7 (PL, X, 286 A – 287 A).

"the man assumed" by the Son of God, he speaks also of the "mixture" of the Spirit, which is the Son considered in His divine nature and in the flesh which He took: *"Naturae se humanae carnis immiscuit."*[25] The mystery of the Incarnation is found inscribed between these two formulae. Neither of them could be considered as giving the precise and adequate definition which would come later. Entirely concerned with his preoccupation of defending the mystery against those who deformed it, the Bishop of Poitiers applied himself above all to defending the contents. However, by the clarification which he makes of the distinction and, at the same time, of the intercommunion or cooperation of the two natures, some of his explanations anticipate those of St. Leo concerning the roles proper to each of the two "forms". . . .

Conclusion. The Incarnation of the Son of God is the central object of the belief which he proposed to expose and defend. . . . He wanted to avenge Christ against the heretics who contested His true origin, and to guard Christ from the cowards who, not daring to deny Him, hardly had the courage to confess their faith in Him. . . .

Christ, Who is the center of the mysteries imposed to our belief, is truly the mystery of the divine condescendence in regard to humanity. It is really "for us and for our salvation" that the Son of God lowered Himself to such a point as to take on our condition of slavery. It is to the consideration of this grandiose and merciful design that St. Hilary clung. It is through Christ that he confounded the rash and the timid who held that the Incarnation of a divine person was inconceivable and incompatible with the primary truths of all religion.

What is still more, the Bishop of Poitiers not only tried to make known in Christ the Eternal Son of God the Father; but he tried to make understood the supreme grandeur which fallen men have in Him—a grandeur assured by the Redeemer Himself. St. Hilary showed a Christ Who, by His personal insertion in the human family, did not propose anything less than to raise all its members to the participation of His life and of His glory in God.

2. T. J. Van Bavel, O.E.S.A.,[1] studies Augustine's Christology comparing it with that of other Latin authors and with Greek Christology. Although his Christology differs little from that of Anselm, he is responsible for introducing in Latin thought the expression "*una persona in Christo.*" Again, he brought into the West the Greek comparison of the hypostatic union to the union of the soul and body in man, as well as the idea that the soul is the intermediary in the union of the Word with the flesh.

Judgments on the Christology of the Bishop of Hippo generally maintain his agreement with the Christian tradition. A comparison of his doctrine

[25] *Ibid.*, II, 26 (PL X, 67 B). Cf. *Tractat. in Psalmum* 54, 2, C.S.E.L., vol XXII, pp. 147–148.

[1] Tarsicius J. Van Bavel, O.E.S.A., is the author of *Recherches sur la christologie de Saint Augustin,* his doctoral dissertation at the University of Fribourg, where it was printed in 1954. This excerpt is from pp. 176–186.

with that of Saint Ambrose reveals no essential differences. Any other assessment would betray an all too superficial knowledge of the texts. Yet regarding Christology, the Bishop of Hippo must be credited with some personal merit, with some importance and value.

Saint Augustine and the Latin Christology. It is striking to observe that Western Christology, a terrain so rich, has been little explored up to now. A synthetic work has flaws and many problems remain to be solved. It was completely natural that Saint Augustine would draw most of his inspiration from the thoughts of his predecessors. To the works of Saint Hilary, of Saint Ambrose and of others, must be added the inestimable factor of the acts of the Councils. We can never value their influence enough, but it is difficult to define this influence in a given case. Thus most of the elements encountered in the Christology of Saint Augustine are the appanage from his Western predecessors.

We must now sum up what is original in his doctrine, either in the further development of another's thought or in the departure from traditional ideas.

The Latin writers were very much aware of the unity of person and of the two natures in Christ. Tertullian, because of his training as a jurist, even created a terminology surpassing that of his own era. The fact that his terminology went unsanctioned for a long time illustrates clearly the isolation which has encircled Tertullian the "montanist." But such isolation is neither the only nor the principal reason why the term "persona" was so long avoided in Christology. The primary reason lies in the philological order: the evolution of the meaning of the word itself. We must also take account of the inconsistency of the terminology of the Greeks, upon whom the most outstanding Western thinkers relied, and we must likewise take note of the danger that is run by confusing the unity in the Christ with the unity in the Holy Trinity when applying the terminology of the Trinity to Christological matter.

The West had to wait for Saint Augustine to reintroduce *una persona.* Saint Hilary was unfamiliar with it, and Saint Ambrose used *persona* in the modern sense only once for Christ.[2] Nor is the term found in other pre-Augustine writers. The late appearance of this terminology in the Bishop's writings shows that he himself did not accept it on the authority of Tertullian. Only Augustine's contemporary, Saint Jerome, used "persona" with more or less precision,[3] and thus, strictly speaking, the Bishop of Hippo could have depended on the Ascetic of Bethlehem. Or must we think of a translation from the Greek where *una persona* is given as the equivalent to "*en prosōpon.*"?[4] It is improbable because the texts hint that the *una per-*

[2] *Expl. ps.* 61, 5 (CSEL 64, 380).

[3] *Comm. in Zachariam* II, 7 (ML 25, 1458): "Non Iesum dividimus, nec duas personas in unam possumus facere personam. . ." Cf. *Ibid.* I, 3 (ML 25, 1436). *Comm. in Matth.* II, 14, (ML 26, 102). *Ep.* 120, 9 (CSEL 55, 498). *Comm. in Hieremiam* III, 52 (CSEL 59, 188). It is perhaps important to recall that in his youth Saint Jerome had heard the teaching of Apollinaris.

[4] Theodore of Mopsuestia speaks a great deal about the unity of person in the Christ, for example, *In Ev. Iohannis* V, 29–30 (ed.-version Voste, pp. 80–81). . . . Did Saint

sona of Saint Augustine is the result of personal and laborious efforts. We discover, in fact, stages in the evolution of his terminology:

a) the Christ-Man bears the person of Wisdom.

b) the person of the Word assumes a human nature in the unity of his person.

c) Christ is one person in two natures.

The slow evolution confirms that *una persona* did not yet belong to the depository of tradition. Thanks to the Bishop of Hippo, the term has been placed there. None will be astonished that the Doctor of Grace greatly contributed to the treatise on the grace of Christ: the union by grace was one of his principal ideas. But how new was the idea? Although the Antioch Adoptionists had spoken in similar terms, it is improbable that Saint Augustine had known them and even less likely that he would accept their terminology, considering that their orthodoxy had been long impaired already. Most importantly of all there is a fundamental difference between the Adoptionists' idea of the union of grace qualifying the union itself and the Augustinian notion that union through grace does not bear upon the nature of the union. For him grace is the principle by which the union is accomplished, and this idea has generally found great favor in the West. There were Latin writers who had discussed the predestination of Christ, and it is probable that Saint Augustine was familiar with works by Theodore of Mopsuestia in which we find expressions recalling those of the African Bishop.[5]

Saint Augustine energetically insisted upon the Hypostatic Union as the principle of the fullness of grace and of the impeccability of the Christ-Man. Up to that point, the Fathers had looked into the virginal conception of Christ as the source of His holiness and His *impeccantia.*

Again the Bishop of Hippo disavowed the opinion that the Baptism of Christ would have brought with it a totally special infusion of the Holy Spirit. We are not yet certain of the meanings attributed to the Baptism of Christ by some other Fathers, but it appears that they did not escape a certain ambiguity, even a dualism. Saint Augustine refused to take this side, instead held that the fullness of the grace of the Christ-Man derives directly from the Hypostatic Union which is the highest grace that can exist. It brings, with it, as necessary consequences, all the other graces which raise the Christ-Man up to his state which Augustinian terminology calls "the similarity of the flesh of sin." These points have strongly influenced the prescholastic doctrine where they are introduced almost without change.

Saint Augustine abandoned tradition by opposing an exaggerated spiritualization of the human nature of Christ in heaven. Hilary is said to have written: "It is not that the human nature be done away with in Christ. . . . It concerns rather a transformation such that the flesh may be

Augustine know Theodore of Mopsuestia? In the course of the Pelagian controversy, Julian of Eclanum appealed to Saint John Chrysostome, to Saint Basil, and to Theodore. Augustine (C. *Iul. o. i.* III, 111. ML 45, 1295) simply replies: "Utinam horum fidem teneres. . . ."

[5] *In Ev. Iohannis* XVI, 14 (ed.-version Voste, p. 212). . . .

truly considered as absorbed by the spirit, and the human nature by the divine nature."[6] But these two assertions were precisely irreconcilable in the eyes of the African Bishop who always upheld the integrity of the human nature of Christ, including His corporality, even in heavenly glory. Although his views have been severely criticized, we think that Saint Augustine's opinion may equally be considered an improvement and a return to the biblical conceptions.

The African doctor has not contributed very much to the progress of the doctrine concerning the affections of Christ. Christ's power over His affections and His participation in our affections were ideas deeply anchored in tradition. But explicit affirmations of the reality of Christ's affections have certainly had a great influence, and the reserved attitude of Augustine about the abandonment of Christ on the cross has probably helped eliminate a dangerous interpretation.

It goes differently with the human knowledge of Christ. The Bishop of Hippo is keenly aware of its exceptional grandeur. If omniscience, beatific vision, and advancement in wisdom are not harmoniously elaborated by him, he has nevertheless delivered to posterity all the elements for systematizing the doctrine (excepting only the concept of experimental knowledge).

Saint Augustine and the Greek Christology. It will always be hard to establish connections between Saint Augustine and the Greek Fathers. This is particularly true regarding Christology because Latin Theology had already assimilated almost all the elements of Greek Christology. Origen, Saint Athanasius, and the Cappadocians played the greatest role in the process. . . . The points common to Latin and Greek Christology are consequently so numerous that there remain only two elements which the Bishop of Hippo can certainly be said to have borrowed from the Greeks: first, the comparison of the Hypostatic Union with the union of soul and body in man; and secondly, the notion of soul as intermediary of the union of the Word with the flesh. These ideas were not adopted by Western Christology up until the appearance of the famous comparison in Augustine after four hundred. It is difficult to tell where he found it. From the Greek writings he knew, probably only Letter 101. of Saint Gregory of Nazianzus exerted influence.[7] In the letter, however, the idea is weakly developed. After Nazianzus, one is reduced to pure conjectures; one could think of Saint Gregory of Nyssa or of Theodore of Mopsuestia.

The concept of the intermediary soul is already encountered in 393, and the translation of Origin's *De Principiis* and Saint Gregory of Nazianzus *Orationes* (in which the theme is very frequent) are subsequent to this date. Hence we estimate again that a still young Augustine had in his hands the translation of Letter 101 of Saint Gregory of Nazianzus,[8] because significantly the first time Augustine

[6] J. Lecuyer, "Le sacerdoce royal des chrétiens selon Saint Hilaire de Poitiers."—*L'Annee Théologique* 10 (1949), pp. 314–315. Cf. H. J. Schoeps, *Vom himmlischen Fleisch Christi, Eine dogmengeschichtliche Untersuchung* (Tübingen, 1951), pp. 16–18.

[7] *Ep.* 101 (MG 37, 180).

[8] *Ep.* 101 (MG 37, 188), where one finds explicitly that the union between the Word and the soul has a certain priority because it is a union between two spiritual beings

touches on the idea is, like Gregory, when refuting Apollinarism. It is quite interesting to note that those two Greek ideas have survived up into Scholasticism. The Augustinian influence could have something to do with it.

The Character of Saint Augustine's Christology. The Christological doctrine of Saint Augustine is firmly traditional, consequently entailing many weaknesses inherent in the theology of its time. The clear ideas (for example, those of personality and of communication of idioms) sometimes suffer in the manner of expression. Augustine does not always succeed in detaching himself from the hold of conventional thought, as happens in his opinion on the affections of Christ. The originality of his doctrine, limited as it is, suffices nevertheless to give a distinctive character to his Christology; its main idea is that the human nature of Christ has enjoyed all the perfections of which it was capable. His reflections on the human nature of Christ are more developed than those of his predecessors. Never did he doubt the existence of a real human soul in Christ, and thus his Christology gives room for a real psychology of Christ. His position lies between Saint Hilary and Saint Ambrose. He approaches Hilary in raising the human nature of Christ well above the ordinary condition of men without slipping into exaggeration. At the same time, Augustine never wholly adopts Ambrose's realism (for which the Bishop of Milan was indebted to the Greek Fathers who combatted the Arians). . . . Saint Ambrose speaks of ignorance, of growth in wisdom, of abandonment, of regeneration of the Christ-Man, and he attributes them to the human nature of Christ. The Bishop of Hippo takes a different course. He places the human nature of Christ at the summit of humanity as the principle of all grace, exempt from the shameful consequences of original sin, safe from immoderate affections and enjoying the fullness of knowledge.

Soon after Saint Augustine's death, the Nestorian controversy burst forth. The invitation to the Council of Ephesus, addressed personally to the Bishop by Emperor Theodosius III, arrived too late at Hippo. It is regretable because, in view of the admirable soundness of his Christology, Saint Augustine would have been the very man needed in that hour. On this account his influence over the East ought to remain limited to some quotations in the Greek Christological florilegium. But if his Eastern influence was almost non-existent, his influence on the West decisively determined the course of evolution. Even some semi-Pelagians, who did not sympathize with him, appealed to Augustine's incontestable authority in Christological questions. It was Vincent of Lérins who composed the first "Summa Theologica" of Augustinian theology.[9] For this reason there seems a certain continuity between the thoughts of the Bishop of Hippo and that of the pre-Scholastics.

---

closer to one another than the Word and the body. Thus, the union with the flesh is accomplished by the intermediary of the soul.

[9] *Excerpta sanctae memoriae Vincentii Lirinensis insulae presbyteri ex universo beatae recordationis Augustini episcopi in unum collecta*, ed. J. Madoz (Madrid, 1940), pp. 103, 25–29).

3. E. Portalié, S.J.,[1] discards as false some interpretations of Augustine's soteriology. He maintains that Augustine's works show his thought in harmony with the Catholic dogma of Redemption. He analyzes four aspects of Augustinian teaching on the matter: Christ's mediation, His sacrifice, His deliverance of man from the bondage of Satan, and His moral influence. The Augustinian synthesis on Redemption greatly influenced Western soteriology.

The Problem. In the interpretation of Augustine's theory on the Redemption it is easy to establish how closely the teaching on salvation is linked to that on the Savior: His soteriology depends on his soterology.

Abelard, since he thought that Augustine portrayed Christ purely as a man morally united by grace to the Divinity, believed that the Redemption consisted solely in the influence of His lessons and examples. All Catholic theologians, on the contrary, having recognized the true Man-God in the writings of the holy doctor, find there also the Catholic dogma of salvation, that is, the expiation of our sins on the cross by an innocent victim substituted for the guilty human race. Until recently Calvinists and Lutherans, who believed in the divinity of Christ, admitted the same interpretation. But the recent breaches opened in the doctrine of the divinity of Christ have caused these new Nestorians to return to Abelard's theory of moral redemption. Many critics have dared to attribute their rationalistic concept to Augustine. The word *expiation* is no longer used and *substitution* makes way for the "solidarity of the human family." Christ, they say, has certainly died for us (*hyper hēmōn*) because His examples of virtue are salutary for us, but He has not suffered in our place (*anti hēmōn*). Some, if they admit that Augustine talked of the Redemption, make fun of it and maintain that he understood a ransom paid not to God but to the devil to deliver us from his enslavement.

Harnack avoids this excess. He recognized that in Augustine "Jesus is represented to us as the mediator, the victim, and the priest through whom we are ransomed and reconciled with the Divinity, so much so that His death, as the Church preaches, is the sure fundation of our redemption."[2] But he attempts to deprive this admission of all value by ascribing these three thoughts to Augustine: (1) Reconciliation with God is much less important than redemption from the devil. (2) The lesson of humility given by Christ surpasses by far this redemption and constitutes the true work of Christ. (3) Besides, only negative results (such as the pardon of sins) are attributed to this redemption, not a positive justification. . . .

Solution of the Problem. There is no obscurity in Augustine's soteriologi-

---

[1] Eugene Portalié, S.J., was born in 1852, and died in 1909. He was professor of Positive Theology at the Institute Catholique of Toulouse. He was a frequent contributor to the Jesuit periodical *Etudes.* This excerpt was taken from R. J. Bastian's translation of his DTC article on Augustine. The translation in book-format is entitled *A Guide to the Thought of St. Augustine* (Chicago: Regnery Co., 1960) pp. 161–175.

[2] Harnack, *History of Dogma, V,* 131.

cal teaching. Our examination of its characteristics will be limited to four points: (1) the mediator; (2) the sacrifice, the principal act of His mediation; (3) the deliverance from the devil which is consequent upon it; and (4) the moral influence of Christ.

1) *Mediator.* In what sense does St. Augustine attribute the role of mediator to the humanity of Christ? This assertion, inspired by the First Epistle to Timothy (2:5)—a favorite text of the great doctor—causes surprise at first. In the *Confessions* he says: "He is mediator inasmuch as He is man; inasmuch as He is the Word He is not an intermediary because He is equal to God, . . ."[3] and consequently equally far removed from us: "He is not mediator because He is equal to the Father, for by this He is as far removed from us as the Father is. How can there be any mediation where there is the same degree of remoteness?"[4] Again: "Christ is the mediator between man and God not as God but as man. . . ."[5] Because of this insistence Scheel blames Augustine for sacrificing the role of the Word: must not the mediator be the Man-God so as to be between the two extremes?[6] Undoubtedly that is true, and that was Augustine's understanding. Two observations will clarify his thought.

In the first place, Augustine wishes to exclude the role of mediator from the divine nature, not from the person of the Word. Since the word *Christ* designates the person of the Word subsisting in two natures absolutely independent of one another, he asks himself which one of the two, the human or the divine, can and must perform the acts of satisfaction and expiation. Now it is clear that these acts do not fall under the purview of the divine nature. The human nature, however, does not act except as informed by the person of the Word. It is therefore the Man-God who appeases the Father and saves us. That is the exact thought of the holy doctor: "We would not have been delivered through that one mediator . . . unless He were also God."[7] This role of the Word and the humanity in the Redemption is admirably explained in *Sermon 127:* "From what He has of Himself He is the Son of God; from what He has of us He is the Son of Man. He has received the lesser part from us; He has given us the greater part. For He also died because He is the Son of Man, not because He is the Son of God. Nevertheless the Son of God died, although He died according to the flesh and not according to the Word. . . . Therefore because He died, He died of what He had of us; because we live, we live from what we have of Him."[8]

Another observation is that Augustine conceived the work of the mediator under a double aspect. His double role is to appease God in the name of humanity, and, in his divine capacity, to convert the heart of man. Now there is a profound distinction underlying these two missions of Christ. The first, the appeasing of God, is the work of

[3] CX, 43, 68 (32, 808) (the author uses standard abbreviations for the works of Augustine, but also his own, listed on p. 331 of his work).
[4] DGrC II, 28, 33 (44, 402). Cf. DCD IX, 15, 2 (41, 269); S 293, 7 (38, 1332).
[5] EnP 103, 8 (37, 1384).
[6] Scheel, *Anschauung Augustins,* pp. 318–319.
[7] En 108, 28 (40, 282).
[8] S 127, 9 (38, 710).

the MAN-God, of the Just One par excellence. (The expression *Homo-Deus* seems to be peculiar to Augustine.) The conversion of man is the work of the GOD-man. It is the love of God (before the Incarnation), coming down to us until it clothes itself with our nature, which will win us over by the sight of this self-abasement—not of the humanity, for that is ineffably exalted, but of the Word in the humanity. These two viewpoints are essential for an understanding of Augustine's teaching. In *On the Trinity* he says: "The one cleansing bath for the wicked and the proud is the blood of the Just One and the humility of God."[9] The blood of the Just One is for expiation; the humility (the abasement of God in the humanity) is to convert our pride.

2) *Sacrifice.* The question here is whether the Redemption was, in Augustine's eyes, an expiatory sacrifice offered by Christ to His Father by means of a substitution. The answer is so clearly, so constantly formulated in all the works of the holy doctor that some people will be surprised at a question brought up by recent critics. For Augustine . . . the first act—and the principal act—of the mediation of Christ is the expiation of our sins and our reconciliation with God through the sacrifice of Calvary, following Ephesians (5:2): "He delivered Himself for us as an offering and sacrifice to God."[10]

a) *Three principles.* There are three principles at the basis of this fundamental dogma. The first is the concept of sin not only as a moral imperfection of the sinner but especially as an injury of the divine right, an offense against God and an outrage to His majesty. The second principle is the theory of the satisfaction due to God, a theory developed chiefly in the teaching on penance of which it is the foundation. Lastly, there is the principle of substitution (vicarious satisfaction) in virtue of which Christ offers Himself and is accepted by His Father as a victim of the sins of the entire human race for whom He thus obtains pardon. Augustine affirms all this simultaneously without distinct analysis, but with a preciseness which leaves no room for doubt: "Christ, though guiltless, assumed our punishment that He might thus cancel our guilt and do away with our punishment."[11] He addresses the terrible reproaches of the Apostle to those who see only a moral influence in the cross: "The carnal man . . . does not perceive . . . what grace the cross of Christ bestows upon those who believe; he thinks that on the cross He acted in this way only that He might leave us . . . an example to be imitated."[12]

b) *Scriptural sources.* Augustine finds the scriptural sources of this dogma in various texts. The first is the words of Jesus at the Last Supper: "And therefore He said, 'This is My blood which shall be shed for many unto the remission of sins.'"[13] Another source is the epistles of St. Paul, the preacher of the cross. Thus, explaining the Second Epistle to the Corinthians (5:20), he says: "He made Him who

[9] DT IV, 2, 4 (42, 889).
[10] Cf. S 152, 9 (38, 824).
[11] CF XIV, 4 (42, 297).
[12] JE 98, 3 (35, 1881–1882). Cf. JE 79, 2 (35, 183).
[13] DPB II, 30, 49 (44, 181).

had not known sin, that is, Christ, sin for our sake, a sacrifice for sins through which we can be reconciled."[14] For Augustine the dogma was really an echo of the ancient prophecies. *On the Agreement of the Evangelists* (chap. 31) shows how Isaiah (chaps. 52–54) applies to Christ, especially the words: "He was wounded for our sins . . . by His bruises we are healed."[15] Augustine adds: "He assumed our crimes, but not as one who had committed them."[16] Lastly, Augustine sees the dogma as the fulfillment of the noble figure of the paschal lamb, following St. Paul in the First Epistle to the Corinthians (1:7).[17]

When we have such precise affirmations which become more accurate as they multiply, it is inconceivable that certain critics were able to attribute the origin of this redemptive idea to St. Anselm. . . . The best Protestant critics, the ones furthest removed from dogmatic presuppositions, have shown all the incongruous elements in an assertion which adduces the German custom of wergild as the origin for a belief long before studied by St. Augustine and even formulated earlier by such Fathers as Tertullian and Cyprian. Even more, Harnack does not hesitate to affirm that, even before St. Paul, the very earliest form of Christianity was based on the expiatory sacrifice of the dying Christ.

c) *Redemptive act.* The redemptive act of Christ is the death on the cross. For Augustine, this death is: (1) A true sacrifice: "By his death, namely by the one true sacrifice offered for us, He cleansed, abolished, and wiped out . . . whatever fault there was."[18] (2) The unique sacrifice prefigured by all the ancient sacrifices: "In all those various kinds of sacrifices is understood that one sacrifice and that single victim on the cross, our Lord."[19] (3) A sacrifice perpetuated in the sacrifice of the altar which is offered throughout the entire world according to the prophecy of Malachias: "All false sacrifices have made way for this greatest and true sacrifice."[20] (4) A sacrifice consisting essentially in the death of Christ decreed by His Father. Nowhere in Augustine, however, can one find a trace of the exaggerations of Protestant scholasticism according to which Jesus on the cross was truly cursed by His Father and suffered the very torments of hell. . . .

d) *Multiple role of Jesus.* The great doctor explains the multiple role of Jesus in this sacrifice. He appears first as priest and sacrificer. Sin is wiped out "through the one sacrifice of the true mediator-priest."[21] Second, He is at the same time the victim and priest because it is He Himself who offers His life and delivers His body to the torments: "He the offerer, He also the offering."[22] And precisely because this

[14] En 41, 13 (40, 253).

[15] DCns I, 31, 47 (34, 1065). Cf. EnP 68, 9–10 (6, 848–849).

[16] EnP 44, 7 (36, 498). Cf. EnP 31, 18 (36, 270).

[17] Cf. DDoC II, 41, 62 (34, 64); EnP 39, 13 (36, 43).

[18] DT IV, 13, 17 (42, 899). Cf. DT IV., 14, 19 (42, 901) for the four elements of this sacrifice.

[19] EnP 74, 12 (36, 955).

[20] DCD X, 20 (41, 298).

[21] DGnL X, 14, 25 (34, 419).

[22] DCD X, 20 (41, 298). Cf. DT IV, 14, 19 (42, 901).

is a free offering of Himself, the death inflicted by the tormentors is transformed into a sacrifice: Christ was offered because He willed it. "And He proceeded to the suffering of death, a voluntary death, not because He had to but because He freely chose it."[23] Augustine also refers the reader to Ephesians (5:2). Third, Augustine shows Christ victorious and triumphant: "A victor and a victim, and therefore a victor because a victim, and therefore a priest because a sacrifice, changing us from servants to sons."[24] Finally, he represents Him interceding in heaven for us, as the great high priest in the Holy of Holies.[25]

e) *Fruits of Christ's satisfaction.* The first benefit of Christ's satisfaction is undoubtedly the forgiveness of sins,[26] the pardon of all sins, even those committed after baptism. "His blood . . . has blotted out all the sins of the guilty; so great a price paid has redeemed all the captives."[27] But St. Augustine is not less insistent on the positive gifts of reconciliation with God, which he expressed in many ways: It is a grace analogous to that of Jesus Christ which is assured us,[28] an incorporation into Christ, whose members all the faithful become: "Through His blood . . . they are joined to the body of Christ."[29] It is a divine adoption, hindered until then by our faults: "The Only-begotten came to loose our sins which prevented us from being adopted by God."[30] He puts the same thought more vigorously: "When about to make men Gods, God became man."[31] . . .

f) *Extent of Christ's Redemption.* According to Augustine, the Redemption of Christ is universal in extent and allows no exception: "The shedding of innocent blood has blotted out all the sins of the guilty; so great a price paid has redeemed all the captives."[32] Thus all sins are expiated, even those committed after baptism, . . . All the captives are ransomed, even infants who die without receiving baptism. Augustine affirms this expressly.[33] Mention must be made of Augustine's argument which closes off all loopholes to the Jansenists.[34] He reasons thus: Jesus Christ has died for all without exception. Therefore all without exception are sinners: "All therefore, without exception, were dead in sin, and for all the dead there died the only person who lived."[35] That is Augustine's mature thought. When he stated that the effects of the Redemption were restricted to the elect, he has to be understood as speaking of efficacious graces which are not given to all. Augustine's sermons can leave no doubt. . . . "The blood of your Lord, if you will it, is given for you,

[23] S 152, 9 (38, 824).
[24] CX, 43, 69 (32, 808).
[25] CEP II, 7–8 (43, 59).
[26] CF XIX, 7 (42, 353).
[27] EnP 129, 3 (37, 1697).
[28] DPB 26, 39 (44, 131).
[29] JE 53, 6 (35, 1771).
[30] JE 2, 13 (35, 1394).
[31] S 192, 1, 1 (38, 1012).
[32] EnP 129, 3 (37, 1697).
[33] CJ III, 25, 58 (44, 732).
[34] CJ VI, 4, 8 (44, 825); OJ II, 175 (45, 1217).
[35] DCD XX, 6, 1 (41, 665).

if you do not will it, it is not given for you. . . . This is the important point, that He gave it once and for all. The blood of Christ is salvation to those who wish it, punishment to those who refuse."[36] "The true and apostolic opinion is that Christ is the Savior of all men."[37] As for the angels, Augustine would have been afraid to favor the Origenist belief in the ultimate salvation of the demons even if he had not already left them outside the plan of the Redemption. He merely mentions that the death of Christ has reunited just men and the good angels in the single city of God, in which the elect will replace the fallen angels.[38]

3) *Deliverance from Satan.* Has St. Augustine pictured the Redemption as a ransom paid to the devil and not to God? Like other Fathers, Augustine was accused of this idea as if the devil had acquired the right to hold humanity in slavery through sin so that the blood of Christ, instead of being offered to God, would have been the price paid to the devil. This is an odious concept, inspired by Eastern Gnosticism, which St. Gregory of Nazianzus was already stigmatizing as an injustice to God.[39] Whatever the other Fathers might have thought, however, was this Augustine's true conception of the Redemption? It is correct to admit that he himself described the enslavement by the devil, to whom men were sold: "They could sell themselves, but they could not redeem themselves."[40] He affirms that the blood of Christ has been the price of our redemption. He talks of the trap set for the devil on the cross. The body of Christ was the bait with which he was taken, and so forth.[41] But a careful examination of the meaning of these images makes it painstakingly clear that this staging is only a way of dramatizing the overthrow of the devil and our deliverance. Augustine's teaching is not only foreign to the gross conception of a ransom paid to the devil, but it gives the key to expressions used by some other Fathers. Some proofs of this follow.

Augustine never expressed the thought that Christ had dealings with the devil, that He was the mediator between man and the devil, and that His blood was offered to the devil. He acknowledges only one mediation, that between men and the Father,[42] and one redemption in the proper meaning of the term, that which redeems us from the wrath of God: "All humanity can in no way be justified and redeemed from the just wrath of God, that is, from punishment, except by faith and the sacrament of the blood of Christ."[43] The expiation of sins by the sacrifice offered to the Father is the central idea of the Redemption and of Christianity for the Doctor of Hippo, as the texts quoted above show. To pretend with Harnack that this reconciliation with God is only of secondary importance is to deprive the facts of all meaning.

In addition, our deliverance from

---

[36] S 344, 4 (39, 1515).

[37] S 292, 4 (38, 1322). Cf. J. B. Faure, his notes on chapter 47 of the *Enchiridion;* Stentrup, *De Verbo incarnato, Soteriologia,* I ,387–416.

[38] En 61–62 (40, 260–261).

[39] Gregory of Nazianzus, *Oratio* XLV, 22, *P.G.,* XXXVI, 654.

[40] EnP 95, 5 (37, 1231).

[41] Cf. S 263, 1 (38, 1210); S 134, 5, 6 (38, 745).

[42] Cf. En 108 (40, 282); DPS 8, 15 (44, 971).

[43] DNG 2, 2 (44, 249).

the devil is always presented as a simple consequence of the expiation and reconciliation with God, not as the result of a ransom paid to the devil. This principle is of primary importance. Far from putting some underhanded dealings with the devil in the spotlight, Augustine everywhere shows that the devil has been vanquished precisely because God received satisfaction and forgave man: "The devil is conquered . . . by the mediator between God and men, Jesus Christ, by whom we are reconciled to God once our sins are washed away. For only by sin are men separated from God."[44]

St. Augustine's theory on the overthrow of the devil positively excludes any idea of ransom. This theory is developed in Book XIII of *On the Trinity*.[45] The whole section should be read and pondered, in particular the following principles: (1) The devil had no claim on us. What some people have considered such a claim is really just a permission from God to chastise sinners. The devil was merely the executioner, not the master. (2) No ransom was therefore due, for the remission of sins by God includes our freedom: "If therefore the commission of sins subjugated man to the devil through the just wrath of God, certainly the forgiveness of sins through the gracious reconciliation of God snatched man away from the devil."[46] (3) This pardon could be gratuitous without any reparation, but it was more becoming that the divine justice should be satisfied and that the devil lose his dominion in consequence of his injustice. This is the reason for the Passion: Jesus dies for those who are guilty; the devil is the unjust slayer of this Innocent One; he is punished and loses his dominion over his victims. "What is this justice, then, by which the devil was conquered?"—Certainly this would be the time to speak of ransom, but Augustine's answer is far different.—"What is it if not the justice of Jesus Christ? And how was he conquered? Because, although he could find nothing worthy of death in Him, he nevertheless killed Him. And therefore it is right that the sinners whom he held should be sent away free."[47] This explanation recurs again and again: "He spilled the blood of the Innocent One and was ordered to depart from the guilty."[48] You have destroyed Him whom you ought not; return that which you were holding."[49] Still more energetically he says of the devil: "He was able to spill that blood, but he was not worthy to drink of it. And because he spilled the blood of one who was not guilty, he was ordered to return the guilty. For He spilled His blood for this purpose, that He might take away our sins. . . . Those were the bonds of the captives, but He came and bound the strong one up with the chains of His Passion."[50] The devil therefore merely takes the part of one who is vanquished and chastised. It is in this sense that the cross was a trap for him:

[44] DCD X, 22 (41, 300). Cf. DT IV, 13, 17 (42, 899); DPB II, 30, 49 (44, 180); JE 53, 6 (35, 1771); S 363, 2 (39, 1635).
[45] DT XIII, 12, 16 (42, 1026).
[46] *Ibid.*
[47] *Ibid.*, 14, 18 (42, 1027–1028).
[48] S 130, 2 (38, 726).
[49] S 134, 5, 6 (38, 745).
[50] S 130, 2 (38, 726).

"It was a trap set for you, and you were taken by that in which you had rejoiced."[51]

But, one might object, Augustine affirms that Jesus has ransomed us from the devil. Yes, but he says also that Jesus has ransomed us from the slavery of sin,[52] from hell,[53] and from death.[54] Does anyone suppose that He paid a ransom to sin, to death, and to hell?

4) *Moral influence of Jesus.* According to Augustine, in what does the moral influence of Christ consist? After the forgiveness of men by God the mediator must achieve a second victory, the restoration of the hearts of men to God. Without exception, no one among the Fathers has developed the moral aspect of the Incarnation with as much insistence as Augustine. Here also we find an utterly personal sign of his teaching: his thesis on the humility of God in the Incarnation is one of his most profound conceptions. Catholic theologians have left to the mystics meditation on this aspect of the work of Christ found in St. Augustine. Protestant critics, on the contrary, especially in these latter days (many probably because the theory of expiation was less pleasing to them, but many also who wish to retain it), have made the great Augustinian thesis of the "humble Christ" crystal clear. It will suffice here to give an accurate statement of the thought of the Doctor of Hippo.

In the divine plan humility is the fundamental lesson of the Incarnation. Consequently, even in his most theoretical works, Augustine unites the twofold purpose of this mystery: expiation offered to the heavenly Father and humility which was restored to its former state by the unfathomable humiliations of the Word made man. This is the characteristic of the person of Jesus Christ which left the deepest impression upon his soul as it did upon the soul of St. Paul, the apostle of the "emptied-out Christ." . . . There is no doubt that the Incarnation is the great proof for Augustine of the love of God for us. It is this love which will lead our hearts to love the humility of God, which in turn, because it is made known through such self-abasement, destroys our pride. "The ideal image of humility in grandeur," says the celebrated critic [Harnack], "is what conquered Augustine. Pride is sin. Humility is the source and strength of all good. From the humiliations of Christ he drew this new sentiment which he implanted in the Church, the cult of humility."[55] That is certainly the impression which the following text of *On the Trinity* gives. Humility is presented as the great salvific mystery: "It is profitable to believe and keep implanted firmly and unshakably in the heart that the humility by which God was born of a woman and led to death by mortal hands with such insults is the medicine most apt to heal the swelling of our pride and the most sublime sacrament for loosing the bonds of sin."[56]

It is precisely because of His humility that Jesus is the way. In the *Confessions* Augustine recounts how the

---

[51] S 134, 5, 6 (38, 745).
[52] S 30, 1, 1 (30, 188).
[53] S 344, 4 (39, 1515).
[54] DNG 24, 26 (44, 260).
[55] Harnack, *History of Dogma, V,* 132.
[56] DT VIII, 5, 7 (42, 952).

role of Jesus as the way of souls but only through humility was revealed to him at a time when he considered Jesus only as an outstanding man: "For I was not humble enough to embrace the humble Jesus, my Lord, nor did I know what lesson His weakness would teach me. For Your Word . . . built Himself a humble home of our clay whereby He intended to detach from themselves those who would be subjected and bring them over to Himself, healing their pride and fostering their love."[57] A little later, speaking of his former pride, he exclaims: "Where was that charity building on the foundation of the humility which is Christ Jesus."[58] This is the ordinary theme of his Christmas sermons: "Recognize the teaching of such humility. . . . Your human pride oppresses you so much that only the divine humility can raise you up."

He attributes this humility to the Word, the divine person, and not to the humanity. God surely cannot humble Himself in His divine nature, but one cannot miss the great lesson of God consenting to be united to a created nature. God alone could have mastered this virtue. "The way to this humility springs from a different source; it comes from Christ. The way is from Him who, although He was mighty, became humble. . . . What else did He teach if not this humility? Not without reason does He say: 'I am the Way. . . .' Through such humility, therefore, we approach God."[59] Thus Augustine exalts the lesson of humility less in the life and passion of the Savior than in the fundamental fact of the Incarnation, decreed and brought to fulfillment by the Word. What a profound statement is that in which he shows Christ as conqueror because in Him God is humbly united to a human nature: "He who conquered was both man and God. He conquered thus, born of a Virgin, because He did not rule that humanity as He rules other holy men, but was humbly united to it."[60]

Conclusion. An exact résumé of the Augustinian theory on the Redemption is provided in the *Enchiridion.* Harnack comments on it as the summation of his system. Let the reader judge for himself: "Since sin had created a great chasm between the human race and God, it was necessary that a mediator who alone was born, lived, and was put to death without sin should reconcile us to God even to obtaining the resurrection of the flesh into everlasting life . . ." (This is the primary purpose of the Incarnation: reparation and reconciliation with God.) ". . . in order that human pride might be rebuked and healed through the humility of God; that man might be shown how far he had departed from God; . . ." (This is the secondary end of the Incarnation: the moral influence of the humble Christ—an important task, but ranking below that of reconciliation. Once this is affirmed, there is no danger of rationalism or Abelardianism . . .) ". . . that the fountain of grace might be opened by the only-begotten Son of God assuming the form of a servant, a form which had no prior merits . . ." (This is the result of the redemptive work, which

[57] C VII, 18, 24 (32, 745). Cf. C VII, 19–20, 25–26 (32, 746–747).
[58] C VII, 20, 26 (32, 747).
[59] EnP 31, 18 (36, 270).
[60] DT XIII, 18, 23 (42, 1033). Cf. EnP 8, 11 (36, 114); EnP 18, 15 (36, 163); E 205, 11 (33, 946); DGrC II, 40, 46 (44, 409).

is not just pardon and deliverance, but sanctification through a grace like to that of the Incarnation.) ". . . that the promised resurrection of the body might also be foreshadowed in the Redeemer Himself . . ." (This is the role of the Resurrection, a guarantee of the future triumph of which we are assured by the reconciliation of Christ.) ". . . and that the devil might be conquered by the same nature which he took delight in having deceived."[61] (Thus deliverance from the devil is represented as a victory over him, achieved by human nature in consequence of its reconciliation with God. There is not a word about a ransom paid to the devil.)

4. J. N. D. Kelly[1] maintains that the Latin Fathers, following the framework of Tertullian's Christology in its broad lines, preserved a balanced orthodox perspective. Although Leo's Tome lacks originality, it went a long way towards meeting the points of view of the two Eastern schools of thought. Western Soteriology conformed broadly to the pattern observed in the East, with greater emphasis on the Lord's death as sacrifice. Hilary is the pioneer of the theology of satisfaction. Ambrose emphasizes the theory of a transaction with Satan. It is Augustine who sums up all the insights and passes them on to the Middle Ages.

Christology. So far (up to 449), Tertullian excepted, the West had made little or no contribution to Christological theory, but the importance which Leo's *Tome* was to assume makes it desirable to glance at the Latin fathers. In general they reproduce the framework of ideas, and even the formulae, inherited from Tertullian. If they seem to lack the speculative interest of the East, this is to some extent explained by the remarkable success with which Tertullian's theory held both the aspects which reflection was showing to be necessary to a sound Christology in balance.

For Hilary, for example, the two natures of Christ (he regularly uses the term *natura*) are united in one Person.[2] Christ is true man and true God, one but comprising two natures in His unity.[3] Each nature is complete, the humanity possessing a rational soul[4]—this is insisted upon in reply to the Arian habit of referring the Lord's experiences of emotion and suffering to the Logos[5]—and the union entails no change or confusion.[6] Further, while Hilary does not hesitate to speak[7] of the humanity as "the man assumed," he regards[8] the Person of the Incarnate as identical with the Person of the Word: "He Who is in the form of a

---

[61] En 108 (40, 282).

[1] Cf. Ch. 1, n. 5. This excerpt has been taken from his book *Early Christian Doctrines,* selectively, from pp. 334–338 and 386–390.

[2] *De trin.* 9, 14.

[3] *Ibid.,* 9, 3.

[4] *Ibid.,* 10, 19.

[5] Cf. *Ibid.,* 10, 50–60.

[6] *Tract. in ps.* 138, 2.

[7] E.g. *Ibid.,* 68, 25.

[8] *De trin.* 9, 14; cf. *Ibid.,* 10, 22.

servant is none other than He Who is in the form of God." This Pauline imagery suggested to him the self-emptying (*evacuatio* or *exinanitio*) which the Incarnation must have involved. This does not consist, as he sees it,[9] in the Word's surrendering any of His powers or ceasing to be what He essentially is (*evacuatio formae non est abolitio naturae*), but rather in His contracting or limiting Himself to human conditions. In other words, he relinquishes, during His earthly career, the glory appropriate to "the form of God." Alongside this, however, should be set Hilary's treatment of the Lord's experiences of pain, weakness, human emotion, etc. These experiences, he teaches,[10] were perfectly genuine, but they were strictly unnatural to Him: "He had a body susceptible of suffering, and so suffered, but His nature was not capable of pain." The point is that, Christ's body having been conceived by the Holy Spirit, it was not really earthly but heavenly (*corpus coeleste*),[11] and was raised above human weaknesses; hence if He consented to succumb to them, He was making a concession, by the free act of His will, to what was expected of Him.[12] Similarly the glory of the Transfiguration and the walking on the sea were not strictly miraculous, but were natural to such a body as His.[13] Thus, side by side with his conviction of the reality of the human nature, there was a decidedly Docetic strain in Hilary's thought.

Ambrose stood even closer than Hilary to the Latin Christological tradition. "It is one Son of God," he stated,[14] Who speaks in both, for both natures are in one and the same subject" (*in cedem*). He refers[15] to "the twin substances . . . of divinity and flesh." The human nature, of course, includes a rational soul,[16] and the distinction between the two natures is sharply maintained.[17] The Person being indivisibly one, he can make use of the "communication of idioms," remarking,[18] for example, "The Lord of majesty is said to have been crucified because, participating in both natures, the human and the divine, He endured His passion in the human nature."

Along similar lines Augustine taught[19] that "Christ is one Person of twofold substance (*una persona geminae substantiae*), being both God and man." Mediator between God and man, He "conjoins both natures in oneness of Person;"[20] in Christ there are two substances, but one Person."[21] The humanity was absolutely real,[22] and of course complete: "there was a

[9] *Ibid.*, 9, 4; 9, 14; 11, 48; 12, 6.
[10] *Ibid.*, 10, 23–32; 10, 35.
[11] *Ibid.*, 10, 18.
[12] *Ibid.*, 10, 24; 10, 35.
[13] *Ibid.*, 10, 23.
[14] *De fide* 2, 77.
[15] *De fide* 3, 65.
[16] *De incarn. dom sacram.* 64 ff.; 76.
[17] *De fide* 2, 77; *de incarn. dom. sacram.* 23.
[18] *De fide* 2, 58.
[19] *C. Maxim. Ar.* 2 ,10, 2.
[20] *Ep.* 137, 9.
[21] *Serm.* 130, 3.
[22] *De agon. Chr.* 20; 24.

human soul in Christ, not just the non-rational part of it, but the rational part we call the mind."[23] It was the rational soul, indeed, which provided the point of union between the Word and the flesh.[24] Yet, while the human nature was real, the fact that it was born from a pure virgin preserved it from original sin;[25] nor was it susceptible, despite the Gospel statements which seem to suggest the contrary, to human ignorance.[26] It was characteristic of Augustine to speak of it as "the man," referring[27] to "the man" whom the Son of God carried or assumed. While this usage, however, indicates that he assigned the humanity a relative independence, he makes it plain[28] that it never existed apart from the Word. Thus the two natures are united in one Person, the Person of the Word. "Into unity with His Person," he wrote,[29] "the form of God remaining invisible Christ took the visible form of a man," and in so doing He "neither lost nor diminished the form of God."[30] Because of this union, he affirmed,[31] predicates appropriate to the one nature can be freely applied to the other, so that the Son of God can correctly be said to have been crucified and buried, and the son of man to have come down from heaven. To illustrate the unity he often invoked[32] the comparison of soul and body, which together constitute a single man.

The Christology which appears in Leo's *Tome* has no special originality; it reflects and codifies with masterly precision the ideas of his predecessors. The following are the chief points he was concerned to bring out. First, the Person of the God-man is identical with that of the divine Word. As he expressed it,[33] "He Who became man in the form of a servant is He Who in the form of God created man." Though describing the Incarnation as a "self-emptying" (*exinanitio*), he claimed[34] that it involved no diminution of the Word's omnipotence; He descended from His throne in heaven, but did not surrender His Father's glory. Secondly, the divine and human natures coexist in this one Person without mixture or confusion. Rather, in uniting to form one Person each retains its natural properties unimpaired (*salva . . . proprietate utriusque naturae et substantiae*), so that, just as the form of God does not do away with the form of a servant so the form of a servant does not diminish the form of God.[35] Indeed, the redemption required that "one and the same mediator between God and men, the man Jesus Christ, should be able both to die in respect of the one and not

[23] *Tract. in ev. Ioh.* 23, 6: cf. ib. 47, 9.
[24] *Ep.* 137, 8; 140, 12.
[25] *Enchir.* 34; 41.
[26] *De trin.* 1, 23; *enarr. in ps.* 6, 1.
[27] *De agon. Chr.* 12; 20; 21; 22; 25.
[28] *De trin.* 13, 22.
[29] *C. Maxim. Ar.* 1, 19.
[30] *Enchir.* 35.
[31] *C. serm. Ar.* 8.
[32] E.g. *serm.* 186, 1; *tract. in ev. Ioh.* 19, 15.
[33] *Ep.* 28, 3 (Leo's "Tome").
[34] *Ibid.*, 4.
[35] *Ibid.*, 3.

to die in respect of the other." Thirdly, the natures are separate principles of operation, although they always act in concert with each other. So we have the famous sentence, "Each form accomplishes in concert with the other what is appropriate to it, the Word performing what belongs to the Word, and the flesh carrying out what belongs to the flesh"[36] Lastly, the oneness of the Person postulates the legitimacy of the "communication of idioms." We can affirm, for example, that the Son of God was crucified and buried, and also that the Son of Man came down from heaven.

These four theses may not have probed the Christological problem very deeply; it is obvious that they left the issues which puzzled Greek theologians largely untouched. They had the merit, however, of setting out the factors demanding recognition fairly and squarely. Moreover, they went a long way towards meeting the points of view of both the schools of thought struggling for supremacy in the East. Antiochenes could recognize their own theology in Leo's vigorous affirmation of the duality in Christ, and of the reality and independence of the two natures. Some of his sentences, indeed, particularly the one cited above, were to prove stones of stumbling to Alexandrian Christologians. Nevertheless these latter, too, could see the essentials of their standpoint vindicated in the Pope's unerring grasp of the identity of the Person of the Incarnate with that of the eternal Word. As he expressed it in a Christmas sermon,[37] it is one and the same Son of God Who exists in both natures, taking what is ours to Himself without losing what is His own."

Soteriology. Western thought on the redemption conformed broadly to the pattern we have observed in the East, with even greater emphasis on the Lord's death as a sacrifice. The physical theory found support chiefly among thinkers who were subject to Greek influences. Hilary, for example, can write,[38] "It was we who needed that God should become flesh and dwell in us, that is, by taking a single flesh to Himself should inhabit flesh in its entirety." The Platonic conception of human nature as a universal clearly lies in the background here. We can see it again in his statement,[39] "for the sake of the human race the Son of God was born from the Virgin and Holy Spirit . . . so that by becoming man He might take the nature of flesh to Himself from the Virgin, and so the body of the human race as a whole might be sanctified in Him through association with this mixture." The same Platonic realism inspires Victorinus when he writes,[40] "When He took flesh, He took the universal idea of flesh (*universalem logon carnis*); for as a result the whole power of flesh triumphed in His flesh. . . . Similarly He took the universal idea of soul. . . . Therefore man as a whole was assumed, and having been assumed was liberated. For human nature as a whole was in Him, flesh as a whole and soul as a whole, and they were lifted to the cross and purged

[36] *Ibid.*, 4.
[37] *Serm.* 27, 1.
[38] *De trin.* 2, 25.
[39] *Ibid.*, 2, 24: cf. *tract. in ps.* 51. 16.
[40] *C. Ar.* 3, 3.

through God the Word, the universal of all universals." Elsewhere[41] he argues that, since Christ's body is "catholic," i.e. universal as opposed to particular, all individual human bodies were crucified in it, and His sufferings have a universal quality.

The theory of a transaction with Satan enjoyed considerable currency. In the hands of Ambrose the emphasis is generally on the Devil's rights and the compensation justly owing to him in requital for surrendering mankind. The Devil, he states,[42] held us in possession, our sins being the purchase money by which he had bought us, and required a price if he was to release us; the price was Christ's blood, which had to be paid to our previous purchaser. Sometimes he suggests[43] that, when Christ paid over what was owing to the Devil, He transferred the debt to Himself, with the result that we changed our creditor, although He has, in fact, most generously forgiven the debt. Ambrose is not afraid[44] to dwell on, and elaborate the details of, the deception worked on the Devil, who would of course never have accepted Christ's blood had he known Who He really was. On the other hand, we find examples of the milder version of the theory, according to which the transaction consisted not so much in the satisfaction of the Devil's supposed rights as in his proper punishment for going beyond them. Hilary, for example, points out[45] that Satan condemned himself when he inflicted death, the punishment for sin, on the sinless author of life. Quite apart from that, so far from resting on justice, the sovereignty exercised by the powers of evil over the human race was only established by their wicked usurpation.[46] Ambrosiaster develops the same theme, teaching[47] that the Devil sinned when he slew the innocent One Who knew no sin. When Christ was crucified, he overreached himself, and lost the authority by which he held men captive on account of Adam's sin.[48] When the principalities and powers who seduced the first man laid hands on the Saviour, they put themselves in the wrong, and were justly penalized by being deprived of the souls they kept in prison.[49]

It is Christ's passion and death, however, which particularly interest these writers. Hilary, for example, states[50] that "the Lord was smitten, taking our sins upon Himself and suffering in our stead . . . so that in Him, smitten even unto the weakness of crucifixion and death, health might be restored to us through His resurrection from the dead." Being "the second Adam from heaven," He has assumed the nature of the first Adam, and so can identify Himself with us and save us. If this is the language of recapitulation, Hilary passes easily to that of sacrifice, stressing the voluntary character of what Christ accomplished. "He offered Himself to the death of the accursed

---

[41] *In Gal.* 2, 6, 14.
[42] *Ep.* 72, 8: cf. *de Iac. et vit. beat.* 1, 12; *expos. ev. Luc.* 7, 117.
[43] *Ep.* 41, 7 f.
[44] E.g. *expos. ev. Luc.* 2, 3; 4, 12; 4, 16.
[45] *Tract. in ps.* 68, 8.
[46] *Ibid.*, 2, 31.
[47] *In Rom.* 7, 4.
[48] *In. Rom.* 8, 4.
[49] *In Col.* 2, 15.
[50] *Tract. in ps.* 68, 23.

in order to abolish the curse of the Law by offering Himself of His own free will to God the Father as a sacrifice. . . . To God the Father, Who spurned the sacrifices of the Law, He offered the acceptable sacrifice of the body He had assumed . . . procuring the complete salvation of the human race by the oblation of his holy and perfect sacrifice."[51] It was by His blood, he emphasizes,[52] and by His passion, death and resurrection that Christ redeemed us. The effect of His death was to destroy the sentence of death passed on us,[53] to expiate our sins,[54] and to reconcile us to God.[55] Though these are incidental remarks, they give substance to the claim that Hilary must be regarded as one of the pioneers of the theology of satisfaction. We come across similar ideas, expressed in terms of redemption and substitution rather than sacrifice, in his contemporary Victorinus. He speaks[56] of Christ redeeming (*mercaretur*) man by His passion and death, pointing out[57] that these only avail to procure remission of sins because the victim is the Son of God. He gave Himself, he states,[58] to death and the cross in our stead, thereby delivering us from our sins.

Ambrose elaborates a theory of Christ's death as a sacrifice offered to satisfy the claims of divine justice. He sees it prefigured in the slaughter of Abel,[59] as also in the oblations prescribed by the Jewish Law.[60] It is a sacrifice performed once for all,[61] its effect being that through Christ's blood our sins are washed away.[62] Christ has destroyed the sentence of death which was against us, and death itself as well.[63] Ambrose explains[64] how this was accomplished: "Jesus took flesh so as to abolish the curse of sinful flesh, and was made a curse in our stead so that the curse might be swallowed up in blessing. . . . He took death, too, upon Himself that the sentence might be carried out, so that He might satisfy the judgment that sinful flesh should be cursed even unto death. So nothing was done contrary to God's sentence, since its terms were implemented." The second Adam died, he adds,[65] in order that, "since the divine decrees cannot be broken, the person punished might be changed, not the sentence of punishment" (*persona magis quam sententia mutaretur*). Here the idea of recapitulation is combined with that of substitution; because He shares human nature, Christ can substitute Himself for sinful men and endure their punishment in their place.

---

51 *Ibid.*, 53, 13.
52 *Ibid.*, 135, 15.
53 *De trin.* 1, 13.
54 *Tract in ps.* 64, 4.
55 *Ibid.*, 129, 9.
56 *C. Ar.* 1, 45.
57 *Ibid.*, 1, 35.
58 *In Gal.* 1, 2, 20.
59 *De incarn. dom. sacram.* 4.
60 *De spir. sanct.* 1, 4.
61 *Expos. ev. Luc.* 10, 8.
62 E.g. *enarr. in ps.* 39, 2; 14; 17.
63 *De fid.* 3, 13; 3, 84.
64 *De fuga saec.* 44.
65 *Expos. ev. Luc.* 4, 7.

"What," he exclaims,[66] "was the purpose of the incarnation but this, that the flesh which had sinned should be redeemed by itself?" Ambrose describes[67] Christ's sacrifice as propitiatory, but recognized[68] both the love of the Son Who gave Himself and the love of the Father Who gave Him. He also brings out the unique fitness of Christ to be our redeemer, both because of His sinlessness and because of the excellence of His Person.[69]

The sacrificial interpretation of the Lord's death is regular in the other Latin writers of the period. Ambrosiaster often recalls[70] that Christ died for us and our sins, offering thereby a sweet-smelling sacrifice. The whole value of this oblation, he indicates, lay in the love and obedience displayed in it. According to Pelagius,[71] Jesus Christ "was alone found fit to be offered as a spotless sacrifice on behalf of all who were dead in sins." God had decreed death to sinners, and by dying Christ was able at once to maintain that decree and to exempt mankind from its effects.[72] A point which Pelagius tries to bring out[73] is that Christ's life could reasonably be offered in place of ours because, being innocent, He did not already deserve death on His own account. Jerome, too, although his ideas were unsystematic to a degree, recognized[74] that Christ "endured in our stead the penalty we ought to have suffered for our crimes." No one, he claimed,[75] can draw near to God apart from the blood of Christ.

All these thoughts, with some fresh ones of his own, were woven together into a loose but effective unity by Augustine. It was his special role, in this as in other aspects of the faith, to sum up the theological insights of the West, and pass them on, with the impress of his genius and authority, to the Middle Ages. . . .

5. J. Tixeront[1] examines the contribution to Christology of the later Latin Fathers. Regarding the basic problem of Christ's unity, Boethius must be credited with the introducing of consciousness and freedom in the definition of personality, Fulgentius and Gregory threw light on secondary questions. Regarding the doctrine of Redemption, the realistic theory seems to have been the more generally accepted, with Christ substituting and expiating for all men.

At the very time when, in the East, Leontius of Byzantium was trying to analyze philosophically the notion of *person,* Boethius made the same at-

66 *De incarn. dom. sacram.* 56.
67 *De Abrah.* 1, 16; *de offic.* 3, 102.
68 *De Is. et an.* 46; *de Iac.* 1, 25; *de spir. sanct.* 1, 129.
69 *In ps.* 118, 6, 22.
70 *In Rom.* 5, 6–10; *in Eph.* 5, 2.
71 *In 2 Cor.* 5, 15.
72 *In Rom.* 3, 25.
73 *Ibid.,* 3, 24; *in Gal.* 3, 13.
74 *In Is.* 53, 5–7.
75 *In Eph.* 2, 14.
1 Cf. Ch. 4. a. 4, n. 1. This excerpt is from *op. cit.,* selectively, from pp. 337–347.

tempt in Rome and upheld his conclusions against Nestorianism and Monophysitism. These researches are noted in the *Liber de persona et duabus naturis contra Eutychen et Nestorium,* addressed to John, a deacon of Rome. There Boethius gives the Latin equivalent of the Greek words *ousia, ousiōsis, hypostasis prosōpon* (III); what he gives are mainly carefully worked-out definitions of nature and person. The first is as follows: *Natura est unamquamque rem informans specifica differentia* (I, col. 1342); the second is well known; *Persona est naturae rationalis individua substantia* (III, col. 1343). It asserts that only individual and intelligent substances can be persons. No doubt, the introduction of "intelligence" and "liberty" into the concept of person marked a real progress; however, Boethius' definition did not sufficiently assert that, to be physically a person, an individual substance must form an independent and separate whole, and it is only by means of a rather broad interpretation of the word *individua*[2] that philosophers and theologians have succeeded in preserving its classical character.

By means of these notions, Boethius refutes (IV–VI) Nestorius and Eutyches, and explains (VII) how Jesus Christ is both *of* and *in* two natures (*Christum in utrisque et ex utrisque naturis consistere*), these two ways of speaking being equally accurate, if properly understood. The eighth and last chapter states that the Savior assumed something of each of the three states of Adam—before the Fall, after the Fall and in the state in which he would have been, had he not sinned; from the first, Jesus took the physical functions, such as drinking, eating, etc., from the second, suffering and death; and from the third, confirmation in grace.

The duality of nature results in a duality of operation and will, as St. Leo had noted in his letter to Flavian. He returns to the subject in his LVIth sermon, n. 2. . . . Maximus of Turin also dwells on the same conclusion . . .[3] and we have seen with what perfect agreement the whole West, at Pope Agatho's request, asserted the same doctrine. In the letter written by this Pope to Constantine Pogonatus we find this doctrine stated with fullness and accuracy.[4]

As the problems raised by Nestorianism, Monophysitism, and Monothelitism brought on the intervention of the Latin Church in the East, so that Church had also to concern herself with certain secondary problems connected therewith.

Count Reginus asked St. Fulgentius what view he should take of the incorruptibility of Christ's body, concerning which the Alexandrian Monophysites were then disputing among themselves. St. Fulgentius answered[5] that there is a corruption of the soul and a corruption of the body, and that even in this latter we must distinguish between a corruption that produces sin and is accompanied by sin, and another that is a mere punishment of sin. Jesus Christ could not experience

[2] *Individuum est quod est indivisum in se et divisum a quocumque alio.*
[3] *Sermo* CVII, col. 743.
[4] Cf. above, p. 143.
[5] *Epist.* XVIII.

a corruption of the soul, nor concupiscence; but He *did* experience the needs and infirmities that are in us as a consequence of sin, such as hunger, thirst, and death; nay, His body would have been dissolved in the grave (*corruptio putredinis*), had it not been preserved from that fate by His speedy resurrection. In the treatise which he sent to Thrasamond (III, 31), the Saint adds that this preservation was becoming to Christ's dignity. Moreover, these weaknesses and infirmities, as well as the motions of indifferent passions, were in Him both voluntary and natural, because He might have dispensed Himself from them: "veras quidem sed voluntarias habuit."[6]

After the error of the Aphthardocetae, that of the Agnoetae drew the attention of the Latin theologians. . . . St. Gregory's († 604) two letters to Eulogius of Alexandria deny that Christ, as man, was subject to ignorance, and answer certain objections.[7] Before his time, however, the author of the treatise *De Trinitate,* which is ascribed to Vigilius of Tapsus, had apparently granted that Jesus Christ, as man, could be ignorant;[8] and, while teaching that the Savior's soul possessed a full knowledge of His divinity,[9] St. Fulgentius deemed the advance of the Christ-child in knowledge real.[10] But Cassiodorus,[11] following in the steps of St. Augustine, had already decided the question in connection with *Mark* XIII, 32, in the same sense as St. Gregory, and St. Gregory's authority carried the general assent of those writers who took their inspiration from him. This was the conclusion adopted by St. Isidore of Seville and St. Julian of Toledo.[12] As to Bede, he taught not only that Jesus knew the day and hour of judgment, but also that the divine Child's progress in wisdom and grace was purely external, the Savior revealing little by little to the eyes of men the grace and wisdom of which He was full from the moment of His conception.[13]

Unlike the dogma of the Incarnation, that of the Redemption was never studied and treated for its own sake in ancient theology; hence we must not be surprised to find, in the authors whose doctrine we are reviewing, hardly more than a repetition of what had been said before.[14]

However, the physical or mystical theory—which sees in the fact of the Incarnation itself a principle of renewal for the human nature that is thus united to the divine nature—a theory scarcely noticed by other Latin theologians, is set forth by St. Leo. . . . Most of the authors of this period espouse the realistic theory, which regards the Passion of our Lord as the real cause of our salvation. Independently of its objective truth, this theory was more accessible to the uncouth intelligences that had to be won over

6 *Epist.* XVIII, 10; *Ad Trasimundum,* III, 25.
7 These are letters X, 35 and 39. . . .
8 *De trinit.,* XI, col. 306.
9 *Epist.* XIV, 29, 30, 31; cf. 33.
10 *Ad Trasimund.,* III, 18; 1, 8.
11 *In psalm.* IX, vers. 40.
12 St. Isidore, *Sentent.,* I, 27, 1; St. Julian, *Prognostic.,* III, 1.
13 *In Matth.,* chap. XXIV, col. 104; *Homil.* I, 12, col. 67. . . .
14 Cf. J. Riviere, *Le dogme de la Rédemption,* chap, XVI, XVII (English translation).

to the Gospel, and more capable of making a deep impression upon them. St. Gregory in particular set it forth fully and with much success; some details found in other writers are also worth noticing.

Most of the authors with whom we are concerned begin by affirming man's inability to extricate himself from the bonds of sin; in order to do this, they say, one must be innocent and free, whereas all men were and still are captives and sinners.[15] The merits of the saints were of no avail;[16] even the angelic nature would not have suffered, for that nature is fallen.[17] What, then, was needed? God Himself must take our nature, our whole nature, and by raising it up, make it capable of wiping out the sins of the world. . . . The restoration of the human race could not take place, then, except through a Man-God. Was it sufficient for the Word to become incarnate? No, for although the Incarnation, according to a beautiful thought of St. Gregory,[18] is by itself a perpetual sacrifice, the expiation of sin demanded that he who came to annihilate it and its consequences should be positively punished. Therefore "sicut propter redemptionem mundi illum [Christum] decuit nasci, ita et pati oportuit."[19] Thus, the Man-God suffered, because He was our representative and contained all of us, as it were, in Himself. He was in some way our representative by the fact of the Incarnation, since He thereby assumed our nature; but He did much more than that by voluntarily taking upon Himself the responsibility for our sins, and the punishment due to them. This is the idea of penal substitution; we find it everywhere: "Causam omnium suam fecit [Christus]," says Cassiodorus.[20] "Quoniam peccata non habuit [Christus] propria," St. Fulgentius writes, "portare dignatus est aliena";[21] and St. Gregory: "Poenam culpae nostrae [Christus] sine culpa suscepit."[22] This being the case, Jesus Christ is justly punished by the Father for our faults. He is delivered to Satan, *i.e.*, Pilate and the Jews,[23] as we ourselves ought to have been. Through His death, He who was innocent paid the debt that weighed upon us. . . .[24] His blood is the ransom and price of our freedom.[25] Henceforth the divine wrath is assuaged, and, while man finds in Christ's example lessons of sanctity, God is obliged, as it were, to put a stop to the effects of His justice. . . .[26]

Cassiodorus observed that this appeasement of the divine wrath and

[15] Cassian, *De incarn.*, IV, 12; V, 15.
[16] St. Leo, *Sermo* LXIV, 2.
[17] St. Fulgentius, *Ad Trasimund.*, II, 2.
[18] *Moral.*, I, 32.
[19] St. Isid., *De fide cath. contra Iud.*, I, 5, 11.
[20] *In psalm.* XXI, vers. 28.
[21] *Ad Trasimund.*, III, 29; *De fide,* 12.
[22] *Moral.*, XIII, 35; III, 26–29; IV, 56; IX, 61. St. Isidore, *Sentent.*, I, 14, 12.
[23] St. Greg., Moral., III, 26–29.
[24] St. Greg., *In evangel. homil.* XXXIX, 8; *Moral.*, XVII, 47; cf. St. Isid., *Sentent.*, I, 14, 12.
[25] Bede, *Homil.*, II, 1, col. 138; cf. St. Leo, *Sermo* LXII, 3.
[26] St. Greg., *Moral,* IX, 61 cf. XXIV, 6. Cf. St. Leo, (*Sermo* LXXVII, 2).

God's merciful attitude towards us go back, to some extent, to the moment of the Incarnation, when the Father gave up Christ as priest and victim.[27] These words suggest another point of view from which Patristic writers consider the death of Jesus. That death is a sacrifice;[28] it is a necessary sacrifice, as St. Gregory observes, because the fault could not be wiped out except by a sacrifice, the victim of which was, not an irrational animal or a guilty man, but one spotless and holy;[29] the sacrifice of which Jesus Christ is both priest and victim.[30] He has offered His life as a sacrifice: "Fecit pro nobis sacrificium, corpus suum exhibuit pro peccatoribus victimam sine peccato."[31] He offered it freely, for He was not compelled to suffer.[32] Owing to His sacrifice, which was offered especially for our sins, we have been delivered from our faults, freed from death, and reconciled to God.[33] According to a famous phrase of St. Leo, cited by Cassiodorus, all men have been crucified, all have died, all have been buried and raised again in Christ.[34]

In the preceding exposition we have considered the death of Christ from the human point of view, as a remedy for the fall, and from God's point of view, as an expiation of sin demanded by His justice and a means of restoring man to His friendship. Satan also is concerned in this mystery. Man was his captive through sin, and Redemption snatches that captive away from him. Does this take place through force or through justice? Through justice. Following in Origen's footsteps, St. Ambrose had represented the blood of Christ as a price paid to the devil for our redemption. Later that explanation was forgotten among the Latin theologians, who adopted the theory of the abuse of power, which had had St. Augustine's preference, and is expressed several times by St. Leo. God could have made use of His omnipotence to snatch us away from Satan; but He did not do so; He willed that everything should be done according to the demands of justice. "Magis uteretur iustitia rationis quam potestate virtutis;"[35] moreover, it was fitting that mankind should should free itself, as it were, by its own efforts, and that Satan should be conquered by that same nature over which he had triumphed. . . .[36] Therefore the Divine Logos becomes incarnate; He assumes our infirmities and weaknesses, thereby deceiving the devil, who regards Jesus as an ordinary man, persecutes Him, and finally puts Him to death as though the Savior was his and deserved such a punishment. This is an abuse of

27 *In psalm.* LXIV, vers. 3.
28 Cassian, *De coenob. instit.*, III, 3.
29 *Moral.*, XVII, 46.
30 St. Prosper, *In psalm.* CXXXII, vers. 2; cf. St. Fulg., *Epist.* XIV, 37; *Ad Trasimund*, III, 30; St. Leo, *Sermo* LXVIII, 38.
31 St. Greg., *Moral.*, XVII, 46.
32 St. Prosper, *In psalm.* CVIII, vers. 5; CIII, vers. 19; Cassiodorus, *In psalm.* LXXXVII, vers. 5.
33 St. Leo, *Sermo* LIV, 3; St. Fulg., *Ad Trasimund.*, I, 15; Bede, *In I Ioann.*, IV, col. 108; *In Ioann.*, III, col. 671.
34 St. Leo, *Epist.* CLXV, 5; Cassiodorus, *In psalm.* LIV, conclusio.
35 *Sermo* LXIV, 2; XXII, 3; XXVIII, 3; LVI, 1.
36 *Sermo* LXIII, 1.

power for which Satan deserves to be punished. Since he has unjustly struck one who was innocent, he shall lose his claims over those who are guilty, and sinners shall become free: "Per iniustitiam plus petendi, totius debiti summa vacuatur."[37] We find the same ideas, on the whole, in Fulgentius Ferrandus,[38] St. Caesarius,[39] Cassiodorus,[40] St. Gregory[41] and St. Isidore. . . .[42]

[37] *Sermo* XXII, 3, 4; LXI, 4; LXIV, 2; LXIX, 3, 4.
[38] *Epist.* III, 5.
[39] *Homilia III de paschate,* col. 1049.
[40] *In psalm.* LIV, conclusio.
[41] *Moral.,* XVII, 46, 47. It will be observed that in this passage St. Gregory calls Satan's power *almost just.* St. Isidore qualifies his statements in a similar way.
[42] *Sentent.,* I, 14, 12.

VI

CHRIST IN MEDIEVAL THOUGHT

1. B. J. Otten, S.J.,[1] examines the Christological and soteriological errors of the early Middle Ages and points out that these errors were not really new. Christology had been fully developed and settled in Patristic times. The same errors were now given new forms. Adoptionism, revived in Spain in the eighth century, flourished again under Abelard's influence. He was led to it by his misconception of the hypostatic union. The same Abelard misconstructed the doctrine of Redemption because of his ideas on original sin.

There is no doctrine of our holy faith that was so thoroughly investigated during Patristic times as that of the Incarnation. And for this fact two reasons may be assigned. First, the doctrine is so fundamental that with it

[1] Bernard J. Otten, S.J., was professor of Dogmatic Theology and the History of Dogmas at St. Louis University, Mo., when he published his well-known *Manual of the History of Dogmas* (St. Louis, Mo., and London: B. Herder Book Co., 1918). It is from this book that this excerpt is taken, selectively, from pp. 170–175, 196–198.

Christianity must either stand or fall. Secondly, no other doctrine was so fiercely and so constantly attacked by men of heretical tendencies who called in question, now one, now another truth connected with this central mystery of Christian belief. As a consequence, when the Patristic age came to a close, Christology had been fully developed, and at the same time there seemed to be no room left for new heresies to spring up along the lines of Christological teaching. Nor did really new heresies arise in this matter during all the centuries that followed, but some old errors were revived and presented in a new form. One or two of them may be briefly noted, before we proceed to review the Christology of the Scholastics.

Some Christological Errors. Spanish Adoptionism, which was really a recrudescence of the Nestorian heresy, was condemned by the Council of Frankford in 794. However, in one form or another, traces of it continued to appear for hundreds of years after its formal condemnation. Thus Roscelin contended that, as nature and person are identical, one must necessarily admit a human person in Christ, since it is of faith that He has a human nature. His error, which is Nestorianism pure and simple, was combatted by St. Anselm, in his treatise *De Fide Trinitatis.* "The Word made flesh," St. Anselm argues, "assumed another nature, not another person. For when the term man is used, it signifies the nature which is common to all men; but when we denominate in the concrete this or that man by the name of Jesus, we designate the person, having together with nature an aggregate of properties by which man, taken in a general sense, becomes an individual and is distinguished from other individuals. And Christ is only one such individual; hence He is only one person."

However, it was principally by Abelard and his school that Adoptionism was revived. This revival seems to have been the outcome of a wrong conception of the hypostatic union, through which the humanity of Christ was assumed into the unity of person. According to Abelard, the hypostatic union is neither intrinsic nor substantial. A truly substantial union, he contends, would lead to an identification of the humanity with the Godhead of the Word, and thus introduce a created and finite person into the Trinity. Hence such expressions as God is man, this man is God, must always be taken in an improper or figurative sense. The connection between subject and predicate in these propositions is purely accidental; it does not imply a communication of properties in any true meaning of the term.

It was this misconception of the nature of the hypostatic union that gave rise to the doctrinal error known in history as *Christological Nihilism.* Its teaching is summed up in the phrase, *Christus in quantum homo non est aliquid*—Christ as man is not anything. It was not meant as a denial of the reality of Christ's body or soul, but of the substantial union between His human nature and the person of the Word, by reason of which the one can in the concrete be predicated of the other. The Word took a real body and a real soul, but did not assume them into the unity of person. They are realities, but not a substantial reality of the Word Incarnate. They are in the Word, but not one with the Word. The Son of God clothed Himself with the humanity as with a garment, that He might appear to men; He used the humanity as an instrument, that He might perform human actions. Hence the expression, *Deus factus est homo,* can only mean, *Deus accepit hominem;* and the corresponding expression, *Deus est homo,* merely stands for, *Deus est habens hominem.*

Furthermore, the better to uphold this peculiar view of the hypostatic union, not a few of its defenders denied that Christ's human soul and body were united so as to form a complete human substance. For the result of such a union would necessarily be an individual substance of rational nature, and therefore a person. But in Christ there is no human person, and consequently there can be no complete human substance. The two constituent elements of such a substance are there, but in a state of separation. Hence the Word Incarnate is in no sense a new reality; He is only the recipient of a new *modus—habitu inventus ut homo.*

Logically this view of the humanity of Christ excludes all filiation, so that Christ as man is neither the Son of God by nature nor by adoption; and not a few theologians of the school of Abelard drew that inference. If the humanity was not even a complete rational substance, adoption in the true sense of the word was obviously out of the question. For adoption means the free assumption of an extraneous person to the right of inheritance; but where there is no complete rational substance, there is no person.

Although this Christological error was most widespread in France, owing to the many disciples and admirers of Abelard, it found followers also in other countries of Europe. Abbot Gerhoh of Reichersberg, who was one of its most formidable opponents, relates that when he visited Rome under Honorius II (1124–1130), he met there a certain Luitolf who openly taught that Christ as man was the adopted son of the Father; and also a canon of the Lateran by the name of Adam, who held that Christ was partly God and partly man. In Germany similar views were defended by Folmar, Abbot of Triefenstein near Wuerzburg, who went even so far as to assert that Jesus Christ was neither the Son of God nor equal to God, and that it would be unlawful to accord him divine honors. It was against Folmar that Gerhoh wrote his treatise *De Gloria et Honore Filii Hominis,* in which he goes to the other extreme of teaching that the divine attributes had been communicated to the humanity of Christ, not only by way of predication, but in reality and in being, that is, in a Eutychian sense.

These Adoptionist errors, propagated by the disciples of Abelard, were discussed at the Council of Tours in 1163, and again at the Council of Sens in 1164; but without definite results. A few years later, however, Pope Alexander III condemned them in three successive letters, in the last of which, addressed to William of Champeaux, then archbishop of Rheims, he says: "Since Christ is perfect God and perfect man, it is strange that some should go so far in their temerity as to assert that Christ as man is not anything (*non sit aliquid*). In order that such an abuse may not creep into the Church of God, we, by these Apostolic Letters, command Your Fraternity to interdict under anathema, by Our Authority, the presumptuous assertion that Christ is not anything; because as He is true God, so is He also true man, subsisting in a rational soul and human flesh."[2]

This condemnation put an end to all theological discussion on the controverted point, and the last traces of Adoptionism gradually disappeared. Later Scholastics qualified the statement, *Christus in quantum homo non est aliquid,* simply as heretical;[3] and *a fortiori* that as man He is not the natural Son of God. However in the fourteenth century another form of Adoptionism made its appearance, which seems to have been originated by Durandus. He admitted that, in virtue of the eternal generation of the Word, Christ as man was the natural Son of the Father; but he thought that over and above this, in view of the rights conferred on the humanity of Christ by the hypostatic union, He might also be called the adopted son of God. Similar views were held by Gabriel Biel and other Nominalists. Although never condemned by the Church, these peculiar opinions are generally regarded as untenable. . . .

Some Soteriological Errors. The teaching of the Fathers on the redemption of the world . . . was taken over in its entirety by the Scholastics; and, excepting a few minor points, was without further development incorporated in their theological system. . . .

Abelard and his school fell into a very serious error regarding original sin. They looked upon it not as a moral stain implying guilt, but as a mere liability to punishment. Human nature, according to them, was not intrinsically vitiated, and therefore stood in no need of restoration. Nothing was required but a remission of the punishment which rested heavily upon the race on account of the sin committed by the common ancestor. And for this the Son of God need not have become man.

Such a view of original sin necessarily led to a misapprehension of the redemptive work of the Savior. It was the example of right living that mankind needed, not the healing touch of a divine physician. And this formed the burden of Abelard's soteriological teaching, as appears from many parts of his works. Thus he writes: "It seems to us that in this we are justified and reconciled to God, in the blood of Christ, that, through a singular grace conferred on us, the Son took our nature, and persevered in instructing us by word and example even till death, drawing us so closely to Him by the bonds of love, that, inflamed by the thought of so great a benefit of divine grace, we might in our charity not be afraid to bear all for His sake. . . . Hence our redemption is that exceeding great love of Christ which He showed forth in His sufferings; for thereby we were not only set free from the servitude of sin, but also acquired the true liberty of the children of God; so that now we do all things, not through fear but through love."[4]

The enlightenment that comes to us from Christ's instructions, the encouragement afforded by His heroic example, the graces obtained for us by His prayer—these, according to Abelard, constitute the work of redemption. "When God caused His Son to become man, He made Him subject to the law which was common to all

[2] Mansi, 21, 1081C; DB, 393.
[3] Cf. Thomas, *Sum. Theol.* III, q. 2, a. 6.
[4] In *Epist. ad Rom.,* c. 5. Cf. *Theol. Christ.* I, 4.

men. Hence it was necessary that He should love His neighbor as Himself, and infuse into us the grace of His charity, both by instructing us and by praying for us."[5]

These vagaries of Abelard were at once strongly attacked by William of Saint Thierry and by St. Bernard. William went to the root of the error by pointing out that original sin is in the true sense of the term a vitiation of human nature, and that the nature so vitiated needed more than example and instruction to raise it from its moral degradation. It was the death of the God-man that wrought the redemption. Christ's death was a vicarious satisfaction for sin. He was in truth the second Adam, by whom spiritual life was restored to the fallen race.

St. Bernard's refutation follows the same line of thought. "The original fault," he says, "was in truth a grievous sin, which infected not only the person of Adam but the entire race."[6] God thought it proper that the redemption should be wrought by the outpouring of blood. "Why, you ask, should He effect by the outpouring of blood what He could have effected by instruction? Ask Him. For me it is enough that so it was decreed."[7] Yet it was not death as such, but rather the obedient will that was efficacious: "Not death, but the ready will of Him who died was acceptable; and so by that death He overcame death, effected our salvation, and restored us to innocence."[8] Christ accepted His sufferings and death freely; but we had urgent need of them for our redemption. "For human perversity can indeed kill, but it has no power to restore life. . . . He alone could in such wise lay down His life, who by His own power rose from the dead."[9]

2. L. Richard[1] believes that Anselm's rationalism led him to his characteristic doctrine on the necessity of the Incarnation and Redemption. His *Cur Deus Homo*, however, represents the most systematic and coherent presentation of the teachings of his age on the subject. Richard considers unjustified Harnack's accusation of anthropomorphism, but he admits that Anselm's views regarding God's motive in the Incarnation are not based on the Scripture. He neglects to consider the doctrine of our vocation in Christ which sees the Incarnation also as a source of grace.

Cur Deus Homo.[2] Saint Anselm was the famous representative of a young intellectualism which put great truth in the value of reason at the same time that it was deeply imbued with faith. He pushed as far as

[5] *Loc. cit.*

[6] In *Hebd. Sanct.* IV, n. 7.

[7] Abelard, *De Error,* c. 5.

[8] *Ibid.*

[9] In *Hebd. Sanct.* IV, n. 3.

[1] Cf. Ch. 1, n. 11. This excerpt is taken from *op. cit.,* pp. 175–183.

[2] In the following pages, the numbers in parentheses refer to the book and chapter of this work. Since the edition prepared by Dom Gerberon in the seventeenth century and reproduced in *PL,* 158, 359–432, Dom. F. S. Schmitt has published the *Cur Deus Homo* (in 1929) as fascicle 18 of "Florilegium Patristicum," which serves as a prelude to his critical edition of the complete works. The treatise under discussion appears in the second

possible St. Augustine's axiom: *fides quaerens intellectum* ("faith seeking understanding"). One must first believe, then seek to understand what faith proposes. The great doctor's faith was so deeply rooted in his soul that he did not distinguish clearly what came from reason and what from revelation. Not only did he prove the existence of God, but he also wished to demonstrate, by necessary arguments, that God is triune. In the *Cur Deus Homo* (which is drawn up in the form of a dialogue), he tried to prove, starting with the idea of God and the universal fact of sin, that God had to become incarnate and die for the salvation of mankind. St. Anselm is Augustinian in his concept of man and his sin, and also in his way of asking the question: "Cur Deus homo?" ("Why the God-man?") only in dependence on sin. But whereas the theology of St. Augustine always safeguarded the absolute independence of the divine gifts, St. Anselm, in his conception of God, affirmed a very definite optimism:

> In God there is not the least possibility of any disagreement, and the weakest reason, if it is not overcome by any greater one, is accompanied by necessity (1, 10).

It is true that "necessity improperly so called" corresponds to the immutability of the plan of divine love for men: "It is necessary that the goodness of God complete what it begins in man, although every good that God does is a grace on his part" (2, 5). It is therefore unthinkable that the entire human race could not attain its end, the eternal vision of God. Since it is impossible for man to reach this goal because of the state of sin in which he enters the world and to which he adds his own faults, there must be a reparation from sin.

To show what this reparation must be, St. Anselm first analyzes sin. Every created will must submit itself to the will of God and thus render to him the honor which is his due. By sinning—that is, by acting against a divine command—the will no longer renders glory to God and therefore contracts a debt in regard to the divine justice.

St. Anselm admits that the creature can certainly not give anything to God or take anything away from him. This "extrinsic" glory which it owes to him is the order of the universe which the creature, depending on its share in it, can either respect or disturb. But in escaping the divine will which commands, the created will falls back under the divine will which punishes in order to establish order, unless it offers a satisfaction which restores to God the honor which it has refused him. "It is necessary that either satisfaction or punishment follow sin" (1, 15).

> It is impossible for God to lose honor: Either the sinner spontaneously renders what he owes [this is satis-

volume of this latter work (Rome, 1940; 2nd ed., Edinburgh, 1946). The chapter divisions are slightly different in the editions of Gerberon and Schmitt, and will be noted in their proper places in the notes below. Cf. P. Richard, O.S.B., *De satisfactione Christi. In tractatum S. Anselmi "Cur Deus homo" dissertatio historico-dogmatica* (Louvain, 1914). More recently a Protestant theologian, J. McIntyre, has made a penetrating and often justly severe study of the criticisms made of St. Anselm by the "liberal" school: *St. Anselm and his critics. A Re-interpretation of the "Cur Deus homo"* (Edinburgh: Oliver and Boyd, 1954). He has been particularly careful to place the treatise in the methodological perspective of the "Credo ut intelligam" and in the literary genre of "Dialogue."

faction], or God takes it from the sinner against the latter's will [this is punishment] (1, 14).

Since satisfaction must render to God the honor refused by sin, it must be proportional to the sin and must be something which is not otherwise due. But it is absolutely impossible for man to do this, since the evil of his sin is so great, since such great disorder has been introduced by him into mankind and into the universe. By way of sin, man ruined all that God proposed to do in mankind, all human nature is corrupted, and "it is impossible for a sinner to justify a sinner" (1, 23). Although St. Anselm does not say in so many words that sin is in some way an infinite evil, he shows that it cannot be offset by any created thing. One must not commit the least sin, even to save the entire world from destruction. "You do not make satisfaction unless you render something superior to that for which you should not have committed sin" (1, 21), consequently something superior to every created thing. It is then absolutely impossible; God alone can accomplish this reparation. And yet it is mankind which must offer this satisfaction for sin. Therefore there must be a God-man.

How was the God-man to make satisfaction? He could not do it by means of what he owes to God in every way, independently of sin—that is, by acts of obedience and love throughout his life. On the other hand, being innocent, he was not subject to death. Therefore it was by a completely free acceptance of the cross that he made satisfaction, and this satisfaction had an infinite value because it proceeded from a God made man. It also had a meritorious value; and since, St. Anselm claims, Christ did not have to merit for himself, it is we, his brethren who benefit from his merit by the grace of pardon.[3] Such, in brief, are the doctrine and the argumentation of this work, which was to have such a profound influence on all theology.

In this work of reflection on the mystery, it is clear that St. Anselm received the dogma through the tradition of the Latin church, which stressed the sacrifice offered by Christ for sins. On the other hand, he neglects the Greek view which puts the emphasis of the incarnation as the principle of deification. While it is true that he invokes the solidarity of nature with Adam to explain the transmission of original sin and the loss of original justice, nevertheless, in explaining our redemption, he does not have recourse to our solidarity in Christ nor to St. Augustine's theology of the Mystical Body. On the other hand, he is faithful to the theme of the victory of Christ, who fought against sin, death and the devil in order to deliver us from their tyranny; and he deserves credit for having definitely brushed aside the theory (which was still presented in his day and which must have been deeply repugnant to him) of the "abuse of power," which attributed to the devil a right over sinful man. "God owes the devil only punishment, man owes him only conflict. All that had

[3] The idea of *merit,* in the strict sense, remained in the background in St. Anselm's writings, as compared to the notion of *satisfaction;* the former word is used only in 2, 20 (2, 19 in Schmitt's edition). . . .

been demanded of man he owed to God, not to the devil" (2, 20).[4]

Clearly distinguishing satisfaction and punishment, he brings a precision which is consistent with the teaching of the Fathers on expiation but which had never been clearly set forth. The acceptance of death by the innocent Christ has a value of satisfaction as regards God and merit regarding us, but this death is not for him a punishment by which the divine vengeance vents itself on the innocent in order to spare the guilty (1, 8–10; 2, 19). On this point, St. Anselm will, in general, be followed by the Scholastics. Luther and Calvin, on the contrary, will do nothing but exaggerate the doctrine of expiation, and this setback makes it easier to realize the progress made by St. Anselm.

To describe the work of Christ, he uses the term *satisfaction,* which the Fathers had not used but with which they were familiar. In Roman law it signified the compensation offered by the delinquent or offender to obtain remission of a penalty incurred or forgiveness for the injury done. We might make a useful comparison with the *Wergeld* of German law, which is a money compensation offered by the guilty person to obtain remission of punishment. It has at times been said that St. Anselm's doctrine was based on this practice. It is possible that our doctor saw an analogy there, but the ancient penitential practice of the Church already provided him with the *term* satisfaction. Tertullian had been the first to borrow it from Roman law to signify the ensemble of painful acts imposed on the sinner to obtain from God remission of his fault and of the eternal punishment due to his sin. When this term passed into the language of the Church, it was imbued with a more spiritual sense, since the initiative of the pardon comes from the mercy of God, and the satisfaction of the sinner had no value apart from his interior disposition. Nevertheless satisfaction remained strictly personal; and since it was the work of penitents, the Fathers scarcely dreamed of saying that Christ performed any himself. At most only one text of St. Ambrose has been cited in this regard. But the meaning of the word was soon to become wider. In the Leonine Sacramentary it designated the mediation of the saints for the benefit of sinners: "Whatever our sins may be . . . , grant, in your kindness, that they may never prevail over the abundant satisfaction of the saints for us."[5] Obviously the satisfaction of the saints meant their merits and their intercession for sinners. This new meaning for the term satisfaction prepared historically for its application to the work of Christ, which was accomplished in the Mozarabic Sacramentary.[6] But it was clearly St. Anselm's treatise which settled

[4] 2, 19 in Schmitt's edition. It should be noted that this old theme survived among the *Schoolmen* despite the refutations of Peter Lombard (III, 20, 5) and his followers. . . . It was also prominent in the Byzantine East despite the efforts of St. John Damascene and Photius. . . .

[5] VIII (April), xxxv; *PL,* 55, 33; ed. Mohlberg, no. 136. Besides six uses of this kind, we also see that the eucharistic sacrifice *satisfies* for the soul of a deceased person (XXXIII [October], 11; *PL,* 55, 135; ed. Mohlberg, 1142).

[6] *Inlatio* [*Preface*] *in Cena Domini, Liber mozarabicus sacramentorum* (manuscript of the ninth century), ed. Ferotin (1912), §64, col. 237: ". . . Who . . . deigned to send your Son . . . , making him our redemption, making him our redeemer; repairing in him for us the perfection of satisfaction and salvation." . . .

the theological fortune of this use of the word. What is important, besides, is that it is justified. The term satisfaction aptly expresses the spiritual value of the obedience of Christ making up for the disobedience of the first man, which had involved the downfall of his race. That is a doctrinal viewpoint which is rooted in Scripture and Tradition.[7]

Nevertheless *Cur Deus Homo* has been the object of much criticism. The great Scholastic doctors especially upbraided St. Anselm for claiming to demonstrate the necessity of the incarnation. Where he speaks of necessity, they see only great fittingness. Thus they stress the gratuitousness of the redemption and the incarnation. They also show that our Savior could have merited our salvation otherwise than by his death. But was St. Anselm really wrong in thinking that God permits evil in his work only if he can draw at least an equivalent good from it? And does this do away with the gratuitousness of the divine gift? If, at these heights, St. Anselm's thought can be called into question, we must admit that it lacked neither force nor elevation.

Protestant historians criticise St. Anselm's doctrine from an entirely different viewpoint, thinking to attack Catholicism itself in it. According to Harnack, "Anselm places the divine attributes in a state of intolerable variance."[8] His doctrine would suppose a conflict between the divine attributes of justice and goodness; with the divine goodness unchangeably willing the salvation of mankind and his justice demanding adequate satisfaction, the incarnation is presented as mediating between the divine attributes—an anthropomorphic concept and one not much in conformity with Scripture.

But this is a false interpretation of St. Anselm's thought. He explicitly states that the creature neither gives anything to God nor takes anything away from him, that God's honor is only the order and beauty of the universe preserved or restored by the creature faithful to God's will. The divine goodness takes all the initiative in Christ's work of redemption, the divine creditor himself gives mankind the means of discharging its duties towards him: "God the Father says to man: 'Take my Son and give him for yourself.' "[9]

We must admit, however, that St. Anselm presents the incarnation as resulting immediately from the demands of the rights of God. In this he is not faithful to the teaching of Scripture which presents it as initiated by the divine mercy; for it is in consequence of this complete gift that all glory is given to God by mankind. Also, there is no opposition between the divine attributes. But in order that this could be seen, he had to show in the redemption the initiative of the Love who gives and forgives, and this is what St. Anselm does not emphasize enough. He tells us that after sin there must necessarily be punishment or satisfaction. But we must answer that there

[7] We may note that, among the few Scripture texts quoted by St. Anselm, several are concerned with Christ's meritorious act of obedience in accepting the cross: Isaiah 53:7; Matthew 26:39 and 42; Romans 5:19; John 6:38; 14:30; 18:11; Philippians 2:8; Hebrews 5:8.

[8] *Outlines of the History of Dogma,* trans. E. K. Mitchell (New York: Funk and Wagnalls, 1893), p. 427.

[9] 2, 20 in Schmitt's edition.

can be grace of pardon and conversion. Certainly man will have to make satisfaction, but he can do it only by grace, and the first gift from which all graces come is Christ. St. Anselm speaks to us very seldom about grace. Further, he does not give a good explanation how the satisfaction of Christ becomes ours, how the merits of Christ—which, he assures us, were unprofitable for himself (as if Christ did not merit his own glorification!)—are applied to us. This is because he too often forgets, in his *Cur Deus Homo,* the great doctrine of our vocation in Christ, of the incarnation as a source of grace. This is perhaps the most serious defect in this powerful work. How true it is that speculative thought finds it difficult to express all the fullness of the living faith. In short, St. Anselm strongly emphasized one aspect of redemption, that which answered to God's right to be glorified by his creature, and it was from this point of view that he analyzed the evil of sin and the work of Christ, which is a perfect satisfaction.

3. H. M. Manteau-Bonamy, O.P.,[1] discusses the Christology of Aquinas as it developed during three marked stages of his thought: as a young professor reflecting on Lombard's *Sentences,* as author of the *Summa Contra Gentiles,* and in his masterpiece the *Summa Theologica.* It is here that his vision of the Incarnation revived and enlightened the most authentic tradition in the Church. Here the Incarnation is no longer a union resulting from an ascent of the human nature toward the Person of the Word, but it is a mystery already accomplished by which the Word substitutes in humanity.

The Commentary on the Sentences (1256). With regard to the problem of the Incarnation, St. Thomas, as a young commentator on the *Sentences,* had his attention fixed continually upon the "three opinions."[2] True, only the second opinion (the so-called opinion of the "composite person") had been generally accepted since the end of the twelfth century. But the Angelic Doctor went to greater pains than anyone else to stress the importance of this position, by comparing it often with the two others, particularly with the first opinion. He accepted the Augustinian tradition which St. Anselm had taken up again.

The theologians of the thirteenth century never ceased repeating that in the Incarnation it was extremely *fitting* that the eternally begotten Son should assume a nature produced by generation. And St. Thomas brought out this same point in his *Commentary on the*

[1] H. M. Manteau-Bonamy, O.P., is a well-known Dominican theologian born in Poitiers, France. He is presently attached to the Dominican House of Studies in Paris. He has published several articles in *Bulletin de la Societé Francaise de études marials,* in *Revue Thomiste,* etc. He is the author of *Maternité divine et Incarnation,* Vries, 1964, and of *The Mystery of the Incarnation* in *The Historical and Mystical Christ,* ed. by A. M. Henry, v. V of *Theology Library* (Chicago, 1958). It is from pages 41–53 of this last book that this excerpt has been taken.

[2] The three opinions recorded by Peter Lombard are: 1) The "supposit assumed" by the Word. 2) The "composite person." 3) "The Word clothed with humanity" (opinion of Abelard).

Sentences. We should note, however, that St. Anselm's doctrine had been weakened. They no longer said it was *necessary* that the Son of God become incarnate, but only that it was supremely *fitting.*

The theological problem of the Incarnation was now seen as follows: on the one hand was the divine aspect, and on the other was the human aspect; how was the *union* of the divine and the human accomplished solely in the divine Person of the Word, in conformity with the Catholic Faith? . . .

Inasmuch as the divine Person is *immutable,* the Incarnation could be accomplished only by the ascent of the begotten human nature toward this Person. The mission of the Word is strictly a Trinitarian problem; the conception and assumption of the human nature constitute the Christological problem. . . .

Against the first opinion, St. Thomas specified: *that which* was assumed was not a reality that existed by itself, even though it was a reality, namely a perfectly constituted human nature. On the other hand, the second opinion appeared to present some difficulties. After all, was not the fundamental problem that of unifying everything in the divine Word and thus safeguarding His absolute simplicity? Hence the term "composite person" seemed an equivocal expression to all the theologians of that time. This second opinion was adopted strictly as an opinion. And yet it was better than the other two because it was the only one that explained the affirmations of our faith: "This man is God"—"God is this man"—"the man did not become God; but it is a fact that this man is God," etc., according to the law of the communication of idioms.

And what of the psychological and corporeal conditions of Christ? Since the Incarnation must be explained in terms of an (instantaneous) *ascent* of the human toward the Person of the Word, it is supremely fitting to consider the humanity as being already endowed with all sorts of perfections both natural and supernatural (the natural perfections of unclouded knowledge, the spontaneity that belongs to man in willing and acting, the absence of corporeal defects, etc.; the supernatural perfections of habitual grace, the virtues, and the gifts) and that this endowment be prior (logically) to the *union* which perfects all things in Christ. In short, we must acknowledge that in Christ all the qualities were present that were requisite for a nature destined from the first instant of its formation to the supreme dignity of *existing only in dependence upon the Word.*

This is a very brief summary of the doctrine of the young St. Thomas Aquinas, which was the faithful echo of his contemporaries' views.

From the Commentary on the Sentences to the Summa Theologiae. As the commentator on the *Sentences,* St. Thomas paid close attention to everything Scripture, the Fathers, and the Councils had to say. Alas! when the young professor first taught in Paris (1254–1259), his only sources of reference were a few Patristic texts, and then they were texts that had passed through several hands before reaching Peter Lombard and his commentators. But at the end of 1259 St. Thomas returned to Italy, and continued to teach there until 1267–1268. It was his good fortune, as early as 1259–1260, to discover a number of conciliar and Patristic collections recently brought from the East, which were rightly or wrongly attributed to various Fathers of Greece, Asia Minor, or Egypt. From then on, the Angelic Doctor made it his first task to study the thought of these authors as revealed in the newly found texts.

In his *Summa contra Gentiles* (Book IV, 28 ff.), he set up—with the help of these writings and those of St. Augustine's which were already known—a critical catalogue of the various heresies, at the end of which he set forth the true position of the Catholic Faith (Chapter 39). One of these heresies seemed to hold greater interest for him than the others, and he gave special attention to it. This was the heresy of Photinus which was given first place because it perhaps seemed to him to be one of the farthest removed from the Catholic religion. Perhaps, too, it gave him an opportunity to reflect more deeply upon the Christology of St. John, St. Paul, and the Cappadocian and Alexandrian Fathers. . . .

Thenceforth, in St. Thomas' mind, the name of Photinus was connected with all errors which placed primary emphasis on the perfecting of man or his elevation toward God in the person of Christ. This position seemed to him diametrically opposed to that of the Manichaeans and of Valentinus who saw only the downward movement of the divine into the human.

But as between the pure becoming of man that Photinus preached and pure "kenosis" (the annihilation of the divine in the human) of the Manichaeans, the Angelic Doctor found a golden mean: *the Word descended into the human by taking the human to Himself*. This conclusion seemed so rich and fruitful to him that it became the focal point of his *Summa Theologiae,* the point to which he referred all questions concerning the mystery of Christ in order to solve them. St. Thomas consciously revived the most authentic Tradition of the Church that had been inaugurated by the sacred writers, and that made up the heart of the thinking of St. Ignatius of Antioch, St. Athanasius, St. Cyril, St. Hilary of Poitiers, St. Augustine, St. Leo of Byzantium, and St. John Damascene.

The Summa Theologiae (IIIa Pars, 1272–1273). In his *Summa Theologiae,* St. Thomas no longer viewed the Incarnation, as he did in the *Sentences,* from the viewpoint of an ascent of the human toward the Person of the Word, from which ascent union would result. He affirmed the *mystery as already accomplished,* that is, he affirmed the hypostatic union. The Incarnation as he saw it was primarily a mystery of unity; and it is in this unity, guaranteed by the divine Person, that the theologian must take rational cognizance of the duality of natures: divine and human. In other words, he aproached the mystery from the point of view of the Word in His function of subsisting in humanity.

It became clear that if there was no human person in Christ this was due not to a deficiency but to a superabundance. For when it is affirmed at the outset that the divine Person subsists in the human nature, the conclusion necessarily follows: there is no human person properly so-called. This was a far cry from the argumentation of the *Sentences* in which the absence of the human person had been explained as follows: the nature was assumed by the Word before having attained to its own proper subsistence at the end of the process of human generation.

After studying the three "opinions" one after the other, St. Thomas declared that far from being opinions—that is, positions that men were more or less free to take or leave—the first and the third "opinions" were formal heresies which revived those of Nestorius and Photinus, whereas the second was the true teaching of the Catholic Faith. St. Thomas' assurance on this point can readily be understood if we remember that the second opinion comes from the Greek Fathers through St. John Damascene. When the expression "composite Word" is thus reinstated in its unitary context it regains all the primitive power and truth which it could not have with Peter Lombard and his commentators, who were of a dualistic turn of mind.

Hence, the human nature of Christ was compared to an instrument that the Word came to take up; but at the same time it was firmly maintained that the Word subsists in the human nature and communicates to it His personal existence. While the notion of instrument is inadmissible in the view of Nestorius, it became—when thus understood—the best help for our limited minds, dazzled by the unfathomable mystery of the hypostatic union. Nestorius, and Photinus even more than he, considered the Incarnation as the ultimate perfection of man existing by himself within the Word; whereas we must follow the Councils in considering the Incarnation as the mystery of a "God who truly became man."

The great originality of the *Summa* also consists in giving a theological explanation of the hypostatic union without allowing *generation* to intervene. From the point of view of the divine Person the union is not restricted to the Son alone, since each of the divine Persons has equal power to subsist in the human; from the point of view of the nature assumed, the fact of generation is not essential, inasmuch as the Word could just as well have assumed an angelic as a human nature.

The task of the author of the *Summa,* therefore, was to distinguish the multiple problems posed by this great mystery of our faith. After having considered the profound fitness of the Incarnation—which is the fitness of divine mercy in the face of the disorder to which Adam's sin had reduced the human race—he went right to the heart of the matter: what the hypostatic union is and what is explained through it (IIIa, q. 2–26). Then, by means of this study of what cannot not be, he set out to explain the conditions in which the Incarnation was in fact realized. That is the theological problem of the life of Jesus from His conception in the womb of the Virgin Mary until His death, His Resurrection, and His glorious Ascension which includes the study of the Mother of God and the study of the Redemption (IIIa, q. 27–59).

When the Angelic Doctor's plan for his treatise on the Incarnation is compared with that of Peter Lombard, we can see the wisdom of the former's choice: the whole work is centered on the hypostatic union as the light that allows us to penetrate a mystery that must necessarily remain obscure to us here below. . . .

The entire treatise gravitates around the hypostatic union, which is its indisputable foundation. The theologian gives the reasons for the union after it has been realized and not during the process of realization. Thus St. Thomas perfected the Anselmian tradition by correcting it, as his forceful words show:

> The mystery of the Incarnation is not to be looked upon as an ascent, as

> it were, of a man already existing and mounting up to the dignity of the union, as the heretic Photinus maintained. Rather is it to be considered as a descent, by reason of the perfect Word of God taking unto Himself the imperfection of our nature, according to Jn. 6:38: *I have come down from heaven.*[3]

To show that everything that must be attributed to Christ in accordance with His condition as man (grace, virtues, gifts, knowledge, etc.) is an *effective consequence* of the hypostatic union, St. Thomas continues:

> But the mystery of the Incarnation is considered as a condescension of the fullness of the Godhead into human nature rather than as the promotion of human nature, already existing, as it were, to the Godhead. Therefore in the man Christ there was perfection of spiritual life from the very beginning.[4]

This gives us a vivid picture of St. Thomas' profound thought toward the end of his life. Not only must we deny all *real* becoming of man into God, but if we want to explain this ineffable mystery without danger of error we must even stop thinking of it as a simple ascent of the human toward the Word. We must always keep the following point of view: through the Incarnation, the divine Word descended deep within human nature by taking it to Himself. It is impossible to lay too much stress on this fundamental point of the Christology of St. Thomas Aquinas.

Thus the fitness of the Incarnation and its fundamental motive, discussed in the first question of the *Tertia Pars* really constitute the marrow of the entire *Summa:* the intimate diffusion of the absolute Goodness which is God, a diffusion accomplished in the most superlative way since it culminates in making a created nature subsist in a divine Person, for the purpose of the Redemption.

> But because for us and for our salvation, uniting the human nature to His Person, He (the Son of God) became the child of a woman, for this reason do we say that He was born in the flesh.[5]

St. Thomas took this affirmation of St. Cyril's and made it his own, because, after the example of the Greek Fathers, he understood very well that "in (Christ) dwells all the fullness of the Godhead bodily" (Col. 2:9); and that in consequence of this not only did the Savior Himself as man but also all the members of His "body which is the Church" benefit from divine graces and favors. By a unique right, the God-man, the first among His brothers, possesses the perfection of holiness, of knowledge, and of power that can bring all men back to God.

The Holiness of Christ. Christ possesses grace at once in a measure and beyond measure. His sanctifying grace, like that of every other man, is measured by His personal nature, but this grace is far from being the foundation of His union with God. For the sanctifying grace of Christ results from the hypostatic union, and it is in this sense that St. Augustine writes that "grace is in a certain respect natural in Christ-the-man."

---

[3] IIIa, q. 33, a. 3, ad 3.
[4] IIIa, q. 34, a. 1, ad 1.
[5] IIIa, q. 35, a. 2, ad 2.

On the other hand, Christ possesses grace without measure if we consider His power as sanctifier. As God, Christ can give grace in His own right; He can even give the Holy Spirit. As man, it belongs to Him to do this instrumentally, for His humanity was from the beginning the instrument of the Godhead, conjoined to it forever. . . .

The Knowledge of Christ. It is because He is the Word made man that it is fitting to claim for Christ the knowledge proper to man: the knowledge that is acquired through the senses, and the knowledge that belongs only to the blessed in heaven, which He had even before the glorification of His body. . . .

The Marks of the State of the God-man. It is easy for us to realize that when the Son of God assumed a body and came into the world to make full satisfaction for the sins of the human race He had to take on "bodily defects, to wit, death, hunger, thirst, etc." He was also obliged to experience such states of soul as sensible pain, sadness, fear, astonishment, etc., with the exception of ignorance.

This is the doctrine of St. Augustine . . . In addition, the Angelic Doctor carried the thought of the Bishop of Hippo further by showing that the human will of Christ could have been in opposition to the divine will, since it possessed the natural and spontaneous tendency to avoid all pain and suffering. And yet the consciously and freely expressed will of Jesus could never contravene the will of His Father, that is the will of the Blessed Trinity as a whole. From this came the possibility of our Savior's meriting for Himself something that He did not yet have, namely the glory of His body and the worship that is due to His body; and of meriting for us, His members, all the graces that we need.

Christ, the Sole Mediator Between God and Men. . . . Christ was not only a priest. He was also a perfect offering; for He was at once an offering for sin, a peace offering, and a holocaust.

That is why His priesthood was established first of all to expiate the sins of the world. It is the mark of His priesthood that it is the source of all other priesthoods: the priesthood of the Old Law which was the figure of His own, and the priesthood of the New Law, which He keeps alive and efficacious in His own Person. . . .

If we are to hold fast to the essentials of the mystery of the Incarnation, we cannot unfold the riches of the *Summa Theologiae* all at once. It suffices to say that the reader who understands that the Incarnation is above all the mystery of the divine Person of the Son descending deep within human nature and taking it to Himself has penetrated the thought of the Angelic Doctor on our Savior and has grasped what matters most. . . .

4. F. Ferrier[1] points out that Scotus' views on the motive of the Incarnation have no basis in the early fathers of the Church. They originated in the Middle Ages, and Scotus' merit is to have popularized them and won acceptance for them. In him they are a logical consequence of his abstract analysis of God's activity. Ferrier also brings up the objection that they

[1] Cf. Ch. 4, n. 1. This excerpt is from *op. cit.,* pp. 104–114.

are not scripturally established. Their defenders attempt to read into scriptural texts, especially Pauline, ideas which the inspired writers never envisaged.

As we begin to reflect on the purpose of the Father in willing the Incarnation of the Word, we quite naturally ask ourselves whether, granted that Christ came on earth, as we know he did, in order to redeem us from sin and its consequences, and that in redeeming us he was fufilling the Father's will perfectly, God also willed the Incarnation in any case, apart altogether from man's sin. Did God will the Incarnation for its own sake, as an end in itself, or merely for the sake of redeeming man and restoring him to the privileged status of adopted sonship which he had shamefully lost? We all know that the one and only divine purpose for the Incarnation given in the Scriptures is our redemption from sin and death by the sacrifice and death of Christ on the cross. The Scriptures teach that in sending his Son into the world to die for us the Father manifested the wonder of his love for us: "God so loved the world, that he gave up his only-begotten Son, so that those who believe in him may not perish, but have eternal life" (John 3. 16). But would we be correct in thinking that a completely "gratuitous" and uncalled-for Incarnation, willed by God apart altogether from any considerations of man's needs, would redound to the glory of God more splendidly than an Incarnation willed simply for the purpose of rescuing man from sin? Does it seem likely that the Incarnation was willed by God, as it were, contingently, that is, just to meet the situation brought about by the contingency of Adam's sin?

The famous Franciscan thelogian Duns Scotus († 1308) considered that God decreed the Incarnation of the Word for its own sake and apart altogether from man's sin, for he willed that the Word Incarnate should be King of heaven and earth, the supreme Mediator between the Father and all created things. He questioned the adequacy of the view of St. Thomas, that God only willed the Incarnation of the Word and the majesty of Christ as the supreme Mediator between the Father and all created beings merely as a means to rectify evil, or merely to redeem man from sin. He argued that the Father predestined Christ to glory "as the first born of many creatures" absolutely in his decree to create the world; the ultimate purpose for which God willed to create the universe must have been that the Word Incarnate should be glorified as the Lord of all created things. Thus, for Scotus, God willed to create man ultimately for the greater honor and glory of Christ himself: he did not will Christ to be man merely to redeem sinners. Scotus argued that if the Incarnation had been willed by the Father solely as a remedy against sin, or as an atonement for sin to the Father, God's supreme gift, the most excellent of all his works, the God-man, would be little more than a sort of by-product in his plan of creation, just "occasioned," as it were, by the chance perversity of man rebelling against God. In other words, a purely redemptive Incarnation would only be a kind of divine afterthought to remedy evil, and not the supreme purpose of God's creative plan. The glory of created things must necessarily be inferior to that of the Word Incarnate, so that God would not have willed the Incarnation of the Word merely for the sake of any good he wished to bestow on man. God must always will a good to men solely that he might in doing good to men glorify his Incarnate Word. For Scotus, then, Christ is the centerpiece of all created things, and the supreme purpose of creation as such; he is not just a means God "improvised" to save fallen man from his own sins and the evils he had brought upon himself by his sins.

Scotus considered that he was defending a view that had the support of many early doctors of the Church, but in fact his theory was comparatively new for it originated in the Middle Ages, having been suggested by Honorius of Autun († 1152), who argued that sin, the greatest of evils, cannot have been the occasion for the Father willing the Incarnation itself, but only for the Father willing the death of the Incarnate Word as a satisfaction for sin. Scotus popularized and won acceptance for this view so that it has come to be known as the Franciscan view about the divine purpose of the Incarnation. Before Scotus' time it was favored by the Franciscan Alexander of Hales, and the Dominican St. Albert the Great, and it was taught later by the Franciscan missionary, St. Bernardine of Siena. It was developed later by Denis the Carthusian, Suarez the Jesuit theologian, and particularly the great Bishop of Geneva, St. Francis de Sales, with whose name it deserves to be particularly associated nowadays. The cardinal tenet of the Salesian theology is that the God-man is at the center of God's plan of creation, for God created man for the sake of Christ. The God-man is, then, the starting point and the final purpose of all creation: simply speaking, God willed Christ and all things solely for Christ.

The modern defenders of this view find support for these arguments from reason in the texts of Scripture, especially those of St. Paul, in which the absolute sovereignty of Christ over all creatures is set forth. The captivity Epistles of St. Paul contain a number of well-known expressions which, it is claimed, support the idea that God willed all created things solely for the glory of Christ. For example, in the Epistle to the Colossians we read: "He is the true likeness of the God we cannot see; his is that first birth which precedes every act of creation. Yes, in him all created things took their being, heavenly and earthly, visible and invisible" (1. 15–17).

Against this Scotist-Salesian view, which has the support of many eminent theologians today, is what we may call the older view of those who link the Incarnation with Christ's redemptive mission, saying that the Word became a man simply to redeem us from sin. These theologians follow St. Thomas. . . . The Thomist view is undoubtedly easier to understand and to explain, and it lacks a certain imaginative appeal which the Scotist and Salesian view possesses. The view of St. Francis de Sales no doubt appeals to many theologians because of the emphasis it puts on the gratuitous nature of God's greatest gift to man, and because it enables us to see more readily that God's creative plan was not "upset" in any way by man's sin.

St. Bonaventure, the greatest of the medieval Franciscan Doctors, seems to have preferred the view St. Thomas defended. St. Thomas considered that we owe the Incarnation solely to the free act of God by which he willed to save man from sin, so that we cannot have any means of knowing whether he had decided to send his Son as man apart from what he has revealed to us. St. Bonaventure said exactly the same: "Whatever depends on the will of God alone, and is in no way demanded by a creature, can only be known to us if revealed in Scripture by which the will of God has been made known to us,"[2] and he rejected the other view, which to him was an innovation, as anthropomorphic in character because allowing too much to a mere argument of convenience.

It seems that the supporters of the Scotist-Salesian view make the mistake of reading into the texts of St. Paul on the sovereignty of Christ ideas which St. Paul himself never envisaged. In the passages quoted St. Paul is explaining that, as the Word of God, Christ is the exemplar of all created things, and that he created as one with the Father and the Holy Spirit. We cannot argue from what he says about God creating that he was writing about creation as such without considering either the possibility or the fact of Adam's sin: on the contrary the contexts show in every case that he is just stating that position Christ holds *in the present order of things,* which is one of creation followed by redemption. In the long exordium which precedes the text we have cited from the Epistle to the Colossians, as in that at the beginning of the Epistle to the Ephesians, St. Paul is writing about the Christ who is our redeemer. In Ephesians, he says that the resurrection is the manifestation of God's will to exalt Christ above the angels, which proves that "God has put everything under his dominion" (1. 22); but we know that Christ merited the glory of his resurrection by his death.

It is very difficult to accept the claims of the Franciscan writer, Fr. P. Chrysostome,[3] that the Scotist view can be found in the traditional teaching of the Fathers of the Church. Msgr. Michel, . . . has sifted the texts of the Fathers put forward by Fr. Chrysostome, and concluded that the patristic support claimed is far from being substantiated.[4] Many passages from the Fathers have to be misconstructed and wrenched from their contexts to make them serve even as favorable to the Scotist view. Texts, quoted to support the idea that God willed the Incarnation absolutely for its own sake, in fact treat of the equality of the Word with God the Father as two Persons of the Trinity. When Clement of Alexandria, Origen and St Ambrose comment on the scriptural theme that the Word is the eternal, subsistent Word equal to the Father, it is impossible to conclude from their commentaries on these texts that they must have been dealing with the will of the Father for the Incarnation of the Word, nor his purpose in willing to create the universe. It is equally false to conclude that because, in commenting on these texts, they do not always mention that Christ became a man to redeem sinners, the Fathers held that the Word would have become a man if Adam had never sinned. A point which is not mentioned by a writer because he is not dealing with it at all is not necessarily absent from his mind. In any case it is absolutely certain that all the Fathers

---

[2] St. Bonaventure, *Commentary on the Sentences,* 3, dist. 1, art. 2, qu. 2.
[3] *Le Motif de l'Incarnation et les principaux thomists contemporaines.*
[4] *Incarnation,* DTC, cc. 1445 ff.

held that the Word did become man to redeem us from sin . . .

It is interesting to ask how Duns Scotus came to envisage his idea of a separate Incarnation for its own sake. His theory was probably the logical consequence of his having followed a purely abstract way of thinking and reasoning in analysing the manner in which God acts. But in making his analysis Scotus failed to avoid the danger which besets us all of thinking of God in an anthropomorphic manner. When a man examines some course of activity, he is forced to analyse, and split up in his mind into separate parts, his motives for acting, the incentives which prompted him to act, and the various aspects of the end he hoped to achieve by his activity. This way of analysing activities is valid and necessary on the purely human level, and it forms an integral part of any study in psychology. But it is invalid if it is applied vigorously to God whose activity and thinking are of a transcending simplicity. This is why St. Thomas warns us that "God's understanding of a cause is not the cause of his understanding the effect, *for God just sees the effect in its cause;* in the same way, the willing of an end is not the cause of God willing the means. God only wills that the means should be ordered to the end. In other words, God wills that this should be for the sake of that, he does not will this because he wills that."[5] The way in which we have to think of the decision to act as being anterior to the act itself is one of the major difficulties we experience in trying to think of God's activity in the world, for we find difficulty in thinking of God, who is Being outside time, except as though he is and acts in some way in time. The analysis of God's activity into "moments" and into numerous "separate acts" of mind and will, some being for the sake of others, is no more valid if applied to God's willing to create or send his Son on earth as man, than it is if applied to the interior acts of God's life in the Trinity, that is, to the Generation of the Word and the Spiration of the Holy Spirit. Care has to be taken from the start to ensure that, in the analogies we use to think of the Persons in the Trinity, we are excluding all temporal relationships; the human terms we use to refer to the Father, Son and Holy Spirit will inevitably be meaningless if they are thought to imply temporal succession in God. The same is true if, in analysing God's purposes in willing the Incarnation of his Son, we think that God's willing of Christ's glory is the cause of his willing to create man.

Scotus was mistaken in treating Adam's sin as a kind of intrusion or misfortune which upset the first set of plans God had made for man's happiness. In creating Adam and Eve, God knew that Adam would sin; he also knew that he had willed to redeem fallen man by the passion and death of his Son, and that by the obedience of his death he would merit the supreme glory for himself as the Lord of all things in heaven and earth. God made a progressive revelation of his plan, but there was no progress in his plan. He gradually unfolded in a temporal sequence of different stages his one divine plan which we see realized as one long history. We should not lose sight of the absolute simplicity either of God's Being, or of the acts of his mind and will, for both his Being and

[5] St. Thomas Aquinas, *Summa Theologica,* 1, qu. 19, art. 5.

his Activity transcend human being and activity. We must keep in mind the basic metaphysical principle that God does not know things, as we do, because they exist; on the contrary, things exist in the way they do, and are linked with each other as they are, because God knows them in the simplicity of his own Being.

Further, Scotus' theory that God wills the Incarnation of the Word just for its own sake as a good in itself that Christ may be the head of all creation, only makes sense if it is correct to think of God's will in the kind of way we think of our human acts of will. Scotus thought that, if Adam had never sinned, Christ would still have been predestined in the same way to be the Lord of all creation, for it is more perfect for him to have this title in a sinless order than to come to its possession as it were by chance, through man having fallen into sin. But Scotus forgets that the greatest of all Christ's titles is that of "Redeemer of the human race": in the present order Christ is far more gloriously the Lord of the universe, which he not only created as God but also redeemed as the Word Incarnate, than he would have been in a sinless order of things. Thus to say that man's sin was the foreseen occasion of God willing the Incarnation is not in any way to lessen the glory God willed to Christ as his own Son. All the works of God are a manifestation of his love. As God is love his works necessarily express his love for his creatures. Thus God did not need to will the Incarnation to express the reality of his love for us. We cannot use the old principle that "the good gives of its very self" to show that the only gift of God that God could wish as good or perfect in itself is the Incarnate Word, for outside himself God cannot will any effect as good or perfect in itself. The divine self-communication is only good and perfect in itself within the bosom of the Trinity. The self-communication of God in the hypostatic union cannot be perfected in itself for the limitations of a mortal thing, even Christ's human nature, impose limits on the created gifts God can make of himself to us.

There could be no gain in glory to the Word coming from creatures which could make his Incarnation as a creature a good to be willed by God for its own sake. On the contrary, an Incarnation, even in a sinless human nature, would always be a "dispossession" of his own divine glory which could never be restored or "made up to God" by any limited finite glorification he received from creatures. God willed to create all creatures for himself in his own *divine* being. Scotus exaggerated in saying that man's sin was a kind of unfortunate chance event of man's early history, which he conceived as taking God, as it were, by surprise. God knew that sin was an intrinsic possibility to any created being, man or angel, because of its limitations, so it is not correct to talk as though, in the traditional view, God willed the Incarnation on the chance and almost unforeseen occasion of this unfortunate event taking place. Thus Scotus' way of looking at the Thomist doctrine shows up the anthropomorphic way of his thinking about God's will which St. Thomas sedulously avoided. For St. Thomas sinful man aspires for deliverance from sin and help from God, and God's will that the Word should be Incarnate to save man shows that God willed the God-man as a good which is perfect in relation to the work of redeeming man from his fallen condition. Christ has the supreme glory of being the Lord and Head of redeemed man, and thus Christ is the supreme manifestation of God to man in his actual state of sinfulness. But a God-man would not be the highest manifestation of God possible to sinless man, for in fact God destined man to see God as he is in himself in the inner life of the Trinity. . . .

5. H. A. Oberman[1] points out how the kerygma of the Incarnation for Gabriel Biel is based on the exinanition of God without entailing a sacrifice on God's part. He notes an unresolved tension between Biel's concern to protect the concreteness of Christ's humanity and his preoccupation to uphold God's utter immutability. According to him, Biel's soteriological views differ from those of Anselm. His emphasis is directed to the active obedience of Christ and not to the passivity of his death. This approach influenced greatly the evaluation of the efficacy of Christ's sacrifice.

Biel's Understanding of the Incarnation: Kenosis and Extracalvinisticum. When we turn to the christological statements in the *Sermones,*[2] we still have to be extremely cautious not to reach too hasty conclusions. These passages usually are cast in a traditional garb which makes it hard to discern Biel's own mind behind the formulation. But judging on the grounds of his selection of traditional statements, we seem to find here a further elaboration of the accident-substance simile as applied to the relation of the human nature and the divine person, a simile suggested by Scotus and Occam and mentioned but not discussed at length in Biel's commentary on the *Sentences.*[3]

As in the *Sentences,* the reality of the personal union is repeatedly stressed. Humanity and not man is assumed by the divine Person, and this humanity does not become the Word but is carried by it. Its relation now to the Word is that of the white color of the milk to the milk itself: the color is not the milk—but, as we would add—only an accident of the milk. The accident-substance example excludes at the one hand the possibility of a confusion of the two natures. At the other hand it stresses the real relation between the two, whereas it does not admit of a Nestorian duality through parallelism.

On the one hand we may therefore say that the kerygma of the Incarnation

---

[1] Heiko Augustinus Oberman is a native of Utrecht, Holland. He is presently Director of the Institute for Reformation History at the University of Tubingen. He was formerly Wenn Professor of Ecclesiastical History at Harvard Divinity School. He coedited with W. J. Courtenay *Canonis Misee Expositio Resolutissima Gabrielis Biel* (Franz Steiner Verlag, Wiesbaden, I, 1963), II, 1965. He is the author of *Forerunners of the Reformation* (Holt, Rinehart, 1966), and *The Harvest of Medieval Theology* (Harvard University Press, 1963). It is from pages 264–270 of this last work that this excerpt is taken.

[2] His *Sermones* are compiled in five works, I to V respectively: *Sermones Dominicales de Tempore,* (Hagenau, 1510); *Sermones de Festivitatibus Christi,* (Hagenau, 1510); *Sermones de Festivitatibus Gloriose Virginis Marie,* (Hagenau, 1910); *Sermones de Sanctis,* (Basel, 1519); and *Passionis Dominicae Sermo Historialis,* (Antverpiae, 1556).

[3] His Commentary to the Sentences was published in Tubingen in 1501 under the title of *Epithoma pariter at collectorium circa quattuor sententiarum librom.*

is for Biel clearly based in the exinanition and condescension of God: God became man and sacrificed his glory to assume the miseries of the human condition. On the other hand the accident-substance example functions at places in such a way that the Incarnation does not seem to entail a sacrifice on God's part, since the human nature is only the accident of the divine Person.

We see how this interpretation functions when Biel describes in one sermon what is for him the heart of the mystery of the Incarnation. This proves to be not the humanity, but the divinity of Christ; not the internal *kenosis,* but the fact that the immutable God became man without diminution or loss as regards any of his attributes. What would later be called the *extracalvinisticum*—the existence of the second *person* of the Trinity *et extra carnem,* and erroneously seen as an innovation on the part of John Calvin—tempers here the kenotic understanding of the Incarnation. . . .

In Chapter Seven, we noted how important it is for Biel in connection with the *fiducia* of the Christian that Christ can be shown to be a real man. And in that context we noted a tension between fiducial hope and emphasis on the divine nature of Christ.[4] In the present context we encounter this again in the unresolved tension between a decided concern, shared with Scotus and Occam, to protect the concreteness of the human nature of Christ—and therefore a real exinanition of God precisely *in* the Incarnation—and the other pole of Biel's understanding of the human nature as merely external and accidental, expressed in his emphasis on the immutability of God, *notwithstanding* the Incarnation. The preponderance of this latter interpretation appears, as we shall see, from Biel's discussion of the *fiducia* of the Christian with respect to the Virgin Mary.[5]

Biel's Modification of Anselm: Centrality of the Life, not the Death of Christ. The focal points of the work of Christ in Biel's theology can be best expressed with the titles "physician" and "instructor"; the decisive actions of Christ were his institution of the sacraments and his proclamation of the new law. Thus the *viator* is provided with the energy and the knowledge to escape the prison broken open by the absolute obedience of Christ. Therefore when we deal especially with the

[4] In Chapter seven Dr. Oberman pointed out how in Biel's thought Christian fiducial hope "would stand or fall with the true humanity of Christ" (p. 235). According to him Biel bases the security of hope on God's love for man irrevocably demonstrated in the exinanition of the Incarnation. "The kenosis brings forth the response of love, so that the fact that He did not empty himself for his own sake, but *pro nobis* evokes in us the security of faith, *fiducia*" (p. 225). This way God provided in his first advent a reliable object for the hope of the *viator.* Oberman notes, therefore, how for Biel "the fiducial hope of the viator is not so much evoked by the crucified Christ as by the Christ of the exinanition. "It rests on the kerygma of the Incarnation and Ascension of Jesus Christ" (pp. 233, 235).

[5] Dr. Oberman notes in Chapter IX, III, *Fiducia in the Virgin Mary,* how in the discussion of the Christian's fiducial hope in Mary, Biel gives as reason for the greater or deeper trust that the Christian might have in Mary rather than in Christ the fact that Christ's humanity is "not pure humanity," since it is uniquely united to the godhead. The contrast of Mary with Christ is that of a *homo purus* and a *homo deus.* "As man's pure nature is represented in the Virgin Mary and has been elevated above the ranks of the angels, no doubt is left that human creatures at some time will join their ranks" (p. 315).

meaning which the passion of Christ has for Biel, it is not because Christ's role as mediator and victor is to be more emphasized than his role of physician or teacher, but because the victory of Christ is the precondition for the efficacy of his other roles.

Structurally Biel preserves the argument of Anselm's *Cur deus homo*. The *necessitas* motif is omitted, of course, in view of the other possibilities open to God *de potentia absoluta,* but the main structure of Anselm's argumentation looms up time and again.[6]

Apart from the rejection of the necessity of Christ's self-sacrifice, there are two more significant changes which are intimately related. The death of Christ does not seem to have the same centrality and significance for Biel as it has for Anselm. Expressed in terms current since late sixteenth-century orthodoxy, Biel stresses more the *obedientia activa*—Christ's fulfillment of the law throughout his life—than the *obedientia passiva*—his expiatory death for the sin of mankind.[7]

The passion of Christ is a continual suffering that began at the moment of his birth, the flight to Egypt, and the poverty of his youth. Christ's death on the cross is only the culmination of a whole life dedicated to obedience and fulfillment of the law. Death was incidental; for what God required of his son was perseverance in righteousness and truth.

This is more than a traditional declaration of the spontaneity of Christ's offer. Biel is primarily interested in the quality of Christ's life, tested and exemplified in his death. And although the propitiation motif is by no means absent, one surmises that the imitation-of-Christ ideal shapes Biel's presentation of Christ's passion. The God-directed Anselmian interpretation of Calvary is markedly less characteristic of Biel's position than the man-directed Abelardian understand- of the work of Christ.

This observation leads us to another related point. The emphasis on the paradigmatic significance of the life and death of Christ determines also the evaluation of the fruits of Christ's obedience and sacrifice. According to what we have called the second eternal decree, the *viator* has to fulfill the law and meet certain set standards of justice. In the life of Christ, especially in the incarnation but also in the passion, a love of God is revealed that has a profound impact on the *viator*. Nevertheless, one cannot profit from the work of Christ without a spontaneous love for God above everything else. The sufficiency of the work of Christ is seen as a sufficient revelation of God's will; in other words it is viewed as a testament.

The sacrifice of Christ is also sufficient with respect to the remission of sins of baptized children who are redeemed by the work of Christ *alone*. With respect to adults, however, the work of Christ alone is not sufficient: "Though the passion of Christ is the principal merit on account of which grace is infused, the kingdom opened and glory granted, yet it is never the sole and complete meritorious cause."

---

[6] The chosen way of redemption is, however, *congruentissimus* and based on God's wisdom. . . . On the structure of Anselm's argumentation see the clear presentation by Krijn Strijd, *Structuur en inhoud van Anselmus' "Cur Deus Homo"* (Assen, 1958), esp. p. 70 ff. With a summary in English and extensive bibliography, p. 301 ff.

[7] Cf. Heinrich Heppe and Ernst Bizer, *Die Dogmatik der evangelisch-reformierten Kirche* 2 ed. (Neukirchen, 1958), pp. 358, 369 ff.

And again: "If we do not add our merits to those of Christ, the merits of Christ will not only be insufficient, but nonexistent."

Imitation of the Christus Victor. The same imitation motif which we surmised behind Biel's primary interest in the *obedientia activa* seems here to lead him to statements that according to late medieval doctrinal standards can hardly be called orthodox. What Biel actually wants to express is not that the work of Christ as such is insufficient, but that the intention of his work can be frustrated by the disobedience of the *viator*. This possibility of frustration is the counterpart of the *pro nobis* theme. Christ not only gained a victory over the devil and thus liberated mankind, but he also showed those who are freed from prison the way out and home.

In the first sense, Christ as *victor,* the work of Christ is complete and sufficient. In the second sense, Christ as example or as *dux,* the work of Christ awaits completion pending the decision of the freed *viator* to follow and imitate him.

The same sermon from which we quoted the bold statement that the work of Christ is even less than insufficient unless complemented by human merits suggests that this is to be understood within the imitation context, and therefore indicates that the work of Christ will prove to be of no avail on judgment day for the unconverted sinner. The passion of Christ, sufficient in itself, will be efficacious only for the elect who indeed imitate Christ and follow him as their leader.

It is in the *Christus Victor* theme that Biel expresses the sufficiency of the work of Christ. His victory over devil and hell is complete: the power of the devil to incarcerate those who are informed by faith and love is broken once and for all. As *victor* he becomes the *dux* who leads (*eduxit*) the innocent children and the saints of the Old Covenant out of their prison.

The *Christus Victor* concept though not the dominant theme of Biel's kerygma, proves to be the systematic key to Biel's Christology since here the disparate lines we noted above suddenly converge. The first of these lines was the emphasis on the divinity of Christ. While the body of the Son of Man lies in its grave, it is the Son of God, in hypostatic union with the soul of Christ but no longer true man, who descends to break open the gates of Hell. Second, it is through Christ's complete fulfillment of the law, his *obedientia activa,* that the devil cannot hold Christ in his power, a reverberation of the early Christian image of the fish and the hook. And third, we see how Christ's work can be sufficient and complete for baptized children, while for the common *viator,* swayed between fear and hope, Christ is only a *dux* to be followed in trial and error.

Finally, Biel's pastoral advice, in light of the *Christus Victor* idea, speaks for itself: the most powerful weapon and strongest antidote against attacks of the devil is the cross. . . . We need only add that resurrection and ascension follow the victory over hell and the devil as its result, reward, and evidence; and as such they are definitely more important than Calvary.

It is clear that Biel's Christology exemplifies the compatibility of the imitation-of-Christ ideal with the *Christus Victor* motif. Nevertheless these two themes should be distinguished; they can be discerned as pointing respectively to the insufficiency and to the sufficiency of the work of Christ. Whereas passive obedience belongs in the context of an Anselmian interpretation of the work of Christ, Biel stresses active obedience together with an Abelardian interest in the impact on mankind of the work of Christ.

It is the active obedience of Christ that serves as an explanation of the victory over the devil. *The Christus Victor motif provides the systematic key to Biel's Christology.* The *viator* must first reap the fruits of the victory of the *Christus Victor*. To the degree to which the *viator* imitates Christ's active obedience, to this degree he too will overcome the powers of devil and hell.

6. J. Meyendorff[1] points out how Gregory Palamas, a fourteenth-century Byzantine saint and theologian, thought of Redemption in terms of death and life, corruption and immortality. Loyal to Patristic tradition he did not view it as "satisfaction" to divine justice, but rather as reconciliation with a living God. Man's deification is a direct consequence of the historical work of Christ. It was Palamas' doctrine of deification that led him to pose the christological problem proper. In what sense was Christ's humanity deified?

Before studying Palamas' thought about deification . . . we should briefly analyze his conception of the work of Christ, which in his view was at the center of human history. His *Homily 16* is devoted to this subject, and is in fact a theological treatise on Redemption.

The Redemption. The Son of God made man "was born of a woman to put on the nature which he had created and which had been corrupted by the counsel of the Evil One; he was born of a woman who was a virgin to create a new man." Thus of his free will he made himself like unto us, in our weakness and our mortality, but he brought in himself the germ of a new life: "Having become son of man and having assumed mortality . . . he transformed men into sons of God, having made them share the divine immortality." . . . Thus the whole work of redemption is conceived in terms of death-life, corruption-immortality. . . . The transmission of Adam's sin was essentially understood by Palamas as a hereditary corruption entailing *at the same time* mortality of the flesh and sinfulness; the voluntary death and resurrection of Christ delivered man from this vicious circle of death and sin. "By a single death, that of his own flesh, and by a single resur-

[1] John Meyendorff is a Russian Orthodox priest professor at St. Vladimir's Orthodox Seminary in Tuckahoe, N.Y. He was Lecturer of Byzantine Theology in the Dumbarton Oaks Research Library and is the author of many studies in his field, published in different Byzantine reviews. His work on St. Gregory Palamas includes *The Doctrine of Grace in St. Gregory Palamas* and *Introduction a l'étude de Gregoire Palamas.* It is from the translation of the last one *A Study of Gregory Palamas* tr. by G. Lawrence, (London: Faith Press, 1964) that this excerpt has been taken, selectively, from pp. 158–159, 175, 180–184.

rection, that of that same flesh, he has healed us from a double death and delivered us from a double captivity, that of our soul and that of our body"; "by his bodily death he has struck down the one who, in death, reigned over soul and body." "For us he suffered a death which he did not deserve . . . to ransom us from slavery to the Devil, and to death, death of the soul and death of the body. . . ."

The death of Christ was above all necessary to break the corrupted heredity of "the old man"; it was a sacrifice of purification, in the Biblical sense of that term. "A sacrifice was necessary," wrote Palamas, "to reconcile us with the heavenly Father and to sanctify us, we who had been soiled by contact with the Evil One. . . . And we need not only a resurrection of the soul, but also the resurrection of the flesh." The loyally Patristic line of the soteriology of Gregory uses throughout expressions derived from St. Paul and from the Byzantine liturgy, especially the Sunday liturgy. For him, redemption is not a "satisfaction" granted to divine justice, but a reconciliation of human nature, fallen and mortal, with a living God. By accepting that his own Son, in the flesh of the old Adam, dies on the cross, and by communicating his own life to man in Jesus, God reestablished his own legitimate power and suppressed the deadly usurpation of the Devil; the Trinity again became accessible to man in immediate, direct and intimate fashion. Palamas uses phrases about this subject which clearly show his existential approach to the Christian mystery: "If the Word of God had not been incarnate, the Father would not have in plain fact manifested himself as Father, nor the Son in plain fact as Son, nor the Holy Spirit as proceeding also from the Father; then God would not have revealed himself in his essential and hypostatic existence, but only as an *energy* contemplated in creatures, as used to be said by the wise ones of old . . . and is said now by the partisans of Barlaam and Akindynos." The doctrine of deification is for Palamas a direct consequence of the historical work of Christ; without him, divine life would have remained inaccessible to man. . . .

It is the supernatural character of deifying grace that Palamas wishes to stress; it is the divine way itself, infinite and uncreated, which appears to us, and *really becomes ours*. This divine mystery into which God allows us to penetrate, this union which he makes accessible to us, is the Mystery of the Church, the Body of Christ. There is no other way of "knowing God in God" but to be grafted by the new birth of baptism on to the Body of the Incarnate Word. The Saints are those "who are born of God by the Word through grace in the Spirit and who keep the likeness to God, their Father." They are in truth "God," "since in all birth that which is begotten is identical with the begetter; that which is born of the flesh is flesh, and that which is born of the Spirit is Spirit" (John 3:6).[2]

Real Deification. Palamas expressed this "identity with the Father" in striking phrases which shocked his adversaries. However his essential thought is borrowed from St. Maximus: man "becomes by participation (*methexei*) that which the Archetype is as cause"

[2] *Apology, Coisl.* 99, *fol.* 131–v.

(*kat' aitian or physei*),[3] he becomes "God by grace" (*chäriti* or *thesei*).[4] As a result the life of God becomes his life, and God's existence his existence. . . .

The Christological problem. Palamas' doctrine of deification led him to pose a Christological problem about which he was in conflict with his adversaries. If the Saints possess "one single *energy*" with Christ, if they "become uncreated" and receive the divine life, if their bodies and their souls produce works which, in our Lord's own words, are "greater" than those which he himself accomplished (John 14:12), one may ask whether the Saints do not identify themselves entirely with God, and whether their created humanity is not absorbed by the divine life. That is the objection which his adversaries raised against him, though they themselves found no other solution than the participation of man in the divine essence, which, for Palamas, did signify total absorption of the human by the divine. That is a problem in Gregory's theology to which we shall return. For the moment it is enough to state the essential Christological assumptions which determined Palamas' thought about deification.

To defend the nominalist positions which he had inherited from Barlaam, Akindynos had recourse to a Christological argument. How, he asks, can one say that participation in Christ confers an uncreated grace, when the humanity of Jesus—in which we participate—was itself created? To assert the contrary would be Monophysite heresy. For Akindynos, the concept of "nature" was a static notion, and the uncreated character properly belonging to the divine nature could not, clearly, be communicated even by participation. "The Lord, One of the Holy Trinity," he writes in an important Christological passage inspired by the Council of Chalcedon, "having become man, has preserved inalienable and invisible his own divinity; he did not transform his own nature into ours with which he united, nor did he transform the nature in which he clothed himself into his own, although he deified it; on the contrary, after the union, the one remained uncreated as before, and the other created, and the two together constituted the incarnate Son of God, man and God; but if such a transformation was to take place, should it not have occurred in him? *A fortiori* (in dwelling) in all the others, he preserved the inalienability of his dignity; and just as, being incorruptible, he could submit himself to corruption . . . so, when he lets himself be seen by the bodily eyes of the holy contemplatives . . . he takes on a certain aspect of such visible (created) beings."[5] This exposition, though verbally accurate, is however incomplete in so far as it does not take into account the "communication of the idioms" as defined by Leontius of Byzantium and St. Maximus the Confessor, and in that it does not allow any real content to the two references it makes to that communication, "although he deified it" and "both together constitute the

[3] *Tr.* I, 3, 39; Maximus, *Opusc. theol. et pol., P.G.* XCL, 33C; *Amb.*, 1084C, 1345D, etc.
[4] *Tr.* II, 3, 52, 68; *Tr.* III, 1, 25; *Theophanes, col.* 948C, etc.
[5] *Against Palamas,* II, *Monac. gr.* 223, *fol.* 163–163v.

Son of God." But the very basis of Palamas' conception of deification was formed from the doctrine of St. Cyril of Alexandria concerning the "appropriation" of the flesh by the Son of God, and from the ideas of St. Maximus about the "communication of idioms." On the other hand Barlaam's, and the other fourteenth century humanists' nominalist thought led to a return towards Nestorianism: humanity and divinity, inalienable natures impermeable one by the other, are in a purely external relation of juxtaposition; deification and grace are created entities, for that reason essentially different from the divine nature, and belonging to the domain of symbols; the participation in God through essence which they sometimes allowed in order to answer Palamas' arguments, leads them on the other hand necessarily to Monophysitism. So it is the Orthodox position, situated at an equal distance away from the two main Christological heresies, that Palamas studies to defend, expressing this doctrine in terms which are almost always borrowed from St. Maximus the Confessor.

There are two main points which he stresses:

1. Humanity and divinity are *united in the hypostasis* of Christ, Son of God.
2. Sanctifying and deifying grace does really reach us by virtue of the "communication of idioms" starting from the *humanity* of Christ, "source of deification," and not only from his divinity.

Hypostatic union and divine energies. The "hypostatic union" of divinity and humanity in Jesus Christ is the very foundation of salvation, and therefore of deification: in Christ, humanity has already participated in the uncreated life of God, because the "flesh" has truly become "the flesh of God." Akindynos, "in wishing to show that deification is something created," "has dared to cite as an example the deification of (the humanity) put on by the Master and to declare that it too was created."[6] Did not the life of that humanity of Christ come from the hypostasis of the Son to which it belonged *as his own?* That is the whole argument of St. Cyril against Nestorius: "The Son of God," Palamas writes, "*is one* with the humanity which he put on, for in his hypostasis he is united with the firstfruits of humanity; that is why we apply to him appellations which derive from humanity, and he grants his appellations to humanity: however, he is not one with every man who receives grace, as he is one with his own humanity: with each (Christian) he is united through *energy* and by grace, and not by the hypostasis; that is why there is only one Christ, because there is only one sole and indivisible hypostasis of the Word of God. . . ."[7] It is therefore the *life of the Word* which deifies the human nature of Christ, and it is *that very life* which, in Christ, is accessible to us, for otherwise our salvation would not have been realized. "What connection should we have with Christ, if he had made a temple in the firstfruits taken from men, without making us temples of his divinity?[8] God in his completeness was incarnate, even though all the divine hypostases were not incarnate; he has united one of the three hypostases with our 'mixture'

[6] *Letter to Athanasius, Coisl.* 98, *fol.* 13.
[7] *Against Akindynos,* III, 6, *Coisl.* 98, *fol.* 73v; cf. *Tr.* II, 3, 21.
[8] Ibid., *fol.* 74v.

(*tō hēmeterō phyrāmati*), not through essence, but by the hypostasis; thus God in his completeness deifies those who are worthy of this, by uniting himself with them not through the hypostasis—that belonged to Christ alone—nor through the essence, but through a small part of the uncreated *energies* and the uncreated divinity . . . while yet being entirely present in each."[9] Palamas indignantly rejects the imputation that he had said that the *humanity* of Christ was uncreated; that would be to disregard the difference between hypostatic union and essential union; the latter assumes a "mixture" (*phyrmon*) of the two natures in Christ, and the participation of all in the essence of the divinity: "If the deifying gift, the deification accorded to the saints . . . is the divine essence and hypostasis, all the Saints are equal to Christ," and the deity becomes "polyhypostatic" (*muriupostatos*).[10] Thus, the humanity proper to Christ "became heavenly not by nature but by dignity, and because of its hypostatic union with the Word of God."[11] So, in Palamite terminology, we have here a clear distinction between the concepts of "essential union," "hypostatic union" and union through the *energies;* for him, these three modes of union are simply established on traditional Chalcedonian and post-Chalcedonian Christology, and on the doctrine of the *communication of idioms.*

The "Body of God." Though Christ alone united *in his hypostasis* divinity and humanity, he communicates to all Christians the *divine energy*—in other words, sanctifying grace—of which he is the source. This he can do in that he has made himself like to men by making *his* their whole nature; therefore it is as Son of God become man that he communicates the divine life. Palamas expresses that soteriological reality in his mystical doctrine of the Body of Christ which, because it is truly the "Body of God," can communicate the divine life: "The Lord, even as man, had received and possessed the divine *energy* and grace."[12] His deified flesh had received and communicates the eternal glory of the Deity; that is what is represented on the Icons and worshipped in so far as it manifests the Divinity of Christ, and it is that too which is offered to us in the sacrament of the Eucharist. "This bread," Palamas writes, "is as a veil between us and the mystery of Divinity (Heb. 10:20), and by this flesh our community is raised to heaven; that is where this Bread truly dwells (cf. John 6:36 ff.); and we enter into the Holy of Holies by the pure offering of the Body of Christ."[13]

So Palamas' doctrine of deification is only one aspect of his christology and ecclesiology. It avoids the snags on which the Messalians—the Pelagians of the East—struck, and those other snags on which the humanists were wrecked. While uniting himself fully with man, God remained inapproachable in his essence; the union of the two *natures* without mixture is only accomplished in the hypostasis of the Son of God become man; but, by grafting themselves sacramentally

[9] Ibid., V, 26, *fol.* 145v.
[10] *Against Gregoras,* IV, *Coisl.* 100, *fol.* 285; *Theophanes,* 941A.
[11] *Against Akindynos,* III, 5, *Coisl.* 98, *fol.* 72v.
[12] Ibid., III, 7, *fol.* 75.
[13] *Hom.* 56, ed. Oikonomos, p. 205.

on to his Person, men can participate in the divine life in a way that is both real and distinct from the union of essences; essential union would make them "equal to Christ," multiply indefinitely the number of the divine hypostases, abolish all distance between the Creator and created beings, transform a voluntary act (*energeía*) of the living God into the inevitable property of an impersonal essence, and finally absorb all activity proper to man in the divine Absolute.

VII

CHRIST IN THE REFORMERS

1. P. Althaus[1] admires in Luther's profession of faith in Christ a decisive element not fully emphasized in Christological orthodoxy. The content of this faith is not so much what Christ is in and for Himself, as what He is "for me." Luther's vision of Christ's union with the Father is not so much of a metaphysical unity of nature, as of a union of persons. He recognizes the salvific will of the Father in the will and actions of Christ. Hence, Christology is for him soteriology. Upon deeper examination, Althaus admits the presence of some contradictions in Luther's two-nature Christology.

[1] Paul Althaus was born in Obershagen in 1888. He taught at the universities of Gottingen, Rostock and mainly at Erlangen. His brilliant works include essays and volumes on all fields of theology, from *Outline of Ethics (Grundriss der Ethik)*, to *Fundamentals of Dogmatics (Grundriss der Dogmatik)*, *The Theology of Faith (Theologie des Glaubens)*, to *Eschatology (Die Letzten Dinge)*. He is particularly known for his works on Pauline and Lutheran Theology: *Paul and Luther on the Nature of Man (Paulus und Luther über die Manschen)*, *The Epistle to the Romans (Der Römenbrief)*, *Luther's Doctrine of Justification and Its Present Critics*, etc. It is from his book *The Theology of Martin Luther* tr. by R. C. Schultz, (Philadelphia: Fortress Press, 1966) that this excerpt is taken from pp. 179–198.

The Reception of the Ancient Dogmas. I believe in Jesus Christ: this is the confession of faith in the Christian tradition which Luther received. Luther felt that the words "I believe" by themselves assert that Jesus Christ is God. For faith is a relationship to God. "If I should say to someone, 'I believe in you and I place my trust and the confidence of my heart in you,' that one must be my god.[2]

Luther understands the confession that Christ is God in terms of the christological dogma of the ancient church. He expressly accepts the great ecumenical creeds of Greek and Latin theology. Apart from individual concepts he expresses no criticism of the traditional christological dogmas. He agrees with Athanasius and rejects Arius. His Christmas song, "All Praise to Thee, O Jesus Christ," adores the miracle of the incarnation of the Eternal Son in the style of Greek christology. He particularly emphasizes that no power of reason is able to comprehend the paradox of the incarnation. The Creator has become a creature. Luther without reservation uses the traditional terminology of the "two natures" and of their unification in the one person of the Lord to describe the mystery of Jesus Christ. He adopts the ancient doctrine of the communication of attributes, that is, of the exchange of attributes between the two natures in the person of Christ and expands it in his doctrine of the Lord's Supper. He is as much concerned with the true deity of Christ as Athanasius or Anselm was and in the same sense as they. "If Christ is divested of his deity, there remains no help against God's wrath and no rescue from his judgment."[3] "We Christians must know this: If God himself is not involved and does not add his weight to the scale, our side of the balance will sink to the ground. By this I mean that if it were true that it was not God but only a man who died for us, then we would be lost. But when God's own death and the dead God lie in the balance pan of the scale it falls down and we are lifted up."[4]

Luther also follows the traditional way of establishing the true deity of Christ. The word of God, the Holy Scripture, as well as Jesus' own witness to himself (here the accounts in the Gospel of John are decisive), and the miracles which have been reported to us all teach that Jesus Christ is true God.[5] The authority of Scripture thus guarantees the true deity of Christ. There is the additional consideration that the kind of works attributed to Christ and even now experienced as coming from him are not merely human but divine works. Furthermore, Christ could not be our redeemer if he were not the true and eternal God. The proof from Scripture, however, remains decisive and primary. Everything new which Luther has to say in christology presupposes the certainty of Christ's deity and incarnation in the sense of the ancient dogmas. Faith in

[2] *WA* 37, 42, (*WA* stands for Althaus' references to the critical edition of Luther's Work. *LW* stands for Luther's Works as published by the Concordia Pub. House and Fortress Press.)

[3] *WA* 46, 555; *LW* 22, 22.

[4] *WA* 50, 590. In *WA* 49, 252, Luther also speaks of the "weight" of the Deity. "The Word [that is, the Son of God] who was in the beginning must do it Himself; He is the weight who tramples sin and death under foot and eternally devours them."

[5] E.g., *WA* 10,[1,1], 181. *WA* 37, 40.

Christ to this extent rests on the recognition of the authority of God's word, of the Holy Scripture. And to this extent Schleiermacher calls on Luther for support when he maintains: "The authority of the Holy Scripture cannot establish faith in Christ; rather this faith must be presupposed in order to grant a particular authority to Holy Scripture."[6] One may not modernize Luther at this point.

The New Element in Luther's Christology. There is a new emphasis in Luther's doctrine of Christ, even though he accepts the old doctrine. With all orthodox theologians of the church, he accepts the deity of Jesus Christ. However, he gives new and deeper insight into the meaning and significance for man of the fact that Jesus Christ is true God. No other theologian since the time of the New Testament has so deeply and powerfully expressed the meaning and significance of this fact. Luther's new approach to christology depends on the search for salvation which brought him to Christ.

That is, of course, also true of the earlier forms of christology. Ancient Greek Christianity was particularly motivated by concern for the immortal life of God which redeems from corruption and from death. For this reason, Greek christology thinks of Christ primarily as the One who through his incarnation and resurrection shares the immortal life of God with human beings. This understanding of salvation corresponds to the statements made about Christ. Western Christianity has been determined by the search for freedom from the guilt and the power of sin. The decisive statements about Christ therefore speak of him as having atoned for sin and now through the sacraments, granting the power of grace for a holy life.

Luther also knows these emphases in the doctrine of salvation; and for this reason the corresponding forms of christology continue to be living elements in his own thought. At the center of his theology, however, the concern for salvation assumes a new form. What does God intend to do with us sinful men? What is his relationship to me? How does he feel about me? This is therefore no longer a concern about God's incorruptible and unfading life, his power, his atoning and saving grace; rather Luther is concerned about God Himself, his will, and his heart. For Luther everything depends on the answer to this question about salvation. He finds the answer in Jesus Christ. For this reason, the decisive thing about Christ is that God has opened his heart to us in the person, activity, and history of Jesus Christ and thus gives us certainty about how he feels about us and what he intends to do with us. This is the new meaning and importance of the deity of Jesus Christ for Luther. Christ is "the mirror of God's fatherly heart,"[7] in whom God himself appears to us. We can say that before Luther, the church and its theologians were primarily concerned with the divine in Christ. They looked for his divine nature, his divine life, and for the divine significance of his satisfaction. Luther, however, looks and finds God the Father himself in person in Jesus Christ.

---

[6] *The Christian Faith,* ed. and trans. H. R. Mackintosh, J. S. Stewart, *et al.* (Edinburgh: T. and T. Clark, 1928), p. 591. [The translation is my own.—Trans.]

[7] *WA* 30^I^, 192; *BC*, 419, 65.

Thereby Luther's christology takes on Johannine characteristics. The great words of Christ recorded in John such as, "Whoever sees me has seen the Father" [14:9] are the ultimate text of his christology. Luther, however, views Paul and John as in perfect agreement at this point. . . .

Luther finds the Father in the man Jesus Christ and nowhere else. The will of the Father is revealed to him in the attitude and activity of the historical Jesus. . . . For Luther, Christ's coming into the world and his activity and life in this world are inseparably bound together; they are a totality. . . .

Luther never tired of centering his own attention and, through his sermons, his congregation's attention on the humanity of Christ. . . . Unlike the "Jesus-piety" of the latter nineteenth and early twentieth centuries, Luther is not interested in Jesus as a great "religious personality" but in recognizing the Father in his Son, in knowing God himself. Jesus is the Son of the Father. . . . We ascend from the viewing of Jesus to the Father, that is, "through the heart of Christ to the heart of God." . . . Luther can speak of "penetrating" as well as of "ascending"; what counts is that we do not stop with the humanity of Christ but that, through knowing Jesus as a man, we penetrate (*durchdringen*) to the heart of God.[8] Both concepts say the same thing. The "logic" of this "ascent" and "penetration" is this: Because Jesus Christ is the Son of the Father, his activities in relationship to men (as described in the Bible) are nothing else than what the Father himself wills and does. Therefore his activity is the basis on which we know the will of the Father.

Since this certainty about the Father's will is so decisive for Luther's understanding of salvation, everything ultimately rests on the will and the attitude toward men that is made known through Jesus' coming and activity. . . . Luther felt that everything in the incarnation of the Eternal Son ultimately shows his love and therewith also the Father's love. . . . It is the one thing which finally matters: God is for us! Luther can therefore characterize the difference between true faith in Christ and a merely historical faith which knows the history of Jesus Christ by saying that true and saving faith recognizes the love of God the Father and his will to save me.[9]

We dare not confuse Luther's method of beginning with the man

[8] Luther discusses the way in which we must "penetrate" to the heart of God in a letter which he wrote to Spalatin in 1519. . . . "However, he should keep this [humanity of Christ] before his eyes, either while it is suffering or while it is nursing [*sugentem*], until the sweetness of its goodness fills him. He should not stop with this, however, but should penetrate it and think: 'Behold at this time and at that time, he did not do his own will but the will of God the Father.' Then the will of the Father, which he shows to us in the humanity of Christ, begins to be pleasing and acceptable to us." *WA,* Br 1, 329.

Emanuel Hirsch, *Hilfsbuch zum Studium der Dogmatik* (Berlin: de Gruyter, 1937), p. 27. Hirsch has translated *sugentem* as though it meant that the humanity elevated itself. But Luther uses *sugentem* not *surgentem* and *sugere* means "to nurse." Luther therefore advises us to look to the infant Jesus as he nurses at his mother's breast. The manger and the cross are placed beside one another as two images for the way in which Christ emptied himself.

[9] This faith which apprehends Christ "understands the love of God the Father who wants to redeem and save you through Christ, delivered up for your sins." *WA* 39^{I}, 45; *LW* 34, 110.

Jesus and then ascending from him to God with what modern theology has characterized as "christology from below toward above [*von unten nach oben*]." It would be equally dangerous to confuse it with Ritschl's attempt to overcome the doctrine of the two natures by beginning with the man Jesus on the grounds that his earthly, historical life reveals to us the characteristics of God. First, Luther's beginning with the man Jesus does not mean that he needs his human characteristics to reassure himself of the fact that Christ is really God or that God is present in him. For Luther, the deity of Christ is assured through the witness both of Scripture and of the church. When Luther leads us to look at the man Jesus, he is not concerned with showing us that Jesus is God but with showing us what He is, that is, with giving us certainty about the character and the heart of God. One may not therefore quote Luther in support of the modern method of coming to know the deity of Christ.

Second, Luther's view of the man Jesus goes far beyond anything that modern theology would understand under that phrase. Particularly, Luther presupposes the dogma that the Son has become man and that he bears the sins of mankind on the cross—. . . The so-called "metaphysical" christology is thus already included or presupposed in the humanity of Christ. And the mere historical fact of the cross does not, as such, reveal the love of Christ and of God, but does so only within the "word of the cross," that is, when it is interpreted in the dogma of the cross. . . .

Luther also directs us to follow in the way "from below to above" in order to know Christ, that is, God in Christ. This way leads from Christ as a man to Christ as God and thereby to God. . . .

This man Jesus, together with everything he does for our sake and all that he shows us of himself is God's son; therefore, he is God and at one with the will of the Father. The deity and sonship of Christ are now of decisive importance for Luther because he knows that Christ's will is God's will and that Christ's work takes place according to God's will and under his good pleasure. Since Luther's ultimate concern is completely personal, that is, he is concerned with God's gracious will for us, he also emphasizes that Christ's person is God and is united with God. This unity is found in the unity of his will with God's will and in the Son's obedience to the Father. . . .

Through all this, Luther changes the basic character of "knowing Christ." . . . For Luther, however, the understanding of the deity and humanity of Christ found in the ancient christological formulas is not yet the decisive thing about Christ's deity; and such knowledge is not yet true knowledge of Christ but only its presupposition. . . . The content of faith in Jesus Christ for Luther is that "He is my Lord" or, in other words, not what Christ is in and for himself, but rather what he is for me.

We might also express this by saying that the true knowledge of Christ consists in recognizing and grasping God's will for me in Christ's will for me and God's work to save me in Christ's work for me. . . .

Christological orthodoxy is not yet true faith in Christ. True knowledge of Christ begins only when the heart sees Christ and the Father as completely one, when it takes them together and thus recognizes and grasps the presence of the Father with his word, heart, will, in the word, heart, will, of Jesus Christ. Such a man becomes completely certain of the heart of God through and for the sake of Jesus. The devil cannot bear that. For such a man has really found God and is now completely removed from the power of Satan. . . . It is not the "metaphysical" unity of the two natures but rather the personal unity of the Son with the Father, of the man Jesus with the eternal God, that is ultimately decisive in the matter of salvation. . . . "I know of no other God except the one called Jesus Christ."[10] To be certain of this is to believe in Jesus Christ. This unity of Jesus with God and of God with Jesus, the presence of the heart and will of God in Jesus, is the "deity of Christ" in the fullest sense.

Thus Luther involved the deity in the humanity with a boldness previously unheard of in theology. More accurately, it is not merely the deity or divine nature but God himself who is personally involved. The fact that Luther views God and man outside of Christ as "further apart than heaven and earth" did not hinder him. God is this man, and this man is the presence of God for us. Basically, Luther thereby transcends the doctrine of the two natures as inadequate. It says far too little and does not say what is decisive. Luther is ultimately concerned not with the relationship of the divine and the human nature but with the relationship of the person of Jesus to the person of the Father. Luther thus takes the deity of Christ and his incarnation more seriously than anyone since the New Testament writers themselves.

According to Luther, this also means that the knowledge of God's metaphysical attributes is not ultimately decisive for a man who is seeking salvation (as essential as these attributes are to God's deity); the ultimate decisive factor is knowledge of God's personal nature and activity. . . . God opens his personal being to us only in the human person of Jesus.

The significance of this for the subjective side of our knowledge of Christ is: subjective knowledge of Christ does not consist in intellectual and theoretical character, but like its content, is the completely personal, practical, existential, and vital grasping of Christ with the "heart" and with the whole person. It is not enough to accept the eternal deity of Christ because of the authority of Scripture and the church. . . . This means that true faith in Jesus Christ is characterized by the fact that it relates Christ and his work to the believer's own existence with its "for me" and "for us."[11] . . . Christology is basically soteriology. Christ is known only in his works and I know his work only when I know it has taken place for me. Thus according to Luther, the doctrine of the person of Christ and the doctrine of his works cannot be separated from each other; they are one in such a way that I can grasp the meaning of Christ's work only in its significance for me. Faith in Christ

[10] "There is no other God apart from this Christ who has become our light and sun. . . . He and no one else is the true God. It is he, I say, who has enlightened us through his gospel." *WA* 31^I^, 63.

[11] *WA* 39^I^, 45 f.; *LW* 34, 110 f. "You do not yet have Christ, even though you know that he is God and man. You truly have him only when you believe that this altogether pure and innocent person has been granted to you by the Father as your High Priest and Redeemer, yes, as your slave." *WA* 40^I^, 448; *LW* 26, 288.

is thus one and the same as justifying faith.[12] Salutary knowledge of Christ is thoroughly personal not only in terms of its content, that is, of God's personal relationship to me, but also according to its method. I know only when I am personally involved in grasping and in accepting Christ as my Lord and only when I risk everything on him. The only significant knowledge of Christ does not precede being overcome and brought to complete trust in him but first comes into existence in and with such trust.

This understanding of Jesus Christ presupposes and is bound to the fact that he is present for us. He is present for us through the word about him. We have him in no other way, for he is now in heaven with the Father. He does not come down to us in person but only in the gospel. And this gospel does not merely bring him to us but also teaches us to know him for what he is. Christ's humanity is as such also a veiling of the deity. If he would come to us today in his historical reality we would not recognize him as the Son in his deity. This must first be revealed to us. And this takes place through the gospel. We need the apostolic word about him which bears witness to who he is. We have him only in faith in his presence in the gospel. Thus the basis of faith is not the "historical Jesus" by himself (Christ's "flesh") but that Christ who is preached in the apostolic witness. Luther does not know Christ apart from the witness of faith which Scripture and Christianity give to him.[13] This is so indispensable for the knowledge of Christ that Luther can say, God wishes the spoken word to be revered more than Christ's humanity.

The Two-Nature Christology in Luther. As we have already pointed out, Luther adopts the traditional dogmatic doctrine of the two natures. . . . Luther teaches the impersonality of the human nature of Christ (*an-* or *enhypostasis*).[14]

How is it possible for Luther to maintain the true humanity of Christ under these circumstances? He teaches that Jesus Christ, according to his human nature, also possessed the attributes of the divine majesty, that is, that even the child Jesus was omniscient, omnipotent, and omnipresent. Luther thus does not understand Christ's emptying himself in the incarnation to mean that he left his deity or essential characteristics of it in heaven. Luther does not agree with the exegetes of the early church who understood Philippians 2:6 f. ("He emptied himself") as describing an act of the pre-existent Christ at the time of the incarnation; rather he under-

---

[12] "The papists therefore have not called upon the Son of God in true faith, that is not as the one through whom alone we have forgiveness of sins and eternal life. Since they trust also in their works, they do not pray to the true God." *WA* 39^II^, 278.

[13] *WA* 10^III^, 349, *LW* 51, 114. (This is quoted in Chap. 6, n. 1.) "Christ is known only through his word. Without the word, his flesh would be of no benefit to me even though it came today." *WA* 10^III^, 210. "Thus He comes to us through the gospel. Yes, it is far better that he comes through the gospel than that he would now enter in through the door; for you would not even know him even though he came in. If you believe then you have; if you do not believe then you do not have." *WA* 10^III^, 92.

[14] *WA* 39^II^, 93 f. (Thesis 11 f., 116 ff.) Luther rejects Augustine's formulation: "The divine Person assumes a man" (otherwise there would be two persons in Christ); instead he says: "The divine Person assumes the human nature." Cf. Loofs, *Leitfaden zum Studium der Dogmengeschichte* (4th ed., 1906), p. 286, n. 9.

stands it as describing the attitude of the incarnate earthly Christ.[15] Christ did not empty himself once for all; rather he constantly emptied himself throughout his entire earthly life. He did not give up the "form of God" and take on "the form of a servant" once for all at the time of the incarnation; rather the man Jesus possessed the form of God at all times and could have used it and brought it to bear, but at every point he laid it aside and made himself the servant of all rather than their Lord. . . .

Luther's understanding of Christ's emptying of himself in the Philippians passage reveals the full depth of his christology. . . . One can say that the incarnation is a progressive event, an always new act of Christ. Here we are dealing with the fact that he gave up not only the use of the so-called metaphysical attributes which the divine nature communicated to the human nature but also that he did not draw the conclusions from his ethical superiority of righteousness, and goodness. Unlike G. Thomasius, the nineteenth century kenotic theologian, Luther does not distinguish between different kinds of attributes but takes them all together as the form of God. . . . The incarnation is completed in the cross of Christ. It is thus no longer only the metaphysical presupposition of Christ's work of salvation but the completion of that work itself. The work of salvation is not something different from an emptying which had previously taken place, but occurs in Christ's on-going emptying of himself. Christ's emptying is continued in Christians. Christ's attitude and activity is their example. Thus Luther's understanding of the incarnation and of the emptying determines and permeates his ethics. . . .

However, all our admiration of this understanding of Christ's emptying of himself, cannot keep us from asking whether Luther's presupposition that the man Jesus had the attributes of the divine majesty available to him can be reconciled with the biblical picture of the historical Christ, or even with the strong emphasis on the Lord's true humanity which we find elsewhere in Luther's own theology. In some of his statements Luther, in spite of everything, seeks to preserve the true humanity of the historical Jesus. An example is his interpretation of Luke 2:40 and 52, "Jesus increased in wisdom." . . . There is no question that Luther with these thoughts stands in the tradition of Antiochian christology.[16] These ideas do not, however, agree very well with his acceptance of the doctrine that human nature did not have its own human person (*anhypostasis*). For these thoughts presuppose an independent personal life of the man Jesus which is more and more moved by the Spirit of God. On the other hand, taken as dogmatic statements they are only a very small concession. The contradiction between

---

[15] Luther's interpretation is followed by Calvin, by the older Lutheran exegetes until J. A. Bengel, also by modern exegetes, e.g., A. Schlatter, and by dogmaticians such as A. Ritschl and Werner Elert.

[16] Cf. Luther's position with that of Theodore of Mopsuestia, particularly the citations in Loofs, *op. cit.*, p. 282. Theodore also teaches that the indwelling of the Logos became more perfect in the course of Jesus' ethical development. There is also precedent in Theodore for Luther's description of Christ's humanity as the "tool and house of the Deity." *WA* $10^{I,1}$, 447. Cf. Loofs, *op. cit.*, pp. 280, 282 and R. Seeberg, *Lehrbuch der Dogmengeschichte* 3rd ed.; (Leipzig. Deichert, 1933) II, 187 ff.

Luther's understanding of the *genus majestaticum* [the doctrine that Jesus, according to his human nature, possessed all divine power and attributes at his birth] as the presupposition of Christ's emptying himself within history remains for the most part in contradiction to the genuine picture of the man Jesus.

And yet the *genus majestaticum* is not Luther's final christological statement. He transcends it when he makes statements which point in the direction of a *genus tapeinoticon* [the doctrine that God in Christ shared the weakness, suffering, and humiliation of Jesus]. Luther holds that the deity of Christ, because of the incarnation and of its personal unity with the humanity, enters into the uttermost depths of its suffering. God suffers in Christ. However Luther did not teach "patripassionism" [that the Father suffered], as the modalists did, but "deipassionism" [that God suffered].[17] He always regarded God's suffering as an incomprehensible mystery. It is a constant stumbling block to reason and even the angels cannot fully understand it. For it means nothing else than that God is at once completely above and completely below. He is the creator and the Lord and yet at the same time the lowest creature and a servant subject to all men, yes, even to the devil. This man Jesus who bears the wrath of God, the sin of the world, all earthly trouble, yes, hell itself, is at the same time the highest God. The mystery of Christ cannot be expressed without these paradoxes. . . .

Luther's basic christological confession (that the Father's heart and will are present in Christ) will always be significant. However, his dogmatic theory which describes Christ as true God and true man is not unified within itself but displays contradictions. Theology had to go beyond it.

2. L. Richard[1] agrees with G. Aulén in giving credit to Luther for reviving in the doctrine of redemption the vision which the primitive Church had of Christ as Victor over the forces of evil. However, he contradicts Aulén's view that Luther denied the aspect of Christ's expiatory sacrifice mounting up to God. Regarding Luther's teachings, he finds his rejection of the efficacious renewal of many by the Spirit of Christ in contradiction to Pauline thought. He also sees Luther's ideas on penal substitution carried to a point of excess.

. . . In the drama of his religious life in conflict with a passionate nature, Luther strongly resented man's powerlessness to free himself from sin by his own efforts, his own works, even by the asceticism of the monastic life. He found in the writings of St. Paul and St. Augustine the truth of gratuitous salvation in Jesus Christ, in which we were asked and given to believe, in opposition to a theology which tended towards semi-Pelagianism. Was this

[17] In a disputation of 1540, Luther on the basis of his understanding of the communication of attributes, rejects the opinion that the deity did not suffer in Christ. "What Christ has suffered should also be attributed to God for they are one." *WA* 39^{II}, 121.

[1] Cf. Ch. 1, 7, note 1, on Richard. This excerpt is from *op. cit.*, pp. 208–214.

not fidelity to the word of God?[2] Luther never claimed to revise the creed of the apostolic faith, the mysteries of the Trinity and the redemptive incarnation. What he claimed to renew, solely on the basis of Scripture, was the concept of justification by faith alone and, consequently, the Christian concept of the sacraments, the Church and the priesthood. Therefore it was on these points in particular that the controversies of that time were based and, as a consequence, the definitions of the Council of Trent.

It has been admitted for a long time, by Protestants as well as Catholics, that Luther, in taking up the expressions of Scripture and Tradition concerning the mystery of the redemption, remained faithful to St. Anselm's concept and attacked only the emphasis on expiation by the substitution of Christ for guilty mankind. It is only in our time that Lutheran historians and theologians, by a careful study of the writings of the father of the Reformation, have revived the question. For them Luther, by the intuition which dominated his entire message, would have accomplished a veritable revolution in the history of Christianity. He would have rediscovered the original meaning of the divine *agape*—as opposed to the *caritas* of St. Augustine, which is a precarious synthesis of *erōs* and *agape* in which the latter becomes corrupted—and that of redemption as the pure initiation of divine love, as the victorious work in which God, in Jesus Christ, triumphs over the forces of evil without demanding any payment in return to him from this Christ acting as head of mankind.

It must be admitted, on the testimony of the texts, that Luther's initial intuitions concerning *agape,* redemption and even justification, are genuinely Christian. But it is certainly unfortunate that, on other points, Luther did not remain more faithful to St. Paul who taught that man is efficaciously renewed by the Spirit of Christ. It is equally regrettable that, in order to express his basically Christian intuition, he kept the general outlines of thought of the nominalist teachers, whose Pelagian tendencies he so strongly rejected. The "imputing" of the justice of Christ to sinners and, conversely, the imputing of all sins to the innocent Christ by God. His rejection of the Scholastic concept of human nature led him to refuse to admit that fallen man had any active capacity for receiving the divine gift, for cooperating with the prevenient grace of God.

Luther first of all rediscovered the original meaning of the redemption as the victorious action of God in Jesus Christ as he triumphed over the forces of evil: sin, death, Satan. This is what he says in his *Small* and *Large Catechisms* and in his commentaries on the Epistle to the Galatians. . . .

This downward aim, we are told, would exclude the reverse aim which mounts up from Christ to God and which is expressed in the doctrine of sacrificial offering and of satisfaction.

Certainly, we admit, Luther also insisted on the sacrifice of the cross, and

[2] The decree *De Justificatione,* from the sixth session of the Council of Trent, stated this definitely and in detail. According to the Protestant historian Harnack, "it is doubtful that the Reformation would have taken place if this decree had been issued by, for example, the Council of the Lateran (1512) and had really penetrated into the flesh and blood of the Church" (*Lehrbuch der Dogmengeschichte* [1910], II, 711).

so much so that he valued it apart from any idea of sacrifice in the celebration of the Last Supper. But for him, Aulén says, to speak of the sacrifice of the cross was to express only "how much the atoning work (if the phrase may be used) *costs* God," who handed over his beloved Son to death; for "Luther refused to admit any sacrifice offered by man to God, in order to influence him as it were from below"[3]—an opinion also held by St. Thomas.[4] But would Luther himself have denied that "Christ handed himself over for us as an oblation and an acceptable sacrifice to God" (Eph 5:2)?

Luther also took up the expressions concerning the merit and satisfaction of Christ. But he did not retain their traditional meaning if it is true that, for him, the merit of Christ is "in close association with the idea of God's grace."[5] Christ's human action, his obedience to the Father, would then have no value! But did not St. Paul concede a meritorious value to Christ's human obedience when he wrote that, taking the form of a slave, "he became obedient unto the death of the cross, and that for that reason God has exalted him" (Phil 2:8–11)?

By the satisfaction of Christ, on the other hand, Luther understood the expiation which the Father made him accomplish in his passion, treating him as the substitute for guilty mankind.

> We must not represent Christ to ourselves as an innocent private person (as the Scholastics, Jerome and others have done), a person holy and just in himself. It is true that Jesus Christ is a very pure person, but you must not stop there. You have not yet understood, even if you know that he is God and man. But you will truly understand him if you believe that this very pure and innocent person was given to you by the Father to be pontiff and savior, or rather to be your slave who, laying aside his innocence and holiness, puts on your sinful person, your death and your curse, becomes a victim and an accursed one for you, in order to deliver you from the curse of the law.[6]

In this dramatic presentation, certainly the idea which emerges is that of satisfaction to divine justice by penal substitution of Christ, the new Adam, for guilty mankind—a substitution accepted by the victim thus chosen. But we must go still further, for such a concept logically demands that Christ endure on the cross the true punishment of sin, which is the pain of loss. Luther, therefore, implies that, on the cross, Christ had to experience the anguish of the damned. Substitution also works the other way, for the imputing of the justice of Christ justifies the sinners who believe in him. Certainly, for Luther, the substitution of Christ for guilty mankind is based on the union effected between him and mankind by the incarnation. But he pushes the assimilation of Christ to sinful mankind too far, since Jesus becomes for God the universal sinner, the cursed one, without ceasing to be

---

[3] G. Aulén, *Christus Victor,* p. 133.

[4] Cf., for example, III, q. 22, a. 3 and ad 1; q. 48, a. 6 and ad 1; q. 49, a. 1 and ad 1, taking care to read the first objections of these articles.

[5] G. Aulén, *op. cit.,* p. 134.

[6] Luther, *A Commentary on St. Paul's Epistle to the Galatians,* rev. and completed trans. based on the "Middleton" text, prepared by P. S. Watson (London: James Clarke & Co., 1953), p. 279.

innocent! On the other hand, he minimizes the assimilation of the believer to Christ, since the justice which is imputed to him by God does not justify him internally. Now, it is certainly the teaching of St. Paul that Christ delivered us from the wrath of God which hangs over sinners; but it is highly debatable whether we can interpret St. Paul as saying that Christ delivered us from it by submitting to it in our place.[7] St. Paul never taught that the wrath of God, which is "upon . . . every man who does evil" (Rom 2:9), was also visited upon Christ.

In treating the primitive doctrine of the victory of Christ over the hostile powers—among which he counted not only sin, death and Satan but also the Law and the wrath of God—Luther, in Aulén's judgment, expressed himself "not less vigorously than Paul himself."[8] But it is indeed dangerous to exceed the apostle in this way. According to him, the mission of the Savior proceeded solely from the *agape* of God, from the divine blessing. Now

> Luther presents us here an antinomy, a conflict, between the Divine curse, the Wrath, and the Divine blessing, the Love . . . ; in Luther the opposition is presented in a far more acute form [than in the Latin theory] . . . For the Latin theory, the satisfaction made by Christ is primarily a rationally conceived compromise between the demand for punishment and the remission of punishment. . . . But in Luther every trace of this rationalism has disappeared; it disappears because the dualistic outlook is maintained, and because the victory over the Curse and the Wrath is in the fullest sense God's victory. . . . Thus the Love of God breaks through the Wrath.[9]

Aulén also says that, "in Luther, (the Wrath of God) is set forth as operative in the present,"[10] contrary to the Scholastic position. St. Paul, on the other hand, seems to hold that if the wrath of God is already present "upon . . . every man who does evil" (Rom 2:9), then it is above all eschatological:

> Through your hardness and the unrepentance of your heart, you amass a treasure of wrath for the day of wrath, on which the just judgment of God is to be revealed (Rom 2:5).[11]

Despite Luther's excesses and strained oppositions, it is useful to hear him vigorously recalling, in opposition to declining Scholasticism, the vision which the primitive Church had of the divine victory of Christ over the forces of evil: sin, death and Satan. Unfortunately, it was not this lesson which was best retained, for three centuries, by orthodox Protestantism, which clung instead to the doctrine of satisfaction by accepted penal substitution.

Calvin professed the same doctrine and set it forth in his *Institutes of the Christian Religion,* placing the clarity

[7] St. Paul in no way teaches that Christ on the cross was a victim of "the wrath of God" . . . a wrath directed against a guilty world which is above all eschatological . . . The wrath of God is his reaction against the spurning of his love, . . . which is first, which is merciful, which is the principle of reconciliation . . . Never does St. Paul present Christ as an object of the wrath of God.

[8] G. Aulén, *op. cit.,* p. 128; cf. pp. 124–125 and 136.

[9] *Ibid.,* p. 131.

[10] *Ibid.,* p. 130.

[11] Cf. F. Ménégoz, "Rédemption," (Rev. Hist. et Philos. Relig., XX (1940), 1921).

and spread of the French language at the service of the Reformation. He was even more explicit on the pain of loss suffered by Christ on the cross.

> Not only was his body handed over as the price of our redemption, but there was another more worthy and more excellent price, that of enduring the dreadful torments which the damned and the lost must feel. . . . However we do not wish to imply by this that God was ever either hostile or angry with his Christ. . . . But we say that he bore the weight of God's vengeance inasmuch as he was struck and afflicted by him and experienced all the signs which God shows to sinners when he is angry with them and punishes them.

The Protestant theologians of the seventeenth century did little more than systematize the doctrine of Luther and Calvin.

3. F. Wendel[1] maintains that while Calvin's Christology is orthodox, when compared with that of Luther, it appears to be less persistent in the tendency to underline the unity of the Christ. This is clear in the presence of difficulties concerning the consequences of that union, especially in regard to the "communication of idioms." He expressly rejects Luther's views on Christ's ubiquity. What is known as "extra Calvinisticum" clearly reveals his thought concerning the separateness and respective characteristics of the two natures. He envisions Christ's work in the roles of prophet, king, and sacrificial priest.

Christ and His Work of Redemption. From the fundamental and substantial unity of the Old and New Testaments, one might draw the conclusion that the work of Christ is not of such fundamental importance as theological tradition has attributed to it. It is the diametrically opposite conclusion at which Calvin arrives, precisely because he does not confine the work and the action of Christ within the New Testament, but sees their intervention quite as much in the Old Covenant. The Biblical witness as a whole is to be regarded as witness to Christ, and theology has no other purpose than the guidance of believers in this quest of the Christ through all the Biblical writings. Calvin's Christocentrism, it cannot be said too often, is as definite and as clearly expressed as that of Luther. But naturally this is more evident in the chapters of the *Institutes* which are specially devoted to Christ and his redemptive work than it is elsewhere.

Calvin had made the traditional trinitarian teaching his own, without the slightest reservation. The same attachment to the dogmatic tradition is prominent in his Christology. What is original in his contribution to this never touches the fundamental affirmations of the Councils of the ancient

---

[1] Professor François Wendel, the Dean of the Faculty of Protestant Theology at Strasbourg, is considered one of the world's outstanding experts on the history and literature of the Reformation. It is from his book *Calvin: The Origins and Development of His Religious Thought* (tr. by Philip Mairet, New York and Evanston: Harper and Row, 1963) that this excerpt has been taken from pp. 215–232.

Church. He adopts in full the dogma of the two natures of Christ and the current explanations of the relation between the two natures. "So much and more was it necessary," he writes, "that he who was to be our Mediator should be true God and man."[2] Indeed, for any contact to be established between the most holy God and sinful man, it was necessary for God to come right down to man, since man would never, of his own strength, have been able to raise himself up to God. "The majesty of God is too high," said Calvin, "for us to say that mortal men could attain to it, seeing that they can do no more than crawl over the earth like little worms."[3] That, of course, is the state of man since the Fall. But Calvin had no very high opinion of humanity even before the original sin. . . . Even before the Fall. contact with God could be made only so far as God's goodness willed to lower itself so far as man. All the more certainly, since then, has man been incapable of reaching up to God, and this is confirmed, in Calvin's eyes, seeing that the angels themselves, though they have preserved the image of God in them, have need "of a leader, through their relation to whom they were given strength to adhere to God for ever."[4]

Sin has, indeed, a double consequence: man becomes an object of horror to God and, conversely, man acquires a horror of God and hates him, for the divine righteousness fills him with fear. Thus the man enslaved to sin cannot take up any other attitude towards God but that of escape from him, be it only by denying him, which is also a manner of hiding from him. But Christian doctrine tells us that to reestablish contact with God, and for men to become his children again, there is need of a Mediator and that this mediator is Christ. It is just this, according to Calvin, which distinguishes Christianity from the other religions—its having affirmed the necessity of an "intermediary."[5] But of what nature could such a Mediator be? We read in the *Institutes:*

> Not without reason did St Paul, when pointing to Jesus Christ as Mediator, expressly refer to him as man.

In other words, Jesus Christ was fully man, and nothing human was unknown to him excepting sin. . . . He observes elsewhere, "Jesus Christ was not only man as to his body but as to his soul also. He was subject to passions, fears and sorrows, as we see him to have been. And since he thus willed to take a human soul, why should he not have had the qualities that pertain to the nature of souls?"[6] Only it must be added that though Christ knew these infirmities, it was because he was

---

[2] *Inst.* 11, 12, 1.

[3] *Inst.,* 11, 6, 4. Cf. among numerous similar passages, the Course upon Hosea, *Opp.,* 42, 264: 'Deum a nobis quaeri non posse, nisi in mediatore Christo. . . . Nisi Christus se medium nobis offerat qua via possemus ad Deum accedere?' or again, the sermon on I Ephesians 1.1–3: "Without this Mediator, it is certain that we are all foreclosed [by God] and the majesty of God ought to make the hairs of our head stand on end." *Opp.,* 51, 256.

[4] *Inst.,* 11, 12, 1.; cf. Commentary on Colossians 1.20, *Opp.,* 52, 89 and the *Reply to the Brothers of Cologne, Opp.,* 9, 338; *Opusc.,* 2023 f.

[5] Commentary upon Acts 17.8: "Here are the principal marks by which our faith is distinguished from that of the pagans; namely, that it holds up Christ alone as mediator, that it teaches that men must look to him alone for their salvation." *Opp.,* 48, 406.

[6] Sermon on Luke 2:50–2, *Opp.,* 46, 487 f.

fully willing to know them, and could have been exempt from them. His voluntary abasement was for no other purpose than to give us greater access to him, "so that we might communicate his benefits to all." That Christ was truly man was moreover an indispensable condition of our salvation. Never should we have been able to contemplate the glory of God face to face had it not been hidden under the veil of humanity. By consenting to the incarnation of his Son, God meant to show us his compassion. Besides, this incarnation humiliates our pride by showing us that God had to lower himself so far to us. But it is something more also: to us it has the value of a pledge, a guarantee of reconciliation. . . . His character as Mediator introduces even into his humanity an irreducible duality, but that is the condition of his saving work. On the one hand, he was "the spotless lamb of God," and on the other he was "a sinner, guilty and accursed" in order to substitute himself for us in the reconciliation with God. . . .[7]

However, reconciliation with God presupposes that the disobedience which was the origin of sin has been replaced by obedience—such an obedience as could satisfy the judgment of God. For it was necessary—to use the terms employed by Calvin—to pay what was owing for sin. Here, then, according to the formula that had become traditional, sin appears as a debt that must be paid if we are to be redeemed before God. But no man, reduced to his own resources, could have discharged such a debt—Jesus no more than any other if he had been no more than a man. God himself had to intervene. . . . We have good right to regard this as a classic expression of the doctrine of satisfaction as it had been current ever since St Anselm. Everything in it is exactly in balance and harmony. Man had rendered himself guilty of sin and had offended God in such a manner that he was doomed to death. So that justice should be done, man had to expiate his sin. But man was incapable, by his own strength, of overcoming death: God alone could do so, but he had to take on human nature, so that it should indeed be man who expiated sin. It is by a kind of necessity of justice, then, that the Redeemer of mankind had to be both man and God.[8]

Whenever Calvin comes to speak of the person of the Christ, he takes care to place emphasis simultaneously upon the unity of the God-man and upon the distinction between the two natures. In the measure that he insists upon their unity, we might once again make an easy comparison with Luther, but if so, we just as quickly perceive that in Luther's case the tendency to underline the unity of the Christ is far more pronounced than in Calvin's, so much so that Luther has sometimes been accused of monophysitism. For Calvin, as for him, it is a necessity of the faith never in the least degree to separate God from Christ. And yet Calvin affirms equally and more clearly still, that the distinction between the two natures is indispensable if we do not want to end by admitting a change in the divinity itself, brought about by the fact of the incarnation and necessarily equivalent to a diminution of it. This is a very important aspect of

[7] Commentary on Galatians 3.13, *Opp.*, 50, 210.
[8] See, for example, *Inst.*, 11, 12, 2.

Calvin's theological thought, and perhaps what is most original in it.

He had no difficulty in finding passages of Scripture which seem to him to confirm both the unity of the two natures and the distinction between them. . . . He rejects, equally, the error that would attribute two persons to Christ, and that which would mix all together and "make the divine essence into humanity." . . . He compares the two natures of the Christ to the two eyes of man: "Each eye can have its vision separately; but when we are looking at anything . . . our vision, which in itself is divided, joins up and unites in order to give itself as a whole to the object that is put before it."

What mattered above all to Calvin was to avoid anything that might be interpreted as a confusion of the divinity with the humanity, even at the center of the personality of Christ. From the very beginnings of his theological reflections he had felt the necessity of safeguarding the divinity of Christ from any contamination by humanity. Certainly Christ was both true God and true man and he conjoined the two natures in a single person, but that was not an exception, not even a unique exception, to the absolute transcendence of the divinity. The *Institutes* of 1536 were already concerned to show, by the simile of man as a composition of body and soul, that the two parts of a whole could perfectly well preserve the properties peculiar to each of them. Calvin made his terminology more precise in the *Confession of the Trinity* of 1537, which was written during the controversies with Caroli.[9] Two years later the second edition of the *Institutes* provided the definitive text. . . .[10]

Thus far, Calvin had confined himself to a correct exposition of the traditional teaching about the two natures of the Christ and the unity of his person, such as Luther also had admitted. But a difficulty was not long in presenting itself with regard to the consequences one could draw from this double affirmation. In the course of his controversy with Zwingli over the Eucharist, Luther had been led to ascribe a considerable importance to the "communication of idioms" or properties. . . . Zwingli, on the other hand, claims that what the Scripture affirms of the Christ according to his humanity and which belongs only to his divinity, is told in but an inadequate manner and that consequently there could not be, properly speaking, any communication of the *idiomata*. Calvin's constant care to make a difference, as clearly as possible, between the divinity and the humanity ought to have led him to similar conclusions. Yet he does not reject the communication of the idioms as such. "The Scripture," he says in a passage of 1536 which was maintained in all the subsequent editions, "speaks according to this form of Jesus Christ . . ." But in 1543 he introduced, a little further on, a passage which reveals his real tendencies, in the course of a polemic against heresy: "We must beware of the raging madness of Eutyches, who, in trying to demonstrate the unity of the persons[11] in Jesus Christ, destroyed both natures. . . ." Yet while he emphatically affirms the unity of Christ's divinity with his humanity, Calvin

[9] *Opp.*, 9, 703–10; see, in particular, 706. . . .
[10] *Inst.*, 11, 14, 1 and commentary on Matthew 24, *Opp.*, 45, 672.
[11] The Latin text has, more correctly, "unitatem personae."

cannot go further into the question of the communication of the idioms without much hesitation, and whenever he thinks he can concede something on this point, he automatically attaches the reservation that, in the person of Christ, divinity and humanity keep their own characteristics without reacting upon one another any more than is required for the existence of this union *sui generis,* and for the mediation of which it is the bearer. . . . This was the case, according to Calvin (who is here following Irenaeus), with respect to the passion and the death of Jesus. And he explains by this same distinction the Scriptural passages which raise the question of progress in the knowledge of Jesus, or of his ignorance. . . .

Similarly the divine nature preserves its properties, and more especially its ubiquity, in which Calvin, contrary to Luther, denies that the human nature participated. Here again we find Calvin's constant preoccupation that nothing should be allowed to diminish the divinity or divest it of any of its privileges. The divinity of the Christ fills all things; it is not bound to his humanity, although it dwells in that humanity. In other terms, the divinity is not dependent on the humanity even in the smallest degree. It is true that the Christ came down to our level by assuming human nature, but he "put off none of his majesty, neither lessened nor diminished himself in his eternal glory."[12] . . . In a famous passage in the *Institutes* of 1559 . . . Calvin summed up, in paradoxical form, the whole of his thought on this subject.[13] . . . But even in 1536 Calvin had expressed the same opinion with a singular clarity, this time in respect of the Lord's Supper, which had been the occasion of controversies about the ubiquity. . . . These are the clearest formulations of what has since been called the *extra calvinisticum:* they vividly define the very basis of Calvinist thinking concerning the essential separateness of the two natures and the maintenance of their respective characteristics. While Luther had taken the unity of the person of Christ as his point of departure and, by extending the traditional notions of communication of the idioms and of the ubiquity, finished by admitting the ubiquity not only of the divine, but also of the human nature of the Christ, Calvin took his stand upon the immutability and incommunicability of the divinity, and thence arrived logically—or at least apparently so—at very different conclusions. He retained the ubiquity of the single divine nature, which he even accentuated to some degree. But he categorically rejected the ubiquity of the body of the Christ, for the same reasons that made him dismiss anything tending towards the deification of man, even in the person of Jesus Christ. Great as is the importance he attributes to the humanity of Christ and to its necessity for the work of salvation, we can say with M. Dominicé that "this humanity of the Christ has value for him only by its union with the divine nature,"[14] but upon condition that we keep in mind the distinction between the two natures and Calvin's unilateral interest in the divine nature and its exaltation. . . . He relied upon this attitude in his

[12] Sermon on Ephesians 1:15–18, *Opp.,* 51, 318.
[13] *Inst.,* 11, 13, 4.
[14] Dominicé, *L'Humanité de Jesus,* p. 48.

belated polemic against the Lutheran advocates of the bodily presence of Christ in the Eucharistic elements. If we place ourselves at the point of view of Christological doctrine we may, however, wonder whether by thus accentuating the distinction between the two natures, he did not endanger the fundamental unity of the person of Christ, and whether some of the affirmations he made would not tend towards somewhat unorthodox conclusions.

Returning to what is properly called the work of Christ, Calvin sought to sum up the different aspects of this in his doctrine of the three offices or ministries of Christ, as prophet, as king and as sacrificial priest. . . . It is possible that he derived this idea first from Bucer, who had alluded to it in his *Evangelical Commentary*.[15] The importance that Calvin, for his part, attached to this triple mission of the Christ is shown by the place he assigned to it, between the exposition of the Incarnation and that of Christ's work of salvation. He defines the three functions of Christ and their meaning in a few sentences: "That prophetic dignity with which we say that Jesus Christ was invested means this: we know that every part of perfect wisdom is contained in the sum of the doctrine that he taught."[16] The kingdom of Christ is neither earthly nor carnal, but spiritual. . . . The rulership of Christ extends not only over the good, it includes also the wicked and is charged with the breaking of their rebellion. . . . This is the reason that Calvin advances to justify the sacerdotal office of the Christ: "As for the sacrifice, we have briefly to note that the purpose and use of this is that Jesus Christ wins favour for us and renders us acceptable to God by his holiness, inasmuch as he is a spotless Mediator. . . . But this sacrifice of Christ consists in his passion and his death, voluntarily assumed in a spirit of obedience, instead and in place of sinful humanity. . . ." However, this is not a sort of settlement of accounts in the juridical sense. What matters to Calvin, and what he, like Luther, sees as the deepest reason for the reconciliation with God, is that the Christ "did and accomplished this by the whole course of his obedience. . . . Although, properly speaking, there can be no question of any obedience by Christ, except according to his human nature, it was the whole of Jesus Christ, in his capacity of mediator, who submitted himself to the Father and who, by his obedience, obtained for us the divine reconciliation.[17] But then a question presents itself: How could the obedience and the suffering of Christ be of such value that they could bring about the salvation of all the elect? . . . The arguments adduced by Lutheran theology may well have seemed to him to rest upon the doctrine of the communication of idioms, though that was not expressly mentioned. Calvin's interest in this question was awakened rather late, hardly

[15] Bucer, *Enarrationes in Evangelia,* 1536, p. 606: "Rex regum Christus est, summus sacerdos, et prophetarum caput." We can trace this back to Eusebius, *Hist. Eccles.,* 1, 3, 9: the first allusion to the triple function of the Christ. Upon the attitude of Luther, cf. J. V. Walter, *Die Theologie Luthers,* pp. 235 ff. J. F. Jansen, *Calvin's Doctrine of the Work of Christ* (London, 1956), tries to minimize the part played by the three offices in Calvin's theology.

[16] *Inst.,* 11, 15, 2.

[17] Commentary upon Micah, 5.4, *Opp.,* 43, 371.

before the controversy with Lelius Socinius in 1555. Socinius asked Calvin to explain how God could have been determined by the merits of Christ, when he had decided to save men by an act of his free and sovereign will. . . . Calvin answered this in a special memorandum, and it was this reply that he afterwards inserted in the *Institutes*. . . .[18]

This amounted to saying that the Christ was able to deserve our salvation only because God would have it so. There is identity between this point of view and that of Duns Scotus. Here again we may wonder whether, by thus depriving the obedience and the passion of Christ of any value independent of the divine will, Calvin did not too much diminish the humanity of the Christ to the advantage of the divinity. Was he not yielding, perhaps unconsciously, to the tendency which had led him to exalt the divine nature one-sidedly, even in the person of Christ? Be that as it may, his thought on this point is closely correlated to the position he had taken up in regard to the distinction between the two natures. We should note, however, that upon occasion Calvin knew how to attribute a certain autonomy to Christ, as in the following passage: "Our Lord Jesus Christ did not have the office of enlightening us in the faith and of reforming our hearts today, only inasmuch as he is our mediator and inasmuch as he is a minister of God, but because he has that also of himself."[19]

An analogous attitude predominates also in Calvin's explanations of the relation between the redemptive work of Christ and predestination. The question arises, in fact, and Calvin faced it, whether the simultaneous affirmation of predestination and of redemption by means of the incarnation and death of the Son of God does not contain an internal contradiction. From the moment that God had predetermined some men to salvation and others to reprobation for all eternity, where is the need for any intervention by the Christ, either to communicate their salvation, or still less to obtain it for them? It looks at first sight as though the decree of election must exclude any need for redemption. That, of course, could no more be the opinion of Calvin than of the theologians before him who had bent their backs over the same problem. On the contrary, it proved possible and quite legitimate to resume the position he had taken up in the *Institutes* of 1543 and that he had developed afterwards, by saying that "the work of salvation is as unthinkable, apart from its relations with election, as would be an election eternal in itself; the history of salvation unfolds itself in relation with election, and completes the latter." . . .[20]

. . . The remission of sins and the reconciliation of men to God by the sacrifice of Christ correspond effectively with the reality of things, but represent only one aspect of it. . . .

We must therefore consider two aspects of the question separately: on the one hand, the fact that God loved us before the creation of the world, and that despite the Fall he still loves us because we continue to be his crea-

[18] *Responsio ad aliquot L. Socini senensis quaestiones, Opp.*, 10a, 160–5; *Inst.*, 11, 17, 1–5.

[19] Sermon on Ephesians 6:19–24, *Opp.*, 51, 859.

[20] P. Jacobs, *Prädestination und Verantwortlichkeit bei Calvin,* Neukirchen, 1937, p. 78 f.; E. Emmen, *De Christologie van Calvijn,* pp. 57 ff.

tures; and, on the other, the fact that our iniquity is hated by God and separates us from him, until the sacrifice of Christ dispels that hatred, and Christ, in uniting us with himself, reunites us with God. . . . It is by Christ, then, and by him alone that we can enter anew into contact with God . . . He is the indispensable instrument that God uses to attract his elect to him. His office as Mediator is closely connected with the Incarnation; yet, in order to call the elect under the old Covenant, he was Mediator even before his manifestation in the flesh,[21] and he remains so after his death. . . .[22]

The sacrifice offered in time by the Christ modifies, at least considered from the human point of view, the attitude of God himself towards men. In reality, that attitude is unchanged and immutable; it cannot therefore be influenced *a posteriori* by the work of Christ. That work is limited to the removal of the obstacle that prevents the divine love from making its way to men. The initiative remains moreover with God. . . .

Christ's work of salvation thus appears as the necessary consequence of the eternal decree of election. Redemption is included in predestination and founded upon it, as Duns Scotus had taught before. It is the means or instrument chosen from all eternity. This does not mean, however, that in Calvin's view Christ the Mediator was reduced to the fulfilment of a merely instrumental part. The Christ took part in the election, because he is one of the three Persons of the Holy Trinity. Election, then, is in this sense also founded upon Christ. Being the Mediator, he has rendered election effectual, for by his sacrifice he has appeased the wrath of God and has restored to its efficacy the love that God had dedicated to the elect of all eternity. In doing this he conformed himself to the divine will, which had freely chosen this means of salvation, but was his will, equally with that of the Father and that of the Holy Spirit.

4. R. S. Franks[1] points out how both Zwingli and Melanchthon reject the Anselmian doctrine of the absolute necessity on the part of God to demand satisfaction. The thought has no place in Zwingli's concept of God's utter sovereignty. His ideas and emphasis on righteousness project themselves in Christology: Christ is our righteousness. Melanchthon's work, clearer and more finished, remains the basis of subsequent Protestant theology. He recognizes in Christ the roles of prophet and king, but he emphasizes that of victim which placates the divine wrath and reconciles man with God.

Zwingli. Zwingli . . . has on the one hand much in common with Erasmus, on the other much also with Luther. To the influence of Erasmus he directly owed the humanistic strain, which characterises all his theological work, and markedly differentiates it from that of Luther, whose early train-

[21] Sermon on Daniel 8:16–27 and 9:17–18, *Opp.*, 41, 504 and 557 ff.

[22] Sermon on I Timothy 2:5–6, *Opp.*, 53, 167.

[1] Robert S. Franks was sometime a scholar of St. John's College in Cambridge, and Principal Emeritus of Western College in Bristol, England. He authored several theological

ing was in the Occamist scholasticism. What Zwingli has in common with Luther is his return from the mediaeval theology to the Pauline Gospel of justification. Yet even here there was a difference; Luther was led back to the Pauline Gospel above all through his own subjective experience, and thus his final apprehension of it centered in the essentially subjective doctrine of justification by faith. Zwingli, who always emphasized his independence of Luther, came to Paul in the first place rather in the spirit of Erasmus than in that of Luther, in so far as his fundamental desire was to go back to the original sources of Christianity, and understand the Divine revelation in the Scriptures. As the result of his search indeed he found in the sources, not a philosophy like Erasmus, but a Gospel like Luther: nevertheless the difference of starting-point between him and Luther led him to make central not the subjective experience of justification but the objective Gospel itself. No doubt justification and the Gospel are only two aspects of the same thing, and the difference between Zwingli and Luther is only one of emphasis. Yet there is a difference, which difference was more accentuated still, when Zwingli in his later theology went back behind the Gospel and made the sovereignty of God his fundamental theological principle.

Another difference between Luther and Zwingli lies in the fact that Zwingli was by nature, what Luther never was, viz. a systematic theologian.

We shall take our account of the ideas of Zwingli from the "Commentarius de vera et falsa religione" (1525),[2] which is the completest systematic presentation of the Zwinglian theology. . . .

Zwingli has already, in his introductory paragraph on the term religion, identified true religion with Christianity. . . . He insists on the religious unity of God and Christ. All that has been said of union with God is true of union with Christ, who is the God-man. Everything, however, cannot be treated at once, and the knowledge of God naturally precedes the knowledge of Christ.

"Just as grace is only rightly known, when guilt is established by the law, as Paul says,[3] that is, when guilt is known as measured by the law; so also Christ, Who is the pledge of grace, nay, Who is grace itself, is only rightly taught and known, when we have seen our guilt and learned that through its intervention, the way of ascending to heaven is closed for us. . . . To know Christ rightly we must, therefore, first rightly know ourselves" (p. 675).

"Christ then is the certainty and pledge of the grace of God. This will be clear as follows: We said in our consideration of man, that his condition was so desperate that . . . how could he . . . hope ever to be numbered among those above? But God was good, and pitying His work formed a plan to undo such a terrible fate. [Yet] His justice being sacrosanct must needs remain no less untouched and unshaken than His mercy. . . ."

---

works, among them *The Atonement* and *A History of the Doctrine of the Work of Christ*. It is from this latter book published in 1962 under the title *The Work of Christ* (London: Thomas Nelson and Sons, Ltd.) that this excerpt has been taken, selectively, from pp. 307–326.

[2] "Corpus Reformatorum," vol xc, pp. 570ff.

[3] Rom. 7:25.

Zwingli insists that the ecclesiastical satisfactions are insufficient. It is only lack of self-knowledge that prevents the recognition of this.

"At last, therefore, wishing to help our hopeless cause, our Creator sent, to satisfy His justice by sacrificing Himself for us, not an angel, not a man, but His own Son, and Him invested with flesh, that neither His majesty might prevent us from intercourse with Him nor His humility cast us down from hope. For that He is God and the Son of God, who has been sent as our Trustee and Mediator, supports our hope. For what can He not do or has He not, who is God? But that He is man, promises familiarity, friendship, yea relationship and community with us; for what can He deny, who is our brother, who partakes of our infirmity? Unheard of and unexpected as was the event, it was yet intended and ordained from the beginning of human misery. For as God created man by His Son, so by Him also He determined to restore him, when fallen into death, by the Same, that creation and restoration might be of One and the Same" (p. 681).

Christ then is the woman's seed, promised in Gen. 3:15, who should break the serpent's head. In the temptation the devil sought to overcome Him, but Christ won the victory. Having failed here the devil raised the Jews against Him.[4]

Zwingli then draws a comparison between the first and the second Adam. . . . The contrasts drawn by Paul in Rom. 5:15–21, show again how our disease was cured by contrary remedies, and how the Divine justice was placated for us by the righteousness of Christ alone, Who is our righteousness, as He is our life. . . .

Christ, then, at the fitting time became incarnate in the womb of a pure virgin by the fertilizing power of the Holy Spirit alone without the co-operation of the male. There were two reasons why He should be thus born of a virgin: (1) His Divinity could not bear contact with the taint of sin; (2) as a victim He needed to be pure from all stain. . . .

That sins are forgiven in Christ's name, is the most joyful news ever heard. "In Christ's name" means "by the power or might of Christ." The Gospel, however, includes besides forgiveness the duty of repentance. The whole work of redemption would be purposeless, if man were not made better thereby. Christ's blood washes away our sin, but with the condition that we should become new creatures. Zwingli says, in verbal agreement with Luther: "The whole life of the Christian man is repentance. For when is it that we do not sin?" (p. 695). . . . The Church (loc. 13) is nothing but Christ's people. . . . Faith is a reality, and in it the spirit confides in the death of Christ, and requires no external assurance. Baptism is a symbol pledging us to a life in accordance with the rule of Christ. In the Lord's Supper we joyfully prove our trust in Christ's death and thank Him for our redemption. . . .

As regards Zwingli's doctrine of the work of Christ we note that, while he makes use of the Irenaean motive that creation and redemption must be by one hand, and while he develops ideas like those of Augustine on the contrary correspondence between the sin of Adam and the obedience of Christ,

[4] Lk. 22:53.

his main doctrine is a modification of the Anselmic doctrine of satisfaction of the same kind as found in Luther. Zwingli in a very thorough-going way elaborates the thought of the need of the reconciliation of mercy and justice, and substitutes the Divine justice for the Divine honor as the attribute in God demanding satisfaction. On the other hand he lays great stress on the subjective aspect of the work of Christ, and its connection with the Gospel: "Christ is the assurance and pledge of the grace of God" (p. 676).

It is to be observed that Zwingli, like Luther, abandons Anselm upon the point of the absolute necessity of satisfaction; the necessity was ultimately that of the Divine decree. God did not need to treat with the devil, and might have refashioned man by His sovereign power. Zwingli even suggests that His ultimate purpose, so far as we can understand it, was that of assuaging conscience. It is true that Zwingli has, except in the "Commentarius," nowhere spoken of the necessity of satisfaction as less than absolute, or suggested that it was subjective rather than objective.[5] Yet it is to be observed that such views fundamentally agree with his doctrine of God, who is so absolutely infinite, as to be above all reach of man's understanding. On this showing, even though satisfaction be a rational necessity from the human, it need not be from the Divine, point of view.

We ask in conclusion: has Zwingli furnished the simplification of theology on the basis of Scripture demanded by Occam? . . . Zwingli may be said to have fulfilled the demand of Occam, as neither Erasmus nor Luther had done. Nevertheless, while Zwingli is undoubtedly superior to Erasmus, because more Scriptural, his advantage over Luther in simplicity is at the expense of a real loss. Luther's paradoxes carry the promise of a final synthesis, completer than that of Zwingli. Luther has inherited the gains of the Scotist and Occamist criticism with its keen eye for the antinomies in Christianity, while Zwingli shows a tendency to return to the Thomist type of theology, which the Nominalist criticism has declared in the end to amount to no more than a unity of aggregation. Such a unity of aggregation is indeed plainly exhibited by Zwingli's doctrine of the work of Christ, which brings together patristic, mediaeval, and new evangelical material: nor, although all is viewed in connection with the doctrine that Christ is our righteousness, is the synthesis of the different elements with this doctrine so intimate as in the parallels in Luther.

Melanchthon. With Melanchthon . . . we pass from the Reformers themselves to the theologians of the Reformation. Melanchthon, like Zwingli, was a humanist; it was his work to unite the traditions of Erasmus and of Luther. He has great importance for the history of the Reformation itself, in that under the influence of Luther he drew up the "Augsburg Confession" (1530), and also published his great "Apology" for it (1531). . . .

The importance of Melanchthon for our doctrine, however, lies not in the "Augsburg Confession" or in the "Apology" but in the final edition of his "Loci Theologici" (1559), in which he has developed his own theology more independently of Luther. The first edition of this great work (1521),

[5] Cf. Ritschl, "Justification and Reconciliation," English trans., vol. 1, p. 204.

like the "Confession" and the "Apology," reflected more strictly Luther's ideas. . . . In the first edition he thoroughly shares Luther's irrationalism. Christian doctrine is altogether different from philosophy and human reason. . . . In the last edition[6] philosophy is, however, at least allowed a usefulness in the explication of theology. . . . In the first edition Melanchthon intentionally devotes attention only to the practical doctrines of the Reformation; in the last he enlarges his view to take in their metaphysical presuppositions, both theological[7] and Christological. . . .

In order therefore to present Melanchthon not merely as the interpreter of Luther, but in his own individuality, we take our account of his theology from the final edition of the "Loci." . . .

While the first edition of the "Loci" contains the famous passage, "This it is to know Christ, to know His benefits, not, as they (the Schoolmen) teach, His natures, and the modes of the Incarnation" (p. 63), the last edition returns distinctly to the scholastic view of the basis of theology. The doctrines of the Trinity and of the Incarnation are introduced as depending on the Scripture and the tradition of the Church (loc. I Of God); while the doctrine of God as Creator has also a rational basis, in that it can be demonstrated from His work in the world (loc. II Of the Creation).

The Son is the Eternal Logos, who has assumed human nature. God has sent Him to be a Redeemer and placate His wrath against sin (I, p .20). His office also includes the work of teaching according to the command of the Father (p. 34). But Melanchthon does not expand the doctrine of Christ's office, but after a recognition of the Augustinian doctrine of original sin (p. 86) proceeds to his central theme of law and Gospel. . . .

The law, Melanchthon repeats, has promises, but upon condition. But of the Gospel he further says:

"Quite other is the promise proper to the Gospel. It has not as ground the condition of the law; it does not promise because of the fulfilment of the law, but freely for Christ's sake. . . . Remission and reconciliation or justification are freely given us, that is, not in accordance with our worth; and yet there needed to be a victim on our behalf, therefore Christ was given us and was made a sacrifice, that for His sake we might certainly conclude that we please the Father" (p. 166). . . .

The sum of the Gospel is contained in the doctrine of grace and justification (loc. VIII), which exhibits the proper benefit of Christ. To neglect it is to transform Christianity into philosophy, to extenuate sin in human nature. . . .

To be justified by faith in Christ signifies to obtain forgiveness not because of our own virtues, but because of the Mediator, the Son of God" (p. 178).

Faith, then, beholds Christ sitting at God's right hand and interceding for us, views Him as Mediator, and applies His mediatorship to our needs. Faith is, therefore, not merely a historical knowledge, though historical knowledge is implied: it is trust (*fiducia*).

"Faith looks upon Christ, Who must be acknowledged as the Son of the

[6] Final ed., ed. Detzer, 1827, vol. i. pp. xvi, 4, 5.

[7] "Theological" in the strict sense, i.e. belonging to the doctrine of God.

Eternal God, crucified for us, and raised again, etc. . . ."

Melanchthon adds a section on the kingdom of Christ (loc. xv).

"The Gospel clearly teaches that the kingdom of Christ is spiritual, that is, that Christ sits at the right hand of the Father and makes intercession for us, and gives remission of sins and the Holy Spirit to the Church, that is, to those that believe in Him and call upon God in trust upon Him; and that He sanctifies them, that He may raise them up at the last day to life and glory eternal. And that we may obtain these benefits, there has been ordained the ministry of the Gospel, by which men are called to the knowledge of Christ; and the Holy Spirit is efficacious, etc." (II, p. 58) . . .

His theology is undoubtedly founded on Luther's, and retains from him the synthetic view of justification, which is the characteristic and central Protestant doctrine. . . .

Compared with Zwingli, Melanchthon has on the whole the advantage both as regards matter and form; of matter, in so far as he reproduces Luther, who is superior to Zwingli; of form, in so far as his doctrine is clearer and more finished than that of the Swiss humanist. . . .

Melanchthon has made the necessary preparation for a new Protestant doctrine of the work of Christ. To the new complex of practical doctrines a new conception of the work of Christ must correspond: to this new conception, however, Melanchthon himself has not yet attained. In his "Loci" his references to the work of Christ are of the most general character, and are mostly introduced only with immediate practical reference to the doctrine of justification. Such references as there are, however, suggest a reduction of Luther's variety of doctrine to one fixed type. Though Melanchthon recognizes the work of Christ as a teacher and also refers to His reign and intercession, the principal point in His work appears to be that as a sacrifice or victim He propitiates the Divine wrath against sinners. In other works Melanchthon develops this last view into a doctrine like that which we have found in Zwingli, modifying the Anselmic theory of satisfaction, and laying great stress on the reconciliation of mercy and justice. Thus in his "Enarratio Symboli Nicæni,"[8] he treats on these lines of the impulsive and final causes of the Incarnation. He says:

"This decree was made by the most free counsel of God, nor do we so repeat its causes, as if anything were thereby detracted from the freedom of will in God, but it is certain that this decree was made with an admirable wisdom and with the preservation of the order of justice and mercy. Consequently we inquire into its congruous causes whatsoever. Now the first is not obscure. Although God received the human race by His mercy for the sake of His Son's intercession, yet God, since He is just, willed that His justice should be satisfied. So by a wonderful harmonization of justice and mercy the reconciliation was established. And since the human race had sinned, it befitted the order of justice that one of the human race should pay the penalty, which was the ransom of the rest. It is therefore clear enough why this sacrifice should be a man. The second reason, why He should be God, is the infinite evil of

[8] Thomasius, "Christi Person und Werk," vol. iii, p. 314.

sin; that He might be a ransom of infinite goodness and an equivalent, this Mediator is also God. Thirdly, no created power could alone have borne the wrath of God, and in so great stress of pains have given true praise to Divine justice. This is the secret and great cause, which the devout do not neglect to consider. For in the punishment, which must be a placation, the praise of justice must be rendered to the Punisher: a created power, however, could not have overcome death and restored to us righteousness and life eternal. And since the Mediator must needs be the perpetual guardian of the Church, hearing it at all times and present with the saints everywhere —it is evident that a created power could not be present nor see the groans of our hearts. These things belong only to the Mediator."

It is observable from the above extract, that Melanchthon, like Zwingli and Luther, rejects the Anselmic doctrine of an absolute necessity of satisfaction.

5. R. S. Paul[1] discusses the reasons why the so-called theory of penal substitution seems to have made its appearance at the time of the Reformers, and, particularly why this theory became the quasi-orthodox doctrine of Atonement for Protestantism. He suggests that biblical reflection and historical factors may account for its appearance at that time. An examination of the confessional statements which followed the Reformers fails to show exclusive acceptance of the theory. He concludes that the events that accelerated the need to formulate Calvinist doctrine more precisely played a decisive role.

[The reading] of the Westminster Confession's *Shorter Catechism* . . . [leads into the] consideration of the way in which the doctrine of the Atonement developed after the time of the Reformers, first in the doctrinal statements of the Reformation and then in its later representative theologians. In the first place, however, let us understand the historical problems with which we are involved.

Two facts stand out regarding the doctrine in its relationship to the history of the churches of the Reformation. First, the "penal" explanation and its descriptive imagery seem to make their appearance at the time of the Reformers, and secondly, although the ideas of sacrifice and ransom, victory, and example occur in the Reformers themselves and continue to crop up from time to time in later Protestants, it was the theory of penal substitution which from the middle of the sixteenth century to the middle years of the nineteenth century became the quasi-orthodox doctrine for the greater part of Protestantism. This poses two historical questions—why did that particular thoery of redemption make its appearance at the time of the Reformation and, since it appears only as one

---

[1] Robert S. Paul, native of England, is at present Waldo Professor of Church History at the Hartford Seminary Foundation. He has authored several theological and historical works: *The Lord Protector, Religion and Politics in the Life of Oliver Cromwell, The Atonement and the Sacraments*. It is from this last book (New York, Nashville: Abingdon Press, 1960) that this excerpt has been taken from pp. 109–114.

theory among others in the Reformers themselves (in view of the features that it soon began to assume), why did it become so universally adhered to by Protestants?

It is not my intention to dwell too long upon the first question, although in itself it would provide a fascinating subject for research. To some extent the particular accent may have been brought into being, or at least helped forward, by the Reformation's emphasis upon the individual's responsibility before God, although I am sure that this is an argument which can be pushed too far. Perhaps there are more solid grounds for tracing the theory to the Bible itself and to the literal interpretation that Protestantism adopted in its claim to biblical authority. No less a modern biblical scholar than Vincent Taylor has pointed out how near the New Testament teaching concerning the representative work of Christ comes to a substitutionary doctrine of the Atonement. "In fact," he observes, "a theologian who retires to a doctrinal fortress guarded by such ordinance as Mark 10:45, Romans 6:10f, 2 Corinthians 5:14, 21, Galatians 3:13, and I Timothy 2:5f, is more difficult to dislodge than many New Testament students imagine."[2]

Even so, it is doubtful whether the legal and penal categories would have been taken up if they had not been living categories in the thought of that time. We have to remember that the Reformation took place when feudal society was breaking down. The concepts of "law," as something defined by the State, and of the individual's responsibility before law were ideas which belonged to the new order. Crime was conceived not so much as the breaking of a personal relationship, an affront to the suzerain's honor as it was under feudalism, but it was a sin against the law, and the state was beginning to be regarded as the upholder of the law and its avenger. But even if these factors in the new society were present to stimulate a particular interpretation of the Atonement once it had made its appearance, why did the penal theory become paramount in Protestant theology?

No clear answer to the question is given in the Confessions. For Lutheranism the *Augsburg Confession* of 1530 simply affirms that men are justified freely "for Christ's sake through faith, when they believe that they are received into favor, and their sins forgiven for Christ's sake, who by his death hath satisfied for our sins."[3] It needs to be read alongside Luther's *Shorter Catechism* where, in expounding the christological articles of the Creed, the catechism speaks of Christ "who has redeemed me, a lost and condemned man, secured and delivered me [even] from all sins, from death, and from the power of the devil, not with gold or silver, but with his holy, precious blood, and with his innocent sufferings and death."[4] No attempt is made to present a theory of atonement —if anything the terms used are more in line with the "classic" view than with the penal theory—but the catechism simply states what Christ has achieved for us. It has been pointed out that Philip Melanchthon in the

[2] Vincent Taylor, *The Atonement in New Testament Teaching* (2nd ed.; Epworth Press, 1945), p. 197.

[3] *The Creeds of Christendom,* ed. Philip Schaff (New York: Harper and Bros., 1877), III, art. iv, p. 10.

[4] *Ibid.,* III, art. ii, answer p. 79.

later editions of his *Loci Communes* appears to have passed over the ransom images that are to be found in Luther and to have concentrated upon the penal theory which rapidly became normative for Protestant theology. But whatever the prestige of Melanchthon as the systematizer of Lutheranism, the doctrinal statements of the Confession as such are not bound to one theory.

It is, however, to Calvinist theology that we must look to trace the development of ideas about the Atonement in the Anglo-Saxon world, but here again we find that the doctrinal statements of early Calvinism are far less bound to a particular theory of the Atonement than we might suppose. The *Heidelberg Catechism* of the Palatinate Churches (1563) declares that Christ is ordained of God "to be our chief Prophet and Teacher, who fully reveals to us the secret counsel and will of God concerning our redemption; and our only High Priest, who by the one sacrifice of his body has redeemed us."[5] The identification of the believer with Christ is made explicit, for by faith the member confessed himself to be "a partaker of his anointing; in order that I also may confess his name, may present myself a living sacrifice of thankfulness to him, and may with a free conscience fight against sin and the devil in this life, and hereafter in eternity, reign with him over all creatures." Christ is "Lord" because, not with silver or gold, "but with his precious blood he has redeemed and purchased us, body and soul, from the power of the devil, to be his own." In all this we can notice a strong ethical element with very little that could be regarded as exclusively distinctive of the penal theory, but this emphasis does appear in the catechism's answer to the question what is meant by the word "suffered" in respect of Christ. It says that "all the time he lived on earth, but especially at the end of his life, he bore, in body and soul, the wrath of God against the sin of the whole human race, in order that by his passion, as the only atoning sacrifice, he might redeem our body and soul from everlasting damnation, and obtain for us the grace of God, righteousness, and eternal life." Similarly in explanation of the clauses in the Creed it declares that he suffered under Pilate in order to "deliver us from the severe judgment of God to which we were exposed." He was crucified in order to take on himself "the curse which lay upon me, because the death of the cross was accursed of God." He descended into hell so that "in my greatest temptations I may be assured that Christ, my Lord, by his inexpressible anguish, pains, and terrors which he suffered in his soul on the cross and before, has redeemed me from the anguish and torment of hell." Among the benefits that come to us from his sacrifice, "our old man is with him crucified, slain, and buried; so that the evil lusts of the flesh may no more reign in us, but that we may offer ourselves unto him a sacrifice of thanksgiving."

The penal idea is here, particularly in its concentration upon the sufferings of Christ and in the idea that our Lord's passion is an atoning sacrifice to the wrath of God, but it is certainly no more pronounced than other biblical images which we discover in Calvin. There is the same emphasis upon ethical identity with Christ and upon

[5] Schaff, *op. cit.,* III, answer 31, p. 317.

the sacrificial aspect of Christ's death. Indeed, one of the striking things about the Calvinist Confessions and Catechisms is the fact that although the penal theory of the Atonement appears in them, it is not elaborated and certainly does not assume the importance that it does in later theology. The *Scottish Confession* of 1560 states that "our Lord *Jesus* offered himself a voluntary Sacrifice unto his Father for us,"[6] and that in his descent into hell and resurrection from the dead, he rose again for our justification and destroyed him who was "the Author of death"—statements which would be as conformable to a sacrificial or "classic" theory of atonement as they would be to one of penal substitution.

Perhaps the penal emphasis falls as strongly in the *Westminster Confession* of 1647 as anywhere—later in point of time, and therefore presumably much more under the influence of "protestant scholasticism." In this Confession it is said that our Lord willingly undertook the Father's appointment to be the Mediator, that he "endured most grievous torments immediately in his soul, and most painful sufferings in his body," and that "by his perfect obedience and sacrifice of himself, which he through the eternal Spirit once offered up unto God, hath fully satisfied the justice of his Father, and purchased not only reconciliation, but an everlasting inheritance in the kingdom of heaven, for all those whom the Father hath given unto him." Even here, however, the theory of penal substitution does not appear in "splendid isolation" and is mixed with the ideas of obedience and sacrifice that we found in the *Institutes:*

> Christ, by his obedience and death, did fully discharge the debt of all those that are thus justified, and did make a proper, real, and full satisfaction to his Father's justice in their behalf. Yet inasmuch as he was given by the Father for them, and his obedience and satisfaction accepted in their stead, and both freely, not for any thing in them, their justification is only of free grace; that both the exact justice and rich grace of God might be glorified in the justification of sinners.[7]

This statement is supported by the *Shorter Catechism* of the *Westminster Confession* where it is said that our Lord fulfills the office of Priest to us "in his once offering up of himself a sacrifice to satisfy divine justice, and reconcile us to God, and in making continual intercession for us." Although the catechism speaks of him suffering "the wrath of God, and the cursed death of the cross,"[8] it stresses equally the free grace of God in Christ and the assurance of his love.[9]

In comparison with this we must mention the extreme reticence of the Anglican *Thirty-Nine Articles* on the subject of the Atonement. They simply state that our Lord was "crucified, dead, and buried, to reconcile his Father to us, and to be a sacrifice, not only for original guilt, but also for actual sins of men."[10] True, reconciliation and sacrifice are the terms used, but an unwillingness to be committed theologically does not always pay good

---

[6] *Ibid.,* III, art. ix, 446 (cf. art. viii).
[7] *Ibid.,* III, 626–27 (XI, iii).
[8] *Ibid.,* III, 681 (ques. 25, 27).
[9] *Ibid.,* III, 683 (ques. 33–36).
[10] *Ibid.,* III, 488; art. ii.

dividends, for it is hard to avoid the impression that in the phrase "to reconcile his Father *to us*" the Anglican Church aligned itself with one of the least attractive and least biblical aspects of the penal theory.

The fact which is made clear, however, from an examination of the confessional statements is that there was no one generally accepted doctrine of the Atonement contained in them, and all the biblical images find expression. On the other hand we do notice a tendency to use the legal and penal ideas which would certainly help to swing Protestant theology into that line of thinking. Nevertheless, it is evident that if a strict doctrine of election, an increasingly rigid Biblicism, and the categories of thought in society were to bring the penal theory more and more into the center of Protestant theology, there were elements within the Confessions themselves which might have redressed the balance if events had not accelerated the need to formulate Calvinist doctrine more precisely. . . .

The events that caused this doctrinal retraction centered in the doctrinal struggle that was going on within Protestantism itself. Just as the radical criticism offered to the Reformers by the Anabaptists led to a stiffening in the doctrines of Church and Sacraments, so the challenge offered by the Arminians to the Calvinist doctrine of Election, and the still more radical criticism levelled by the Socinians, led to retrenchment along the whole front of Christian doctrine by those who had inherited the work of the Reformers and regarded themselves as the guardians of the Reformed teaching.

VIII

CHRISTOLOGY IN THE SIXTEENTH THROUGH THE NINETEENTH CENTURIES

Protestant Authors

1. L. Perriraz[1] analyzes the background of the Christological views of Socinianism and Arminianism in the seventeenth century. They preclude the rationalist criticism of the following century. Socinus' rationalism renounces all mystical and sentimental elements. Christ's divinity in the Nicaean sense is rejected. Arminianism, influenced by both Arianism and Socinianism, follows the same line of thought. Rationalist Criticism eventually undermined Protestant Scholasticism. Pietism failed as an effort to remedy the deficits of Orthodoxy.

One might think that by the sixteenth century orthodox Christology had been acknowledged by all. This was true generally speaking, although Arianism had had supporters through the Middle Ages. Without this survival of

[1] Louis Perriraz is a distinguished Protestant pastor and theologian, professor of History of Modern Theology at the University of Lausanne. He is the author of *Histoire de la Théologie Protestante aux XVIIIme et XIXme siècles*. It is from the third volume *Le Probléme Christologique* (Editions Henri Messeiller, Neuchatel: 1956) that this excerpt has been taken from pp. 24–34.

Arius' thinking, which had undergone change over the centuries, one would not understand the outbreak of thoughts contrary to the reigning orthodoxy, which one sees appearing in the sixteenth century with the Socinians and the Arminians, who prelude the rationalistic criticism of the eighteenth century.

Socinianism is the work of Lélius Socinus (Sozzini) and his nephew Faustus, who formed a very rigid organization. . . . (Lélius' death in 1562 and the unexpected death of Faustus in 1604 did not stop the development of the sect, which had spread widely (and) its principles, slightly modified, are found once again as the sharpest weapons of the rationalists, deists and atheists of the eighteenth century.

Socinianism teaches that man must obey his reason and follow its natural light which suffices to lead him to the truth. It acknowledges a revelation, but this more on account of the ignorance of man than of his need for redemption. This ignorance exists because of the contradictory manifestations of the divine will, which the intelligence of man never arrives at knowing. That is why it is necessary that God Himself manifests what He wishes and requires from His creatures. Consequently, the good is that which God wishes, not the absolute good. This is what Scripture teaches, where the notion of the good varies depending on whether one is speaking of the Old or New Testament. If moral law is the law of the world, it is presented differently by different authors and moments in history, and this law comes from the arbitrary will of God.

However, since man has not obeyed God and has exposed himself to condemnation, God has raised out of the heart of the human race a man born of a virgin, whose pure and holy life gave the example of perfect obedience, whose death was that of a martyr, and whose sacrifice confirmed the truth of his teachings. The courageous and magnificent death of Christ raised Him to a divine stage, and led Him to sit at the right of the Father, to rule over the world, and to receive the prayers of those who love Him.

To complete this rapid sketch of a movement whose importance has never been recognized, let us borrow from the Racovian Catechism, several pieces of information on the internal organization of this doctrine, without forgetting as Harnack remarks, that this work dates from the time when the Socinian Church was already established, and does not reflect the original form of the doctrine.

First of all, it must be kept in mind that Socinianism presupposes the great anti-ecclesiastical movement of the Middle Ages, which the Socinians, influenced by the Reformation, strove to organize. Humanist, and Pelagian, the movement knew how to skillfully use critical thought stirred up by the doctrines of the Church, especially that of the philosophy of Duns Scotus. From this it developed its anti-trinitarian and anti-catholic attitndes. Actually many from the beginning of the fifteenth century began to rebel against the authority of the Church and its dogma, due to religious or scientific reasons. It was the meeting of scholasticism and the Renaissance, of reason and art, which would reappear in modern times to the detriment of religion. Socinianism tried to coordinate all of this.

According to the Racovian Catechism, religion is a full knowledge of a doctrine of salvation, which is the road of eternal life shown by God in Jesus Christ. This is what the New Testament says (the source and norm of truth), where God has revealed His will and the road of salvation. For Socinus, faith alone does not suffice; the intelligence must comprehend, because religion is the business of reason. Thus, the doctrine of Socinus is a rationalism which renounces every mystical or sentimental element. . . .

We are thus led to Christ whose divinity Socinianism cannot accept in an orthodox sense. In the Gospels, Christ is a mortal man, although more than an ordinary man, since He became immortal, and was "the one" from God from His birth. Sanctified and sent into the world, clothed with the wisdom and the power of God, then raised to God after His resurrection, He was divine by the power that was in Him. This conforms to the Scriptures and to Exegesis.

In brief the Socinian doctrine is presented as follows: In accordance with His free decree, God decided to bring men to eternal life. For this He raised the man Jesus, provided from his birth with divine powers, and who as a prophet, announced to man the perfect divine law, deepening and explaining the Decalogue. He proclaimed promises of eternal life, and gave example of a perfect moral life, consummated by his death. He went beyond the Old Testament, corrected Moses, and added new laws. With the promise of the Holy Spirit, he offered a strong aid for their observance and assured pardon to those who repent. All this implies faith and obedience toward the Savior. By his resurrection, Jesus assured those who followed him deliverance from sin, the gift of the Holy Spirit and eternal life. But there is nothing mystical in all this, neither in the concept of faith nor in that of the sacraments. These are two very simple acts, one of initiation (baptism), the other of remembrance (Holy Communion).

For Socinus and his followers it is not a question of divinity or connaturality in the Nicaean sense, nor of Trinity or of two natures in Christ. Christ remains a man. The Socinians admit that by virtue of his natural qualities and spiritual gifts bestowed upon him at the moment of his baptism, he possessed a perfect knowledge of the divine will, which he revealed to the world in his teaching. But it is the Father who must remain the object of our adoration. If one wishes to adore the son, he must not forget that it is the Father that we adore in Him, and he must renounce this, if this gesture be detrimental to the worship we owe to the Father.

As Strauss has remarked, this view recalls that of Catholics regarding saints and angels.

Persecuted in Germany and in Poland, Socinianism took refuge in Holland, England, and especially in Transylvania. Everywhere, by the efforts of its distinguished men, it spread the elements of a freer culture, of a theology which broke with the reigning orthodoxy. Their action is felt in the formation of the rationalistic criticism of the English Deists and influenced the evolution of Arminianism, which so strongly troubled the life of the Dutch Church in one of the country's gravest hours.

In their fight against the despotism of Spain (a fight which was political and religious at the same time), the people of the Netherlands had adopted Calvinism under the most rigid form. The *Confessio belgica* and the *Catechism of Heidelberg* which had been imposed on the Church of the United Provinces, did not please all and provoked an opposition which became very serious with James Arminius, a professor at Leyden. Contrary to the views of the strict Calvinists, of whom Francis Gomar, a colleague of Arminius, was the chief speaker, Arminius made salvation depend on an act of faith, therefore on freedom. For him predestination was a Catholic idea and should be rejected as much as the authority of the Pope. He insisted on the dignity of man that God himself respected as in the Scriptures.

These remarks were not lacking in pertinence, but the Arminians hurt the good image of their views by adopting a eudaemonism contrary to the holiness of the Christian life.

To defend his point of view, Arminius adopted a criticism of Scripture and dogma inspired by rationalist philosophy. He was followed by his colleague Episcopius, by the jurist Hugo de Groot and others. . . . This led them to attack the dogma of the Trinity. If Arminius declared that he wished no change in the dogma, this was not true of Episcopius, who emphasized the subordination of the son to the Father, or of Clêricus and Vorstius, who had been drawn towards Unitarianism through the influence of Arianism and Socinianism.

Thus while orthodox dogma sought to establish itself in Protestant scholasticism, rationalist criticism, which little by little came to undermine it, grew and intensified itself. It must be mentioned that the excesses of the scholastics whose theories were sometimes a defiance to the most valid principles of reason, furnished the weapons for the critique that one sees appearing during the first decades of the seventeenth century.

It is true that at first criticism directed itself only to the books of the Bible. It sought to establish a method of examination more consistent with a sense of history, which was born and grew parallel to the sense of human dignity, during the Reformation. . . . In Holland, the theologian Cock (Coccejus), sought to unite history with divine action, and considered the Old Testament as a collection of types of Jesus, which presented themselves in a more or less distinct manner according to time or occasion.

These ideas which one will see reborn in the nineteenth century with Heugstenberg, and which enjoy definite favor in certain contemporary milieus, undermined the basis of Calvinist dogma in the seventeenth century.

The same effect resulted from the efforts of George Calixtus to bring together the churches and from those of Gottfried Arnold to discover the healthy spiritual tradition of the Church in the heresies themselves.

These men did not intend to undermine the Christological dogma, but all of these investigations created doubts about its value and gave weapons to the enemies of the Church. The progress of Cartesianism and of rational explanations, united to a better knowledge of antiquity, created this situation of confusion which developed in the middle of the eighteenth century, a situation characterized by the triumph of rationalism and the complete destruction of orthodoxy. . . .

Pietism, which was an effort to remedy the deficits of orthodox piety and to diminish the role of reason in behalf of that of the heart, implied, as a consequence, a certain scorn for dogma and theological discussions. By insisting on the human nature of

Christ, on his sufferings and his death, it attracted attention to these elements neglected by orthodoxy. In doing so, however, it lent a hand to those like Spalding, who considered as secondary the dogmas of the Trinity, the two natures of Christ and original sin. This gave grounds to doubt whether the official doctrine was in conformity with primitive Christianity, and whether a better constructed exegesis would not give a different image of Christ.

But despite its force and its ardor, pietism did not make any positive contribution to the dogmatic treasury of the Church. It fell very early into sentimental effusions and by the end of the century, returned to the old ways, and to the old formulas which responded so little to the fundamental inspirations from which it came. In the nineteenth century it mingled with the Awakening, which was animated by the same spirit.

The story is quite different with rationalism, born in the Renaissance and strengthened by the philosophy of Descartes. . . . It certainly brought beneficial effects delivering man from oppressive guardianship, both juridic and religious. But it was less successful in the manner in which it attacked Christian dogma, and in particular, the Christological dogma.

Penetrated, perhaps unconsciously, with the principles of Socinianism, it saw Jesus as a superior man who was filled with the Holy Spirit and whose life and doctrine were a model for those who believed in him. In his essays on Rationalism, Rohr considers the founder of Christianity as a purely human apparition. Jesus is a man in the full sense of the word, a product of his environment and his age, yet one who surpassed all men in wisdom, virtue and piety. He was the true hero of humanity. His origin was natural, and that which the Gospels report of his birth belongs to the world of myths and legends, and his divinity consists of his dignity.

Rohr and his followers were convinced that they presented a life of Christ more beautiful and sublime than orthodoxy, because in their eyes, that which made the grandeur of man was not his heavenly origin but his free and personal activity. Jesus is shown truly great by the fact that he possessed divine wisdom, and also because he acted in a perfectly moral manner.

These views of Rohr express the convictions of all the rationalists, from Semler to Wegscheider and to Paulus. But aside from these men who still show a certain respect for the person of Jesus, there were those who allowed themselves to be carried away by invectives and blasphemies, as the English deists, the French encyclopedists and certain German rationalists, such as Reimarus, author of the famous *Wolfinbüttler Fragmente*.

In its desire to reject the past, while preserving the ethics of the Gospels, rationalism did not realize that the doctrine which relied only on individual reason threatened to collapse Because Christian life in its plenitude cannot develop independently of Christ.

It is this thought which still gives value to orthodoxy. Its followers strove as much as they could to save the doctrines of the past, but under the blows of rationalistic criticism, they no longer knew what had to be kept and what had to be rejected. While Rheinhard maintained the impersonal character of the human nature in Christ, others conceived this union as a mere friendship. This would do away with his immortality. Rheinhard himself questions the divine powers that Jesus possessed before his birth . . . and in his infancy. It is only at the mature age that Jesus was endowed with this power.

But if the personality of Christ came from God, all this supranaturalism which took the place of orthodoxy meant nothing. Thus the different sides were asked to leave their subtilities and to go back to the Bible (not seeing that the scriptures are not a systematic treatise, and are in need of a definite doctrine to interpret them wisely). This is what is questioned by the rationalism inspired by Spinoza and his *Theological and Political Treatise.*

A study more detailed than that which was elaborated here, would give us a better understanding of the confusion in the ecclesiastical environment in the second half of the eighteenth century. The imprecisions which hindered the ancient school of Tübingen from formulating the great Protestant dogma of justification by faith show the measure of trouble of their age.

It is not then to theological circles that one should turn for a new vision of the work and nature of Jesus . . . The remedy was brought by the idealistic currents at the end of the eighteenth century, which broke down at the same time the old orthodoxy, and the rationalist platitudes, to give dignity and grandeur to religion and Christianity.

However, if the work of a Hamann or a Herder is remarkable, if German romanticism has renewed the source of piety and prepared the views of the Awakening that one sees appearing at the end of the Napoleonic Era, it is only from a true theological movement that a deep restoration of the Christian dogma can be achieved. This was exactly what was devised by Fredric Schleiermacher, who presented himself to the men of his time as the prophet of the new era. . . .

2. L. Perriraz[1] reviews the fundamental principles of Schleiermacher's *The Christian Faith* as applied to his Christology. He points out the roots of his failures. He sacrificed too much of the contents of faith to the spirit of the times. Although his positive Christian convictions tried to make themselves felt in his speculations, he reduced Christ to an idealization of what is best in mankind. Redemption is nothing else than victory of the consciousness of God in man over the lower consciousness. It is a mere natural, psychological process which can be accomplished without the intervention of anyone from above.

Inasmuch as the Christological formula is an integral part of the theological scheme, it is difficult to discuss it without knowing the views that an author has had in general on religious and theological questions. Therefore, if we want to know what Schleiermacher thought of the person of the Savior, we must go back to the thoughts and intuitions which dominate his work. His *The Christian Faith,* which appeared in 1821, reveals to us

[1] Cf. n. 1 of this Chapter. This excerpt is from *op. cit.,* pp. 36–47.

both his method and his principles which became those of modern theology in opposition to orthodox theology.

The work begins with a definition of religion (a feeling of absolute dependence), and then goes on to a definition of Christianity (a monotheistic religion, teleological, at the center of which is redemption brought by Jesus Christ).

This is the main point in Christianity and the common ground of all the communities which call themselves Christian.

It follows that if for some their consciousness is not always in dependence on Christ, they can find redemption, however, in the Christian sense, if they place themselves in the framework of the Christian community.

Thus, the starting point of Schleiermacher is neither a dogma of the Church nor the image of Jesus transmitted by historical tradition, which would have led him to accede to an influence alien to his own religious experience. This starting point is rather that personal experience which, in the midst of the community of which he played a part, regenerated his soul. His life was transformed by the ideal of the redemption which the community saw. Thus he accomplished communion with God through Jesus Christ and in that way found the experience of redemption which assured him peace, strength and happiness.

It must be said that the consciousness of the individual is always stretched out toward this ideal, but when it wishes to attempt to realize it by its own means, it comes into contact with the power of evil and only succeeds in attaining victory by uniting itself with community.

Here, we find again the profound thought of Schleiermacher for whom religion is a life which is only realized in its fullness in communion with God. And this life, always threatened by the offensive recurrences of sin, only finds its bloom in the framework of the society of believers where the individual experiences the delivering power of Christ.

It is on these principles that Schleiermacher formulates his Christology.

As a general proposition, belief in God is given to us only in our union with the Redeemer, whose perfection symbolizes free activity in contrast to free receptivity, expression of the need of redemption of the believers. And so, according to this, in order to be a Christian, one must desire communion with Christ.

Thus, in Christian life there are two things to consider: on the one hand, the work of the Redeemer, and on the other hand, the receptiveness of the believers. It is the former which concerns us here.

The activity of the Redeemer depends on his particular dignity. For Schleiermacher, this dignity is characterized by the fact that the universe, destined to realize the perfect, divine life, has found its completion in him. Perfection and activity are intimately united in him, and we cannot separate them, except for didactic necessity.

For our theologian, the person of Christ appears as the prototype of the divine life, the one in which the spontaneity of the new life, which he tried to create in the world, is powerfully manifested. In Christ, the prototype became historic, and all the instances of his life carry the same stamp of perfection. This character is determined in him by the power of his consciousness of God which pervades all his acts and all his thoughts.

This is why the believer receives from the image of Christ, possessed by the Christian community, the impression of the perfection and sanctity of Jesus Christ, which gives power to conquer sin. Thus, Christ becomes for each member of the community the master of life, the inspiration for every good work.

What has been the connection of this prototype with history?

From a human point of view, Jesus developed like any other individual, but his consciousness of God is only accounted for by an action of the Creator climaxing his creation. From the beginning of his life, this strength was in him and governed his whole development. He was not hindered by the environment in which he grew up, and every perceptible impression evoked his consciousness of God in an harmonious way. He was raised, without harm to his innocence, to the total, spiritual control of life by the sole strength of his consciousness of God.

However, adds our author, we can not say that he possessed from his childhood a perfect knowledge of God, which would have made his childhood an illusion, and his life as a man an appearance. The history of Jesus is not understood without the influence of his environment and without the adaptation of the ideas of his time.

But, to this purely human character, we must add that which constitutes his dignity as prototype.

At all times in his development, he was freed from struggles and conflicts which hinder the lives of men, in other words, from everything which conditions the advent of sin in the world. Every perceptible impression as every work he accomplished, manifested the harmony of his consciousness intimately united to God.

The formation of his consciousness of God from childhood to full maturity, when his spiritual perfection manifested itself, can be described as a transition from innocence to perfection. And this innocence was not the act of an exterior protection but rather that of the consciousness of God that Jesus possessed in an original way.

If the dignity of Christ consists in the spiritual function of the consciousness of God, he alone possessed this consciousness which was a divine essence in him (*Sein Gottes*).

In other men, consciousness is hindered by lower consciousness which shows that in them this consciousness of God is not a divine essence. The latter only exists in man through Jesus Christ. "In his personal consciousness, the consciousness of God lived constantly, and determined exclusively each moment of his life. This perfect co-existence of the Supreme Being in him is his particular essence and his most profound identity."

In this way, the Redeemer was similar to other men by his human nature and different from all of them by the strength of his religious consciousness. In as much as sin is not a complete disturbance of human nature, it is possible to reconcile this nature with an harmonious and holy development of the Redeemer. This is why Jesus has not at all been affected by the deficiencies of human nature. Similar to other men and completely different from all of them, he possessed a personal dignity because of the indwelling of God in him.

It is in this way that the consciousness of God became divine essence in the world, and Christ became the intermediary of all revelation of God to mankind, in that he represents and carries in himself a new creation, a new state of the consciousness of God. A second Adam, he is the spiritual life which expands and propagates itself—a kind of spiritual thriving or bearing of fruit (*Befruchtung*). The advent of Adam and that of Christ are two correlative instances of the same eternal wisdom of God and occur in a series incomprehensible to us (Rom. 5: 12–29).

As a result of this, ecclesiastical formulas are to be reexamined according to the forsaid principles.

We cannot retain the dogma of the two natures, since it is not possible to speak of the nature of God. God is spirit and the word nature implies diversity and passivity. This concept could be used in the context of paganism, but not in that of the spirit in which one would not know how to compose a unity of different natures; to attempt it would lead to the destruction of the unity or of the natures.

Christ distinguishes himself from us by the strength of his religious consciousness and his absolute sanctity. "The Word has been made Flesh." "God was, in Christ, reconciling the world with Himself." It is in this way that God became man.

But, in this union of the divine and the human in Christ, only the divine was active, carrying human nature along in its activity. On the other hand, the consciousness of God in Christ had to bend to human nature which also had its role to play in the work of Christ. How did Schleiermacher express this connection?

For him, the activity of God is eternal, and as in him determination and activity are identical, the result is that in the scheme of eternity, everything in God appeared at the same time. But for us who live in time, the determinations of God are successive, and show themselves to us in the creation of man or in the birth and work of Jesus Christ. From this point of view, we can say that the person of Christ has always been in the process of becoming and involved in the creation of the world (*Christus sei auch als menschliche Person, schon immer mit der Welt zugleich werdend gewesen.* [Gl. II p. 68, édit. de 1830]).

What is more, the human person in Christ was not impersonal, which would have been an imperfection, because this nature is a unity suitable to form a person, and has its own existence in the changing stream of human nature. The formation of the individual is an act which appears as the accomplishment of this nature communicating to him an active strength. Thus, the seed of the consciousness of God is found in all men; otherwise, how could it have developed? This seed also existed in the man Jesus, but a supernatural intervention made him Christ the Savior, which imperfectly expresses the dogma of the miraculous birth.

But if the human nature cannot be disregarded—let us repeat again—it was the divine element, which was the active agent in Jesus—the element which was also present in conditions considered as passive such as prayer or adoration. Everything in him has its origin in the divine essence, even acts which are perfectly human. Sanctity and absolute perfection are the two attributes which express his manner of being and the relations within him of the divine and the human. In him, the possibility of conquering sin, which is so weak in men, remains constant, since his consciousness of God perfectly dominated the impulses of the flesh at all stages of his development.

That is why, in spite of the temptations he suffered, he never sinned.

For Schleiermacher, the work accomplished by Christ is in strict relation with the stated principles; it is both redeeming and reconciliating.

The former is brought about by the sanctity and the perfection of Christ. It consists in liberating our consciousness of God which is hindered by the flesh. In believing in Christ, we attain his holiness, or in other words, the mastery of the consciousness of God in ourselves. The activity of God, which is both creative and preserving, is the same as that of Christ which recreated our personality. Thus, the renewed consciousness of God becomes a new principle of life which regenerates all the manifestations of human nature.

On the other hand, the activity of Christ is reconciliating in that it reestablishes the normal connection with God, in this way bringing about happiness (*Seligkeit*) which is nothing but communicated perfection. The interior and exterior obstacles remain, but as stimulants; the consciousness of sin still exists as part of human nature; but the personal, egotistical life dies, man is made anew, because Christ is at the center of his life.

It is thus that Jesus Christ accomplished his work—prophetic, priestly and kingly—all at the same time. By his life and his death, he communicates to man the new strength which allows victory over the powers of destruction. This is a point of view of solidarity which we often see reappearing around the nineteenth century.

What must we think of this doctrine which has had a profound influence on a great number of theologians and thinkers until our time? It has been judged in very diverse ways, some considering it as a mutilation of biblical testimony, others proclaiming it as a magnificent interpretation of the evangelical message.

Let us try to judge clearly, and to do so let us ask if the way in which Schleiermacher presents the advent of the Redeemer and his work corresponds to the principles which are the foundation of his dogmatics.

We are told that this advent was a miracle, the manifestation of the personal and redeeming will of God. But is the word miracle used properly here? In a conception of the world where everything is ruled by the eternal laws of the cosmos, the so-called miraculous act can only be a manifestation of the laws, which amounts to saying that it is not a miracle. As a result of this, the advent of Jesus can only conform to the natural scheme of things. And yet it seems that in spite of the sometimes obscure expressions of his thoughts, Schleiermacher opened the way to a much more religious conception of the miracle, considered not as a disparagement of the natural laws of the universe, but as an event where the power and love of God shines forth to the soul of the believer.

But there is more. If we refer to thesis 96 and the following ones in his *The Christian Faith,* we learn that in Jesus Christ divine essence and human nature are united in one and the same person, and that in this union, the divine alone was active, the human remaining passive and receptive. In other words, that which distinguishes Christ from other men is the predominance of his consciousness of God, by which he became the prototype of a perfect human nature.

These assertions recall those of the Council of Chalcedon which were taken up again by the reformers and the basis of the orthodox doctrine. Has Schleiermacher only given another form to this doctrine or did he want something else?

Apparently, the identification is perfect, and Schleiermacher would not have permitted to place the sincerity of his intentions in doubt. But here again the principles at the base of his religious philosophy have brought about a very strong deviation in the manner of justifying the experiences of piety.

Let us now deal with the nearest one.

Christ is the Redeemer. In him, the consciousness of God has always been the inspiration for his acts, in other words, the obstacle which, in other men, obstructed the expansion of the perception of God (the feeling of absolute dependence) did not exist in Him. The opposition of the lower consciousness to the consciousness of God has, in fact, been suppressed by the mastery of the latter.

But is the perception of God, in Christ, manifested in all spheres of life? It is difficult to say. This is why Schleiermacher teaches that the character of the model only corresponds to the religious sphere alone. Jesus did not play a role in the political, scientific or esthetic spheres, but only in the one connecting man with God.

How are we to understand this? Jesus developed like other men and grew up in the same circumstances, but without any struggle or any conflict between good and evil. But Schleiermacher says also that the possibility of sinning is in every man, that it always accompanies good because, by virtue of its early development, the lower consciousness in all men gets a start which in some way remains the necessary condition for the development of the consciousness of God. He tells us also that the consciousness of God never appears in the pure state, but that it is always linked to the determinations of the lower consciousness.

Thus, if Jesus fully lived an authentic life of man, his consciousness of God could only have expanded in the framework common to other men, and would have found itself in close quarters with the obstacles and limitations which the perceptible world places in the development of the life of the Spirit; he would also have had to suffer the obstacles which were encountered in his life. Is it not this which lets us understand the well-known passage from the Epistle to the Hebrews 5,8: "He learned obedience by the things which he suffered."

It sounds good to say that the Redeemer was always led by the consciousness of God and protected by it from the weaknesses which assail other men. But we cannot see how these assertions can be brought into the framework of the system, nor how they can be reconciled with others which are completely opposed.

Let us not forget that the thinking of Schleiermacher is "Monist": God is involved in the world, the Spirit in the material and the spiritual perception only develops in its union with the lower consciousness. Absolutely no real being can escape this general law, and if Christ truly lived the life of man, he must have bent to the circumstances of history. As in all men, his lower consciousness appeared first, which leads us to say that he knew sin, without which he would not have known grace.

If we maintain the assertions of our thinker for whom Christ has always been in possession of the fullness of his consciousness of God, the historical life of Christ is only an appearance, and we fall into "docetism."

In order to make his formulation of thought more acceptable, Schleiermacher distinguishes between the historical advent and the intimate nature of the Redeemer, only the first being affected by the circumstances of life on earth, the second remaining unchanged. In other words, Schleiermacher distinguishes between the ideal Christ, the Christ of faith, and the Christ of history.

This distinction which was familiar to German idealism is difficult to accept for those who take historical facts seriously. The evangelical accounts show us a Christ in whom the divine nature is demonstrated in all his actions and in all his words, which explains the astonishment and the admiration of the witnesses of his life. It seems sometimes that for Schleiermacher the intimate nature of the individual is not shown in his actions, as if it exceeded the frameworks of his life. In this case, the profound nature of Jesus would go beyond history, an ideal produced by the imagination. But if the believer must be elevated to the perfect stature of Christ, how will he attain this?

We know that for Schleiermacher the consciousness of God is hindered in all men by the lower consciousness. But, by virtue of his original perfection, man succeeds in making his consciousness of God triumph, because the feeling of the divine pushes him to go beyond himself. The need for ascension is the profound law of the spiritual life. But, all things considered, the ideal Christ who was not affected by any of the circumstances of his time, is only the idealization of the highest and the best in mankind. The ideal Christ, conjured up by German idealism, is nothing but the exaltation of the most beautiful moral qualities of mankind.

Thus, if we examine the propositions of our theologian closely, it is very difficult to find once again the Christ of the Gospels in the marvelous description which he has drawn of the Redeemer.

But can we even say that such a Christ was necessary? For those reading *The Christian Faith,* there would be no doubt of it. It is because an individual is a member of the community that the individual has the experiences of a power which allows the superior consciousness to triumph over the consciousness of sin, power of perfection and holiness which is that of Christ. It is the action of Christ which gives way to the perception of God freeing it from the hindrances of the lower consciousness, and which elicits the blooming of the spiritual life.

However, if we consult the philosophical principles on which *The Christian Faith* rests, we will see that theses 59 to 61, on the original perfection of the world and that of man, teach that the world and man were created in such a way that perfection is implied in the creative act which gave them birth and which their development will demonstrate. The individual possesses within himself not only the idea of eternity but also that of perfection. The world was perfect from its origin, not that sin was absent from it, but in that its latent powers were to lead it to perfection by the simple forces which ruled it. It is by the evolution of powers hidden in the heart of man that the consciousness of God will end by assuring its domination over the impulses of the lower consciousness.

We now find ourselves in the presence of a profound dualism between the religious philosophy of Schleiermacher and his Christian experiences.

If the consciousness of God develops under the action of the inherent laws of his nature and if perfection is involved in the original nature of man, we cannot very well see which role we can attribute to Christ. It is here that one measures the distance which separates Schleiermacher from the reformers.

This leads us to two conclusions.

On the one hand, as we saw previously, redemption, as Schleiermacher expressed it, was involved in the work of creation, the consciousness of God being an inclination implanted in human nature and done in order to expand in various forms according to the times and the individuals. Here, the point of view of Scripture has been surpassed, although we can find expressions and ideas in Paul which are quite close to those of Schleiermacher. If, for the latter, redemption is the completion of creation which brings to the open, little by little, the forces hidden in it from its origin, for the apostle, the day of the Lord, the great day of redemption and reconciliation, will reveal that which has been hidden in the world from the beginning. For Schleiermacher, as for Paul, creation has, from the beginning, stretched out toward the realization of the Kingdom of God.

However, the manner of presenting things reveals an irreducible antithesis between our theologian and the authors of the New Testament for whom Christ is a supernatural manifestation of the redemptive will of God. In his essence he is unfamiliar to our nature. For the evangelists and the apostles, there is a radical dualism between sin and grace; grace did not manifest itself by a slow evolution, but it made itself apparent in the midst of a sinful world when the time was right.

On the other hand, as a result of all that has been said, the thought of Schleiermacher fluctuates between two contrasting conceptions which he sought to unite as closely as possible. Thus, in his speculative views, he intermingled his positive Christian convictions. Everywhere, he strived to assert them, and this is seen in pages where we know full well that the author is writing not with his head alone, but with his heart enlightened by his Christian experience. This must have impelled him, in spite of the errors that we have pointed out, to make a very great place for the person of Christ, or rather, the central place, in his doctrine and therefore to oppose rationalism.

He was led at first by a regard for history, because in contrast to the idealism of his time, he taught that the active forces in the life of mankind are facts and not ideas, persons and not theories. This is why religion does not allow itself to be taught like the sciences, but is communicated from person to person as a living reality. It was in the communion of Jesus Christ that his disciples experienced the power of his spirit and the reality of God.

Schleiermacher made these experiments from his childhood and he repeated them at all stages of his life.[2] The communion with Christ which the believer finds in the midst of the

[2] Cf. *Letters to St. Luke.*

Christian community expresses well the experience which he encountered in the Moravian church which he served most faithfully. Therefore, in his eyes, the person of Christ remains in the center of every specifically Christian conception. It is on this basis that Christology rests, not on the deductions of a philosophy inherited from romanticism. But Schleiermacher sacrificed too much to the spirit of the times by viewing redemption as a mere victory of the consciousness of God over the lower consciousness, which reduced it to a natural, psychological process which was able to fulfill itself, without anyone's help, since it is in the nature of things. That is why his disciples and his friends sought in different ways to establish a Christology more clearly established on a Scriptural basis, and more consistent with the notion of religious consciousness. . . .

3. C. Welch[1] suggests among the reasons for the revival of interest in Christology in Protestantism in the last century, Schleiermacher's call for Christocentrism, Hegel's claim to having recovered and exalted the truth of the Incarnation, and, paradoxically, Strauss' *Life of Jesus* which dramatically challenged the biblical foundations for the original picture of Christ. In his *General Introduction* to the works of Thomasius, Dorner, and Biedermann, Welch offers excellent insights on their distinctiveness and differences. The key problem for all alike was the metaphysical being of Christ with his humanity as a pivot of reconstruction. Reflections on Christ's humanity involve concentration on his unique consciousness.

According to a common schema of classification, Thomasius, Dorner and Biedermann respectively belong to the three major types of German theology in their time—"neo-Lutheranism," "mediating theology," and "speculative theology." . . .

. . . The three authors have much to recommend them as "representative" thinkers in addition to being central individuals in three varying tendencies of the thought of that period. Both Thomasius and Dorner have affinities with the revival theology in their appeal to the claim of religious experience and their participation in the broad trend toward reappropriating "ecclesiastical" or orthodox doctrine;

[1] Claude Welch was born in Genoa City, Wisconsin, in 1922. He is a well-known Protestant scholar who has taught at Princeton and at the Yale Divinity School and Graduate School. He is presently Berg Professor of Religious Thought and Chairman of the Department of Religious Thought at the University of Pennsylvania. He has authored and co-authored many theological works; such as, *The Reality of the Church, In This Name: The Doctrine of the Trinity in Contemporary Theology, Protestant Christianity Interpreted Through Its Development,* "Theology," in *Religion* (edited by Paul Ramsey). It is from *God and Incarnation in Mid-Nineteenth Century German Theology: Thomasius, Dorner and Biedermann,* edited by him (Library of Protestant Thought, Oxford University Press, 1965) that this exerpt is taken, *General Introduction,* pp. 4–12. Although Dr. Welch's *Introduction* is not intended to be either an historical account of a full evaluation of the Christologies of the authors concerned, but rather a commentary to be read along with the translations of their original works, nevertheless his excellent insights and remarks are most illustrative.

and the Erlangen theology with which Thomasius was associated embodies the confessionalist mood in a mild and flexible form. . . .

The Christological problem is a natural common focus . . . not only because of the central place it holds in the work of Thomasius, Dorner and Biedermann, or of the distinctiveness of what each has to say concerning it, or of the fact that they are in vigorous debate with one another and that we thus have in their writings a vivid cross-section of theological exploration, but also because the question of Christ has a peculiar pre-eminence in the Protestant thought of the mid-nineteenth century. On the whole, in the questions of the meaning of religion, and of the nature of religious knowledge (or revelation and faith), the theology of the period tends to build on the foundations laid in the first part of the century, notably by Schleiermacher, Hegel and Coleridge. In a striking way, however, the Christological question both claims attention and takes on new dimensions during the middle period. Doubtless this is due partly to Schleiermacher's call for a Christocentric principle, *i.e.* for everything in theology to be directly related to the redemption accomplished in Jesus of Nazareth, and due also to Hegel's claim to have recovered and exalted the truth of the concept of the incarnation. Certainly this development is evoked in another way by the dramatic thrust given by Strauss's *Life of Jesus* against the entire traditional picture of Christ. In any event, preoccupation with Christology is evident in various ways. Not only is there the sudden flourishing of kenotic theories and the spirited controversy that ensued in German theology. The question of Christ also lies at the heart of the work of the most seminal theological minds in Britain and America, F. D. Maurice and Horace Bushnell. In quite another vein, and at the same time, the Christ of orthodoxy was being rejected by the emerging unitarianism and transcendentalism (*cf.* Emerson's Divinity School address). And at the end of the period, Ritschl's demand for a Christology (and theology) without metaphysics, one exclusively of "value judgments" and not of theoretical judgments, as well as one grounded wholly in the historical career of Jesus, marks the turn to a distinguishably new theological scene.[2]

Within the spectrum of Christological concerns, the key problem for Dorner, Biedermann and Thomasius alike is "metaphysical"; it is the question of the being of God in the historical person Jesus Christ, or in the language of the classical doctrine, of the union of God and man in the God-man. Thus the matter is first of all that of the "person" rather than of the "work." Both Thomasius and Dorner insist, to be sure, on the inseparability and even the unity of person and work, so that the uniting of God and man in Christ is itself his redemptive activity. But when Ritschl, for example, would put it the other way around and say that the meaning of

---

[2] One would not contend that Christology as an item of doctrine was the problem for Kierkegaard in the way it was for these others, yet for him the paradox of the God-man and the absolute qualitative distinction it embodies is the essential counter to the "System's" confusion of time and eternity and thus its abolition of Christianity; and no less Christological is the problem of contemporaneity with Christ.

Christ is strictly contained in his purpose and act, then Dorner finds him guilty of leaving only an "accidental" significance for the person. The structure of Thomasius's whole *Dogmatik* emerges directly out of his further elaboration of the theory of incarnation. And for Biedermann, the doctrine of God-manhood is just where all the difficulties of the classical theology come to sharpest focus, and the decisive question is the relation of the Christian principle to the historical figure Jesus. Second, the problem is not conceived as centrally an historical one—either as the radical question whether and how the figure of Jesus can be laid hold of at all by historical research (though that question was already acutely raised by Strauss) or as the problem of a relation of faith to an individual in history, as posed by Kierkegaard. Nor is there a disposition here to abandon the problematic of divine and human "natures" in favor of a Christology of "event" or of divine and human "histories," though perhaps openings for some such turn can be found in both Biedermann and Dorner.

The question of the uniting of deity and humanity, however, has been shaped for these thinkers in a critically new (one may say "historical") way. Whether in relation to the new biblical criticism and the "quest for the historical Jesus," or to rationalism's earlier demand for the human figure instead of the attributes of divinity, or to romanticism's taste for individuality, or to other factors—the humanity of Jesus has become the pivot of reconstruction. The question could no longer be, as it had been for so long: Given the fullness of deity in Christ, how can the genuineness of the humanity be maintained? Now it is rather: Given the integrity of the human existence, how is it possible to speak of the presence of the divine? It is still a question of the mode of union of divine and human being (or, for Biedermann, of the truth of this idea in the concepts of absolute and finite spirit), but now with the complicating factor that the reality and completeness of the human existence are above all not to be prejudiced. Further, the view of humanity involves a concentration on the particular consciousness of Christ—thus more generally reflecting the notion of personality as centering in self-consciousness, and in turn the question of the relation of modern concepts of personality to the traditional language of *persona* and *substantia* in both Christological and trinitarian doctrine. On the other hand, the question of the person of Christ is also inseparable from a re-examination of the nature of the divine and its relation generally to the human; and Dorner and Biedermann in particular believed the nineteenth century to have opened valuable new perspectives at just this point.

The Christological reconstructions of Thomasius, Dorner and Biedermann thus take shape in response to a reconsideration of both the divine and the human poles, and they emerge as radically different answers. For Thomasius the answer is an actual "kenosis of the Logos," a "withdrawal to potence" by the second person of the Trinity in order that his incarnate life could be identical with a genuinely human existence.[3] For Dorner the solution must be found in a new ap-

[3] This also requires a trinitarian conception in which each of the "persons" is a center of self-consciousness. . . . Thomasius was neither the first exponent of the new kenoticism

preciation of the inner homogeneity or compatibility of divine and human and in a uniting of God and man that genuinely "becomes" in the humanly historical life of Christ. For Biedermann the truth emerges from a right relating of the "Christian principle" to the religious self-consciousness of Jesus through the materials provided by the concepts of absolute and finite spirit.

Hegel and Schleiermacher were the great figures under whose shadow the German theology of the whole nineteenth century developed, who laid the foundations and opened new possibilities for construction. But the problems, for the mid-nineteenth century, were given their more precise configuration by David Friedrich Strauss and Ludwig Feuerbach.[4] Strauss, at least in the first and fourth editions of his *Life of Jesus,* radically put in question the historical object of faith, Jesus Christ. Feuerbach put in question the metaphysical object. These two questions together—whether faith in the revelation of God can be attached to the historical individual (either because the Gospel portrait is essentially mythological, or because it is inappropriate for the absolute to manifest itself fully in a single individual), and whether the idea of God is not itself altogether a projection of the human consciousness—form "the deeply disturbing background of the theological history of all the succeeding decades."[5] Yet the matter can be stated thus only in principle. For in the mid-nineteenth century it was Strauss's questions far more than those of Feuerbach that were accepted as pertinent, and it was also Strauss who first split asunder the Hegelian identification of the content of religion and philosophy. Of our three theologians, only Biedermann took Feuerbach seriously, and in this the other two are typical of the period. Next to Schleiermacher and Hegel, it was peculiarly Strauss who became a point of departure for all three men—and to note the differing ways in which this occurred will offer further insight into their theological stances and their position in the nineteenth century as a whole.

For Thomasius, the immediate impetus was given not so much by the *Life of Jesus* as by the vigorous criticism of orthodox Christology in the *Glaubenslehre,* where the story of the "struggle with modern science [*Wissenschaft*]" included some harsh words concerning the "contradictions" in the Lutheran Christological development.[6] In Thomasius's first major publication

(that was probably Sartorius), nor the most extreme (that was Gess); but he was its most important defender, and in his articulation one sees not only the thrust of the movement but also, more clearly than anywhere else, the theory's presuppositions and possibilities. For rigor and vigor in working out the implications of the conception, Thomasius (and the German kenoticism in general) makes the later nineteenth-century British ventures into kenoticism look pallid indeed. It is all very well to praise the imprecision or vagueness of the British kenoticism as theological modesty and restraint before a mystery, but the presuppositions on which the kenotic theory can really emerge are precisely those that demand pursuit to the limit of the metaphysical and even the psychological questions.

[4] Strauss, *The Life of Jesus* (New York, 1860); and *Die christliche Glaubenslehre in ihrer geschichtlichen Entwicklung und in ihrem Kampf mit der modernen Wissenschaft* (Tübingen, 1840–41). Feuerbach, *Das Wesen des Christenthums,* 1841 (*The Essence of Christianity,* New York, 1957); and *Das Wesen der Religion,* 1851.

[5] Karl Barth, *Die protestantische Theologie im 19. Jahrhundert* (Zürich, 1947), 509.

[6] It was not, to be sure, Strauss alone but also Baur and Dorner to whom Thomasius sought to reply in the *Beiträge.* . . .

after assuming a theological professorship we see him replying as one for whom the vital demand is to reaffirm and re-establish the classical doctrine, but by a truer discernment of its intention and a positive renewal of its development.[7] Here he embodies the tenor of the "Erlangen theology" as a whole, with its desire to combine faithfulness to the Lutheran confessions with genuine scholarship and theological progress, and its fusion of Schleiermacher, revival theology and biblicism. The development of the new mood and direction was already under way when Thomasius arrived, and reflected a general renewal, with a confessional orientation, in the Lutheran church in Bavaria. But it was Thomasius, along with Hofmann,[8] who brought the Erlangen school to its characteristic expression, and Thomasius was for thirty years a center of its theology. His book on the Lutheran Church's confession "in consequence of its principle" (1848) was his formal effort to show how the teachings of that church's confessions in general, and the Formula of Concord in particular, grow from Luther's doctrine of justification by faith, as an "organic life-principle of the church. . . .

Applied specifically to the Christological reconstruction, this means that the kenotic theory is to be firmly attached to the Lutheran Christological developments of the sixteenth and seventeen centuries, as the continuation of their most basic inner drives but also as the completion and even the correction that removes the grounds for the old and new attacks. At the same time, in Thomasius's defense of the whole Christology, the Schleiermacherian insistence on religious consciousness as the source of doctrine emerges as a powerful reinforcement of the voice of tradition. Throughout the *Dogmatik,* "scriptural proof" and the witness of "eccleciastical consensus" follow the theological argument in which doctrine is developed out of the "deep inner grounds and life-roots," *i.e.* the living experience of communion with God.

Was it Strauss also who provided the occasion for I. A. Dorner's Christological studies? Here the situation is

---

[7] Born July 26, 1802, Thomasius became professor at Erlangen in 1842, after seventeen years as pastor near and in Nürnberg. During the latter part of that time he had also taught religion in the Gymnasium and published an influential outline for religious instruction, which was reprinted as late as 1901: *Grundlinien zum Religionsunterricht an den mittleren und oberen Klassen gelehrter Schulen* (Nürnberg, 1839). His university study (1821–25) had been carried on for a year and a half at Erlangen; for another year and a half at Halle, where he was generally repelled by the then dominant rationalism, though attracted by the conservative Knapp; and for one year at Berlin, where both Hegel and Schleiermacher were at the height of their influence, where he also heard Marheinke with appreciation, and where he developed what was to be a continuing close relationship with Tholuck. The whole of his teaching career was spent at Erlangen. He died January 24, 1875.

[8] Johann Christian Konrad von Hofmann (1810–77), who was at Erlangen in lesser posts from 1835 to 1842, and as professor from 1845. In his *Schriftbeweis* (3 v., Nördlingen, 1852; 2nd ed. 1857), which Thomasius often cites, he exhibits the characteristic interweaving of experiential and scriptural authority, and the conviction that it is especially in the Lutheran confessions that scriptural and experiential Christianity is to be recognized. Others in the school, whose influence extends into the twentieth century, included H. Schmid, K. A. G. von Zezschwitz, Theodosius Harnack and F. H. R. Frank.

different, for Dorner was a contemporary of Strauss at Tübingen, as both student and tutor, and the first portion of what was to be his masterpiece, the *History of the Development of the Doctrine of the Person of Christ,* appeared in the Tübingen quarterly in the same year that Strauss issued the second volume of the *Life of Jesus* (1836).[9] Yet through the completion of the history and its revision and expansion (1846–56), Dorner's argument developed with a keen view to the contentions both of Strauss and of Baur's history of the Trinity and the incarnation.[10] Like Thomasius, Dorner seeks to validate the intent of classical Christology against any finally negative judgment such as that of Strauss, but at the same time in a "critical" way that shared many of the objections of Strauss and Baur. The Christological development is not to be seen as the working out of a more or less unilinear tendency, but as a dialectic of factors in imbalance and disproportion, out of which the adequate formulation is yet to be wrought. Obviously Hegel stands in the background of this view of history, and the influence of his dialectic is also present in Dorner's systematic structures. . . .

More basic for Dorner than Hegel, however, is Schleiermacher. It is not too much to say that Schleiermacher's ideal of the "prince of the church" (or philosopher-priest), the Christian who combines the highest and most universal attainment in scholarship with the fullest responsible leadership in the church, was also Dorner's. The "religious" and the "*wissenschaftlich*" interests are twin authorities of legitimate theological development. . . .

Of our three theologians, Biedermann most directly begins his work from the problems posed by Strauss, and he is also the most self-conscious and explicit in relating his efforts to Schleiermacher, Hegel and Kant. Somewhat younger than either Thomasius or Dorner, he was just completing his university studies at the time of the publication of Strauss's *Glaubenslehre* and Feuerbach's *Essence of Christianity,* and he had already been deeply struck by the former's putting of the historical question in the *Life of Jesus.*[11] In his first major publication, on the struggle be-

---

[9] Born June 20, 1809, Dorner took his entire university training at Tübingen (1827–32), which for the students in the *Stift* had a rigorously prescribed four-year theological course. Baur, who was at that time coming under the influence of Hegel, was one of his teachers. After assisting his father in a parish for two years, Dorner became a tutor (*Repetent*) at Tübingen (1834) and then associate (*ausserordentlicher*) professor in 1838. Beginning with a call to Kiel (1839), he made an exceptionally wide tour of teaching posts, going to Königsberg (1843), Bonn (1847), and Göttingen (1853) before finally being appointed at Berlin (1862) as both professor and member of the superior church council. The former post he resigned in 1883, the latter in 1884, because of ill health. He died July 8, 1884.

[10] F. C. Baur, *Die christliche Lehre von der Dreieinigkeit und Menschwerdung Gottes in ihrer geschichtlichen Entwicklung* 3 v., (Tübingen, 1841–43).

[11] Born March 2, 1819, Biedermann studied first at Basel (1837–39) and then at Berlin (1839–41), especially with the "speculative theologians" Wilhelm Vatke and Philipp Marheineke (the latter was the greatest of the early Hegelian theologians). He was at first negative toward Schleiermacher, but after experiencing the impact of Strauss's book he moved on at Berlin to immerse himself in the study of Hegel and Schleiermacher together. Returning to Basel, he took a parish in 1843 (so that he could marry), and also helped found and edit a journal called *The Church of the Present* (1845–50). In

tween philosophy and theology, we see him absorbed in the language and the problematic of the "younger Hegelians." It was even possible for him to be attacked as Feuerbachian. Biedermann says in his theological recollections, however, that he had never been much impressed by Feuerbach, because of the latter's naturalism and sheer sensationalist epistemology, to which Biedermann was from the first diametrically opposed.[12] It was Strauss who most acutely exposed the theoretical need into which the church had fallen, and who served as the bridge to Hegel for Biedermann (typically, just because of the bitterness and hostility toward Strauss in nearly all ecclesiastical circles, Biedermann was particularly open in expressing gratitude to him). With respect to Christology, as Biedermann saw it, Strauss was and is correct on the side of the negative critique: the Christian principle cannot be identified with the historical individual Jesus. But Strauss never fulfilled the promise of speculative construction, and he never overcame the characteristic tendency of modern speculative philosophy to make Jesus merely accidental to the Christian principle—and Biedermann was quite unwilling to settle either for a mere idea casually related to Christ or for a substitution (as in Strauss) of the race for the individual.

Behind and beyond Strauss it was Hegel to whom, as Biedermann put it, he owed a great part of the nourishment of his philosophical thinking, and whose language permeates his *Dogmatik* . . .

In the specifically Christological construction also, one finds Biedermann attempting to overcome the weaknesses of both Hegel and Schleiermacher. From the former is indeed to be drawn the conception of absolute and finite spirit, through which the old stumbling block of viewing divinity and humanity as two antithetical sorts of spiritual essences is overcome, and from him also comes the conception of the "self-actualization" of the Christian principle; from Schleiermacher there is the concentration on the religious self-consciousness of Jesus as the locus of that self-actualization, and the insistence on the person of Christ as the source of the efficacy of the principle in history. But neither Hegel nor Schleiermacher is able finally to escape critical ambiguities at the point of the relation between principle and person. Thus for the question of the historical object of faith, as well as for the question of the metaphysical object, a more inclusive, deeper and more fruitful view must be attained.

The systems of Biedermann and Dorner appeared chronologically at the end of their period. By the 1880's it was already clear that neither they nor Thomasius represented the theological wave of the future. To be sure, kenotic Christology was to enjoy a (largely

---

1850, in spite of opposition from the conservative church party, he was appointed *ausserordentlichen* at Zürich, and was full professor in dogmatics, from 1860 until his death on January 25, 1885.

[12] *Ausgewählte Vorträge und Aufsätze,* "Erinnerungen." Biedermann had been attacked, e.g., for referring to the religious object as man's "universal essence," but he explains that he meant something quite different from Feuerbach's infinitized consciousness, *viz.* the essential and creative ground, which is represented in Christian terms as God the Creator and Father. It was this attack which brought forth his *Unsere junghegelsche Weltanschauung oder der sogenannte neueste Pantheismus* (1849).

independent) popularity in Britain around the turn of the century; the influence of idealism continued to be powerful outside of Germany; Dorner's theological temper was embodied in various strands of liberalism; and continuities of many sorts could be identified. Yet Dorner was correct when, in letters to Martensen at the time of the publication of his *System,* he predicted that his work as a whole would not be acclaimed by the rising theological generation.[13] It was not so much the strict Lutheran confessionalists or the biblicists—whom he noted as sure to be dissatisfied with what he had done, in spite of his own sense of nearness to the Lutheran spirit and his intention to be truly biblical—but quite another sort of theological mood, which he recognized, that stood against his effort, and also against those of Biedermann and Thomasius. Albrecht Ritschl was the new representative man, the one who tried to accomplish what the new theology most deeply wanted accomplished, *viz.* a cutting loose from the spirit of "speculation," and even from the metaphysical in theology, and a turning to the "practical" as a new foundation and form for theology.[14] All the mid-nineteenth century's powerful systems for uniting the dogmatic and the philosophical were to be left behind. Thus also the Christological question as an "objective" or "metaphysical" matter was to be given up in favor of other modes of posing the question of Christ, restricted to "historical" or "value" or "existential" judgments. Whether in this, or in the larger turn away from the "objective," the new theology was an advance or a retreat, whether it more fruitfully met or merely evaded the questions put to theology in the nineteenth century, is another kind of question, which is not to be discussed here.

4. J. Peter[1] criticizes three views of Christ prevalent at the turn of the century: the view that He did not exist, the view of incompatibility between the "Jesus of history" and the "Jesus of faith," and the view of consistent eschatology. The first is totally unsound. The second has rendered some valuable contribution, but a reexamination of its grounds has resulted in a general rejection. Schweitzer's picture of Jesus as a self-deceived visionary influenced some, but has failed in the long course.

No one will question the statement that the figure of Jesus dominates the New Testament. It is true that only four of the twenty-seven books give anything approaching an orderly account of his life; but the material in these four amounts to all but a half of the total, and the other books are

---

[13] Letters of July 3, 1878, and May 11, 1879; *Briefwechsel,* II, 352 f., 390.

[14] On this point *cf.* esp. Ritschl, *Theologie und Metaphysik* (1881); also W. Herrmann, *Die Metaphysik in der Theologie* (1876) and *Die Religion im Verhältnis zum Welterkennen und zur Sittlichkeit* (1879).

[1] The Rev. James F. Peter is the Federal Supervisor of Religious Broadcasts for the Australian Broadcasting Commission. He is a member of the Executive Board of the Australian Council of Churches, and was formerly Professor of Theology and Caldwell-Morrow Lecturer in Church History at the University of Queensland. It is from his book *Finding the Historical Jesus* (New York: Harper and Row, 1965) that this excerpt is taken, selectively, from pp. 23–49.

just as plainly concerned to give their readers information about Jesus or his significance. Nor will any one question the further statement that those who wrote in the New Testament supposed that they were writing about a historical figure. . . .

We shall review (three) of the positions which have been taken up during the last hundred years. We shall at the same time be noticing the significant literature and disclosing factors for which any who attempt to understand the historical Jesus must show regard. . . .

The View that Jesus did not Exist. Our consideration of attitudes towards the historical soundness of the New Testament picture will obey the dictates of logic, if not those of contemporary interest, and begin with the view that Jesus did not exist at all.[2]

During the last century many have put forward this view, including some scholars of considerable renown. Today it is practically a lost debate, although present-day advocates of this view are not unknown.[3]

To deny the existence of Jesus involves discounting a considerable amount of evidence which suggests that he did exist, and it may be sufficient treatment of the view here to remind ourselves of what that evidence is.[4]

There are the Gospels themselves . . . There are the other books of the New Testament. . . . There is the existence of a body of early Christian literature . . . some of which was

[2] The use of the term "Christ-myth" in this connection is to be distinguished from its use by a few recent writers (chief among them Fritz Buri) who, though regarding historical knowledge about Jesus as irrelevant, do not deny his existence.

[3] The following constitute the most influential presentations of this view. Bruno Bauer, *Christus und die Cäsaren. Der Ursprung des Christentums aus dem romischen Griechentum* (Berlin, 1877). Bauer's earlier position was that the actual existence of Jesus is problematical, and only of significance as awakening into life the Messianic idea; the transition may be seen in his *Kritik der evangelischen Geschichte der Synoptiker* (Leipzig, 1841–2) and *Kritik der Evangelien und Geschichte ihres Ursprungs* (Berlin, 1850–1851). Albert Kalthoff, *Das Christusproblem. Grundlinien zu einer Sozialtheologie* (Leipzig, 1902); *Die Entstehung des Christentums. Neue Beitrage zum Christusproblem* (Leipzig, 1904); E. T. *The Rise of Christianity* (London, 1907). As with Bauer, this is a later development; cf. *Das Leben Jesu* (Berlin, 1880), which presents a view similar to that of contemporary liberals. Arthur Drews, *The Christ Myth; Witnesses to the Historicity of Jesus.* J. M. Robertson, *Pagan Christs; Christianity and Mythology.* William Benjamin Smith, *Der Vorchristliche Jesus* (1906), only portions of which have been included in the E. T., *The Pre-Christian Jesus.* Prosper Alfaric, *Pour comprendre la vie de Jésus* (1929). P.-L. Couchoud, *Jésus . . .* (1924). Some present-day Russian writers (whose scholarly integrity may be doubted) have taken up the cudgels on behalf of this view. The recent editing by Addison Gulick of a MS of W. B. Smith, *The Birth of the Gospel; A Study of the Origin and Purport of the Primitive Allegory of the Jesus* (New York: Philosophical Library Inc., 1957), and the presentation by Gulick of a copy to the Library of the University of Queensland show that some people still have an interest in the propagation of this view.

[4] Notable among treatments of the evidence are: Johannes Weiss, *Jesus: Mythos oder Geschichte* (Tübingen: J. C. B. Mohr, 1910); F. C. Conybeare, *The Historical Christ* (London: Watts & Co., 1914); Joseph Klausner, *Jesus of Nazareth* (London: George Allen & Unwin Ltd., 1925); Maurice Goguel, *La Vie de Jésus* (Paris: Payot, 1932); E. T., *Life of Jesus* (London: George Allen & Unwin Ltd., 1933); Ch. Guignebert, *Jésus* (Paris, 1933); E. T., *Jesus* (1935); Roderic Dunkerlery, *Beyond the Gospels* (Harmondsworth: Penguin Books Ltd., 1957).

written before some of the New Testament . . . as well as . . . the recently discovered documents from Nag-Hammadi . . . all this literature, so varied in content, style and intention . . . must be recognized as evidence of a widespread conviction that such a man existed.

There is non-Christian evidence in the form of passing references made to him in the writings of contemporary historians: Josephus and Tacitus[5] Suetonius[6] . . . and the early second century correspondence between Pliny the Younger and the Emperor Trajan,[7] are evidence for the existence of the Christian movement, and to that extent bear upon the question whether Jesus himself actually existed.

There are references to Jesus in the Talmud. Günther Bornkamm considers that it "betrays no independent knowledge whatever and is nothing but a polemical and tendentious misrepresentation of the Christian tradition."[8] Ethelbert Stauffer thinks differently, and uses the Talmud quite extensively (along with other non-biblical evidence) in his chronological account of the life of Jesus.[9] The truth lies between these two, and in the attitude of Joseph Klausner who remarks that though the references are "very few" and "of little historical value, since they partake rather of the nature of vituperation and polemic against the founder of a hated party than of objective accounts," they are evidence that this founder of a hated party did actually exist.[10]

Others may advance additional lines of evidence; Dunkerley, for example, wants to attach some value to what is said about Jesus in Moslem tradition, but the evidence to be advanced along the five lines already mentioned is such that even what Conybeare called "a mere preposterous superfetation of a disordered imagination"[11] cannot shift.

Before leaving consideration of this view we shall note—not only because of their interest but also because of their bearing upon any judgment that we ourselves may make concerning the New Testament picture of Jesus—three opinions which are held concerning its origin.

According to Conybeare the blame for the emergence of such a view must be laid at the door of orthodoxy which, he says,

> by refusing to apply in the field of so-called sacred history the canons by which in other fields truth is discerned from falsehood, by beatifying credulous ignorance and anathematizing scholarship and common sense, has surrounded the figure of Jesus with such a nimbus of improbability that

---

[5] xviii, iii, 3; xx, ix, 1. See Dunkerley, *op. cit.*, pp. 35–47. Cf. Conybeare, *op. cit.*, p. 156, and Klausner, *op. cit.*, p. 556, on the suspected additions. The references to Jesus in Josephus' *Jewish War* occur only in the Slavonic version. For Tacitus, *Annales* XV, 44.

[6] *The Twelve Caesars,* xxv, dealing with Claudius, who reigned from 41 to 54.

[7] *Plinii et Trajani Epistulae,* xcvi, xcvii.

[8] G. Bornkamm, *Jesus of Nazareth,* trans. I. and F. McLuskey with J. M. Robinson (New York: Harper & Row, 1960), p. 28.

[9] E. Stauffer, *Jesus and His Story,* trans. Dorothea M. Barton (London: S.C.M. Press Ltd., 1960), *passim.*

[10] Klausner, *op. cit.*, pp. 18–19. He points out on p. 46 that the first generation of the Tannaim do not seem to have shown the same bitterness as was later displayed.

[11] Conybeare, *op. cit.*, pp. 195–6.

it seems not absurd to some critics of today to deny that he ever lived.[12]

The laity, he says in another place, "are so justly suspicious of the evasions and *arrière-pensées* of orthodox apologists that they are ready to accept any wild and unscholarly theory that labels itself Rationalist. . . .

In Sydney Cave's opinion, the blame must be laid at the door of those (especially in the latter half of the nineteenth century) who were unwilling to accept anything in the Gospels which gave Jesus more than human greatness . . .[13]

We may sum up the situation by saying that three factors played their part in the production of this extraordinary view: an inadequate consideration of the data by those who held the view, a conservatism which would allow critical thought no place at all, and a criticism which, suspicious of all conservative presuppositions, remained blind to its own. They must be guarded against continually in every attempt to find the historical Jesus.

The View of Liberalism. At the dawn of this century there was published in Germany a series of lectures which were "both a symptom and a source of influence: a symptom of the direction in which liberal Protestantism had been and was still travelling, and the source of an influence which was widely exerted upon liberal theology during the first two decades of the twentieth century."[14]

These were the lectures of Adolf von Harnack on "The Essence of Christianity,"[15] and they are regarded by many as the classical exposition of the view we are now to consider.

As far as the picture of Jesus is concerned, the liberal view may be characterized broadly as the "Jesus of history" movement—not that it alone of the estimates of the person of Jesus takes note of the fact that he lived in history, nor that all those classed as belonging to the movement agree in what they say about Jesus; the phrase is used generally to designate those who consider that there is incompatibility between "the Jesus of history" and "the Christ of the creeds," and that it is the former to whom we must go.[16]

The liberal position in regard to the New Testament picture regards Jesus as one who, himself enjoying a more than ordinary experience of God through trusting completely in him, taught others to do the same, and gathered about himself a band of disciples. After the hostility of the religious leaders of his people had resulted in his being crucified, his disciples, convinced that the influence of so sublime a life could not be ended there, felt him to be still alive and continued in the fellowship which they had known during his life-time. Before

[12] Conybeare, *op. cit.*, p. 1, see also pp. 128, 168.

[13] Sydney Cave, *What Shall We Say of Christ?* (London: Hodder & Stoughton Ltd., 1932), p. 23. This opinion had earlier been expressed by Albert Schweitzer, *The Quest of the Historical Jesus* (third English edition, London: A. and C. Black Ltd., 1954), pp. 305, 318.

[14] G. V. Jones, "Harnack's *Das Wesen des Christentums,*" *The Expository Times,* vol. LXVI (1954–55), p. 100.

[15] Adolf von Harnack's *Das Wesen des Christentums,* (Leipzig: 1900). An E. T. published a year later had the title *What is Christianity?*

[16] Not all who make such a distinction belong to this school. Some note an incompatibility, but claim that it is the latter to whom we must turn.

long there grew up within this fellowship beliefs concerning him which were without historical basis. His deeds of service for others became miracles of healing, the experience of his continuing influence became the story that he had left his grave on the third day, and the recognition of the unusually close fellowship with God which he had enjoyed became the conviction that he was in fact a divine being, while the extension of the fellowship to include Gentiles meant that these brought with them ideas of divinity with which they quickly proceeded to overlay the Master of beloved memory. When the time came for some of the fellowship to write accounts of his life and of the early Church, all these tendencies, which by now had so played their part that some of those who wrote had never known a Gospel free of them, were reflected in the accounts they gave of the historical events. And the tendencies thus enshrined in the New Testament were carried to further extremes by the Fathers, whose creeds represent degrees of metaphysical speculation undreamed of by Jesus and his first followers.

Among those who have felt that the Jesus of history can and should be separated from the Christ of faith, there have been many different shades of opinion. Some consider that the chief perverter of the simple Galilean Gospel was the apostle Paul, others that later creeds, ostensibly based on his statements, misrepresent him; some hold that the New Testament picture of Jesus, though unhistorical, is to be recognized as an honest, and to some extent successful attempt to express his greatness, others that this picture displays a manner of distortion deplorable and culpable; some insist that the early Church's formulae need filling with new content, others that there can be no advance toward the truth until all the old forms of expression are scrapped completely. But the underlying thesis of liberal thinkers is recognizably the same; their point of view has had and continues to have a wide influence, and many of them have made to the life of the Church at large, as well as to Christian scholarship, contributions of outstanding value.

Those who contended for such a view were able to cite a number of supporting factors.

a) Christian thinking generally has always been anxious to assert that Jesus was fully human. "Consubstantial with us concerning the manhood," says the Chalcedonian Symbol: a man as we are men. Therefore, it was considered on this view, he was limited as we are limited: to think otherwise is to deny that Jesus was truly a man. This concern for the Savior's real humanity led on to the conviction that errors must have crept into those passages in the New Testament which suggest that Jesus possessed powers not possessed by us; hence nothing but good would follow the removal of such errors.

b) It is very often the case that adoration of a hero gives rise to exaggeration of his character and capabilities. Here, it was thought, is a very likely cause of what appear as distortions in the New Testament picture of Jesus. Remembering the power of his personality or aware of the way in which his influence was still to be felt, his followers could think of no title too great, no rank too exalted, for him, and such they proceeded to ascribe to him. Moreover, the first Christians had little interest in the personal life of Jesus; they regarded his return on the clouds as imminent, and were more concerned with waiting in eager hope for their final redemption.

c) The findings of biblical criticism were held to give added support to this way of thinking; indeed they are still regarded by some as the chief cause of it. It is conceded on all sides that, underlying the Gospels as we have them today, were earlier documents, or at least oral traditions, which the writers used each in his own way. Underlying those documents and traditions there were doubtless others again, and in the process of passing them on embellishment was inevitable. Of particular significance was the fact that the first three Gospels are synoptic in their presentation while it is the fourth Gospel, standing apart from the synoptic tradition and of later date, which records the most extravagant claims made for, or by, Jesus. . . .

d) The whole outlook of the age which saw the zenith of liberalism tended to favor the production of a Savior like him whom this movement unfolded. The idea of the innate goodness of men carried with it the idea that all men needed was an example of the highest and best and they would quickly follow it, while the accrediting to him of supernatural powers was an affront to an age characterized by a spirit of scientific enquiry and self-determination.

This, then, is the liberal view, and the grounds upon which it chiefly rested; and there can be no denying its wide influence, the Herculean labors of biblical criticism and theological enquiry which it inspired, and the admirable qualities of Christian character among its supporters. Nor can there be any denying that it gives rise to questions of historiographical procedure which no assessment of the New Testament picture of Jesus can afford to neglect.

Nonetheless, a re-examination of the grounds upon which this position rested has resulted in a general departure from it.

a) To say that Jesus was a man is not to say that he must fit precisely the mould which what we know of men causes us to construct . . . as George Tyrrell said of Harnack, the Christ that they see "looking back through nineteen centuries of Catholic darkness, is only the reflection of a liberal Protestant face seen at the bottom of a deep well."[17]

The knowledge that is to be gained concerning the unusual powers possessed by some men (even some Western civilized men, to say nothing of their greater incidence among Eastern and primitive peoples), in the way of exorcism, telepathy, psycho-kinesis and all that is called generally "extra-sensory perception," might have caused liberal theologians to be rather less confident in their assertions as to what a man, *qua* man, could or could not have done; while the case of Jesus in particular should have led them to wonder whether F. W. Robertson was not right when he remarked "exceptional manifestations of psychic and spiritual force . . . were only to be expected in a being of exceptional elevation and fullest capacity."[18]

b) It is questionable whether the worship which his first followers gave

[17] George Tyrrell, *Christianity at the Cross-roads,* p. 44; cited by D. M. Baillie, *God Was in Christ,* p. 40.

[18] This statement occurs in one of Robertson's sermons, the precise reference of which I have mislaid.

to Jesus would have led them to the sort of misrepresentation which the liberal theologians attributed to them. More than fifty years ago P. T. Forsyth pointed out:

> We could not speak of Jesus with any respect if his influence not only could not protect his first followers from idolatry in placing him where they did—beside God in their worship—but actually prompted that idolatry. . . .[19]

Nor can we accept unquestioningly the allegation that the New Testament writers had no real interest in the life which Jesus lived. . . . We may not regard them as such in every particular, but we are bound to notice that their motives included a desire to have certain things about Jesus put accurately. We are bound to notice also that a similar desire underlay the later refusal to admit certain "Gospels" to the canon.

c) While criticism of the New Testament has done much to disclose the nature of its writings and in particular to show how the Gospels are related to each other and to earlier documents (or traditions), it is not generally conceded now, as was once declared so confidently, that a chronological progression in dogma is discernible. Instead, it is considered that the Christ of the creeds is implicit in even the earliest of the New Testament writings, and that "the riddle of the New Testament" lies in the figure of Jesus himself. As Hoskyns and Davey say in their book with that title:

> Any historical reconstruction which leaves an unbridgeable gap between the faith of the primitive Church and the historical Jesus must be both inadequate and uncritical: inadequate, because it leaves the origin of the Church unexplained, and uncritical because a critical sifting of the evidence of the New Testament points towards the life and death of Jesus as the ground of primitive Christian faith, and points in no other direction.[20]

"There was," G. S. Duncan remarks, "a naive readiness among many critics to believe that only the earliest sources could be trusted as history."[21]

The possible consequences of such a line of argument were stated forcefully by Schweitzer, whose remarks concerning Schmiedel and von Soden can be applied to liberal thinkers generally . . .[22]

. . . It is this basing of the life of Jesus on an ideal picture which is not derived from the Gospels, but stands complete in advance, which has led Cullmann to speak of the liberal position as a continuing form of Docetism.[23]

---

[19] P. T. Forsyth, *The Person and Place of Jesus Christ* (London: Hodder & Stoughton Ltd., 1909), p. 207.

[20] E. Hoskyns and N. Davey, *The Riddle of the New Testament* (second edition; London: Faber & Faber Ltd., 1936), p. 170.

[21] G. S. Duncan, *Jesus, Son of Man.* (London: Nisbet & Co. Ltd., 1948), p. 15.

[22] Albert Schweitzer, *op. cit.*, p. 305. Cf. his statement concerning Kalthoff: "The Christ of Kalthoff is nothing else than the Jesus of those whom he combats in such lofty fashion: the only difference is that he draws his figure of Christ in red ink on blotting paper, and because it is red in color and smudgy in outline, wants to make out that it is something new" (*ibid.*, p. 318).

[23] Oscar Cullmann, *Christ and Time* (London: S.C.M. Press Ltd., 1951), p. 129.

d) There is a marked difference between the general outlook of the heyday of liberalism and that of our own day . . . liberalism has in the last score or so of years suffered a decline.

The View of Consistent Eschatology. The liberal position suffered a severe shock at the hands of Albert Schweitzer, who, Bornkamm says, "has erected its memorial, but at the same time delivered its funeral oration."[24]

Whether it is right to conclude, as some have done, that Schweitzer is alone responsible, or more responsible than others for loosening the stranglehold which liberalism had upon Christian scholarship is beyond our present interest. We shall concern ourselves with the view put forward by Schweitzer himself, and the way in which his presentation made possible a new approach to the question of the historical Jesus.

Schweitzer's view can be found in his *Sketch* of the life of Jesus, published in 1901.[25] But it finds more forceful expression in a book which appeared ten years later (and which he intended at first to be only a supplement to the earlier one).[26] This was *The Quest of the Historical Jesus.*[27]

Few writers, over the years since the publication of Schweitzer's *Quest,* have failed to be influenced by him and, though not many of his followers have accepted his contentions in their entirety, Schweitzer himself has not offered any substantial modification of his position. "The decision in favor of eschatology is hardly likely to be questioned again," he has written more recently, although, because of "the difficulties it raises for the traditional Christian faith," the eschatological solution has not succeeded in dominating the latest writing on the life of Jesus, and is not within sight of doing so.[28]

The first eighteen of the twenty chapters of Schweitzer's best-known book are taken up with a survey of eighteenth and nineteenth century attempts to portray the historical Jesus.[29] He considers that these attempts had made it clear, at the end of the nineteenth century, that (accepting the Marcan hypothesis of synoptic origins) the only possible alternatives are a thorough-going scepticism or a thor-

---

[24] Günther Bornkamm, *op. cit.,* p. 13. Schweitzer, no less than those he criticized, used the Gospels as sources for a chronological biography.

[25] *Das Messianitäts- und Leidensgeheimnis. Eine Skizze des Lebens Jesu* (Tübingen: J. C. B. Mohr, 1901). The E. T., *The Mystery of the Kingdom of God, The Secret Jesus' Messiahship and Passion,* was not published until 1925 (London: A. & C. Black).

[26] A. Schweitzer, *Out of My Life and Thought,* trans. C. T. Campion (New York: The New American Library of World Literature, Inc., 1953), p. 30.

[27] *Von Reimarus zu Wrede* (Tübingen: J. C. B. Mohr, 1906). The E. T., *The Quest of the Historical Jesus; A Critical Study of its Progress from Reimarus to Wrede,* was published in 1910 (London: A. & C. Black). A second, and revised German edition was published in 1913 under the title, *Geschichte der Leben-Jesu-Forschung,* but this has not been translated. The Third English Edition of 1954 differs from the edition of 1910 by the inclusion of an Introduction.

[28] Introduction to *The Quest of the Historical Jesus,* Third English edition, p. xiv.

[29] Hence the title of the book. H. S. Reimarus wrote in 1778 and W. Wrede in 1901. Schweitzer concerns himself almost exclusively with attempts which appeared in German.

ough-going eschatology:[30] either we must regard the picture of Jesus based on the Marcan narrative as the creation of the evangelist or we must accept it, with the eschatological utterances, as a true picture of Jesus.

Of the alternatives, Schweitzer accepts the second and regards Jesus as a visionary, the product of Jewish apocalypticism, convinced that he was the Messiah, and proclaiming from the outset the immediate advent of the kingdom of God. In this expectation he sent out the Twelve and, when their return showed that his expectation was disappointed, he concluded that his own death was necessary for the ushering in of the kingdom. Believing this, Jesus set out for Jerusalem intending to suffer death at the hands of the authorities, and (for so he now considered it to be the will of God) to have concentrated upon himself the sufferings which he had always considered to form part of the mystery of the kingdom of God. He died, believing that he was fulfilling the purposes of God, giving his life for the "many" predestined to share in the kingdom.

At no stage, Schweitzer considers, did Jesus voluntarily disclose the secret of his Messiahship: it was wrung but in a state of ecstasy in which he from him by the pressure of events. At the Transfiguration the three disciples did not learn it from his lips, shared; and Peter's declaration of his Messiahship in the presence of the other disciples at Caesarea Philippi (which in Schweitzer's view took place *after* the Transfiguration) was a betrayal of the confidence given him on the earlier occasion. The triumphal entry into Jerusalem was not an occasion when Jesus was recognized generally as the Messiah; he entered as the prophet Elijah (for to assume a general recognition of the Messiahship at this point makes unintelligible the subsequent happenings of Passion Week). It was precisely the communication of his Messiahship which constituted Judas' betrayal; and it was the priests' going among the crowd telling of this which changed the crowd so quickly from their view of him as a prophet worthy of honor to that of him as a blasphemer deserving of death.

This, according to Schweitzer, is the historical Jesus, "to our time a stranger and an enigma," but one who "means something to our world because a mighty spiritual force streams forth from him and flows through our time also."[31]

There is no doubt that Schweitzer's protest against the attitude that was common among scholars, and against the ideology which underlay it, was as timely as it was telling. But neither its timeliness nor the fascinating manner of his presentation of it should blind us to the defects in Schweitzer's position.

Much in the Gospels shows that Jesus was far from being concerned exclusively with the coming kingdom and that, on the contrary, he saw life in this present world as a good gift of God, to be enjoyed by his children with thankfulness. . . .

Nor is Jesus altogether "to our time

---

[30] German, *konsequente Eschatologie.* It is this which (in order to avoid confusion with other views taking account of the eschatological emphasis in the New Testament) has caused this position to be called that of "thoroughgoing" or "consistent" eschatology.

[31] *The Quest of the Historical Jesus,* p. 397.

a stranger and an enigma." Efforts to make him "by a popular historical treatment" into a figure "sympathetic and universally intelligible to the multitude"[32] must face the criticisms which Schweitzer advances; but the fact remains that there is much which makes a strong appeal to every age, and shows his teaching to be not, as Schweitzer contended, only an *Interimsethik* but a teaching relevant to the life we know now. . . .

In the third place, Schweitzer's presentation is unsatisfactory because of the limitations of his exegesis, which practically begins and ends with Matthew, and in Matthew with the sayings in 10:23 and 11:12. Thus he concentrates attention upon those aspects of Jesus' life and teaching which appear to have been a source of puzzlement to the very people who were sufficiently drawn to him to seek to preserve a record of what he said and did.

There is on Schweitzer's part an assumption that Jesus accepted without question or amendment the ideas of an apocalyptic Messiah which prevailed in Judaism. The essential weakness of Schweitzer's method, says Richard R. Niebuhr, is that

> he rests his whole explanation upon a reference to the spirit or mentality of the age. He allows no originality or creativity to individuals and groups within a given generation . . .[33]

Nowhere is the limited nature of Schweitzer's exegesis more apparent than in his neglect of the place given in the New Testament to the Resurrection.

> They (Schweitzer and his disciple Werner) regard as the mid-point of the process the future coming of the Messianic age, whereas the mid-point of time in the entire New Testament and *already for Jesus* is rather the historical work of Jesus himself . . . It is simply not true that Primitive Christianity has the same eschatological orientation as does Judaism . . . The primary thing is not the eschatological expectation, but this conviction concerning the resurrection . . . [34]

A further defect of this view is its assumption that Jesus' recognition of his own death as the decisive point in the divine plan of salvation excludes the possibility of a time interval between this death and the Parousia. Morgenthaler has remarked that the saying in Matthew 10 (upon which Schweitzer leans so heavily) is to be read "as an expectation for the near future, but not for the very near future,"[35] while Cullmann points out that there are a number of sayings[36] which show that such an interval (whether he expected it to be a short one or a long one is not essential) is precisely what Jesus anticipated.[37]

That Jesus did not believe history would come to an end shortly after his

---

[32] *Op. cit.*, p. 397.

[33] Richard R. Niebuhr, *Resurrection and Historical Reason; A Study of Theological Method* (New York: Charles Scribner's Sons, 1957), p. 133.

[34] O. Cullmann, *Christ and Time*, pp. 85–6.

[35] Morgenthaler, *Kommendes Reich* cited by Herbert G. Wood, *The Expository Times*, vol. LXV (1953–4), p. 208.

[36] E.g., Mark 14:62; 13:10; 2:18; 14:28.

[37] Cullman, *Christ and Time*, pp. 149–50. Cullman mentions the sayings indicated, and refers to W. G. Kummel, *Verheissung und Erfüllung*, 1945, and W. Michaelis, *Der Herr verzieht nicht seine Verheissung*, 1942.

death is maintained also by C. H. Dodd.[38] . . .

Brunner points out:

> The imminent expectation of the Parousia in the whole of the New Testament pales into insignificance before the belief that in Jesus Christ the New Age had already dawned . . .[39]

While such defects as these preclude acceptance of the view of consistent eschatology, it is possible to appreciate a number of things which our consideration of that view has brought to light. . . .

Schweitzer's presentation has served to remind us that our best understanding of the teaching of Jesus and the events of his life will come as we place them against the background of first century Palestine. . . .

We can be grateful too for Schweitzer's demonstration that the tradition of the life of Jesus enshrined in the Gospels is not something easily divided into sections, any of which can then be discarded at will. . . .

Again, Schweitzer made it plain that any adequate representation of the historical Jesus has to take account of the "other-worldly" factor in his thought and teaching. . . .

A term which has been made popular in this connection, and which has helped towards clarification of the matter, is that of C. H. Dodd, who speaks of "realized eschatology" (as opposed to "futurist eschatology"):[40] although history still goes on, and the end is yet to be, the meaning of history has been revealed in the decisive event which has already taken place.[41]

Finally, there is in Schweitzer's presentation a severe criticism of the common notion that dogmatism of any kind must spell the end of historicity. . . .[42]

We need not . . . accept or discuss the "dogmatic, therefore historical" contention; it is enough to be reminded that a statement is not necessarily false because it is in accord with some idea which the writer is known, or believed, to hold.

All these factors—both those which weigh against Schweitzer's position and those which show the lasting values in it—have done much to open up for us a situation in which the question of the historical Jesus can be approached in a less biased way. . . .

5. G. Aulén[1] analyses the views on Atonement of Orthodox Protestantism, of authors of the Enlightenment, and of nineteenth-century theologians. Orthodoxy returned to the typical Latin outlook. The Enlightenment directed its attack to this doctrine, but not to regain the classic approach,

---

[38] C. H. Dodd, *The Parables of the Kingdom* (revised edition; London: Collins [Fontana Books] 1961), pp. 82, 115.

[39] E. Brunner, *Die christliche Lehre von Schöpfung und Erlösung* (Zurich: Zwingli-Verlag, 1950), p. 310. E. T., p. 262.

[40] A. M. Hunter suggests "inaugurated" as a better term than "realized." "The Interpretation of the Parables", *The Expository Times*, vol. LXIX (1957–8), p. 102.

[41] C. H. Dodd, *The Apostolic Preaching and its Developments* (new edition reset; London: Hodder & Stoughton Ltd., 1944), appendix, "Eschatology and History," pp. 79–96.

[42] *The Quest of the Historical Jesus*, p. 385.

[1] Gustaf Emmanuel Aulén was born in Sweden in 1879. He taught Systematic Theology at the Universities of Upsala and Lund, becoming bishop of Strängnäs in 1933. He was

but in behalf of a subjective, anthropomorphic approach. Schleiermacher's views followed this humanistic type of soteriology. For him Atonement consists in the deepening of the soul's consciousness in God, which follows salvation or "moral uplift." Ritschl in Germany and Rashdall in England, with their characteristics and differences, follow to a great extent the same line of thought.

The Doctrine of the Atonement in Protestant Orthodoxy. The typical Latin outlook on the Atonement . . . regained control of Protestant theology long before this found a definite expression (of its own). . .

The doctrine of the Atonement in Lutheran Orthodoxy is not simply identical with that of Anselm; but the differences must not be exaggerated, and they do not in the least involve any departure from the essential Latin type . . .

The broad similarity of this doctrine with that of Anselm consists primarily in the fact that the whole conception is dominated by the idea of Satisfaction; the satisfaction is treated as a rational necessity, the only possible method by which Atonement can be effected. Protestant Orthodoxy thus follows Anselm more closely than the usual mediaeval teaching. It states the problem in the same way; it repeats the contention that the payment of the satisfaction is the only alternative to a condonation of laxity. One or the other there must be; either a love which in forgiving violates the demands of justice, or else satisfaction. No other alternative is regarded as conceivable.

The divergence of the Protestant doctrine from that of Anselm is often held to consist largely in this: that it treats the satisfaction made by Christ as being also an endurance of punishment; the sin of man had deserved punishment, punishment is the inexorable demand of justice, and, therefore, Christ endures it instead of men. . . .

The idea of God which underlies it is, above all, that of a Justice which imposes its law and demands satisfaction; only within these limits is the Divine Love allowed to operate, and there is a suggestion that the idea of the Divine Love is regarded with some suspicion, as though it needed to be watched lest it should infringe on the demands of justice. . . .

It is true, of course, that the act of God in justifying man is treated as an act of His Mercy as much as of His Justice. God's *gratia* is shown in His readiness to accept the satisfaction offered by Another, and impute it to sinful men. . . .

At the same time it is clear that God's work in the Atonement is to be represented, not by a continuous line, as in the New Testament, the Fathers, and Luther, but, as in Anselm, by a broken line; for the compensation is paid by Christ as man, from man's

---

perhaps the foremost dogmatic theologian of the Swedish Church. He was the editor of *Svensk Teologisk Kvartalskift,* and the author of a number of books, of which the most important are *Den allmänneliga kristna tron* (1923). E. T. *The Faith of the Christian Church, Den kristna gudsbilden* (1927). It is from his book, *Den kristna försoningstanken,* translated into English with the title of *Christus Victor* (New York: Macmillan Co., 1954) that this excerpt has been taken from pp. 128–142.

side, in man's stead. It would, indeed, be unfair to say that God is regularly represented as simply the recipient of the atoning work, or that His attitude is changed thereby; for the Atonement is regarded, as it had been by Anselm, as having its origin in God's will, springing, as was so often said, out of the Divine mercy as well as of the Divine justice. Nevertheless, it remains true that the Divine operation in the Atonement was regarded as interrupted by the compensation paid from the human side, from below. . . .

Thus the doctrine of the Atonement in Protestant Orthodoxy belongs indisputably to the Latin type, and it forms the clearest and most logical of all the expressions of that type. During this period the classic idea of the Atonement is completely suppressed in the realm of theology; for, though the phrases and images which belong properly to it still occur occasionally, they are mere reminiscences, and play no part at all in the theological result. . . .

The Arrival of the "Subjective" or Humanistic Doctrine. The doctrine of the Atonement came to be regarded as the palladium of Orthodox Protestantism; only the doctrine of the verbal inspiration of the Bible can be compared with it in importance from this point of view . . .

Therefore the assault of the Enlightenment on the Orthodox theology concentrated itself on the doctrine of the Atonement. It was subjected to a fierce theological criticism, partly similar to that of the Nominalists three centuries before; the difference was that the theologians of the Enlightenment had no respect for the church authority which the doctrine enjoyed. In the course of the eighteenth century, the doctrine became in a measure disintegrated by the assaults made upon it; but in the nineteenth century it enjoyed something of a revival, and, though it failed to regain the leadership of the theological world, it recovered sufficient strength to maintain the controversy, and to give rise to a number of mediating theories.

The decline of the doctrine really begins with Pietism, for, . . . it is here that the first definite signs appear of a movement in the subjectivist direction . . . The most important point of all, in view of the future, was that the watchword of Pietism was New Birth (*Wiedergeburt*) rather than Justification—that is to say, the word chosen was one that described a subjective process.

But for the theologians of the Enlightenment, the controversy against the "Orthodox" doctrine of the Atonement became a matter of primary concern. The criticism of the Latin theory had begun with Abelard, and had never been completely silenced; now it dominated the situation. All the bases of the Orthodox theory were challenged. A "more human" idea of the Atonement was propounded, to replace the accepted "juridical" treatment. The idea of sin was made relative; sin was regarded as a state of imperfection. The doctrine of retributive punishment was scouted, for punishment could only be ameliorative. Above all, these theologians desired to uproot the "anthropomorphic" features and "relics of Judaism" from the conception of God; the idea of God that lay behind the Orthodox doctrine of the Atonement was inconsistent with the "simple teaching" of Jesus, and the love of the Heavenly Father. It was therefore intolerable that God should be thought of as needing to be "propitiated" through a satisfaction offered to Him. The death of Jesus could not rightly be interpreted in this way—so far all agreed; it was understood in various ways, as a seal set upon His teaching, as a vindication of the moral order of the universe, as a lofty example, as a symbolical expression of God's readiness to be reconciled. Only in some such sense could the work of Christ rightly be connected with the Atonement.

It was an axiom of the enlightenment that God's attitude to the world must, always and unalterably, be one of benevolence and goodwill; such language was preferred to the word Love. Therefore, so far as God was concerned, no Atonement was needed. It is therefore a little surprising that, side by side with this emphasis on God's unchanging goodwill, the idea appears of a certain influence exerted upon God from man's side. Man repents and amends his life, and God in turn responds by rewarding man's amendment with an increase of happiness. The ruling idea is therefore essentially anthropocentric and moralistic. . . .

The Nineteenth Century. The nineteenth century is characterised by a continuous conflict between the "subjective" and the "objective" views of the Atonement. The latter had survived the assaults of the Enlightenment, and had succeeded in gathering its forces to make a more vigorous resistance; but the hegemony lay with the other side. It is true that, from Schleiermacher onwards, the theology of the Enlightenment was not simply reproduced; it was criticized as shallow; and an endeavor was made to deepen it. Yet these theologians show a closer continuity with the Enlightenment than they themselves believed; this is true not least of Schleiermacher himself. There was the same humanistic and anthropomorphic outlook in their teaching on the Atonement as in their theology in general.

The feature which first arrests our attention in Schleiermacher is his distinction between *Erlösung* and *Versöhnung,* Salvation and Atonement. Salvation takes the primary place; it is effected as the individual's sense of God grows stronger. Atonement, reconciliation, is the sense of blessedness, which follows on a deepened consciousness of God. This distinction was of special importance in nineteenth-century theology, and it well illustrates the anthropocentric outlook. Schleiermacher says quite plainly that the change in the spiritual life which comes to pass as the soul's consciousness of God is deepened, is the real meaning of that which is called Atonement.

It is particularly interesting to note the order in which the two ideas, Salvation and Atonement, are arranged. Wherever the classic idea of the Atonement is dominant, the two coincide; alike in the early church and in Luther, Salvation is Atonement, and Atonement is Salvation. With the Latin doctrine the case is different; Atonement is treated as prior to Salvation, a preliminary to it, making the subsequent process of salvation possible. But Schleiermacher reverses the order; Salvation (the change in the spiritual life) comes first, and Atonement (Reconciliation) follows as its completion.

It would be possible to object that this comparison is misleading, because the terms in question are being used in different senses. Even so, it has its value. It shows that the change in the meaning of the terms follows directly upon the change of order. Schleiermacher, with his anthropocentric outlook, interprets salvation primarily as a *Lebenserhöhung,* or moral uplift; Atonement, or Reconciliation, becomes essentially a sense of being at home in the cosmos, gained through the uplift of the soul, or a new attitude to life, characterised by harmony with the universe. Man comes to understand that all things are dependent on God, and, therefore, that which seems to disturb the harmony of things does so only in appearance. It might be said that "Atonement" in this sense means that man is reconciled with his situation and his environment. The subjectivity of the whole conception is in any case evident.

The place of Christ and Christ's work in this scheme is consistent with the rest. The anthropocentric attitude is not modified when He comes into consideration. Christ is regarded as the starting-point of the influences that work towards the strengthening of man's consciousness of God, because He is the embodiment of the ideal of religion, the Pattern Man, who has an absolutely perfect and blessed consciousness of God. But it is not necessary for our purpose to go more fully into Schleiermacher's dialectically interesting discussion of the Latin doctrine of the Atonement and of earlier forms of teaching. God is not regarded as having any direct relation to the process of man's Reconciliation, except in so far as He is the ultimate sanction of man's sense of "absolute dependence." When all is governed by universal causality, there is no room for an Atonement in the sense of the removal of an alienation between God and man. No such alienation can be believed to exist, since the active hostility of the Divine Love towards evil has faded away and the dualistic outlook has been banished by the monism which dominates the view. In so far as this is used to explain God's relation to Christ and His work, the prevailing idea is that Christ is treated as the Head of the human race, and that God's attitude to mankind is influenced by the fact that He sees mankind in the light which radiates from Christ.

Ritschl, in his great work *Rechtfertigung und Versöhnung,* maintains essentially the same line of thought. Like all the writers of this school, he gives us a vigorous criticism of the "juridical" doctrine of the Atonement; but he is blind to the significance of the classic idea, and summarily dismisses its imagery whenever it comes under discussion. The title of his book shows an anxiety to do better justice to the Reformation than Schleiermacher had done; "Justification" in his title takes the place of Schleiermacher's "Salvation." Nevertheless, the line of thought is closely parallel. The central point for Ritschl is that man gives up his mistrust of God, which had been based on a misunderstanding of God's character, and is dissipated by the sight of Christ's faithfulness to His vocation even unto death; this human faithfulness is a revelation of the Divine Love. As with Schleiermacher, Atonement follows subsequently, as the result of man's new relation to God, and signifies primarily a new relation to the world, characterised by *Selbstbehauptung,* self-realisation, and mastery of the world. Here, too, the anthropocentric nature of the idea is plain.

The latest work of importance belonging to this general type is *The Idea of Atonement in Christian Theology,* by Dr. Rashdall. He, too, works with the distinction of "objective" and "subjective" views of the

Atonement. By the former he means a theory following the lines of the Latin doctrine; the "subjective" view he traces back particularly to Abelard, who in this exposition of the subject receives quite a disproportionate share of attention. It is a surprise to find Abelard's theory described as "entirely in harmony with the earlier tradition of the church" (p. 443). Abelard's thought is summed up as follows: "He sees that God can only be supposed to forgive by making the sinner better, and thereby removing any demand for punishment" (p. 359).

No doubt Rashdall may be regarded as comparing favorably with Continental theologians of a similar tendency, in so far as he follows the praiseworthy English tradition in giving a greater place to the Incarnation than the German writers whom we have discussed. Nevertheless, it cannot be said that he gives adequate expression to the Christian idea of the Incarnation; like other idealistic writers, he allows the highest human to shade off into the Divine, and thus obscures the distinction between the Divine and the human. Christ reveals God, because He exhibits the ideal manhood (*cf.* pp. 447 *ff.*). But it is particularly important to see that the question of Salvation is treated by him just as much from the ethical point of view as by Schleiermacher. The following are typical phrases: "The death of Christ justifies us, inasmuch as through it charity is stirred up in our hearts" (p. 438); "the efficacy of Christ's death is attributed to the moral effects which it produces" (p. 443); Christ has taught us "to think of God as a Father who will forgive men their sins if and in proportion as they have repented of them" (p. 461); and "in the two parables of the prodigal son and the Pharisee and the publican, we have the fullest expression of this fundamental idea—that God forgives the truly penitent freely and without any other condition than that of true penitence" (p. 26).

The weakness of this exposition is not to be found in the language about the ethical effects of the Divine forgiveness on human lives; on the contrary, this is its strength. Its weakness is that the forgiving and atoning work of God is *made dependent upon* the ethical in human lives; consequently, the Divine Love is not clearly set forth as a free, spontaneous love. Wherever there is such a view of the Divine Love, as not called forth by the worthiness or goodness of men, but as bestowing value on men by the very fact that they are loved by God, the work of the Divine forgiveness always appears as prior to ethical regeneration, not dependent upon or proportioned to human repentance or any other conditions on man's side. It is this primacy of the Divine Love which is the basis of the classic idea of the Atonement as God's own work.

I will now give just one instance of an attempt to mediate by way of compromise between the Latin and the humanistic types of view, which were for the most part in violent opposition to one another during the nineteenth century. It is taken from an essay by the Swedish Archbishop Ekman, which in its day (1906) attracted much attention. It shows how deeply the anthropocentric habit of thought had sunk in, even among those who were anxious not to lose touch with the Latin theory of the Atonement, which was regarded as the church teaching. The Archbishop's leading idea is that "it is simply the conversion of men that effects the

Atonement"; hence "God gives up His displeasure against a man, and reverses His sentence of judgment, when the man confesses his sin and asks for pardon, recognises that he has rightly deserved to suffer for his sin, and earnestly applies himself to do God's will." This line of thought is followed out thus: the conversion of the human race is the Atonement of mankind; and such a conversion has taken place representatively in Jesus Christ. He is "the true man," He "stands forth as the Head of mankind, and to plead man's cause." This influences God's attitude: "Let us imagine a nation which is universally despised, but among it is a noble hero, who exercises a mighty influence on the nation; then we become reconciled in our thought towards this nation. There radiates from the hero a reconciling light over the nation. . . . So, in the midst of mankind God sees Jesus Christ. He sees a ruman radiance which scatters its beams over the human race. He sees streaks of truth, purity, and righteousness spreading among men. He sees in the body of mankind a new heart, whose strong pulse is spreading new life through the veins of the body. . . . He has then no further displeasure with mankind seen as a whole, He no longer despairs of mankind, He reconciles Himself with mankind."

The significant thing is that this last passage, which is intended to conserve what is essential in the "objective" doctrine of the Atonement, contains not the faintest idea of an Atonement effected by God Himself. The approach of man to God is altogether an approach "from below"; Christ as "the true man" may be conceived to exercise influence on God's thought of mankind and His relation to mankind; God sees "a human radiance" illuminating the human race, and therefore reconciles Himself with mankind.

If our sketch of the third of the three main types of Atonement-doctrine has left a less clear impression on the reader's mind than the other two, this is not altogether due to the brevity of our description of it; there is a lack of definite outline in the type itself. This lack of definiteness is reflected in the name which it commonly bears —the "subjective" doctrine. It would, of course, be absurd so to press this word as to imply that this teaching leaves God wholly out of account and so makes the idea of a true Atonement meaningless; but it is true that in this view the emphasis is shifted from that which may be held to be done for men by God or by Christ to that which is done in men and by men.

In order to understand this third type of view, it is important to see that its character is determined by its opposition to the Latin theory. It criticises especially the notion that God needs in any sense to be reconciled or that His attitude to mankind should be changed; any such assertion is inconsistent with His love. Hence the Love of God is maintained, with a denial of any sort of tension or opposition between God's mercy and His justice. The question then becomes, whether the Divine Love is so set forth as to conserve the deepest elements of the Christian faith, or whether there is loss of something essential through over-simplification. . . . I will add just one point. The "subjective" view is anxious to show how there cannot be any influence exerted upon God so as to propitiate Him or change His attitude towards man. Yet at the same time this view assumes, even to a greater extent than the Latin view, just such an influence upon God from man's side. For the extent to which "atonement" is effected depends upon that which is done in and by men, on their penitence, their conversion; therefore God's attitude to men is really made to depend on man's attitude to God. The case is not different when Christ and His work come under consideration. The effect of Christ's work is that God, seeing the character of Christ, and His place as the Representative Man, gains a new and more hopeful view of humanity.

Catholic Authors

1. K. Adam[1] discusses the theories regarding the hypostatic union in Catholic thought after Trent. The merit of the Thomistic position lies in ensuring the closest union between the divinity and humanity of Christ, at the price, however, of the totality of the latter. The followers of Scotus preserved Christ's humanity in its fullness but their negative concept of personality is inadmissible. Different views on the transcendence and immanence of God account for this diversity of opinions. The author favors Suarez's over Molina's views.

The influences of . . . theories by which early Scholasticism attempted to comprehend the mystery of the hypostatic union, persisted into High Scholasticism . . . It was not until after the Council of Trent that late scholastic theology turned to the task of clarifying and deepening the . . . theories, mostly with the aid of such Aristotelian concepts as essence and existence . . . Theologians sought to answer the question of the ultimate basis for unity in the constitution of Christ.

The Solution of the Thomist school. Fundamentally, their solution depends upon the position taken up by the various schools of thought within the Church with regard to the relationship between person and nature, and essence and existence. They are all agreed that the distinction between person and nature, essence and existence, is not merely a logical, but above all a virtual, distinction, that is, one founded upon fact (*cum fundamento in re*), even though such a distinction is not readily to be established in the concrete reality of phenomena. A virtual distinction is one that becomes apparent only after thinking about certain given facts. The question that divides the various schools of thought within the Church is rather this: Is the distinction between person and nature simply a virtual one of this kind, or is it more profound, is it a substantial distinction, as between one thing and another? If the latter, then the "existence as a person" can in substance be detached from the human nature. This nature would remain undiminished, *integra,* even if it had no person. In this case, the Logos would be united to the human nature by the simple suspension of the human existence as person, or, more precisely, by the suspension in the very act of union of the human mode of sub-

[1] Cf. Ch. 1, n. 4. This excerpt is from *op. cit.,* pp. 221–233.

sistence, while its place would be taken by the divine existence as person. According to this theory, the union takes place by way of subtraction; the being of the person is subtracted from the human person. The real point of unity is, then, what the Logos puts in the place of the suspended and withdrawn human mode of subsistence, that is, the autonomy of the second divine person, or, in Scholastic terms, the divine *esse existentiae*. This doctrine was mainly put forward by the Thomist school founded by the Dominican Bañez (d. 1604), which was based upon certain fundamental doctrines of St. Thomas Aquinas. His view was that its union with the self of the Logos caused the human nature to give up its own mode of subsistence, its own peculiar mode of self-possession and self-belonging. It no longer belongs to itself, but to the self of the Logos. This is where it has its ultimate resting place, its proper autonomy. The independent sense of identity, which transforms ordinary human nature in general into an individual concrete man, is attained in an infinitely higher sense by the human nature that is integrated into the identity of the Logos. Being thus assumed into the absolute autonomy of the Logos, it appropriates to itself the Logos' absolute power of reality and might of existence. It no longer exists in and by itself, but by this power of existence of the Logos. And thus the *unio in persona* becomes more profoundly a *unio ad esse, ad existentiam*. This is possible because in the Thomist scheme a real distinction persists not only between nature and person but also between essence and existence; they are distinct as potency and act, the mere possibility of being and realized being, are distinct. Hence the humanity of Jesus is able to receive the absolute power of reality of the Logos, as well as its personality. The Logos extends its divine power of being to it, and takes it up in its might. Its own power of existence, its own *existere,* is of itself suspended or, rather, assumed into the absolute and autonomous reality of the Logos.

The advantage of the Thomist explanation is in its ability to establish the closest unity of the humanity of Jesus with the person of the Logos without in any way diminishing or harming the human nature itself. But in depriving the human nature of its highest and ultimate stage of existence, the *esse existentiae,* it is inadequate. Its opponents are in a position to maintain that Thomism does in fact diminish the human nature; they have only to regard this *esse existentiae* as the essential characteristic of nature and essence, and to assume that person and nature, essence and existence, are only virtually distinct from each other, and not detachable from each other. On the other hand the Thomist theory appears to divinize the human nature in so far as its existence is also the existence of the Logos. Since in the Logos existence is identical with the divine nature, the conclusion would not be far to seek that the human nature came into possession of the divine essence as well as the divine existence.

The Solution of Duns Scotus. The sharpest refutation of the Thomist explanation came from Duns Scotus . . . and his school. Duns Scotus taught that the nature and person and the nature and existence of created things are not really distinct, but rather that their separation is only virtual. And therefore the assumption must be made that in Christ there is, as well as the two natures, also a dual mode of existence, human and divine, created and uncreated. Where, then, does Scotus locate the point of unity of the two natures in Christ? If the human nature of Jesus does not exist in the eternal existence of the Logos, but possesses a human existence, what joins it with the Logos in a substantial union, what is to be understood by the existence as person which the human nature has from the Logos? Duns Scotus has recourse to the following explanation: To the created personality, being a person is something wholly negative. To the creature, it simply means the *negatio dependentiae actualis et aptitudinalis.* Being a person simply means that the created being does not belong to another subject either in fact (*independentia actualis*) or potentially (*independentia aptitudinalis*). Every individual rational nature is thus without any further ado and without the approach of another substantial perfection a person, as long as it remains belonging to itself, and is not united to any higher hypostasis. The moment a created being united to a higher hypostasis is released from this higher hypostasis, it would promptly return to being a person again. In the created being, its being as person is something purely negative, a state of not-being-dependent, or of not-being-potentially-dependent. In contrast, however, it is something positive in God, because God, as an entity in himself, an *ens a se,* is the absolute autonomy of all being. This autonomy is his nature. It is the source of his abundant perfections. If this definition of the person of the Creator is applied to Christ, Scotus' theory would argue that the human nature, in being assumed into the unity of person of the Son of God, would lose its being as a person in so far as it loses its actual and potential independence, its *independentia actualis et aptitudinalis*—i.e., to the extent that it is no longer independent. It loses nothing positive but only its negative independence and incommunicability with regard to another hypostasis. By means of God's omnipotence, a human nature is integrated into the divine person "after the fashion of a part." This integrated part, however, with the exception of its lost independence, preserves the fullness of its specific human mode of being, and thus its human existence, which is an essential part of this specific mode of being. There is only one person in Christ, but a dual existence. Unlike the Thomist theory, Scotus does not regard the being as person as a real *modus subsistendi,* which would be the addition of a positive reality to the human nature; it is something negative, freedom from all dependence. And in so far as human nature loses this independence to the Logos, this Logos is its person, endowing it with its own incommunicability and autonomy. The existence itself belongs as a positive mode of being not to the identity as person but to the human nature. This is how it preserves Christ's humanity, even in the hypostatic union. To this extent we must say that Christ's humanity is no longer an independent human person, in so far as it has surrendered its independence to the Logos. But by virtue of its nature, it exists through its own created existence, and not through the uncreated existence of the divine Word.

The advantage of Duns Scotus' theory is that it preserves Christ's full humanity in every conceivable form. The identity of our nature with Jesus' humanity, the *homoousios hēmin* is consistently maintained. But we have doubts about its depletion of the concept of person. St. Thomas Aquinas, whose authority Duns Scotus too recognizes, describes "person" as the "most perfect in the entire nature"—he is referring to what subsists in a rational nature (*Summa Theologica,* I, qu. 29, a. 3). Now this expresses something absolutely positive: the autonomy is primary; the independence is only secondary, since the autonomy is its prerequisite. A further weakness in Duns Scotus' conception is that it is unable to say clearly what really does inextricably unite divinity and humanity in Christ. The union does not bring about the slightest change in the human nature of Jesus. Similarly, the Logos also remains unchanged in every respect. So what really takes place in the hypostatic union? After all, the God-man is a substantial essence, a substantial synthesis of the divine and human natures. But how can a substantial essence arise if nothing substantial takes place in either part of the synthesis? Scotus would reply: The true union is brought about by the absolute and immutable will of God, an all-embracing transcendental power. It is God's will that this concrete human nature should belong not to itself but to the Logos. And God's almighty will has its effect. So we may conclude that its only correlative can be a substantial union.

As we shall see, this divine will remained in all it wrought strictly transcendent. Scotist thought is disposed to ensure this transcendence of the divine and supernatural in every respect, unlike Thomism, which recognizes the immanence of the divine. Because the divine will that constantly integrates the humanity of Jesus into the Logos is entirely transcendent, it can be known only by faith. So the incarnation is purely the object of faith. There is nothing in the miracle that has its place in the world of experience. On the strictly empirical level of experience, Christ in his human figure appears just like the rest of us. Only our faith has any knowledge of his divine mystery.

The Scotist and Thomist Doctrines. The theory of supernatural and divine transcendence at the bottom of Duns Scotus' doctrine is the stamp of his entire system, just as on the other hand Thomism is marked by the contrasting doctrine of the immanence of the divine in things earthly. This is the crucial point where, in our judgment, the two schools clearly part company. . . . In the Thomist view of Christ, too, the purely human, natural being of Christ is so penetrated and animated by the divine power of the Logos that its true reality is the same as that of the Logos. But in the Scotist view, the Logos and its activities remain strictly transcendent. All that is to be seen and experienced of Christ the man is purely human. Only our faith knows that in his metaphysical depths this man Jesus belongs not to himself but to the Logos.

The Solution of the Molinist School. The Scotist doctrine was revised, or rather deepened, by certain theologians who were adherents not so much of the Scotist school as of Molinism. They were mostly members of the Society of Jesus. Tiphanus, Franzelin, and Pesch maintain that the Logos assumed complete human nature in the further sense that not only the individual human existence but also the being of the human person belongs at least virtually to the human nature. The person, then, is not negative, but something positive. But it is only virtually distinct from the nature. The moment the humanity of Jesus would be released from the hypostatic union, it would be able to exist as a separate created being, in its own power, and be a person. Nothing is taken away from Christ's human nature by its assumption into the Logos. Whatsoever belongs to human nature forms part of it even after the incarnation. Hence the Thomist theory of subtraction is untenable. What has happened in the incarnation is simply that the selfsame intact human nature has been assumed into the divine hypostasis, and that from this moment on it no longer belongs to itself but to the Logos. But in this process the human personality is by no means completely cancelled out. Because it belongs to the human nature, it is still there, virtually, and is not extinguished or destroyed by the divine person, but assumed into it. This assumption does not imply the destruction of the human self, but its exaltation. In Scholastic terms, it is not a *defectus ad imperfectum,* but a *profectus ad perfectum,* a tremendous transfiguration into the divine. This process of perfection is possible because human nature, like every created nature, on account of its *potentia oboedientialis,* is ordinated towards union with the divine. The hypostatic union is the fulfillment of the deepest longing that lies like an undeveloped seed in created nature, the longing for the most real union and unity with God. This is why there is nothing in any way unnatural about the process of incarnation. Indeed, it is much rather the fulfillment of what the Creator from the beginning planted in nature as its ultimate culminating potentiality.

The Solution of Suárez. It was Suárez (d. 1617) who put forward a theory mediating between the two opposing conceptions of the Thomist and Scotist schools. He too follows Scotus in the doctrine that nature and existence are in reality the same, and that therefore in Christ a dual existence is to be assumed. So the point of unity of the two natures in Christ cannot lie in the uncreated existence of the Logos, as the Thomist theory would have it. To this extent, Suárez follows the Scotist school. But he labors to avoid the evil conclusions that would arise if the Scotist principles were applied unmodified to Christology. To this end he makes use of the Thomist distinction between person and nature. Certainly nature and existence can be separated only conceptually. But person and nature can be distinguished in reality, *realiter.* Existence as person brings with it its own peculiar reality, distinct from that of nature. This reality is to be conceived after the fashion of modal accidents. In distinction to absolute accidents, modal accidents are those conditions of being (*quidditates*) that could not be conceived as existing without having a substance as bearer. They are the necessary forms of appearance of a substance. Such modal accidents, for example, would be the form, the figure, the movement, of a body. They are not mere relationships, because they are real effects of real activities, and are themselves in turn the causes of real effects. Movement, for example, is a real factor in the production of speed, just as is the mass of a body. The reality that makes of nature a person is to be conceived after the fashion of these modal accidents.

Only this reality would not be an accidental mode, but substantial, because its ultimate perfection is rendered in autonomy, in substantiality. According to Suárez, this would make a person out of nature only by adding to nature the *modus per se existendi,* the mode by which nature itself has its autonomous existence, the *modus substantialis.* And thus the person is not, as Scotus assumed, something negative, but a positive perfection, since it is not yet contained in the individual nature as such. This was the way by which Suárez tried to improve Scotus' concept of the person. By the hypostatic union of Christ's human nature with the Logos, whereby the Logos appropriates the human nature to itself and becomes its bearer, it loses its natural *modus substantialis.* It gives something up, something certainly real, but not its *existentia,* as the Thomists would have it, not the highest stage of its ordination in being, but simply a mode of being, the *modus per se existendi.* And the place of this natural mode is taken not by the eternal mode of being of the Logos itself, as the Thomists would have it, but by a new mode created by divine omnipotence, the *modus unionis,* which binds the two natures together. This new mode too is a *modus substantialis,* and it contains the basis of unity of the two natures in Christ. The role played by the eternal will of God in the Scotist system is in this case taken over by something real, created, the *modus unionis.* This is a rejection of the Thomist explanation, which acknowledged the ultimate basis of Christ's unity in the "*existere.*" Here, we have a bond of unity that is not uncreated but created, the supernaturally created *modus unionis.* This disposes of the danger of divinizing Christ's humanity. Suárez attempts to improve upon Scotus by giving up his negative conception of the being of the person as *independentia,* and ascribing to it a positive created reality. This brings the further advantage of being able to establish a positive bond of unity in Christ in so far as the union of both natures is not brought about by the will of God alone, but also by means of the real, supernaturally created *modus unionis,* which takes the place of the natural *modus per se existendi* that has been abolished in the incarnation, and which by this very substitution inextricably unites the human nature with the Logos. Suárez believes that this gives him the advantage over Thomism, for in his system Christ's human nature is not directly taken up into the divine existence and essence, and thus divinized, but preserves its own relative autonomy and its peculiar characteristics as a created being.

The objection to Suárez's theory is that, given his presuppositions, the concept of a *modus substantialis* is not tenable. Suárez does not assume any real distinction between essence and existence. And so existence is already given with nature. The conclusion then would be that the *modus per se existendi* of which Suárez speaks cannot be a mode of substance, but only of accident. For in Scholastic ontology, everything that is a subsequent addition to being is an accident, *Omne, quod sequitur ad esse rei, est ei accidentale* (Thomas Aquinas, *Summa contra Gentes,* I, 22). Now, it is true, in the case we have been discussing there does not seem to be any justification for the objection. If we assume that the being at issue here is divine being, then it cannot be said of it that its mode of subsistence is a "subsequent addition." Rather it is already included in divine being, indeed, it is the culmination of divine being. So Suárez's theory does in fact appear to have cleared away all doubts that could be raised against the Thomist and Scotist conceptions. Objections to Suárez's theory itself are only of a terminological nature, for the expression *modus substantialis* is an unusual one in Scholastic usage.

2. L. Richard[1] notes that Trent did not have to issue any direct definition concerning the doctrine of the redemption itself, since the reformers did not attack the dogma as such. Trent's statements are directed to aspects of the redemption, such as the meaning of justification, the merit of the justified Christian, and the sacrifice of the Mass. Regarding the doctrine of penal substitution, Richard points out how Protestant and some Catholic authors went too far in their interpretations of Christ's abandonment by the Father. The cult of the Sacred Heart in the seventeenth century was a response to Jansenism.

The Council of Trent. . . . Protestantism did not attack the dogma of the redemption. The Council of Trent, therefore, did not have to define it directly. The solemn magisterium of the Church ordinarily intervenes only in cases of necessity, and most often to condemn heresies or to set aside errors which affect the deposit of faith. Faith in Jesus Christ, the Son of God incarnate, born of the Virgin Mary, dead on the cross and risen for our salvation is so deeply rooted in the Christian conscience that there is no need to define it anew. . . .

But, in the face of Protestant errors regarding justification, the merit of the justified Christian or the sacrifice of the Mass, the Council was in fact induced to present very explicitly the Catholic doctrine of redemption.

Recalling the dogma of original sin, the Council declared that:

> men were slaves of sin and under the power of the devil and death to such an extent that neither the Gentiles with their natural powers nor even the Jews with the Mosaic Law could be free. . . . This is why the Father of mercies sent his Son, Christ Jesus, to men . . . so that he might redeem the Jews who were under the law and that the Gentiles also might be able to obtain justice without having sought it, and that all might be able to receive adoption as sons (D.B., 793–794) . . .

Treating the causes of justification, "which is not just the remission of sins but the sanctification and renewal of the interior man," the Council declared that:

> the efficient cause of this justification is the merciful God . . . , and the meritorious cause is his beloved Son, our Lord Jesus Christ, who, when we were enemies, because of the very great love which he had for us, and through his holy passion on the tree of the cross, merited justification for us and made satisfaction to God the Father for us (D.B., 799).

The Council likewise defined that "original sin can be taken away only

[1] Ch. 1, n. 7. This excerpt is from *op. cit.,* pp. 229–244.

by the merit of the one mediator, our Lord Jesus Christ, who reconciled us to God in his blood" (D.B., 790).

Treating the merits of the justified man, which come in the first place from the grace and merits of Christ, the Council made this important statement on the subject of redemption:

> Christ Jesus, as the head of his members [Eph 4:5] and the vine with regard to the branches [Jn 15:5], exercises his action [*virtutem influat*] on the justified themselves, and this salutary force always precedes, accompanies and follows their works (D.B., 809).

Likewise the doctrinal statement on the sacrament of Penance asserted:

> Whereas by making satisfaction we suffer for our sins, we are conformed to Jesus Christ who has made satisfaction for our sins and from whom comes everything that we can do . . .[2]

These texts of the Council, although in summary form, give the essential truths: the absolute powerlessness of sinful man to free himself from sin, the initiative of divine mercy, the grace of salvation which comes to us through Jesus Christ, the Word made flesh for us. To describe the redeeming work of Christ, the Council sanctified the ideas of merit and satisfaction: Christ merited justification for us; he made satisfaction for us to God. This merit is based on the charity which animates him for our sake and makes him accept the passion and the death of the cross. It will be noticed that the Council, following St. Thomas, placed the idea of merit before that of satisfaction. Christ merited to us (in the dative: *nobis*), which shows Christ as the meritorious cause for our sake: *causa meritoria.* On the other hand he is said to have satisfied for us, *pro nobis,* to God the Father. "*For* us" certainly means "in our favor," but it also means "in our place," as our head. . . . This is not because we have no more to satisfy for our part; but what we cannot do—offer God a glorification which compensates for our sins—he has done, so that henceforth we might be able to do it in him and through him, as the Council declared. Likewise we will have to merit; but our merits proceed first from his prevenient and concomitant grace, and it is Christ himself who gives this grace. Meritorious causality is accomplished in the present efficacy of Christ.

If the Council adopted expressions of merit and satisfaction to describe the work of Christ, it is not at all because it abandoned the ancient words redemption and sacrifice. [It also used] the word "ransom" (D.B., 794); and to define, against the Protestants,

[2] Thus the same term is used to denote the satisfaction of Christ for our sins in his passion, and the satisfaction of the sinful and penitent Christian—which takes all its value from that of Christ . . . But it is clear that these works of satisfaction have no place in the satisfaction which Christ accomplished by the sufferings of his passion, sufferings which had nothing punitive or medicinal about them. What they have in common with our sufferings is, as St. Thomas says (III, q. 48, a. 2), that the act of making satisfaction to God who has been offended by sin consists in offering him something which he loves more than he hates sin. This is what Christ, as the head of mankind in its act of returning to God, accomplished fully by the perfection of his charity when he accepted his passion which was brought about by the sins of mankind. This is what he alone could do, but what we can do by his grace if we are united to him. (Cf. L. Richard, "Sens théologique due mot satisfaction," Rev. Sc. Rel., VII [1927] 87–93.)

that the Mass is a true sacrifice, it had to recall that "Christ offered himself to God the Father once on the altar of the cross, by dying [*morte intercedente*], in order to accomplish an eternal redemption" (D.B., 938).[3] . . .

Expiation by Penal Substitution. Both Scripture and Tradition affirm that Christ, by obedience to his Father and love for men, expiated in his passion for the latter by accepting death, the penalty of their sins, though he himself was innocent and the beloved son.

But with the help of the nominalist theology and the extreme comparison of the "abandonment" of Christ to mystical abandonment, the idea of penal substitution led some to attribute to Christ, who was "burdened with the sins of men" and "abandoned by his Father" during the passion, the feeling of divine reprobation, the experience of the pain of loss. Protestant theology . . . ended in this interpretation. But we find it presented, with certain reservations, by the Catholic preachers of the seventeenth century: Bossuet, Bourdaloue[4] and a number of spiritual authors who did not, however, derive it from the masters of the Reformation. We shall cite only this passage from a sermon of Bourdaloue:

> Jesus Christ in himself is the Holy of Holies, the Beloved of the Father . . . ; but we do not take care that on Calvary he ceased, so to speak, to be all this, and that, in place of these qualities, which were obscured and as it were eclipsed for a time, he was reduced to being what Scripture calls a curse for men, *factus pro nobis maledictum,* to being the victim for sin, *propitiatio pro peccatis,* and—since St. Paul said it, I will say it after him—to being the tool of sin and sin itself: *Eum qui non noverat peccatum, pro nobis peccatum fecit.* . . .

It was only natural that these masters of the pulpit form a school; therefore we find similar developments during the eighteenth, nineteenth and even the twentieth centuries. We cite one spiritual author as an example:

> Nothing would have been done for our salvation if Jesus had not been substituted for all sinners and if God, in accepting this substitution, had not consented to consider him as the universal sinner and to strike all human iniquities in him.[5]

[3] In his constitution *Cum Quorundam* (August 7, 1555) condemning those who deny the Trinity, Paul IV used the words "redeem" and "reconcile" (D.B., 993).

Since the time of the Council of Trent, the solemn magisterium has had no occasion for giving a complete treatment of the mystery of the redemption, although some of its pronouncements have touched upon it, as in the case of Jansenism. . . . However, the Vatican Council had placed this subject on its agenda.

[4] Bossuet, "Carême de Louvre, Sermon du Vendredi Saint"; Bourdaloue, "Premier sermon sur la Passion de Jésus-Christ." Numerous quotations from more recent authors will be found in J. Riviére, *Le dogme de la rédemption, Etude théologique* (3rd ed.), pp. 227–240.

[5] J. Corne, *Le mystère de Notre Seigneur Jésus-Christ,* Vol. IV, *Le sacrifice de Jésus* (Paris, n.d.), quoted by J. Rivière, *op. cit.,* p. 232. Some more important names may also be quoted; for example, J. J. Olier, who speaks of "the penitent Jesus" in his beautiful chapter on the virtue of penance (*Introd. à la vie et aux vertus chrétiennes,* chap. 7); P. Grou (*L'intérieur de Jésus et de Marie,* Part I, chap. 55, 59, and 61); C. L. Gay (*Elévations sur la vie et la doctrine de N.S.J.C.,* 89th elevation). A decree of the Holy Office (July 15, 1893) condemned the use of the name "penitent" when speaking of Jesus or of his Heart, even under the form of "poenitens pro nobis" (J. de Guibert,

More pronounced and more surprising for a justly famous philosopher and theologian, the same tendency can be shown to exist even up to a very recent period: "He endured, in a manner possible to the immaculate Son of God and man, the pain of hell."[6]

This oratorical theology is doubtless intended to make us realize all the horror which Christ experienced for sin, an undeniable truth on which it is important to meditate. But in working out the scriptural and traditional idea of the expiation of Christ in this way, one distorts the Gospel meaning, just as, in the patristic age, some were able to falsify the idea of ransom in the theory of the rights of the devil. The texts of St. Paul which are cited do not, in fact, mean that Christ experienced the effect of the "wrath" of God which "falls on every man who does evil." As Cornelius à Lapide (eighteenth century) said in appealing to the commentaries on the Fathers, that would be

> an intolerable blasphemy, unknown in past centuries. Christ could not conceive God as angry with him. Indeed he knew he loved God his Father and that he was very dear to the Father.[7]

We must not forget that the word of Christ on the cross (Mk 15:34) was the first verse of Psalm 22 which expresses the sorrowful cry and the filial confidence in God of the just man oppressed by his enemies and abandoned by all. The idea of an abandonment in which Jesus would experience in his soul the effect of the wrath of God is completely foreign to patristic tradition, as well as to that of the great doctors of the thirteenth century.

The better theologians of the sixteenth century—both the Dominicans, with Cajetan, and the Jesuits, with Robert Bellarmine and Suárez—remained faithful to the doctrine of the great doctors of the thirteenth century; and when they encountered this new expression of abandonment, they rejected it.[8]

St. John of the Cross and St. Francis de Sales were certainly true theologians and even doctors of the Church, but one still feels that their spiritual experience or that of the souls whom they directed dominated in part their analysis of the internal sufferings of Christ, which led them to believe that his Father expressly took away spiritual consolation. However, their thought remained moderate. St. Francis de Sales especially knew how to avoid the exaggerations noted above, while retaining the exact idea which inspired the movement of communing in the moral sufferings of the Savior:

> Our divine Savior was incomparably afflicted in his civil life, being condemned as guilty of treason against God and man; . . . in his natural life, dying in the most cruel and sensible torments that heart could conceive; in his spiritual life enduring sorrow, fears,

---

Documenta ecclesiastica christianae perfectionis studium spectantia [Rome, 1931], no. 1028).

[6] G. Rabeau, "Agonie du Christ," in *Catholicisme,* col. 228.

[7] *In Hebr.,* 5:7, ed. Vivès, XIX (1868), p. 394 f.

[8] Bellarmine, *De septem verbis,* II, 1; *Opera Omnia,* ed. Vivès (1875), VIII, 512–513; Suárez, *In IIIam, q.* 46, *a.* 8, *Disp. XXXIII,* section I, 1–3 and section II, 4–5; *Opera Omnia,* ed. Vivès, XIX, 530–531 and 533–534; cf. Maldonatus, in *Math.,* 27:46 (Mayence, 1862), I, 471f.

> terrors, anguish, abandonment, internal oppressions. . . . For though the supreme portion of his soul did sovereignly enjoy eternal glory, yet love hindered this glory from spreading its delicious influence into the feelings, or the imagination, or the inferior reason, leaving thus his whole heart at the mercy of sorrow and anguish.[9] . . .

To enumerate the sufferings of Christ completely apart from the divine punishment of sin, and every impression of abandonment by God which resembled a temporal loss, is not to minimize the depth and the purity of his internal suffering, inspired by his unselfish redemptive charity. Jesus certainly was perfectly aware that he was the beloved Son sent for the salvation of men. But at the same time he suffered physically and morally from the sinful world. Fully aware of his responsibility for the salvation of mankind, he had to experience, before the brilliant victory over the powers of darkness, the supreme anguish of the salvation of the world and to triumph over it by his unfailing hope.[10]

Devotion to the Sacred Heart of Jesus. . . . The cult properly so-called of the Sacred Heart was outlined in the twelfth and thirteenth centuries by the mystics who, from the wound in the side, penetrated to the heart of the Savior. At first a private devotion, from a St. Gertrude, for example, to a St. Francis de Sales, it became public especially through the work of St. John Eudes and St. Margaret Mary Alacoque. The Holy See solemnly approved it by instituting a feast for Poland (in 1765), later extending it to the universal Church in 1856 under Pius IX. This devotion and cult have been, in the seventeenth century and thereafter, like a response of Catholic faith and piety to the Jansenist movement which tended to narrow the universal extension of the redemptive love or to disavow its depth.

The purpose of the cult is to honor, under the figure of his fleshly heart, the redeeming love of our Lord Jesus Christ, and, more especially, his love for man which impelled him to spend himself and sacrifice himself for their salvation. . . .

Thus the cult of the Sacred Heart of Jesus proposes, in a way accessible to all, the fundamental mystery of our

---

[9] *Treatise on the Love of God,* book IX, chap. 5. For St. John of the Cross, cf. *The Ascent of Mount Carmel,* book II, chap. 6, trans. E. Allison Peers (Westminster: Newman, 1945), I, 84.

[10] Various works have contributed to the defense of the doctrine which we have just presented in opposition to the misleading ideas referred to above: F. Prat, *The Theology of Saint Paul,* II, 180–213; J. Rivière, *Le dogme de la rédemption, Etude théologique,* pp. 227–261 and 576–577; G. Jouassard, *L'abandon du Christ par son Père durant sa Passion d'après la tradition patristique et les Docteurs du XIIIe siècle* (thesis of the Theology Faculty at Lyons, 1923, unpublished except for the chapters which appeared in periodicals . . .); R.T.A. Murphy, O.P., has repeated the subject of the thesis which he prepared at the Angelicum, *The Dereliction of Christ on the Cross* (Washington, 1940) and concerning which one may consult P. Benoit, Rev. Bib. LIV (1947), 301–303; S. Lyonnet, *Theologica biblica Novi Testamenti, De Peccato et Redemptione* (Rome, 1956 [reprinted under the title *Quaestiones de Soteriologia N.T.*]), Appendix, "Expiatio penalis," pp. 250–264; L. Mahieu, "L'abandon du Christ sur la croix," *MSR* (Lille), II (1945), 209–242; Philippe de la Trinité, "Dieu de colère ou Dieu de l'amour," in *Amour et Violence* (=*Et. Carmél.,* 1946, pp. 105–128). These works contain numerous exaggerations which sound exegesis and sound theology should have cast aside for good.

faith: the mystery of the love of God, love which the Father shows by giving his Son in the redemptive incarnation and which Christ himself prolongs by handing himself over to the death of the cross for us and by giving himself to us in the Eucharist in order to share with us his sacrifice and his life. . . .

Note: This treatment of the redemption in the successive stages of Tradition did not dwell on the Eastern witnesses after the patristic period. Our information in this field is rather limited. Furthermore, it does not seem that the development of its ideas were stated as clearly as in the West. The living tradition of the liturgy kept alive the meaning of the mystery of the redemption in its rich complexity, without that kind of clarity, which St. Anselm's synthesis effected among the Latins. Since the nineteenth century, however, attempts at a more systematic formulation have appeared, either as a reaction against the "juridicism" of St. Anselm or because of certain Platonic or Neoplatonic tendencies of Oriental orthodoxy (*sophiology*). The influence of classical Protestantism (*kenotism*) and at times even liberal Protestantism on Russian theology has not been negligible in this respect. For a preliminary examination, the reader may refer to J. Rivière, *Le dogme de la Rédemption dans la théologie contemporaine* (pp. 78–96, where various works are reviewed), to the Russian theologian S. Boulgakof, *Du Verbe Incarné* (Paris: Aubier, 1943), pp. 269–346 and *passim*, and to P. Henry, S.J., "Kénose," in *DBS*, col. 142–156.

3. H. N. Oxenham[1] examines the doctrine of the Atonement in some controversial Catholic authors of the seventeenth and eighteenth centuries. He maintains that Malebranche represents in this point what he considers to be the Patristic and Catholic tradition, while Arnauld adopted the Thomist viewpoint. Gunther in Germany also rejected the juristic view of vicarious satisfaction, siding with the Scotist approach. The primary object of the Incarnation is for him the infusion of divine life in man.

The Atonement did not . . . become a subject of direct controversy at the Reformation, nor has it, except in some few instances in Germany to be noticed presently, been distinctively handled by later Catholic theologians. For the most part they either follow the patristic method, as Thomassin and Petavius, or, more generally, the Scholastic, adopting either the Thomist or Scotist system under various modifications. Among Thomists may be reckoned Suárez, Vasquez, Gregory de Valentia, Dominic à Soto, and Tournely; among Scotists, Medina, De Lugo, Frassen, and Henno. All alike introduce the doctrine as falling under that of the Incarnation. Petavius, out of sixteen books on the Incarnation, devotes one chapter only to the satisfaction and three to the priesthood of Christ. Thomassin gives half of one book to His satisfaction and the whole of the next to His

[1] Henry Nutcombe Oxenham, Late Scholar of Balliol College, Oxford, is the author of *The Catholic Doctrine of the Atonement* (London: W. H. Allen Co., 1895). This excerpt is taken from pp. 271–289.

priesthood, which, however, includes an exposition of the doctrine of the Eucharist . . . One or two specimens shall be given both of the scientific and devotional treatment of the subject during the seventeenth and eighteenth centuries; and, as the Parisian Sorbonne was at that time the great theological school of the Church, they shall be taken from the works of . . . its professors.

And first we may notice a famous controversy carried on in France between two of the most distinguished writers of the seventeenth century. Among the many questions, philosophical and theological, on which Malebranche and Arnauld were opposed to each other, one was that . . . on the motive of the Incarnation.[2] In his *Treatise on Nature and Grace,* the great Oratorian maintains that Jesus Christ, though His birth among men occurred in the fullness of time, is, in the eternal counsels, the Beginning of the ways of God, the Firstborn of all creation, and the predestined Model whereon our humanity was formed after the image of His. The Word and Wisdom of God, foreseeing among all possible creatures none other that was worthy, offered Himself, to establish as Sovereign Priest an everlasting worship in honor of His Father and to present a victim deserving of His acceptance. The world was created for the sake of the Church, that is of Christ who is its Head, and man was formed after the image of Christ to be the ornament of this visible temple. So far Malebranche said no more than had often been said before him. But he goes on to observe, that it was requisite for the fulfillment of this design that man should be subject on earth not only to trials and afflictions, but to the movements of concupiscence, in order to illustrate the victories of grace; and that the sin of the first man was *necessary,* because for making the elect merit that glory which shall be one day theirs, no means could be comparable to leaving them for a while immersed in sin (*de les laisser tous envelopper dans le pêche, pour leur faire à tous miséricorde en Jésus Christ*), inasmuch as the glory they acquire by resisting concupiscence through the grace of Christ is greater than any other. This need not, and perhaps did not mean more than St. Paul's statement, that God has concluded all under sin, or in unbelief, that He may have mercy upon all;[3] or than the somewhat poetical exclamation of the Roman ritual, *O certe necessarium Adae peccatum quod Christi morte deletum est.* Indeed Malebranche seems to have moulded his language on such expressions as these. Still he certainly laid himself open to the retort, which was actually made, that on this theory the Fall was not simply permitted but predestined by God, and that "humanity was sacrificed for Christ, not Christ for humanity." Arnauld, however, by no means contented himself with objecting to this part of his opponent's system. He appealed to the authority of Aquinas—which is of course on his side—against the Scotist idea of the Incarnation, as independent of the Fall; and, with less prudence, asserted in reliance on Thomassin—what is unques-

[2] See Malebranche, *Traité de la Nature et de la Grace;* Arnauld replied in his *Réflexions Philosophiques et Théologiques.*

[3] Rom 11: 32; Gal 3: 22.

tionably incorrect—that the Fathers are unanimous in making the decree of the Incarnation depend on the prevision of sin. It was not to be expected that theologians, whose characteristic principle it was to grudge the universality of redemption, should appreciate what must have appeared to them the very superfluous charity of assuming a nature which did not need to be redeemed. And Arnauld, highly as we may and must respect him as a man and a writer, was, unhappily, deeply imbued with the theological idiosyncracies of his school. He seems on some points to have had the better of his antagonist . . . But, on the whole, we may fairly consider Malebranche as representing in this dispute the patristic and Catholic tradition, while the great champion of Jansenism, like the Lutherans and Calvinists before him, adopts the narrower system which had found favor with some of the Schoolmen . . .

One later specimen shall be adduced, also from a professor of the Sorbonne, of the theological treatment of the subject.[4] Robbe, the author of a *Treatise on the Mystery of the Incarnate Word,* after successively repudiating Wicliffe's notion of an absolute *à priori* necessity for the Incarnation, Raymund Lully's of a necessity assuming the Fall, and that of the Calvinists (borrowed from St. Anselm) of a necessity assuming the restoration of fallen man, decides, against Scotus, that it was necessary for *condign* satisfaction, because no other could be equivalent or *ex alias indebitis.* He adds, against the Socinians, that it was a true and proper satisfaction. Nor was it only sufficient but superabundant. Any act of Christ, or any single drop of His Blood, would have been *sufficient* for our redemption, from the dignity of His Person, but not *efficient* unless He had so designed it. The sacrifice was really offered *ad alterum,* because offered to the whole Trinity. The author further argues, against Vasquez, Medina, and others, that it was *ex propriis* and *ex alias indebitis,* because acts belong to the person, not the nature of the agent. Under this last head the question is asked, whether the satisfaction of Christ required any agreement on God's part to accept it, or whether He was bound as a matter of justice to do so? The necessity of an agreement is denied by St. Bonaventure, Scotus, and others (among whom must be reckoned Tournely), but affirmed by Suárez, whose opinion Robbe adopts, considering it clear from Scripture (Heb. 10) that there was in fact such an agreement, and thinking further that it was requisite, because the offending parties might have been fairly called on to make satisfaction themselves. Christ was our Head by arrangement (*pacto*) and not, like the first Adam, by nature. He satisfied in strict justice, inasmuch as His satisfaction was adequate and more than adequate, but to accept it for us was a matter not of justice but of mercy.

And now let us take [an] example from the same century, of the hortatory and devotional rather than scientific treatment of the subject, which for that very reason will be in one sense a surer test of the habitual manner of looking at it. [It] will be found, like the theological treatises of Petavius and Thomassin, to bear out the remark . . . that, while the scholastic formula of satisfaction was retained

[4] *Tractatus de Mysterio Verbi Incarnati,* auctore J. M. Robbe. Parisiis, 1762.

as one method of expressing the mystery of atonement, the idea of sacrifice was that most predominant in Catholic teaching and devotion.

In illustration of this we may refer, in the first place, to a *Treatise on the Priesthood and Sacrifice of Jesus Christ,* in four books, by Leonard de Massiot, a French Benedictine of the learned Congregation of St. Maur.[5] The author begins by tracing out the idea and obligation of sacrifice, as the supreme act of homage to God, and as including, since the introduction of sin into the world, an additional character of reparation; and shows how both the interior and exterior sacrifice are most perfectly realized in Christ. The second book deals with the sacrifice and priesthood of Christ, in its unity, perpetuity, and continuation in the Eucharist. The whole mystical Body is offered with Him on the Cross, which is the common altar of all mankind. In the third book the effects of His sacrifices are considered, under the classification of satisfaction, merit, overcoming the power of sin and Satan, and confounding pride by humility. The last half of the book is occupied with the treatment of the Eucharist, as an abiding memorial of the benefits wrought by Christ, a sacrifice of praise and thanksgiving, a mystery of unity, a sign of the union of the faithful, and a mystery of faith. The fourth book, which is much the longest, continues in detail the consideration of the priesthood of Christ, as communicated to His Church in the Eucharist. To return to the chapter on satisfaction, the writer relies chiefly on St. Anselm's argument for the impossibility of man making satisfaction for himself, and on Aquinas for the sufficiency of that wrought by Christ, as giving to God something more pleasing than what He had lost by sin, owing to the charity with which Christ endured the pains of His passion, the excellence of His life, and the dignity of His Person. His voluntary temporal death, it is added, was of far greater value than our eternal death could be. Our personal satisfactions are not superseded by His, but must be united with it. . . .

It will at once be seen that with these writers—and they are but a specimen of many more—the dominant idea, as with the Fathers, is that of Sacrifice, which comprehends more than the notions of satisfaction only, or of the payment of a debt. It includes and exhausts them, but it includes a great deal more. We may further observe that this idea is habitually viewed in connection with its perpetuation in the Eucharist. . . .

And here it will be well to give some notice of German Catholics . . . stepping into the place occupied before the French Revolution by the doctors of the Sorbonne. . . .

We cannot pass over in silence . . . Günther. With his philosophical system, which is said to be very obscurely expressed, I have no acquaintance, nor indeed is this the place for examining it. The following is the simplest account I can give of his theory of the Atonement.[6] . . . Günther's system implies, if I understand him rightly, the Scotist idea of the Incarnation being decreed before the prevision of the Fall. Its primary object is the infusion

[5] *Traité du Sacerdoce et du Sacrifice de Jésus Christ.* Par L. de Massiot. (Poitiers, 1708.)

[6] Günther, *Die Incarnationstheorie.* (Wien, 1829.) His Philosophical Works were placed on the Roman Index.

of divine life into man, or his regeneration to eternal life. The death of Christ is "not the moving but the mediating cause" of redemption; or, in other words, God is not gracious to us because Christ died, but Christ died for us because God is gracious. The juristic view of vicarious satisfaction is rejected, on the ground that justice requires the punishment of the guilty, and can least of all be satisfied by the supreme injustice of punishing the innocent instead. That would be a direct contradiction. Some other explanation must therefore be found for the Sacrifice of the death of Christ. God will only forgive sin to those who are willing to be reformed; but for this man needs practical proclamation of the heinousness of sin, which is given, as in a picture, by the death of Christ. But the ground of sin lies not only in ignorance or unbelief, but in the infirmity of a perverted will, and the work of redemption, therefore, must be something beyond a mere outward exhibition; it must consist in the real communication and implanting of a new nature, to reunite the soul with God. The redeeming power must, then, be sought in the *life* of Christ, but it can only be imparted through His death. The Son of God took, in His Incarnation, a human body under the conditions of fallen nature transmitted from Adam though without sin. This body of death He offered up to God, pouring out the earthly blood and animal soul or life;[7] and thus He satisfied justice and opened the hands of love. The necessity for His death does not rest on any attribute of the Divine nature, for God is Love, but on some quality of human nature, which as yet we cannot fully comprehend, but which is indicated by the statement of Scripture, that "without shedding of blood there is no remission," for the soul is in the blood and the blood is that which atones for the soul. It is clear that this theory lays a special stress on the Incarnation, and views the death of Christ chiefly as a channel for conveying the benefits of the Incarnation to us, but the precise meaning of the latter portion of it I do not profess to understand. . . .

4. I. Tubaldo[1] reexamines the Christology of Rosmini, a nineteenth century Italian philosopher and theologian. After reviewing his basic philosophical concepts and theorizing on what he calls the Rosminian twofold effect action of the Word in the Incarnation, he questions the accusation that Rosmini be either Monophysist or Nestorian in his thinking. He recognizes that there are difficulties and obscurities in Rosmini's thought, yet there remains the possibility of positive hypotheses regarding his Christological doctrine.

Rosmini is not an unknown personality today. His philosophical thought has been the subject of many studies. As a result many prejudices about him have been debarred, and many erroneous views have been dispelled.

---

[7] This may remind the reader of some similar expressions of Origen's.

[1] This excerpt is taken from *La Dottrina Cristologica di Antonio Rosmini,* the Doctoral Dissertation of Ignio Tubaldo (Milano: S.A.L.E. "Sodalitas," Domodossola, 1954), selectively, from pp. 5–6, 188–189, 166–172.

But while his philosophy is nowadays more objectively known and more calmly evaluated, his theology remains obscure, difficult as it might be to distinguish in him the philosopher from the theologian. This distinction is particularly difficult regarding his Christological thought. . . .

The Incarnation of the Word does not occupy a marginal place in his system. Christ is for him not only life of the soul, but also soul of thought. Redemption is not only a rebirth in God, but also a rebirth in the world. It is a revaluation of the things created by God, hence a renewal and a new direction of thought. God and wisdom and Christ the philosopher is the binomial raised by the Incarnation.

The student of Rosmini has before him . . . the task of examining deeply and calmly his entire thought . . . These considerations have guided us and given us the key and method of investigation. We have reviewed the philosophy of Rosmini, especially those concepts which directly touch upon the subject of our consideration, namely, the concepts of man, soul, faculty and person. This is the only way to do justice to his Christological thought. There are several studies on the subject, the most recent being D. Biancardi's publication: *La Personalita dogmatica di Cristo nelle opere di A. Rosmini* (Mantua, 1942). Biancardi's conclusion that Rosmini's thought was in the line of Monophysism was startling. It is for this reason that we have undertaken a reexamination of the issue. It is both impossible and unfair to discuss Rosmini's doctrine of the Incarnation only on the basis of its controversial aspects, limiting oneself to the examination of his Christological proposition condemned by the Holy Office (Proposition 27). The Christological doctrine of Rosmini is not limited to that. It has a much greater ambit and life. . . .

An unprejudiced study of his work will prove constructive, even if it does not dispell all the shadows present in his Christological thought. One of the reasons for this obscurity is the fact that Rosmini never treated *ex professo* the subject of the hypostatic union. He dealt with it only in an accidental manner . . .

A deeper examination of some of his philosophical concepts, bearing importance on the subject of our investigation, throws new light on elements unrecognized by previous research. This is particularly true regarding his concept of faculty, and particularly of will as nature, and his concept of the supremacy of the will.

The Rosminian philosophical concept of person is understandable and meaningful only when considered in connection with the concept of soul as a feeling or a radical activity and not in connection with the concept of consciousness. This proves how uninformed and inconsistent is the parallelism of the names Rosmini-Gunther, which is so much in vogue.

Person is conceived as activity, but as activity which is essential to the soul and to man as a subject. It is activity which emanates from the will, with this understood as nature and not merely as faculty. This activity, therefore, cannot be understood in terms of actual operation or *actus secundus* of the scholastics, but as the intrinsic and ontological constituent of man as a subject.

The concept of person is by no means a marginal element in the Rosminian system, but an integral and harmonious one. It is associated with the concept of the soul and it is explained exclusively in connection with it.

The Word by becoming Incarnate became the person of Christ. Rosmini's statement regarding *the fact* of the Incarnation has never been questioned. Questions arise with his explanation of *the way* in which the hypostatic union occurred.

The conclusion, drastic as it might be, that the union consists in a dynamic link, does not exclude the possibility of other hypotheses. The reason for this lies precisely in the very fact that Rosmini's Christology is not incomplete.

The opinion that Rosmini thought in terms of a double effect causality of the Word in the Incarnation has not been explored before. It guided us in our study. . . .

Rosmini's thought proceeds in the following manner. The Word became incarnate, through the work of the Holy Spirit by producing a twofold effect, the sanctification of the human nature and the union of the two natures. The first effect consists of a rapture by the Holy Spirit and an objective communication of the Word. This renders possible the second effect . . .

The first effect . . . is stated by Rosmini in the first half of the condemned proposition which reads: "the human will was completely enraptured by the Holy Spirit to adhere to the objective Being (*esse*), that is to the Word." With these words Rosmini describes the first logical moment of the Incarnation. He is not yet speaking of the Incarnation proper, but only of the preamble to it. The expression "adherence of the human will to the objective Being" cannot be understood as a more or less explicit affirmation of Nestorianism (with its mere moral union of natures), since Rosmini is not yet speaking about the union itself, that is about the second effect. He is talking about the first effect, that is, about the sanctification of the human will, . . . the adherence to the Word as to an object, not as to a subject . . .

What is important and difficult to understand in Rosmini's thought is the second effect. . . . The hypostatic union consists precisely, if not exclusively, in the second effect: *misit in mundum,* that is, in the mission of the Word into the predestined human individual. It is helpful to keep in mind the main passage in which Rosmini explains how the mission of the Word to a human nature took place. The passage occurs in his Introduction and Commentary to the Gospel of St. John . . . "So that it (*the will*) gave completely to Him, control of the man, and the Word personally took this control, thus becoming Incarnate. . . . Hence the human will ceases to be personal in the man. This will is person in other men. In Christ it remains nature." . . . It was from this passage that Proposition 27 was excerpted. We interpret this text in the following manner. . . . It states how the Incarnation as such took place after the sanctification of humanity. It expresses the manner in which the Word became the supreme active principle and therefore, person in Christ (this was the second effect) . . .

That the second effect occurs through the mediacy of the first is easily shown by the form in which Rosmini expresses himself. The Holy Spirit, he says, enraptures totally the human will, making it so adhere to the objective *esse* that it would be logical that a totally sanctified will would be totally possessed by the same Word . . . The first effect sanctifies the will; the second one puts the human will under the influence of the Word.

Does the Incarnation consist only in "the placing of the human will under the influence of the Word?"

Human personality consists in the will in as much as this stands for the activity or dynamism of the subject, and in as much as it remains independent, that is supreme. Since we find in Christ a human will, not annihilated, but simply dependent from the Word (for the Word assumed its control), this will ceases to be itself the constitutive of the person. . . .

These Rosminian expressions may lend strong credence to the opinion that in Christ the human will is not a person simply because it depends on the Word, and that, therefore, the hypostatic union consists only in the fact that the human will is under the influence of the Word. According to this the link uniting the two natures is a mere dynamic link, insufficient to establish a real union.

However, to rest with this conclusion (we wanted to see how far a conclusion could be stretched) would be, in our estimation, superficial and never final.

It is quite certain that in Rosmini's thought the first effect brings about sanctification (and predestination) of the human nature. It is also certain that the second effect brings about the hypostatic union (*misit in mundum*). But is it so certain that for Rosmini the second effect consists only in having the human nature depend on the Word? Could it not be that this dependence is an effect of the union itself? A more penetrating study does not exclude the possibility of this interpretation. . . .

The true problem consists, therefore, in finding out if in Rosmini's thought the Word becomes the supreme principle of activity only because it moves and directs his human nature, or because of a prior effect. . . .

IX

CHRIST IN ORTHODOX CHRISTOLOGY

1. M. Jugie[1] discusses various positions taken by Byzantine theologians regarding the hypostatic union, after the schism of 1054. Some of these seemed to have favored a Monophysite view, while others took a position close to Nestorianism. Both alternatives were condemned by synods. Another major debate in the twelfth century centered upon the interpretation of Christ's words "the Father is greater than I." All the interpretations were free of heresy and the condemnation of some of them was done only for political reasons.

Since the final split of 1054 there has been no controversy between East and West regarding the doctrine of the Incarnation. There have been, however, differences of opinion among the Orthodox theologians themselves on the issue of the union of the two natures in the Word.

[1] Martin Jugie is a well known French expert in Orthodox theology. Born in 1878 he has taught at the Pontifical Oriental Institute in Rome, at the Institut Catholique de Lyons, at the Lateran University and at the Propaganda Fide College in Rome. He is the author of many works: *Nestorius, Oeuvres Complètes de Georges Scholarios, De Processione Spiritus Sancti, Histoire du canon de l'Ancien Testament dans l'Eglise greque et l'Eglise russe,* etc. It is from his book *Theologia Dogmatica Christianorum Orientalium,* v. II (Paris, 1933) that this excerpt has been taken from pp. 651–657.

The doctrinal debates at the end of the eleventh and throughout the twelfth centuries touched more or less directly upon the hypostatic union.

The first issue was raised by John of Italy, the Philosopher. It dealt with the manner in which human nature assumed by Christ was understood to have been deified, whether truly in itself or merely on account of its closeness to the Word, by its adoption. We do not know exactly what position was taken by John or how he explained the whole problem.[2] His followers split into the two alternatives mentioned above.

The first alternative was defended by a certain monk, named Nilus who persuaded many Armenians of Constantinople to follow his erroneous views. We do not know what the precise nature of his teachings was. However, from the scarce information provided in Anna Comnena's *Alexias,* we are able to see that his language and expressions reflect traces of Monophysitism and even Eutychianism.[3]

The other alternative was defended by Eustratius, metropolitan of Nicaea, who left for us some explanation of his views. In the course of his debate with the Armenians regarding the two natures in Christ his effort to emphasize the distinction between divinity and humanity, seems to have led him close to Nestorianism. He taught:

1. The human nature in Christ is always, and necessarily, and essentially in a condition of servitude, and it adores like a servant the inaccessible divinity, ministering to it in its actions, addressing and readdressing itself to its creator.

2. The same nature was subject to progress and moral growth, and it was not endowed with perfection from the beginning.

3. It was on account of his union with the Word in one person, that the man in Jesus, a servant according to his nature, was given to be a son and heir. This has also been granted to others, although not in the same manner, since he alone subsists in the Word, and alone was made his inseparable temple, holy and immaculate and truly worthy of God.

4. The man in Christ deserves indeed praise in as much as, having a nature capable of sin, he abstained from malice and remained in purity.[4]

Eustratius did not make public the proceedings of two debates with the Armenians in which the above views were expressed. Somehow, however, they became known and he was accused of heresy in 1117. He had to appear before a synod, at which he submitted by condemning and rejecting all dubious propositions. The rejection of the following ones is worth noting: "If anyone would say that

[2] John of Italy was condemned at a synod held in Constantinople in 1082. The acts of this synod have been published by Th. Uspenskii in *Izviestia Instituti archeologici russici Constantinopolitani,* II (1897), pp. 30–66.

[3] *Alexias,* 1, X, P.G., CXXXI, cols. 697–700. Anna accuses Nilus of ignorance regarding the nature of the hypostatic union, but she fails to give any details about his position. The *Synodicum* is silent about him . . . From this we argue that his error consisted more in poor choice of language than in content. He was condemned at a synod under Nicholas III Gramaticus shortly after the synod against John the Italian, c. 1086. Cf. Th. Uspenskii, "Bogoslovskoe i pholosophskoe dvigenie v Vizantii XI i XII viekov," in *Jurnal ministertsva narodnago prosviechtcheniia,* CCLXXVII (1891), St. Petersburg, pp. 145–47.

[4] Cf. the edition of A. Demetracopulo *Ecclesiastical Library,* pp. 11–15, and *Athenian,* IV (1873), pp. 227–233. Cf. also *cod. Dionys. Anthon. 120,* fol. 705–707.

that which was assumed was merely the High Priest and not simply Christ, let him be anathema." "If anyone would divide Christ, who is One after the union, segregating on one side God the Word, and on the other side that which was assumed, and does not glorify this One with the same glory and dignity, on account of the hypostatic union, as only one son after the Incarnation, let him be discarded from the adoption of sons, promised by the Savior." "If anyone would say that the assumed nature was perfected and purged and deified progressively, and not at the moment of the union, a union by which the Word of God subsists in it, let him not share the union of God!" "If any one would call servant the one who freed us from servitude, and would not believe that He was made indeed according to the form of servant, but now is not a servant, inasmuch as we obtained freedom through Him . . . let that one lose that freedom for which our Lord suffered to be called servant."[5]

From all this we can understand the sense in which the followers of John of Italy understood the proposition: *the humanity of Christ was deified by its position.* . . . If not intentionally, at least in manner of expression, they appear to lean toward a Nestorian or Adoptionist view, thus departing from the common teaching of Byzantine doctrine as understood by John of Damascus and other Greek Fathers.

Regarding the title "servant" *doulos* attributed to Christ, the Damascene had already discussed it and rejected it because it was suggestive of Nestorianism.[6] Other Byzantine authors after him also discussed the title, especially Gennadius Scholarius, whose position was similar to that of John of Damascus.[7]

In 1156 a new debate was provoked by Soterichus Panteugenus, a deacon from Constantinople, elected patriarch of Antioch. He, fearful of Nestorianism, would not endorse the idea that the Incarnate Word, as man, would offer unto Himself, as God, the sacrifice of the cross. He maintained that this sacrifice was offered by the Incarnate Word to the Father and to the Holy Spirit, or to the Father alone. This question with other issues regarding the reality of the sacrifice of the Mass was discussed and judged at two synods held in 1156 and 1158. The decision was found in the very words of St. Basil's liturgy *You who are offering and are offered and are received.*

The doctrine of the mystery of the Incarnation was also indirectly touched upon in the debate of 1166 on the meaning of Christ's words in the Gospel: *the Father is greater than I* (John 14:26). There were several interpretations, each claiming the authority of the Fathers: 1) Some maintained that the Father was said to be greater than the Son because He is the principle of the Son. 2) The Emperor, Manuel I Comnenus, and with him almost all the bishops, preferred to say that the Son is inferior to the Father in as much as He is a man, with all human attributes includ-

[5] *Ibid.* Nicetas Seides wrote a polemic dissertation against the novelty of Eustratius dedicated to Alex Comnenus. This dissertation has been preserved in the *Codex Atheniensis* 483. Cf. Th. Upsenskii, *op. cit.*, pp. 147–152. The error of Eustratius was recorded in the *Synodicum* under two anathematisms. His name, however, was withheld . . .

[6] *De Fide Orthodoxa,* 1, III, ch. XXI, P.G., CXIV, c. 1085.

[7] *Oeuvres completes,* III, pp. 363–368.

ing non-sinful passions. 3) Others saw the inferiority of the Son, not so much from the viewpoint of his humanity as from the humiliation of the Word by which he did not hesitate to become man and hide his majesty. 4) Others still suggested a more subtle explanation, saying that when Christ made that statement, he made a certain mental restriction considering his human nature as it is in itself, abstracting from the hypostatic union. St. John Damascene had said something similar in his *De Fide Orthodoxa:* "What we say about ignorance can be equally said about servitude regarding the flesh of Christ, if not united to the Word of God, that is, if, by precisions and subtle considerations, we separate that which is created from that which is uncreated. But since it is irrevocably united in a hypostatic manner, in what sense can it be servant?"[8] 5) Others, finally, and also in the footsteps of the Damascene, interpreted Christ's words in the sense that He is the head of the mystical body, the mediator who takes our place. According to St. John of Damascus, Christ ascribed to himself certain roles, on account of a particular extrinsic appropriation intended by God, which he calls *prosopic* (impersonating), inasmuch as he took our place and substituted for us.[9]

Out of these five interpretations, the synod of Constantinople of 1166 approved only the first two, giving preference to the second one. The other three were rejected under anathema.[10] A new synod, held in 1170, condemned and excommunicated Constantine, the metropolitan of Corcyre, and John Irenikus, a monk. Both had continued to defend the fourth interpretation. Their names were recorded under those anathematized in the *Synodicum* of Orthodoxy. . . .

It seems that the above mentioned synods rejected and condemned the last three interpretations, not so much out of conviction as to please Manuel, the Emperor. There is nothing truly heretical in them, regardless of judgment on their intrinsic probability. It is no wonder, therefore, if later theologians such as Michael IV Autorianus, Ecumenical Patriarch (1207–1214), wanted to rectify the issue, removing the anathemas from the *Synodicum.*[11] This, however, did not come to pass. . . .

---

[8] *De Fide Orthodoxa,* 1, III, ch. XXI, CXIV, c. 1085 B.

[9] *Ibid.,* cc. 1092–1093; 1, IV, ch. XVIII, cc. 1185–1189.

[10] Cf. John Cinnamus, *Historiarum,* 1, VI, ii, P.G., CXXXIII, cc. 616–624, who maintains that Demetrius from Lamp, a village in Asia, was responsible for the controversy; Nicetas Acominatus, *Treasure of Orthodoxy,* v, XXXV, excerpts of which have been published by A. Mai, *Scriptorum Veterum Nova Collectio,* IV, pp. 1–96, P.G., CXL, cc. 201–282 . . . ; L. Petit, "Documents inedits sur le concile de 1166 et ses derniers adversaires," in Vizantiiskii Vremennik, XI (1904), nn. 3–4 . . . ; Manuel Comnenus, *Edictum de Controversia, quatenus Pater major Christo sit,* P.G. CXXXIII, cc. 773–786 where the different views are clearly discussed; Th. Uspenskii in *Jurnal ministertsva,* CCLXXXVII, pp. 304–315, and in *Ocerki po istorii vizant. obrazovannosti,* (St. Petersburg, 1891), pp. 236–243; . . . Michael Glykam, *Chapters on the Difficulties of Sacred Scripture,* II, ch. LXXIX, pp. 275–315; . . . V. Grumel "Le Napisanie o pravej vêrê de Constantin le Philosophe," in *Echos d'Orient,* XXVIII (1929), pp. 183–294.

[11] Cf. A. Heisenberg, *Neue Quellen zur Geschichte des lateinischen Kaisertums und der Kirchenunion. III. Der Dericht des Nikolaos Mesarites über die politischen und Kirchlichen. Ereignisse des Jahres 1214,* (Munich, 1923) (*Sitzungsber. der bayer. Akad. der Wissensch. Philos. philol. und hist. Klasse,* 3 Abhand.), pp. 11—19.

2. F. Gavin[1] examines the views of four recent Greek Orthodox theologians concerning the motive of the Incarnation, and sees two of them, those of Rhôsse and Kephala, leaning towards the Scotist position, while those of Mesolora and Androutsos prefer the Thomist approach. He points out how the Greek theologians distinguish two meanings of Redemption: an objective one, as a deliverance of fallen man from sin, and a subjective one, as the personal appropriation of this achievement by the individual, through the Holy Spirit.

The Causes and Purpose of the Incarnation. It is clear that Rhôsse's definitions of Christianity as a "mutual relationship of fellowship between God and man, the result of Divine energy and as well of human receptivity and co-operation,"[2] and of Christian Dogma, as "the teachings of the Christian Faith concerning the operations of God," as well as his whole treatment of the subject of Revelation, would suggest his alignment on the Scotist side in the questions concerning the Incarnation. "The possibility and necessity of the Incarnation of the Word of God," he says, "lies both in the right concept of God held in general by Theism, according to which God is not only the transcendent Being, but as well the immanent Being, possessing both absolute and relative attributes, and also lies in the nature and aim (skopos) of man, created according to the image of God, that in mutual fellowship with Him man might become like Him and finally achieve entire perfection. This perfection of man is bound up with the perfecting of religion, and the necessity of perfecting religion involves necessarily the Incarnation of which there would be not only a perfect imparting of divine truth, power, and life, but also a perfect human vehicle to receive this imparted (divine truth, power, and life). . . . Hence the Incarnation of the Word would have been necessary for the perfection of man even without (man's) sin. Still more did it become necessary because of the fact of sin, since man did slip into sin by the wrong use of his reason and free will. So because of this sin of the human race Divine Revelation in religion (that is, the Incarnation) attains its destined end, the perfection of man, not directly, but by the Redemption of man from sin. Hence the Divine Revelation, before leading man on to perfection, has first to redeem him from sin by means of the Incarnation of the Word by whom the world and man were created, and by whom man's perfection is achieved. Hence the idea of the God-man and its actualization in the Word of God in that Person in the historic person of Jesus Christ is at once the Miracle and the loftiest miracle. But it is not in opposition to the human mind in its healthy state, but is rather demanded by it as necessary

[1] Rev. Frank Gavin was professor of ecclesiastical history at the General Theological Seminary of New York. It is from his book, *Some Aspects of Contemporary Greek Orthodox Thought* (Milwaukee: Morehouse Publishing Co., and London: A. R. Mowbray, 1923) that this excerpt has been taken from pp. 172–177 and 201–202.

[2] *Dogmatikē,* p. 21.

for man's perfection."[3] By this Rhôsse means that the Incarnation would have taken place in any case, but the fact of sin determined some of the conditions by which its purpose would be achieved. Man in his "healthy state" still required the completion of his nature and capacities by the Incarnation; far more in his state of sin did he require it.

Kephala leans rather to the Scotist side in his interpretation of the Incarnation, though not in such a complete and thorough way as does Rhôsse. "The coming of a Savior and Redeemer was the common expectation of all peoples," Jews as well as Gentiles.[4] His coming "appears absolutely necessary . . . to stabilize the shaken hopes of people, to inspire religious reverence, to fill the void in men's hearts, to satisfy the longings of the spirit, to quicken political and moral life, and to reform and regenerate man corrupted by sin."[5] Kephala is not absolutely Scotist in his treatment of the causes and purpose of the Incarnation, as is seen in the quotation above, yet his emphasis on the work of our Lord as completing and fulfilling human needs,[6] his list of the characteristic notes of the Savior's character and work,[7] his enumeration of the objects and purposes of the Incarnation,[8] are all consistent with a Scotist point of view. Revelation "is necessary . . . because of the conditions into which the human race had fallen, with man's spiritual faculties darkened and his highest destiny forgotten. Through Revelation God leads the race into the way of truth and lifts it from its prostrate condition."[9] Our Lord's work was "to give eternal life to those who believed in Him, and to teach them to know and worship in spirit and in truth the one true God, and Jesus Christ whom He had sent."[10] Since "man without knowledge of God is an incomprehensible mystery, without fellowship with Him something inexplicable[11] . . . (for God made man for the purpose of constituting him a sharer in His own Goodness and blessedness),[12] . . . He sent His Son to turn man from the folly of his way, to lead him to his heavenly Father, and teach him his destiny on earth."[13] He sums up our Lord's purpose in the words: "The mission of the Savior was the glory of God—by making known the true God, whom mankind because

---

[3] Rhôsse, *op. cit.*, pp. 465–466 . . . It will be seen that this passage is bound up with Rhôsse's whole contention as to the subject of Revelation, of which it is the conclusion. It is in line with one phase of St. Irenaeus' thought, his doctrine of the *anakephalaiōsis*. Cf. Rhôsse, *op. cit.*, p. 464 where he employs the chief text for this doctrine (Eph. 1, 10).

[4] Kephala, *Christologia*, pp. 10, 11–17; revelation to and expectation by the Gentiles, pp. 17–21.

[5] *Ibid.*, p. 23.

[6] "Since the desire of eternal life is innate, it is true," *ibid.*, p. 29, and in Jesus this desire had its satisfaction and fulfilment (*ibid.*, pp. 32–34).

[7] E.g., His divine character, words, deeds fulfilment of prophesies, miracles; submission to Him of angels, men, and nature; His Church, the results of Faith, etc. (*ibid.*, pp. 34–37).

[8] He came "to save man from ignorance, doubt, despair, hatred," etc. (*ibid.*, p. 37).

[9] *Ibid.*, p. 129.

[10] *Ibid.*, p. 175.

[11] *Ibid.*, p. 176.

[12] *Ibid.*, p. 177.

[13] *Ibid.*

of sin had forgotten, and by turning man from the folly of his way."[14] Kephala seems then to waver between the Scotist and Thomist theories, but his greatest emphasis seems to be on our Lord as the complement and fulfillment of man's needs and aspirations, and as the complete Revelation supplanting and fulfilling that which had gone before. He does not deal directly with the question whether or not God the Son would have become Incarnate had not man sinned, but the implication drawn from the general tenor of his thought, is that Kephala is more Scotist than Thomist.

Mesolora is more explicitly Thomist in his treatment of the subject.[15] "Man, as a rational creature endowed with free will, has been and is under a special providence of God[16] who does not desire the death of a sinner—for the first parents did not fall of their own proper volition nor with full consciousness (of their act). Consequently . . . man did not lose completely the image of God, but there remained in him traces of good. For this reason his salvation and rehabilitation were possible . . . The way and means of reconciliation of man with God were found through the mediatorship of the Son and Word of God."[17] The appearance of the Incarnate God "was the greatest evidence of God's special providence for the salvation of man."[18] "The Old Testament describes the causes of the sin and fall of man, teaching that man could not by his own powers (alone) achieve redemption and deliverance from evil, for the recognition of which fact alone were the Law and the Prophets given, (and) to serve to prepare the way for salvation . . . It was necessary that the Eternal Word of God by whom the world was created, should take flesh in order to save the lost sheep."[19] According to Mesolora, sin was the cause of the Incarnation, the purpose of which was to save sinful mankind.

This same doctrine is clearly and definitely taught by Androutsos. "Man having fallen under the power of sin and the Devil, was unable to be saved and to have fellowship with God, but was under condemnation to destruction and eternal death. This destruction of the human race the Creator would not allow, and in His mercy, His love for men, and His kindness[20] (or by what other name His love for sinful man may be called) formed the means of deliverance from evil, and planned to send His Son into the world for the salvation of men. This plan of God was conceived before the foundation of the world, eternally . . .

[14] *Ibid.*, p. 179.

[15] He devotes pp. 199–242 of vol. III. of his *Symbolikē* to the Incarnation. His definitions (p. 204, note 1) are most valuable: the subject of Our Lord and His work may be termed "divine economy," for from it we learn that God in a divine and mysterious way arranged (*ōkonomēse*) the salvation of man; "His redemptive work may also be called "the Incarnate economy" (*ensarkon oikonomian*); Redemption "(*apolytrōsis*)" "in its wider meaning, signifies all the means which God uses to effect the removal of sin," and "Christology" . . . treats of Christ the Saviour.

[16] This passage links up with his treatment of "the Divine Providence and Governance of the world" (pp. 185–191) and "Foreknowledge and Foreordination" (pp. 192–199) immediately preceding.

[17] *Op. cit.*, III. p. 199.

[18] *Op. cit.*, III. p. 200.

[19] *Ibid.*, p. 204.

[20] Cf. Eph. 2, 4; Tit. 3, 5.

Hence it is called 'foreknowledge,' 'foreordination,' 'purpose,' 'the mystery of His Will,'[21] and the like. The conception of God as unchanging and above time demands that this will of God be eternal—in His determining the redemption of the world in Christ Jesus in His eternal aspect in relation to Creation. This will the Son and Word of God carried out, becoming Incarnate 'in the fullness of time.' "[22] . . . Androutsos goes on to say: "The cause of Incarnation of Jesus Christ is . . . the restoration (*anastasis* = "resurrection") of fallen man, to which Holy Scripture bears witness in many places,[23] . . . and which the Church describes in the words 'who for us men and for our salvation came down from Heaven.' "[24] Androutsos states the Scotist contention and says of it: "This theory has no foundation in Scripture, but has the explicit statements of weighty Fathers against it. The antithesis between the second Adam and the first in the New Testament does not show that the coming of the Savior was necessary to complete the works of creation. The words in Eph. 1, 10 take for granted the disruption of the unity of the world through sin, and in 1 Cor. 15, 43 Christ is termed 'the heavenly' (Adam) because of the Resurrection and not because of His Incarnation. Of the Fathers, St. Irenaeus[25] says: 'The Word would not have been Incarnate had it not been for the salvation of flesh'; St. Ambrose said that the *causa incarnationis* was *ut caro quae peccaverat, per se redimeretur.*[26] Rightly Augustine observed: *si homo non periisset, filius hominus non venisset.*"[27] . . .

Redemption, Atonement, and Salvation. The work of Our Lord in making atonement for man, in achieving his redemption, and propitiating the Divine Justice has, as has been shown above, a universal, complete, and final character. The Greek theologians distinguish two meanings of Redemption: objectively, it is the deliverance of fallen man from sin, and subjectively, the personal appropriation of this great achievement by the individual, through the Holy Spirit.[28] "Redemption," says Mesolora, "in its widest meaning includes the whole Revelation of God. His Providence and His particular activity directed towards the salvation of man. In general, all the works of God to the end of removing sin, from the Fall of man on, are called 'redemption,' which is, negatively, the deliverance from sin, and positively, the sanctification of man. Redemption includes three things—(a) the doctrine of Our Lord as Redeemer of the world; (b) the doctrine of His redemptive work applied to men by Grace and adoption; and (c) the doctrine of the continuity, preservation, and functioning of the Church founded by Him."[29] In another connection he says: "The Atone-

21 Eph. 1, 9, 11; 3, 9, 11; Rom. 16, 25; Col. 1, 26.
22 (Gal. 4, 4.) Androutsos, *Dogmatikē*, pp. 165–166.
23 E.g., St. John, 3, 16; 12, 47; 2 Cor. 5, 19; 1 Tim. 1, 15; St. Luke 19, 10.
24 *Op. cit.*, p. 168.
25 *Adv. Haer.*, V, 14, 1.
26 *De incarnationis dominicae sacramento,* 6, 56.
27 *Serm.* 174, 2, 2, and cf. *ibid.*, 175, 1. Androutsos, *op. cit.*, pp. 168–169 and notes.
28 Cf. Androutsos, *op. cit.*, p. 167; Mesolora, *op. cit.*, III, p. 204, note 1.
29 *Op. cit.*, III. p. 229, note 1.

ment, through the death of our Lord on the Cross, did not render sin non-existent, nor does it take away the consequences and burden of it, for this is in entire opposition to the ethical order of the universe and to the Holiness of God. Atonement and Redemption removed only the middle wall of partition separating man from God, and procured eternal life. The merit of Christ lies for us in the forgiveness of sins and union with God. This was attained objectively through the Sacrifice of the Cross; it is accomplished subjectively in each of us by his own appropriation of the Grace flowing from the Cross, and the life of faith. . . . As Christ died to sin to make satisfaction to the divine righteousness, so each man must die to sin, having the life and suffering of the Savior as his example. Only one who strives and conquers in this struggle,—through the life-giving Grace of God revealed completely in the death on the Cross of the Only Begotten Son of God, and through the exercise of his own free will coöperating with it,—is redeemed justified, sanctified, and saved. . . ."[30] In Androutsos' words: "The death of the Cross established fellowship between God and man in the sense that there was no obstacle on God's side for the rehabilitation of man, and the way of salvation and eternal life was opened up to man. But in order for man to lay hold of and make these good things his own it is necessary that God should extend to him a helping hand; man having fallen into the depth of destruction through sin cannot raise himself up. . . . He stands in need of divine assistance throughout. . . . The whole doctrine of Grace, the Church, and the Sacraments . . . is concerned with the appropriation of the redemptive work"[31] of our Lord.

3. A. Guirgis Waheeb[1] maintains that it is on account of differences in philosophy and in manner of expression that Christological variances exist between Chalcedonians and non-Chalcedonians. The Coptic Church prefers a more mystical approach to the question of the union of divinity and humanity in Christ. In line with the non-Chalcedonian view, however, it maintains, allegedly more in conformity with Scripture, "two natures before, but only one after the union." This one nature is, in this opinion, synonymous with essence, hypostasis and person. This approach, however, is not the same as that of Eutyches.

Two points might first be noted concerning our Church: It is a very conservative Church, and it is a deeply spiritual, even a mystical Church. On the whole our people have been very religious, not only since they embraced Christianity, but for many prior centuries, actually since the beginning of their civilization, before history began. Religious feeling is in-

[30] *Op. cit.*, pp. 231–232, note I.

[31] Androutsos, *op. cit.*, p. 218.

[1] A. Guirgis Waheeb is professor at the Coptic Theological Seminary of Cairo. This article, entitled "The Christology of the Coptic Church," is from the address delivered by the author at the *Evangelische Akademie.* It appeared in *Orthodoxy* (Winter of 1961), pp. 252–256.

herited in our nation, its love runs in our blood. We do not dare to change and we do not like to change. We stick to the principles of Christianity preserved in our Church. We are brought up to carefully preserve our faith and hand it on to the younger generation without any alteration, i.e., in its very early and pure form, according to our Lord's words in the Apocalypse: "That which ye have, hold fast till I come." (Rev 2:25)

Secondly, the Coptic Church is deeply spiritual, even mystical. Her spiritual leaders and thinkers had to deal with philosophy, but they hesitate to mingle philosophy with religion because it is a source of heresy and potential danger. Most of the heretics were pious men who mixed religion with their own philosophy. Philosophy is important for theologians who must be able to follow philosophical thinking and influence philosophers with the precepts of religion. But to read philosophy or even to discuss philosophical problems is one thing, but to change religion into philosophy is another thing altogether. It is a mistake to think that philosophical terms and expressions could confine theological meanings, which are purely divine. Philosophical expressions are not always fit to express all that philosophers mean to say and therefore new terms are created by some philosophers, others may use the same term with a diverted or completely different meaning. It is not the same thing with our divine religion. Is it not needful in our religion, not to depend on philosophical terms in understanding and conceiving a divine fact especially if this fact is concerned with the divine essence or the divine nature of our Lord?

I dare to state that the whole controversy between Roman Catholics, Protestants, and the Chalcedonian Orthodox Churches on the one hand and the Monophysites of the non-Chalcedonian Orthodox Churches on the other, is a pure philosophical controversy, raised because of the right term the Christians should use to express their belief in respect of the kind of union existing between the Godhood and the manhood of our Lord and Savior.

We people of the east are most fearful of using philosophical terms to define a divine meaning. The non-Chalcedonian Orthodox Churches believe in the Godhead of Christ as well as in his manhood. But Christ is to them one nature. This may seem contradictory. Whatever the rational contradictions may be, our Church does not see any contradiction in her profession concerning the nature of Christ.

There is always a mystical and a spiritual solution that dissolves and overcomes all contradictions. Because of this mystical experience we do not always ask why and how.

There are many mysteries in our religion which we accept with deep acquiescence just because they are revealed by God. We believe in them contrary to the evidence of our senses and to our material mind if we use the word, just because they are proved to be from God. As we believe in God and in his omnipotence, so we believe in the other mysteries of our religion without any need to ask why and how. A philosophical mind cannot agree to this mystical faith. But a philosophical mind is not in fact a true religious mind. It rather believes in its own capacities and measures. Religion to a philosophical mind is a science that could be treated on the same basis as any other branch of human knowledge. A philosophical mind applies to religion the same scientific method. Here enters into religious analysis classification, philosophy and so on, in order to make it more reasonable and acceptable to a philosophical mind. Alas, with this kind of treatment we cannot penetrate the spirit of our religion. Where reason interferes, mystical experience disappears. We have to use our minds up to a point beyond which we should leave our minds for the guidance of mystical experience.

The Orthodox faith, according to our profession is that our Lord is perfect in his godhood and perfect in his manhood. However, we cannot dare to say that he is God and man together. For this expression means separation. He is rather God incarnated. The Godhead and the manhood are united in him in complete union, i.e., in essence, hypostasis and nature. There is no separation or division between the Godhood and manhood of our Lord. From the very moment of the descent of the divine Word in the Virgin's womb, the second Person of the blessed Trinity took to himself from St Mary's blood, a human body with a human reasonable soul, and made himself one with the manhood he took from the holy Virgin. The one born from St Mary, therefore, is God incarnate, one essence, one person, one hypostasis, one nature. Or we may say that he is one nature out of two natures. In other words we may speak of two natures before the union took place, but after the union there is but one nature, one nature that has the properties of two natures.

Hence the union in which the non-Chalcedonian Orthodox Churches believe differs essentially from the kind of union which Eutyches professed. Eutyches said that our Lord is one nature, but his union is based on a notion that the manhood of Christ is totally absorbed in his divinity and completely vanished like a drop of vinegar in the ocean. Eutyches in fact denies the real existence of the manhood of Christ.

Contrary to Eutyches the non-Chalcedonian Orthodox Churches profess that Christ is one nature in which are completely preserved all the human properties as well as all the divine properties without confusion, without mixture and without alteration, a profession with which the Coptic priest cries out while reciting at the consignation in the liturgy holding up the paten with his hands: "Amen, Amen, Amen, I believe, I believe and confess till the last breath that this is the life-giving flesh which thine only-begotten Son our Lord and our God and our Savior Jesus Christ took from our Lady and Mistress of us all, the Mother of God, the holy Mary. He made it one with his divinity without mingling and without confusion and without alteration . . . I believe that his divinity was not separated from his humanity for a single moment nor for the twinkling of an eye."

The Godhood then is preserved, the manhood is also preserved. However, Christ is of two natures but he is not two natures after the union as Pope Dioscorus of Alexandria said. The Godhead did not mix with the manhood, nor were they confused or changed to one another. The Godhead and the manhood are united not in the sense of a mere combination or connection or junction, but they are united in the real sense of the word union. But how does it happen? How do the properties of Godhead and manhood unite in one nature without mixture, without confusion and without alteration, we do not know. How it is that Christ has the properties of the two natures, but not the two natures, we do not know either. This may be illogical and contradictory. There is one thing of which we are sure: we believe in a kind of union that surpasses all human understanding and imagination. In a mystical experience we would overcome all contradictions.

This union is a real union. We may speak sometimes of a divine nature and a human nature, but this separation is in our minds only. In fact there are not two natures after the union. It did not happen that a divine nature and a human nature separated from each other, came together in union. What happened was that the second Person of the blessed Trinity came down and dwelt in the Virgin's womb and made for himself a human body with a human soul as the Gospel of St John declares: "And the Word became flesh" (1:14). There is no other word that could more emphatically denote the complete union than "became." The Holy Spirit could have inspired another expression, but it did not. There is no duality here between two natures; there is but one nature. This is a real proof of the union in the sense which we understand.

The union between the Godhead and the manhood in Christ is likened to the union between soul and body in man. Although the soul and body differ from each other in essence yet the union existing between them made from them but one nature to which we refer by the expression "human nature." Another likeness which may be clearer: the union existing between coal and fire in a firebrand. However, the union in Christ cannot be likened or compared with any kind of union that we know in our human experience. It is a union that has no equal.

Once more I repeat: we believe in one nature. This nature is not the Godhead alone or the manhood alone. It is one nature that has the properties of the two natures without mixing, without confusion and without alteration.

So it appears that the difference between our profession and the profession of the Chalcedonian Churches is insignificant. It is a matter of expressing the same meaning and the same theological fact. I believe that this is true to a great extent. Still, we have our reasons to stick to our traditional expression: "one nature of the Logos incarnated," one nature of two natures, one nature that has the properties of the two natures without mixing, without confusion, without alteration. These reasons may be summed up in the following points.

There is no biblical text which proves that Christ is of two natures after the union. On the contrary all biblical texts are on our side. We may mention but a few as examples: St John explicitly says "And the Word became flesh and dwelt among us."[3] In the Book of Revelation, our Lord declares "I am the first and the last, and the living One, and I was dead, and behold I am alive for evermore and have the keys of death and of Hades" (Rev 1:17–18). The (independent) pronoun *I* in this passage shows no duality. It is he who is the first and the last and it is he who was dead. The same meaning is clear in John 3: 13: "And no man hath ascended into heaven, but he that descended out of heaven, (even) the Son of Man which is in heaven." The *he* is the One that is in heaven, and he is the Son of Man on earth. Always the same thing. One essence, one hypostasis, one nature.

St Paul, speaking to the bishops of Ephesus claims the same union, saying: "Take heed unto yourselves and to all the flock, in the which the Holy Ghost hath made you bishops, to feed the Church of God, which he purchased with his own blood." (Acts 20:28) How could the apostle say that the blood shed is the blood of God if there were duality in Christ in any sense?

The same apostle states in his first epistle to the Corinthians "For had they known it they would not have crucified the Lord of glory" (I Cor 2:8). Then the crucified one is the Lord of glory himself. Once more there is no duality.

The same fact is quite clear from other passages. "As great as is the mystery of the Godhood, he who was manifested in the flesh" (I Tim 3:16) ". . . being in the form of God, thought it not robbery to be equal with God, but made himself of no reputation, and took upon him the form of a servant, and was made in the likeness of men; and being found in fashion as a man, he humbled himself and became obedient unto death, even the death of the cross" (Philippians 2:6–8).

Other passages are: Matt 3:17; John 1:18; 3:16; 8:58; I Cor 8:6; 10:4; Gal 4:4; Ephes 4:8–11; Tit 2:13.

In addition to the lack of biblical evidence for the doctrine of two natures, we hold that doctrine to be a dangerous expression. It implies duality, or even a kind of separation between Godhood and manhood. Otherwise there is no sense in insisting on the expression "two natures" since there is union. Second, the expression does not denote a real union but rather, expresses the existence of two separate natures coming together or combined together. Consequently such an expression opens the way for Nestorianism which the Chalcedonian Churches surely condemn as a heresy against our Christian faith.

If there were two natures united together in Christ after the union, then Redemption of Christ was an act of his humanity, for it is the flesh that was crucified. Consequently that Redemption of Christ had no power to save the human race. In fact, its value lies in the fact that the one who was crucified is the Word incarnate. Surely the Godhead did not suffer crucifixion, yet the Godhead gave the crucifixion its infinite value and capacity to save all the human race. The expression "one nature that has the properties of the two natures" saves our belief in the redemption of our Lord. The expression of two natures implies the possibility of a crucifixion of the flesh of Christ, not of Christ himself. All passages of the Scriptures are against such interpretation. The blood, St Paul said, is the blood of God: ". . . the Church of God which he hath purchased with his own blood." (Acts 20:28)

The expression "two natures" cannot explain the dogma professed by the adherents of Chalcedon that our Lady is the Mother of God. On the contrary, the Chalcedonian expression implies the possibility of the Nestorian heresy which all the Protestants in their diverse sects accept: that St Mary is not the Mother of God. The expression that Jesus Christ is in one nature can easily explain this fact because the one born from Mary is not merely the man Jesus but the Word incarnate.

These are the reasons why the Coptic Church refuses to use the expression "two natures" and sticks to its traditional expression "one nature" which St. Athanasius the Great and St Cyril of Alexandria professed, and why the non-Chalcedonian Orthodox Churches refuse to acknowledge the Tome of Leo of Rome and the Chalcedonian definition, for they explicitly profess the existence of two natures after the union.

This is our position today. I am convinced that the Chalcedonian formula is far from being a Nestorian profession, and that the non-Chalcedonian profession is far from Eutychianism. Therefore, we do not abandon hope that one day all Churches will have not only the same faith but also the same profession and the same theological terms and expressions.

4. K. V. Sarkissian[1] begins his study by establishing how from the beginning it was on doctrinal grounds that the Armenian theologians rejected the Chalcedonian formula of the two natures in Christ. He maintains that their position has remained unchanged throughout the course of centuries. He admits that what is needed for possible common understanding of the mystery is a common language, a deeper realization that, in the reality of Christ, it was God who descended to man, and that after all, faith is more important than formulas.

Speaking about the historical experience of the Armenian people, Henri Gregoire, the highly renowned Belgian Byzantinist, says: *"la querelle des deux natures en Jesus-Christ fut sa tragedie."*[2] For more than one reason, this statement can be extended to the whole Christian East. Bitter controversies, mutual accusations of heresy followed by anathemas, harmful enmities and disastrous persecutions have affected our past history to a point where we have lost the clear understanding of our respective attitudes towards Christology, and all our relationships in history have been marked with a strong trend of polemics which, at its best, resulted in the recognition of certain formulae as absolute and, therefore, unchangeable at any cost.

If our present ecumenical era, with its new spirit of openness towards each other, will not open our eyes to new visions and a new and deeper understanding of our respective positions, then, indeed, we must confess that we have lost a God-given opportunity for a new witness to the unity and mission of the Church to which

[1] Karekin V. Sarkissian is a Bishop of the Armenian Apostolic Church, of the Catholicosate of Cilicia. He is attached to the Armenian Theological Seminary of Antelias, Lebanon. This article is a reprint of his address entitled *The Doctrine of the Person of Christ in the Armenian Church,* delivered at an unofficial consultation held at the University of Aarhus, Denmark in August 1964. It was first published in the *Greek Orthodox Theological Review,* X (Winter of 1964–1965), pp. 108–109.

[2] Sirapie Der Nersessian, *Armenia and the Byzantine Empire* (Cambridge, Mass., 1947), Preface, p. xix.

we have the firm consciousness of belonging together.

It is in this spirit of a fresh approach to our respective attitudes that I would like to set forth as clearly as possible the fundamental positions of the Armenian Church in the past by offering to your consideration and evaluation some statements of genuine authority within the Armenian Church with regard to the understanding of the unity of the Two Natures in Christ.

First of all, let us begin with a confessional statement which enjoys the highest authority in the Armenian Church as it is always publicly professed by candidates for the Holy Orders at the Ordination and Consecration Services.

> We believe that One of the Three Persons, God the Word, begotten of the Father before the ages, in time descended in the Virgin Mary, the Theotokos, took of her blood (i.e. substance) and united it with His Godhead; for nine months He waited in the womb of the Immaculate Virgin and (thus) the perfect God became perfect man with soul, spirit and flesh. One person, one prosopon and one united nature: God became man without undergoing change and alteration, He was conceived without human seed and was born immaculate. As there is no beginning for His Godhead, so there is no end for his manhood. (For Jesus Christ is the same yesterday and today, and the same for ever.)
>
> We believe that our Lord Jesus Christ walked about on the earth. At the age of thirty years He came to be baptized. The Father bore witness from above by saying: "This is my beloved son," and the Holy Spirit in the likeness of a dove descended upon Him. He was tempted by Satan but overcame him. He preached salvation to men. He laboured bodily and underwent fatigue, hunger and thirst. Then He voluntarily suffered, was crucified and died bodily and remained alive through His Godhead. The body was placed in the tomb being united with the Godhead; by the soul He descended into hell with the unseparable Godhead.[3]

Our purpose will be to try to show how this understanding of the doctrine of the person of Christ was reached. But, at this juncture, a historical fact must be taken into account before any doctrinal inquiry and analysis.

Now, it must be accepted that the Armenian Church did not react to the Council of Chalcedon only upon the instigation and under the influence of the Syrians in the beginning of the sixth century. Nor were they misled because of the deficiency of their language in its capacity to render correctly the subtleties of the Greek expressions. Neither did they exploit the doctrinal issues for purely political and nationalistic purposes. In fact, they dealt with the Council of Chalcedon on doctrinal ground, and as early as the fifth century, as will be shown now.

We are in possession of two doctrinal documents of the fifth century which make it clear how the Armenian Church understood the union of the Two Natures.

1) The first document is a treatise ascribed to Moses of Khoren or Khorenatsi, the famous Armenian historiographer.[4] Speaking against those who separate Christ in two, he asserts

[3] See the *Book of Daily Offices,* where this Confession appears always on the first page.
[4] The authenticity of this attribution is well assessed nowadays on scholarly grounds.

very strongly the idea of unity right from the beginning by saying that it is possible for *many* elements to join together and to be united in *one* nature. Man is composed of earthly and spiritual elements, but he has one nature. The two are not confused in him; that is to say, the flesh is not soul and the soul is not flesh. Each maintains its own properties. The distinctness of the two is not destroyed by their union. Likewise, the Incarnation also must be understood in the same manner. We must confess Christ One in His nature because it is said "the Word became flesh" and that "He took the form of a servant." The meaning of the Scriptures is clear: that which was taken by the Word was that which He did not have. Therefore, the two, the Word and the flesh, which were separate before the Incarnation, became one after the Incarnation.

Arguing against those who consider the union of the *Two Natures* impossible, he says that they have no right to assert the unity of the *persons.*[5]

> It is said (in the Scriptures) 'He who was in the form of God took the form of a Servant.' You see, it says form *and* form; which form is then absorbed in the mixture according to their confession? For (if they think that) the union of the whole results in confusion, then they have to understand the same for *the persons.* Indeed, their sayings are ridiculous... because, as in the legendary tales, they create one head and two tails![6]

He urges his opponents to give up their separatist attitude and confess the union of the Two Natures or to deny altogether the whole Incarnation.

It is not difficult to detect the influence of the Alexandrian theological tradition all through the text of the whole treatise.

2) The second document, which is a longer exposition than Khorenatsi's treatise and which deals with the subject on biblical and theological ground, rather than philosophical as was the case in the previous document, comes to us from St. John Mandakouni, a fifth century Church Father whose treatise is written in a remarkably pastoral and eirenical spirit.

This is an attempt *"to demonstrate,"* as the title itself suggests so pointedly, why it is right to confess the Saviour *"of two natures"* (ek duo physeon) or *"one nature"* (mia physis). There is no place here for the least doubt that the doctrine of the Council of Chalcedon is directly aimed at in this treatise.

Here, again, we find a strong plea for maintaining firm the unity of the Two Natures in Christ the "how" of which remains above our human understanding.

There are two points which he refutes categorically: The first is the very idea of union as understood by those who in fact separate Christ in two. For him the union is a genuinely real one and not a sheer principle of union or simply an indwelling of the Word in the flesh. "Some consider that the descending (the Incarnation) was

---

[5] The Armenian word is "demk" which generally corresponds to *prosopon.* Here, however, it stands for *hypostasis,* because obviously in this passage Khorenatsi tries to show that for those who say *Two Natures in One Person* this latter expression becomes an empty notion if its authors cannot conceive a unity in nature.

[6] See *Book of Letters* (Tiflis, 1901), pp. 24–25.

in appearance and not in truth." They believe that Christ became man in the sense that He inhabited the flesh by "complaisance and will."[7]

Here, in fact, he attacks the ideas propounded in the name of Theodore of Mopsuestia who was much more influential in the bordering countries of Armenia, the Syriac-speaking Christian world, than Nestorius or any other Antiochene theologian.

For him Christ assumed the human nature in its integral reality and united it to Himself inseparably and thus made it *His own.*

Secondly, he criticizes the Dyophysite position for its dualistic interpretation of Christ's life on the earth. The distinctness of the Two Natures has led the Dyophysite thinkers so far as to give each *nature* the meaning of a *person.* It is this *hypostasized* understanding of Christ's natures, as the Tome of Leo formulates it so sharply, that has always been fiercely opposed by the non-Chalcedonians.

Mandakouni's interpretation of the Dyophysite position goes as far as to see in it the teaching not of two *persons,* but of two *individuals* in Christ. Thus, he compares the two Natures to Peter and John walking along in the same direction, but on parallel roads. . . .

Obviously, this is an exaggeration of the Chalcedonian understanding of Christ's natures. However, it is also an eloquent testimony to the kind of interpretation in which the dualistic conception—the stress put on the Two Natures—has been the stumbling block for the non-Chalcedonians. . . .

The union has such an intimate character that through the act of the Incarnation "The Word is the Word of the flesh and the flesh is the flesh of the word."[8]

These two fifth-century documents are sufficient to give us a clue to the way of Christological thinking in which the Armenian Church was engaged in the last quarter of the fifth century.[9] In these two documents we are given an idea about the doctrinal basis upon which the Armenian Church took its official stand vis-à-vis the Council of Chalcedon in the beginning of the sixth century (506/8).

To confess Christ *"One Nature"* or *"Two Natures"* was the fundamental principle which guided the later theologians in their expositions of the doctrine of Christ's person as well as in their defense, through polemical writings, of this Christology which they cherished wholeheartedly all along their history.

During the subsequent centuries, the position of the Armenian Church remained unchanged. The heads of the Church as well as the Church divines (i.e. the vardapets) suspected Chalcedon on the grounds of its dual-

[7] *Book of Letters,* p. 33.

[8] One can easily recognize in this expression a striking similarity with St. Cyril's 11th Anathema which runs as follows: "If anyone does not confess the flesh of our Lord to be life-giving and *the own flesh of the Word Himself* conjoined to Him in dignity, or having a more divine indwelling, and not rather life-giving, as we affirm, because it became the own flesh of the Word who had strength to quicken all things, be he anathema." T. H. Bindly, *The Oecumenical Documents of Faith,* p. 215, fourth edition (London, 1950). See the Greek text, *ibid.,* pp. 114–115; the Armenian version in *Book of Letters,* p. 405.

[9] It must be noted also that the translation into Armenian of Timothy Aeluros' *Refutation of the Council of Chalcedon and the Tome of Leo* (480–484) gave a strong move to the Armenian theologians in their fight against the Council of Chalcedon.

istic conception of Christ's person always being associated with the teaching of Nestorius.

It would take me too far if I tried to present the later stages of the Armenian position in detail. Therefore, I would confine my presentation to some cases where the Armenian Church leaders and theologians were engaged in correspondence with the Greek Church Fathers and, thus, the Armenian theologians were prompted to present the teaching of their church in the context of an *encounter* as is the case of our present consultations.[10]

1) In answering a letter sent by Photius, the Patriarch of Constantinople, to the Armenian Catholicos, Zacharia (855–877), Vardapet Sahag, surnamed "Meroud," deals at a considerable length with the problem of the union of the Two Natures.[11]

To Photius' invitation to the Armenians to accept the Council of Chalcedon as the Fourth Ecumenical Council, he answers:

> Our Fathers rejected the Council of Chalcedon and preached Christ the Son to the world as 'One of Two Natures' united without confusion and without separation. They (i.e. the Chalcedonians) divided Him in two natures and operations and wills, thus following the Nestorian false teachings. But they describe Him also as united in order to win the simple-minded by showing them that they were far away from the Nestorian heresy (p. 284)

What is that unity which the Chalcedonians have in mind? The unity of the *person.* But Vardapet Sahag, together with all the Armenian theologians, finds absurd this unity of *person* without the unity of the *nature.* That idea of unity, in his reckoning, is a clever and disguised escape from the Nestorian teaching which the Chalcedonians condemn by name. It is with this view that he collates passages from Nestorius and Pope Leo in order to show the affinity of their respective christological doctrines.

> What communion there exists between Chalcedon and Cyril? For the latter said 'One united Nature of Two,' according to the Holy Council of Ephesus (431). Chalcedon decreed two separate natures. (pp. 285–286)...

He aims specifically at the Chalcedonian definition when he says:

> The Council of Chalcedon said 'One Person and Two Natures in Christ' in order not to ascribe to God the Word the sufferings. This is ridiculous. For it was on the same point that the impious Nestorius erred when he opposed the Great Cyril. (p. 290)

And in order to show how the union was intimate he brings forth the example of the gold put in fire.

Again he argues against those who affirm that the natures are separated and the persons are united:

[10] We have a most valuable symposium of doctrinal letters exchanged between the Armenian Church Fathers and the Leaders of other churches, such as the Greek, Syrian and Gregorian Fathers. It is called *The Book of Letters* . . . The basic document for our inquiry will be this collection of letters. There are several other writings of Armenian theologians dealing specifically with the Council of Chalcedon and its christological teaching. But I felt that a thorough study of them would not [be] in its right place in the immediate purpose of this consultation.

[11] See *Book of Letters,* pp. 283–294.

> For, if the union of the natures results in confusion, as they say, the same then must happen to the persons which they say to be one.... (p. 291)

2) Again, in another correspondence which took place in the 10th century between Theodore, the Greek Metropolitan of Melitene, and Khatchig, the Armenian Catholicos, we find the same type of arguments put forward against the Council of Chalcedon and, particularly, against the formula of Two Natures. This time another theologian, by the name of Samuel, drafted the answer letter in the name of the Catholicos. He says:

> We do not agree with the new teaching of the Council of Chalcedon and of the Tome of Leo which state two natures in God the Word Incarnate. We confess Christ not God alone, neither man alone, and not God and man separated one from the other, but 'God made man.' And as He is Only-Begotten Son of the Father, so also He is the Only-born of the mother, One Son; and as One Son, one Christ; and as One Christ, One Person; and as One Person, one prosopon; and as one prosopon, one will; and as one will, also one operation; and as one operation, one nature; as He truly is: *One Nature*. . . .

In order to explain the character of the union, the author brings forth the following analogy: The union, he says, must not be conceived as "One and one which have come together with the same dignity, but like a harp with the harper to whom is united in concord the movement of its will; or like the light of a lamp which is united with the rays of the sun and which cannot be separated from them and cannot shine forth with the distinct rays of its own. Likewise, the human essence united with the divine inseparably, does not operate separately according to its own power. For, the stronger overcomes the weaker by uniting it to itself and divinizing it."[12]

I could go on along this line by bringing forth many other passages taken from the Armenian Church Fathers and doctrinal statements. But I think it is sufficient for our immediate purpose to stop here and to consider the implications of the views expressed in the passages already quoted and briefly commented on.

What can we draw of these citations as significant aspects and conclusions with a view of mutual understanding?

1) First of all, we, both sides, need *a common language*. For, in all these passages one could easily perceive that for the Armenian theologians the word *nature* meant a concrete reality; and, as Samuel Vardapet said, it actually meant "the perfect man." Therefore, to use the expression "Two Natures" in this concrete sense of the term, gives easily way to the conception of division in Christ. This fear of theirs has been justified because of the Tome of Leo where the natures are described as self-consistent entities with their proper operations. This way of thinking in Christology, indeed, was not far from what Nestorius had taught. Thus, the "Nestorianizing" tendency of the Council of Chalcedon was bitterly resented and fiercely opposed by those churches who eagerly maintained firm the teaching of the Council of Ephesus (431). And it must be admitted that before they showed the affinity between Chalcedonism and Nestorianism it was the Nestorians

[12] *Book of Letters*, p. 315.

themselves who welcomed the Council of Chalcedon seeing in it the vindication of their position. There is ample evidence to this effect in the 5th and 6th century Armenian Church history, particularly in its relationship with the Syriac-speaking Christianity of Mesopotamia and Persia.

If the term *nature* were taken in an abstract sense, that is to say, as denoting the properties pertaining to Godhead and manhood in Christ, then it would have been more easily understood. In that case, however, one could legitimately but not necessarily speak of more than *two natures* . . . Nevertheless, it would have been a happier expression and more acceptable one than the "Two Natures" in the Leonine sense of the term.

2) The second point is that the basic reality of utmost significance in the whole understanding of Christ's person is that it was God who became man. The whole meaning of the Incarnation is that God assumed the human nature in its entirety. The central, initiative action was God's. It was He who descended from above and united to Himself what belonged to man in order to save humanity from the death of sin. *"And the Word became flesh."* This is the fundamental, essential and unique fact which has served the non-Chalcedonians of all times as the basis of their Christology and a watchword for their position. From the times of St. Athanasius and St. Cyril up to our present time the strong emphasis has always been put on this biblical affirmation.

Doctrinally, this affirmation has developed in the conception of the closest, most intimate, inseparable yet unconfused union of the divine and human natures in Christ, and to such a point that the flesh has become God's flesh through which He suffered, was crucified and dead and buried. The subject, so to speak, was always God the Word. The human nature did not stand in itself alone in Christ, but was assumed by God and made His own. It is in this respect that one can say that God suffered. "We confess, therefore," says Saint Nerses IV, the greatest Armenian Church Father and theologian with a strong sense of ecumenical spirit, "Christ as God and Man, but we do not mean division by this, God forbid!, because He Himself suffered and did not suffer; since by His divine nature He was immutable and impassible, but in His human body He suffered and died. Consequently, those who say that it was one who suffered and another who did not suffer, fall into error. Thus it was none other than the Word who suffered and embraced death in His body; because the same Word Himself who was impassible and incorporeal consented to become passible in order to save humanity by His Passion."[13]

Going on further, St. Nerses speaks about the relationship between the two natures in the following passage:

> Thus the nature of Christ is said to be one, not confused, but two natures ineffably united with each other. If it were not so, then we should have to consider not only two natures in Christ but three, two human natures, that is, soul and body, and one divine nature. But according to the writings

[13] *The Profession of Faith of the Armenian Church by St. Nerses Shnorhali,* pp. 37–38. Translated with introduction and comment by Terenig Vartabed Poladian (Boston, Mass., 1941).

of the Fathers, after the union the duality in the sense of separatedness disappeared.[14]

3) If we are able to look further and deeper than what pure history gives us, in other words, if we can transcend certain historical formulations which have caused misunderstandings, without ignoring them or minimizing their significance, and grasp in a new effort of faithful obedience to Christ our faith in the Incarnation as such, I believe we have a firm common ground to stand on and make manifest our communion in faith. After all, faith is deeper and far more important than the formula which is a certain pattern of communication.

The subsequent history of Chalcedon with all its efforts aiming at a conciliation between the Chalcedonian and non-Chalcedonian Churches has taught us that a rapprochement and a common understanding are possible if the problem is dealt with in itself, being distinguished from other problems of cultural, political or national character.

I should like to conclude this presentation with the challenging words of Catholicos Nerses IV:

> Therefore, if *'One Nature'* is said for the indissoluble and indivisble union and not for the confusion, and *'Two Natures'* is said as being unconfused, immutable and indivisible, *both are within the bounds of orthodoxy.*[15]

If this statement could be made in the twelfth century, what conclusions can we draw from it in the twentieth century?

This is the real challenge we face in common.

5. S. S. Harakas[1] finds Bulgakov's positive presentation of the Chalcedonian faith in terms of this doctrine of God-Manhood original yet conservative, logical yet mystical, with much to commend it. It is in Bulgakov's deeper analysis of his God-Manhood doctrine from the viewpoint of Sophiology—that is, the theology of the Wisdom of God—that the author sees grounds for criticism from orthodox theologians.

The life of Father Sergius Bulgakov was a true spiritual odyssey. His was a life full of the pulse of his times and he lived and thought fully during his lifetime. Here before us we do not have a tradition-encrusted man who knew nothing more than his Church and its Theology, but rather, a true citizen of this world and age who found his life's meaning in the Orthodox Church after having searched everywhere else for it.[2]

---

[14] Terenig Vartabed Poladian, *op. cit.,* pp. 40–41.

[15] See *Profession of Faith,* p. 41.

[1] Stanley S. Harakas is a Greek Orthodox priest associated with St. Basil's Church in Peabody, Mass. He is a frequent contributor to the *Greek Orthodox Theological Review.* It is from his article "Sergius Bulgakov and His Teaching" (VII, Summer of 1961, Winter of 1961–1962) that this excerpt is taken, selectively, from pp. 92–99.

[2] The following biographical information is, in part, taken from a private letter to the author from the Very Rev. Alexander Schmemann, Professor of Church History and Liturgics at St. Vladimir's Orthodox Theological Seminary in New York, dated April 15, 1959, who was a student of Father Bulgakov for five years. In part the information is

"The late . . . Father Bulgakov belonged to the generation of Russian 'Intelligentsia' that went to the Church via Atheism and Marxism. A son of a priest, he lost his faith in his student years, went to Germany, studied philosophy and political economy, joined Marxism and upon his return to Russia, taught political economy. However, soon enough (his mind being deeply 'religious' in spite of his atheism; his acceptance of Marxism, the result of a search for absolute values), he felt dissatisfied with Marxist philosophy. In the beginning of the century, with a group of Russian Marxists and former positivists (Berdyaev, Struve, Frank) he began the movement first from 'Marxism to Idealism' (the title of a famous symposium, published by the group) and then to historic Christianity and to the Church. In 1910–15 he was one of the leaders of the Moscow Academy of Religious Philosophy, the living center of the 'return' of the intelligentsia to religion."[3] By 1917 he had become one of the leading laymen of the Russian Orthodox Church, taking a leading role in the great Sobor of 1917–18. "It was only at the height of the revolution when Bulgakoff, threatened with arrest and no longer living in his own apartment, was finally ordained."[4] He was then exiled by the Soviet Government. Since 1925 he was Professor of Dogmatic Theology at St. Sergius' Orthodox Theological Institute in Paris. "It is in Paris that he wrote almost all of his theological works . . . his Sophiology raised a theological storm in the Russian Church, and was condemned by the Patriarchal Church in Moscow in 1937."[5] In 1940 the position of Dean was created and Bulgakov received the title and remained in that position until his death in 1944.[6]

As can be seen . . . the life of Sergius Bulgakov was a true spiritual and intellectual journey . . .

What was it that caused this . . . change from an atheistic Marxist to an Eastern Orthodox Theologian and Priest? . . . The change became unavoidable because of intellectual dialectics, and a clear understanding that the right path of social idealism leads directly to religious faith. . . .

This return to Christianity and Eastern Orthodoxy was carried on with a good intellectual conscience.[7] . . .

There was a two-fold foundation and basis, however, at the root and in the development of this odyssey. The first was a deep inner desire and necessity. The second was the answer in Christianity which satisfied that desire. The fundamental desire and motive which led him into this spiritual and intellectual odyssey was the search for a "general outlook on life, an en-

---

taken from Donald A. Lowrie, *St. Sergius in Paris, The Orthodox Theological Institute,* (New York: Macmillan, 1951). Information concerning Prof. Schmemann is also found in the above mentioned book—esp. 93–94.

[3] Alexander Schmemann, *private letter,* permission granted to quote in note of April 21, 1959.

[4] Lowrie, *ibid.,* p. 63.

[5] Schmemann, *private letter.* See Lowrie, *ibid.,* concerning this unfortunate situation, in which politics played a major role (pp. 54–55). But it was to be clearly understood that Bulgakov arguing for the freedom of the Eastern Orthodox Theologian made a clear distinction between Doctrine of the Church and private theological opinion. (Lowrie, 52–53).

[6] Lowrie, *ibid.,* p. 43.

[7] *Ibid.,* p. 363.

deavor to connect dogmatic or theoretical ideas and practical conclusions, to give answers to the 'cursed questions' . . . a complete answer to all the questions which had tormented me during my life."[8]

And what was at the heart of that 'complete answer'? Essentially it was the doctrine of man as the image of God, this being seen in the Incarnation. For Christ is 'God-Man,' and the whole of mankind participates in this God-Manhood.[9] This doctrine of the God-Manhood is the key to studying the emphasis of Sergius Bulgakov on the doctrines of the Eastern Orthodox Church. Practically all areas to which he forcefully applied his mind were interpreted in terms of the doctrine of God-Manhood. This is the golden thread that runs through nearly all that he has written, for the teaching of the God-Manhood defines the whole relationship of God to man and his place as a center and representative of the whole of nature. . . .

The Incarnation. As we noted in the preceding lines, the pervading doctrine in the theology of Sergius Bulgakov is the doctrine of the God-Manhood. It is based on the Chalcedonian dogma of the person and nature of Christ. Yet Fr. Bulgakov managed to find significance in that doctrine which awaited expression in his writings. He notes: 'The relation of the two natures in Christ is there (Chalcedon) defined not positively, but in a series of negations: *inconfuse, inmutabiliter, indivise, inseparabiliter* . . . For all its great and fundamental significance for Christian Faith, it cannot be denied that this definition confronts theological thought with fresh difficulties. It is, in fact, thereby invited to go beyond the negations of Chalcedon to the affirmations there tacitly assumed.'[10]

Bulgakov's starting point is this proposition: for God to become incarnate, there must be some common point between God and Man. "The union of the two natures, the divine and the human, must be something more than the mere mechanical conjunction of two alien principles. That would be a metaphysical impossibility"[11] he says. What is the solution? He finds it in two apparently contradictory phrases: 'Divine God-Manhood' and 'Creaturely God-Manhood.' Divine God-Manhood is that which is in God's nature which is the image of God in man. It is the primordial manhood in God in the image of which God created Man. Conversely, the Creaturely God-Manhood is the divinity in man.

In one place he summarizes this clearly and succinctly in the following words: "Man as having God's image is god-like, and God as having His image in man is man-like. There exists a positive relationship between God and man which may be defined as God-Manhood."[12] This is the metaphysical explanation of the Incarnation—since Divinity is the prototype of humanity and humanity is the image of Divinity, both man and God have common points. In a sense, both man and God are theandric. Thus Bulga-

[8] *Ibid.*, p. 364.
[9] *Ibid.*, p. 364.
[10] Bulgakov, *The Wisdom of God* (New York: Paisley Press, 1937) p. 128.
[11] *Ibid.*, p. 132.
[12] *Social Teaching in Modern Russian Orthodox Theology* (Seabury Western Theological Seminary, Evanston, Ill.: 1934) p. 13.

kov writes: "Human nature is elsewhere to be found only in the possession of a human person, and seems to admit of no other owner. From this we must infer that, since the person of the Word found it possible to live in the human nature as well as in its own, therefore it is itself in some sense a human person too. It must be somehow co-natural with God, but also with Man, that is, with God-man. . . . While man on his side, must be naturally capable of receiving and making room for the divine person instead of the human. . . . The Incarnation thus appears to postulate on its hypostatic side at least, some original analogy between divine and human personality, which yet does not overthrow all the essential difference between them. And this is found in the relation between type and prototype. The personal spirit of man has its divine uncreated origin from 'the spirit of God' (Genesis 2). It is a spark of the divine, . . . and though his present state of sin obscures his memory of his heavenly birth, yet he has something in him which asks for God-manhood. . . . If man, the creature is by destiny thus theandric, the Word, on the other hand, who is his Prototype, is the everlasting God-man. . . . Thus it was possible for the person of a created human nature to so realize its original God-manhood. Since from all eternity, the person of the Word was somehow human, it was possible for it, in becoming the person of a created human nature, to elevate without destroying it . . . and so we confess Christ to be perfect God and perfect Man, and the human compound in Him to be maintained entire, for there is sufficient metaphysical ground for the possibility of the Word's descent into humanity."[13]

The original, yet conservative, logical yet mystical, fresh yet ancient theological position here briefly outlined has much to commend it and, alone, this certainly would have received serious consideration and evaluation in modern Orthodox Theology. But Bulgakov did not remain satisfied with this interpretation and he went further in his analysis of God-manhood and he came up with the rather unique and quite strange theological concept of the Wisdom or Sophia of God to which we now turn our attention.

The Wisdom (Sophia) of God. The word used by Bulgakov to label his further thought in this area of doctrine and theology, I believe, was an unfortunate one. The term 'Wisdom of God' already had specific content in the traditional doctrine of God as one of the attributes of the one God. Thus, the term itself was calculated to bring confusion. But its Greek translation, or rather, the transliteration into English, German and Russian of the Greek word for wisdom, 'sophia,' was even more unfortunate. In his book, *The Wisdom of God,* Bulgakov recognized this. He writes: ". . . the Western reader has already become acquainted with such words as 'Sophia' and 'Sophiology.' For him, of course, these words are tinged with the peculiar exotic oriental flavor of 'gnosis,' and, indeed, smacks of every sort of rubbish and superstition."[14] Yet Bulgakov was convinced that he was neither peculiar nor heretical. He felt that the Sophiological doctrine had "pro-

[13] *The Wisdom of God,* pp. 129, 130, 131.
[14] *Ibid.,* p. 28.

found bearing on the very 'essence of Christianity.' "[15] Neither was he conscious of any heresy. He writes in the same place that "the sophiological point of view brings to bear upon *all* Christian teaching and dogma, beginning with the doctrine of the Holy Trinity and the Incarnation and ending with the questions of practical everyday Christianity in our own time, a special interpretation. It is untrue to affirm that the development of the doctrine of the Wisdom of God leads to the denial or undermining of any part of Christian dogma. Exactly the reverse is true. Sophiology accepts all the dogmas acknowledged as genuine by the Orthodox Church. . . ."[16]

What then is this Sophiology in the theology of Sergius Bulgakov? The best approach to understand it is to return to what he has written regarding Divine and creaturely God-Manhood. "Man as having God's image is god-like, and God as having His image in man is man-like. There exists a positive relation between God and man which may be defined as God-Manhood."[17] The attempt to define this God-manhood, to locate it and describe it, both in God and in man is Sophiology. Thus he writes, "The central point from which sophiology proceeds is that of the relation between *God* and *the world,* or, what is practically the same thing, between *God* and *man*. In other words, we are faced with the question of the meaning and significance of God-manhood"[18] "The dogma of God-manhood is precisely the main theme of sophiology, which in fact represents nothing but its full dogmatic elucidation."[19] Basically what is this God-manhood? Bulgakov will answer: "The image of God in God Himself or (in other words) His holy Wisdom (Sophia)"[20] The Wisdom of God, or Sophia, is to be found, therefore, in both God and in man. In God it is His divine life and glory and in man it is the ground of creation.

The divine Sophia is divine nature. Thus, the Divinity in God constitutes the Divine Sophia. . . .[21] To the question "how is this Divinity or Sophia related to the triune God," he answers: "The tri-hypostatic God possesses, indeed, but one Godhead, Sophia; possesses it in such a way that at the same time it belongs to each of the Persons, in accordance with the properties distinguishing each of these persons."[22] This Godhead, this Sophia in God, therefore, as understood by Bulgakov, is conceived ontologically as a living, "loving substance, ground and 'principle' "[23] Thus the persons of the Holy Trinity are founded on a single principle and ground, which Bulgakov chooses to call 'Divine Sophia.'

---

[15] *Ibid.*

[16] *Ibid.,* p. 29.

[17] *Social Teaching . . . ,* p. 13.

[18] *Wisdom of God,* p. 30.

[19] *Ibid.,* p. 34.

[20] *Social Teaching . . . ,* p. 13.

[21] *The Wisdom of God,* p. 56.

[22] *Ibid.*

[23] *Ibid.,* p. 59 and pp. 87–88. ". . . we must once for all remove the common scholastic misunderstanding which makes of Wisdom no more than a particular 'property' or quality, comprised in the definition of God, and therefore devoid of proper subsistence. . . . We must insist on the full ontological reality of Ousia-Sophia."

What we have described thus far is Bulgakov's concept of Divine Sophia. But his doctrine of Sophia has another aspect, 'Creaturely Sophia.' This is the image of God in the world and especially in man. He follows the Aristotelian and Platonic concepts used in some patristic thought when he sees the creation of the world as creation on the basis of the divine prototypes in the nature of God Himself. "God creates the world, as it were, out of Himself, out of the abundance of His own resources . . . (the) world only receives according to the mode proper to it, the divine principle of life. . . . God contained within Himself. "God creates the world, as it were, the divine prototypes, *paradeigmata,* the destinies, *proorismoi,* of all creatures; so that the world bears within it the image and, as it were, the reflection of the divine prototype."[24] The application to Bulgakov's Sophiology is obvious. The image of God in the world and in man, primarily, is to be understood as the image of the Sophia of God. Divine Sophia is the prototype of the world. Fashioned after the Sophia of God, the world and man constitute the creaturely sophia. Thus to say that man is created in God's image is to note a true identity between man (the image) and God (the prototype). This leads Bulgakov to speak of the 'divinity' of man and the 'humanity' of God.

The doctrines of Sophiology have not been accepted in the theological thought of the present day theologians of the Orthodox Church. Perhaps the greatest criticism leveled against it is that which is related to God's freedom in creation. This position would have God forced to create the world as it is and in no other way. God's freedom is made subject to an 'Aristotelian entelechy.'

[24] *Ibid.,* p. 99.

X

CONTEMPORARY CHRISTOLOGY

PROTESTANT AUTHORS

1. T. F. Torrance[1] notes that Barth champions the orthodox side of modern theology by taking the Incarnation literally as the coming of the Son of God into human existence and history—at the other pole of Bultmann's view of the Incarnation as a mythological construct. For Barth, Christ is the center of all truth. To know Him man needs more than science; he needs wisdom. Parallel to Barth's refusal to develop any doctrine about the Logos independent from his unity with humanity is his refusal to consider man and culture independently from Christ.

The Centrality of the Incarnation. For more than a hundred years the New Testament documents had been subjected to the most searching scrutiny any documents have ever known, and out of it came an immense focus

[1] Thomas F. Torrance was born in 1913. He was educated at the universities of Edinburgh and Basel. He is a minister of the Church of Scotland, and professor of Dogma at the University of Edinburgh. He has authored several theological books and articles. *The Doctrine of Grace in the Apostolic Fathers* is perhaps the most known. It is from his book *Karl Barth: An Introduction to His Early Theology 1910–1931* (London: SCM Press Ltd., 1962) that this excerpt has been taken pp. 204–217.

of attention upon the historical Jesus Christ. But during this period in which Christianity became assimilated to culture, and theology became subservient to general scientific and philosophical ideas, biblical and theological research took over methods that were developed in the empirical investigation of creaturely objectivity and applied them to its own task, but it also took over even more than the natural sciences the philosophical presuppositions that were still attached to these methods. It was ultimately through relation to these philosophical presuppositions that Protestant theology sought its justification as a respectable academic pursuit. In this development biblical and theological research could only produce 'a historical Jesus' that was basically an expression of the contemporary culture, a 'Jesus' dressed up in the clothes of the nineteenth and twentieth century—that line of development reached its peak and its dénouement round about 1910. . . .

The immense research of modern times into the New Testament has concentrated our attention upon the historical Jesus Christ in the most intense way, but it failed to retain the historical Jesus, for, owing to its philosophical presuppositions, it lost him in the depths of its own subjectivity. Now, however, with the re-orientation of Protestant theology, the historical Jesus Christ is being interpreted out of himself, out of the concrete act of God in Jesus Christ, and not out of our own creative spirituality. Hence in our day there has arisen a powerful Christology which interprets the object of its thought in terms of its own objective rationality and, because it is able to give the historical Jesus Christ the saving significance that it finds in him in his objective reality, the historical Jesus is not dissolved away but stands before us as the supreme act of God in the midst of history.

Here we reach the great water-shed of modern theology, in the doctrine of the *Incarnation.* On one side of that water-shed the Incarnation is taken seriously as the coming of the Son of God into human existence and history, as the Being of God in space and time at work for us and our salvation, in the atoning life and death and resurrection of Jesus Christ. Here, where theological language is certainly employed in its analogical character, it is language deriving from and reposing upon objective reality, the concrete act of God in Jesus Christ. That supplies the basic frame of reference for all theological doctrines and gives them their realist character. It is here that Karl Barth, standing in the center of the whole Christian tradition from the earliest times to the present, has given us massive and formidable articulation of the substance of the Christian faith, and in so doing he has laid it more squarely than ever upon its solid foundation.

On the other side of the watershed the Incarnation is regarded as a mythological construct designed to express in an objectified manner the creative spirituality of the early Christians. Behind this lies a horror for the notion of the Being of God in space and time and therefore for the concrete act of God in the objective historical reality of Jesus Christ. Hence, everything is given a fundamentally symbolic interpretation, not symbolic of an objective reality, but symbolic of a subjective state or of a basic self-understanding of man over against God. The rejection of the Incarnation as the real advent and presence and activity of God in space and time, supplies the frame of reference for a re-interpretation of all other doctrines and gives them anthropocentric character, for they have to be 'demythologized' of their objective content and transposed into determinants of existentialist self-understanding. It is here that Rudolf Bultmann stands in the center of an anachronistic reaction that moves away from the center of the Christian faith out on to the marginal areas of gnostic speculation and self-redemption, and in doing so he has provided modern theology with the same testing-point which the Church had to face in the fourth and in the fifteenth centuries when it was challenged to take seriously the Being and Act of God himself in his revelation.

There are two basic issues here. On the one hand, it is the very substance of the Christian faith that is at stake, and on the other hand, it is the fundamental nature of scientific method, in its critical and methodological renunciation of prior understanding, that is at stake. This is the great watershed of modern theology: either we take the one way or the other—there is no third alternative. That does not mean to say that one must wholly follow Barth on the one hand or wholly follow Bultmann on the other, but that one must go either in the direction taken by Barth or in the direction taken by Bultmann. The way of Barth leads to the establishment of Christianity on its own solid God-given foundations and to the pursuit of theology as a free science in its own right; the way of Bultmann leads to the dissolution of Christianity in secular culture and to the pursuit of theology as an expression of a reactionary, existentialist way of life.

A recent statement of Barth, published in the *Christian Century* sums up well his own reaction to the challenge of Bultmann.[2]

"Among the undertakings which I have seen my theological contemporaries pursue and complete, Rudolf Bultmann's 'demythologization' of the New Testament has occupied me most of all—less because of its concrete problematic propositions than because it seemed to me a highly impressive resumption of the theme and method of the type of theology fostered by Schleiermacher; Bultmann's work thus gave me occasion to submit to a new consideration, examination and sharpening [of] my own point of departure acquired 40 years ago in a deviation from the Schleiermacherian tradition. I could not in conclusion follow Bultmann in respect to his particular thesis and much less still in respect to his fundamental method, in which I saw theology in spite of all safeguards being led anew into Egyptian or Babylonian captivity to a particular philosophy. From association with the young theological generation studying in Basel it seemed to me as if the interest in a decidedly existentialist interpretation, for a while devouring everything else, as in former days the interest in an historical-critical interpretation did likewise, would soon diminish. Yet from another perspective the situation can appear different, and I would not be surprised if existentialist interpretation should still have a noteworthy future in the diverse forms given it by Bultmann's disciples. What is certain is that one must be grateful to Bultmann for the warning that the not yet completed emancipation of theology will not be so easy as

[2] *The Christian Century,* Jan. 20, 1960, p. 74f.

some (including very likely, some of my readers and friends) would have it. To me it is significant that present-day Old Testament scholars, especially in regard to the old, yet always new, theme of 'faith and history,' are on the whole on much better ground than the authoritative New Testament men, who to my amazement have armed themselves with swords and staves and once again undertaken the search for the 'historical Jesus'—a search in which I now as before prefer not to participate."

That does not of course mean that Barth has no concern for the real historical Jesus Christ or is sceptical about successful research into what the New Testament has to say of him, but that the attempt to find a 'Jesus' apart from his Gospel, a Jesus apart from the concrete act of God in him, a 'Jesus' that can be constructed out of the historical records by means of criteria derived from secular sources alone, is a failure to understand the New Testament. The real, objective, historical Jesus is the Jesus Christ who cannot be separated from his self-revelation or from his Gospel, for that Revelation and Gospel are part of the one historical Jesus Christ who is to be understood out of himself, and in accordance with his own being and nature. To use the language of John Calvin, it is not a 'bare Christ' or 'naked Christ' that is the object of our faith, but 'Christ clothed with his Gospel,' 'Christ clothed with his acts and promises,' the 'whole Christ,' for that is the only Jesus Christ there ever was, and is and ever will be. Any other 'Christ' would only be a construct of our imagination or an objectification of our own creative spirituality.

If this whole Jesus Christ is the proper object of our faith, then scientific exegesis and interpretation of the New Testament must be accompanied by and tested by the critical and constructive inquiry of dogmatics, through which we allow Jesus Christ in his objective, historical and divine reality to disclose himself to us and to speak to us the very Word of God which he is himself.[3]

Jesus Christ and Culture. If Jesus Christ is only man and not God himself in human existence, if the Incarnation is only an objectified construct of our religious self-consciousness, then Christianity is only a transient expression of human culture that emerged out of the stream of time and will be submerged again as the course of civilization advances on in its great achievements, and theology becomes only an ideological interpretation of the structures of man's historical existence and self-understanding. But if Jesus Christ is the one Word of God become flesh, the very Son of God come into our human existence in space and time, for us and for our salvation, then as the one Truth of God he is the center of all truth and the creative source of all that is good and beautiful and true, and of all true culture. A dogmatic theology that takes its inquiry seriously cannot stop short of inquiring into the relevance of the concrete act of God in Jesus Christ for our redemption, but must go on to inquire into its relevance for all creation. It cannot stop short of the significance of Jesus Christ for the life

[3] Cf. John McIntyre, *Anselm and His Critics*, p. 55: "Theological interpretation is an essential part of the determination of the facts which constitute the Christian faith, and so-called impartial historical criticism is by itself unqualified to achieve that end."

of the Church but must go on to inquire into his universal and cosmic significance, and therefore into the relation of the Church to the world, and of its mission to universal human activity. If in Jesus Christ God himself became man and has entered into our historical and creaturely existence, within its continuities and rhythms and operations, and has forever bound it up with his own eternal Being as Creator and Savior, then all things in heaven and earth, and all knowledge and truth and art, are made to pivot upon this axis: Jesus Christ as the one Truth of God and the Light of life. But the obverse of that fact is also inescapable, that the one Truth of God, in its creative and saving work, has taken the way of the historical Jesus Christ in the midst of all historical reality. Therefore it is here, in the historical reality of Jesus Christ, and indeed in his *humanity*, that we are to discern the one Truth of God at work in and behind all truth.[4]

It is for this reason that Barth finds the word *scientia* too narrow to convey the full significance of the knowledge of Jesus Christ as the Truth of God. It requires to be enlarged through what the Old Testament called 'wisdom,' the *sophia* of the Greeks or the *sapientia* of the Latins. This gives us a concept of knowledge and wisdom that embraces the entire existence of man. The Truth which we know in Jesus Christ is the Light of life; it is Truth by which we can live and which throws its light upon the whole of our being, upon all its moments and activities and aspirations. To live by this Truth is the meaning of Christian knowledge—it is to live in the light of the knowledge of God, to live with an enlightened reason, and therefore to be sure of our own existence and of the ground and goal of all that happens.

"A quite tremendous extension of the field of vision is indicated by this," Barth says. "To know this object in its truth means in truth to know no more and no less than all things, even man, even oneself, the cosmos and the world. The Truth of Jesus Christ is not one Truth among others; it is *the* Truth, the universal Truth that creates all truth as surely as it is the Truth of God, the *prima veritas* which is also the *summa veritas*. For in Jesus Christ God has created all things, He has created all of us. We do not exist apart from Him, but in Him, whether we are aware of it or not; and the whole cosmos exists not apart from Him but in Him, borne by Him, the Almighty Word. To know Him is to know all. To be touched and gripped by the Spirit in this realm means being led into all truth."[5]

We will not attempt to follow out in detail the way in which Barth relates the voice of Christ to the cosmos, or the Truth of Christ to the universe of truths which concerns us in the cultural life of man. It will be sufficient to indicate how, on the ground of the Incarnation, Barth refuses to develop any abstract doctrine of the Logos of God apart from his unity with the humanity of Jesus Christ, or any abstract doctrine of man, that is, an independent anthropology, but only a doctrine of man in his essential reality and wholeness in relation to God,

---

[4] Cf. Barth's essay 'Philosophie und Theologie' in *Philosophie und Christliche Existenz,* pp. 94f, 101f, and *Church Dogmatics* IV.3 § 69.2 'The Light of Life.'

[5] *Dogmatics in Outline,* p. 26.

and to his fellow-man, and so to the world at large.

Just as in his doctrine of creation, Barth expounds the Covenant of Grace as the internal presupposition and ground of creation, and expounds the creation as the external presupposition and ground of the Covenant, so he thinks of Jesus Christ, the concrete fulfilment of the Covenant, in a constitutive relation both to the eternal election of God and to the whole of creation, for in him all things are gathered up and reconciled and made good in the divine good-pleasure. It is therefore only in Jesus Christ that we can understand the essential nature of the creaturely world and only in him that we can see properly and discern the ultimate meaning of all creaturely being and continuity and activity. It is in his great reconciling work that God has finally made good his work of creation, and therefore it is in the faithfulness of God incarnate in Jesus Christ that we can understand the independent distinctiveness of creation, its terrestrial truth, and its constant meaning, which persist in spite of all sin and corruption for the sake of the divine glory which in Jesus Christ overflows for all that God has made. Jesus Christ is the final establishment of the creation of God, and therefore it is only in and through him that the meaning of creaturely being and the rhythm of its continuity can have their fulfilment. Hence we are summoned to the praise of the Creator, which we cannot yield without enjoying and taking in earnest creaturely existence within the limits allotted to it by God's grace, and under the final affirmation of it by God's concrete act in Jesus Christ.

And yet, as in his doctrine of creation, Barth does not develop an ontology of creation or an independent cosmology as the prior understanding for theological interpretation of God's special work of redemption, so he refuses to develop a phenomenological understanding of man's creaturely actuality or his historico-existential structures as a general frame of reference for a new assimilation of theology to culture. Because Jesus Christ is the one Truth behind all truth, and the creative source of all culture, that does not allow us to detach theological activity from its proper object, the Being of God in his revelation, and to drag it down within the ideological circle of man's independent interpretations of the cultural patterns in his existence. A genuine theology can never be assimilated to any attempt to give meaning to man's life from some point of view determined by man himself, and therefore partaking of the sin and revolt of man from the source of all creaturely being and meaning in the one Truth of God.

Barth's refusal to take that course is dictated not only by propriety of theological method, but by sheer respect for the purpose of God revealed in creation and redemption, that man shall have completeness, unity and wholeness in his sphere as creature, as God is complete and whole in his own sphere. Respect for the creature and its creaturely activities will not allow its meaning to be distorted by an ideology developed out of man apart from Christ, or by one in which man in his independence seeks to transcend his creatureliness in order to ensure some place for himself in the divine. Therefore the *diastasis* which Barth was concerned for so many years to reveal between theology and culture was not only in the interests of good theology but in the interests of good culture, that is to say, of the proper fulfilment and enjoyment of full creaturely being and activity in its own determinate reality and truth. Far from manifesting any element of Philistinism, Barth's Christological theology carries with it the profoundest sense of God's affirming and supporting and guaranteeing and protecting of all that he has made, of his establishment of the creature in a mode of being and structured life of its own, within the limits allotted to it as a creature, and therefore in dependence upon the grace of God, but therefore also in the freedom of a reality to which God gives independent creaturely being and to which he gives glory—and so constancy and permanence—through sharing with it his own eternal glory.

Where Jesus Christ is really known as God in his turning toward man to be man's God, and as man who is the object of the eternal love of God, and therefore as God's man, there can only be the utmost reverence for human life and respect for human activity. It is the Incarnation, the fact that God has become man, and a man, in Jesus Christ in the midst of creation, that reveals that man is the center and crowning point of all God's ways and works in creation. There he is constituted by God as his covenant-partner, and called to a life on the boundary between heaven and earth where the meaning and goal of all his activity is found in divine support and affirmation, in divine concurrence and blessing, and where man can fulfil his life by being faithful to the creaturely world of men and nature in which God has placed him as well as by being faithful to the heavenly Father through filial love and obedience. In this way all the ways and works of man in his faithfulness on earth belong to the praise and rejoicing of creation in the Creator. Hence Barth can speak of the fulfilment of man's creaturely life and activity as the external aspect, and of the fulfilment of his Redemption in Jesus Christ as the internal aspect, of God's eternal purpose of grace. . . .

. . . The proclamation of the Gospel in the world awakens an *echo* in the external voices of the world which seem to take up its message and reflect it in ways and manners of its own. The self-revelation of Christ did not take place in a dark and empty and indefinite sphere, but in one which has real existence, fulness, form and brightness, thanks to the creative will and work of God. . . .

Theology is not . . . primarily concerned with the lights and truths of the creaturely world as they reflect and echo the Light and Truth of God, but we are concerned with human knowing and human understanding and human articulating of the one Truth and Light of God in Jesus Christ. It is here, then, in theology, perhaps above all, that we are to see the positive relation between the God of all grace and man as his covenant-partner, between God's sovereign togetherness with man and man's free togetherness with God. . . .

None of Barth's contemporaries discerns or appreciates more the positive relation of his theology to historic culture than Hans Urs von Balthasar. It is therefore fitting to end this study with a fine tribute from him to Barth.

"Barth's theology is beautiful, not merely in the external sense that Barth writes well. He does write well because he combines two things, passion and concrete positivity. It is passion for the subject-matter of theology and concrete positivity appropriate to the exciting nature of that subject-matter. Concrete positivity means to be engrossed in the object—it means objectivity. And Barth's object is God as he has revealed himself to the world in Jesus Christ according to the biblical witness. Because Barth—with Calvin, as against Luther—looks away altogether from the state of faith itself to its material content, because he commits himself to a strict theological objectivism ("faith lives from its object"), and thereby differentiates himself in the sharpest way from the Neo-Protestantism of Schleiermacher, he speaks well and without any suspicion of pietistic edifying. The subject-matter is edifying in itself, for it is so gripping and so demanding upon the whole man that here true objectivity coincides with an emotion that pulses through everything and has no independent expression of its own. Barth's theology is thus given a form and a presentation that mark it off from the all too disinterested objectivism of many a Catholic dogmatics. This combination of passion and objectivity is the reason for the beauty of Barth's theology. Who else in recent decades has known how to expound the Scriptures without becoming unduly exegetical or biblicist, without lapsing into tendentious constructions or pastoral rhetoric, but has concentrated so entirely upon the Word that it alone shines forth in its fulness and glory? And who is there who with unflagging energy has drawn a longer breath, taken a longer look and sustained it, as the subject-matter developed and presented itself before him in its vast extent? One would have to go back to St Thomas to find again this freedom from tension and narrowness, such unrivalled superiority in comprehension and in generosity—generosity which, with Barth, is not seldom charged with humour, but which acquires, above all, a pronounced taste for the proper tempo and rhythm of thought. Barth knows how to convince us that for him Christianity is an altogether triumphant matter. It is not merely because he has the gift of style that he writes well, but that above all he bears testimony, utterly objective testimony to a matter which, since it is about God, has the best style and the finest manuscript."[6]

2. H. Ridderbos[1] analyzes Bultmann's mythological interpretation of God's redemptive work in Christ's death and resurrection, and maintains that it is fundamentally unacceptable. It plays havoc with the New Testament message. Bultmann's basic thesis is the modern dogma of the impene-

[6] Hans Urs von Balthasar. *Karl Barth, Darstellung und Deutung seiner Theologie,* p. 35 f.

[1] Dr. Herman Ridderbos served as minister of the Reformed Churches in the Netherlands from 1934 to 1943 when he became professor of New Testament Studies at the Theological Seminary of Kampen. He is the editor of the *Reformed Weekly* (Kampen), one of the leading ecclesiastical periodicals in the Netherlands. He is the author of many scholarly publications: *Paul and Jesus, The Origin and General Character of Paul's Preaching of Christ, The History of Redemption and Holy Scripture, The Coming of the Kingdom, Galatians,* etc. It is from his monograph *Bultmann* (tr. by David H. Freeman, Philadelphia: Presbyterian and Reformed Publishing Co., 1960) that this excerpt has been taken pp. 17, 23–36.

trability of the natural world-order. His interpretation of the resurrection is controlled by the superstition that only that which can be ascertained by history can actually occur in time.

In the first place, according to Bultmann, the New Testament is, in more than one respect, of a mythological character. And if the New Testament proclamation is to be made intelligible for modern man, this mythological character must be removed. In particular this is true of the New Testament view of the world and of the history of redemption. . . . Accordingly the entire conception of the history of redemption in the New Testament bears a mythical character when viewed as the outcome of a struggle between supernatural powers, a struggle in which the Son of God descended from heavenly regions to dispute with the devil, to bring forgiveness, to inaugurate a new world era by his resurrection, and then, by returning to heaven, to bring the cosmic fulfillment of his redemptive work.

The significance of God's redemptive work in Christ's death and resurrection. . . . Jesus Christ, as the Son of God, as a pre-existent divine essence, is a mythical figure. He is, however, at the same time an historical person whose life ended on the cross. The historical and the mythical are interwoven in an unusual manner. The question is whether the mythological manner of speaking would not simply express for our faith, the supernatural *importance* of the historical person and his history. The issue is clear enough with respect to the utterances concerning his pre-existence and virgin birth. Faith here speaks in the language of mythology concerning the significance of Jesus. Such a concept is incomprehensible from the standpoint of the possibilities of this world. Mythically stated: He is of eternity, he is the Son of God.

The same argument is pertinent to Christ's crucifixion. This center of the Christian kerygma also appears in mythological form. The pre-existent Son of God is crucified; he is the sacrifice whose blood atones for our sins, and frees us from death. And this mythological conception, in which ideas of sacrifice and a juridical theory of satisfaction are mixed is useless to us. Even the New Testament does not exhaust the meaning of Christ in the pardon of former sins. Rather, the New Testament would say that the cross of Christ frees the believer from the *power* of sin and opens for him the way to a sacrifice or dedication of his life. To believe in the cross does not mean that we see a mythical event which took place in the external world. It means that we accept the cross of Christ as our own and permit ourselves to be crucified with Christ. When purged of all mythological content, the cosmic and eschatological significance ascribed to the cross in the New Testament, is reduced to the fact that the cross has a dimension which extends to all men ("the cosmic dimension") and that it becomes, again and again present ("the eschatological dimension"). Basically, mythological language wishes only to give expression to the lasting significance (*Bedeutsamkeit*) of historical events. The preaching of the cross confronts a person with the question as to whether he will also permit himself to be crucified with Christ, abandoning the flesh and surrendering himself to the "invisible," to what is not at man's disposal.

How can we know, however, that the historical event of the cross has this lasting redemptive significance? Does this depend upon the meaning of Jesus' person? For the contemporaries of Jesus this was certainly so.

They experienced the significance of the cross on the basis of their personal connection with the person of Jesus. For us this is no longer possible. And in the New Testament the crucified one is not proclaimed in such a manner, and the significance of his cross is not derived from his historical life. It was derived from the fact that the crucified one is at the same time the resurrected one. The cross and the resurrection in the New Testament proclamation belong with each other and constitute a unity.

What can we do with the mythological story of the resurrection? We can no longer accept it as a miraculous event which supplies us with the objective proof of Christ's significance. It is true that it is so thought of repeatedly in the New Testament (Acts 17:31). And Paul also tries to establish with certainty the resurrection as a historical event by enumerating the eye witnesses (I Corinthians 15:3–8). But this argumentation is fatal. The return of the dead to life is a mythical event; the resurrection cannot be established by witnesses as an objective fact, a guarantee of faith; the resurrection itself is an object of faith. It can be an object of faith only because it appears in our existence and makes the significance of the cross clear. Christ's death on the cross is not limited to himself, but in the surrender of faith it is repeatedly effectual in the acquisition of freedom, in putting off the works of darkness, in the return of man to his proper self. The resurrection is, therefore, not a mythical event, but it establishes itself in the concrete life of the believer. Faith in the resurrection is nothing but the faith that the salvation of God works itself out in the cross. It is not faith in Christ which is primary, rather it is faith in the cross which comes first. It is not because the cross is the cross of Christ that it is the redemptive act, but because the cross accomplishes redemption, in our existence, the cross is the cross of Christ. Otherwise the cross would be the tragic end of a noble man.

The question—How do we know that the historical event of the cross has divine redemptive significance?—can in the last analysis find no other answer: because it is proclaimed together with the resurrection, and because in this proclamation, the crucified one is encountered by us as the resurrected one. Faith in the Word of the resurrection is the real faith in the resurrection. *The fact of the resurrection is nothing other than the origin of the faith in the resurrected one,* in which the proclamation has its origin. The fact of the resurrection, as the resurrection of Christ, is *not* an historical event. The only historical fact that can be approached is the belief in the resurrection of the early disciples. The matter in which this originated can be made intelligible only to a certain degree from an historical point of view, e.g., visionary experiences, etc. The faith in the resurrection is important, however, not in its historical origin, but as the (*eschatological*) event repeatedly brought about by the proclamation of the Word. Faith and the Word by which faith becomes effective, belong to the eschatological event. In the proclamation both the cross and the resurrection are present. The encounter with the resurrected one occurs only in the proclaimed Word.

Does this interpretation of the New Testament's proclamation remove all remnants of mythology? Not if every utterance concerning the action of God is to be understood in a mythological sense. Such a redemptive action of God, is, however, no longer a miraculous supernatural event, but an event that is carried out in the closed historical border of space and time: in the person of Jesus, as a concrete historical man; in the sober proclamation of the person and the fate of Jesus of Nazareth; in the apostles, intelligible in their historical humanity; in the church, as a sociological phenomenon. But all such events are at the same time eschatological events, because there occurs, indemonstrably for science, but certainly for faith, the transition from the "the life according to the flesh" to "the life in freedom." The fact that this is not demonstrable insures the scandalous character of the Christian proclamation and insures it against the reproach of being mythological. The divine is not human, the heavenly is not earthly as in myth, but the presence of God in history is maintained in its paradoxical character. This is the unmythological sense or meaning of the great *kerygma*: "The Word became flesh."

Criticism

In General. Anyone carefully viewing Bultmann's program to *de-mythologize* the New Testament ought to be truly aware that it contains a frontal attack upon the manner in which the church of all ages has confessed its faith. And anyone who takes cognizance of Bultmann's larger theological works, his analysis of the first three Gospels, his book on Jesus, his commentary upon the Gospel of John, his writing on primitive Christianity, and his miscellaneous publications, is only confirmed in this impression. Undoubtedly, in the subjective sense of the word, Bultmann is not a ruthless critic like many of his modern predecessors. He desperately attempts to retain the kernel of the Christian faith. In Bultmann there is evidence of the tremendous struggle between the Christian faith and modern scientific thought. He rejects any compromise between faith and science, in which the results of the latter are denied or remain unreconciled to the content of faith. The thought of Bultmann can be viewed as a reaction against neo-orthodoxy, as the latter has developed since the end of the first world war, especially in Western Europe. . . . Bultmann's recognition of the necessity to conquer any dualism between faith and science is, in spite of many difficulties, an imperative demand.

Many Christians are involved in an un-Christian dualism. The quesion is, however, how far has Bultmann succeeded in solving the problem without doing violence to faith and to the established results of science.

Two methods can be employed. The *result* of de-mythologizing can be brought to light. One can try too, to test the validity of its theological and philosophical premises. We must not shun the second approach. Yet it is important to realize what is at stake in the conflict for and against Bultmann's *Entmythologisierungsprogram*. One of Bultmann's severest critics asks what remains in Bultmann of the

Christ of the Apostle's Creed. He concludes that Jesus Christ "was not conceived by the Holy Ghost, not born of the Virgin Mary. He did suffer under Pontius Pilate, He was crucified, He did not descend into hell and did not rise again on the third day from the dead; He did not ascend into heaven and does not sit on the right hand of God the Father, and will not come to judge the living and the dead." These words are devoid of any literal meaning, they are mythological, and do not denote any historical objective reality. This is true not only of Christology but is equally true of the Trinity, the substitutionary sacrifice of Christ, justification as the free pardoning from the guilt of sin, and the work of the Holy Spirit. All this is merely an "objectifying" imagination; it is of sole importance that we understand how faith can speak therein concerning itself. . . .

Bultmann's Mythological Interpretation of the History of Redemption

His Definition of the Mythical. To understand Bultmann's theological position in its entirety it is important to comprehend his conception of myth and of mythical thinking. Bultmann does not offer any systematic conceptual definition of these notions. In a more or less casual manner (in a note) he says the following: "the mythological is the manner of representation in which something which does not belong to this world, the divine, appears as something human; in which something belonging to the transcendent world appears as if it belonged to this world. For example, God's exaltation or elevation above the world is thought of as a spatial distance."[2] . . .

. . . In one of his recent "concluding" publications, Bultmann has again expressed himself quite clearly. Mythical thinking relates certain appearances and events to supernatural divine powers. In contrast scientific thought can deal only with the closed relationship of natural causes and effects. And this is true not only of science of nature, but also of the scientific conception of the personal life of man. A person who has outgrown mythical thought knows himself as a unity and recognizes his feelings, thoughts, and volitions, ascribing them to himself and no longer to the in-working of demonic or divine powers . . .

Myth and the New Testament Concept of God. In our opinion the *entmythologisierung* of the New Testament, based upon this concept of myth, plays havoc with the very heart of the New Testament message. . . . What makes Bultmann's interpretation of the New Testament fundamentally unacceptable—is his New Testament concept of God, or rather of the preaching of the entire Scripture with respect to God. In Bultmann's theology, the world and human personality retain their own independence and are completely shut off from God. At the very most, only something which occurs within this closed order can be *understood* by faith as an act of God. In the New Testament, however, *God is the Lord* of the world, not only because he is its creator, and because

[2] "Mythologisch ist die Vorstellungsweise, in der das Unweltliche, Göttliche als Weltliches, Menschliches, das Jenseitige als Diesseitiges erscheint, in der z.B. Gottes Jenseitigkeit als räumliche Ferne gedacht wird," *Kerygma und Mythos* I, p. 23.

from moment to moment he leads or directs the history of the world according to his council, but in particular because, in Christ, God acts in a unique manner with the world. He descends into history so that the coming of Christ is the middle point of an entire redemptive history which embraces the life of the world from the beginning to its end. And this all occurs not because of the world but because of God and for the honor of his name. The entire view which the New Testament (even as the Old) gives of the world, man, and history bears a theocentric character. It is for this reason that the *de-mythologizing* of the New Testament, proposed by Bultmann and his followers, signifies a destruction of this view of God. It can correctly be said that at the same moment in which one eliminates "myth" from the New Testament, not only is there no longer any room for Christ as the son of God, but the very conception of God is different; namely, God becomes a distant, non-active, majestic God. In contrast the New Testament speaks of a living God who acts in the history of the world and enters into human existence. This and this only is the legitimate interpretation of the Johannine expression, "the word became flesh and dwelt among us." This is also the meaning of the name Immanuel: "God is with us." Anyone exchanging this for Bultmann's conception loses hold of the kernel of the New Testament kerygma; he loses hold of the revelation of who God is and how God acts.

What we have said is equally true of Bultmann's interpretation of New Testament Christology. When he says that the statements concerning Christ's pre-existence and his virgin birth simply express in a mythical way the importance of Christ's historical person for our faith, Bultmann does not have any other foundation for this affirmation than the dogma of a closed world-order that will not admit of an "intervention from above." Of course it is true that Bultmann and his followers[3] appeal to exegetical considerations: The task of *de-mythologizing* is given to us by the New Testament itself insofar as certain New Testament *mythologoumena* do not agree with each other; for example, the idea that Christ is born of a virgin is in conflict with the idea of Christ's pre-existence.[4] But it is not [at] all evident that pre-existence and the virgin birth are in conflict with each other. Paul speaks in Philippians 2 of Christ's divine pre-existence and of his becoming a man in one breath. The idea of the virgin birth points to the way in which the Son of God assumed his human nature. What gives offense is not the inner contradiction of the idea but the idea itself, that of the pre-existence of a historical person as well as that of the virgin birth. The basis for criticism is not found in exegesis but in a modern dogma. Moreover, this modern dogma of the absolute separation of God and the world and the rendering independent of the world with respect to God, is in conflict with the essence of the New Testament kerygma because the latter is motivated by faith in the sovereignty of God over the cosmos. This de-mythologizing of Christology is there-

[3] Thus, for example, Hartlich and Sachs, in opposition to Barth, *Kerygma and Mythos* II, p. 114.

[4] *Kerygma und Mythos I,* p. 24.

fore a destruction of Christology because it not only affects the New Testament view of the world but it also does violence to the New Testament revelation of God.

Myth and the Witness of the Resurrection. What we have said is equally clear with respect to Bultmann's view of the resurrection of Christ. According to the definition proposed by Hartlich and Sachs, which Bultmann accepts, the mythological is that which cannot really happen because it cannot be established by the general laws of science. Miracles are impossible, the resurrection of Christ must be viewed as impossible. For it cannot be established as an objective fact by any number of witnesses. In Bultmann's opinion the Pauline argumentation in I Corinthians 15:3–8, where the eye witnesses are summarized, is fatal. It would make the resurrection a *beglaubigendes Mirakel.* Instead of the resurrection as an objective fact Bultmann posits the faith in the resurrection as the origin of the Christian kerygma.

Karl Barth in his severe criticism of Bultmann's interpretation of the New Testament proclamation of the resurrection[5] has correctly pointed out that this conception is controlled by a concept of reality that rests upon a superstition; namely, upon the superstition that only that which is objectively ascertainable by historical science can actually occur in time. Bultmann, Barth writes, rejects the report of what occurred in the forty days after Jesus' resurrection, because he cannot arrange its content insofar as it concerns the living Christ (and not only the faith of his disciples) under the "historical facts," in his limited sense of the word. Bultmann is, according to Barth, certainly right in this. No one can scientifically establish the resurrection of Christ. But Bultmann is incorrect when he draws the conclusion that the event portrayed did not occur. Why is it impossible for such an event to happen? Events can occur which are much more certainly real than anything which the "historian" as such can establish, and according to Barth we have evidence that the resurrection of Christ is just such an event.

This criticism is justified. It exposes the concept of reality on which Bultmann's de-mythologizing process proceeds. The latter is not only in conflict with the preaching of the New Testament, which because it is based upon a totally different conception of God also is characterized by an entirely different concept of reality, but this de-mythologizing also encloses the origin of the Christian proclamation and of the Christian Church in an impenetrable and mysterious obscurity. If Christ be not risen then the Christian proclamation and the Christian Church did not start with the resurrection but with the faith in the resurrection. The resurrection did not give rise to faith during this forty-day period, but faith gave rise to the resurrection. Or again to employ the words of Barth: "Nothing happened between Him and them; there was not a new and basic meeting between Him and them which in its newness was all decisive and out of which their faith arose. To be sure, at one moment they really penetrated to the mystery of the cross—but they were *alone*. Their faith did not have any basis upon which it was founded as faith before anything else. It stood sovereign in itself. The

[5] *Kirchliche Dogmatik* III, 2, pp. 531–537.

'deed of God' was thereby identical with the fact that they believed. And that it happened that they believed is the real content of the Easter history, the Easter time, that is the content of the Christian proclamation, the ground of existence of the church and of the sacraments. Jesus himself was not risen."

These words are of significance because they are appropriate to let us see the nature of the historical puzzle which this interpretation of Christ's resurrection involves us in. If Christ did not rise from the dead and this story is a myth, the question confronting us is how this myth originated. It is undeniable that this "myth" originated several days after the death of Jesus. A very abrupt change had to take place in the thoughts and deliberations of the disciples with respect to their dead Master. To think of this as the mythical formation of the significance (*Bedeutsamkeit*), which the disciples abruptly ascribed to Jesus' crucifixion without any new fact as its basis, a fact which originated outside of themselves, is a postulate that is dictated by Bultmann's concept of reality, but which is at the same time absolutely unintelligible from an historical point of view. It is especially incomprehensible if one remembers that this resurrection witness, in the primary sense of an eye witness (compare Acts 1:21, 22 ff.) was the starting point and center of the Christian proclamation and formed the foundation of Christian certainty.

Moreover, if after the passage of time such a new and spontaneous certainty occurred in his disciples with respect to Jesus' death, how can this assume the form of faith in the resurrection? Undoubtedly, Peter, John, Paul and all the disciples lived in a different concept of reality than Bultmann and his followers, and they were more susceptible to belief in such wonders, about which Hartlich and Sachs (with the approval of Bultmann) must declare, upon the basis of their definition of a myth, that they could not really happen. But this does not prove that we can ascribe to these disciples individual or collective hallucinations. What is here called myth was related to or concerned with an historical person, a person whose death had been witnessed three days before. In this respect the situation differs from that of heathendom, which concerns itself with various primeval heroes, or with a mythical figure whom no one had ever seen. And, in addition, what was projected or rendered objective was not only reality for the faith of the disciples, but it was also reality for their eyes, ears, and hands. In other words if this faith is considered to be a spontaneous occurrence without any factual basis upon which the disciples based their certainty, then it is not enough to point to the peculiar and uncritical nature of their world picture and conception of reality; in addition one must in this case also conclude that they were under the sway of an abnormal psychological condition. It is a puzzle how one can then consider this faith and the proclamation based upon it as the permanent starting point of the Christian faith. It is a puzzle that such an interpretation would be more attractive to a modern man than the proclamation of the real resurrection of Christ.

And finally when Bultmann and his followers speak about this mythological projection or objectivization they appeal repeatedly to the conception of the first Christians, as children of their time. It is impossible for us to enter into all the details involved at this point.[6] It is clear, however, that this so-called historical explanation fails exactly where it ought to possess the most demonstrable force, i.e., in its explanation of the faith in the resurrection. It is just in this decisive and central starting point of the Christian kerygma that the explanation of the *history of religion* in our opinion fails entirely. For the disciples were Jews, and it is an undeniable fact that to Judaism the figure of the dying and resurrected Messiah was entirely alien. There is no point of contact in contemporary Jewish conceptions in which the disciples could seek the return of Jesus from death to life. And yet some such point of contact must be present if the method of the *history of religion* is to hold. Of course one can appeal to the Greek conceptions concerning the "dying and rising Gods" such as they are found for example in some Hellenistic cultus-myths. But, even laying aside the fundamental difference in nature between these cultus-myths and the resurrection of Jesus from the dead, it is clear that the faith of Peter and John and of the church at Jerusalem in Jesus as the risen Savior was not derived from Greek myths. One might contend that after Jesus' death various religious motives entered which were foreign to the congregation of early Christians. But this cannot remove the fundamental fact that before such was possible, the disciples, and with them the early church at Jerusalem, already lived in the certainty of the resurrection of Christ.

If the faith and the preaching of Jesus as the resurrected does not rest upon the reality of his resurrection from the dead, we are faced with an historical riddle. The miracle is removed, but a riddle is set forth in its place. One denies the resurrection of Christ and posits the unexplainable mythical figure of the Christ of the early church in its place. But this has nothing to do with an exposition of the New Testament, nor with an interpretation which could not eliminate the real character of the New Testament proclamation. What is maintained by Bultmann in our opinion is nothing but a faith in the impenetrability of the natural world-order, a thesis which is in flagrant conflict with the central message of the New Testament.

3. R. A. Killen[1] maintains that Tillich's Christology implies a definite departure from Scripture. The Pauline doctrine of the Incarnation is interpreted in terms of a mythical manifestation of essential God-Manhood within existence. According to this the only person in Christ is the human person of Jesus who gradually became the Christ by his self-

[6] In this connection I would like to make mention of my writing *Paulus en Jezus* 1952, pp. 83 to 129 (English edition *Paul and Jesus,* pp. 80 to 130, 1958, Presbyterian and Reformed Publishing Company, Nutley, N.J.). In this work I have treated the absolute untenability of this affirmation with respect to the New Testament proclamation of Jesus as the Son of God, the Lord, who descended from the heavens, the creator of the cosmos. In this connection I have treated Bultmann's appeal to the pre-Christian gnostic myth.

[1] Dr. R. Allan Killen is the author of *The Ontological Theology of Paul Tillich* (J. H. Kok, N. V. Kampen, 1956). It is from Ch. X of this book, n. 5 *The Doctrine of Christ,* that this excerpt has been taken from pp. 257–265.

surrender to the God-Man from heaven. The author thinks that Tillich's view of Christ as only the center of history does away with the scriptural vision of Christ as Lord of all history and salvation. His ontological theology fails to establish the uniqueness of Christ.

Tillich is to be commended for the stress which he places upon Christ and for his insistence that Christ forms the middle point of history. That he has renamed the Biblical term the "new creature" the New Being does indicate a certain departure from the Scriptures but still the stress upon the new reality experienced in regeneration is an emphasis upon an important phase of salvation.

Nevertheless the view which Tillich has of Christ, that is his doctrine of Christ, is very different from that presented in the Scriptures. He does not believe that the second person of the Trinity, God the Son, has come down from heaven and taken upon Himself a full human nature, become flesh and become a man. He writes in the article called, "A Reinterpretation of the Doctrine of the Atonement" (in which perhaps he gives his clearest exposition of his view of the Incarnation), "I am becoming increasingly suspicious, . . . that many people employed the concept of Incarnation in a mythological and superstitious manner: it implies for them the transmutation or metamorphosis of *a* divine being into *a* human being, a polytheistic myth which we find in all paganism, and incompatible with the fundamental truth of prophetic revelation. The God who creates, sustains and transcends all beings, is not himself *a* being, not even the highest."[2] From such a statement it is clear Tillich flatly rejects the idea that in the Incarnation a heavenly person, that is of God the son, actually became man. He writes, "When the Christian Church rejected Arianism, it rejected at the same time the conception of the Incarnation as the transmutation of a divine being into a human being."[3] Tillich admits that there may be a biblical inclination to describe the historical Jesus "in terms of a semi-mythological character."[4] Phil. 2:5–11 speaks, he says, of "the pre-existent spiritual being who resigns his divine form and power, and takes the form of a servant, and is raised by God on high to receive a name which is above every name—this being who makes a moral decision in His pre-existent state is certainly not God himself, but a divine being. The decision 'not to snatch at equality with God but to empty himself' occurs in a suprahistorical, mythological sphere . . ." And he continues, "the distinction of the three spheres [Pre-existent, servant, and raised] is mythical, using three modes of time for the destiny of the divine being."[5] In John 1:1–14 Tillich says there is a similar description of the Logos who was with God, of his function in creation, and his entering a world which did not recognize him, but, "the mythological ele-

[2] Paul Tillich, "A Reinterpretation of the Doctrine of Incarnation"; *Church Quarterly Review,* Jan.Mar. 1949, p. 134.

[3] *Ibid.,* p. 135.

[4] *Loc. cit.*

[5] *Loc. cit.*

ment is reduced to a great extent by the categories Logos, Life and Light."[6] In John the divine being spoken of *"is a divine principle in which the mythological implications of pre-existence have been overcome* to such an extent that the later Logos doctrine could develop from it. It represents a definite step beyond Paul."[7]

Surely it is strange reasoning on Tillich's part to go from Paul to the Gospel of John in order to prove a dying away of the mythical elements in the idea of the Incarnation! John 1. states clearly "the word became flesh." In John 3:17 we read, "God sent his son into the world," in Jn 17:5, "And now, O Father, glorify me with thine own self with the glory which I had with thee before the world began." No one can read this Gospel without seeing clearly that it teaches the heavenly origin of Jesus Christ! Tillich's fantastic attempt to prove from John that Jesus Christ did not first exist as a heavenly person, indicates how difficult is his task to prove Jesus was not a heavenly person. He concludes his argument, "It follows from this that the biblical interpretation of the Incarnation does not imply that God as such becomes man . . ."[8]

In I Cor. 15:45–49, Tillich argues that Paul presents three stages: 1. The heavenly man who is spiritual and immortal before his coming. 2. The physical man Adam subject to death. 3. The heavenly man, who overcomes death. "The emphasis which Paul lays on the sequence of these stages in a polemic form, indicates that he struggles for the historical manifestation of the man from above after Adam's fall, an idea which did not exist and could not exist in the pagan form of a myth of the "original man."[9] Tillich is trying to reason that his idea of an original God-man, that is of man as he was in his essential state before his fall, is what Paul was endeavoring to express here but could not make clear! There are three stages: There was *first* man as essential being before he fell or "the heavenly man who is spiritual and immortal"—though "essential being as such is merely potential and not actual"[10] and therefore never really existed—and in that condition man was united with God. There is *second* man as he exists or "the physical man Adam subject to death." There is *third,* the Incarnation, in which the Logos principle in God became united with the essential being of man as it was in the mind of God, to form the God-man, and the God-man in turn became united with a man called Jesus. To express this anthropologically, Jesus so completely surrendered himself to God that he could become united with this "essential God-manhood."[11] Tillich simply says, "The Incarnation is the manifestation of essential God-manhood within existence."[12] And therefore he can conclude: *"the proposition that*

---

[6] *Loc. cit.*

[7] *Loc. cit.;* Italics ours.

[8] *Ibid.,* p. 136.

[9] *Loc. cit.*

[10] *Ibid.,* p. 142.

[11] *Ibid.,* p. 143. "To essential man belongs the unity of his finiteness with his infinity, and it is precisely this unity which I call Godmanhood." It is this which the Logos accomplished before he united with Jesus.

[12] *Ibid.,* p. 146.

God became man, or became flesh, is definitely unbiblical."[13] What Paul is expressing is the myth of essential being becoming united with existential being when Jesus became Christ!

It is not necessary to go any further to show the entire difference of Tillich's theory of the Incarnation from that presented in the Scriptures. Phil. 2:5–11, John 1:1–14, 1 Cor. 15–49 are all denied their clear unequivocal meaning by him and reinterpreted by the superimposition of this theory of essential being. Tillich is presenting a theory of the restoration of the unity between finite man and the Infinite which was lost by man's assertion of himself in order to exist. Perhaps the best simile to express his view of the prehistoric fall is that of the unconscious struggles of the babe in its mother's womb before it is born. Can the babe be held responsible for what it does in coming to birth. Surely not! Yet Tillich insists that man in the state of "dreaming innocence" asserted himself and fell *before* he came to self-conscious existence, and that all, including Adam, are responsible for this "original sin"! To lay upon man the responsibility of what occurred in a period of "dreaming innocence," before self-consciousness was attained, is surely an injustice. When the Fall is thus removed from history original sin becomes a necessity and therefore not a responsibility. If the idea of the imputation of Adam's sin to his offspring is a stumbling block to man's finite reason, this solution of Tillich's only makes the stumbling block all the greater! An act of rebellion committed in conscious revolt by Adam in the time of innocence, is entirely different from something done in unconsciousness. This explanation makes the imputation of Adam's sin to mankind only harder to understand.

Tillich's claim that Jesus was a human person brings him into conflict with the Reformed Confessions, which teach that Christ is a divine person. The Westminster Confession for example says, "The Son of God, the second person in the Trinity, being very and eternal God, of one substance and equal with the Father, did, when the fullness of time was come take upon him man's nature, with all the essential properties and common infirmities thereof . . ."[14]

It is not necessary for our immediate purpose to go into the difficult problem of the human nature assumed by Christ. The general view of Calvinistic Reformed theologians, and our own, is that Christ assumed an impersonal human nature. . . . The most important point for us is that the confessions clearly teach that the Second Person of the Trinity assumed a complete human nature or as the Westminster Confession describes it "man's nature with all the essential properties and common infirmities thereof," and as the Confessio Belgica expresses it "became like unto man, really assuming the true human nature, with all its infirmities, sin excepted . . ."[15] This occurred in such a manner that "there are not two sons of God, but two natures united in one person." The human nature had no subsistence apart from the Son of God with His divine nature—an idea often expressed by the word *anhypostasis*. But Tillich

[13] *Ibid.*, p. 139. Italics ours.
[14] The Westminster Confession of Faith, VIII: 2.
[15] The Confession of Faith as revised at Dordrecht. Art. 18 and 19.

clearly teaches on the one hand that no divine person did descend from heaven, and on the other hand that a human person called Jesus existed first apart from any union with the divine nature in any sense. Jesus surrendered himself completely in a process of submission which extended through his life—the Cross for Tillich begins in Christ's life of self-surrender long before his death—and finally became completely united with the God-Man from heaven at the Cross.

Tillich is forced by his definition of God as Infinite and Absolute, and the corollary which he deduces from this that God cannot be a person, to find the person of his "Jesus who became the Christ" in the man Jesus. That the Scripture presents no such view he actually must admit since he himself says that there is in Paul in particular, and also still in John, a "myth" of Christ as a person come from heaven. . . .

With his theory of Christ as the center of History Tillich makes a separation between Jesus Christ and the history of salvation. The Scriptures regard Him not simply as the center but also as the Lord of History. "No man hath seen God at any time, the only begotten Son which is in the bosom of the Father He hath declared Him."[16] He has and does reveal God the Father in history. . . . He was controlling and developing the progressive history of salvation from the Fall to the Cross and until His return. The picture given in the Scriptures is that Christ is the Lord of history, "upholding all things by the word of His power," and active in it both in the creation—"by whom all things are made"—and in the history of salvation as it developed in such events as the Ark, the Covenant with Israel, the revelation through the prophets as they searched, "what or what manner of time the Spirit of Christ which was in them did signify of the sufferings of Christ and the glory that should follow,"[17] and that today He holds the stars of the seven Churches in His hand, and that He will come again for His own.

The history of salvation is not confined to an event in the year 33 A.D., even though all salvation rests upon the satisfaction offered for sin in the death of Christ upon the Cross, but has an historical development which started with Adam and Eve . . . and continues till Christ hath put all enemies under His feet, judged the quick and the dead, and delivered the kingdom again to God the Father.[18]

There is no substitutionary atonement offered by Christ for sin in Tillich's view. He only reunites what was separated—that is he unites essential God-manhood and man—first however doing this for himself since he was a fallible, erring man[19] and in doing this also accomplishing it for man. Christ experienced the "strange work of God's love," as God, united with Jesus

---

[16] Jn. 1 : 18.

[17] Peter. 1 : 11.

[18] 1 Cor. 15 : 24–28.

[19] "A Reinterpretation of the Doctrine of the Incarnation," p. 145. "It is not wise to attempt to express the character of the New Being in Christ in negative and static terms such as 'lack of sin' or 'lack of error.' " It is to be expected that Volume II of *Systematic Theology* will reveal Tillich's view of the problem of the sinlessness of Christ. He certainly considers that Christ could err but tries to separate error from sin. Error is due to finiteness, sin to hybris or pride and concupiscence, and Jesus as human was finite, but still he showed no pride because he constantly surrendered himself to God, according to Tillich.

Christ, took the strange work of love upon himself.[20] "The Cross of Christ is the symbol of the divine love, participating in the destruction into which it throws him who acts against love: This is the meaning of Atonement." But such is not, we must point out, the substitutionary Atonement presented in the Bible in which there is a real satisfaction for sin. The scripture says: "He shall see the travail of his soul and shall be satisfied . . . for he shall bear their iniquities."[21] "For he hath made him to be sin for us who knew no sin; that we might be made the righteousness of God in him."[22]

With his teaching that a man called Jesus finally by self-surrender became the Christ, Tillich places himself in a position from which it is difficult for him to maintain that his views are superior to those of Buddhism. . . . [Regarding] "Eschatology," it would be difficult for him to maintain any real sort of conscious future existence, when he says the subject-object relationship will cease in the future life. When such a close union with the Ultimate is claimed, the Buddhist theory of Nirvana appears more consistent.

When it is said that it is difficult for him to defend himself against Buddhism, this is meant in the sense that the Buddhist is in a position to claim equal finality and importance for his view of Buddha, as Tillich does for his view of Christ, as the center of history and the bringer of the New Being. The Buddhist claims, just as does Tillich, that his founder was a man who finally became deified. The weakest point, in other words, in Tillich's view of Christ, and that which makes him most vulnerable, is that he only has a man who became deified. Since such a religion as Buddhism has the same, wherein lies the difference? . . .

Tillich himself sees much in Buddhism with which he can agree. In his *Systematic Theology* Volume 1 he refers to Buddhism in several places.[23] He considers that it had, at least in its earlier forms, a realization of the Ultimate or Being-Itself,[24] and classes it as a form of mystical monotheism.[25] According to him it has a god, is monotheistic, and shows indications of trinitarian thinking—even if it does not have a trinity—to the extent that there is more than one principle in the Buddhist All.[26] At the same time it fails to reach the level of "exclusive monotheism," since in Buddhism God may be absolute and universal but never becomes concrete.[27] In contrast, in the event of Jesus becoming the Christ, Christianity presents an explanation of how the absolute and the relative, the universal and the concrete, have been united in the union of the Logos principle in God with a man called Jesus, in such a manner that he became "the Christ" and can be regarded as a divine person. Buddhism, Tillich claims, has an ecstatic experience of the Ultimate but cannot have a final revelation—that is a single revelation of the union of the uni-

---

[20] *Love, Power and Justice,* p. 113.
[21] Isaiah 53:11; Gal. 3:13.
[22] 2 Cor. 5:21, Cf. 1 Peter 2:15; 3:18.
[23] *Ibid.,* p. 16, 113, 132, 220, 229.
[24] *Ibid.,* p. 132, 229.
[25] *Ibid.,* p. 229.
[26] *Loc. cit.*
[27] *Loc. cit.*

versal and the concrete, and of God and man—which can form the central point of reference for all other revelations. In contrast to this, "There is no revelation in the history of the Church whose point of reference is not Jesus as the Christ."[28]

Tillich's strongest point of defence is that Buddhism makes the creation in itself evil, while he holds that there is evil in creation only because of man's sin. If he had not placed sin beyond the responsibility of man, in a period of "dreaming innocence," his position would be much stronger at this point. Since he does place original sin before existence, he makes it essentially a necessity. His view of Non-Being makes evil also a necessity for creation—God would be the Unmoved Mover except for Non-Being.

It is hard to see in what way the Christ Tillich presents unites the universal and the concrete in any more real manner than could be claimed by the Buddhist for Buddha. Such an argument as Tillich presents for Christ, as uniting the Universal and the concrete, could be equally well applied to any other religious figure who has become deified in the eyes of his followers. His one strong point here is that the Scriptures do speak of the Logos coming down from heaven. In other words he can find material in the Bible which can be used by "demythologization" and "interpretation" to support his theory of the deification of the man Jesus. But he can only make the Scriptures fit his theory by the application of such methods, though of course these methods are open to most definite criticism. The Buddhist could introduce the theory of the one and the many, and apply it to Buddha equally well. Tillich applies the theory of the one and the many to the Bible, and by means of "demythologization" and "interpretation" makes the Bible support the theory.

If Tillich reasons that the New Being is unique in that it excludes all other appearances as the New Being—nothing else can be the New Being in contrast—he argues in a circle and bases his reasoning upon the acceptance of his own definition of the New Being. Such an argument cannot be claimed to prove anything, and certainly is worthless as a means to distinguish and defend his view against the possible claims of any other religion.

Tillich's inability to defend the Christ which he presents as the center of history against the possible claims of such a religion as Buddhism, has been dealt with in some detail, in order to show the particular weakness of his Christology. There is a real danger, because his arguments for the uniqueness of Christ are so weak and unsatisfactory, that some of his successors may find some other religion just as compatible with his ontology, and retain his ontology while rejecting the Christ whom he presents.

4. W. N. Pittenger[1] views Brunner's Christology as the expression of most extreme neo-orthodoxy. He sees him rejecting as rationalization any

---

[28] *Ibid.*, p. 132.

[29] *Ibid.*

[1] W. Norman Pittenger, S.T.D., was born in Bogota, N.J., in 1905. He was Charles Lewis Gomph Professor of Christian Apologetics at the General Theological Seminary in

theological discussion of the Incarnation. His Christology is primarily concerned with Soteriology. The Word of God is God's announcing for our salvation his own name and his own person. Christ is *The Only One,* the Word of God to be encountered exclusively by faith and not to be measured as a historical figure. Jesus becomes an accidental, and an almost irrelevant, element in the revelation of the Word, with Incarnation and atonement outside the "historical process."

Emil Brunner and Karl Barth have separated over the question of general revelation; and they have other very decided differences, for example about whether or not there is ultimate salvation for all men. However, their position as the most eminent of the dialectic theologians remains firm, and their differences do not seem to affect seriously the general outline of the doctrine of Christ which is characteristic of the entire modern school that has been so profoundly influenced by them. . . . I shall attempt a critical evaluation of the classical statement of this Christology in Brunner's work *Der Mittler.*[2] I have chosen this volume in preference to half-a-dozen others . . . because it has been enormously influential and . . . still represents, despite its author's not very significant changes in view since its appearance, the most "extreme" statement of neo-orthodox Christology. . . .

The place of Christ in this theology may briefly be summarized as follows: He is the once-for-all, the absolutely and entirely unique revelation of God to man, the Word of God. This Christ, says Brunner, is the single meeting place of Deity and humanity, "the human life in which God wills to meet. man." Apart from this one spot, as we have seen, there is no *real* revelation, only "indirect" and in some sense corrupt intimations. Yet the revelation in Christ is not really in the historic figure of Jesus; for it is "not the actual fact which is made known through history" which is the revelation but rather "the invisible secret of the person of Jesus, hidden behind the veils of history and human life, not the Christ after the flesh but the Christ after the Spirit." . . . With Brunner the historic figure is almost meaningless apart from faith, yet curiously enough he, like others of the "school," while denying the continuity on which the patristic outlook rested, still speak of Christ as "the Word made flesh," and ventures to apply to him the language of Chalcedonian orthodoxy.

A Christology of Salvation. Brunner's doctrine of Christ is primarily concerned with soteriology in the strict sense of forgiveness of sin, a characteristic which of course marks most of German theology from the time of Luther. The Word of God is understood to be "the Word of salvation," or

New York, and is presently teaching at King's College, Cambridge, England. He also chairmaned the Theological Commission of the World Council of Churches in 1961–62. He has authored many theological works, among them *Christian Sacrifices, Theology and Reality,* etc. It is from his book, *The Word Incarnate* (New York: Harper and Bros., 1959) that this excerpt has been taken, selectively, from pp. 132 to 145.

[2] Translated by Olive Wyon and published with the English title of *The Mediator* (New York: Macmillan, 1934).

"the Word of grace," or "the gracious Word which conveys mercy and pardon." An almost complete lack of interest in any of the cosmological questions which may be raised about the Word of God is evident in Brunner's treatment of the history of the *Logos* conception. This "spoken Word of the Creator" is essentially "the Word which is salvation"; and Brunner permits no metaphysical speculation to deflect him from his main concern. The Word of God as an eternal person in the Godhead is described in traditional language as "the process of self-communication existing eternally in God," but we discover that the self-communication which is predicated of him, so far as the *world* is concerned, is largely confined to the "speaking of God's name" to man—that is to say, the revealing for salvation of God's person as love to those who are called to this knowledge. The Word is that in which or in whom God "expresses himself," but the expression seems to be almost exclusively soteriological. It is the speaking of God's pardon and his forgiving love. Therefore the Christian faith is above all else the knowledge of God as the one who saves. In fact, he is the God known in religious experience and of a very special sort of religious experience, much as Brunner and all of his colleagues would fight shy of the description and attack any view which was based on "experience."

It is God's Word who speaks that salvation. In this sense there is combined with the soteriological emphasis an almost verbal sense of revelation. Presumably all God does is *speak;* one might ask if he ever is said to do more than talk about himself. The traditional Catholic teaching of infused grace is of course explicitly denied as a doctrine which reduces Christianity to a materialistic or sub-personal level; this would introduce "process" and hence make Christianity a species of general revelation and not the absolutely once-for-all self-disclosure of God. As a result, we are left with the feeling that at heart the Christian faith is for Brunner a sort of "conversation piece," but one which is remarkably one-sided for God does all the talking and man all the listening.

For Brunner, then, the Word is primarily if not solely what God says to us; it is God's announcing for our salvation of his own name and his own person. All that man can do in the presence of that Word is to listen to what is said, and then accept or refuse, although this choice seems finally in God's hands, none the less. The speaking of the Word is an imperative, a challenge, man's inescapable moment of crisis and decision. Upon it hangs spiritual life and upon it hangs spiritual death. It is God, crashing into our human world with his *either-or. . . .*

Christ the 'Only One,' the Word. But in Christ there is the once-for-all revelation. He is no prophet; to him the prophets looked forward, even if unconsciously. He is the Word in person. He does not announce the message from God; he *is* the Message. He is utterly unique, not merely in what Brunner calls "the modern sense" of that word, which for him would mean only one who is the climax of a series which is "relative and gradual." He is unique in that he is "the *Only One* . . . who can have no equal." He is utterly different from us in principle; we are mere creatures, he is the very Word of God, God himself. He comes to us "from beyond the frontier of creaturely existence, because he comes to us from the side of God, from the bosom of God, from within him, from the mystery of the divine self-existence." . . .

We can only raise here the questions, How does man recognize Christ for what he is claimed to be, if apart from him there is absolutely no knowledge of God which may be trusted? Does not this position destroy the whole basis for the Christian doctrine of Christ as God-man? Is it not true that unless our every experience of goodness, truth, and beauty, our every profound insight, and even something of the message of the great non-Christian religions, have some measure of revelatory value, the Christian faith is really without foundation in the basic order of the world? . . .

. . . Christ's distinction from the prophets, as a matter of definition, rests "in the fact that in him person and Word, indeed the essential divine Word, the mysterious Word, the Word from the other side, are all one." . . . In a sentence that could be unexceptionable, but for Brunner has a peculiar meaning, "In the fact that the Christian worships a man as the supreme authority, he expresses the absolute and unique mystery that this man is God."

But the Jesus of history is not the object of faith. Brunner compares this conception of Christ with the Christologies of the nineteenth and early twentieth centuries. He is especially critical of doctrines resting upon "disposition," as in Ritschl and Herrmann, or upon "piety," as in Schleiermacher. Against these theories of Christ's nature and work, which he calls "humanistic" theories, and against all their successors in the same tradition, he declared that this widespread "perception that the life of Jesus expressed perfect love, the perception of his ethical and religious temper, and the trust which this inspires, is not connected with faith at all; it is simply an opinion, in accordance with the general human ethical standard."

That Jesus was such-and-such a man is for many of the dialectical writers no revelation at all, no Word of God speaking salvation to the soul of man. For Brunner such a starting-point would mean that faith was centered in a contingent historical figure and not in the Word of God. A Christology like Ritschl's and Herrmann's would, he believes, keep Jesus entirely in the sphere of human history; but the doctrine of Christ's deity "means that in him God is acting, that his forgiveness is the forgiveness of God, his divine proxy, his authority, the secret of his person. Not because he shows forth perfect love does God show himself in him. . . . Only because and in so far as he is recognized as the One who comes to us from the inmost heart of the mystery of God, does his love really tell us something about God which otherwise we would not know." How right and how wrong is Brunner's teaching here! Christ is not to be compared with any other figure in history, by standards of our own making; if we do so, we reduce him to the purely contingent, and there is then in him no revelation at all. Christ is himself the supreme standard. Yet on the other hand, the life of the historic Jesus as portrayed in the Gospels can be measured and studied; but for Brunner it is not this historic figure who matters at all for faith, but the Word striking us in and through him, and that Word is without any comparison with others.

The Historic Jesus the Incognito for the Word. Following this train of thought, the "neo-orthodox" school has been prepared in some of its exponents to say frankly that the historic figure of Jesus of Nazareth, as contingent and "accidental," is almost irrelevant for the revelation of the Word of God. The revelation of God, while it is thus in some sense connected or related with history, is not in nor of history; the relation or connection is as a tangent to a circle's periphery. At this point, we must note the concept of the super-historical, *urgeschichte*. This is a realm that apparently has some loose connection with the historic event-level which we know in the time process, but as we have indicated, it touches that level only at a tangent. It is indeed in some sense the locus of the "facts" of religious faith, but it is reached only by a faith which is itself the work of God in man, and which cuts across and supersedes the "facts" in so far as they are historical and hence "contingent."

By the use of this concept Brunner is able to accept the most extreme and radical, even sceptical views, of the New Testament and of Christian origins, and at the same time to claim that Christ as Word of God may be accepted with the certainty of faith. One way in which the dialectic theologians have put this is by saying that the *personality* of Jesus as existing in time and space is human: his *person*, which does not exist in time and space, is divine. . . . It is doubtless in line with this view that the 'school' feels that Christ can have no connection with other events. Indeed he is not an event nor the culmination of event but the *end* of event, the *end* of all process, the intersection of history and eternity; he is, so to speak, the "fullfilment" of history by being the abrogation of it.

The Incarnation and Atonement cannot then be "dated," says Brunner, for they are not really part of the historic process. That they actually happened, that human guilt was "expiated" (to use his own phrase), and that man's sin was covered through Christ's sacrifice, "is not anything which can be conceived from the point of view of history." Attempts to prove anything about Christ from history must therefore fail; faith alone can perceive the truth. That certain things are true and actually did happen is of course given to faith; but Brunner's denial of any real relationship of time and eternity finally reduces him to the expedient of affirming that "it would be absurd to say that in the year thirty the Atonement of the world took place. But we can say: this event, which those who know history tell us probably took place about the year thirty, is the same as that which we know through faith as the divine act of Atonement."

Just what this wriggling has gained him is not very clear; for the dilemma remains quite obvious. Either by a certain series of actual historic events man was brought close to God, or he was not; and while scientific history cannot interpret those events in what we might call spiritual regard, for faith alone can know who Jesus Christ is, the event itself when so interpreted by faith *is* the Incarnation and the Atonement. This Incarnation and Atonement can hardly have taken place in some supra-historical realm about which *nothing* is known or can be known apart from faith. . . .

Salvation therefore rests upon knowledge of the Christ of faith, the secret of his person. Thus the claims made by the historical personality for himself (except perhaps the assertion of Messiahship, to which Brunner seems to cling) are of no real value, and acceptance of them is not salvation. The decisive fact is "what his significance really is, and not what he felt about it." That is certainly true. But Brunner makes such a sharp contrast between this historical figure and the Christ of faith, that it is difficult to see how companionship with one led to faith in the other, even with the belief in the Resurrection.

Brunner is indeed very clear that the inner life and the psychology of Jesus are of no importance for faith; his self-consciousness is not the center of the Christian religion; his being sent by God to man is. And apart from the acceptance of him as such, in that moment of crisis when he confronts man, there is no hope. This is man's ultimate necessity, upon which depends life and death, heaven and hell. It is the moment of choice.

For man "expiation" of his guilt is necessary; he is sunk in sin since the Fall and cannot rise by his own efforts. The Word by his Incarnation and Atonement reveals man's present plight and when known by faith redeems man. This is "our redemption and our life, as well as our humiliation and death." One without the other is false. Yet we may remark in passing that with this whole outlook on the nature of the world and history, and the relation of these to God, it is doubtful if the Word *can* in any genuine sense redeem his creation. If God never touches his world except tangentially, if there is an absolute and ultimate dualism, and if even in the great act of Redemption God has not actually "entered" into his world to save it, that creation has not really been brought back to him. "God does not redeem what he has not assumed"; and at the very heart of this theology, in Christ himself, there is a gap between the historic and the divine, God and man, which is not bridged. Brunner says that "the Son of God assumed the whole of humanity," but it is an assertion which really finds no place in his system.

The Christian Revelation and Redemption. What is revelation and Redemption, as Brunner understands them? Briefly, they are that God sent his Son, so that man's self-will is broken and God's secret name may be known and honored. There is no trace of man's becoming in any vital sense a sharer of the divine nature. . . . The act of revelation and redemption is essentially the *disclosure* of the love of God, the *announcement* of his love; one of the ends of revelation and redemption is the making known of this love towards men. But once again, this is not through word spoken on earth nor life lived among us, nor is this redemption through event in history; it is through, and in super-historic transaction grasped by faith. . . . God's self-giving, then, might seem to reduce itself merely to an announcement to us; but this is qualified by making it an announcement in *deed.* Here we have the ring of common historical Christianity, but our satisfaction is spoiled by the absolute refusal of any love towards the human Jesus as the deed thus embodying the divine in the sphere of history. Devotion can only be directed to the Word, not to the historic personality. . . .

The Error of Formal Christology. Brunner is insistent that there should be no theoretical discussion of the Incarnation; that is, as to the *how* of it and of the resultant Atonement. He quotes Melancthon's aphorism that the knowledge of Christ is the knowledge of his benefits, not of his natures; and he severely castigates those who attempt to develop some theory of the mode of union of the divine and human in our Lord. Such a union is known only to faith; it is the result of the impact of the Word upon the helpless soul of man. For this reason, there is in *The Mediator* no attempt to work out a formal Christology, which might in some fashion "explain" the mystery of the Incarnation by bringing it within the ambit of human experience or by hinting at some means by which it may have been achieved. All such efforts, Brunner believes, reduce Christ to our human standards and limitations, try to fit him into our categories, and therefore deny his uniqueness, his imperative call upon our faith, and his demand for a decision in our life.

Christological speculation is rationalization, according to Brunner; it turns "a necessity for decision into a need for explanation." "A relation produced by the authoritative personal presence of the Word of God is turned into a magico-material substantial presence. The doctrine of the two natures becomes the object of purely external, theoretical, semi-scientific discussion and explanation." In this way, any real attempt to understand how the Word became flesh is dismissed as the worst of errors. Men can do one thing only when faced with him—accept without any question and without any attempt to reason. They are passive recipients of a message from God, a message which is God, coming to them *ab extra,* from outside themselves and from outside the world which they know in their own experience. How then they can know the message to be from God is another question . . . the theologians of this school seem to land back in the very subjectivism which they so violently denounce, for their recourse to faith and their frequent reference to the *testimonium Spiritus Sancti* do not really save them from the epistemological problem. . . .

In one place Brunner writes that the "humanity of the Son of God means that he has really come, it means the contingency and the uniqueness of the revelation," while "the divinity of the Son of Man means the eternity of the Word, the personal presence of the eternal God in him." It may seem that in words like these the Swiss theologian approaches the emphases which mark the traditional Christian view of the Incarnation. But the hope is false, for an analysis of these phrases in the light of the remainder of his work shows that almost every one of them is used in some sense which differs radically from the traditional view.

There is indeed but the slightest connection between this "neo-orthodox" Christology and that which is reflected in the Apologists and Fathers of the Church, although Brunner endeavors to show that St. Irenaeus, his favorite patristic writer, held a position like his own. . . .

A study of this Christology appears to bear out the conclusion that despite certain important emphases which are corrective of liberal Protestant errors, the developed position of the "neo-orthodox" as represented by Brunner is thoroughly unsatisfactory. There is nothing in it of that profound conviction of man as God's son (even when estranged from God by sin) which roots back in the Galilean Gospel and which alone makes belief in the God-man a living possibility. There is nothing of the sacramental point of view which follows from the acceptance of Christ and his extended presence in his mystical Body as the concentration in a thoroughly human mode of an eternal self-donation of God to his world. As this theology sees him, Christ is utterly unrelated, prodigious, miraculous; a bolt from the blue into this wicked world. He astonishes and shocks us by his strangeness; he is in no way congruous with the rest of our experience and knowledge; he makes nonsense of all we have thought God has partially revealed of himself to men, for he is the denial not the fulfilment of it.

This kind of doctrine of Christ seems to me to crystallize an irrational philosophy, a sceptical epistemology, and a dualistic theology. While it is true that the "neo-orthodox" theology was valuable in emphasizing once again the great fact of God's transcendent majesty and glory, it has obtained its victory at the expense of destroying the significance of the world which God loved enough to "enter" and redeem. It is a hard saying, but I believe that this theology is much farther from the Christian gospel than the liberal school which it so despises. . . .

5. L. Malevez, S.J.,[1] analyzes Oscar Cullmann's thesis of assertive and exclusive functional theology and Christology in the Scriptures and finds it unfaithful to the authentic spirit of the Bible. He goes on to point out the unorthodox implications which that view would suggest. He sees Dupont's functionalism as not exclusive. However, it is exaggerated and misleading. Functionalism in the Scriptures is relative and presupposes some basic ontological judgments.

The expression "functional theology" has various meanings among modern theologians. Some use it to describe our subjective religious representations. Most authors, however, apply this term to the object of our representations, God. They say God has manifested himself to us, not in himself, but in his exterior functions, especially in the salvific function exercised through Christ. It is in this sense that we will treat of functional theology here.

We are not concerned here, however, with the objective functional theology of Rudolf Bultmann, who says that our faith attains God only as he wishes to relate himself to us as our judge and liberator. For Bultmann the reality of the Christian salvific event is singularly reduced; for him Christ's person contains no mystery, no divine union. We will concentrate here on that type of functional theology that sees in Christ some real identity with God.

Cullmann's Christology. Oscar Cullmann's functional Christology claims our first attention. According to him the Christology of the first Christian communities is the fruit of reflection on the historical Jesus. Because the

[1] Léopold Malevez, S.J., is professor of Dogmatic Theology at the Jesuit College of St. Albert at Louvaine-Eegenhoven. He is the author of many theological studies. His book *The Christian Message and Myth: The Theology of Rudolf Bultmann* is a recognized Catholic critique of Bultmann's work. This is a condensation of his article "Nouveau Testament et théologie fonctionnelle" published in English in *Theology Digest,* Spring 1962, pp. 77–83. Oscar Cullmann's reply to this article was also published in *Theological Digest,* Autumn 1962, pp. 215–219.

entire Old Testament referred to him, Jesus was thought of as having been at work before his earthly life. As the bearer of revelation par excellence, he must have been the very source of revelation. Remembering that in Genesis all was created by the "Word of God," these communities saw that in creation Christ made the first revelation and took the first step in the history of salvation. A parallel to Gen 1 is seen in the opening of John's Gospel, where the Word, as the mediator of revelation, is again said to "create everything." This early Christian notion of pre-existence demanded a purely dynamic and functional Christ. It is true that he is God in a true sense; but he pre-exists only as principle of things and as source of revelation. Christian documents cannot and do not recognize in him any reality within God independent of his revealing function. John considers the pre-existence of the Word only in strict connection with his external action; the pre-existence of Jesus is the first step of the history of Jesus.

This exclusively functional notion of the pre-existent Christ is clear from his Christian titles: In the New Testament, the question, "Who is Christ?" does not primarily ask, "What is his nature?" but, "What is his function in the history of salvation?" The Christology in the New Testament is a history. When Christianity came into contact with the Greek world, the Church was forced to ask the question of natures. Simply by allowing it to be asked, she introduced a speculation that was foreign to the New Testament. Let us consider in this connection three of his biblical titles: Lord, Word, and Son of God.

Lord, Word, Son of God. "Lord" (*Kyrios*) designates the divine sovereignty of Jesus in the present period of salvation history, Cullmann finds; but it is also used of Christ's mediatorship of creation, and so applies to Christ's pre-existent state. In both applications, however, it signifies only that Christ and the Father are one in their sovereignty over the world.

The title "Word" (*Logos*) Cullmann assigns exclusively to Jesus' pre-existence. The remote Old Testament context from which it comes considers the Word of God as an independent entity through whose mediation the creative activity of God is exercised. This Word, considered as God not in himself but in his communication of himself to the world, influenced Christianity directly but not via later Judaism. It is true that the Judaism of Sirach, Qumran, and rabbinism, under the influence of pagan Hellenism, considers the Word, or Wisdom, as a "part of God"; but even here the functional character of the Word is not weakened. It exists in the action by which God reveals himself to the world. And it is this aspect of the older biblical view, preserved also in later Judaism, that appears in the *Logos* of John.

John's original contribution is the formerly unheard-of notion of a Word addressed by God to the world, which became incarnate to an earthly life. And this addition to the basic notion actually strengthens the functional concept of the Word. Cullmann does recognize in the Prologue an ascent beyond creation and revelation to the being of the Word with God. But he shows that, although Christ is neither a creature nor an emanation from God, he is different. For God can be conceived apart from his act of revealing; the *Logos* cannot.

In the title "Son of God" John also

implicitly touches upon the question of the relation of essence between God and Christ, independently of the Incarnation. John's answer remains, according to Cullmann: Their unity is their oneness in the act of revelation. Though one may speak of the Father without reference to revelation, one may speak of the Son only in reference to it. Subsequent speculation on the "being" of the Son is merely philosophical, Cullmann claims, and goes beyond what is contained in the sources. He even seems to consider a kind of disappearance of the Son when he has finished his salvific work at the end of time.

Assertive and Exclusive. Absolutely speaking, Cullmann could have confined himself to saying that the writings of the New Testament do not speculate on the divine condition of the Son, apart from his external function. (He could have been "assertive but not exclusive.") To this he could then add: When we undertake to reconstruct a specifically *biblical* theology, we should, because of this silence of Scripture, refrain from introducing a consideration of the independent existence of the Word. This position might raise certain questions concerning the methodology of theology, but at least it would not exclude the Nicene theology's legitimate development. Pierre Benoit, O.P., seems to understand Cullmann in this way; otherwise his unreserved approbation of Cullmann's functionalism is inexplicable. But Cullmann's theology is assertive *and* exclusive, and this is the way it was understood by A. Grillmeier, S.J.

If Scripture closes the way to a concept of the Son that goes beyond his creative and revealing action, then the Nicene *homoousios* is condemned in advance; for to say of the Son, in the Nicene sense, that he is "consubstantial with the Father" is to say that he enjoys with respect to the created universe the same independence as the Father. The post-Nicene theoretician may concede that the Son does not exist without freely positing the eternal act of creation in time, and that the act of creation is not really distinct in the Son from the act of existing (the classical doctrine of the divine simplicity). But he cannot say that the Son exhausts his reality in creative activity. He observes that the eternal union of the Son with the creative act does not formally depend on his condition as Son. With respect to union with the free creative act, the Father is in no way different from the Son. Cullmann holds that Scripture attributes to the Son a relation of union and a necessary identification with the creative act, which is verified in him alone. But if Cullmann were right, Scripture would be calling into question the divinity of the Son.

Catholic Reactions. Catholic exegetes consider Chalcedon's Christology a fully legitimate evolution, for the New Testament does not *exclude* the idea of a *Logos* which proceeds in God independently of his revealing function. Some Catholics admit, however, that the New Testament scarcely envisages the Son of God in any other way than in his salvific function. Moreover, the pre-existent Christ owes his title *Logos* to his function as revealer of God to men. Cullmann cites Jacques Dupont, O.S.B., and M.-E. Boismard, O.P., among the Catholic exegetes who accept functionalism, but regrettably neglects to note their differences from his own thinking.

Dupont says that John's theology is not one of essences, but that it is functional. He bases this interpretation of John's *Logos* on its purely Jewish inspiration. He acknowledges no influence of Greek philosophy in John's application of *Logos* to Christ. In 1 Jn 1:12 John tells us that he has seen and touched the word of life, the vivifying Word. In Apc 19:11–16 he draws on the Old Testament in calling Christ the avenging or exterminating Word, an eschatological function. In the Prologue, John identifies Jesus with the *creative* Word of God, not to tell us the Word is the person of Jesus, but to show the Word's action in the universe. Nevertheless, Dupont does not neglect to recall that according to John this creative Word was at the beginning with God, and was God. That the *Logos* is with God and that He is God means that He is a divine being whose existence and procession in God are independent of his work of creation.

Assertive, not Exclusive. Dupont sees in "Son of God" a title more expressive of the mission of Jesus than of his divine nature. But he admits that John occasionally goes beyond this manner of seeing Christ and acknowledges a sonship that is independent of Christ's mission; for example, in 1:18 Christ is called the only-begotten God. Dupont's interpretation, therefore, turns out not so exclusively functional as some of his expressions would lead one to think. Unlike Cullmann's, his functionalism is "assertive, not exclusive." It has to do particularly with the concept of the Word: That the Word was generated by intellectual procession, as later theologians will say, is neither asserted in John's Prologue nor excluded by it. Rather, Christ is called the Word because He is the revealer and the creator. Hence, "the Word was made flesh" indicates the antithesis between man's frailty and the Word which lasts forever. "Flesh" does not indicate man's nature but his wretched condition. "Flesh" is opposed, not to the *nature* of the Word, but to the *condition* of the Word—the Word of God. John is not thinking of the Greek theology of the Incarnation—the union of two natures in one person—but of the concrete Christ. Dupont also gives a functional interpretation to the titles Light, Life, and Truth, and to the glory Christ received from his Father.

Boismard agrees up to a point with Dupont's functional interpretation, but for him the exterior function is expressly attached to the interior nature of Christ. His sonship is functional because He makes sons; but He makes us sons precisely because He is himself the Son of God. Generalizing from this, Boismard interprets John as saying that the revealing function of Christ is also founded on the essence of Christ as the Word in whom God thought of himself and expressed himself independently of any eventual revelation. This interpretation of John is based on the Sapiential books, which speak of Wisdom in God before God's creative work and independently of it. Hence, Boismard can be ranked as a functional theologian only in a very broad sense.

Biblical Theology Functional? The instances of functional theology we have just examined are Christological. But according to their authors, the functionalism that applies here applies to the whole biblical doctrine of God. They assert this, but do not prove it. In my opinion, there is no proof that biblical theology is functional; and functionalism is not a characteristic by which Scripture can be distinguished from natural theology. Admittedly Scripture has a way of looking at God that is not that of natural theology. But to consider God not in himself but in his free activity, as Scripture does, is also the perspective of natural theology, in which God can be known only from the works of his creation, not directly in himself. So if Scripture is functional, metaphysical theology is too.

One might attempt to distinguish Scripture from natural theology by saying that Scripture stops at God as author of salvation history, whereas metaphysics proceeds from God's causality in the universe to investigate his essential attributes. But this too is inadequate. Scripture develops scantily the essential attributes of God, but what it does say gives them substantially the same sense as natural theology. Scripture mentions:

divine nature—2 Pt 1:4
divinity—Rom 1:20
eternity—Rom 16:26, Apc 1:4–8, 16:5, Rom 1:20
invisibility—Rom 1:20, Col 1:15, 1 Tim 1:17, Heb 11:27
incorruptibility—Rom 1:23, 1 Tim 1:17
blessedness—1 Tim 1:11, 6:15
one who cannot be tempted—Jas 1:13
God is not unjust—Heb 6:10, Rom 3:5, 9:14
no one is good but only God—Mk 10:18
God alone is wise—Rom 16:27

None of these expressions refers either explicitly or implicity to the work of creation. We have reason to believe that they are to be understood in the sense the Greek mind and natural reason would give them. They are judgments of essence, as Karl Rahner remarks, and not of existence. They are not the judgments of purely functional theology; to understand them it is not absolutely necessary to refer to the special history of salvation.

Opposing function to essence, therefore, does not distinguish Scripture from natural theology. The distinction lies rather in this: The God of natural theology is a necessity; the God of Scripture is a mystery. Philosophy asks itself not so much, "What is He?" as, "What is it that He *cannot but be*?" It arrives at his attributes from the principle of non-contradiction. This characteristic of rational necessity is present in natural theology's basic observation that God is *creator,* and freely so, and in the discovery of his attributes.

Scriptural God a Savior. Scripture also shows us the freedom of God's attitude toward man and toward creative activity. But it especially stresses that this free creation is inspired by a loving desire to save, a desire of which natural thought can have no presentiment. Only revelation can show forth the peculiar character of this gratuitous love. It is an absolute initiative, upsetting and surprising, recognizable only in faith.

Scripture does not present the interventions of God in history as illustrations of already known abstract properties. Rather, through God's actions we are introduced to a knowledge of his highest attributes which, accepted in faith, enrich and interpenetrate our natural knowledge on an altogether new plane. Scripture, as we have seen above, is aware of the natural meaning of the divine perfections, but more often the natural meaning is assumed into the revealed meaning.

We borrow Rahner's examples. When Scripture says that God is the just judge, we see, beyond the justice known by reason, the historical condemnation of sin in the flesh of Christ, made sin for us (2 Cor 5:21). The reaction of the all-holy God to sin exceeds our understanding here, as does its converse, God's patient longanimity (Rom 2:4). Divine omniscience in Sacred Scripture does not mean principally God's knowledge of himself nor that which he exercises in his creative causality, but rather God's look which pierces to the heart of man to judge him and at the same time to be merciful to him through the gratuitous event of the death of his Son (Mt 6:4–6). Finally, the infinite power of God belongs to that free and suprarational action of God in the history of salvation which could have made of the stones children of Abraham (Mt 3:9), which is at work in the resurrection of Christ (Act 2:24) and in the conversion of the rebellious.

The originality of biblical theology is to be defined, then, by the fact that its content does not express a rational necessity. It is not distinguished by its functionalism nor by the absence of determinations of the divine essence. Scripture does not merely call up these ontological determinations in express fashion from time to time; it also, when speaking of God in his supernatural, salvific function, shows something of his being. God's acts in Scripture show that *for us* He is a *mystery* of love, but through this they hint at what he is in himself. This scriptural knowledge of God's being remains a knowledge through representations of him borrowed from the world where God deploys his creative actions. But through all these media it is God that we see.

God Is the End. Scripture thus shows us God's being by showing us his saving action, and even positively invites us to seek his essence in his action. The culmination of God's intervention in our history is to be at the end "when all things are made subject to him; then the Son himself will also be made subject to him who subjected all things to him, that God may be all in all" (1 Cor 15:28). Cullmann's very disputable interpretation of this text is that it denotes the end of the function of the Word and hence, perhaps, of his being. A better interpretation is that beyond Christ and his salutary work is the excellence and grandeur of God, whose instrument Christ is. Christianity's aspiration is to bring the Christian to a love of God in himself, in his abyss and his darkness. An absolute functional theology would have to hold such a desire suspect and not conformed to Scripture. But it would seem to be the absolute functional theology that is more in danger of being unfaithful to the authentic spirit of the Bible.

Limits of Functional Theology. The biblical doctrine of God, then, does not appear to be wholly functional. This now gives us a valuable basis for judging a functional theology of Christ or of the Spirit. If Scripture presented God exclusively in a functional perspective, the presumption would be strong in favor of a Trinity not immanent but "economic"—one in which distinction arises because of different functions in different phases of the economy of salvation. But since Scripture does not so present God, the way remains open for an immanent Trinity, and also for a Christology that is not absolutely functional.

We still must determine whether in fact New Testament Christology is rigorously functional. Dupont's exegesis called forth reservations from Boismard, and it suggests some other remarks. Recall first that Dupont never called into question the divine Son as a person independent of his creative and revealing functions. Nevertheless, some aspects of his functionalism seem exaggerated. Although the New Testament formulas that express Christ's divinity are always at least implicitly connected with his messianic action, it remains no less true that at the source of this saving action the fully divine ontological reality is discernible. For John the very thing that makes Christ's mission possible is his communion with the Father in eternal sonship. Taken in their most natural sense, the texts say that Christ enlightens because he is himself light, in a plenitude that is received but is equal to that of the Father. He gives life, divinizes, makes us children of God because he is himself above the condition of creatures: God-Son but God. If this is St. John's thought, he is not "philosophizing" in Greek fashion or any other; and yet he is expressing himself "ontologically," as would any mind attempting to express a power rooted in the inherent essence of its possessor.

Dupont betrays an effort to purify his treatment of John's thought from all metaphysical contamination. It is true that if metaphysics is a science of the rational necessities of being, these will hardly be found in John or anywhere else in Scripture. But to Dupont metaphysics means any knowledge of "natures." And thus we have exegetes, like cherubs before the Ark, guarding Scripture from the intrusions of ontology. The guard is useless and too late. Ontology is already within the sanctuary, without profaning it. Dupont admits a divine being independent of creation. What more is required to constitute an ontological judgment? Were one to grant, with Cullmann, that John thinks of the Word exclusively as linked with revelation and the Incarnation, one is still saying: God determines himself for the communication of himself to the world. And this is an ontological judgment.

Functional and Ontological. As a matter of fact, neither ontology nor the designation of natures is a peculiar property of the Greek mind. They are the very structure without which the mind cannot express its slightest content. Dupont says that John's "The Word was made flesh" does not establish what will later be the theological concept of the Incarnation; he claims that there is no idea here of the union of two natures, but simply a concrete designation of Jesus. But it seems strange to posit such opposition between John and later theologians. After all, what does Chalcedon say but that the divine person who is the Word has taken our human condition without becoming thereby two subjects.

We must finally confront Cullmann's extreme form of functionalism, which sees the divine being of the Word to be merely the result of the warping influence of the Greek mind. To hold with Cullmann that "We cannot say 'Son' except in relation to God's revelation" results in a modalist theology of the Trinity—hence the gravity of the dispute. Does Cullmann think of the Son as a person distinct from the Father? It is probable, but not certain, that he does. But it is certain that for him the New Testament gives the Son divine rank. This seems sufficient to shake his functionalism.

Response to Cullmann. It is the

undisputed doctrine of both Testaments that the God of the Bible enjoys a sovereign liberty with respect to creation and the history of salvation. And according to the New Testament, creation has its source in a free, divine predestination in Christ. Is it right to say, then, that Scripture makes sovereign mastery of the universe the privilege of the Father, and gives no indication that it is shared with the Son? After all, John tells us that the Son has received the power to create, since all things were made by him. The fact that He has *received* this power distinguishes him from the Father. But having received it, He truly possesses it as fully as does the Father, unlimited and unweakened. If the Son is divine, how can limits be put to his free creative power?

If, as a matter of fact, the Son in John has the attributes of the divinity, as Cullmann admits, he must also possess in John's thought all the liberty of the God of Scripture with respect to creation. In making explicit the liberty of a nature with respect to its activities, later theological development is not under the impulse of Hellenistic tendencies; but, to use Cullmann's phrase, it reacts to the pressure of tendencies native to Christianity: the fully biblical idea of the sovereign liberty of God in the contingent work of salvation. The Nicene and Chalcedonian theology is an altogether natural interpretation of John's thought. Extreme functionalism, on the contrary, does violence to the biblical concept of creation.

Moreover, in evolving a theology of the Son as independent of creation in his meaning and his existence, Christian dogma served precisely the better interests of that salvation-history which Cullmann rightly calls the heart of the message. If the Son is not God, if He does not have all the attributes of God, such as liberty with respect to the created world, then he has not divinized us, nor saved us; no history of salvation remains; no salvation remains.

6. R. P. Martin[1] introduces his study of the "New Quest of the Historical Jesus" with a survey of the background and authors leading to the contemporary debate. He discusses Käsemann's views as departing from the classic Bultmannian position, with Bornkamm carrying the debate a stage further. Ernst Fuchs swings away more decisively and Robinson precises the nature of the new quest as distinct from nineteenth-century attempts and from the Bultmannian approach. The new quest is presented as possible, legitimate and even necessary. Martin's criticism is that the new quest leans toward Docetism, overemphasizes existentialism, and shows narrow criteria in its judgments over authenticity.

[1] Ralph P. Martin is presently Lecturer in New Testament Studies in the University of Manchester, England. He has been Lecturer in Theology in London Bible College, and was recently Visiting Professor of New Testament in Bethel College, St. Paul, Minnesota. He has authored *The Epistle to the Philippians, An Early Christian Confession,* and *Worship in the Early Church.* It is from *The Quest of the Historical Jesus* (edited by Carl F. H. Henry, Grand Rapids, Michigan: Eerdmans Publishing Co., 1966) that this excerpt is taken from pp. 25–45.

One of the most vigorous currents in mid-twentieth century theology is a recent description[2] of the New Quest debate, which in 1964 entered its tenth year. The title, "The New Quest of the Historical Jesus," fixes attention upon one of the most heavily documented themes of modern biblical and theological scholarship; and equally it exposes the critical nature of this discussion. For all participants agree that this is no peripheral matter lying far away on the extremities of Christian teaching, and of speculative interest only; but, on the contrary, it concerns the center and substance of the Church's proclamation: *the person of Jesus Christ as the preached Word of God, and His relation to history.*

Background to the Debate. To trace back the current debate to its sources is a complex business, for many tributaries flow into the main stream at the point where it rises. Indeed, it is not easy to fix precisely the place at which the origins of the controversy lie. Perhaps the chief determinants which shaped the rise and development of the new movement are the Deist challenge to the orthodox Christian faith in Europe, the influence of the Ritschlian theology with its ambivalent attitude to Gospel history, the rise of new methods of historical science and enquiry, the relentless probings of biblical criticism which placed question marks against many of the age-old, time-honored assumptions and convictions of the Church; and (as a later factor) the influence of existentialist philosophy upon Christian thinkers.

Subsequent events have confirmed three factors . . . to be important as far as twentieth-century biblical studies in the life of Jesus are concerned. Prior to the arrival of these methods which were applied to the Gospel materials, no one seemed in doubt that a portrait of Jesus as a figure of first-century Palestine could be sketched by a careful and sympathetic drawing together of the Gospel data. . . . The main European examples of *Lives of Jesus* were collected and critically examined by Albert Schweitzer. . . . "There is nothing more negative than the result of the critical study of the Life of Jesus" (*The Quest of the Historical Jesus,* tr. W. Montgomery [New York: Macmillan, 1910], p. 398). His own attempt in a concluding chapter to make good the deficiency and to depict Jesus as an apocalyptic visionary, the deluded victim of a fixed eschatological program which, in the end, crushed Him in despair and failure, did not escape the same verdict.

Schweitzer's book marks the end of an era. Already at the turn of the century the stage was being prepared for some new and dramatic changes. . . .

As far as the study of the Gospels as historical records of Jesus' earthly life is concerned, the development of scholarly attitudes and estimates may be conveniently traced to a point of new departure in H. J. Holtzmann's *Die synoptischen Evangelien,* published in Leipzig in 1863, which gave a classic statement of the so-called "Marcan hypothesis," *viz.*, that Mark's

[2] The present writer owes this quotation—and some valuable guidance as to procedure and bibliographical control—to J. Benjamin Bederbaugh's comprehensive survey, "The First Decade of the New Quest of the Historical Jesus" (*The Lutheran Quarterly,* 16 [Aug. 1964], pp. 239ff.).

Gospel as the foundation-document underlying the other Synoptic Gospels contains a clear, factual, unembellished record of the life and public career of Jesus. . . .

Holtzmann was motivated by a *theological* concern to defend the liberal estimate of the historical Jesus against the mythical interpretation of Strauss. And Holtzmann's vindication of Mark's priority and historicity held the field until the turn of the century, when three powerful forces were at work which ultimately assailed and destroyed the Holtzmann doctrine as far as German scholarship was involved. These new approaches to Synoptic history may be tabulated.

a) Wilhelm Wrede's discussion (in 1901) of the messianic secret in the Gospels, chiefly in Mark's Gospel, concluded that Mark is *not* a record of unvarnished history, portraying Jesus "as He actually was," but a dogmatic treatise, in which the doctrine of the messianic secret is imposed upon the historical materials.

b) K. L. Schmidt considered (in 1919) "The framework of the story of Jesus," and, by an analysis of the sections (*pericopae*) of the Gospel material in a firm critical manner, came to a startling verdict:

> As a whole there is no life of Jesus in the sense of a developing biography, no chronological sketch of Jesus' history, but only single stories (*pericopae*), which are put into a framework (*Der Rahmen der Geschichte Jesu*, p. 317).

c) The doctrine of *Sitz im Leben* (the principle that each section of Gospel teaching and narrative may be suggestively placed in the setting of its historical context, when we have regard to its literary form and theological content) was taken by the early practitioners of the "form critical method" a stage farther than that of a purely literary exercise. From an analysis of the "types" or "forms" (*Gattungen*) of the literary materials of the Gospels—into such categories as "miracle-stories," "conflict-stories," "biographical *apophthegmata*" or "tales"—some of the form critics moved on to appraisal, and gave a critical judgment on the historical worth of the data. . . . By this judgment on the historical value of Synoptic incidents, what the Church has traditionally regarded as authentic, factual, episodic history is evaporated into an idealized reconstruction invented by the later Church of the apostolic era. The *Sitz im Leben Jesu* is transformed into *Sitz im Leben der alten Kirche* by a stroke of the form critic's pen; and Gospel history is subsumed under the ominous category of *Gemeindetheologie*.

The name of Rudolf Bultmann occurs, in this discussion. . . . Accepting J. M. Robinson's revised estimate of Bultmann's skepticism concerning the historical Jesus, we may use his words to summarize the situation which was the immediate background of and precursor to the new quest debate:

> [Bultmann's] form-critical analyses corroborated the view that a Life-of-Jesus research after the style of the nineteenth century is impossible, and his existential interpretation undermined the thesis that such a Life-of-Jesus research was legitimate *Kerygma und historischer Jesus* [1960], pp. 10f.).

Dr. Robinson adds, providing us with an entree to the debate, "Therefore it is not surprising that the critical restudy of his [Bultmann's] position by his pupils should begin here" (*A New Quest of the Historical Jesus* [London: SCM Press, 1959], p. 12).

The Course of the "New Quest" Debate

The situation in 1953–54 may be summed up in the following manner. Under the direct influence of form criticism and Bultmann's kerygmatic-existentialist theology, German left-wing scholarship had made an hiatus between the Jesus of history and the Christ of the Church's proclamation. The historical Jesus was regarded as an eschatological prophet *simpliciter* who announced the imminent arrival of the kingdom in non-messianic categories and called for a radical repentance and "decision" in the light of the kingdom's near realization.

A decade of debate in reaction to this minimal interpretation of the life and ministry of Jesus was set afoot by a series of continental articles, the chief impetus being provided by Ernst Käsemann's address to the "old Marburgers" in October, 1953 (published in *Zeitschrift für Theologie and Kirche*, Vol. 51 [1954], pp. 125–153).

E. Käsemann. Käsemann shares many of Bultmann's presuppositions. Chiefly, his approach to the Gospel records is controlled by the view that biography and the revealing of traits of personality are not to be found therein. Nevertheless, Käsemann exhibits a definite move away from the classic Bultmannian position in three ways:

a) Although he grants that it is not possible to construct a Life-of-Jesus containing exact chronological data, a detailed *curriculum vitae* with stages of psychological development ("The Problem of the Historical Jesus," in *Essays on New Testament Themes* [London: SCM Press, 1964], p. 45), he is unwilling to admit a "disengagement of interest from the earthly Jesus" (p. 46). . . .

Käsemann shows himself sensitive to the danger of Docetism with its denial of interest in the earthly Jesus; and shows a more open regard for the possibility of recovering the historical Jesus whose preaching (he is anxious to show) is in continuity with the Church's proclamation.

b) It is the preaching of Jesus which Käsemann highlights as the distinctive element in the Gospel data. . . .

> Our investigation has led to the conclusion that we must look for the distinctive element in the earthly Jesus in his preaching and interpret both his other activities and his destiny in the light of this preaching (p. 44). . . .

c) Here is a decisive break with Bultmann's thesis of a disjunction between the eschatological announcement of a future kingdom which Jesus simply heralded and the Christian proclamation that Jesus is the Messiah and inaugurator of God's reign on earth. To be sure, Käsemann doubts whether Jesus claimed messianic status (*ibid.*, p. 38), but the evidence he adduces shows that this is the only title which properly fits Him. The evidence forms a fivefold pattern: Jesus' authority is seen in His overriding the venerable Mosaic Torah—an assumption of authority in the Sermon on the Mount which no rabbi or Jewish prophet would ever have made; His freedom in dealing with the Sabbath rules and with the prescriptions for ceremonial purity and dietary regulations (e.g., Mark 7); His masterful dealing with demoniacs, which thereby destroyed the basis of classical demonology; His immediate apprehension of God's will for human life, evidenced by His possession of the Spirit (Matt. 12:28) and use of such asseverations as *Amen* which "signifies an extreme and immediate certainty, such as is conveyed by inspiration" (*ibid.*, p. 42); and, most persuasively, Jesus' status *vis-à-vis* John the Baptist. John ushered in the turning point of the ages (*Aeonenwende*), and announced the advent of God's reign in the coming of Jesus. "Evidently, [Jesus is] he who brings with his Gospel the kingdom itself"; and so in Jesus Christ the kingdom arrived, and was not simply announced as proximate.

Käsemann's original propositions were received sympathetically (cf. the literature in Robinson, *A New Quest,* pp. 13f.), and were carried forward by significant contributions.

Günther Bornkamm. Bornkamm's distinction is a notable one. His *Jesus of Nazareth,* (London: Hodder and Stoughton, 1960) is offered as an appraisal of Jesus' life, ministry, and challenge from within the Bultmannian school. And it takes the debate a stage farther. An assessment of Bornkamm's contribution is provided in the following.

> Käsemann accepts as authentic, evidence concerning the *teaching* of Jesus, and concerning one aspect of his *work,* that of dealing with demoniacs. Bornkamm goes on to other aspects of Jesus' work (especially in his dealings with people) and makes a tentative beginning in regard to the *altitude* of Jesus. He deals with the significance of Jesus' forgiveness of sins and his table-fellowship with publicans and sinners (W. R. Farmer and Norman Perrin, *Religion in Life,* Vol. 29 [1959–60], p. 93).

A representative statement in Bornkamm's volume bears out this estimate:

> Quite clearly what the Gospels report concerning the message, the deeds, and the history of Jesus is still distinguished by an authenticity, a freshness, and a distinctiveness not in any way effaced by the Church's Easter faith. These features point us directly to the earthly figure of Jesus (*op. cit.*, p. 24).

Ernst Fuchs. Fuchs marks the most violent swing-away from the traditional Bultmannian position. For him the outstanding trait of Jesus' ministry was His readiness to consort with tax-collectors and sinners and to share meals with them. This act was no simple illustration of sociability or condescension. It means, rather:

> Jesus forwent the publication of his own private eschatological experiences; rather he determined only to draw the consequences from them and to begin here on earth with the work of God visible only in heaven! This is why he celebrates his meal . . . This conduct (*Verhalten*) is neither that of a prophet nor that of a sage, but rather the conduct of a man who dares to act in God's stead, by (as must always be added) calling near to him sinners who apart from him would have to flee from God (Fuchs, *Studies of the Historical Jesus,* as quoted by Robinson, *A New Quest,* pp. 14f.). . . .

Jesus, furthermore, envisaged after the death of John the possibility of His own suffering and death; and thus read into John's martyrdom a personal significance for His own life and destiny.

With Fuch's treatment two important novelties within the Bultmann school are clearly to be seen. First, in his use of John's death as having a significance for Jesus, Fuchs is adopting a psychologizing method, which the Bultmann school have hitherto eschewed. Secondly, the relation between the message Jesus preached (and its ensuing behavioral pattern) and the kerygma of the apostolic Church is one of intimate association. For Jesus' message is the implicit declaration of His own self-understanding as One who acted *in loco Dei*, which became explicit in the post-Easter proclamation of the Church. There is no disjunction between the two, as Bultmann had insisted; but rather a linear continuity. Bultmann, in a later response to his errant disciple, criticizes the "relapse into the historical-psychological interpretation" which Fuchs has adopted, a relapse which is reprehensible, according to Bultmann, because it "describes Jesus' attitude as a phenomenon perceptible to the objectifying historian" ("The Primitive Christian Kerygma and the Historical Jesus," in Braaten and Harrisville, *The Historical Jesus*, Nashville, 1964, pp. 32f.). In fact, in an earlier response (*Zeitschrift für Theologie und Kirche*, Vol. 54 [1957], pp. 244–54), Bultmann had conceded some elements of Fuchs' construction of Jesus' attitude to sinners and consciousness of His mission, but had shied away from any biographical-psychological interpretation, especially of Jesus' understanding of His death.

James M. Robinson. Robinson, the chronicler of the "new quest" debate, is responsible for the introduction of this new phase of New Testament science to the English-speaking world. The position which he adopted in 1959 (in *A New Quest*) was characterized by the statement of three theses:

a) The quest of the historical Jesus still remaining to be carried out is a *new* quest. Its "newness" is a double one: first, in relation to the nineteenth-century attempt to reconstruct the Jesus of history, and second, in relation to Bultmann's wedge between the Christ of kerygma and Jesus of Galilee. The new quest has an approach which differs from that of the nineteenth-century quest, and it employs a more refined methodology. . . .

. . . Nineteenth-century historiography was a pliable instrument for this task, for history was, at that time, regarded as a descriptive science on a par with the natural sciences (cf. E. Troeltsch in *Hastings Encyclopedia of Religion and Ethics,* Vol. VI, 716ff.) and thereby concerned with "brute facts" and unembellished biographical details.

The newer treatment sees history as an existential undertaking on the part of the historian, who is no detached and impartial observer standing outside the stream of the historical process which he seeks to interpret (Robinson, *op. cit.*, pp. 76f.). . . . There are now two ways of access to the person of the Church's Lord: the *via kerygmatica,* by which the proclamation of Christ in the Church presents an understanding of Jesus which it presupposes to be a continuation of His own self-understanding; and the *via historica* which, by using the modern historiography of Dilthey, Collingwood, and Bloch, takes up the non-kerygmatic material of the Gospel to reconstruct the self-understanding of the Jesus of history.

Examination of the Gospels by critical methods . . . excludes all elements in the Gospels which are kerygmatic or confessional, all material which can be paralleled in apocalyptic or rabbinic contemporary Judaism, and all possibly doubtful Aramaic *Logia* which could be considered on other grounds as the inauthentic creation of the early Church in Palestine (for example, the name "Lord" [*kyrios,* Aramaic *Mar (an)*]). Sayings of Jesus such as those contrasting humiliation and exaltation (e.g., Matt. 23:12; Luke 18:14. See also Anderson, *Jesus and Christian Origins* [New York: Oxford, 1964], pp. 241–306) reveal an authentic understanding of existence on His part. Later these became "mythologized" in the apostolic kerygma as Christ's pre-existence, incarnation, and enthronement (Phil. 2:5–11; I Tim. 3:16; I Pet. 3:18–22). Here, it is claimed, is a direct continuity between pre- and post-Easter situations, an illustration of the claim of the new quest that, by an uncovering of Jesus' understanding of existence, "the historical Jesus confronts us with existential decision, just as the kerygma does" (Robinson, *op. cit.,* p. 77).

Secondly, in relation to Bultmann's disavowal of interest in the Jesus of history and his driving a wedge between the Christ proclaimed in the kerygma and the Jesus of Galilee, the new quest seeks to reopen the lines of communication between history and kerygma.

b) and c) Robinson's second and third theses assert that the quest is "possible," "legitimate," and even "necessary," though the grounds of legitimacy and necessity are clearly not the same as those of the nineteenth-century quest. . . .

Bultmann affirms a historical continuity between the two [Jesus and Kerygma] but qualifies this by remarking that continuity is not identity. . . . Thus, he avers, there is no "essential relationship" (*sachliches Verhältnis*) between Jesus and the apostolic Christ; the first is the proclaimer of the kingdom to come, the second is the proclaimed, heavenly Lord, dressed up in mythological garb, the bearer of the saving Word in the Church's contemporary preaching.

Professor Robinson, responding to this statement in a clear, forthright fashion, sets out the issue between him (representing the post-Bultmannian "wing") and Bultmann himself. In a 1962 article in the *Journal of the Bible and Religion* (Vol. 30 [1962], pp. 198–208), he seeks a justification for positing a closer relation than Bultmann was willing to allow between the Jesus-portrait in the Gospels and the kerygmatic Christ. . . .

In a word, whereas Bultmann drives a wedge between Jesus' preaching, which is regarded as simply preparatory for the later kerygma, Robinson argues that already in Jesus' message there is implicit "a structure corresponding to the kerygma's reference to the once-for-all event of cross and resurrection" (*ibid.,* p. 206). Robinson counters the criticism that his view is a reversion to the nineteenth-century quest—"a complete capitulation to the heirs of Schweitzer"[3] or that it falls into the trap of psychologism (a judgment passed by Bultmann on Fuchs' view). Aware of these pressures, Robinson has modified his earlier view, which based an existential understanding of Jesus' message upon His selfhood (*Selbstverständnis*).

---

[3] Paul W. Meyer, *Novum Testamentum,* Vol. 4 (1960), p. 133. Cf. the critical question of Harvey and Ogden: "Are not both quests seeking the same object—the inner life of Jesus?" (*loc cit.,* p. 236).

This position was criticized by Harvey and Ogden:

> Is the new quest for the *existentiell* selfhood of Jesus different from the old quest for the 'inner life" of Jesus, his "personality"? And if it is impossible to recover Jesus' "inner life"—as Robinson claims—is it any easier to recover Jesus' *existentiell* selfhood? (*loc. cit.*, pp. 222ff., 234).

Instead of "understanding of self," Robinson now prefers to speak of "understanding of existence" (*Existenzverständnis*) (*Journal of the Bible and Religion,* Vol. 30 [1962], p. 208, n. 36).

But he is still faced with the same double embarrassment even with a change of terminology. . . .

Later discussion has faced the issue of this disjunction. As a further indication of the waning of Bultmann's influence, "post-Bultmannians" like Käsemann are moving in the direction of a more positive attitude to history by an acceptance of a *Heilsgeschichtlich* scheme, that is, a view that the history which the New Testament records "discloses" is the redemptive purpose and acts of God, which are temporal and factual, yet invested with an eschatological significance. This respectful attitude to history has long been maintained by Oscar Cullmann, Joachim Jeremias, W. D. Davies and Alan Richardson, and has received fresh stimulus from the work of such scholars as W. Pannenberg and G. E. Wright.

At the opposite end of the scale, other scholars are taking a negative attitude to Gospel history and seeking to ground the Christian claim and challenge in a more purely philosophical interpretation of the Christ-event. Schubert M. Ogden (*Christ Without Myth,* New York, Harper, 1961) and Paul van Buren (*The Secular Meaning of the Gospel,* New York, Macmillan, 1963) are willing apparently to detach the Christian kerygma from its historical moorings and to equate it with a call to existential decision.

A singular fact is that no contribution from within the Anglo-American evangelical section of the Church has striven to wrestle with this disjunction; and to offer an evangelical perspective from which the inter-relation of history and kerygma may be appraised. . . .

By way of final summary we shall offer certain criticisms of the principles and program of the new quest; and in this way point out certain basic evangelical *credenda* which may be submitted as important in any satisfactory solution which seeks to resolve the tension between the Gospel picture of Jesus as the proclaimer and the post-Easter proclaimed message of the Lord of the Church.[4]

Some Questionable Assumptions of the New Quest

The Interest of the Evangelists in the Human Jesus. New Testament scholarship in the post-World War II period had grown accustomed to the

[4] Strangely, what pass for evangelical emphases in this debate are shared by Roman Catholic scholars; in particular, our closing section is indebted to Raymond E. Brown's perceptive critique in "After Bultmann, What?—An Introduction to the Post-Bultmannians" (*Catholic Biblical Quarterly,* 26:1 [Jan. 1964], pp. 153–178). Worthy of special mention, too, is the Roman Catholic-Protestant symposium *Faith, Reason, and the Gospels,* ed. John J. Heaney, S.J., (Westminster, Maryland: Newman Press, 1961).

assertion—often stated as an *ipse dixit* of unquestioned certainty—that the early Christian had no interest in biographical details of the earthly Jesus; and that the Evangelists did not write their Gospels as "Lives of Christ" in the sense of modern psychological studies of human personalities.

The absence of the latter intention in the Evangelists' purpose may be freely granted (cf. John 20:30, 31); but it may be seriously doubted that there was no interest in the human Jesus. British scholars (like T. W. Manson, Vincent Taylor and A. M. Hunter) have argued that this Christian interest in the details of our Lord's earthly ministry and the high value placed upon His teaching (reflected in Paul's letters) are part and parcel of apostolic Christianity; and it is a priori unlikely that the first generations of Gentile believers were content to commit their lives to a mythological Lord whose "history" was (on the form critical claim) as uncertain and adventitious as that of the cult divinities of the Hellenistic mystery religions. . . .

The Danger of Docetism. The recent discussion, insofar as it shares the presupposition of Bultmann's radical dealing with Gospel sources, still is bedeviled by the threatened danger of Docetism. . . .

The fear is widespread, among Bultmann's critics and those who see the new quest as sharing his methodological approach, of so evaporating the Jesus of Galilee and Jerusalem that His place is taken in a theological schema by a cipher, a symbol, a formula, or an idea, dignified as it may be by a title like the "Christ-event" or "metahistorical reality." . . . The same criticism has been applied to Bultmann's later writings. . . .

A Preoccupation with Existentialism. The historiography of the Bultmannian and post-Bultmannian school reflects a too one-sided preoccupation with existentialism. There are two applications of this line of criticism which may be brought forward.

First, the type of human person whom the new questers envisage as representing "modern man" is one who struggles for the meaning of existence. The image in which modern man is made is that of Augustine's "existential man,"—singling out but one element of Augustine's teaching—caught in the dilemma of discovering his true life over against an inauthentic existence and torn by inner anxiety and conflict, and obsessed by *cor inquietum* whose plaintive confession is, "I was at strife with myself, and rent asunder by myself" (*Confessions,* viii. 10.22).

The New Testament is interpreted as providing the answer to such an existential predicament. But the question has been raised whether this interpretation both of man's need and the New Testament answer does not unduly narrow the latter and force it on to a Procrustean bed of existential philosophy. . . .

Raymond E. Brown has written: "Is not the hypothetical man who encounters the Jesus of the new quest too much a creature of volition and anxiety in search of freedom and love, and too little a rational creature with an insatiable desire to know?" (*Catholic Biblical Quarterly,* Vol. 26 [1964], p. 25). . . .

Secondly, an existentialist interpretation of the Gospels falls into the same trap as the earlier quest of the historical Jesus, namely, that of constructing its own image of Jesus. T. W. Manson has pointedly remarked on this consequence of the adopting of an a priori approach to the New Testament:

> It is easy to laugh at those who, a couple of generations ago, saw in Jesus a good nineteenth-century liberal humanist with a simple faith in a paternal deity. It is less easy to see the joke when the Jesus of history is a twentieth-century existentialist, a kind of pre-existent "Heidegger" ("The Life of Jesus," in *The Background of the New Testament and its Eschatology*, ed. W. D. Davies and D. Daube, [Cambridge University Press, 1956], p. 220).

Too Narrow Criteria for Authenticity. . . . One can legitimately protest that these criteria for authenticity are too narrowly conceived. Raymond E. Brown justly objects: "The minimalest rules used to isolate authentic material in the Gospels would be applicable if the Gospels were written to deceive" (*op. cit.*, p. 27).

Besides this general comment on the hyper-skeptical approach adopted by the new questers, further comment may be made on the specific criteria. . . .

a) Negatively, we may remark that "since Jesus was proclaiming a message himself, we would expect many of his words to have a kerygmatic ring. Since Jesus was a Jew, we would expect many of his words to have parallels in Jewish literature" (*ibid.*). The question here turns upon responsibility for the burden of proof. James Robinson wishes to place it squarely on the shoulders of those who maintain that we should accept statements attributed to Jesus unless it can be conclusively shown that they are inauthentic. But this skeptical approach to the Gospel data which implies that we are duty-bound to justify every saying of the incarnate Lord must be resisted.

b) On a positive level, two important observations of Gospel hermeneutic must be registered. The one is that of Brown, who calls attention to the attested phenomenon that some of the *dicta* of characters in the Gospels (in particular, the Fourth Gospel—and of Jesus *par excellence*) contain what may be called the germinant principle. That is, statements made during the ministry of Jesus are presented with a signification appropriate to the ministry, yet also holding a much deeper meaning appropriate to a post-Easter insight. . . .

The New Quest and the Fourth Gospel. The enigmatic nature of some of Jesus' kerygmatic teaching and the incidents which accompanied and exemplified it is clearly to be seen in John's Gospel. . . .

The Fourth Gospel contains two further elements in addition to these instances of Jesus' words and actions which took on new significance in the post-Easter period: it professes to contain eyewitness testimony (19:35; 20:30; 21:24, 25) and it records the promise of the Holy Spirit whose function will be to awaken the disciples' memory to what the earthly Jesus said (14:26). It is true that eyewitness testimony in the Gospels has been recently re-evaluated and its value minimized (D. E. Nineham, *Journal of Theological Studies,* Vol. 9–11 [1958–1960]). But to overlook the presence of men and women in the apostolic Church whose personal reminiscences and recollections of what Jesus looked like, said and did, we may safely presume, is an oversight or denial which must be corrected. The alternative is the assumption that the original disciples and followers of Jesus were spirited away after Pentecost—a possibility too ludicrous to contemplate!

It is also true that John's Gospel is dismissed, in the recent debate, as a piece of dogmatic *Tendenz* which makes no claim to historical veracity. Thus G. Ebeling writes of the Fourth Gospel: "a historical account in the strict sense is not expected of it" (*The Nature of Faith* [Eng. tr., New York: Collins, 1961], p. 50). Oscar Cullmann's discussion on 'L'évangile Johannique et l'historie du Salut' (*NTS*, 11:2, Jan. 1965) is a welcome reaction.

The new questers have as yet shown little appreciation of the so-called "new look" on the Fourth Gospel, as A. M. Hunter (*The Gospel According to John*, 1965), C. H. Dodd (*Historical Tradition in the Fourth Gospel*, 1963), J. A. T. Robinson (in *The Roads Converge* [ed. P. Gardiner-Smith], 1963), and R. E. Brown (*CBQ* 24, 1962, pp. 1–14) have outlined it. Brown comments: "A reintroduction of some of this Johannine material into the new quest would perhaps give body to its sketch of the historical Jesus" (*CBQ*, 26, 1964, p. 29).

Conclusion

There are some slight indications that the men of the "new quest" are moving farther away from Bultmann's historical radicalism and apparent uninterest in the historical Jesus; and this determination not to lose contact with the historicity of Jesus has been applauded by other, non-Bultmannian participants in the debate. At the same time, others (like Conzelmann and Ogden) have advocated a more thorough-going application of the Bultmannian methodology and have disdained the aim of the new quest. . . .

7. D. M. Baillie[1] criticizes three views of contemporary Protestant Christology. He finds the terms misleading or at least inadequate in the position which presents the Incarnation on the basis of the old concepts of "anhypostasia" or "en-hypostasia" (impersonal or in-personal humanity of Christ). The theory of the divine self-emptying (kenosis), understood precisely as a solution to the problem of Christology, does not bear examination. Heim's doctrine of Christ as God appointed leader demanding obedience is not the answer. It ignores the basic Christological issue: How is Christ related to God?

I propose to discuss certain lines of Christological thought that have been prominent in modern theology. There seem to me to be three trends of thought that call for examination and criticism in the interests of our present purpose. First, there are the endeavours of various theologians to work out the meaning of the Incarnation on the basis of *Anhypostasia*, the old conception that in Christ there was no distinct human personality, but

[1] Donald M. Baillie died in 1954. He had been Forwood Lecturer in the Philosophy of Religion at the University of Liverpool. He had also taught at St. Mary's College and was Professor of Systematic Theology at the University of St. Andrews. It is from his book *God Was in Christ* (New York: Charles Scribner's Sons, 1948) that this excerpt has been taken, selectively, from pp. 85–104.

divine Personality assuming human nature. Second, there are the endeavours to build a Christology on the idea of the divine Kenosis—the so-called Kenotic theories. Third, there is the very distinctive Christology of Karl Heim, which works with the ideas of Leadership and Lordship.

I
Anhypostasia

Several modern theologians have taken up and sought to work out in modern terms the ancient doctrine that Christ is not a human person, but a divine Person who assumed human nature without assuming human personality—the doctrine that gave rise to the familiar phrase, "the impersonal humanity of Christ." . . .

Now it is notoriously difficult to determine what precisely this doctrine meant when it was first enunciated and accepted by the Church. Unless we are careful we shall find ourselves understanding it in a sense very difficult to distinguish from the Apollinarianism which had already been condemned, or in a sense very similar to the Monothelite heresy which was subsequently condemned. It is easy to understand its negative bearing, as a repudiation of what was taken to be the Nestorian position. But it is highly doubtful whether the phrase "impersonal humanity" conveys what was intended, just as it is likely that *hypostasis* and *persona* did not mean just what we mean by either *person* or *personality*. And few theologians now would defend the phrase or would hesitate to speak of Jesus as a man, a human person. H. R. Mackintosh wrote: "If we are not to trust our intuitive perception that the Christ we read of in the Gospels is an individual man, it is hard to say what perception could be trusted."[2] R. C. Moberly wrote: "Human nature which is not personal is not human nature."[3] . . .

I find it . . . difficult to understand Professor Hodgson when, without tying himself to such language as "the impersonal humanity of Christ" or "not a man but Man," he declares nevertheless that the doctrine underlying these phrases is "essential to any adequate Christology."[4] "We should . . . think of the Incarnation as the entry by One who is divine upon an experience of life under certain conditions, namely, those which are involved in being the subject of experiences mediated through a body in this world of space and time; for to be subject of such experiences is to be human."[5] "What we mean by manhood in its most spiritual essence, its *nous* (to use Apollinarius' term), is to be the self-conscious subject of experiences mediated through a human body," and "the Incarnation is to be thought of as the entry upon experience of such a life by the divine Logos."[6] Professor Hodgson's aim here is, having replaced the philosophy of "substance" by sound modern philosophy of the self as "subject," to restate the catholic doctrine of the Incarnation in modern terms. But the Christology which he reaches seems to me

[2] H. R. Mackintosh *The Doctrine of the Person of Jesus Christ,* p. 390.
[3] R. C. Moberly, *Atonement and Personality,* p. 92.
[4] Leonard Hodgson, in *Essays on the Trinity and the Incarnation,* edited by Rawlison, p. 383.
[5] *Ibid.,* p. 379.
[6] *Ibid.,* p. 387.

to be a restatement in modern terms, not of the catholic doctrine, but rather of the Apollinarian heresy. . . . Doubtlessly Apollinarius interpreted the working of this in a much more docetic way than would Professor Hodgson: he assimilated the humanity of the incarnate life to the life of God, whereas Professor Hodgson would give a very human account of it. Yet I would submit, with the greatest respect, that the latter's theory seems very like an unconscious acceptance of the Apollinarianism with which Cyril's doctrine has so often been charged. The only "mind," he seems to teach, that was in the incarnate Christ was the divine mind of the Second Person of the Trinity, which entered on a human experience by functioning through a human body. Does this mean that the Son of God changed into a man? It is impossible to believe that Professor Hodgson would wish to put it in that way. But if Jesus was not a man at all, but simply the divine Son of God having experience through a human body, so that the only "subject" of the experience was God the Son, there seems to be no room left for what we surely find in the Gospel story: Jesus as a man having experience of God in faith and prayer, where God is not the "subject" but the object.[7] . . .

Some years ago Dr. H. M. Relton wrote a scholarly and suggestive essay in Christology,[8] in which, recognizing that "impersonal humanity" is a meaningless phrase, he passed from *anhypostasia* to the *enhypostasia* proposed by Leontius of Byzantium and John of Damascus: the idea that the humanity of Christ, while not impersonal, can be described as not having *independent* personality, but being personal in the Logos. The human nature is personalized in the Divine Logos which assumes it, and is thus not impersonal (*anhypostasia*) but "in-personal" (*enhypostasia*). Dr. Relton soundly argues that "without God, human personality is incomplete, and that He alone can supply it with that which alone can help it to its full realization." From this it is a natural conclusion that the manhood of Christ is not less personal but more fully personal than that of any other man, because of its complete union with God, and certainly Dr. Relton regards Him as not only "Man" but *a* man in the fullest sense. This is a real contribution, and I find it very congenial and instructive. But I cannot help feeling that it is a pity to express it in terms of *enhypostasia*. It is difficult to see why this term, with all its associations, should be used at all unless it is meant to indicate that, even if the human nature of Christ is "personalized" in the hypostatic union, the "subject" is always and exclusively the Second Person of the Trinity; and that would at once bring back all our difficulties as regards Jesus having a human experience of God.

Moreover, there seems to be no

[7] I do not question that there may be a sense in which God has experience of God or God as subject has experience of God as object. That may, as has often been said, be one of the truths enshrined in the doctrine of the Trinity. But surely that was not what was happening in the Incarnation, in those parts of our Lord's experience which we may describe as His faith in God and His praying to God.

[8] H. M. Relton, *A Study in Christology*. Dr. Relton is not the first to develop this idea of *enhypostasia,* as distinct from *anhypostasia,* in Western Christendom. Some of the early Reformed theologians made regular use of the idea. See A. B. Bruce, *The Humiliation of Christ,* App., Sect. iii, note E.

sound reason why we should feel constrained to think in terms of either *anhypostasia* or *enhypostasia* in our Christology. If it is the case (as many at least will agree that it is) that the technical term *hypostasis* or *persona* in the statement of Trinitarian doctrine does not mean just what we mean by "person" in modern speech, the "hypostatic union" surely cannot be translated *simply* as "personal identity," and it is difficult to put a clear meaning into the idea of one *hypostasis* or *persona* of the Trinity taking the place of a human center of consciousness in a human life. If, on the other hand, we maintain that Jesus was in every sense a human person with a human center of consciousness, while being also the Incarnation of the divine Word, the second *persona* of the Trinity, there is no reason why that should be taken as implying the Nestorian heresy of dividing Christ into two persons—a heresy which may have never existed in that form except in the imagination of its opponents, and which Nestorius himself, whatever may have been his errors, almost certainly never entertained.[9]

I do not know whether Father Thornton's Christology in his difficult book, *The Incarnate Lord,* should be classed among modern re-interpretations of the *anhypostasia.* But so far as I can understand his argument, it seems to me, like other views which I have been criticizing, to exclude the possibility of recognizing the Jesus of the Gospel story as a real man. Father Thornton bases his Christology on the idea that the Incarnation is the final stage in the ascending series of organic unifications which the scientists call evolution; so that apparently the relation of Jesus to humanity is somewhat the same kind as the relation of humanity to the merely animal world: "In each new level which appears all the previous levels are representatively taken up and included; so that at the summit of the series man is in some sense a microcosm of the whole, including within himself all levels of the series. The series is thus taken up in man, because he shares the unfinished character of the series. Now if the Incarnation brings creation to its true end in God, this must mean that the cosmic series is gathered up into the human organism of Jesus Christ. . . . As the series is taken up into the human organism, so in Christ the human organism is taken up on the 'level' of deity."[10] But on this view it would surely be impossible to regard Jesus as a man among men, a member of the human species: He would be-

[9] As long ago as 1876 Professor A. B. Bruce had the insight to raise the question: "Were Nestorius and those who thought with him *Nestorians* in the theological sense?" He concluded that it was only by implication, and not by conscious intention, that they occupied the "Nestorian" position of dividing Christ into two persons (*The Humiliation of Christ,* 1st ed., pp. 64f.). Since then this has been more than confirmed through the discovery of a Syriac translation of a work of Nestorius himself which had always been known to the Assyrian (Nestorian) Christians, though unknown to the western world. (An edition with English translation was published in 1915 by G. R. Driver and Leonard Hodgson under the title, *The Bazaar of Heracleides.*) The discovery led to the publication of two excellent little monographs on Nestorius: J. F. Bethune-Baker, *Nestorius and His Teaching* (1908) and Friedrich Loofs, *Nestorius and His Place in the History of Christian Doctrine* (1914). Both of these books defend Nestorius against misinterpretation, and it is now pretty generally agreed among theologians that, whether Nestorius was orthodox or not, he was never a "Nestorian."

[10] L. S. Thornton, *The Incarnate Lord,* p. 225.

long rather to a further stage, and would be a new species. It is vain to reply that man not only belongs to a higher species than all other animals, but is also himself an animal, taking up into himself all the previous stages. For the "animal" in man is a different thing from the animal on lower levels, being transformed by the new unification on the level of spirit. The body of man is different in essential ways from the bodies of other animals; and the mind of a man is very different from the mind of any other animal (even if it is difficult to know precisely where and how to draw the line), so different that we cannot penetrate far into the latter. So far as we do try to penetrate, we speak of "animal psychology," realizing that it is a very different thing from human psychology, and that even its instincts are not the same as the corresponding human instincts. Similarly it seems to me that, on Father Thornton's theory, we should need a "divine psychology" for the interpretation of the mind of Jesus Christ, for His mind would not function as a human mind. Such a Christology would, with the best will in the world, run inevitably into Apollinarianism or Monophysitism or some form of Docetism. The divine and the human are brought together in such a way that the human no longer remains truly human in Christ. His humanity becomes quite different from ours; whereas catholic Christianity has always taught that His humanity is essentially the same as ours, that in respect of his manhood He was of one essence (*homoousioos*) with ourselves. Neither His body nor His mind was *essentially* different from the bodies or minds of other men. He was in every sense a member of the human race.[11] . . .

As regards the conception of *anhypostasia,* I do not question that in its day and in its environment it played a useful and necessary part, mainly as a bulwark against any kind of Adoptionism. . . . The only *anhypostasia* in the case is not a denial of personality, but a denial of independence, and it seems to me to be misleading to call it by that name.

II
KENOSIS

The Kenotic Theory of the Incarnation belongs distinctively to modern times.[12] . . . The beginnings of it in the modern world are sometimes traced to Zinzendorf, but it was only in the nineteenth century that the idea was taken up and elaborated theologically as a theory of the Incarnation, mainly on the European continent. During the last half century it has played a considerable part in British theology, and has been adopted by a good many prominent divines in [England] country as a basis for Christology. . . .

It is easy to see why this theory be-

[11] My criticism of Fr. Thornton's view is, I think, fundamentally the same as the criticism made by Dr. J. K. Mozley in a passage to which I feel myself directly indebted. See Mozley, *The Doctrine of the Incarnation,* pp. 146 f.

[12] On the question whether support can be found in the Patristic age for the Kenotic Theory, see J. M. Creed, *The Divinity of Jesus Christ,* p. 77, and also Creed's essay in *Mysterium Christi,* p. 133. He quotes Thomasius of Erlangen, the founder of modern Kenoticism, as admitting that very little definite support for the theory can be found in Patristic literature; and he quotes Friedrich Loofs of Halle in a similar sense. "The nearest approach to it is to be found in the heresiarch Apollinarius," who said, "Incarnation is self-emptying."

longs peculiarly to the modern world, and why in the modern world it looks at first sight very promising. It is because it apparently enables us to combine a full faith in the deity of Jesus Christ with a completely frank treatment of His life on earth as a human phenomenon, the life of a man. Thus it tackles the Christological problem in the peculiarly sharp form which it has assumed in modern times. . . . Thus we seem to get a real God-man and an intelligible meaning for the Incarnation, thoroughly congruous both with the New Testament idea of the divine condescension and self-emptying and with the modern treatment of the Gospel story and the rediscovery of the "Jesus of history."

Yet I cannot think that this use of the idea of divine self-emptying will bear examination. . . .

1. I am not aware that a good reply has yet been made to the simple question asked by the late Archbishop of Canterbury in objection to the Kenotic Theory. "What was happening," he asked, "to the rest of the universe during the period of our Lord's earthly life? To say that the Infant Jesus was from His cradle exercising providential care over it all is certainly monstrous; but to deny this, and yet to say that the Creative Word was so self-emptied as to have no being except in the Infant Jesus, is to assert that for a certain period of history the world was let loose from the control of the Creative Word."[13] . . .

2. Instead of giving us a doctrine of Incarnation in which Jesus Christ is both God and man, the Kenotic Theory appears to me to give us a story of a temporary theophany, in which He who formerly was God changed Himself temporarily into man, or exchanged His divinity for humanity. This is true even if the Kenoticist maintains the *anhypostasia* in the sense of impersonal humanity. . . . If, however, the Kenoticist gives up the idea of the *anhypostasia,* impersonal humanity, and regards Jesus as in every sense *a* man, a human person (as do some holders of the Kenotic Theory), then the situation becomes still stranger. The Kenoticist would then be involved in saying that He who before the Incarnation had been a divine Being now turned into a man, with human instead of divine attributes, for the time. . . . Surely the relation between the divine and the human in the Incarnation is a deeper mystery than this.[14]

3. The difficulties of the Kenotic Theory become still greater when we go on to ask: Was the *kenosis* merely temporary, confined to the period of the Incarnation of the Son of God, the days of His flesh on earth? The holders of the theory would *logically* have to answer: Yes. . . . Thus, in the Kenotic theory in that specific sense (which is what we are concerned with) He is God and man, not simultaneously in a hypostatic union, but *successively*—first divine, then human, then God again. But if that is really what the theory amounts to—and I do not see how it can otherwise be interpreted—it seems to leave

[13] William Temple, *Christus Veritas,* pp. 142 f.

[14] It is interesting to find Father Bulgakov, of the Eastern Orthodox Church, who himself makes large use of the idea of divine *kenosis* in another way, writing as follows: "It is essential to realize that, contrary to the various kenotic theories of Protestantism, our Lord in His abasement never ceased to be God, the Second Person of the Trinity." Sergius Bulgakov, *The Wisdom of God,* p. 134.

no room at all for the traditional catholic doctrine of the *permanence* of the manhood of Christ, "who, being the eternal Son of God, became man, and so was, *and continueth to be,* God and the man in two distinct natures, and one person *forever.*"[15] . . .

There are other ways in which Christian theology can use the idea of divine *kenosis.* Russian Orthodox thought has made considerable use of the idea, not only in connection with Incarnation and Atonement, but as indicating something which is involved in Creation itself, and even in the Trinity.[16] But that is something quite different from the Kenotic Theory as a Christology, and this last is what I find unacceptable.

III
Leadership and Lordship

Under this heading I propose to examine the Christological theory worked out by Professor Karl Heim of Tübingen in his book entitled *Jesus der Herr.*[17] It seems worthwhile to include this in our study, not only because of the great eminence which Heim has rightly enjoyed as a theologian, but also because of the very distinctive and original nature of his Christology.

Heim takes the notion of Leadership (*Führerschaft*) which is so widespread today, as his clue to a satisfying Christology. The Hellenistic cults of the ancient world created the new religious category of Kyrios which found its true fulfilment in Christ as Lord, and the category of Leadership has a similar significance for today. Thus, according to Heim, we are in a better position today than were our forefathers of the Enlightenment or of the Idealistic period for the understanding of the Lordship of Jesus, because instead of concentrating on true *ideas* we know what it is to give unconditional obedience to a Leader (*Führer*). (This would seem to imply that democracy works against the understanding of New Testament Christianity!) In this fallen world, infected as we are with original sin, it is impossible for us men to rise above the polarity of our earthly experience and to guide our own lives or have any direct knowledge of God. Therefore we need a Leader whom we can unquestioningly follow, and God has given us such a Leader in Jesus. This does not mean that Jesus left behind Him a code to be obeyed. The original apostles seldom quote the words of Jesus for the guidance of themselves or of the Church. Leadership must be something more direct. It must be an I-Thou relationship between the Leader and his followers, giving present guidance at each moment, and the early Christians were conscious of Jesus as a living Lord with whom they were in touch. Can we have the same experience? Yes, we can, and we must, if Jesus is to be our Leader and Lord. We can have it through the Holy Spirit. The Holy Spirit is the encompassing medium or continuum in

[15] *Westminster Shorter Catechism,* Ans. to Q. 21 (my italics).

[16] See Bulgakov, *The Wisdom of God,* pp. 133 ff., and Gorodetzky, *The Humiliated Christ in Modern Russian Thought,* chap. v.

[17] *Jesus der Herr* is the second volume of a tetralogy, the general title of which is *Der evangelische Glaube und das Denken der Gegenwart.* The first volume of the series has been translated into English by Professor E. P. Dickie under the title of *God Transcendent,* but *Jesus der Herr* is not available in English.

which we can have direct contact with Jesus, and it is only in that moment-to-moment contact with our Leader that we can have any knowledge of God at all. We cannot say why it is precisely at that point that we find the leadership we need. For we do not choose our Leader, but He chooses us, and it is not a case of our taking possession of Him in the sense of accepting His ideas, His program, His ethic, as our own. That would turn the I-Thou relationship into an I-It relationship. No, we simply follow our Leader, through direct contact with Him. There is no reason why we should not have such a relationship with Jesus who lived on earth nineteen centuries ago; for the I-Thou relationship is independent of space and time, and transcends all temporal and geographical distances. So Jesus becomes our contemporary, and this direct personal relation to Him is the very essence of Christianity. Thus the relation between God and man is permanently changed since Christ came: not in the sense that we have direct access to God or direct knowledge of Him (to claim that would be to anticipate the final consummation) but in the sense that we have Jesus as a living contemporary, to lead us to God. That is the meaning of having Jesus as Leader, and that is Heim's Christology.

I find it is impossible to study this Christology without the uneasy feeling that the 'leader' category, which it uses as its clue, is not being used in its most worthy sense. Leadership is constantly spoken of today, in many different quarters, and perhaps too much, as one of the great needs of the age. But surely there is a false and a true, and the true leadership is not that which merely demands blind and unintelligent assent and obedience. The true leader 'gives a lead' to the people by endeavouring to 'carry them with him' in an intelligent perception and acceptance of his objectives. He is indeed ahead of them and can see farther, but he is eager to let them see for themselves as much as possible of what he sees. It seems plain that in the moral and religious realm, and even in social and political life apart from very limited and temporary objectives, this is the only kind of leadership that is of any value at all. The other kind, which demands *blind* obedience, has played havoc with human life in our own time. Yet it is this latter that Heim appears to take as his clue to Christology. His thesis, indeed, is that Christ and Christ alone is called to exercise that absolute leadership which has with disastrous consequences been arrogated to themselves by other leaders. He is the one true Leader and Lord. Thus Heim's thesis may be regarded as a valiant Christian retort to those other claims, and it is in that spirit that it was put forward in an environment which made all Christian protest difficult and perilous. But can the category of leadership, as Heim conceives it, yield a sound Christology?

Let us examine his meaning more closely. What does Heim mean when he asks and answers the question whether and why we need a *Führer* in the life of faith? Is he simply asking the old question whether we need an absolute *external* authority in religion? At some points that appears to be what he means; and if he meant an internal authority, why should he have to take so much trouble to prove our need? What he has to prove is the necessity of an actual historical Leader, to lift us above the polarity of our human experience and to guide us to God. And Heim does treat of the actual Jesus of history among His disciples in the days of His flesh: that was the beginning of His leadership. Moreover, it appears in Heim's description as a leadership which demanded, not understanding, but blind and unquestioning acceptance and obedience. He lays the very strongest emphasis on that aspect of the authority of Jesus. Jesus' commands needed no higher legitimation than His own personal injunction. His disciples were to do this and that, not for any reasons which they could share with Him, but solely and simply for His sake, because He asked it ('for my sake'). His endeavor during His ministry was not primarily to give men a doctrine or a world-view, but to bring them into personal relationship with Himself, as the Leader to whom God had given plenipotentiary power. But is not this an extremely one-sided view of our Lord's earthly ministry? It can hardly be questioned that our Lord spent a large part of His time in teaching, and that a great deal of His teaching was not about Himself or His relation to God or to His disciples, but about God's ways and the nature and demands of His kingdom. And on these matters He spoke with an authority very different from the dictatorial authority of the *Führer* who imposes his will and demands blind and unintelligent obedience. Yes, it must be said that even Jesus, speaking with such immense authority, did not approach men in that way. He spoke with the authority of truth, and on that He relied. His endeavor was to make people see the truth for themselves. He did not ask men to give up thinking, but rather seems to have deliberately awakened their minds by asking penetrating questions. According to Bishop Gore: "He shrank from making dogmatic statements. Plainly He preferred to stimulate the minds of His disciples to discover the truth (e.g. the truth about Himself) for themselves."[18] Again: "No teacher ever showed more belief than our Lord in the capacity of the ordinary man to think rightly, if he be only sincere and open-minded. He did not, except rarely, use the dogmatic method. It would seem as if He feared to stunt men's growth from within thereby."[19] That may be a one-sided overstatement, but is it not historically truer than Heim's account of the leadership of Jesus in the days of His flesh?

It is, however, when he comes to Christ's leadership of later generations that Heim's use of the 'leadership' category becomes most confused and confusing. It is not, of course, on Heim's view, by an authoritative code of conduct bequeathed to us that Jesus becomes our Leader, but by a direct I-Thou relationship with us in the present, which is possible through the Holy Spirit. Here we seem to move away entirely from the idea of an *external* authority to something very like the *testimonium Spiritus Sancti internum*. And surely such an inward authority is something very different from the kind of leadership that Heim describes. It certainly calls for unconditional obedience, but it is not *blind* obedience. It is by "enlightening our minds in the knowledge of Christ" that the Holy Spirit calls us to the Christian life. And if Heim describes

[18] Charles Gore, *The Philosophy of the Good Life,* p. 198.
[19] Ibid., in *A New Commentary on Holy Scripture,* p. 286.

this as an I-Thou relationship, transcending time and making Jesus our contemporary, it gives us, plainly, not an external authority but an inward guidance. It is not guidance by 'the Jesus of history' in the limited sense, but by Christ present in our hearts through the Holy Spirit. What kinship has this with the kind of *Führerschaft* which Heim adopts as his clue? It is of the essence of the latter to give an absolute external authority, whose guidance has to be unconditionally obeyed by us even if we do not at all understand it; and it is difficult to see how *such* leadership could be exercised except during the lifetime of the leader, since it does not operate through a general code of conduct that could be handed down. As regards *inward* guidance from moment to moment, I do not see that this can be illustrated at all by the *Führerschaft* familiar in the modern world, unless the guidance is conceived in an automatic and unintelligent manner quite unworthy of the traditional Christian language about the Holy Spirit enlightening our minds in the knowledge of Christ.

If we further pursue the Christological question about Jesus' relation to God, it is exceedingly difficult to clarify Heim's answer. Who and what is this Jesus? And why is He our Leader? His leadership, says Heim, is not eternal, but has both a beginning and an end. It began with the Incarnation, when God, for reasons which we cannot penetrate, appointed this Man to be our Leader. It will come to an end in the final consummation, when the Son will hand over all authority to the Father (as in 1 Cor. xv, 24–8). For the period of Jesus' earthly life, His followers had the Leader with them in the flesh. For the period between that and the final consummation, we have the Leader with us through the Holy Spirit. But if we take all this in the sense which Heim's 'leader' category seems to require, it appears to leave us at two removes from God. We cannot have any knowledge of God except through Jesus, from whom we have to take everything absolutely on trust; and we cannot know Jesus (in this interim period) except through the Holy Spirit. On Heim's principles it would seem necessary to go on to ask: How do we know the Holy Spirit? However deeply true it may be in the traditional catholic sense of the words that we know God in Christ through the Holy Spirit, the meaning becomes different and very problematic on the basis of Heim's Christology. Is the Holy Spirit God? If not, are we left at two removes from contact with God? Or if the Holy Spirit is God, how can we men (who in the polarity of our experience cannot know God directly) know God the Holy Spirit? On Heim's principles it would appear that we should need another absolute leader in the flesh, to distinguish the true from the false for us in this realm of the Spirit of God.

Thus I cannot see that Heim's use of the 'leader' category helps him to answer the Christological question. Indeed, he does not seem to me to answer the Christological question at all. He does not succeed in making clear his doctrine of 'Jesus our Contemporary.' Is Jesus the only person in history who can be 'contemporary' with the people of any or every generation? And is it Deity, or Divinity, that enables Him thus to transcend time? So far as I can discover, that is not what Heim means, but rather that the I-Thou relationship even between two men is possible across the centuries, transcending by its very nature all intervals of time. Yet that would seem to make nonsense of his doctrine of the Holy Spirit. But again—apart from the question of contemporariness—Heim never tell us why Jesus is able to do for men what they cannot do for themselves. Man cannot rise above the 'polarity' of our human experience and come to know God for himself. How was Jesus able to do it? And therefore how is He qualified to be our Leader? It is 'personality,' according to Heim, that qualifies for leadership. What then of the personality of Jesus Christ? Is it His personality in the human sense, as a phenomenon which can be studied historically, that makes Him Leader? That does not appear to be what Heim means, for He does not make much of 'the Jesus of history' as our guide. Is it then the 'Person' of Christ in a transcendent sense, as defined in catholic dogma? But Heim does not make much use of this either. He gives no answer to the question how this Jesus is related to God, except that God has appointed Him to be our absolute Leader. In this matter he even out-Ritschls the Ritschlian school. The Ritschlians, it might be said, refused to answer the Christological question except on the level of 'value-judgments,' for they made little of the Christological definitions of catholic dogma, which seemed to them to contain alien metaphysics with which Christian faith has nothing to do. But then the Ritschlians built upon the Jesus of history, upon the approach that God makes to us through the human personality that we encounter in the Gospel story. That gave some content to the Ritschlian Christology, taking the place of the rejected metaphysical definitions. But Heim's Christology makes as little of the one as of the other, and seems strangely lacking in positive content as regards either the personality of Jesus or the nature of God.

Catholic Authors

1. R. L. Faricy, S.J.,[1] points out that while Teilhard de Chardin's theology of Redemption recognizes the negative aspect of reparation and expiation for sin, it stresses the positive and constructive element of victory over evil and of unification of a disordered universe. For him, Redemption has cosmic universal significance, with Creation, Incarnation and Redemption understood as structural elements of one single great mystery. The cross is the symbol of this difficult and painful process of creative unification. It is the symbol of Christ's redemptive function, as well as the symbol of Christian existence.

The New Testament theology of the Redemption has a twofold point of view corresponding to what might be called the negative and the positive aspects of the redemption. The negative aspect of the redemption is

[1] Robert L. Faricy, S.J. is professor of Ascetical Theology at the Catholic University of America in Washington, D.C. It is from his article "Teilhard de Chardin's Theology of Redemption" in *Theological Studies* (December 1966) that this excerpt has been taken from pp. 553–579.

Christ's atonement for the sins of the world, "that Christ died for our sins in accordance with the Scriptures."[2] The positive aspect lies in the fact that the Redemption is a victory over the powers of evil. "During our minority we were slaves to the elemental spirits of the universe, but when the term was completed God sent His own Son, born of a woman, born under the law, to purchase freedom for the subjects of the law in order that we might attain the status of sons."[3] "Bearing the human likeness, revealed in human shape, He humbled Himself and in obedience accepted even death —death on a cross. Therefore God raised Him to the heights and bestowed on Him the name above all names, that at the name of Jesus every knee should bow—in heaven, on earth, and in the depths—and every tongue confess, 'Jesus Christ is Lord,' to the glory of the Father."[4] Since the end of the age of the Fathers of the Church, Christian theology of the Redemption has paid more attention to the negative aspect than to the positive. Teilhard de Chardin in his reflections on Christ's Redemption of the world, while not neglecting the ideas of reparation and expiation for sin, stresses the positive aspect.

Teilhard tries to formulate the beginnings of a theology of the redemption that he feels is in the direction of answering the questions and the needs of contemporary man. His theological reflection emphasizes the constructive side of the redemption, the victory over the forces of evil, and it allows more room than most past theology for man's place in the redemptive process, more room for active as well as passive human participation in the Redemption of the world. Teilhard sees past views as giving great stress to the dark side, the negative aspect of the Redemption; he himself tentatively suggests a point of view that gives more stress to the positive aspect. . . .

The Redemption. Christ's death was much more than a historical accident or a consequence of evil in the world and much more than simply an example for Christians. Christ's death marks "the complete immersion of the Divine Unity in the ultimate depths of multiplicity." The coming of Christ into the world by some oblique or indirect route would be incomprehensible. Christ had first to steep Himself in the matter of the cosmos so that He could raise it up to Himself. "It is because Christ has 'inoculated Himself' in matter that He is inseparable from the growth of spirit and so ingrained in the visible world that He could not be uprooted without shaking the foundations of the universe."[5] Christ could not have become the "way out" for the universe and the point of fulfilment for the universe without first becoming immanent in that universe. And to immerse Himself in the experimental world meant to undergo that world with its inevitable evil. Christ could not be Omega without being immanent to, immersed

[2] 1Cor 15:3.

[3] Gal 4:3–5.

[4] Phil 2:8–11. R. Schnackenburg mentions that "Paul's soteriology, which embraces the whole world, needs clarification on more than one point—on the question of its cosmic import (cf. Col 1:20), for example" (*New Testament Today* [tr. D. Askew; London: 1963] p. 75).

[5] "Mon univers" (1924, *OE* 9, 89).

in, the world, and the price of immanence is suffering and death.[6]

We know that God is supremely free as regards His will to create the universe and to become incarnate and to redeem mankind. But God's plan of creation and salvation is perfect, and all the parts of that plan are integrally and perfectly related. As a result, from our standpoint in the experimental world and in the light of divine revelation, all the elements of God's plan appear to us—because of their perfect inter-connection—to have a certain necessity. The Incarnation and the Redemption are so organically a part of God's whole creative plan that in the cosmic perspectives of Teilhard we cannot understand the mysteries of creation and the Incarnation and the Redemption without understanding them as intrinsically interrelated. In spite of the perfect freedom of each of God's salvific acts, we cannot understand "creation without God's immersion in the world through the Incarnation, nor the Incarnation without redemptive compensation."[7] Because we ourselves are part of God's plan and can see that plan only "from the inside," the redemptive Incarnation appears to us as necessarily connected with the creative process. Teilhard by no means contests God's freedom; he does contest a conceptual pluralism that would artificially separate Redemption from Incarnation or either from the creative process. Teilhard's viewpoint is the viewpoint of the Old and New Testaments: the history of salvation begins with creation. And for Teilhard as for St. Paul, Christ's Redemption is the Redemption not just of man but of the universe. Because of the nature of this evolving universe where evil is statistically inevitable at every level, Christ's work of the unification of all things in Himself appears to us as inevitably involving the pain of the Redemption. Christ's work of the redemption of the world was a painful work, a work of suffering, because it included reparation for the sins of the world or—in Teilhard's somewhat esoteric expression—"compensation for statistical disorders."[8] Teilhard sees Christ's redemptive work as also including the "creative pain" of a "specific effort of unification that goes against a kind of inclination or inertia of existence in virtue of which participated being

[6] See "Du cosmos à la cosmogénèse" (1951, *OE* 7, 270–73). See F. X. Durrwell, C.SS.R., *In the Redeeming Christ,* tr. R. Sheed (New York, 1963) pp. 5–7: "It is not just a question of cancelling a debt; condemnation is built into my nature, and the redemption must be accomplished in a physical transformation" (p. 5).

[7] "Comment je vois" (1948, unpublished essay) pp. 20–21. On the ontological distinction and fundamental unity of the order of creation and the order of redemption, see K. Rahner, S.J., *The Christian Commitment,* tr. C. Hastings (New York, 1963) pp. 38–74. Rahner's idea of Christian spirituality, however, is quite different from Teilhard de Chardin's. In making an application of his distinction between the creative and redemptive orders to the life of the Christian, Rahner seems to take the "order of creation" as a category of the Christian's positive approach to the world, the "incarnationalist" component of the Christian life. He seems to consider the "order of redemption" as the category of the "eschatological" component, implying renunciation and flight from the world. For Teilhard, of course, there is only one Christian spirituality, the spirituality of the Cross, and it has both "incarnational" and "eschatological" components. The redemptive order implies both renunciation *and* a constructive approach to the world.

[8] "Comment je vois" (1948, unpublished essay) p. 20.

tends constantly to fall back toward multiplicity."[9] Reparation for evil, compensation for disorder in the world, is the negative aspect of Christ's redemptive effort. But it is the positive aspect of the redemption that is most stressed in Teilhard's perspective: the specific effort of the unification of a disordered world. "Jesus is truly He who bears the sins of the world; moral evil is mysteriously compensated for by suffering. But more fundamentally, Jesus is He who structurally overcomes in Himself, and for all of us, the resistance to spiritual ascent, a resistance that is inherent in matter."[10] Although Teilhard's vision of the whole structure of the universe, a vision that is theological as well as phenomenological, did not take on definite lines until after 1930, he considered the Redemption in terms of unification from the time of his early works. He writes in 1917:

> The principle of unity that saves a guilty creation from returning to dust is Christ. By the force of His attraction, by the light of His moral and spiritual teaching, by the binding power of His very existence, Jesus comes to reestablish at the heart of the world the harmony of efforts and the convergence of all things. When we read the Gospel in a straightforward way we see that no idea translates better for our understanding the redemptive function of the Word than the idea of the unification of all flesh in one same Spirit.[11]

Very early too, Teilhard saw the necessity of understanding Christ's redemptive function as *universal.* In 1920 he writes that "if Christ is to be understood as truly universal, then the Redemption and the Fall must be understood as extending to the whole universe."[12] The idea that Christ's work of redemption is a *universal* work of unification is not without difficulties, as Teilhard well knew. For one thing, it seems to imply a naive notion of the earth as the center of the entire universe. Is the choice of this one small planet among countless possibly inhabited planets an arbitrary choice on the part of the Redeemer as the scene of His painful work of saving the universe? In the face of these and other difficulties, without being able to resolve them all, Teilhard holds firmly to the principle "that there is one Christ in whom all things have their stability. All secondary beliefs must cede to that one fundamental proposition. Christ is everything or He is nothing."[13] Christ the Redeemer is, as Reedemer, also Christ the Unifier, so much so that it is not from Adam that mankind derives its real unity and solidarity but from Christ.[14]

It is, then, the creative and unificative aspect of Christ's redemptive function that Teilhard emphasizes. Again, in 1933, he writes that "the complete and ultimate sense of the Redemption is not only expiation but labor and conquest."[15] And in 1944 and 1945:

---

[9] *Ibid.*

[10] "Christologie et évolution" (1933, unpublished essay) p. 8.

[11] "La lutte contre la multitude" (1917, *Ecrits,* p. 124).

[12] "Note sur le Christ universel" (1920, *OE* 9, 41).

[13] "Chute, rédemption, et géocentricité" (1920, unpublished essay) p. 5. For a discussion of this problem, see C. Davis, *Theology for Today* (New York, 1962) pp. 164–70.

[14] *Ibid.,* pp. 3–4; "Mon univers" (1924, *OE* 9, 109).

[15] "Christologie et évolution" (1933, unpublished essay) p. 8. Cf. however, C. Mooney, S.J., *Teilhard de Chardin and the Mystery of Christ* (New York, 1966) p. 133 "We should expect a very strong affirmation of the negative aspect of Redemption, namely, the

"The suffering Christ, without ever ceasing to be He who carries the sins of the world, and precisely *as such,* is being understood more and more by the faithful as He who carries and supports the weight of the world in its process of evolution."[16] Christ is "He who carries with the sins of the world the whole weight of the world in progress."[17] By His passion and cross Christ did make reparation for the sins of the world, taking them on Himself, and making atonement for them; this is the "negative" aspect of the Redemption. But there is a positive aspect that is brought into relief when the redemption is put into the context of a world in process, in evolution; this positive aspect of the Redemption is the redemptive effort of Christ to unite all things to Himself. Thus, in the context of a world in a state of becoming, in a state of converging evolution, creation and the Incarnation and the Redemption are seen as three complementary facets of one single process: pleromization, the gradual unification of all things in Christ in the fulness of the Pleroma. Creation, considered as "creative union," implies a certain immersion of the Creator in His work. Because the creative process inevitably engenders evil as a secondary statistical effect, a certain redemptive compensation on the part of the Creator is implied. Creation, Incarnation, and Redemption, in the framework of Teilhard's thought, are understood as structural elements of one single great mystery. "Taken in their full sense, creation, Incarnation, and Redemption are not simply facts localized in time and space; they are truly dimensions of the world."[18]

The Cross: Reality and Symbol. Teilhard's views on the cosmic significance of the historical reality of the suffering and death of Christ are summed up in his understanding of what the Cross stands for. Teilhard's idea of the Redemption and what it means for men is condensed in a short but very rich paragraph from *The Divine Milieu.*

> To sum up, Jesus on the Cross is both the symbol and the reality of the immense labor of the centuries which has, little by little, raised up the created spirit and brought it back to the depths of the divine milieu. He represents (and in a true sense, he is) creation, as upheld by God, it reascends the slopes of being, sometimes clinging to things for support, sometimes tearing itself from them in order to pass beyond them, and always compensating, by physical suffering, for the setbacks caused by its moral downfalls.[19]

---

reparation made by Christ for the sins of the world. . . . Yet no such affirmation is anywhere to be found." This statement seems somewhat exaggerated. Mooney makes a good point, however, when immediately after the above statement he criticizes Teilhard for not explicitly stating that Christ's reparation for sin is "a bearing of the weight of man's refusal to love." The notion of sin as a "refusal to love" is implicit in Teilhard's writings, but he never brings it out. See also J. LeBlond, S.J., "Consacrer l'effort humain," *Etudes* 296 (1958) 63–68.

[16] "Introduction à la vie chrétienne" (1944, unpublished essay) p. 8.

[17] "Christianisme et évolution" (1945, unpublished essay) p. 6.

[18] "Quelques vues générales sur l'essence du christianisme" (1939, unpublished essay) p. 2. See "Du cosmos à la cosmogénèse" (1951, *OE* 7, 270–73).

[19] *DM,* p .104.

Christ's suffering and death on the Cross are not simply the suffering and death of an individual nor a simple expiation. The death of Christ was an act of creative power. "Jesus crucified is not a reject: He is not defeated. On the contrary, He carries the weight of the universal course of progress with Him toward God."[20] "The Cross is the symbol and the real act of Christ raising the world with its whole burden of inertia and with all its natural vitality—an act of expiation, but also a hard journey of conquest." In Christ's death on the Cross we see "creation in the category of laborious effort."[21]

The Cross is not "a symbol of sadness, of limitation and repression"; it is the symbol of the difficult and painful effort of creative unification. Christianity does not ask man to live in the shadow of the Cross, but in the fire of its intense zeal.[22] In this life, man remains in what we can call the existential structure of the Cross. It is true that we are already "risen with Christ" by the sacrament of baptism and that our life here is pointed toward our own resurrection just as Christ's passion and death are pointed to and inseparable from His resurrection. But in this life the Christian is in the structure of the Cross; it is the life to come that is to be in the existential framework of Christ's resurrection. The Cross, then, is not only the symbol of Christ's whole redemptive function, but also the symbols of the life of the Christian. In Christ crucified "each man must recognize his own true image. . . . The truth about our situation in this world is that we are here on the Cross."[23] By its birth and by its very nature, Christianity is marked by the sign of the Cross, and it can remain what it is only by identifying itself always more intensely with the meaning of the Cross. What is this meaning of the Cross? What does the Cross mean as a symbol of Christianity and in particular of the life of the Christian? A few years before his death, Teilhard wrote to his superiors in Rome setting forth his own ideas of how Christianity should be understood in the light of contemporary events and attitudes and how it should be presented in the contemporary world. In the brief essay intended for his superiors, Teilhard puts his ideas

---

20 "La signification et la valeur contructrice de la souffrance" (1933, *OE* 6, 66).

21 "Quelques vues générales sur l'essence du christianisme" (1939, unpublished essay) p. 2. J. Danielou, S.J., writes that the earliest sermons about the Cross celebrate its cosmic character, and quotes from a sermon of Gregory of Nyssa (*Catechetical Discourse* 23, 3): "I know thy mystery, O cross, for which thou wast raised up. Indeed, thou wast raised up over the world, to make steady that which was unsteady. One part of thee rises into the heavens, to point to the Word on High; another part stretches to right and left, to put to flight the fearsome power of the adversary and to gather the world together in unity; and one part of thee is planted in the earth, so that thou mayest unite the things that are on the earth and the things in hell with the things that are in heaven" (*Christ and Us,* tr. W. Roberts [New York, 1961] p. 141).

22 *DM,* p. 102; "Christologie et évolution" (1933, unpublished essay) p. 8.

23 "La vie cosmique" (1916, *Ecrits,* p. 56). That man in this world in the structure of the Cross is as true for Teilhard as for St. Augustine, for whom historical humanity, both the heavenly and the earthly "cities," are in the interior of the mystery of the Cross of Christ. See J. McCallin, "Christological Unity of the 'De Civitate Dei,'" *Revue des études augustiniennes* 12 (1966) 85–109.

in the form of an answer to the question: How can we best state today the meaning of the Cross?[24]

> In its traditional and elementary form, and as it is still currently presented in pious books, in sermons, and even in seminary teaching, the Cross is first of all a symbol of reparation and expiation. And, in this interpretation, the Cross is the vehicle and the expression of a whole psychological attitude in which can be recognized at least as tendencies the following elements:
>
> a) the world is viewed as dominated by the catastrophes of evil and death, the normal and chronological consequences of an original Fall;
>
> b) human nature is viewed with suspicion . . . ;
>
> c) there is a general almost Manichean mistrust of anything material. . . .
>
> All this, of course and fortunately, in the context of a powerful love for the crucified Savior. But this love is almost exclusively of the "ascensional" kind, characterized by acts . . . of painful purification and suffering detachment. . . .
>
> This should be changed. . . . The Cross should be to us not just a sign of *escape,* but of forward movement. The Cross should shine before us not just as purifying, but as motivating. Is such a transformation possible without deformation? Yes, I answer emphatically; it is possible and even demanded—if one goes below the surface of things—by all that is most traditional in the Christian spirit.[25]

In Teilhard's theologoy of the Redemption, Christ not only bears the sins of the world, but also the weight of the world in evolution. For Teilhard, then, the Cross is the symbol not only of reparation and expiation, but the symbol of the redemptive unification of the world, of the progress of the world toward Christ-Omega. The Cross is the symbol of the synthesis of the "upward" component of sacrifice and adoring reparation and the "forward" component of progress through laborious effort. This is the Cross that Teilhard venerates; "it is the same Cross" as the Cross of traditional Christian piety, "but much more true." It is not only the symbol of the victory over sin, but "the complete and dynamic symbol of a universe in the state of personalizing evolution."[26]

The notion of the Cross as the symbol of true progress runs through Teilhard's writings. The symbolism applies not only to Christ's redemptive work, but also to the sharing in that redemptive work by the Christian. Christ's suffering and death are not only the model for the Christian; it is Christ's redemptive act that gives meaning and efficacy to man's work in building the world toward Christ. "The Cross, as well as being the expression of what we have to undergo in the way of expiation, is also, and I would say primarily, the expression of the creative but laborious effort of mankind climbing towards Christ who awaits it."[27] The Cross is the symbol

[24] The full title of this unpublished essay is "Ce que le monde attend en ce moment de l'église de Dieu: Une généralisation et un approfondissement du sens de la croix" (1952).

[25] *Ibid.*, p. 4.

[26] *Ibid.*, p. 5. See W. Whitla, "Sin and Redemption in Whitehead and Teilhard de Chardin," *Anglican Theological Review* 47 (1965) 81–93.

[27] "Intégration de l'homme dans l'univers" (1930, unpublished essay) p. 13. See "La vie cosmique" (1916, *Ecrits,* p. 82); "Le prêtre" (1918, *Écrits,* pp. 288–89); "La route de l'ouest" (1932, unpublished essay) p. 15: "The Hindu saint recollects himself and exhausts himself in order to shake loose from the matter in which he is imbedded; the Christian

not only of the dark and regressive aspect of the universe, but also and above all of the luminous and conquering aspect; it is the symbol of progress and victory . . . through difficult labor."[28]

> Towards the peaks, shrouded in mist from our human eyes, whither the Cross beckons us, we rise by a path which is the way of universal progress. The royal road of the Cross is no more nor less than the road of human endeavour supernaturally righted and prolonged. Once we have fully grasped the meaning of the Cross, we are no longer in danger of finding life sad and ugly. We shall simply have become more attentive to its barely comprehensible solemnity.[29]

2. S. P. Schilling[1] finds Rahner's theology profound and greatly influential among contemporary theologians. With demands for new approaches to old formulas, his Christology has both existentialist and essentialist orientations. The author objects to Rahner's explanation of creation and Incarnation in terms of a divine kenosis, that is, of the possibility that the Absolute has in his infinite unrelatedness of divesting himself of himself to become the finite other. He believes that this kenotic view of the ultimate relationship between God and creature might not preserve their distinct identity.

Permeating all of Rahner's thought is a spirit of adventurous questioning to which no area of doctrine or life is closed.[2] . . . Such inquiry is a difficult and dangerous procedure, since it demands a willingness to reformulate old

---

saint recollects and exhausts himself to penetrate and transform that matter. The first seeks to isolate himself from the multiple; the second works to concentrate and to purify it. The Oriental seeks to escape by abandoning time, space, and himself. The Occidental emerges from the plural carrying it with him. Of these two attitudes only the second is capable of expressing to the modern mind the truth, the power, and the attraction of the Cross."

[28] "Introduction a la vie chrétienne" (1944, unpublished essay) p. 8.

[29] *DM*, pp. 103–4. See "The New Spirit" (1942, *FM*, p. 95): the Cross is "the Symbol, the Way, the very Act of progress." In spite of the fact that the Cross occupies such an important position in Teilhard's writings, some theologians continue to criticize him for not giving sufficient place to the Cross. This is hard to understand except as indicating a lack of familiarity with Teilhard's writings. H. Urs von Balthasar objects that Teilhard's Christology seems to leave no place for the Cross; he has other objections to Teilhard's Christology, but this seems to be the main objection; see his "Die Spiritualität Teilhard de Chardin," *Wort und Wahrheit* 18 (1963) 339–50. See also H. Riedlinger, "The Universal Kingship of Christ," tr. T. Westow, in *Who is Jesus of Nazareth?*, ed. E. Schillebeeckx, O.P. (*Concilium* 11 [New York, 1966] pp. 119–27); Riedlinger wonders whether "the absence of a theological treatment of the cross in Teilhard constitutes an irreparable and basic lacuna in his synthesis or whether it can still be inserted as an afterthought" (p. 124). The fact is that this theological treatment of the Cross is not absent in Teilhard.

[1] Sylvester Paul Schilling is a native of Massachusetts. He is presently Professor of Systematic Theology at Boston University School of Theology. He is the author of *Methodism and Society in Theological Perspective* and *Isaiah Speaks*. It is from his book *Contemporary Continental Theologians* (Nashville–New York: Abingdon Press, 1966) that this excerpt has been taken, selectively, from pp. 206–225.

[2] His main work is *Schriften zur Theologie*, Einsiedeln, Zürich, Köln: Benziger Verlag, 1957–62. The first two volumes have been published in English by Taplinger (Helicon)

questions, to raise new ones, and to explore untried solutions whose agreement or disagreement with the established doctrine of the church cannot be known in advance. . . . For example, the Chalcedonian "formula" is—a formula; it is marked by an incompleteness which it "does not resolve but in fact preserves." What is merely conserved or handed down without a fresh, personal effort to understand it, in relation to the source of revelation, "rots as the manna did." We can really preserve the past "in its purity" only by relating it responsibly to the present and the future.[3]

Closely related to Rahner's demand for new approaches is his partially existentialist orientation. . . . Man can be understood only in his wholeness as a being who, aware of being questioned by existence, needs to respond in passionate commitment as well as reflection. Our clearest thought of God and Christ is related to the salvation-event in man. . . .

Nevertheless, Catholic theology in Rahner's view must also be a theology of essence. Though human "nature" is a "remainder concept," it is necessary and objectively justified. There are intrinsic and continuing structures and connections in reality which can in some measure be known and elucidated. Unlike Bultmann, for instance, Rahner believes it is possible to make true statements about the real God whose grace man encounters in salvation, and even about life after death. . . .

Christology. History is "a becoming new which preserves the old." Therefore doctrinal formulas which are historical embodiments of Christian truth should be neither abandoned nor passed on in petrified form. Rahner follows this principle in considering the Incarnation, presupposing but not simply repeating the Chalcedonian declaration.[4] Since the church's Christological dogma has never claimed to be an adequate distillation of biblical teaching there is need for a fresh examination of biblical Christology. Such study would, for one thing, produce a renewed recognition of the humanity of Christ. Rahner finds in the current understanding of the Chalcedonian formula an implicit if unconscious Monophysite tendency which fails to do justice to the New Testament portrayal of the historical Jesus and his role as Messiah and Mediator. Thus the Incarnation becomes "almost a transient episode in God's activity in his world," and the continuing manhood of Christ strongly affirmed at Chalcedon is overlooked. Jesus becomes God among us, but the Jesus who in human freedom becomes our Mediator is left in question. Freedom subjected to the divine nature cannot be the intrinsic personal freedom which is essential to human personality. The real humanity of Christ must therefore be clearly and explicitly asserted.[5]

The Incarnation. Rahner devotes major attention to the meaning of the incarnation, examining it both meta-

---

Press, Baltimore, with the title *Theological Investigations* (I: *God, Christ, Mary and Grace,* tr. Cornelius Ernst, 1961; II: *Man in the Church,* tr. Karl H. Kruger, 1963). In later references this work will be cited as *Schriften* or as *Investigations,* respectively.

[3] *Investigations,* I, 149 f., 7, 10.

[4] *Investigations,* I, 150, 154; *Schriften,* IV, 137.

[5] *Investigations,* I, 155–61, 183 f., 198.

physically and existentially. One of his most profound and difficult essays deals successively with the questions: What does it mean (1) that God has become *man*, and (2) that he has *become* man? In approaching the former, he endeavors to formulate the ontological counterpart to the ontic statements of orthodox Christology, asking how the nature of real being should be conceived to correspond to the church's assertions regarding God, man, and Christ. Which account of ultimate reality is necessarily adapted to these statements? Rahner believes that a sound answer to this question will prevent the mythological impression, often made by the traditional affirmations, that God has clothed himself in the garment of a human nature which only externally envelopes him.

Rahner's basic conviction is that true being, represented by both man and God, is Spirit as such. Man cannot be defined in any way which would specify limits to his nature. All that can be said is that his existence is referred to the incomparable God. Our nature is self-transcendence, limitless reference to the "mystery of fullness." We exist in the decision of accepting or rejecting our own mystery, and the larger mystery to which it refers. The transcendence "which we are and act" makes up our existence and God's, and both as mystery. However, this mystery is not something concealed and to be disclosed, standing next to something already known. Rather it is simply what is there, the given. It is the ultimate horizon of all conceiving, in terms of which we conceive other reality. It is the uniqueness which always distinguishes God, and because of him ourselves.

The reality which is human nature comes to itself by losing itself. This occurs most radically when, yielding itself utterly to the mystery of fullness, it is so expropriated that it becomes the mystery of God Himself. It is accepted by God as *His* reality, thus arriving at the point toward which according to its essence it is always moving. This occurs in the Incarnation. Man *is* in the degree to which he gives himself away. His nature is his potentiality for obedience. The Word of God "assumes" human nature, therefore, when this potentiality is most fully developed. Found thus by infinity, man becomes what he is. His being finds supreme fulfillment when a true man gives himself to God so fully that in him the mystery toward which man's questions point, the question beyond question, becomes present as final answer.

When we ask who fits this description in earthly history—who therefore is the one to whom we can bring the mystery of our own nature—we can turn only to Jesus of Nazareth. Such an event took place and eternally takes place only in Him. We others are too far from God, thinking that we alone understand ourselves. But Jesus knew that only the Father knew His mystery, and therein He understood that only He knew the Father.[6]

What, then, does it mean for God to *become* man? Rahner finds the answer primarily in the concept of *kenosis*. The Word can become flesh because the Absolute has in His infinite unrelatedness the possibility of divesting Himself of Himself to become the finite other. By giving Himself away, God posits the other as his own reality, without having to undergo

[6] *Schriften*, IV, 140–45.

becoming in his own original essence. Differentiation is implicit in God as love; since He wills to have the other as His own, he constitutes it in its genuine reality. As the fullness which gives itself away, He externalizes himself and becomes historical. This original capacity for divine differentiation is the ultimate source of the possibility of creation, in which God gives reality to the other without giving up himself. Therefore rooted in the deepest ground of creation itself is the possibility of its being "assumed" by God, the basis for his possible self-objectification in human history. The immanent self-utterance of God in his eternal fullness is the condition of the self-utterance and self-projection of God in both creation and incarnation.[7]

In Rahner's view the relation of creation and incarnation extends still further, the latter being seen as the goal of the former. The Incarnation of the Word is indeed a unique event in real history. However, it is not merely a subsequent occurrence in a world already finished, a kind of divine afterthought occasioned by human sin and the need of redemption. Ontologically it is the "unambiguous goal of creation as a whole," to which everything prior is preparatory, pointing to the event in which God, while giving being to what is other than He, once for all achieves both the greatest proximity to it and the greatest distance from it. In radically objectifying himself God appears in utmost truth. The history of what he has created thus becomes profoundly his own, and it finds its center and fulfillment in Christ.[8]

Though Rahner devotes his full intellectual powers to Christological speculation, he maintains that a person who misunderstands and therefore rejects the orthodox formulas may nevertheless consummate faith in the incarnation existentially. Many a man, looking at Jesus and his cross, confesses that therein the living God has spoken to him the last and decisive Word, and thus has delivered him from all those factors in his existence which hold him captive to guilt and death. Such a person derives from Jesus the final truth of his life. But his belief is true only if Jesus really is the one whom the faith of the church confesses. Therefore this person believes, whether or not he knows it reflectively, in the Incarnation of the Word of God. Indeed, Christ has been met by many who were unaware that they had encountered the one whose life and death held the secret of their redemption. The grace of the incarnate God is present in every reality worth choosing, as its hidden essence. When therefore a man accepts his existence in quiet patience, in faith, hope, and love *as* the mystery contained in the mystery of eternal love and life, he says yes to something which is what it is because God has actually filled it with the Unmeasured—Himself—since the Word became flesh. Such a person entrusts Himself to Christ without knowing it. "Whoever wholly accepts his manhood . . . has accepted the Son of man, because in Him God has accepted man." We do fulfill the law and love God when we love our neighbor, for God has become this neighbor.[9]

Christology and Anthropology. It

[7] *Schriften,* IV, 145–49.
[8] *Investigations,* I, 164 f.
[9] *Schriften,* IV, 152–54.

should now be apparent that for Rahner the incarnation is the clue to a true understanding of man no less than of God. The fact that God has become man means that Christology is the beginning and end of Christian anthropology, and that such anthropology is inevitably theology. Humanity is not something added on to God, a mere form of appearance; it is His very presence in the world. In Christ's human life we see what our human life really means. Our finitude is that of the Word of God himself. Most profoundly understood, man is seen to *be* because God himself *ek-sists*—projects himself outward, externalizes himself in the other. Through this self-emptying God's existence "receives its value, strength, and reality." Man arises when God, willing to be non-God, lovingly speaks Himself out into the godless nothing. "He has spoken his Word as our flesh into the emptiness of the not-divine and sinful." Man is the abbreviation of the divine Word, the image of God Himself. He is the expression of the bottomless mystery of his ground, in which he eternally participates. Through the incarnation the finite itself has been given an infinite depth. It is no longer an antithesis to the infinite, but that which the infinite has become in order to open to the finite a door into the infinite. Man is therefore forbidden to think poorly of himself, for he would then think poorly of God.[10]

Values. 1. Rahner combines profound respect for the historic positions of the church with enthusiasm for raising unexplored questions and reexamining accepted truths in new contexts. . . . In his explorations he makes constructive use of the methods, theories, and insights of other disciplines, notably philosophy and the sciences. His combination of regard for the old and openness to the new and different has invigorated Roman Catholic thought, advanced Catholic-Protestant understanding, and provided a valuable point of contact between Christian faith and secular culture.

2. Rahner's theology derives great power likewise from its synthesis of existentialist and essentialist features. He is concerned that certain truths of God's revelation so often become unexistential in the day-to-day life of the Christian, but never seriously doubts the objective reference and grounding of such truths. He insists as strenuously as Bultmann that Jesus Christ must be known personally in his power to transform actual existence, but just as firmly contends that such an experience implies that Jesus truly *is* the Christ, whose capacity to save springs from his relation to ultimate reality. . . . The God proclaimed in the New Testament is Creator as well as Redeemer, and those whom He redeems become new creations. . . .

Difficulties. It is questionable whether Rahner's kenotic view of the ultimate relation between God and the finite creation preserves the distinct identities of God and man. He ventures the profound hypothesis that the Absolute, while retaining His own infinite unrelatedness, may freely divest himself of himself, or give Himself away, thereby positing the finite other as His own reality. In this sense God may become the other without having to "become" in His own original essence. Both creation and incarnation spring from this possibility. Creation is the loving self-projection

[10] *Investigations,* I, 183–85, 190–92; *Schriften,* IV, 150–52.

or self-differentiation of God's eternal fullness, and the Word made flesh brings this divine self-emptying to its supreme fulfillment.

This theory is not subject to the fatal objections raised to the nineteenth-century Protestant kenotic Christologies, since Rahner conceives God as giving reality to the finite without surrendering his divinity. However, the similarity between his conception and Hegel's personalistic pantheism suggests another difficulty. In Hegel's dialectical "notion of religion," the subjective, undifferentiated unity of God objectifies itself to produce its finite other, but returns to and fulfills itself in a higher unity which includes differentiation.[11] The question is whether Rahner's view is not ultimately as monistic as Hegel's. Is he any more successful than Hegel in maintaining the full metaphysical identity of man? If the finite is that which the infinite has become, if in its genuine reality it is "constituted" by God, if man is truly God's "own reality,"[12] is not man ultimately a part of God rather than possessing individual identity as a creature of God? Rahner's language seems to imply an affirmative answer, which would in turn raise serious questions regarding the relation of human sin and error to the divine perfection. Further clarification of this issue by Rahner himself is much to be desired. . . .

3. T. H. Clarke, S.J.,[1] discusses various aspects of contemporary Catholic Christology. He sees an effort to integrate dogma with Scripture, the ontological with the functional and with the psychological in Christ, the strictly christological with the soteriological, ecclesiological, sacramental and eschatological. He points to the growing interest to better understand in relevant, contemporary terms the meaning of the realities involved in the scriptural proclamation "the Word Became Man." Studies on Christologies of the past are spurred by the same incentive.

It is an unfortunate, though perhaps inevitable, feature of contemporary theology that the Christ of apologetics is more prominent than the Christ of dogmatics. Concern for relating the Jesus of history to the Christ of Faith, or, to employ more current categories, for integrating the *historisch* and *geschichtlich* elements of the Christ-reality, has overshadowed some excellent work of the past decade in the field of dogmatic Christology. The present essay is an attempt to present a few of the more significant contributions in this field. It is far from being comprehensive, and is confined, for the most part, to Catholic authors. Leaving aside the problems of soteriological and cosmic Christology, it will focus on questions more immediately connected with the dogma of Chalcedon. Even here it will do little

[11] G. W. F. Hegel, *Der Begriff der Religion* (Leipzig: Felix Meiner, 1925), p. 188.
[12] *Schriften,* IV, 148 f.
[1] Cf. Introduction, n. 1. It is from his article "Some Aspects of Current Christology," (originally published in *Thought* and reedited by Joseph E. O'Neill, S.J., in *The Encounter with God,* (New York: Macmillan Co., 1962), that this excerpt has been taken, selectively, from pp. 33–58.

more than sample a very extensive literature. . . .

I

. . . We may look at . . . three phases, patristic, scholastic, modern, or, otherwise expressed, positive, speculative, psychological.

First, considerable attention is being given today to the Christology of ancient Alexandria and Antioch. The Alexandrian Christology is described as a "descending," or *logos-sarx,* Christology. It begins not with the man Jesus but with the eternal Word. Under the influence especially of the Stoic notion of the *logos* as the unique, immanent, hegemonic and vivifying principle in man, Alexandria tends to conceive the eternal Word as assuming the role of this *logos* in Christ. The advantages and disadvantages of such an approach are apparent. The unity of Christ is safeguarded, but at the risk of denying or neglecting the existence, or at least the redemptive significance, of the human mind and will of Christ. One prominent, though controverted, trend today is to stress the limitations rather than the advantages of this approach. In particular Saints Athanasius and Cyril, the two great champions of Alexandrian Christology, are considered by some to have failed to give the human soul of Christ its due place in their soteriology. One might use the phrase, "functional Apollinarism," except that there is question not of positive error but of an understandable inability to exploit this facet of the reality of the God-man.

Discussion of the virtues and defects of the Antiochene school is also part of the present scene. Antiochene Christology is described as "ascending," because it begins with the man Jesus, especially as portrayed in the Synoptics. The phrase *assumptus homo* expresses what is characteristic of this approach: a true, complete man has been assumed by the Word. Opposition to Alexandria is conveyed by the formula: *logos-anthropos.* In Christ the Word and a man are intimately united. Whereas in earlier decades the focus of interest in the Antiochene school was Nestorius, today it is his master, Theodore of Mopsuestia, who is the central figure. . . . What judgment is to be made today of Theodore? Francis Sullivan concluded in his doctoral dissertation that Theodore was truly the father of Nestorianism.[2] John McKenzie, among others, has challenged this verdict.[3] The dispute has more than technical or antiquarian interest. It was no accident that the school of Antioch, and Theodore in particular, should stress the reality and value of the rational and human in the Word Incarnate. For this is exactly what Antioch did in its approach to the word of God in Scripture. Theodore was the champion of literal exegesis in his own day, and is somewhat the darling of exegetes today. Nor was it an accident that Alexandria, more mystical in its Christology, should be mystical also in its approach to Scripture. And so quite apart from the technical questions involved, it is perfectly natural to hear Father McKenzie, that vigorous ex-

[2] F. Sullivan S.J., *The Christology of Theodore of Mopsuestia* (Rome, 1956).

[3] J. McKenzie, S. J., "Annotations on the Christology of Theodore of Mopsuestia," *Theological Studies,* 19 (1958), 345–373; see also the reply of Fr. Sullivan, *ibid.,* 20 (1959), 264–279. Cf. Ch. III, B. A. 3.

ponent of critical exegesis and critic of Origenian hermeneutics, speaking out in defense of Theodore. Just as it was natural for Cardinal Newman, whose theory of the mystical sense of Scripture is more Alexandrian, to characterize Antioch as the very metropolis of heresy.[4] . . .

As we would expect in an age which is engrossed with psychology, personal existence, the subject, Alexandria and Antioch meet today in a concern for the conscious life of the man Jesus. Protestant theologians have for a long time attempted to express the mystery of Christ, especially in what regards the Pauline Kenosis, in psychological terms: But apart from Rosmini, Günther and the effort to refute them in the nineteenth century, Catholic theologians till a few decades ago were less interested in this aspect of Christology. It was the second edition of Paul Galtier's *L'unité du Christ* in 1939 which stimulated reflection on the psychological unity of Christ, especially in terms of the question: how was our Lord humanly aware of His own divinity?[5] . . .

At the opposite extreme from this position we may perhaps place the position of Xiberta, which for some critics comes too close to Eutycheanism for comfort. . . .

Between the positions of Galtier and Xiberta a wide variety of opinions exists, differing both in their metaphysical presuppositions and in their analysis of human consciousness. There are those who maintain that the problem as placed above is a false one.[6] . . . Some go further and attempt to break through a certain dichotomy between the ontological and the psychological which may be at the root of the dilemma. According to this view, knowledge, self-awareness, self-possession, self-disposition, is not a mere adornment or refinement of being, it is being itself, in its fullness. Where being exists in its perfection, in God, it is identically infinite knowledge, infinite self-awareness. And in the hierarchy of creation, the same is true. To be in any full sense is to know, to be aware of self. To be a man is to be aware of oneself as a man. To be humanly the God-man is to be humanly aware of oneself as the God-man. Hence, says Karl Rahner, in virtue of the hypostatic union itself, the human soul of Christ is immediately and consciously in the Word, and the beatific vision is merely the consequence of this consciousness; it is the hypostatic union itself insofar as the hypostatic union is necessarily an *intelligible actu* in the *intelligens actu* of the human soul of Christ. It is the prolongation, if you will, of the hypostatic union in the sphere of intelligence, the knowledge situation connatural with natural divine sonship.

Something should be said also of current opinion on the related question of the human knowledge of Christ in general. There would appear to be a growing uneasiness with the teaching, as commonly understood since St. Thomas, of a triple human knowledge in Christ, beatific, infused, experiential. Particularly obnoxious to many today is the tendency of past ages to extend the object of Christ's infused

---

[4] J. H. Newman, "An essay on the Development of Christian Doctrine" (6th ed.; London, 1888), p. 343.

[5] Cf. excerpt 5 of K. McNamara.

[6] Cf. P. de la Trinite, "A propos de la conscience du Christ; un faux problème théologique," *Ephemerides Carmeliticae,* 11 (1960), 3–52.

knowledge to include areas having directly to do with salvation. Moreover, the theological principle of perfection, which insists on attributing to Christ in His human pilgrimage all the intellectual endowments of angels and men, is being closely scrutinized. How can we do justice to the condition of Christ, as *homo viator,* as like to us in all save sin, as subject of a *kenosis,* as learning obedience by what He suffered (Heb. 5:8), as ignorant of the day of judgment (Matt. 24:36), if for the sake of an abstract principle we burden His human mind in its earthly pilgrimage with types and degrees of knowledge which would appear to have no clearly established soteriological function, which are with difficulty compatible with one another, and which run the danger of reducing the *kenosis* to a purely ontological reality? Moreover, it has been suggested that the principle of perfection, which is quite in place where there is question of moral excellence, was applied to the realm of intellectual excellence by Augustine and others under the influence of a certain Socratic notion that knowledge is virtue. So runs the negative critique. The positive attempts at reconciling what we might call the principle of perfection and the principle of imperfection have focused on the beatific vision and on infused knowledge. As regards the beatific vision, there is first of all the desire to stress the differences rather than the points in common between the immediate vision of God had by the blessed and the immediate vision had by Christ as *viator*. In fact, it has been suggested that not all immediate vision is beatific. The immediate effects of the vision of God are conditioned by the state of the subject. A soul in hell would be tormented, not beatified, by an immediate vision of God. The vision as had by Christ in His mortal, kenotic condition is to be analogously understood. Also with regard to the knowledge of vision, some have gone back to St. Bonaventure for the idea that the vision of all created reality in God was not always actual for the human mind of Christ; a habitual vision sufficed (Karl Adam has gone further and has said "potential"). In this view the ignorance of the day of judgment which Our Lord attributes to Himself is taken to mean: Not even in His knowledge of immediate vision did He have *actual* knowledge of the day of judgment. Such an actual knowledge did not belong to the mission of revelation and salvation given to Christ by His Father.

This tendency to reduce the scope of knowledge of vision is accompanied by a similar tendency regarding infused knowledge. Some theologians today reject the thesis of the presence of infused ideas in the human mind of Christ from the very beginning of His life. They feel that whatever value tradition has given to the doctrine of infused knowledge can be saved by making it consist in a certain supernatural illumination whose role is to "translate," so to speak, the knowledge of vision into the sphere of the communicable and revealable, and thus integrate knowledge of vision with experiential knowledge. . . .

II

A very important aspect of current Christology is concerned with the form in which the content is expressed, and especially with the relationship of the conciliar form, as exemplified in the definition of Chalcedon, with the biblical form. Chalcedon spoke of

Christ as a single divine person in two distinct natures. It terminated its definition by stating that this teaching was in accord with what the prophets and our Lord Himself had taught. But when we turn to Scripture, even to the New Testament, do we find there Chalcedon's doctrine of nature and person? And if not, how are we to look upon Chalcedon? A betrayal? An irrelevancy? A Hellenization of the Gospel? An extension of revelation, legitimate or illegitimate?

The question is, of course, not a new one, but it has entered a new phase, owing especially to Oscar Cullmann's book, *The Christology of the New Testament.*[7] . . . Quite apart from the question of orthodoxy, the statements in question serve to highlight the problem of the relationship of the Church's dogma of the Incarnation to the New Testament statements about Christ. . . .

These are some of the questions which we must put to the Scripture scholars. They come down to this, perhaps: Now that the ghost of the Hellenization of Christianity by St. Paul has been laid and the links of the entire New Testament with the tradition of Israel given their due place, is it not time to stress what Jew and Greek had in common rather than what was peculiar to each? It is not likely that the answer to these questions will show that the problem raised by Cullmann is a completely false one; but perhaps it will help us to place the problem in a still more qualified and accurate way.

When this is done, then the dogmatic theologian, who is concerned with relating the sources of revelation among themselves, will have to put to himself some questions regarding the relationship of Chalcedon and the New Testament. . . .

I know of no one who has undertaken the large task of thus integrally relating the Chalcedonian one-and-many to the scriptural one-and-many, using recent advances in biblical exegesis and theology, including whatever is acceptable in functionalism, using the methods of Grillmeier and Danielou, relying on the basic notions of dogmatic development, the nature of revelation and the senses of Scripture, as tools. Till this is done, we should be grateful, I think, to the exponents of functionalism for the stimulus to doing it they have provided.

III

Even from what we have seen so far, it may be clear that Christology today is not merely repeating well worn formulas or holding the line against critics, but that attempts are being made to move forward our understanding of Christ. Perhaps this forward-moving character of current Christology can best be suggested by enumerating and briefly describing some particular proposals.

First of all, Father Karl Rahner, who in a notable essay has called for a spirit of enterprise in Christology,[8] advances in another article a threefold proposal in meditating on the basic formula: The Word of God became man.[9]

---

[7] Philadelphia, 1959. See the analytical review article of D. Stanley, S.J., in *Theological Studies,* 20 (1959), 409–421. Cf. also in this Ch. L. Malevez' article.

[8] *Theological Investigations,* vol. I (London–Baltimore, 1961), 149–200.

[9] K. Rahner, "Zur Theologie der Menschwerdung," *Catholica,* 12 (1958), 1–16; the article has appeared in French as "Réflexions théologique sur l'Incarnation," *Sciences Ecclésiastiques,* 12 (1960), 5–19.

The *Word* became man—not the Father or the Holy Spirit. *Could* the Father or the Holy Spirit become man? Father Rahner, and with him Father Grillmeier, protest against our too ready acceptance, especially out of reverence for St. Thomas, of the idea that any one or two or all three of the divine persons could assume one or several human natures, singly or together.[10] They suggest that we look again at a stream of early patristic thought according to which the Father, by His personal character, could express Himself visibly and perfectly *ad extra* only through the Son, whose personal character it is to be the perfect expression of the Father within the Godhead, and, should God freely choose to create, to be the perfect expression of the Father *ad extra.* So far as I know, this proposal has remained general, and no one has attempted to argue for it in detail.

The Word became *man.* What is man? We may think, says Father Rahner, that we know what man is, that we can define him as rational animal quite independently of Christ; and our understanding of the Incarnation, which involves a true humanity, is contingent upon our understanding of man. But until we see man in Christ, until we realize that the openness of human nature involves a radical though obediential capacity for hypostatic union, a capacity which has been actuated only in one man but which is present in all men—until we do this, have we really understood the mystery that is man? Can it be that our understanding of man is contingent upon our understanding of the Incarnation? And that there is no adequate anthropology that is not rooted in Christology? Rahner's preoccupation here would seem to be somewhat similar to that of Karl Barth, even though the doctrinal presuppositions would undoubtedly be different. Rahner develops this suggestion somewhat by showing that the meaning of human nature is "to be the castaway, the abandoned, that which perfects itself and reaches its true stature by continually yielding itself to the Incomprehensible. But this occurs most fully, to an unsurpassable degree, in the most radical form possible, if this nature so abandons itself to the mystery of fullness, is so emptied out that it becomes God's own."[11] He also suggests the possibility of what he calls a transcendental deduction of the credibility of Christ which would set out from the dual character of man, who is at once a corporeal, concrete, historic being of earth, and a being of absolute transcendence, and which would aim to show that Christ is the objective correlative of this dual structure of man.

The Word *became* man. What happens to the Word when He *becomes* that which He was not before? The Church tells us against Monophysism, that He does not cease to be what He was, He is not transmuted, for He is immutable. Scholastic theology, working from Aristotelian metaphysics, tells us further that the Word does not even acquire a new relationship; the Incarnation involves a real relationship of the humanity to the Word, but not of the Word to the humanity. We are justified in saying that the Word became man, that the Word is man, because of this unique

[10] A. Grillmeier, art. "Christologie," *Lexicon für Theologie und Kirche,* Vol. 2, col. 1160.

[11] K. Rahner, *Catholica,* 12 (1958), p. 5.

new relationship of the humanity to the Word. But nothing has happened within the Word; the Incarnation is not a new divine experience, but a human experience had by a divine person. A new relationship in the Word would be an increase in perfection which is excluded by the divine immutability. Now neither Father Rahner nor Father Gutwenger are satisfied with this classic conception; they feel, that, among other things, it appears to evacuate the divine *kenosis* of any real content, to reduce the *factum est* to a manner of speaking. Gutwenger's proposal is to speak of a transcendental or structural real relation of God to the world by virtue of the decree of creation (hence also of the Incarnation), a relation identical with the divine essence, hence not violating the divine simplicity, a relation which in its *esse ad,* like the Trinitarian relations, says neither perfection nor imperfection, hence not violating the divine immutability and infinite perfection, and yet a real relation of God to the actual world, which means a certain modification in God without detriment to His immutability.[12] Rahner's proposal, I must confess, escapes my comprehension. His formula is that the Word, who is unchangeable in Himself, is changeable in another. I simply do not understand how this formula says anything which is both true and new. On the other hand, Rahner offers in the course of his argumentation an analogy which could well prove fruitful for our understanding of the Incarnation. Just as our affirmation of trinity in God does not compromise our affirmation of His absolute unity, and just as the concept of divine unity to which we naturally come cannot tell us directly what the trinity might be, so the affirmation of a certain modification in God by the Incarnation need not, he suggests, compromise our affirmation of that immutability which is required by the divine perfection. The analogy, I say, may be a fruitful one, but it hardly seems that we have the fruit as yet. Whereas St. Augustine's employment of the metaphysics of relation helped to a real *intelligentia fidei* regarding the divine trinity and unity, it is not yet clear that we have here such a positive insight into the compatibility of a real *factum est* with the divine immutability. In any case, this is one line of current effort at a better understanding of the Incarnation.

A final group of current studies is concerned with the enduring mediational and instrumental role of the humanity of Christ in our salvation. Here a whole series of questions, most of them traditional, are being examined, and there is a general convergence of answers toward a unified theory. The recent interest in the symbolic aspect of the sacraments, together with the realization of how much symbolism, especially of a liturgical provenance, is present in the Gospels, has led to the conviction that there is a wealth of material awaiting theological exploitation. Both as regards the miracles of Christ in general and as regards the resurrection in particular, there has been a shift from emphasis on the physical and apologetic aspects to emphasis on the symbolic and kerygmatic aspects. The miracles of Christ, especially the resurrection, are signs of the presence of divine grace, the presence of God

[12] E. Gutwenger, *Bewusstsein und Wissen, Christi* (Innsbruck, 1960), pp. 114–121 .

powerfully acting to bring salvation to His people according to a consistent pattern.[13] Karl Rahner has pointed out how theology in recent centuries has neglected the mysteries of the life of Christ prior to His passion; what possibilities are offered in the Gospel accounts of His baptism, temptation, transfiguration, for example, for a more complete speculative Christology. Especially if one favors a Caselian-type view of the presence of the mysteries of the life of Christ in the liturgical mysteries, or at least sees in the mysteries of His life in their very historical occurrence salvific causality not only by way of merit and satisfaction but, to use St. Thomas' phrase, *per modum cuiusdam efficaciae,* the way is prepared for a more adequate explanation of how the grace of Christ, head of His Body which is the Church, comes to His members. There is the further effort, suggested by Karl Rahner, and admirably executed by Juan Alfaro, to show how, notwithstanding the immediate character of the beatific vision, it is, from another point of view, essentially mediated by the humanity of Christ. In summary, the key notions of *sacramentum, instrumentum* and *ordo* are capable of yielding a Christology more perfectly structured in itself, better integrated with the theology of grace, the sacraments, the Church and the last things, and kerygmatically more satisfying.

If one had to sum up the principal efforts and opportunities in current Christology, it might be done in the following terms: First, an effort at integration, an attempt to integrate the conciliar with the scriptural, the ontological and objective with the psychological, subjective and personal, the sphere of being with the sphere of function, the strictly Christological with the soteriological, ecclesiological, sacramental and eschatological. Secondly, an effort at balance, on every level, between the legitimate exigencies of Alexandria and Antioch, the descending and ascending Christologies. Thirdly, an effort at translation, at showing the relevance of the theology of the God-man to modern man's life, and especially at finding in the mystery of the Incarnation the solid basis of that integral Incarnationalism that Christians are seeking today.

4. A. Grillmeier, S.J.,[1] remarks that contemporary theology tends to be more Christocentric, both objectively and subjectively. The study of Christ begins by exhausting first the richness of the Christ-image in the Scriptures—dynamic Christology. Then it goes on to the consideration of His being in a deeper understanding of the classical doctrine of Christ's person—static Christology. The salvation motif serves to cast light upon the being and nature of Christ, and upon his supernatural accomplishment. The author finds a truly relevant contribution to Christology in the studies on the problem of Christ's psychological unity.

[13] Cf. L. Monden, *Le Miracle, signe du salut* (Bruges, 1960); F. Durrwell, *The Resurrection* (New York, 1960).

[1] Cf. Ch. 1, n. 1. This excerpt is taken from *The Figure of Christ in Catholic Theology Today* published in *Theology Today,* v. 1 (Tr. by Peter White and Raymond H. Kelly, Bruce, Milwaukee, 1964), from pp. 66–93.

The course of theological pursuits in recent years gives us occasion to hope that the foundations of a *"Christological Age"* have finally been laid. Though Mariology and ecclesiology have entered into the foreground in recent decades, we have witnessed nonetheless an equally intense effort to examine and deepen the Christ-image. As a matter of fact, Christ, Mary, and the Church constitute in Catholic theology an indivisible unity. They are concentric circles, as it were, about the one order of the Incarnation.

The foregoing is one of the dominant themes in Christology today. It embraces salvation as the *raison d'être* of the Incarnation. The world and history are centered on Christ. Revelation, the saving act of Redemption, preaching, and theology are stamped with Christ or are oriented toward Him. Where something is in a state of flux, Catholic theology, out of long experience and tradition, inquires further into the "substance and being" lying beneath appearances. Catholic theology prefers to linger and rise gradually from its foundations, a characteristic for which it has often been harshly judged. Such inquiries into the roots have marked the Church for centuries, and now new questions centering around the "Person and consciousness of Christ" are being bridged in this spirit. In surveying these problems, we believe we shall be able to shed light upon some of the most important contemporary Christological endeavors both in scientific theology and in the proclamation of the "Good News" by the Church to the world. Much of it is handed-down matter still carrying the clear stamp of the past. This is not surprising in an age of such momentous theological breakthrough as we are witnessing.

I
Salvation as the "Raison d'etre" of the Incarnation

The Christology that has been enshrined in theological manuals has received much criticism from within, in recent decades, and open reproof from without. Complaints are raised against an apparent separation of the doctrine of salvation by Christ from "Christology," considered as the theological study of the Person and nature of Jesus Christ. An overemphasis in Christology on the aged formulae of the old councils has perhaps hindered theologians from fully exhausting the richness of the Christ-image in Holy Scripture and even from seeing its basic contours at all. The Catholic doctrine of Redemption, it is argued, is content with formal consideration of the redemptive work of Jesus Christ (seen as "atonement," "merit," "sacrifice," or "ransoming," etc.), and fails to attend to the actual working out of Redemption portrayed in the biblical "mysteries of the life of Jesus." It is urged that the image of Christ is unquestionably situated much more centrally in Catholic theology and that it performs the intrinsic function of fulfilling and bracing together all of theology's single parts. Consequently, our first questions are subdivided into various individual themes, which appear to fall into two major groupings, of which the one is concerned with "Christocentric perspective" and the other with "redemption as event and history."

1. Christocentric Theology. We can speak of a subjective and an objective Christocentric theology. The first refers to a theological approach or

to a subjective view of the reality of Redemption. The second refers to this reality itself as effected by God.

Subjective Christocentric Theology. The call to shape the whole of theology according to the Christ-image has been raised more distinctly by Karl Barth than by anyone else. . . . A subjective Christocentric theology requires a Christological hermeneutics. . . .[2]

There is also among Catholic theologians a call to shake off a methodology and hermeneutics which have been rightly accused of liberalism. We are asked to shake off pure philology, sterile scientific research, and neutral objectivity, in favor of a "theological," "interested," "engaged," dogmatic and finally *Christocentric* interpretation of Scripture. Hence the recource to patristic exegesis and a pursuit of the "spiritual sense" of scripture.[3] The challenge regularly voices certain criticisms made in the nineteenth century by J. A. Möhler and M. J. Scheeben. Through modern historical thought, through a broadening of our theological methods with the categories of existential philosophy and the incorporation of biblical typology and patristic symbolism, contemporary theology should succeed in opening up this deepened understanding of Scripture and in rousing the whole of theology out of its torpor. According to Henri de Lubac the "spiritual sense" of Holy Scripture coincides with the methods of dogmatic theology. This, basically, was also Scheeben's contention. For there is an inner connection between Scripture, tradition, and the Church. Moreover, the inner dynamism of the spiritual sense leads us to the New Covenant, to the event in history when God's transcendence becomes concrete, palpable for us in Christ, the God-man. Jesus Christ *is* the spiritual sense and content of Scripture. In Him is the unity of the Old Testament and the New brought to its fullness, and in Him is the sense of world history summed up. The methods of pure historical research are not sufficient for deciphering this final sense of Scripture. Such research leads merely to a Christ-image devoid of content, attainable by purely natural research. The inspired character of Scripture and the presence there of divine revelation demand, in the sense of this hermeneutics, that we approach Scripture with an epistemological apriori: We must know beforehand that the full and sole content of revelation is Jesus Christ, the Word of God spoken to us, the crucified and resurrected. The interpretation of Scripture may not prescind in any way from the sense of faith, but must rather possess faith as its true strength, and must allow it to bear fruit. The

---

[2] See L. Malevez, n. 5 of this Chapter, part A.

[3] The literature here is vast, but cf. the *Elenchus* which appeared in *Biblica,* 35 (1954), pp. 7–13; 36 (1955), pp. 5–8; 37 (1956), pp. 8–13. Also A. Kerrigan, O.F.M., *St. Cyril of Alexandria, Interpreter of the Old Testament* (Rome, 1952), pp. 435–461; J. Coppens, *Les harmonies des deux Testaments. Essai sur les divers sens des Ecritures et sur l'unité de la Révélation* (Tournai, 1949); Coppens, "Nouvelles réflexions sur les divers sens des Saintes Ecritures," in *Nouvelle Revue Theologique,* 74 (1952), pp. 3–20; H. de Lubac, *Catholicism* (New York, 1955); and *Histoire et Esprit. L'intelligence de l'Ecriture d'après Origène* (Paris, 1950); and *Der geistige Sinn der Schrift* (Einsiedeln, 1952); R. E. Brown, *The Sensus Plenior of Sacred Scripture* (Roland Park, Md., 1955); F. Buri, "Neuere Literatur zum Problem der Hermeneutik," *Schweizer Theologische Umschau,* 42 (1954), pp. 66–72.

full mystery of Christ includes the *Corpus Mysticum,* the Church. This means that the mystery of Holy Scripture is to be understood only in the spirit of the Church, which is the Holy Spirit. The Holy Spirit was given to the Church in order to lead her to the totality of revelation.

Objective Christocentrism. Today there is thus a demand for an integration of "Christ-thinking" into our theological approach and method. But even more is required, for there is raised the summons to a more intensified, more substantial Christocentrism in the separate branches of theology. A "methodological" centering of the Christ-idea should, it is urged, bear fruit in the specific disciplines themselves. Here we are on more solid ground than we were before, in the discussion of subjective Christocentrism. The question concerning the "motif of the Incarnation," the so-called *praedestinatio Christi,* has not as yet been decided in favor of either the one or the other party, whether Scotist or Thomist. Nonetheless, the thought that history and creation in general are bound up in Christ is winning more and more followers—and here Karl Barth's theology is not the least influential factor.

The current controversy transcends the type of treatment usual in traditional theology and preaching; and at the same time gains in relevance to modern man. The knowledge that the classical passage for the *predestination of Christ* (Col 1:15 ff.) refers precisely to the Word made flesh (and not the preexisting Logos as such) acquires for this idea a strong biblical foundation.

We do not wish to attempt here even to sketch the structure of a Christocentric theology. Serious efforts have already been made elsewhere to complete various theological disciplines in the light of Christology. This has been done with particular effectiveness in the area of sacramental and moral theology.[4] And particular advantages are rendered ecclesiology (together with Mariology) and eschatology when they are given Christocentric orientation.[5] . . . The objective Christocentrism of the Bible has in fact not been harvested, or for the most part even considered by theologians. Theology can and must begin and end with Christ. Today's pursuit of a theology

---

[4] Cf. K. Rahner, "An Outline of Dogmatic Theology," in *Theological Investigations,* I (Baltimore, 1962), pp. 20–38; H. Schillebeeckx, *Christ the Sacrament of Encounter* (New York, 1963). Cf. also J. Fuchs, "Die Liebe als Aufbauprinzip der Moraltheologie. Ein Bericht," *Scholastik,* 29 (1954), pp. 79–87.

[5] Cf. O. Semmelroth, *Kirche als Ursakrament* (Frankfurt, 1955²), and "Die Kirche als 'sichtbare Gestalt der unsichtbaren Gnade,'" *Scholastik,* 28 (1953), pp. 23–29; K. Rahner, "Die ewige Bedeutung der Menschheit Jesu für unser Gottverhältnis," in *Geist und Leben,* 26 (1953), pp. 279–288, and *Schriften zur Theologie,* III, pp. 47–60. Rahner rightly underscores the fact of grace as created, but accidental grace is always (as a communication "of God" to the created soul) simultaneously an "uncreated grace." As such it is most essentially and intrinsically the grace of God become man. Christ did not merely effect it "meritoriously" in a distant point of the past. He remains, in His glorious humanity, the permanent realization of this grace. At the same time every grace has also an ecclesial significance by means of which it orients one toward the Church. Cf. Rahner's "Die Gliedschaft an der Kirche nach der Lehre der Enzyklika Pius XII., 'Mystici Corporis,'" *Zeitschrift für katholische Theologie,* 69 (1947), pp. 128–188, especially 176–188; also in *Theological Investigations,* II, pp. 1–88.

of history—as thorny and untrodden as the path may be—can find substance in these thoughts.

2. Salvation as Event and as History. The traditional direction of Catholic dogmatics, proceeding from Christ's being to His work, can be thoroughly modern and has advantages which cannot be easily foregone. Nevertheless it is proper and necessary to integrate more closely Christ's nature with His work, Christology with soteriology, being with doing. Not that this has been entirely lacking in the past. But when, from the very inception of our Christological efforts, we insist upon knowing the motif of the Incarnation, and ask: "Why did God become man?" then only will we at last cast our inquiry in a soteriological framework. It must not be peripheral; rather it should tend to permeate organically every facet of Catholic doctrine concerning the person of Christ. It is possible, without throwing over what has been handed down, at least to draw the contours of a definitely soteriological image of Christ—and one based upon the words of Holy Scripture. It can be extremely profitable for us to travel the road twice; once from His deed to His being, and again from His being to His work. Before we reiterate the classical doctrine of the person of Christ as expressed in the formulae of the ancient Councils, we should develop the features of the biblical figure of Christ, for they remain as standards for the theology of the Fathers. It will be especially fruitful to allow the salvation motif to cast light upon the being and nature of Christ, upon His natural humanity, and upon His supernatural accomplishment. In this connection it should be made clear that the hypostatic union itself should be taken as the fundamental figure and model of all union with God whatsoever. . . .

Christ as Event and Act. If a doctrine of salvation in Christ is to be developed it should not be limited—unavoidable as this factor may be—to a formal inquiry into the satisfaction, merit, and sacrifice of Christ. For what salvation is, and how it is realized, is defined by God Himself in the Person of Jesus and in the happenings in and around Him. We are referring to the "mysteries of the life of Jesus" . . .

If our formal doctrine of salvation can thus be supplemented by a portrayal of salvation as an actual event it will thereby receive an enriching and deepening fulfillment. Redemptive salvation is an encounter between God and His creation, an event which God sets in motion. It is He who reconciles us with Himself in Christ (2 Cor 5:18). . . . Is it not a question then of an all-embracing event which established creation and the covenant anew, which stretches from the beginnings until the end of history, spanning both protology and eschatology, man's origin and destiny?

3. A Dynamic Christology. With all its new tasks, Catholic theology can still learn about its own past, and can reintegrate that past in a fresh way. Such a synthesis might confront East and West with each other, remolding and vivifying both.[6] . . . What the West can learn from the East is above all an interpretation of the Incarnation which is dynamic and rich in tensions. What the West can give the East is the balance and precision of its Christ-

[6] Cf. the invaluable article by O. Rousseau, O.S.B., "Incarnation et anthropologie en Orient et en Occident," *Irénikon,* 26 (1953), pp. 363–375.

image. Our two-sided idea of man can fulfill itself in both directions. . . .

The Christology of the East [is] a Christology understood as "salvation event." . . . Chalcedon—dedicated to opposing any misunderstanding of the divine *physis* in Christ—expressed not the event but the being: a person (hypostasis) in two natures. We shall see how significant this was to become for the evolution of our interpretation of Christ. But if the formula of Chalcedon is not to lead to a one-sided view of Christ, then it needs to be completed by the living dynamism of the Alexandrian-Cyrillic vision. This does not at all mean that we should return to the old "terminology." But an ideological synthesis is pressingly needed.[7] The Christ-image of Alexandria with its emphasis on Christ's glorious reign as Lord and Word, should extend its light both to East and West. A new emphasis upon Easter elements in our liturgy can only serve to further these things.

II

The Nature and Being of Christ

Asking about Christ, the God-man, is a disinterested question. Yet it will lead of necessity to direct knowledge about the questioner, man himself. Hence we may, in fact must, pose the question of Christ most seriously. Consequently we may not pass over as insignificant the new controversies which are arising over the nature and being of Christ. . . .

Modern Christology and Christ's Unity. Commencing with this fundamental definition [of Chalcedon] which by no means exhausted the whole of dogma concerning Christ, but which made clear its decisive principle, modern Christology strives to define more exactly this singular and most sublime case of a God-man relationship. Modern positions remain very close to the old, classical solutions, even though they employ an advanced terminology and metaphysics.[8] Here we can see what a stimulus Chalcedon actually meant for the history of theology. Alexandrian Christology could not have provided a basis sufficiently broad for theology. The principal question is still that of the definition of this ineffable unity of Christ. One interpretation begins with the idea of a "unified unity," as the Fathers were wont to call it, which sees the humanity of Christ as being one, indeed as being personally one with the *Logos,* bypassing any further inquiry into the metaphysical structure of the unity. This is the Scotist-Tiphanic school of Christology, whose principal concern is the loyal defense of Christ's humanity.[9] Proceeding from the opposite approach, others strive to investi-

[7] Cf. A. Grillmeier, "Der Neu-Chalkedonismus. Um die Berechtigung eines reuen Kapitels in der Dogmengeschichte," *Historisches Jahrbuch,* 77 (1958), pp. 151–166 (B. Altaner-Festschrift).

[8] Cf. here K. Rahner, in *Chalkedon III,* pp. 3–49 (reprinted in *Theological Investigations, I* [Baltimore, 1962], pp. 149–201); cf. also J. Ternus, *Das Seelen-und Bewusstseinsleben Jesu.* For a systematic investigation of the whole problem, cf. *Chalkedon III,* pp. 81–237; and even more recently, R. Haubts, "Probleme der jüngsten Christologie," *Theologische Revue,* 52 (1956), pp. 145, 162, especially pp. 155–158.

[9] The most significant presentation of this Christology in German is that of K. Adam, *Der Christus des Glaubens* (Düsseldorf, 1954) (English tr. *The Christ of Faith* [New York, 1963]). The high value of K. Adam's Christology lies particularly in its biblical basis.

gate the "unifying unity." Naturally the difficulties involved here are enormous, though undeniable headway is being made. Let us take a look at the work of those theologians who have tackled more decisively than anyone else the question of unity in Christ. For these theologians, a fundamental principle is provided by St. Thomas, who maintained that in Christ there is *unum esse,* i.e., one, and only one act of being, of existence. Although there are truly two natures in Christ, He is in the strictest sense "one and the same," metaphysically "one subject" and "one being." But in order to explain this unity, it is necessary to deny any created existence whatever to the humanity of Christ. J. H. Nicolas, O.P., points out, in one of the most recent studies of this school, how close to despair theologians since Cajetan have been in their efforts to elucidate the classical Christology of Thomism.[10] Dom Diepen, O.S.B., has uncovered the fundamental limitations of the thesis according to which the uncreated existence of the *Logos* is identified with the existence of Christ's humanity. It requires an interchange or identification of efficient causality with formal causality. Thomism takes its point of departure in the fact that God is the efficient cause of Christ's humanity. As such, does not God virtually and eminently contain in Himself all that He effects outside Himself? Can the infinite act not become in this way the acts of the very beings He created? P. Nicolas says rightly: "That the form of an effect is given beforehand in the cause does not mean that the effect is constituted through the form of the cause. . . . To cause means to confer being, and if the effect is distinct from the cause, then the being it receives must also be distinct from the being of the cause."[11] Suppose we were to conceive the unity of person in Christ in such a way that the *Logos* takes the assumed nature into His divine existence.[12] This would imply an equation of the personal subsistence of the *Logos* with His divine existence. But "being" is an essential attribute of God and hence is absolutely common to all three Persons, whereas personal subsistence is *proper* to each one. How, then, can the divine *esse* or being be equated with the existence of the humanity of Christ without abrogating essential theological principles of the Trinity and the metaphysical laws of being? Would not this view require divine Being—the being common to all three Persons—to become the formal cause of the humanity of Christ in the strictest sense, because *esse* is not a mere point of reference, but an act?[13] It would be impossible in this way to bind the human nature of Christ to the *Logos* as Person. The whole Trinity would necessarily be incarnated and made the act of a created being. Dom Diepen has rightly invoked against such views the principles of St. Thomas, those principles which St. Thomas used to condemn the pantheism of an Amalric

[10] On the occasion of a study by H. Bouëssé, O.P., *Le Sauveur du Monde,* Part 2, *Le Mystère de l'Incarnation* (Chambéry-Leysee and Paris, 1953). Cf. the review in *Revue Thomiste,* 55 (1955), pp. 179–183.
[11] *Ibid.,* p. 182.
[12] *Ibid.* Nicolas reproduces the thought of Bouëssé with the words, "Le Verbe attire à son exister divin la nature assumée."
[13] *Ibid.,* p. 183.

of Bène.[14] The path of Cajetan and Billot provides no through passage.

Does this render impossible every attempt to explain the unity of being in Christ in the "direction" of formal causality, or better, in that of a "quasi-formal" causality? M. de la Taille, S.J.,[15] makes another attempt by assuming that there is a created existence proper to the humanity of Christ. From the divine act of being, common to all three Persons, comes, as from its efficient cause, the *esse* or "act of being" of this humanity, and it comes forth precisely by way of the Hypostasis, the Person, of the *Logos.* The human nature of Christ is created and maintained as the creaturely existence of the hypostasis of the *Logos.* If there is any quasi-formal relationship, it is to be found only between the "subsistence" of the second Person of God and "His" humanity. The Incarnation must be considered the highest case of God-world relationship, but it is an analogous instance, as is the case of the inhabitation of the Holy Spirit and of the vision of the creature dwelling in God at the end of time. To be sure, there is in the Incarnation, as against these analogous types of this relationship, not merely a difference of degree, but one of essence. The humanity of Christ is "substantially" united to the *Logos*—and united in the unity of the one subsistence and consequently in that of "one subsisting reality" (*una res subsistens*). All other grace brings about only an accidental union with God. The unity of the personal act with the *Logos* is of critical significance for the humanity of Christ. If His humanity finds its autonomy in the *Logos,* the *Logos* in turn becomes, in this humanity, truly a man.[16] Here we have more than a mere orientation, more than an ordering of Christ's humanity to the *Logos.* If the *Logos* "is" in the world in and through the humanity of Christ, then this humanity is subject to an "actuating" by the *Logos,* an "actuating" which may not be considered as efficient causality. Every requirement for the subsistence of a spiritual being is thus fulfilled by the *Logos* in this humanity which is created by the act of the triune personal God. The *Logos* fulfills it by way of a quasi-formal self-communication which thus leads to a singular case of transcendental unity.

Consequently, the "Thomistic" approach of Cajetan must be abandoned, if we wish to explain the metaphysical unity of Christ as that of "one subsisting" reality through the singularity of the act of existence. Nevertheless, the solution—as far as the mystery of the Incarnation permits one at all—is to be sought in the area of (quasi-) formal" causality, for otherwise we can come to no *unum* in the metaphysical sense. Indeed we may admit everything that Dom Diepen asserts in explaining the unity in Christ according to St. Thomas. He is working from the principles of integration, or the integral whole. He knows very well that Deity and humanity are no more "partial substances" in this whole than they

---

[14] According to R. Haubst, *Theologische Revue,* 52 (1956), p. 156.

[15] M. de la Taille, "Actuation créée par l'Acte Incréé," *Recherche de Sciences, Religieuses,* 18 (1928), pp. 253–268; and "Entretien amical d'Eudoxe et du Palamède sur la grâce d'union," *Revue Apologétique,* 48 (1929), pp. 5–26, 129–145; and in *Mysterium fidei* (Paris, 1931³), p. 514 ff.; cf. J. Ternus, in *Chalkedon III,* p. 229 ff.

[16] *Ibid.,* pp. 213–215, 229 f.

are "constituents standing unto themselves." It is a question neither of a synthesis of natures nor of a disparate and heterogeneous conglomeration. "Christ is formally *one* more than anything else because of His one act of subsistence." Christ's human *esse* or act of being is distinct in its very nature from the divine act of being. Yet it forms, with the divine act of being *one being* proportionally as Christ *is* at once God and man, and as His human nature does not *sub*sist for itself. Thus "there is," as Diepen says against Duns Scotus and against Baslism, "in Christ only one unique existence—and this not as if every created existence in Him were eliminated, but because this created existence is integrated into the complete and personal Being of the Son of God."[17] Is the question of the "unifying unity" thereby fully exhausted? We believe the Theory of Actuation has still something further to add here, although metaphysically it may lack some thoroughness and detail. In any case it can make clear for us the fact that the unity of Christ as the actuation of Christ's humanity through the subsistence of the *Logos* contains dialectic elements worthy of our attention. The more interior the union and bond of this humanity with the subsistence of the *Logos,* the more it can be considered as a fully actuated, created, and individuated essence (and this does not mean that it is autonomous). This point may be fittingly directed against the old "synthesis in nature" which succeeded in conceiving of union only by sacrificing the natural and independent mode of operation proper to human nature. Expressed in a dialectical formula the view proposed here can be stated thus: the greater the union of human nature with the *Logos,* the more perfectly actuated is its distinct essence of "being a man." This formula alone does justice to the mystery of the Incarnation, without invoking it as such.[18] For it lays stress upon three things concurrently: "God" "becomes" "man." And therein lies also the kerygmatic significance of this theory—which surely has not as yet been thought through. For in Christ, the God-man, "being a man"—which is not in the order of nature—is carried in its dignity, scope, and overall significance for the economy of salvation, to the level of Christ's personal reality. Forasmuch as grace is a supernatural "actuation" of nature for a supernatural purpose, so is it in fact the actuation of Christ's human "nature." The entire pattern of this nature is bent toward a supernatural end (whereby all rights of nature, as is emphasized today in all theology of grace, are to be preserved). But in Christ is found the highest of all graces, the *gratia unionis creaturae ad subiectum divinum.* Never can anything higher fall to a creature's lot. Hence the Incarnation means the highest actuation, realization, and fulfillment of this human nature in Christ.

The Antitype. This conception of the unity proper to Christ and of His being as God-man is a Christology of unification. A school of theology has taken a stand in opposition to this view, perceiving therein a threat to divine transcendence. It prefers to con-

[17] R. Haubst, *Theologische Revue,* 52 (1956), p. 157.

[18] Cf. K. Rahner, in *Chalkedon III,* p. 15; F. Malmberg, Über den Gottmenschen (Basel-Frieb-Wien, 1960), pp. 27–70; and B. Lonergan, S.J., *De constitutione Christi ontologica et psychologica* (Rome, 1956[1], 1958[2]).

sider itself the custodian of the ancient *Logos-Anthropos* tradition and the doctrine of the *Homo Assumptus.* The leader and champion of this interpretation of Christ was the Franciscan Father Déodat de Basly († 1937). For him the fundamental mistake of the Cyrillic-Thomistic Christology of unification consisted in the falsification of the true relationship between God and creation. Basly saw the true problem, and saw it correctly. There is no doubt that theologians of unification have advanced too precipitously, as we have already pointed out and must continue to point out. But here we encounter a direct and categorically expressed antithesis. It states that a nonabsolute, created thing, whether body or spirit, cannot enter into an intrinsic union of being with the Absolute.[19] It cannot, and may not, come to the *una res subsistens* of the Thomists. Instead, the only possibility of connecting the nonabsolute with the Absolute remains, according to Father Déodat, a *subjonction déitante.* This should preserve both full divine transcendence and the corresponding autonomy of the assumed man (the *Homo Assumptus*). The result is a very loose Christ-image which is open to the accusation of Nestorianism and which needs to be more carefully stated. Following, then, the official condemnation of this interpretation of Christ the ecclesiastical world became publicly aware of a true theological controversy, the background of which is, even for the trained theologian, extremely difficult to see.

In a unique novel, *La Christiade Française* (Paris, 1929), in which even geological sketches are found together with appendices on the patristic doctrine of the *Homo Assumptus,* Father Déodat attempted to represent the God-man relationship in Christ as a "love duel" (*duel d'amour*) of the *Home Assumptus* with the triune God. This love duel is peculiar, however, in that this "assumed man" is "placed below" (*subjoint*) the *Logos,* while the *Logos* is "placed over" (*surjoint*) the assumed man. The "over" and "under" relationship was certainly valid. The dubious part was the suffix: *-joint.* Between both elements there was only an undefined bond, which appeared in further elaborations by the Franciscan to be altogether too loose. The "assumed man" is, as *agens,* completely autonomous. This autonomy means that the *Logos* exercised no influence whatever upon the human knowledge and willing of Jesus. This autonomy alone, Father Déodat claimed, could keep intact the teaching of Chalcedon on the two natures subsisting "inconfusedly" (ασυγύτως) in Christ. Up to this point the doctrine of Father Déodat seemed acceptable to many theologians who subsequently broke definitively with him. But Father Déodat went still further and shifted the weight of the autonomy so emphatically into the humanity of Christ that it is only there, as it were, that the "I" of the *Logos* comes into being. There is in God only "one" individuality, which is that of the one nature. Hence, on the level of the Absolute, which alone can explain the Incarnation as a phenomenon outside of God, the *Logos* is not an autonomous "I."[20] Although the *Logos* is

[19] Cf. Déodat de Basly, O.F.M., "Inopérantes offensives contre l'Assumptus Homo," in *La France Franciscaine,* 17 (1934) pp. 419–473, 456.

[20] I.e., He is not, according to Father Déodat de Basly, "un agisseur agissant des actions qui ne sont que ses actions propres" (*ibid.,* p. 463).

thus certainly placed over (*surjoint*) the *Homo Assumptus,* it is still not placed in this superior position as an autonomous "I" (*Je, Moi*). For the Trinity is, as regards all that is outside of God, only *one* indivisible autonomy. Thus if Christ can be addressed as an "I," a *Je,* a *Moi,* then it must be in virtue of the autonomy of the "assumed man." Only in the latter is there an "I," a *"Je,"* and *"Moi."* The Gospels always show, according to Father Déodat, the *human* "I" of Christ, who stands before the triune God, in His individuality and personality in no essential way different from every other man. Hence the Franciscan adjusts the notion of person to his application of this concept to Christ. "Who, then, in Christ is really the final subject by whom everything must be done or uttered? Who is the final bearer of the being and natures that are in Him?" If we ask these questions of Father Déodat we receive an answer totally different from that of the Christology of unification. With Aquinas, the theologians of unification say that Christ is the Word-become-flesh, the *Logos* in the flesh. Everything is centered in the one and only subject, which is the *Logos.* Thus is Christ not merely an *unus,* an only one, a "one and the same" personal subject, as Chalcedon exclaims with the whole of early tradition (see Denz. 148), but even an *unum* (neuter gender). Thus the unity of Christ in the transcendental metaphysical sense is affirmed and the distinction between the two natures is in no way denied. It is otherwise with Father Déodat de Basly. The *Logos* and the "assumed man" are bound into a type of complex "person" which de Basly defines as a "physical and transcendent whole (*Tout physique et transcendant*)."[21] Christ is a "connecting whole" between what is not absolute (man, soul, body) and the Absolute (God). But the latter may not be regarded here as triune. Above all, the *Logos* may not be taken as a complete, autonomous principle of operation (*parfait Agisseur autonome*).[22] This connecting whole, which is Christ, is thus inwardly in part an absolute which is autonomous only as God (*qua Deus*) but not as *Logos,* and partly a nonabsolute, the *Homo Assumptus,* which enjoys perfect autonomy.[23] Strangely enough, Father Déodat believes that he has, through his exposition, raised himself to a level superior to that of Nestorius and Cyril of Alexandria. In spite of all their differences, they are both, for Déodat, fundamentally the same. They make of Christ, the God-man, a synthesis which exceeds the sum of His "components"; they make Him into a "third being" (*Tiers-être*), as Déodat repeatedly asserts. For Nes-

[21] Déodat de Basly, "Le Moi de Jésus Christ," in *La France Franciscaine,* 12 (1929), pp. 125–160; 325–352), p. 148 f.; and "L'Assumptus Homo, *ibid.,* 11 (1928), (pp. 265–313), pp. 284–286. Father Déodat, referring here to the words of Augustine, "Persona Christi, mixtura Dei et hominis," says "C'est le TOUT, mixtura, qui et la personne du Christ. C'est ni le Verbe, ni l'Assumptus Homo, mais ce TOUT–là que les deux unis, font: persona Christi" (cf. above).

[22] Déodat de Basly, "Inopérantes offensives," in *La France Franciscaine,* 18 (1935), p. 55.

[23] *Ibid.,* 17 (1934), p. 457. Only for this *Tout physique et transcendant* are the *Logos* and the *Homo Assumptus* concurrently "interior." Otherwise, from the standpoint of the latter, "L'Assumptus Homo perfectus est in obliquo le Verbe qui lui est *extrinsèque,* mais qui lui est transcendentalement *surjoint.*"

torius, this *Tiers-être* is composed of *Logos,* regarded as an autonomous individual, and of Christ's human nature. And this *Tiers-être* is concretely "man," i.e., autonomous in Déodat's view. Besides his false notion of the Trinity, Nestorius is to be censured only for this *Tiers-être.* Not a word is uttered concerning Nestorius' faulty conception of the unity between the *Logos* and Christ's humanity. Cyril of Alexandria, on the other hand, does not, we are told, conceive of the second component in Christ as a concrete *homo,* i.e., an autonomous man.[24]

Déodat's own position thus means that in the connecting whole which is Christ, the *Logos* itself, is not to be considered as an *individuum,* as a self-sufficient "I." The *Logos* can act in Christ only as God (*qua Deus*), not as *Logos* (*qua Verbum*). Thus Christ's individuality and autonomy are to be attributed to the *Homo Assumptus.* The latter also becomes the primary subject of words uttered by Christ or addressed to Him. When one says "Christ" in Déodat's sense, he is referring directly (*in recto*) only to the autonomous, individual *Homo Assumptus.* This is not the "whole" as such. The *Homo Assumptus* is only a part, it exists only "in the whole." Only of this "whole" can divine and human things be said. Only because this whole comprises both God and man, and precisely by a "placing over" of the one component and a "placing under" of the other, can divine and human things be attributed to it, and precisely by way of a *réciprocation prédicative.* Father Déodat never wishes to accept the traditional assertions (*communicatio idiomatum*) that this *Homo Assumptus* is the *Logos* or that the *Logos* is man. For he sees there the dreaded identity of the infinite with the finite, of the absolute with the relative.[25] Nor may Mary be named "Mother of God" with logical immediacy and unequivocal meaning. In reference to Christ the term "Mother of God" refers first of all to the bearer of the *Homo Assumptus* as an autonomous *individuum.* With respect to the *Homo Assumptus,* Mary is directly and immediately mother; with respect to the *Logos* she is mother only indirectly, by way of inclusion, *in obliquo.* We must clearly distin-

---

[24] *Ibid.,* 18 (1935) (pp. 33–104), p. 45. . . . Déodat misinterprets here both Nestorius and St. Cyril. In the end he draws very close to Apollinaris. (Cf. P. Galtier, "S. Cyrillus et Apollinnaire," *Gregorianum,* 37 [1956], pp. 584–609.) Both formed their Christ-image according to the principle that two complete dimensions could not grow together into a third. Hence the humanity of Christ must be made into something "incomplete" if it is to serve as a principle. Apollinaris is supposed to have taken from Christ's humanity the soul, whereas Cyril, leaving this intact, took the *autonomy* from His human nature. "Il faut que la réel inabsolut subjoint au Verbe ne soit qu'un réel imparfait, ou (according to Cyril) imparfaitement autonome (!), puisque déjà le Verbe est, lui le un réel parfait (with Apollinaris), ou parfait Agisseur autonome (with Cyril)." (See *La France Franciscaine,* 18 [1935], p. 55.) Nestorius thus unites, according to Father Déodat, two autonomous individuals to make a *Tiers-être,* and Cyril unites the *Logos* as an independent Individual with a nonautonomous humanity. Father Déodat himself wishes to unite an individual, autonomous "assumed man" with the *Logos* for which this *Homo Assumptus* is not individual, not an autonomous dimension. The two are not united to constitute a third which is above the original two and resulting from them, but are "Person" as a totality.

[25] Cf. Déodat de Basly, "L'Assumptus Homo," in *La France Franciscaine,* 11 (1928), p. 282; "Le langage in recto dirait l'identité de l'Infini et d'un fini: suprême erreur." Cf. R. Haubst, *Theologische Revue,* 52 (1956), p. 148.

guish that in Christ God and Man are related to one another as "one thing to another" (*un autre et autre quelqu'un*). Father Déodat attempted to support his doctrine with an appeal to the whole patristic tradition and to his master Duns Scotus.[26] Certain basic assumptions in the latter in fact lean in this direction, e.g., the Scotistic stress upon the wholeness and autonomy of the human spirit as efficient cause in Christ's humanity and on the absolute transcendence of the divine. But Dom Diepen has shown that Déodat goes beyond Scotus. For Scotus decidedly aligned himself to the so-called doctrine of subsistence and in the form expounded by St. Thomas in the renowned second *opinio* in *S.T., III,* q. 2, a. 6.[27]

The judgment of the Church . . . against a follower of Déodat, Father Léon Seiller, O.F.M., showed that extreme *Homo Assumptus*-Christology is not compatible with Catholic theology.[28] There is a genuine value in stressing the autonomy of Christ's humanity, as is to be seen in that type of Christology which is represented today by such theologians as Galtier and K. Adam. But Galtier clearly distinguishes himself from Déodat in building upon the foundation of the theory of subsistence and in assuming a substantial unity between Christ's humanity and the *Logos*—assumptions which Déodat most decidedly shuns. To be sure, the Christology of Galtier also fell under the reproach that it inquires in fact after the "unified unity" in Christ and not after the "unifying unity."[29]

The Christ-Image. What theologians provide as outlines to the Christ-image needs then to be filled out by the theologians themselves and by those who preach to the faithful. . . . Those theologians who hold for the one act of being in Christ also teach a more or less "strict, dynamic hegemony of the *Logos.*" One of the most recent representatives of this point of view attributed an actuating and directing efficient causality to the *Logos* as its own, but not to Christ's humanity.[30] He thinks that an irrevocable principle of the theology of the Trinity seems inapplicable to Christ, the principle namely which asserts that every exterior act of the triune God is common to all three Persons. Now the humanity of Christ, regardless of its union with the *Logos,* remains a creature, an "exterior act," and hence cannot be excluded from the universal law of trinitarian operation. The doctrine of the hegemony of the *Logos,* therefore, has its limitations. The exaggerations which are to be noted in this new theology are a remnant of the old Apollinarist synthesis in nature. They have their origin in a false understanding of the mystery of the Incarnation. For the primary concern of God's intervention in Christ in human history is not to act according to His divine nature. It was not to this end that He brought about the Incarnation. His first intention is to be and act as man in the world. It is for this

[26] In his work, "Sotus Docens," *Supplement à la France Franciscaine,* 17 (1934).

[27] Cf. L. Ott, in *Chalkedon II,* p. p. 906 ff., 913–915; I. Backes, *ibid.,* p. 928.

[28] Cf. Pius XII on his Encyclical on Chalcedon, *Sempiternus Rex* in *Osservatore Romano,* Vol. 13, 9, (1951), n. 212, p. 2. cols. 1–2.

[29] Cf. K. Rahner, in *Chalkedon III,* pp. 11 ff., 32 ff.

[30] Cf. R. Haubst, *Theologische Revue,* 52 (1956), pp. 158–162.

reason that, within the limits set by the Church's *magisterium,* we must consider as highly significant that other Christ-image which emphasizes the *difference* between the divine and the human, or at least strives to see this difference given equal stress with the unity. Paul Galtier therefore insists again and again that the human spiritual life of Jesus was in no way changed as a result of the hypostatic union. There is no "hegemony of the *Logos,*" in Parente's sense, since there can be no personally specific action of the *Logos* upon Christ's humanity. The hypostatic bond between Christ's humanity and the *Logos* proffers no occasion for the divine nature to act directly upon the human. Such a view nevertheless does not preclude the possibility of considering Christ's human nature—precisely in *its* truly human aspects—as an organ or instrument of the divinity.

Thus today, as ever in the past, the coloring varies in the figure attributed to Christ by theologians. All agree that the true synthesis is expressed by the two fundamental Chalcedonian principles. The "inconfused" must always accompany the "undivided." This synthesis is, however, without meaning as long as the above-mentioned dialectical principle which underlies every encounter and union with God is not taken seriously. This principle asserts that the highest union with God implies the highest fulfillment of created essence and being. For this reason it is from the Actuation theory that we can expect Christology to turn with a view to elaborating on Chalcedon. For it seems to hold the greatest promise of opening up the mystery of Christ's God-manhood, and thus of integrating both these great themes in Christology.

III
Person and Consciousness

The true contribution of our time to traditional Christology is the inquiry into the human consciousness of Jesus Christ. Here the psychology of Christ is joined to and builds with and upon the ontology of Christ. Even in the new posing of the question required by this enterprise old tensions and solutions become particularly meaningful. . . .[31]

[31] [See next excerpt] The first direction was led, in recent years, by the following: P. Parente, *L'Io di Cristo* (Brescia, 1951¹, 1952²); M. B. Xiberta, O.Carm., *El Yo de Jesucristo* (Barcelona, 1954); and *Tractatus de Verbo Incarnato I–II;* . . . H. Diepen, O.S.B., in numerous articles in *Revue Thomiste* (1949–1956). In the other direction: besides Déodat de Basly; J. Rivière; Léon Seiller, "Homo Assumptus bei den Kirchenvätern, Ausgewählte Texte," *Wissenschaft Weisheit,* 14 (1951), pp. 84 ff., 160 ff.; esp. "La psychologie humaine du Crist et l'unicité de personne," *Franziskanische Studien,* 31 (1949), pp. 49–76, 246–274; also separately (Paris-Rennes, 1950) (indexed: *AAS* 43 [1951], no. 12; cf. M. Browne, O.P., in *Osservatore Romano,* Vol. 19, 7, 1951). In a moderate way P. Galtier, esp. in *L'unité du Christ. Etre. Personne. Conscience* (Paris, 1939) and in numerous articles (cf. the bibliography in M. B. Xiberta's *Tractatus II,* pp. 671–739). Also K. Adam. For survey and general discussion cf. J. Ternus, "Das Seelen- und Bewusstseinsleben Jesu," in *Chalkedon III,* pp. 81–237. A Perego, "Il 'lumen gloriae' e l'unità psicologica di Cristo," *Divus Thomas,* (Pi), 58 (1955), pp. 90–110, 296–310; R. Haubst, "Probleme der jüngsten Christologie" (cf. note 15); B. Lonergan, *De constitutione Christi* (cf. note 18); and "Christ as Subject: a Reply," *Gregorianum,* 40 (1959), pp. 242–270; J. Galot, S.J., "La

5. K. McNamara[1] analyzes and contrasts the views of Galtier, Parente and Xiberta regarding the problem of the psychological unity of Christ: "Who is the 'I' in Christ's statements?" He agrees with the main criticism raised against Galtier's view, that it bears, at least on account of its language, a striking likeness to the defective Christology of Antioch which did not safeguard Christ's metaphysical unity. He equally objects to Galtier's logical consequence of making the human nature in Christ the sole true agent of its operations.

The aim of the following note is to present readers with an outline of an important controversy in Christology which is currently attracting widespread interest on the Continent. What follows is based mainly on two recent books which owe their origin to the controversy, each representing a substantial contribution to the problem by a theologian of the highest competence. Mgr. Pietro Parente, author of *L'Io di Cristo,*[2] has been until recently Dean of the Faculty of Theology at the University of Propaganda Fide in Rome. Fr. Bartholomew M. Xiberta, author of *El Yo de Jesucristo,*[3] is a distinguished Spanish theologian, professor at the Carmelite Scholasticate in Rome and a recognized authority on the Tract *De Verbo Incarnato.* In *L'Io di Cristo* and *El Yo de Jesucristo* Mgr. Parente and Fr. Xiberta have provided us with commentaries of outstanding merit on many aspects of the theology of the Incarnation. Here, however, we are concerned with these books only from the point of view of the particular problem that evoked them.

I

In Jesus Christ two integral, distinct natures, one divine one human, are indissolubly united in the single divine Person of the Word. This is the substance of the dogma of the Incarnation, defined at the Council of Chalcedon in 451 A.D. In Christ's human nature there exists a human soul, a human intelligence, therefore, which acts according to the same laws as any other human intelligence, but with an altogether unique perfection. Among the acts of that intelligence it is clear that we must include the act of self-consciousness. This is the act by which the soul becomes aware of itself and its existence, not by abstract knowledge derived from a logical process, but by experimental awareness arising from an act of introspection. In what way exactly does Christ as man attain to such a knowledge of His own being? By what process of his human intellect does He become aware of His personal unity in the hypostasis of the Word, with that

psychologie du Christ," *Nouvelle Revue Theologique,* 80 (1958), pp. 337–358; F. Malmberg. *Über den Gottmenschen* (Basel-Frieberg-Wien, 1960), pp. 89–114.

[1] Cf. Ch. 3 N. 5. The present article entitled "The Psychological Unity of Christ: A Problem in Christology" appeared in *The Irish Theological Quarterly* (vol. 23, 1956, pp. 60–69).

[2] Morcelliana, (Brescia, 1951), p. 238.

[3] Herder, (Barcelona, 1954), p. 172.

kind of awareness which each of us has of his own personal unity? This is the question which has come to be known as the problem of Christ's psychological unity or, as is evident from the titles of the two books mentioned above, the problem of the "I" of Christ.

The problem is stated by Fr. Xiberta in the form of three questions.[4] These questions arise from a consideration of Christ's statements as found in the Gospels, e.g. "Before Abraham was made I am,"[5] "I and the Father are one,"[6] "the Father is greater than I."[7] The following are the questions as put by Fr. Xiberta:

I. Who is the "I" that makes these statements, i.e. who is the subject who speaks?

II. What is the content of this "I," in other words what is the total object of consciousness to which belongs the unity in virtue of which the "I" is uttered? Is it the human nature of Christ, from whose lips springs the "I" in the hearing of men? Or is it the divine nature of the Word? Or is it both together?

III. Since the "I" as uttered by Christ has for its immediate source His human nature, how does the human intellect perceive, i.e. have experimental awareness of the Second Person of the Blessed Trinity and its own relationship to it? This third question arises only on the supposition that, in answer to Question II, one admits that the content of the "I," on some occasions at least, includes the divine nature of the Word.

As far as Question I is concerned, one's immediate reaction is likely to be that Catholic theology has long ago given the answer to it, namely that the subject who utters the "I" of Christ is the divine Person of the Word. To affirm that any other subject was in question would surely be tantamount to a denial of the personal identity of Jesus Christ with the Second Person of the Blessed Trinity; to suggest that the human nature was this subject would be to fall into the grossest form of Nestorianism, a division of Christ into two persons. In fact, however, this latter answer has been given by certain theologians, among them no less distinguished a name than that of Fr. Paul Galtier, S.J.[8] It is obvious, therefore, that Question I cannot be summarily dismissed, even though Fr. Galtier's reply may eventually be judged to be out of harmony with the traditional expression of the Incarnation doctrine, if not with its very substance. One need scarcely say that Fr. Galtier has not the least desire to compromise the personal unity of Christ. But while keeping that doctrine in mind, he believes that the complementary aspect of the dogma, namely the integrity and complete freedom of the human nature—its full "autonomy," to use the phrase which is dear to the school of thought of which Fr. Galtier is the leading representative—should, in our thought and expression, be given the emphasis which the genuine patristic tradition accords to it. In this way the ever-present danger of Monophysitism will be avoided. Moreover, by placing in

[4] Op. cit., pp. 132 f.
[5] John 8:58.
[6] John 10:30.
[7] John 14:28.
[8] P. Galtier, *L'Unité du Christ. Etre . . . Personne . . . Conscience,* (Paris, 1939), especially pp. 237–371.

relief the psychological aspect of the dogma, Catholic theologians will make their teaching on Christ more acceptable to the modern mind. A Christ who is presented as endowed with a fully human psychological personality is certain to make a greater appeal to an age that is profoundly interested in problems of psychology. Thus Fr. Galtier may be said to have given a psychological slant to the study of the doctrine of the Incarnation and to that extent to have posed the problem of Christ in new terms.[9]

The starting-point of Fr. Galtier's system is that in any individual human nature one must recognize the existence of a two-fold "I." There is in the first place the substantial "I," the underlying concrete reality which is the acting subject and reveals itself as such to consciousness. As an object of consciousness it enters into and forms part of the second "I," the psychological or empirical "I," which is the sum-total of psychological phenomena which combine to form one complex object of consciousness. The substantial "I" is in a human person identified with metaphysical personality, but it pertains to the person *qua* individual nature not *qua* person. *De facto* it is identified with the person but it does not derive from the person and can accordingly exist apart from it, as it does, in fact, in the human nature of Christ. That nature is a substantial "I," an individual concrete subject in respect of its own activities, but it is not a human person because it has been assumed into personal unity with the Word, which possesses it as its own. In virtue of this relationship, the Word is the ultimate subject of attribution for the human operations, but the human nature alone, as substantial "I," is their sole agent or active subject.[10]

This then is Fr. Galtier's meaning when he replies to Question I in the words "the human nature of Christ," or, in terms which underline the psychological autonomy of that nature and which Fr. Galtier and others propose as its best description, well authenticated by tradition, the "homo assumptus" or "assumed man." Such a view of the human nature is intimately linked to the Scotist concept of the essence-existence relationship and of the formal constitutive of personality. For Galtier, following Scotus, the formal constitutive of personality is not a positive entity but simply the non-assumption of an individual nature by a higher *suppositum*. Hence, the Hypostatic Union, while resulting in a human nature that lacks human personality, does not in itself imply in that nature any reality whereby it is distinguished from a non-assumed human nature. There is no communication of personal existence by the Word to the human nature, no question of the Word supplying *eminenter* the function of an impeded substantial

[9] The same general preoccupations in Christology are to be found in the writings of the late Déodat de Basly, O.F.M. ("L'Assumptus Homo" in *La France Franciscaine* XI, 1928, pp. 265–314; "Le Moi de Jésus Christ," ibid., XII, 1929, pp. 125–60). In fact de Basly's work has been largely responsible for the development of the psychological approach to the Incarnation doctrine. Nevertheless Galtier was the first to attempt the integration of this approach with the classic scheme of traditional theology. In doing so he accepts the fundamental position of de Basly concerning the "I" of Christ, though with certain reservations. Cf. Parente, op. cit., pp. 86 ff., pp. 163, 167; Galtier, op. cit., pp. 309 ff.

[10] Xiberta, op. cit., 34 ff., 132; Parente, op. cit., pp. 168 ff., Galtier, op. cit. pp. 339 ff.

mode of the human nature, no degree of actuation by the Word of the human nature—one or other of which is postulated by the various theories which visualize a real effect in the human nature in virtue of its assumption by the Word. It is obvious that this Scotist concept of Christ's manhood fits in very well not only with the description "assumptus homo," but also with the view of the human nature as the subject which utters the "I" of Christ, and of the Word as non-active, an ultimate subject of attribution whose role in so far as the Hypostatic Union is concerned, is not dynamic but merely static.

It is clear then that the controversy concerning the psychological unity of Christ is not a completely new one, but has its roots in the time-honored philosophical dispute concerning the formal constitutive of personality. There is a sense too in which the controversy goes back to a much earlier period, namely the time of the great Christological conflict between Antioch and Alexandria. For it is quite clear that the advocates of the "assumptus homo" theology are much more indulgent to the Antiochene Christology of the fourth and fifth centuries than are theologians generally, and make corresponding reservations about the Christology of Alexandria, particularly as represented by St. Cyril. Nor is it at all suprising that these old lines of division should reappear in the present controversy, for the Christologies of Antioch and Alexandria owe their special characteristics not to any fortuitous and passing circumstances, but to two distinct approaches which the mystery itself seems constantly to invite, each of them a perennially valid approach, but never altogether free from the danger of exaggeration and consequent error.

II

Mgr. Parente, in his work *L'Io di Cristo,* vigorously rejects Fr. Galtier's contention that the subject by which the "I" of Christ is uttered is the human nature as distinct from the Word, the "assumptus homo" of which Fr. Galtier speaks. This latter description Mgr. Parente considers to be out of harmony with the traditional expression of the dogma of the Incarnation: it is capable of bearing an orthodox meaning, and was in fact used in an orthodox sense by many worthy representatives of the traditional Christology, but it can also have a Nestorian sense, and for that reason was rejected by St. Cyril of Alexandria and later by St. Thomas.[11] The question of language apart, however, Parente considers that Galtier's theory "inevitably compromises" the unity of Christ in all senses. It compromises it in the psychological order (for a reason we shall see presently) and, what is even more serious, it compromises it in the ontological order also. "If in the ontological sphere," he writes, "the Hypostatic Union is reduced, as in Galtier's view, to a mere conjunction of the human nature with the divine, without any real physical bond between the two; if in the psychological sphere the distinction between them is even more sharply drawn and the Word neither acts in that sphere nor is perceived in it in any way, we do not see how one can speak of personal unity in Christ. Personal unity is inconceivable without

[11] Parente, pp. 86–93.

unity of substantial existence and without unity of action at least from the point of view of the person as hegemonic principle."[12]

Mgr. Parente's own reply to Question I is that the only subject by which the "I" of Christ is expressed is the Word, acting through the human nature by way of efficient causality. This reply of Parente is in turn based on a selected theory of the formal constitutive of personality, though Parente contends that, in so far as he affirms that the human nature is not a subject of operation as distinct from the Word, he is merely expressing the substance of the dogma of the Incarnation, independently of any theological explanation.[13] There is no doubt, however, that the concept of the person as operating through the nature by way of *efficient causality* is linked to the theory of personality that is associated with the name of Capreolus. According to this theory the formal constitutive of personality is the possession of connatural existence (human existence, therefore, in the case of a human nature), and accordingly Christ's human nature is not a person because it exists by the communicated *esse* of the word. This is the view which Mgr. Parente proposes as the true interpretation of St. Thomas's thought, and from it he deduces his concept of the Word as efficient cause of the human activities by the following argument: *agere* follows upon *esse*, therefore the Word, since it is the source of existence for the human nature, must constantly direct and control by its activity the actions of the human nature.

Among those Thomists, however, who with Mgr. Parente accept Capreolus's theory of personality, there are some few who will not grant this final link in his chain of argument. Fr. C. V. Heris, for example, the well-known Dominican theologian of the Incarnation, maintains that while the Word, by communicating its existence to the human nature, places the latter in a condition in which it may act, it cannot on that account be said to intervene in the acts of the human nature.[14] It is clear then that Mgr. Parente in speaking of the Person of the Word as the hegemonic principle of the act by which the "I" of Christ is uttered, is basing himself not only on a particular theory of personality but also on an argument from that theory whose validity does not go unquestioned. Nevertheless, in so far as the precise query contained in Question I is concerned, Mgr. Parente's reply will be endorsed by all Thomists and also, one may confidently add, by very many whose allegiance lies elsewhere in the disputed question concerning the formal constitutive of personality.

We pass on now to Questions II and III, which may be taken together. Fr. Galtier's reply (a knowledge of which is necessary for a full understanding of Mgr. Parente's words quoted above) is, as might be expected, largely determined by the same Scotist concept of the Hypostatic Union which influenced him in his reply to Question I. To Question II he answers that the content of the "I" uttered by Christ is the divine and human natures together. The "I" is uttered by the

[12] Ibid., p. 172.

[13] Ibid., pp. 173, 178 f.

[14] *The Mystery of Christ* (Eng. Tr.), Cork, 1950, p. 43. Cf. G. D. Smith, "Notes on Recent Work," *Clergy Review*, August, 1951, pp. 106 f.; Xiberta, pp. 27–9.

human nature as distinct from the Word, but in uttering it the human intelligence has present to it not only the human nature but also the divine. By a reflexive act the human intelligence is experimentally aware of the human nature and all its psychological activities. This act, however, does not attain to a knowledge of the Word. Hence, if left to itself, i.e. independently of the beatific vision, the human mind of Christ would be unaware of its personal existence in the Word, and would therefore be conscious of possessing a human personality which it did not possess in fact. But Christ as man enjoys the beatific vision, and in it knows the Person of the Word and its Hypostatic Union with the human nature. Here we have Fr. Galtier's reply to Question III. The beatific vision is the key to the problem of Christ's psychological unity. Through it Christ as man knows His ontological unity and the divine nature of the Word, and thus is enabled to utter an "I" which is divine as well as human.[15]

Mgr. Parente's solution is altogether different. He is of course in agreement with Fr. Galtier that the "I" of Christ embraces the divine Person of the Word together with the human nature, but there agreement ends. Parente rejects Galtier's explanation of the psychological unity of Christ on two grounds. In the first place he considers that so complicated and indirect a way of preserving that unity cannot be correct: the view that the beatific vision is necessary if Christ in His human consciousness is to be preserved from error about His own mode of subsistence has all the appearances of an artificial construction erected to support an initial false assumption. Secondly, he denies that the beatific vision can be the ground of a true act of self-consciousness: in Galtier's theory the human intellect of Christ would *know* that it subsisted in the Word but would not be *experimentally* aware of it—hence the problem of Christ's psychological unity is still unsolved.

Mgr. Parente then offers his own solution, based on his concept of the Word as the principle of existence in the human nature, and hence as the *principium quod* which regulates the activity of which the human nature is the *principium quo*.

It is Thomistic teaching, he affirms, that the human mind can by its own powers come to a knowledge of its own nature and existence. For a knowledge of its nature a "diligens et subtilis inquisitio" is required, but its *esse* is known by a simple act of reflection on its own activities. This knowledge is not the result of a process of reasoning, but "has the character of an experimental perception, which has for object the substance of the soul in its concrete individual existence." Applying this principle to the Hypostatic Union, Mgr. Parente concludes that Christ in virtue of His created intelligence is directly aware of the personal existence of the Word, which in Him takes the place of a connatural existence. In another way too the self-consciousness of Christ extends to an awareness of the divine Person, viz. by experiencing the hegemonic activity of the latter with respect to the acts of the human nature, which finds itself in the relationship of *instrumentum conjunctum* to the Word. In these two ways, therefore, Christ as man, by His own natural activity independ-

[15] Xiberta, pp. 37 f., 132 f.; Parente, pp. 168 ff.; Galtier, pp. 346 ff.

ently of the beatific vision, perceives His ontological unity and the fact on which it is grounded, and thereby attains to psychological unity also.[16]

III

It is clear that Mgr. Parente's explanation stands at an entirely opposite pole from Fr. Galtier's. Where the latter is especially concerned to preserve the fully human character of Christ's manhood, the former is, before all else, on guard lest the perfect unity of Christ be in any way compromised. And just as Galtier leaves himself open to the charge of Nestorian tendencies, so Parente will have to defend himself against opening the way to a Monophysite or Monothelite view of the Incarnation.

It is not surprising, therefore, to find that Fr. Xiberta, in the book referred to above, seeks to find a middle way between these two theories. In general, however, he is much nearer to Mgr. Parente than to Fr. Galtier. He fully agrees with the former that the "assumptus homo" theology is out of harmony with the picture of Christ that emerges from the Scriptures, and is incompatible with unity of person. The starting-point of that theology is false, viz. the Scotist view of personality as in itself a mere negation. And while the Church has permitted that view to be freely held in the Schools as a philosophical theory, and as a possible explanation of the absence of a human personality in Christ's manhood, the matter takes on a different aspect when the theory is accepted as a datum and made a guiding principle for the interpretation of the Incarnation doctrine as a whole: *parvus error in principio, magnus in fine.* Galtier's view of the Word as a mere subject of attribution in relation to the free acts of Christ's manhood is, he argues, a distortion of the Church's doctrine springing from this Scotist assumption. To find a similar view of the Incarnation we have to go back to the Antiochene theology, where we find, in the writings of Theodore of Mopsuestia and Nestorius, a use of the "communication of idioms" that very much resembles Galtier's. Nestorius's error was not that he denied Our Lady's right to the title "theotokos" in any and every sense, but that he deprived the phrase of its true meaning by allowing it only in a loose sense—in Scholastic language *in obliquo,* not *in recto.* This idea is paralleled by Galtier's theory of the Word as exercising no activity whatever in virtue of the Hypostatic Union itself; as a subject whose only relationship to the human nature it had assumed is that to it must be referred, as ultimately responsible, the activities of which the human nature is the sole cause.[17]

For all this, Fr. Xiberta will not accept Mgr. Parente's theory that the Word acts *by way of efficient causality* to regulate the decision of the human nature. Such a view "does not fail to raise legitimate fears in regard to the exercise of liberty."[18] He therefore attributes a different kind of activity to the Word—a profound and universal influence exercised by it over the human nature, and affecting the latter not only in its *esse* but also in its *agere.* He describes this activity as the "com-

[16] Parente, pp. 180–92.
[17] Xiberta, pp. 108–31.
[18] *Ibid.,* p. 125.

plete sublimation of the human nature" by the person of the Word, as the raising of the human nature "to the highest pinnacle of perfection which its obediential capacity allows." How is this supernaturalization of the human nature effected? Not by the communication of the *esse* of the Word to the human nature, but by the final actuation by the Word of a human nature already constituted as a real entity by its own proper efficient causes. This *plena actuatio* of the human nature is what places it in personal unity with the Word, thereby subjecting it to a supernaturalizing influence that is all-pervading.[19]

This influence is analogous to that exercised in the natural order by the person over its own proper nature. Fr. Xiberta describes as follows this fundamental activity of the person: "In us too there exists between person and nature a perfect convergence in activity: it is I who think with the understanding, see with the eyes, touch with the hands. But this convergence depends altogether on a unity which exists without identity. That unity is the fruit of a profound influence of the whole being on the individual parts, since without such an influence substantial unity is not achieved. From that influence springs in its entirety all that the parts receive in virtue of their insertion into the subject."[20] But in Christ's human nature the person is the Word, therefore to Him we must attribute the corresponding influence over that nature.

Sublimated by this influence, the human intelligence of Christ exercises its act of self-consciousness, and in doing so perceives a twofold object: the human nature in which it exists (and which it could perceive even apart from this sublimation) and the divine nature of the Word, which it apprehends as hypostatically united to that human nature. The Word is apprehended in the first place in a clear knowledge—both acquired and infused—of the *effects* of the Hypostatic Union, and here certainly there is question of experimental awareness, of true self-consciousness. It is apprehended also by another medium—in the beatific vision, which for Fr. Xiberta is the connatural effect of the Hypostatic Union (as opposed to a privilege demanded by it or simply appropriate to it), and, in his opinion, is also the ground of a true act of self-consciousness by the human intellect. Thus Christ is able to utter his "I" with full consciousness of both the eternal and temporal aspects of His own being.[21]

IV

We have here then three very different solutions of the problem of Christ's psychological unity, each championed with vigor, and indeed with ardour, by a distinguished author of international reputation, and backed by a fund of theological erudition. And the list does not end there, as is clear from Fr. Xiberta's survey of the opinions that have been put forward. It is clear that the controversy which Fr. Galtier's thesis has aroused will continue, and that even partial

[19] *Ibid.*, pp. 125, 143. Cf. B. M. Xiberta, *Tractatus de Verbo Incarnato* (Madrid, 1954), Vol. I, pp. 257, 264 ff.

[20] *El Yo de Jesucristo,* p. 128.

[21] *Ibid.*, pp. 152–6.

agreement will be reached only gradually. The question is a complex one, involving long-standing scholastic disputes, rival interpretations of the ancient heresies, and divergent allegiances to the great representatives of Patristic Christology. Most of the points at issue have been referred to explicitly above: the question of the formal constitutive of personality, the relationship of the divine and human natures of Christ in the domain of causality, the kind of knowledge Christ has in the beatific vision, the relative merits of the Alexandrian and Antiochene Christologies, the precise sense of the condemnation of Nestorius of Ephesus. Other problems are clearly implied in the controversy, e.g. the meaning of the Trinitarian law that all action *ad extra* are common to the three divine Persons (the principle to which Fr. Galtier and others appeal in excluding any real effect in the human nature in virtue of its Hypostatic Union to the Second Person), the exact significance of the orthodox doctrine opposed to the Monothelite heresy, the extent to which the categories of non-Scholastic thought, and of modern psychology in particular, should be allowed to modify traditional modes of thought and expression.

Only in respect of one of these controverted problems can the present writer claim any close familiarity with the details of the dispute, viz. the validity of the Christology of the School of Antioch. Fr. Xiberta has pointed to the striking likenesses between the "assumptus homo" theology and the characteristic features of the Antiochene Christology, and there can be little doubt that he is justified in doing so. The Antiochene Christology has had its enthusiastic defenders and, unquestionably, at a critical period it played its considerable part in the work of preserving and transmitting the doctrine of the Incarnation. Nevertheless, it was seriously defective, as it did not sufficiently safeguard the unity of Christ. The reason for this was that it had lost sight of the ontological dependence of the human nature on the person of the Word. Fr. Galtier considers that this principle can be preserved intact by insisting on the fact that the human nature is possessed by the Word. One could not quarrel with this if the idea of possession were not so attenuated as to imply no more than a remote attribution to the Word of the predicates of the human nature. For this was precisely the defective idea that the Antiochene theologians had in mind when they spoke of Mary as being Mother of God "by relation" or "because of the union." And the source of their difficulty here appears to have been the rigid exclusion (inspired by fears of Monophysitism) of any metaphysical penetration of the human nature by the person of the Word—a position that is fully paralleled by the Scotist rejection of any real modification of the human nature of Christ solely in virtue of the Hypostatic Union.

To this point of similarity between Fr. Galtier's Christology and that of the Antiochenes is closely related another, namely an identical concept of the human nature of Christ as in itself the subject or sole true agent of its own operations. Fr. Galtier's concept of the "substantial I" of the human nature would certainly have been endorsed by Theodore and Nestorius, but in them it forms an essential part of a dualism which, in Nestorius at least, went beyond the limits of orthodoxy. To guard against the error of

Nestorius the constant tradition of the Church has canonized the usage that allows but a single "I" in Christ. It is true that the concept of a human "substantial I" which is no more than an individual concrete nature that is truly active and impinges on consciousness, is compatible with the unity of the "ontological I," or person, in Christ. But is it advisable to use language which can so easily obscure the difference between orthodoxy and Nestorianism? One should bear in mind the warning given by the Most Rev. Michael Browne O.P., the present Master-General of the Dominican Order, when, as Master of the Sacred Palace, he wrote apropos of a work which had been placed on the Index: "When the human 'I' of Christ is treated as an autonomous subject, though even only psychologically, so as to exclude from the activity of the assumed human nature the Word as active principle, one runs the risk of affirming implicitly a human ontological 'I,' thus veering towards the erroneous doctrine of Nestorius."[22] It is difficult to see that this admonition does not apply also to Fr. Galtier's theory, though the work to which it directly refers propounded a more extreme dualism than Fr. Galtier would countenance.

In due course the verdict of the *consensus theologorum* will be given in regard to Fr. Galtier's theory of the substantial and psychological "I" of Christ. Even if that verdict should be unfavorable, to Fr. Galtier will still go the credit for having first posed and offered a systematic solution to the problem of Christ's psychological unity.

---

[22] *Osservatore Romano,* July 19, 1951. Cf. Xiberta, op. cit., pp. 61 f.

INDEX